# Grow and Hide

# Grow and Hide

## The History of America's Health Care State

COLLEEN M. GROGAN

# OXFORD
### UNIVERSITY PRESS

Oxford University Press is a department of the University of Oxford. It furthers
the University's objective of excellence in research, scholarship, and education
by publishing worldwide. Oxford is a registered trade mark of Oxford University
Press in the UK and certain other countries.

Published in the United States of America by Oxford University Press
198 Madison Avenue, New York, NY 10016, United States of America.

Library of Congress Cataloging-in-Publication Data
Names: Grogan, Colleen M., author.
Title: Grow and hide : the history of America's health care state /
Colleen M. Grogan.
Other titles: Grow and hide
Description: New York, NY : Oxford University Press, [2023] |
Includes bibliographical references.
Identifiers: LCCN 2023006066 (print) | LCCN 2023006067 (ebook) |
ISBN 9780199812233 (hardback) | ISBN 9780197691557 (epub) |
ISBN 9780197691564 (ebook)
Subjects: LCSH: Medical policy—United States—History. |
Medical policy—United States—History—19th century. |
Medical policy—United States—History—20th century. |
Medical policy—United States—History—21st century.
Classification: LCC RA395.A3 G74 2023 (print) | LCC RA395.A3 (ebook) |
DDC 362.10973—dc23/eng/20230418
LC record available at https://lccn.loc.gov/2023006066
LC ebook record available at https://lccn.loc.gov/2023006067

DOI: 10.1093/oso/9780199812233.001.0001

Printed by Sheridan Books, Inc., United States of America

*To*
*Michael*
*Adelaide, Eleanor & Clara*

# CONTENTS

PART III    THE CONSEQUENCES OF GROW
AND HIDE: 1965–2020

# Introduction

## America's Expanding, Unequal, and Hidden Health Care State

Throughout liberal and conservative regimes, the American government has invested gradually, but quite consistently, in public health protection and prevention, building up the American health care system (hospitals, clinics, laboratories) and various insurance and direct care programs to pay for patient care. Despite this substantial investment, the American public is repeatedly told that the United States has a predominantly private health care system with relatively little government involvement.

When President Obama signed the Affordable Care Act (ACA, also called "Obamacare") in March 2010, guaranteeing coverage for 32 million uninsured Americans, he touted the bill's historic significance. However, he was also quick to assuage fears that the United States was moving away from a private insurance model: "Long after the debate fades away, what will remain standing is not the government-run system some feared, [but instead] . . . legislation [that] built on the private insurance system that we have now and runs straight down the center of American political thought."[1]

When fighting against the ACA, conservatives use similar rhetoric. For example, when candidate Donald Trump argued against Obamacare in a *60 Minutes* interview in 2015, he insisted that "the government's gonna pay for it." Yet, when asked what to do about the uninsured, he quickly focused on private insurance: "[F]or the most it's going to be a private plan . . . with lots of competitors with great companies and they can have their doctors, they can have plans, they can have everything."[2] Most importantly, when asked separately what the government's role in health care should be, gone was any mention of

*Grow and Hide.* Colleen M. Grogan, Oxford University Press. © Oxford University Press 2023.
DOI: 10.1093/oso/9780199812233.003.0001

government payments: "The only way the government should be involved [is] to make sure those companies are financially strong, so that if they have catastrophic events or they make a miscalculation, they have plenty of money," he said. "Other than that, it's private."[3]

In reality, the American health care system was already a predominantly public-funded one before the passage of the ACA, and it had been a predominantly public system for a very long time. In the United States, the terms "private" and "public" are less real descriptors of the health care system and more political frames for "good" and "bad." The great irony is that the United States created a substantial publicly financed system while framing it as the opposite. I call this the Grow-and-Hide Regime. The purpose of this book is to explicate the Grow-and-Hide approach by showing the true extent of public funding in the health care system over time, illuminating why and how that public role has been marginalized, revealing the extreme fragmentation and inequality that results from this Grow-and-Hide Regime, and considering possibilities for reform.

## The American Myth

If we add up all the items that are funded through taxation, public taxpayers cover 60% of national health expenditures (see Figure I.1). While this level of public funding is substantial, it is seldom discussed or portrayed, and it is almost certainly more than 60%. There are four main components of the American Myth, under which policymakers and private actors persistently overcount private funding, and at the same time undercount publicly funded activities.

### Over-representing Private Insurance

As a society, we can structure and pay for our health care system in many ways. For example, we could collectively choose not to use government taxation to offer public insurance or pay for private insurance premiums. Instead, we could act as consumers and pay the premium price directly to private insurance companies, like we do for auto insurance, or reject health insurance altogether and pay for health care services directly "out of pocket." Although this is theoretically possible, it has not been the case for a very long time. Since the 1940s, the federal government has subsidized the purchase of employer-based health insurance, which is the main form of private health insurance in the United States. Yet in the 1960s, when the federal government began reporting private health expenditures, it hid the subsidy and overstated

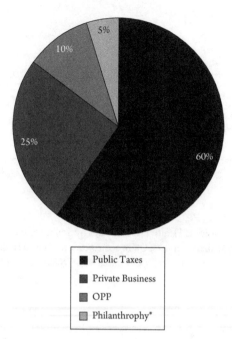

*Figure I.1* National Health Expenditures by Source of Funds, 2019.*

* In the NHE Accounts this category is labeled "Other Private Revenues"; however, it is defined as "all other private sponsors of health care other than private business and households. The most common source of other private funds is philanthropy. . . . For institutions such as hospitals, nursing homes, and HHAs, other private funds also include income from the operation of gift shops, cafeterias, parking lots, educational programs, and investment income." Also included in this category are private investments in research, structures, and equipment. Because private investment amounts are included under the private business category, I refer to this category by its majority funder—Philanthropy. *Source:* Centers for Medicare & Medicaid Services, Office of the Actuary, National Health Statistics Group, "National Health Expenditure Data," Table 19, http://www.cms.hhs.gov/NationalHealthExpendData/.

the role of private spending by lumping private insurance and out-of-pocket payments (OPP) together. As a result, the federal government's presentation of the data suggested that most national health expenditures (NHE) were paid for through private means—from about 75% in 1960 to 54% in 2009 (see Figure I.2).

If out-of-pocket payments are separated from the larger "private" category, the picture of the American health care system changes drastically (see Figure I.3). As out-of-pocket expenditures have declined over time, the government (at the federal, state, and local levels) has picked up a greater share of the health care tab. Of course, the logical explanation for this increase in public funding is the passage of major public insurance programs—Medicare and Medicaid—in 1965. Yet even before 1965, public financing was quite substantial (see Figure I.4).

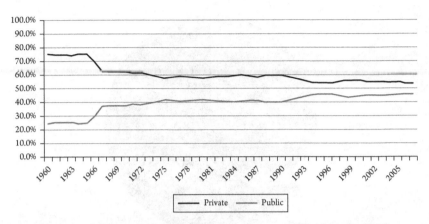

*Figure I.2* Percent of National Health Expenditures by Source of Funds, 1960–2005. *Source:* Centers for Medicare & Medicaid Services, Office of the Actuary, National Health Statistics Group, "National Health Expenditure Data," http://www.cms.hhs.gov/NationalHealthExpendData/.

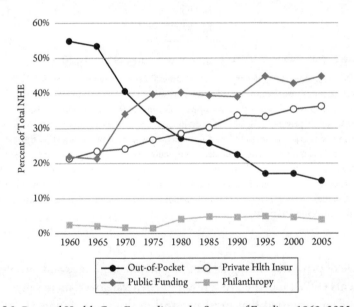

*Figure I.3* Personal Health Care Expenditures by Source of Funding, 1960–2005. *Note:* Public Funding includes: Medicare, Public Assistance, Dept. of Defense, Maternal and Child Health, VA, General Hospital/Medical payments (federal, state & local), and School health. This is arguably a conservative estimate because the following publicly funded sources were not included: workers' compensation, vocational rehabilitation, temporary disability, and public health activity. *Source:* Centers for Medicare & Medicaid Services, Office of the Actuary, National Health Statistics Group, "National Health Expenditure Data," As shown on website when accessed on June 26, 2009 (website: http://www.cms.hhs.gov/NationalHealthExpendData/). As discussed in Chapter 10 herein the Office of the Actuary has changed its methodology and definitions so these data now look different for the same years. Nonetheless, even using current data definitions on the website, the general trend as shown here is still the same.

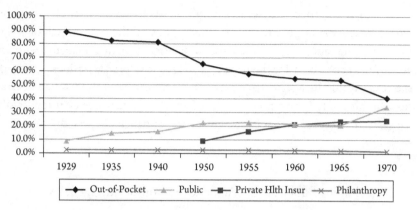

*Figure I.4* Personal Health Care Expenditures by Source of Funding, 1929–1970. *Source for 19291975 data:* R. M. Gibson, "National Health Expenditures, 1978," *Health Care Financing Review* 1, no. 1 (Summer 1979): 1–36; Office of Research, Demonstrations, and Statistics, Health Care Financing Administration: Selected data. Shown in: *Health United States, 1979* (U.S. Department of Health, Education and Welfare, Public Health Service, Office of Health Research, Statistics and Technology, DHEW Pub. No. 80-1232), Table 72, p. 191. *Source for 1980-2005 data:* Centers for Medicare & Medicaid Services, Office of the Actuary, National Health Statistics Group, http://www.cms.hhs.gov/NationalHealthExpendData/02_NationalHealthAccountsHistorical.asp#TopOfPage; Extracted from website on 6/26/09.

Before the passage of these major public insurance programs, the government paid for a considerable proportion of health expenditures through its investment in government-owned hospitals and clinics, its reimbursement of "charity care" patients to private nonprofit hospitals, and the provision of care through public health departments. These same forms of public provision—with public insurance thrown into the mix—still exist today, though they are often overlooked because they are intentionally hidden.

In the post-2010 era, it is extremely difficult to determine the extent of public versus private funding, because the data are no longer categorized according to public and private funds. The federal government's Office of the Actuary presents national health expenditures according to three major categories that obscure public and private financing. For example, through the ACA market-place plans, the federal government subsidizes premiums and cost-sharing for persons up to 400% of poverty, but expenditures for marketplace plans are listed under private nongroup individual insurance. Similarly, when companies offer employer-based health insurance to their employees, the expenditures for these plans are counted under private health insurance even though they are subsidized with public tax funds. Even the major sources of financing for Medicare—the U.S. national health care plan for the elderly—are labeled as "private business and households" to represent Medicare's mandatory payroll tax, where employers and employees contribute.

In sum, if one tried to determine public funds based on taxation, using the federal Actuary's category for "government sponsor," the result would be a significant undercount. And if one tried to determine private financing without government taxation using the Actuary's category for "private business sponsor," the result would be a significant overcount. Importantly, this is not an aberration. In this book, I show how the role of private sector financing is repeatedly suggested to be more than it is, and government financing repeatedly suggested to be less.

## Hiding Public Health Activities in Non-health Agencies

Since the early 1900s, the U.S. government has reiterated a persistent myth that public health is only 3% of national health expenditures. For most of the 20th century, the federal government used a fairly narrow definition to determine "public health activities." Today, official public health expenditures include agency spending at the Food and Drug Administration (FDA), the Centers for Disease Control and Prevention (CDC), and state and local health departments. But what these agencies do, while crucially important, represents only a small amount of overall public health activities.

For example, in the National Health Expenditure Accounts, government spending for public works, air and water pollution abatement, sanitation and sewage treatment, and water supplies is not included under "public health activities." Even if we look only at the federal level and do not include the substantial spending on sanitation and public works at the state and local level, the amount spent on preventive public health in agencies outside of the Department of Health and Human Services (HHS) is significant. The U.S. Environmental Protection Agency's (EPA) budget in 2019 was $8.9 billion. Under the U.S. Department of Housing and Urban Development (HUD), $218 million was allocated in 2019 to the Office of Lead Hazard Control and Healthy Homes (OLHCHH). In the U.S. Department of Energy's budget for 2019, there were numerous "public health" line items related to environmental management that totaled $6.7 billion. Another major agency providing basic primary prevention is the Food Safety and Inspection Service within the U.S. Department of Agriculture (USDA). By its description, the Service "is the *public health agency* in the U.S. Department of Agriculture responsible for ensuring that the nation's commercial supply of meat, poultry, and egg products is safe, wholesome, and correctly labeled and packaged."[4]

Indeed, the USDA runs the largest obesity prevention program in the United States. What used to be America's Food Stamp program, dealing primarily with hunger, changed its name to Supplemental Nutrition Assistance Program

*Table I.1*  **Federal Prevention Programs, 2019**

| Agency | Program | Amount (in millions) |
|---|---|---|
| EPA | All programs | $8,850 |
| HUD | Lead Hazard Control and Healthy Homes | $218 |
| DOE | Environmental Management | $6,732 |
| Subtotal (EPA+HUD+DOE) | | $15,799 |
| USDA | Food and Nutrition Service | $104,872 (2018 budget) |

*Source:* Environmental Protection Agency; U.S. Department of Housing and Urban Development; U.S. Department of Energy; Office of Chief Financial Officer; U.S. Department of Agriculture.

(SNAP) to emphasize its primary public health goal of focusing on nutrition and promoting and providing healthy foods. In 2019, the USDA allocated nearly $73 billion of its budget to SNAP.[5] In addition, the USDA allocated over $20 billion to Child Nutrition Programs (CNPs), which primarily provides support for school lunch and breakfast programs, and roughly $6 billion for the Special Supplemental Nutrition Program for Women, Infants, and Children—better known as WIC. WIC's mission is to "*safeguard* the health of low-income women, infants, and children up to age five who are at nutritional risk by providing nutritious foods to supplement diets, information on healthy eating [including breastfeeding promotion and support], and referrals to health care."[6]

The total USDA public health budget for 2018 equaled $105 billion[7]—above the $98 billion total for HHS, which is listed by the federal Actuary as the total of "public health activities" in the United States (see Table I.1). These programs in the USDA, EPA, HUD, and DOE actively pursue public health objectives and should be counted as such, yet they are not included in official national health expenditure tables.

## Hiding Publicly Funded Medical Treatment under Labels of Prevention

The U.S. government has also promoted a rhetorical myth that makes an arbitrary distinction between prevention and treatment. This part of the American Myth paints prevention as squarely within the realm of the state, and includes population-level concerns (e.g., sanitation, infectious disease control), while painting treatment as within the realm of the private physician, comprising individual-level treatment of the sick.

Since the early 1900s, public health leaders have been involved in a continual project of redefining the field of public health. At the beginning this was partly a reaction to new scientific knowledge, which was prompting a need to move beyond, in their words, "old" notions of public health—focused on sanitation and bacteriology—to a "new" understanding of public health, focusing instead on communicable diseases, and thus necessarily dealing with individual health behaviors (parlance that today includes wearing a mask, washing hands, and social distancing). It also meant screening and testing for communicable diseases and, when cases were positive, providing treatment. Just as with the COVID-19 pandemic, this early conception of public health was built around the idea that while controlling the spread of disease does impact population health, such control depends on the behaviors of individuals, and on positive individuals getting treatment. However, individual-level health care treatment has always been conceived in the United States as squarely in the domain of the medical profession. Here—in what is called "preventive medicine"—numerous tensions arose about the proper domain of public health.

Indeed, the exact role of public health gets murky and difficult to measure, because it sits in such a heavily contested area. For example, from the 1920s through the 1940s, public health leaders had heated debates about whether public health prevention should include medical treatment.[8] In 1926, one of the leading public health figures of the 20th century, Charles-Edward Amory Winslow—the first chair of Yale University's School of Public Health—argued in his presidential address to the American Public Health Association's annual meeting that "public health was at a crossroads." He noted that by focusing on sanitation and bacteriology for the half-century prior, their field had substantially reduced communicable and environmental diseases, but that going forward public health leaders must, when addressing major causes of illness, include dealing with chronic disease. And because effective prevention efforts to address chronic disease demanded a focus on the individual patient, this forced the public health profession to shift its emphasis from the population to individuals.

While the distinction between prevention and cure was clear under the "old" public health that defined itself by sanitation and bacteriology, Winslow pointed out that, even by 1926, the distinction was not so clear. Public health departments, along with voluntary associations (nonprofits in today's terms), had developed visiting nurse associations, school-based clinics, and maternal and child health programs—and they were all referred to and known as "public health prevention." But in their effort to provide effective preventive care, they provided treatment as well. Many treatments *are* prevention: vaccines, prenatal care, cancer screenings, annual exams, and most blood and urine tests, to name just a few. Hence the term "preventive medicine." Winslow was one of the first public health leaders—though certainly not the only one—to publicly acknowledge that the distinction between treatment and prevention is exceedingly difficult. He argued that if public health was to succeed, then prevention and treatment should become indistinguishable: "The attempt to fix the boundaries of the public health program by establishing a distinction between prevention and cure must then in practice lead only to confusion and incertitude."[9]

But Winslow and his allies were the exceptions rather than the norm. A century later, the U.S. government is still attempting to fix the boundaries of public health by asserting the persistent myth that public health is only concerned with prevention and population health, and is distinct from treatment. It uses this strategic framing to hide the reach of public health.

## Hiding Public Subsidies for Health Care Infrastructure

In addition to creating the public health infrastructure necessary to provide prevention and treatment, the U.S. government also invested significant public funds to develop the U.S. health care system. This is the fourth part of the American Myth, which promotes the idea that the development of the U.S. non-profit health care sector was private, despite substantial public investment. Public investment occurs by granting tax-exempt status to the nonprofit sector and granting public subsidies for new construction, technology, and equipment. Although government capital investments are shown in the federal Actuary's national health expenditure tables, this is another area where the portrayal of public funding is seriously misleading.

The U.S. government at both the federal and state level—though primarily at the state level—provides tax-exempt bonds for capital investments to nonprofit health care facilities. While hidden public subsidies for capital investments started in the 1930s, this form of capital health policy shifted in the 1960s to the tax-exempt bond. In addition, through the Medicare program, the federal government provided subsidies to private health care facilities to cover the cost of depreciation and interest. These two policies shifted how nonprofit hospitals financed capital investments and how hospitals thought about the need to raise capital for new investments. These subsidies allowed nonprofit hospitals to invest in the latest technology—a new high-end specialty hospital wing or a new oncology suite—and market these new investments to privately insured Americans with no assurances that the uninsured, or even those with public insurance, could have access to these new facilities. Moreover, while all American taxpayers subsidized capital investments for private nonprofit hospitals, they subsidized those hospitals again when these investments increased health care prices, which in turn increased the tax-exempt premiums people paid for private health insurance.

But, again, these capital investment subsidies have been largely hidden from view. When the actual cost of tax exemptions is not shown to the public, it looks like the private sector is footing the bulk of the bill for capital investments—73% as depicted in the national health expenditure tables. Private health care companies use these portrayals of capital investments to their advantage. For example, a central strategy for the pharmaceutical industry when it was fighting against the Clinton reform plan in the early 1990s was to argue that private investments provide new and advanced innovative technologies, and that government regulations would deprive the American public of lifesaving cures.

In the chapters that follow, I detail the Grow-and-Hide strategy under each aspect of the American Myth. But, first, it is essential to understand what the strategy is; why, how, and by whom it has been pursued; and what consequences have emerged.

## Grow and Hide

> *Another year, another president, another address to Congress calling for a national health care program. It was a familiar scene, one that had played out pretty much the same way since Harry Truman's day, with an enthusiastic launch giving way to shambolic negotiations and then, inevitably, catastrophic failure.*
>
> —Jonathan Cohn, *The Ten Year War*

Most explanations of the American health care system, like Jonathan Cohn's, focus on one question: Why have attempts to pass national health insurance (NHI) in the United States continually failed?[10] President Franklin Roosevelt was the first president to seriously—though briefly—consider national health insurance, when his advisors counseled him to include health security as one of the central pillars under the Social Security Act. Given his health struggles after contracting polio at the age of 39, FDR understood better than most the importance of access to good medical care. Nonetheless, when he assessed that organized medicine's opposition to NHI might jeopardize the entire Social Security Act, he made a political calculation to jettison the idea in order to protect the most important piece of legislation under the New Deal. Looking back on this event, one might logically conclude that the U.S. government failed to act on health care during the 1930s.

But by focusing on NHI, Cohn and others fall into the state-builders' trap—thinking in terms of the ideological categories and framing tactics that state actors at the time gave us. To appease the American Medical Association (AMA), the FDR administration was clear in all official public documents and speeches that the Social Security Act did nothing regarding the provision of medical care. For example, in FDR's 1935 message to Congress, he stated bluntly, "I am not at this time recommending the adoption of so called 'health insurance.'"[11] Yet, in the same speech—in the sentence immediately before, as a matter of fact—FDR recommended "Federal aid to State and local public health agencies and the strengthening of the Federal Public Health Service," investments that became Title VI of the Social Security Act. All the actors involved in building up the U.S. health care system—politicians, federal agency directors and bureaucrats, provider associations (including the AMA and the American Hospital Association), business leaders, and the voluntary health agencies—repeatedly framed the work of the federal Public Health Service and grants-in-aid to state and local public health agencies as distinct from medical treatment. Few have taken seriously how Title VI—or the many other government actions conducted under the rubric of "public health"—impacted the U.S. health care system.

In Parts I and II of the book, I examine what the U.S. government did before 1965 under policies and programs pertaining to "public health and prevention," which provided medical treatment and built up health care infrastructure. In the 1930s and prior, when the U.S. government (federal, state, and local) was supposedly doing very little regarding health care reform, the government actually invested substantial public dollars in hospitals, clinics, school-based health, the health care workforce, and expanding the public health infrastructure. At the turn of the 20th century, as the modern hospital began to establish itself as a place for curative medicine rather than convalescence (or a place to die), the number of hospitals increased dramatically—from 2,000 in 1900 to 7,000 by 1928. They were built with grants, most often from local governments, and nearly half (45%) were maintained by receiving public appropriations.[12]

Although public funding enabled hospitals to grow and spread across the American states, the government's role was (and still is) rarely acknowledged. Instead, not only do we, like Cohn, conclude that when FDR abandoned NHI there was an "absence of government action," but we also conclude that "the private sector took matters into its own hands."[13] I show how the private sector was allowed to gain much power and take matters into its own hands *because* of government action, not the absence of it.

To debunk the American Myth, we must not only critique what the state does, but also deconstruct how policy actors describe the state.[14] We must shift the historical question dramatically—from "Why no government action?" to "Why has the American government significantly expanded health care spending and public provision in every historical period over the last century, and how has the state successfully hidden this public spending from view?"

## Why and How Growth?

*[We need] to make sure that people who can't afford health care have got
health care available to them in a common-sense way. And that's why I'm
such a big backer of expanding community health centers to every poor
county in America.*
                    —President George W. Bush, January 27, 2005, Cleveland, OH

Today, nearly 30 million people receive their health care from community health
centers (CHCs).[15] CHCs are nonprofit organizations that serve residents in
areas designated as "high need." They are built primarily with federal funding
from the Department of Health and Human Services (HHS), and receive most
of their operating revenue from public insurance (Medicaid) and state and local
governmental support. Given the CHC system's public financing, one may think
it is a residual, marginalized program. On the contrary, however, CHCs represent the country's most extensive primary care system. Although the CHC infrastructure received an increase in appropriations under the ACA, it was already
the largest primary care system before the passage of the ACA, with $7 billion in
annual expenditures.[16] CHCs started as a demonstration project in 1965, and although they were maintained over time, CHCs experienced their most dramatic
growth under the George W. Bush administration, when the number of delivery
sites tripled and the number of patients served more than doubled. At the 2000
Republican National Convention, Bush introduced his idea of "compassionate
conservatism." Support for CHCs fit perfectly into this ideology, but it was also
part of a larger pattern under the Grow-and-Hide Regime.

   Robert Mickey argues that this Republican support for CHCs was one component of "a longer-term strategy to build some government programs in order
to shrink other larger programs," such as Medicaid or the push for NHI.[17] This is
true. However, rather than comprising a new strategy, as Mickey suggests, I show
that investing in health care infrastructure and supporting segregated systems of
care emerges out of Grow and Hide, and is a very old bipartisan strategy. But,
first, we need to understand why growth occurs in the first place.

## Why Growth?

The American health care state began in the 19th century, with public health
as its answer to epidemic diseases such as cholera. Public health leaders were
called sanitarians, after their primary focus on sanitary reforms. Although there
were municipal boards of health prior to 1866, that year marked a major shift
because the Metropolitan Board of Health Act eliminated the patronage-linked
health boards and replaced them with a new board, run wholly by leaders with

expertise in sanitary science. The 20 years before this act was passed can best be described as a period of conflict between patronage politics and emerging scientific evidence. Of course, it wasn't just evidence from Europe—showing the importance of clean water and streets without excrement to limit the spread of disease—that eventually enabled the passage of sanitary reforms; it was also a growing coalition of business and civic leaders working in concert with public health leaders. In Chapter 1 I document this political story to illustrate how scientific evidence led to sanitary reforms, and to reveal how creating autonomous, scientific public health agencies—with minimal political interference—was significant in building the public health care state.

Although public health leaders tried repeatedly to use their scientific authority to create a unified health care system, they also used this same argument to disperse public health responsibility across government agencies and onto the private nonprofit sector, which ultimately—and ironically—undermined their scientific authority. In this early period, these nonprofit organizations—including foundations, associations, and local organizations that provided health and social services—were referred to as the voluntary sector, and this sector was central to the development of the American health care state. Understanding how growth occurred—decentralized and in close collaboration with the voluntary sector—is crucially important to understanding how that growth was structurally hidden in the years that followed.

In studying the early development of the public health care state, most historians focus on the role of sanitary and hygienic reforms based on germ theory. This is logical, because these reforms were transformative in reducing mortality and morbidity from a slew of diseases and epidemics common in the 19th century, such as cholera, yellow fever, and the plague. However, another critical foundational effect of the early public health care state was the development of health care infrastructure: hospitals and clinics. The state-voluntary collaboration, with strong business support behind it, played an important role in shaping the health care delivery system. While sanitary reforms provided improvements to population health, state-voluntary investments in the health care system were developed with explicit class and racial bias. A separate delivery system for the indigent was such a central part of the zeitgeist that an alternative was never seriously debated.

Public health leaders at this time were physician scientists who were also leaders in the American Medical Association, and who strongly supported state investments in public health. Even private practice physicians were largely supportive when public health focused on sanitation and hard-to-treat communicable diseases for which private practice had no cure, such as tuberculosis. Yet when the field of public health began to expand its boundaries around 1910 to provide not just preventive care but treatments, private practice physicians lobbied strongly against state involvement, marking the beginning of Grow and Hide.

## Why and How Hidden?

Initially, the main reason for hiding growth in public health investments was the threat of retrenchment (or even stasis) from forces opposed to public health expansions. As mentioned, the opposing force was mainly composed of private physicians who could convince some local, state, and federal politicians (depending on the bill) that such expansions would infringe on private practice. But the opposition was not against all forms of state activity; rather, they were primarily opposed to various forms of public insurance, compulsory insurance, and any expansion of public facilities to provide treatment beyond the indigent. However, because these physicians did support publicly funded treatment for indigents, where to draw the line—between the poor and nonpoor, or the needy and non-needy—was, from a medical perspective, always ambiguous. This ambiguity created the opportunity to hide growth through discursive strategies.

Moreover, even private practice physicians, who eventually took over the leadership of the AMA, supported expansions in public health for areas in which they were uninterested: population health (e.g., sanitation, vaccinations) and communicable diseases (e.g., tuberculosis, venereal disease). The AMA and the American Hospital Association (AHA) also supported infrastructure investments, namely building hospitals, which by the 1920s were considered essential for the practice of curative medicine, and there was widespread support for these aspects of public health.

The AMA was more skeptical when public health interventions moved into health promotion. They strongly supported public health responsibility for indigents and "complicated" cases, such as venereal disease and tuberculosis, but it was this delineating of which specific populations deserved public health (rather than private-sector medicine) that made the tactical framing of who exactly constituted these groups particularly important, and part of what made the government's reach so murky.

It's important to note that stakeholders—for example, business, labor, physicians, hospitals—and even more progressive leaders at the time all supported using the government to provide care to vulnerable and indigent populations. For example, even early advocates for compulsory health insurance argued that this form of insurance was most appropriate for workers and their dependents, whereas a separate system of care was needed for indigents.

***Voluntary Nonprofit Sector.*** As Morgan and Campbell's book *The Delegated Welfare State* describes, when government contracts with the private sector to deliver government-funded services, they delegate important responsibilities, but they also hide under private provision the true extent of the welfare state. Because the tie to the voluntary sector was so close in the early development of the public health care state, the distinctions between the public and voluntary sector were muddied from the beginning. When the government began to increase subsidies to the voluntary sector, the discourse emphasized the role and benefits of private provision, and was almost always silent on the extent of public funding behind this private provision. This process enabled the Grow and Hide approach.

***Federalism.*** Critical to the state's ability to grow and hide public provision is the American federal structure. First, arguing for a decentralized program where the federal government allows funding for local discretion was crucial to the founding of public health state-building, because it was consistent with a strong belief in federalism and its tie to classic liberalism. Because the rhetoric emphasizes local decision-making while saying nothing about the extent of state growth, this approach is promoted, ironically, as minimizing the role of government. Second, funding public health through a federal structure means there are public allocations at each level of government—federal, state, and local. But because the distribution of the costs is shared across government units, *total* public expenditures are hidden from view. Finally, most federal health funding to the states shifted over time to a shared financing approach, which created an additional incentive for growth—if states spent more, their share of federal dollars increased.

***Institutional Fragmentation.*** Because the boundaries of health and public health are quite elastic, and because there was no centralized federal department of health until the 1960s, as public health and health care programs grew, the administrative responsibility for overseeing and implementing programs was distributed across health and non-health agencies. This happened very early when the field of public health shifted from sanitation to a greater emphasis on communicable diseases, and public health leaders advocated for new departments of public health to shed their trash-collection responsibilities and shift them to departments of sanitation. While this practice started with public health, it continued with other more traditional health programs, so much so that by 1940 many states had nearly two dozen different agencies overseeing health care programs. Importantly, this fragmentation has only increased over time. When Medicare and Medicaid were passed in 1965, government reformers built on this complex and fragmented system; and when reformers passed the ACA in 2010, they did the same thing.

## Why Did Discursive Strategies to Hide Growth Continue?

*We've got to quit having the Federal Government try to micromanage health
care and instead set up incentives to the private sector to manage the costs.*
—President Bill Clinton, 1992[18]

My argument to explain the development of the American health care state is consistent with a relatively new wave of scholarship on the state that demonstrates significant state power and authority to intervene in almost every facet of American life.[19] To make this development clear, I provide empirical data about what the state has done at all levels of government over time, and concurrently analyze the statecraft used to define this action. I show how "volunteerism," "democracy," and "private innovation" were used as thematic triggers to encourage Americans' belief in their own political culture as classic liberalism. Ironically, as William Novak points out, assuring the American public's belief in classic liberalism has proven to be "ideologically central to the project of building the American state."[20]

When government investment in the health care system is called "investing in private innovation," as President Clinton did in 1992 while promoting his health reform proposal, it is important to recognize how this framing is done strategically—to increase the legitimacy of state authority and the power of the state to intervene.

Chapter 2 describes the early discursive seeds of Grow and Hide, in the 1910s, when the boundaries of the public health state began to expand, and when, in response to the subsequent opposition, the public health coalition put forth the argument that public health departments are *solely* concerned with population health and prevention, and are distinct from medical care. This process began an intellectual recognition among public health leaders that the distinction between prevention and treatment is a false divide. Nonetheless, in their rhetoric, these same leaders would—then and in the future—utilize the idea of this artificial divide to hide growth.

Chapter 3 focuses on discursive strategy around major health reform efforts prior to the 1930s, which included mobilization for compulsory health insurance, health centers, building hospitals, and other major policy recommendations from the Committee on the Costs of Medical Care (CCMC). A very important finding that helps illuminate why the United States never passed national health insurance relates to public health leaders' lack of interest in insurance reform. Many historians claim that public health leaders, especially those in the federal Public Health Service (PHS), were uninterested in compulsory insurance because they saw it as a turf issue that would undermine their authority. However, I argue that this telling misses a larger strategy at play.

Because public health leaders were central to the project of building the American health care state, and thus knew the true extent of the growth, they were hopeful that the public health care state could eventually create a unified, coordinated health care system. Under this unified system, prevention and health promotion would be valued and prioritized, and everyone would have access to care—if not exactly *equal* access, then access to *some* level of care. In other words, to these leaders, building up a National Health Program—as they outlined in the 1910s, in the CCMC report, and again in 1938—was a much more realistic and sound approach. Chapter 3 details their preference for this alternative strategy prior to the 1930s, and Chapter 4 shows this preference in relation to debates about compulsory insurance during the New Deal period from 1932 to 1940.

The public health leaders advocating for the National Health Program back in 1938 envisioned a federal oversight and coordinating role, administered by the PHS, that would eventually make the components of the plan work in harmony. Some voiced concerns about this incremental method, but the majority involved in the development of health policy at this time supported the National Health Program approach—implemented as separate components by all levels of government over a decade—because they also envisioned it to be more comprehensive and more attuned to improvements in the delivery system, and thus a better alternative to national health insurance. Often overlooked in historical debates about health care reform is the fact that further investment in "state medicine" (as it was called at the time)—where health services were provided essentially free (or heavily subsidized) at facilities funded by the government—was as much a legitimate policy alternative as NHI or voluntary private health insurance, if not more. Because National Health Program proponents envisioned significant government funding of hospitals to mean a public bed was available to a sick person when it was needed, even if the person was unable to pay, the argument for NHI was diminished. Understanding this debate is crucial because it reveals the incentives of public health leaders to continue to incrementally grow and hide the health care system, even when the system became more fragmented, and why they offered only tepid support for NHI.

## Grow and Hide Creates Interests to Continue Grow and Hide

Unfortunately, public health reformers did not foresee how such a fragmented and unequal system would empower private health care interests—especially the hospital industry—to hide government subsidies while blaming the government itself. Because government subsidies to the voluntary sector were largely hidden, voluntary health service organizations (most notably hospitals) were able to emphasize how their expertise, innovation, and even efficiency were—despite significantly higher prices—superior to public provision (such as public hospitals). As a result of this discourse, a uniquely American frame emerged, one that conveyed how significant public investment should be viewed as private. Chapter 5 documents how this frame emerged from the voluntary sector between 1940 and 1965.

Of course, actors who supported the government's role incentivized the government to reveal its public investments so it could claim credit for the subsequent benefits. At times when the political winds shifted toward more support for an explicit government role in the health system, such as Roosevelt's New Deal in the 1930s and Johnson's Great Society in the late 1960s, there were clear efforts among leaders in the public health coalition to reveal public expenditures and the benefits that emerged from those investments. In general, "grow and reveal" represented—during times when broader government reform (usually NHI) looked promising—efforts to argue that government action is not the scary socialist state the opposing actors claim it to be, because the government was already significantly involved in activities the American public not only accepted but desperately wanted, such as local hospitals and access to treatment. Indeed, Chapter 3 shows how public investment in public health and the health system was extensive by 1929, but already substantially hidden from view; Chapter 4 details rhetorical efforts during the New Deal period to reveal this growth.

But when NHI failed, as of course it did during the New Deal, these same state-building leaders would shift back to hidden, residual rhetoric about the role of government in health care. I offer three reasons to explain this reliance on hiding government. First, as described in Chapter 1, it begins with the origins of the public health movement, when physician-scientists and others mobilized for public health, they also fought against patronage control of health agencies, emphasizing the importance of independent scientific agencies and keeping politics out of public health decisions. Thus, as public health leaders were building their public agencies, they were very skeptical of government, due to years of fighting patronage politics and, in their view, repeated experience of "undue political interference." As a result, they also used antigovernment rhetoric to bolster the scientific reputation of their agencies, which—ironically—aided in concealing the role of government.

Second, these same public health leaders and liberal reformers repeatedly made calculated compromises, believing that incremental expansions were better than nothing, even if those expansions were labeled as private to establish state authority. And third, once the Grow-and-Hide strategy took hold, there were strong feedback effects, since public health leaders recognized that further hiding of government subsidies was a good strategy to protect the public subsidies already in place.

While the early compromises were logical, reformers reasoned that when the political winds shifted in their favor, they could advantageously expose government action to help support a more expanded comprehensive reform in the future. But again, what they underestimated was the degree to which private actors could embed the private frame into the American mind.

Hiding growth through private provision is not only politically useful to those favoring growth, but also to the private actors who benefit and then fight for a continued stake in the system. Because private provision increases complexity, private actors can use rhetorical gamesmanship to capitalize on and perpetuate public confusion. For example, the AMA and AHA used "socialism" and "state medicine" to argue against compulsory insurance. However, just as important, they and many other actors used tropes of classic liberalism—"volunteerism," "choice/freedom," and even "democracy"—to describe the health service system they received substantial public subsidies to build. While state actors were actively debating the meaning of hospital subsidies—whether subsidies for hospital construction, for example, should guarantee access to hospital care to all Americans—industry stakeholders were actively changing the language they used to describe the subsidy.

Part II (especially Chapter 5) details the impact of the postwar political backlash on health policy discourse, the rise of this "volunteerism" rhetoric used by private actors, and its impact on building the American health care state, namely significant public expenditures for private, voluntary provision. At first, hospital leaders aggressively sought state grants, and they publicly referred to this funding as supporting public beds or providing needed social benefits. Over time, however, as hospital administrators fought for reimbursement of nonpaying patients, they switched to calling this "charity care," even though they received extensive public subsidies for the care. As a result, the framing of public funding to private, nonprofit facilities shifted from "state medicine" (or "public beds" or "social benefits") to "funding for charity care" in private facilities.[21]

The strategies of private stakeholders were successful in redefining how Americans think about this public investment. Public funding for treatment and public investments in health care infrastructure did not change; what changed was how elites talked about it and the meaning they attached to it. When the public discourse changed, the vision for a National Health Program was lost. Grasping why this vision was lost is crucial to understanding the American Myth's origins and U.S. health policy today. Allowing the term "charity care" to become part of the national health care lexicon helps explain why hospitals in the United States still today indirectly receive public funding to provide services to the uninsured, yet claim they do not. The history of this strategic framing helps explain the absence of any regulation requiring hospitals to provide non-emergency services to uninsured patients, despite these subsidies.

Because government expenditures had by 1950 already increased significantly under an extremely fragmented and unequal system, the structure of this complicated system made it difficult to see the whole of government expenditures, even if one were specifically looking. In Chapter 6 (the end of Part II), I document how extensively the government's role was hidden under this peculiar health care state before 1965. I detail four main areas where the government's role was already ample and yet completely obscured: reporting national health expenditures as primarily private, the extent of medical treatment under the rubric of public health policy, government subsidies for hospital construction, and showing payments for the indigent as public and residual while hiding government's reach to the nonpoor. By 1960, the U.S. government had established, in deep collaboration with the voluntary sector, all the components of the American Myth.

## Consequences of Grow and Hide

Because the health programs passed under the Great Society built on this fragmented and unequal system, it continued to enable the Grow-and-Hide strategy led by the private sector. Elected officials and state agency leaders also often bolstered this voluntary, antigovernment frame by using the same language and providing data consistent with hiding the role of government. In Part III (Chapters 7 through 10), I describe the main consequences of Grow and Hide: fragmentation and the demise of health care planning, profiteering and the financial industry's takeover, and growing inequality while focusing on public expenditures to the poor.

### Fragmentation: The Failure of Health Care Planning

In 1966, during the early days of the Great Society, two planning acts were passed. Public health leaders were again hopeful that these acts would provide an opportunity for the government to plan and rationalize the U.S. health care system. However, because the planning acts also built on the Grow-and-Hide strategy—voluntary, local planning embedded in the private sector—and because the U.S. health care system was already extremely expensive, fragmented, uncoordinated, and unequal, such hopes were quickly dashed. When the largest health planning act in the United States—then and now—was passed in 1974, its ability to effectively plan this unwieldy system was considered dead on arrival.

As detailed in Chapter 7, the private hospital sector was extremely influential in designing the planning acts as voluntary, local, and without government authority, and yet when planning failed, they shifted the blame back on government and reified the planning acts as "government regulation."

## Profiteering: Hiding the Financial Industry's Takeover

By 1980, with the shift in power toward the Republican Party, there was a strong embrace of the "competitive approach." The crafted framing that government regulation in the 1970s had failed—and also the rise of capital markets in the U.S. health care system—enabled this approach. Starting in the late 1960s, government policy shifted from direct government grants funding capital construction for the voluntary hospital system to instead relying on the tax-exempt bond markets.

Chapter 8 explicates U.S. capital health policy from 1965 to 2008—just before the passage of the ACA. I document how public subsidies bolstered and encouraged the private sector's reliance on capital markets, and created an even more bifurcated health care system: the "have" hospitals that cater to private health insurance in more affluent, predominantly white communities secured high credit ratings with access to capital markets; and the "have-not" hospitals that suffered from low credit ratings without easy access to capital served the uninsured and Medicaid patients in less well-off communities that predominantly included people of color.

## Inequality: The Conspicuous Health Care Safety Net

Rather than change capital health policy, the U.S. government instead created more transparent subsidies to support the "health care safety net" (the term's emergence is a result of this bifurcation) while continuing to hide how public funding in health care supports the capital markets and the affluent connected to these markets. Even around 2000, when private equity firms entering the health care space raised concerns among policymakers about the demise of publicly funded health care infrastructure, a politically polarized government said little and did nothing.

Similar to dynamics described in Parts I and II, because the structural components of the health care system were the same—with a heavy reliance on federalism (across multiple levels of government), subsidies to the nonprofit sector, and administrative responsibility across multiple government agencies—the system enabled more Grow and Hide. But unlike the pre-1965 period, wherein the hospital industry and providers argued that they would rationally plan the health care system using the voluntary approach, in the post-1980 period, conservative policymakers and private sector leaders argued that the market, under competition, would best determine the composition of the health care infrastructure. While this raised some questions about public subsidies to the nonprofit sector, most public subsidies were hidden under the rubric of competition. And although the government's role behind significant health care expenditures to the private health care sector remained hidden and rarely discussed, I show in Chapter 9 how investments in the health care safety net were strategically made much more transparent by policymakers, and clearly labeled as public dollars at stake.

Most importantly, because Grow and Hide strategically feeds on fragmentation and inequities, the turn toward competition and capital markets in health care made fragmentation and inequities in the health care system even more severe. The politics of Grow and Hide creates a process whereby policymakers strategically reveal some subsidies while strategically hiding other forms of public funding. While the public discourse around conspicuous public expenditures to poor/low-income Americans reflects a commonly understood partisan divide—with Republicans typically fighting against expansion, and Democrats fighting to maintain or expand benefits—the debate itself contributes toward these expenditures remaining a major bipartisan focus on the political health care agenda. In contrast, from 1980 to the present, neither party has seriously debated capital health policy.

Similar to the Great Society, when health reformers passed the Affordable Care Act (ACA) in 2010, they also expanded coverage on top of the existing U.S. health care system. As a result, while 20 million Americans importantly gained coverage under the ACA, the logic of Grow and Hide was left untouched. I detail in Chapter 10 how the ills of this system perpetuate and deepen under the ACA: (1) capital health policy continues in an even more unregulated form, where private equity firms in the U.S. health care system have increased dramatically, taking advantage of public funding while remaining completely unregulated and hidden from view; (2) the conspicuous Medicaid program continues to expand for some and retract for others, building on current inequities; and (3) the ACA increases fragmentation as it continues to rely on voluntary planning with no real government regulation. That these three ills are allowed to fester and continue to grow and hide, helps explain why the American Myth is alive and well.

# PART I

# THE EMERGENCE OF A PUBLIC HEALTH CARE STATE

## 1860–1930

Although public health is an ancient science, the American health care state accelerated in the 19th century. Municipal boards of health existed prior to 1866, but that year marked a major shift away from patronage-linked health boards towards board's run by leaders with expertise in sanitary science. Scientific evidence helped produce this shift alongside a growing coalition of business and civic leaders working in concert with public health leaders. In Chapter 1, I document this political story, which highlights how the role of scientific evidence in state-led sanitary reforms, and the effort to create autonomous, scientific public health agencies—with minimal political interference—was significant in building the public health care state.

Three main factors are crucial components for understanding how the public health care state grew: (1) federalism, (2) a close collaboration between the state and voluntary sector, and (3) institutional fragmentation. American federalism explains why public health infrastructure developed in a completely decentralized fashion, and patronage politics explains why the public health coalition developed the public health care state in close collaboration with the voluntary sector. Chapter 1 establishes the importance of the state-voluntary collaboration for not only shaping public health but also the U.S. health care system and its strong dependence on private provision.

Chapter 2 describes the early discursive seeds of Grow and Hide, in the 1910s, when the boundaries of the public health state began to expand, and in response to the subsequent opposition from private practice physicians. This process began an intellectual recognition among public health leaders that the distinction between prevention and treatment is a false divide. Nonetheless, in their rhetoric, these same leaders would—then and in the future—utilize the idea of this artificial divide to hide growth. Specifically, the public health coalition argued in public discourse that public health departments are solely concerned with population health and prevention, and distinct from medical care.

Initially, the main reason for hiding growth in public health investments was the threat of retrenchment from forces opposed to public health expansions. However, even private practice physicians, who eventually took over the leadership of the AMA, supported expansions in public health for areas in which they were uninterested: population health (e.g., sanitation, vaccinations) and communicable diseases (e.g., tuberculosis, venereal disease). The AMA and the American Hospital Association (AHA) also supported infrastructure investments, namely building hospitals, which by the 1920s were considered essential for the practice of curative medicine, and there was widespread support for these aspects of public health.

The AMA was more skeptical when public health interventions moved into health promotion. They strongly supported public health responsibility for indigents and "complicated" cases, such as venereal disease and tuberculosis, but it was this delineating of which specific populations deserved public health (rather than private-sector medicine) that made the tactical framing of who exactly constituted these groups particularly important, and part of what made the government's reach so murky.

Chapter 3 focuses on discursive strategy around major health reform efforts prior to the 1930s, which included mobilization for compulsory health insurance, health centers, building hospitals, and other major policy recommendations from the Committee on the Costs of Medical Care (CCMC). A very important finding that helps illuminate why the United States never passed national health insurance relates to public health leaders' lack of interest in insurance reform. Many historians claim that public health leaders, especially those in the federal Public Health Service (PHS), were uninterested in compulsory insurance because they saw it as a turf issue that would undermine their authority. However,

I argue that this telling misses a larger strategy at play. It's important to note that public health stakeholders included not just leaders in PHS, but those business, labor, physicians, hospitals—and even more progressive leaders at the time all supported using the government to provide care to vulnerable and indigent populations. For example, even early advocates for compulsory health insurance argued that this form of insurance was most appropriate for workers and their dependents, whereas a separate system of care was needed for indigents. But, most importantly they supported publicly funded efforts to build the health care system as more important than investing in compulsory health insurance.

# A Conspicuous Public Health Care State

## Science, Federalism, and the Voluntary Sector

The public health care state has developed as completely decentralized, in collaboration with voluntary organizations, and under the banner of "nonpolitical" scientific agencies. The early history of this system explains how and why public health leaders were able to hide its growth in later periods. Understanding this foundational history is important for three reasons. First, the state-voluntary collaboration shaped the U.S. health care system, leaving it fragmented and unequal. Second, leaders in the public health coalition characterized the state's close collaboration with the voluntary sector as "private provision," abetting the beginning of the American Myth and setting the stage for Grow and Hide. And third, this formative history provides insight as to why the mixture of public and private "has been so ubiquitous in American history as to be almost invisible."[1]

## The Power of Science: Building the Public Health Care State

*This age of neglect, carelessness, and skepticism is rapidly passing away, and all over the country can be seen the outcroppings of a genuine faith in the efficacy and importance of sanitary regulations, manifested by the establishment of health boards.*[2]
—Hermann Biggs, Undergraduate Thesis, 1882

Few embodied the scientific imperative and political savvy behind the public health movement better than Hermann M. Biggs, chief medical officer of the New York City Health Department from 1902 to 1913, and commissioner of

*Grow and Hide*. Colleen M. Grogan, Oxford University Press. © Oxford University Press 2023.
DOI: 10.1093/oso/9780199812233.003.0002

health for New York State from 1913 to 1916. Born in 1859 in a small town on Lake Cayuga in upstate New York, Biggs completed a year of medical training at Bellevue Hospital in New York City and then graduated from Cornell College in 1882 with a medical degree. When Biggs graduated, major scientific breakthroughs in bacteriology were occurring. As a young student of science, it is perhaps not surprising that he was fascinated by the major scientific advancements of the day. What may be surprising, though, is the focus of his undergraduate thesis—"Sanitary Regulations and the Duty of the State in Regard to Public Hygiene"—in which he argued that the role of the state in public health was indispensable. Biggs's position, however, was not an aberration. All the leading American medical and sanitary scientists in the late 19th century were strong supporters of state-building for public health. There would eventually be a broader coalition of support, including the backing of the American public, but that took time to acquire.

## Physician Scientists versus Medical Sects

Between the cholera epidemics of 1832, 1849, and 1866, the American public's reaction to the importance of sanitation changed enormously. Cholera is a horrible disease marked by diarrhea, acute spasmodic vomiting, and painful cramps, and as the disease progresses, the afflicted person's face often turns blue and pinched, "his extremities cold and darkened, the skin of his hands and feet drawn and puckered."[3] In 1832, there was nothing the average physician from any medical sect could do to alleviate the pain and eventual death of a well-developed case of cholera. Few physicians, however, were willing to admit this. American medicine in 1832 was populated by multiple competing sects, and the three major medical sects— Regulars (or Allopaths), Eclectics, and Homeopaths—each portrayed their practice as the most effective and scientific, and they disagreed on how to treat illnesses and diseases. The average physician—regardless of the sect—was poorly trained and poorly paid. Virtually anyone could call himself a physician or healer and prescribe treatments and drugs.[4] Quacks of every description flourished during this time, and advertisements for cures and preventives were common (see Illustration 1.1). The medical historian Charles Rosenberg described this situation:

> The conflicting and uniformly unsuccessful modes of treatment followed by the medical profession shook an already insecure public confidence. Some of the poor and unenlightened hid their symptoms as long as they could, unwilling to trust themselves to a physician's care, while even the most credulous displayed an increasing skepticism toward the therapeutic claims of the profession.[5]

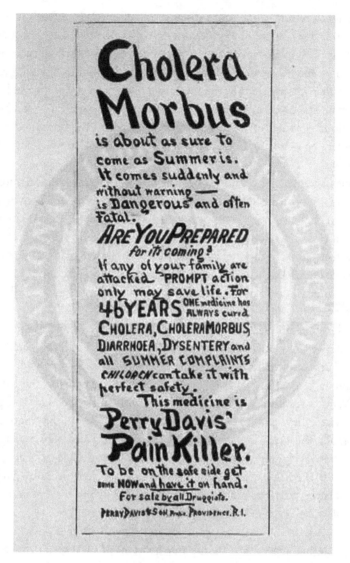

*Illustration 1.1* Example of Advertisements for Cures for Cholera, 1886. *Source: Harper's Weekly.* July 17, 1886. Website: https://virtualny.ashp.cuny.edu/Search/search_res_image2018. html?id=489.

Prior to 1832, the state did very little to fight against epidemics. Most of the leadership response came instead from ad hoc committees organized and led by members of the community. For example, John Powell's history of the yellow fever epidemic in 1793 describes a surrogate government run by a group of self-appointed public-spirited citizens.[6] Although municipal governments grew and became much more established by 1832, there was still a lack of evidence that sanitary reform would curb disease. So, although New York City, for example, did have a Board of Health, its members consisted of just the mayor and non-medical members appointed by the mayor. Even when medical experts became board members, they had no authority to follow through with administrative rulings. As Howard Kramer described in his history of the public health movement, the Board of Health "was a political body, [and] . . . proper sanitary precautions were left unattended."[7] As a result, when the board responded to the cholera epidemic in 1932, and again in 1949, its work was temporary and ineffective.[8]

British scientist John Snow's experiments during the London cholera epidemic of 1854 changed that perspective. His work provided convincing evidence that cholera is transferred person to person by infected fecal matter, which offered a clear set of solutions—most notably, adequate sanitary reforms for clean streets and a pure water supply. Despite these scientific solutions, it took nearly two decades fighting against political opposition and public apathy before the first landmark reform was passed in 1866—a comprehensive health law for New York City.[9]

While 1865 brought the end of the U.S. Civil War and the promise of peace, it also drew into sharp focus the alarming level of disease in America's crowded urban slums. Life-threatening diseases—including typhoid, dysentery, pneumonia, and tuberculosis—were a part of everyday life in the tenements. New York's streets were almost impassable with snow, ice, dirt, and garbage. Many large cities, such as Milwaukee and Providence, still had no water systems at all. The urban population in U.S. cities increased substantially in the 1840s: New York grew from 300,000 to 500,000, and Chicago from 5,000 to 30,000. By 1860, New York City grew to 800,000, and overcrowding in the tenements was a serious problem.[10] Nearly 20,000 people lived in underground windowless cellars.[11] As Kramer put it:

> In external appearance the poorer quarters of the typical American city presented a scene of utmost disorder, filth and confusion. Narrow, unpaved streets became transformed into quagmires when it rained. Rickety tenements, swarming with unwashed humanity, leaned upon one another for support. Inadequate drainage systems failed to carry away sewage, and outside privies bordered almost every thoroughfare. Slaughterhouses and fertilizing plants for their part contaminated the air with an indescribable stench.[12]

Proponents of sanitary reform saw ways in which government could solve the problem, but they faced political opposition, usually because the solution—scientific boards with authority—threatened valuable patronage. For example, in New York City, the health department was overseen by City Inspector Boole, who had no public health expertise and yet was given authority to hire all his subordinates. Again Kramer's description is helpful:

> These positions soon became patronage plums for Tammany Hall . . . the health wardens whose duties were to inspect and remedy unsanitary conditions in their districts were lowly henchmen without any interest in sanitation.[13]

As a result, sanitary-reform proponents focused their efforts on the state legislature. In 1857, the Academy of Medicine petitioned the state legislature to impose public health measures on New York City. While a bill that year was defeated, the following year the state senate appointed a committee of five prominent businessmen to investigate health conditions in New York City. The committee's report recommended a complete reorganization of the health department, replacing political appointments with public health leaders who were qualified physicians. Health bills that included these recommendations were supported by the newly formed New York Sanitary Commission and many business leaders, but were still defeated in 1859 and again in 1860.[14]

Nonetheless, mobilization around these bills helped create a broader coalition for public health reforms, causing concern among Tammany politicians. The New York Citizens' Association—a supporter of the "honest government" movement—was formed in the early 1860s, and also sponsored the Council of Hygiene and Public Health. The council included business leaders, philanthropists, and prominent sanitarians: Elisha Harris, Willard Parker, Stephen Smith, and Alonzo Clark. In response, the city inspector reorganized the Board of Health, adding some physicians as board members and as health wardens to work in free dispensaries in the tenements. However, as the sanitary conditions remained unchanged and even worsened—"the garbage and refuse [becoming] deeper by several inches"—even the city inspector had to admit that there was more filth and associated mortality, to "a point of fearful magnitude."[15] The Draft Riots of 1863 illustrated the level of discord emerging from the failure to improve conditions of tenement life.

In 1864, the Citizens' Association tried again, sending a committee to Albany to pass a health bill for New York City. At the hearings, despite his earlier admission, the city inspector denied all charges regarding the unsanitary conditions of New York City. So the Citizens' Association decided to conduct a survey, with photographs, to provide counter-evidence. Prominent sanitarian Dr. Stephen Smith was in charge of the survey, and presented its findings to the state legislature. The New York Times printed his testimony in its entirety, calling it "one of the most shocking pieces of reading" of our time. Smith testified that "house-slops, refuse, vegetables, decayed fruit, store and shop sweepings, ashes, dead animals, and . . . human excrement" covered the street "to the depth sometimes of two or three feet."[16]

Given this growing opposition, when the cholera epidemic came to New York's shores it was difficult even for the Tammany machine to ignore the helpful potential of sanitary reforms. This situation created a great deal of political pressure, and subsequently the Metropolitan Board of Health Act was passed in 1866.[17] The provisions in the new act were substantial: it eliminated the authority of the city inspector and all existing health boards. It created a new board comprising sanitary experts and four police commissioners to enforce the board's policies across New York City and the broader metropolitan area.[18] To public health reformers, this composition of the new board was critical. In working out the details of the ACT, proponents argued that a proper board of health should consist not of political appointees, "but of medical men trained especially for public health work." As the *Evening Post* put it, the public health bill was a reform in the "right direction," and should be run by "competent persons."[19]

Rosenberg argues that in the history of public health in the United States, there is no event more important than the passage of the Metropolitan Board of Health Act: "For the first time, an American community had successfully organized itself to conquer an epidemic. The tools and concepts of an urban industrial society were beginning to be used in solving this new society's problems."[20]

By all accounts, the board worked efficiently and effectively. In just eight months, the new health board issued and served 31,077 cease and desist orders, which allowed the board to remove 160,000 tons of manure from vacant lots, clean 4,000 yards, empty 771 cisterns, and disinfect 6,418 privies.[21] These sanitary reforms were able to keep the epidemic in check, and in 1866 the deaths per 100,000 population were significantly lower than in the previous cholera epidemics in New York City (see Table 1.1).

These results were very widely noticed, and—most importantly—the positive outcomes were attributed to the new board's work. The public credited the board with saving the city, and even Tammany politicians admitted that the board had proven itself honest and efficient.[22] In 1855, although physician-scientists leading public health boards believed in germ theory and theories of contagion, few private practice physicians did. But after the Metropolitan Board of Health's successful response to the cholera epidemic in 1866, even private physicians began to concede that the low cases of cholera were due to the work of the board, and they began to accept the work of sanitarians under state and municipal boards of health.[23]

The actions of the Metropolitan Board of Health were seminal because they showed the power of sanitary science to prevent disease—not through prayer

Table 1.1  **The Great Epidemics of New York City, 1800–1900**

| Year | Disease | Total Deaths | Deaths per 100,000 |
|------|---------|--------------|--------------------|
| 1832 | Cholera | 3,513 | 1,561 |
| 1849 | Cholera | 5,071 | 1,014 |
| 1851 | Dysentery | 1,173 | 221 |
| 1854 | Cholera | 2,509 | 395 |
| 1866 | Cholera | 1,137 | 113 |
| 1872 | Smallpox | 1,666 | 118 |
| 1875 | Smallpox | 1,899 | 125 |
| 1881 | Diphtheria | 4,894 | 266 |
| 1887 | Diphtheria | 4,509 | 226 |

Source: Wilson G. Smillie, Public Health: Its Promise for the Future (New York: Macmillan, 1955), p. 382. Original Source: Health Bulletin, New York City Department of Health, March 1953, p. 6.

and fasting, as had been done for years with no avail, but through disinfection and quarantine. Rosenberg calls it the "gospel of public health," because even preachers began singing the praises of sanitary medicine. For example, preachers would incorporate hygiene into notions of morality: "What opportunity is there of benefiting the souls of man, while their bodies are thus crowded and packed in such filthy abodes."[24] Given the influence of Christianity on popular belief systems, this new inclusive framing, ironically enough, helped produce not just elite mobilization for the public health movement, but public support as well.[25]

## Federalism and Spreading Boards of Health

The lesson of the Metropolitan Board of Health's work against the cholera epidemic spread quickly to other cities across the United States. After New York City, Chicago established a municipal board of health in 1867, and by the turn of the century most major cities had established health departments with budgets, staff, and significant duties. Nearly all city health departments across the country had professional staff: physicians, bacteriologists, chemists, sanitary engineers, statisticians, and public health inspectors.[26] A survey of municipal health departments conducted by the American Public Health Association in 1912 found that over 60 cities had health departments with programs to control contagious diseases. In addition, with revolutionary developments in microbiology, health department diagnostic laboratories proved invaluable in attacking diphtheria, scarlet fever, and typhoid. As a result, 25 cities invested in diagnostic laboratories and gave their local health department authority to run these laboratories. Moreover, in the majority of cities, health departments also had authority over inspection of general housing conditions and tenement house inspection.[27]

The most important force leading the legislative drive for municipal health departments was the American Social Science Association (ASSA). Formed in 1865 in Boston, it encapsulated the scientific imperative of the broader Progressive movement, whose mission was to "collect all facts, diffuse all knowledge, and stimulate all inquiry, which have a bearing on social welfare."[28] One of the ASSA's key objectives was to secure public health legislation to establish public health infrastructure to prevent disease. Its membership was wide-ranging: not just noted sanitarians and other scientists, but well-known politicians, clergy, philanthropists, and business leaders. As Swenson describes the ASSA, its "membership overlapped all segments of elite society."[29]

I do not mean to imply that municipal health departments sprung up with no opposition. As mentioned, patronage politics was widespread in American cities, and local politicians were not quick to give up coveted positions in city government. Just as the New York City story reveals, establishing scientific health boards run by sanitarians took time, persuasion, and mobilization. For example, it was not until the second outbreak of the bubonic plague in San Francisco that the newly elected mayor, Edward Robeson Taylor, who was also a physician and public health advocate, was able to reform the city health department and replace political appointees with public health professionals.[30] Moreover, the existence of new health departments did not mean there were never subsequent "intrusions" by local politicians. Indeed, such "political interference," as the public health leaders called it, was why they remained vigilant in their insistence that public health departments must be autonomous scientific agencies.

At the same time, there was a growing movement to establish state boards of health. By the time Biggs wrote his thesis in 1882, there were already 27 boards of health, and government investment in public health was building momentum. In 1869, Massachusetts was the first to establish a state board,[31] and the idea diffused quickly across America: in a short four years, four other states created boards (Louisiana, California, Minnesota, and Virginia); five years later, 10 more, and five years after that, another 12.[32]

The intent of these boards was straightforward: to coordinate activities across the state and centralize control. Most boards began as purely advisory to local governments, but they quickly assumed regulatory functions overseeing multiple aspects of public health.[33] Although many local governments opposed state boards due to their imposed regulatory functions,[34] municipal boards of health welcomed state boards because they often fought for increased funding to coordinate and expand local public health efforts.[35]

By 1905, every state in the union had established state boards with substantial administrative reach: (1) to regulate and oversee the training of local health officers and sanitary inspectors; (2) to establish uniform control of communicable disease by instituting reputable "scientific" quarantine procedures; (3) to create and enforce pure food laws; (4) to protect the purity of public waters; (5) to grant licensure of relevant medical professions and trades, such as pharmacists and physicians; and, (6) to collect vital statistics.[36] Health boards across the country also created "schools" and workshops to train sanitary personnel, and they instituted specific rules and procedures personnel must follow. For example, in 1905, New Jersey required all health officers and sanitary inspectors to pass an examination written by its state health board. As a result, the work of the state boards, and the scientific standards required to work as health officers and inspectors, created a new image of scientific authority over the field of public health.[37]

The establishment of municipal diagnostic laboratories marked a significant turning point in American public health state-building. The first laboratory in New York City was made possible by a $50,000 gift from steel magnate Andrew Carnegie.[38] At the opening of the Carnegie Laboratory on May 14, 1885, Professor E. G. Janeway's keynote address (published in the *Journal of the American Medical Association—JAMA*) argued for the necessity of research laboratories to "advance knowledge of the etiology of disease," and strategically mentioned how the German government's investment in medical research was far ahead of the United States:

> The German government has been very far-seeing in this matter, and has subsidized the study of disease. . . . The result of this course is, no doubt, familiar to you all. Germany has taken the lead in this matter, and students from all parts of the world have flocked to her institutions of study.[39]

Hermann Biggs, being in charge of the bacteriological work at Carnegie Laboratory, was able to appeal to the city (through its Board of Estimate and Apportionment) for an allocation of resources to establish the first municipal bacteriological laboratory in the world. The laboratory's purpose was to apply "bacteriological methods in the diagnosis of epidemic cholera and other infectious diseases."[40]

Not only did the laboratory start work on cholera, but Hermann Biggs's longtime friend and colleague, Dr. William Park, was appointed "bacteriological diagnostician of diphtheria," allowing the city to begin work on clinical diagnosis and surveillance of diphtheria as well.

Hearing about new advances in diphtheria, Biggs traveled to Europe in the summer of 1894, and, according to Dr. William Park, "while visiting Europe, [Biggs] heard the address of Roux and Behring on the use of antitoxin in the cure of diphtheria. He was so impressed that he called me to start the production of diphtheria antitoxin immediately."[41] Upon his return, Biggs quickly requested from the city Board of Estimate an additional $30,000 for the production, distribution, and administration of diphtheria antitoxin, which the city promptly granted.[42]

Just one year later, in 1895, the first antitoxin was produced by the New York Health Department laboratory, and it quickly became available for use and placed at the disposal of all hospitals in the city. Furthermore, diphtheria antitoxin was made available to the city's poor without charge. It is difficult to overstate the importance of the diphtheria antitoxin in reducing mortality. Prior to the introduction of the antitoxin in 1895, the diphtheria death rate was over 14 per 10,000 of population; by 1911 this had declined to a rate of 2.7.[43]

Besides its enormous impact on the city's ability to attack this disease, the antitoxin was also hugely important for public health state-building—it represented a critical turning point for showing the world that the United States could be a leader in state-supported scientific medicine. At the time, as Janeway's earlier quote illustrates, most of the advanced research in medicine was still being done in Europe (primarily in Germany).[44] All the great medical scientists of the day— William H. Welch, Hermann Biggs, William Osler—had spent their formative years studying there,[45] and after all, it was the German state that had invested in basic research to develop the diphtheria antitoxin.

Yet, despite the supposedly weak American state, it was across America's federalist system that the development of the antitoxin's application blossomed. Even the German scientist Robert Koch made a note of this. Koch wrote to Biggs that he was "delighted with the work [on diphtheria in New York and said the city was] far in advance of them in the practical management of the disease." In conclusion, he added, "you put us to shame in this work. I do not think the ministry will give us the appropriation required for similar work here, but I shall submit to them the circular on this subject issued by the New York City Health Department."[46] Indeed, establishing government-financed laboratories to diagnose and develop serums and antitoxins began to be viewed as necessary for effective public health work, and the idea quickly spread to other U.S. cities (and eventually to Europe). By the end of 1894, 11 cities were employing the bacteriological diagnosis of diphtheria, and in just a few years, almost every state and nearly all large cities had diagnostic laboratories.[47]

Nearly 30 years later, in 1924, Dr. Welch emphasized in his Sedgwick Memorial Lecture that Biggs's concept "that the public health diagnostic laboratory is an essential part of governmental health organization" was one of the two great sanitary contributions of America.[48]

## The Federal Role

The federal government played an important role in encouraging the development of a federally structured public health state. The Public Health Service was created when President John Adams signed the Act for the Relief of Sick and Disabled Seamen on July 16, 1798.[49] This act created Marine Hospitals to provide medical care to seamen, and to protect U.S. borders from infectious diseases, chiefly through quarantine and fumigation.[50] Prior to 1901, the Marine Hospital Service, which oversaw the Marine Hospitals, primarily served a military function—protecting soldiers and civilian health during wartime and running veterans' hospitals—rather than a federal government agency serving the public. As a result, the best sanitarians and bacteriologists of the 19th century— William Sedgwick, Rudolph Hering, L. H. Taylor, and Stephen Smith, to name just a few—were not part of the federal Marine Hospital Service, but instead served on state boards of health or headed municipal health departments.[51]

Describing the state of sanitary science in the federal government, social scientist William Allen wrote in 1899 that "there is absolutely no one whose business it is to look out for national health interests or to collect and publish national health statistics. In a word, we have at present no national sanitation."[52] Actually, a National Board of Health had been established in 1879, but in a classic story of political infighting, Congress discontinued the board a mere four years later. Most historians have overlooked this event because it is largely viewed as an example of the failure of Americans to create a centralized structure of public health care governance. While this is indisputably true—the United States did not create a centralized health care state—it is also true that this National Board, even though it was eventually dismantled, is an important example of public health care state-building.

The idea of starting a national public health bureau began almost immediately after the American Medical Association (AMA) created a Section on State Medicine and Public Hygiene in 1872.[53] At each of the AMA's annual meetings from 1874 through 1878, leading physician-scientists across the country actively debated the creation of such a national entity. At the time, there were only six boards of health established across the country. As a result, the leaders of this section were of two minds: one group thought a National Board of Health was premature because public opinion and state governments had not yet "been brought to full knowledge as to the indisputable benefits of sanitary initiatives."[54] This group thought it best to fully develop state health boards, believing a federal body would naturally follow. The other group believed the United States needed federal action immediately to spread "the life saving benefits" of sanitation and to more quickly and efficiently disseminate essential knowledge to states about how to set up state boards of health.[55]

Despite disagreement about timing, the consensus regarding the eventual benefits of a national bureau (or department) prompted the AMA to continue deliberations at the annual meetings regarding a national body's appropriate functions and organization. All members argued for agency independence so that it could function on purely scientific grounds and not be subject to the spoils of the patronage system.[56] Scientific independence was a prominent theme across all levels of administration—local, state, and federal—and was paramount among proponents in all their discussions regarding the role of government in developing the public health state.

While there was consensus about the need for autonomy to assure scientific authority, there was disagreement about which organizational structure would provide independence and sustainability. Among these physician-scientists, there was significant concern about the Marine Hospital Service's scientific integrity. At that time, the service was primarily focused on enforcing quarantine and running hospitals for sick veteran seamen; it did not actively incorporate new scientific thought, and it was part of the patronage machine. Especially in the eyes of these elite physician-scientists, the service was run by "inadequately trained, old-school physicians."

Those who were particularly concerned about the Marine Hospital Service lacking scientific rigor argued for creating a separate board of health that would report directly to the Treasury. Others, such as prominent public health leader and physician Stephen Smith, argued that the Marine Hospital Service should be combined with the Army and Navy to develop a new Department of Public Health. Notably, Smith understood the political power of state-building from the ground up. He "foresaw that Congress would lose interest in the National Board of Health, but would continue to support a service agency that had full-time career officers and was incorporated as an integral part of national government machinery."[57]

As it happened, the three existing national departments with medical officers—the Army, Navy, and the Marine Hospital Service—each claimed to be most appropriate to head up the federal charge. The Surgeon General, Dr. John M. Woodworth of the Marine Hospital Service, who designed the Public Health Service seal in 1872 (see Illustration 1.2), was the primary sponsor of a bill passed by the Senate to set up a Bureau of Health, which would include the Marine Hospital Service and use of its "official machinery,"[58] and would have a

*Illustration 1.2*  Seal of the US Public Health Service, designed by John M. Woodworth in 1872

director-general to act as a single head. Dr. John S. Billings, a surgeon in the U.S. Army, proposed an alternative bill that passed the House. This bill proposed the creation of a National Board of Health, to operate entirely independently of the Marine Hospital Service. Both men, who came from very different backgrounds, fought vehemently for the passage of their respective bills.[59]

Billings was considered a physician-scientist and had the backing of the American Public Health Association (APHA), the AMA, and many state boards of health.[60] In contrast, Woodworth had the support of many members of Congress and federal staff—the kinds of people who, according to physician-scientists at the time, let politics get in the way of science, and were not up to the task of running a national agency of sanitary science.[61]

As is often the case in public health history, a catastrophic event pushed the debate into action. When the yellow fever epidemic hit the Mississippi Valley states in 1878, its devastation—over 100,000 people were stricken, and 20,000 died—created widespread demand for federal action. The hardship galvanized the public to demand more of government to prevent disease and protect life, but elites also demanded government action to protect commerce. Especially given that this epidemic occurred not long after the Civil War, commerce in the northern states was much more prosperous than in the South, and state capacity to develop basic sanitation was much more accessible in the North. In contrast, sanitation in southern states was still extremely underdeveloped, and basic sewerage systems and adequate drainage were practically nonexistent. Northern commentators at the time pushed for federal action not just (or perhaps not at all) to help the sick in the South, but to help keep those sick from infecting the North and hindering economic prosperity: "Not only did the non-infected North contribute directly its millions [over $200 million] for the relief of the pest-ridden South, but indirectly it suffered still more because of obstructions to its commerce."[62]

All these factors emboldened the federal government to act, and in 1879 Congress passed the bill sponsored by the APHA and AMA to establish a National Board of Health, with Billings as its chair. The board consisted of seven physicians (each from a different state), and one representative each from the Army, the Navy, the Marine Hospital Service, and the Justice Department. The physicians were a distinguished group. For example, Dr. Henry Bowditch from Massachusetts was a pioneer in state health work; Dr. James Cabell, a professor from the University of Virginia; and Stephen Smith was a leader in New York City who was said to have "done more to advance the public's health than any man in the nation."[63] Ironically, because they favored the development of state boards first, these men had each played a prominent role in calling the establishment of the board premature, but Billings marched ahead nonetheless.[64]

While the National Board of Health was largely ineffective at stopping the yellow fever epidemic or securing quarantine in Louisiana, Billings instituted other measures that profoundly affected public health state-building. Billings received a massive increase in appropriations ($500,000) and spent four years building up a federal scientific structure for public health, which focused on the following four purposes: First, he created the original grant-in-aid system for public health work in the United States, using federal allocations to state and municipal health boards to develop and standardize public health work across the country. Second, he fought for *federal* control of the Quarantine Act. Third, he advocated close collaboration with all ports of the world. And, fourth, he recommended investigations of food and drugs.

Meanwhile, Surgeon General Hamilton was busy planning the board's demise. Just a few days after the Board of Health bill passed, Surgeon General Woodworth collapsed and died. While the cause of death was unknown, Dr. John B. Hamilton, who took over Woodworth's position, insinuated that the conflict with Billings caused Woodworth's death. When answering questions of the Public Health Committee in Congress four years after the death, Hamilton said:

> Doctor Woodworth's death was the result of persecution . . . he was hounded to his grave by some of the same "sanitarians" who became the temporary beneficiaries of that cessation of opposition.[65]

In stark contrast to Billings's endless résumé of responsibilities and leadership roles in government and the scientific community,[66] when Hamilton took office he had no national experience. Instead, he had worked his way up the

Marine Hospital Service ladder as a career officer, primarily working for Marine hospitals in various states. Public health leaders quickly pointed out that he had no "official" sanitary or public health training and was not even a member of the American Public Health Association.[67] Because of his background, the scientific leaders of the new National Board of Health did not take him seriously as a leader, and certainly not as a potential foe. This—combined with the four-year clause for the board's renewal—turned out to be a grave mistake for the board's proponents, since Hamilton was an astute political and administrative strategist.

Although Hamilton had no formal public health training, he understood the steps necessary to operate a federal public health department. Ironically, the initiatives he started in the Marine Hospital Service were the same developments Billings put in place at the National Health Board. Understanding this allowed Hamilton to extinguish the fire behind arguments that a separate national board was needed. For example, when Billings requested an increase in appropriations for the board, Hamilton testified in front of a congressional committee against the board's renewal, based on the argument that the Marine Hospital Service was already doing that which Billings was requesting. To win back the powers of the Marine Hospital Service, Hamilton expanded its role to encompass the 19th-century domains of public health—sanitation, bacteriological research, and the dissemination of standards across the American states. However, thinking ahead, he also incorporated the work of elite physician-scientists:

> Relative to what Dr. Billings says about cholera germs, I desire to invite the attention of the Committee to the Weekly Abstract published a few weeks ago, in which the diagnosis of cholera was made of the cases that occurred in New York, by an officer of my service by the name of Kinyoun, who has spent nearly five years in the study of bacteriology. We have spent several hundred dollars in forming a laboratory in New York, and the diagnosis was made by Drs. Armstrong and Kinyoun, with Dr. Biggs at the Carnegie Laboratory. Full accounts were published in the medical journals.[68]

Hamilton knew he had to increase the scientific stature of the service for it to gain power. Note how he strategically developed relationships with leading physician-scientists of the day, and was quick to highlight these collaborations in his testimony. Ultimately, he argued effectively that the board was duplicative and that it no longer had a monopoly on scientific authority. When Congress subsequently eliminated the National Board of Health, the Marine Hospital Service regained and expanded its powers.

For example, where the National Board dealt with a diverse set of state and local quarantine laws and regulations, in 1893 Congress gave the Marine Hospital

Service full responsibility for foreign and interstate quarantine. Under this new federal mandate, the service emphasized cooperative relationships with state health departments.[69] Building on the work Hamilton mentioned in his testimony, in 1887 the service established a hygienic laboratory at the marine hospital on Staten Island in New York to apply new principles of bacteriology in studying disease across the United States. As official government documents describe its evolution, "this cradle of medical research in the Public Health Service quickly proved its worth, and before the turn of the century, its activities were transferred to headquarters in Washington," and became the National Hygienic Laboratory.[70]

With these new developments, President Theodore Roosevelt increased federal involvement even further from 1901 to 1909. Consistent with the support he'd given earlier in New York, Roosevelt continued to be a major supporter of public health efforts, and he appropriated more funding to prevent the spread of epidemic diseases.[71] In 1901, Dr. Walter Wyman, Surgeon General of the Marine Hospital Service from 1891 to 1911, secured $35,000 in appropriations from Congress to build the Hygienic Laboratory, which resided under the service's new Division of Scientific Research. Dr. Milton J. Rosenau was appointed the director of the laboratory, and several bacteriologists were immediately employed to conduct experiments to determine the cause of yellow fever and other diseases. One year later another law was passed, which changed the title of the Marine Hospital Service to the Public Health and Marine Hospital Service, clearly signaling the federal government's intent to protect the health of the public, not just the health of veterans and military personnel. That same bill increased the scope of the Hygienic Laboratory and appointed an Advisory Board, anointing the laboratory with prestige and scientific authority to advance medical research and, more broadly, to establish authority over infrastructure-building for the United States health care system.

Professor William H. Welch of Johns Hopkins University served as chair of the Advisory Board from 1902 until 1932. Welch was one of the most influential men in American medicine and public health during this time. He started the first school of public health, also at Johns Hopkins, and was one of the elite physician-scientists who believed in a robust public health care state. He was a student of the famous Dr. Robert Koch of Germany, and his writings mirrored those of Biggs:

> It is to be deplored that our National Government has had so little share in this important movement in public hygiene. This Association (APHA) has advocated a plan by which the various states may secure aid from the National Government for the support of public laboratories of hygiene analogous to that in operation in the case of Agricultural Experiment Stations, and it seems to me very desirable

that this or some similar plan should be adopted. Then we are all agreed that our government should have a central sanitary organization in connection with which a laboratory of public hygiene should be established. We can now appeal as never before to the furtherance thereby of commercial interests, a motive which seems to be more efficacious with our legislators than the lives and health of human beings, possibly even more than the welfare of cattle.[72]

Other members included Professor William T. Sedgwick, sanitary engineer, of the Massachusetts Institute of Technology; Professor Victor C. Vaughan, of the University of Michigan, Ann Arbor; Professor Simon Flexner from the University of Pennsylvania, who had headed the plague inquiry for the national government; and Professor Frank Westbrook, who taught pathology and bacteriology at the University of Minnesota.[73] Like Welch, all these men were leaders in public health, medicine, and science, and all advocated for a strong public health care state, which meant departments with autonomy and scientific integrity.

## A Federated Marriage: Public Health State and the Voluntary Sector

The image of Alexis de Tocqueville's 19th-century America—a mobilized mass public enthusiastically engaged in volunteer activities creating a rich and vibrant civic life—may invoke a more idealized notion of America than the nation ever really lived up to.[74] However, voluntary organizations did flourish in the 19th century, and, as time progressed, nowhere was their activity more pronounced than in public health.[75] While the diversity of voluntary organizations belies any airtight categorization, one can usefully think about their development as falling into four main types: (1) private foundations that funded public health initiatives; (2) federated professional associations—such as the American Public Health Association—with local, state, and national offices; (3) federated disease-based organizations, such as local, state, and the National Tuberculosis Association; and (4) community-based service organizations—such as district nursing associations—that rendered direct services.[76]

Although each organizational type played a unique role, they worked together in coalitions to conduct fundraising efforts, develop health programs, build health care facilities, and help the government take on an expanded public health role.[77] There were also powerful business interests behind the state-voluntary public health movement that helped fund many local initiatives, and then pushed for federal action to support widespread dissemination. Importantly, this state-voluntary collaboration worked in concert with the American federal system. At every governmental level—local, state, and federal—there were corresponding voluntary organizations that helped build the public health care state.

## Tuberculosis and Federated State-Building

In 1892, Dr. Lawrence F. Flick and his associates organized the Pennsylvania Society for the Prevention of Tuberculosis to mobilize the public around disease prevention. The success of their efforts spread, and other states also began creating similar voluntary associations. Ohio started a tuberculosis society in 1901, and New York followed suit in 1902. As the number of state tuberculosis associations grew, the question of national coordination became particularly pressing, especially when multiple local associations proposed to represent the United States at the 1904 International Congress on Tuberculosis in Paris.[78]

Dr. S. A. Knopf, a physician-scientist who studied tuberculosis (and much more), published a letter in the *Journal of the American Medical Association* (*JAMA*) calling the two proposed American congresses unsuitable for proper scientific representation, and argued for one national tuberculosis congress to represent America.[79] Prior to publishing the editorial in JAMA, Knopf sent the letter privately to scientific leaders of the field—including William Osler, then a professor of medicine at Johns Hopkins Medical School, and Dr. Edward Janeway, professor of medicine at Bellevue Medical College in New York City— asking for their opinion on the matter. Since these men would be the ones to control the new national congress, there was, unsurprisingly, unanimous agreement that only one congress should represent American medicine and that it should be "composed of good men from each state," lest the conference "be a disgrace to American medicine."[80]

Per Knopf's suggestion, in January 1904 the most prominent medical men from around the country were invited to a conference in Baltimore, with Professor William Welch as chairman. They elected William Osler to head up the committee to represent the United States in Paris. They vowed to create a "United States Society of the Study and Prevention of Tuberculosis," with Dr. Livingston Trudeau as the association's first president, and Osler and Biggs as vice presidents.

Once the National Tuberculosis Association was fully established in 1906, it began to focus on developing state and local associations and standardizing its activities across the United States. In particular, the association offered standardized educational materials at the local level, instructions on appropriate tuberculosis procedures and treatment, and standardized regulations for Tuberculosis quarantine.[81] Between 1904 and 1916, increased appropriations were granted every year at all levels—cities, counties, and states. By 1915, all states had active associations.[82]

Several foundational aspects of the development of state tuberculosis associations are noteworthy. First, the same scientific imperative necessary for the spread of state and local health boards helps explain the spread of local and state tuberculosis (TB) associations. Although the TB associations mobilized the public, the physician-scientists started and led the associations—especially at the national level—and used their status to imbue the movement with scientific integrity. In New York City, for example, Biggs was the first to sign the charter creating the Committee for the Prevention of Tuberculosis, which was part of the Charity Organization Society of New York and eventually renamed the New York Tuberculosis and Health Association.[83] The other nine signers were similarly among the most prominent scientific physicians in the city.

Second, while the tuberculosis associations were instrumental in conducting mass education campaigns and mobilizing the public, these organizations were funded by prominent civic leaders with significant ties to the business community. Within just two weeks, an appeal for donations to support the work of the New York TB Association raised a total of $5,000.[84] When scientific leaders were forming the National Tuberculosis Association and wanted to expand its influence, they could tap into the public health network. At the turn of the 20th century, the vast majority of foundations—backed by wealthy philanthropists—supported local health efforts. The Carnegie and John D. Rockefeller Foundations invested massively to reorganize American medicine, subsidizing research to speed the advance of science, creating public health programs to eradicate disease (especially in the South), and building schools to establish a public health workforce.[85] Indeed, during the first third of the 20th century, the largest U.S. foundations allocated nearly half their gifts to health causes and institutions.[86]

Due in part to the amount of money they gave and the elite network within which they operated, foundations had a significant influence on health policy during this early formative period. The Rockefeller Foundation was particularly active in the South, working with local health departments and the PHS to eradicate disease epidemics.[87] While wealthy philanthropists were often the public face of a foundation (e.g., Andrew Carnegie, John D. Rockefeller), those actually administering the funds and running the programs were usually the same public health leaders working in government or universities.[88] They moved between positions—working for a foundation and moving into government, or working for the government and consulting for multiple associations and foundations.

For example, when the New York Board of Health wanted to revise its sanitary code in 1904, it appointed a special commission whose membership included the following physician-scientists: William Osler and William Welch of Johns Hopkins University, Frank Billings of the University of Chicago, John Musser of the University of Pennsylvania, Theobald Smith of Harvard, Edward

Janeway of Bellevue Medical College, and T. Mitchell Prudden and Emmett Holt of Columbia University and the New York College of Physicians and Surgeons. All these men held office positions in the AMA and the APHA, were appointed to the National Tuberculosis Association, worked with the Rockefeller Foundation on numerous studies, were appointed to advisory commissions associated with foundations such as Milbank Memorial Fund and the Carnegie Foundation, and consulted with the federal and state governments. It is important, too, to note the AMA's support for the government's role in public health during this early period. The editorials in *JAMA* clearly stated this preference, and in an illustration on the cover of *JAMA* in 1912, the editors depicted the government as public health's protector against death by disease (see Illustration 1.3).

All of the major public health leaders worked with foundation staff as consultants or as directors of research. For example, William Welch—was a member of numerous boards and commissions established by the Rockefeller philanthropies. Simon Flexner was director of the Rockefeller Institute for Medical Research, and Abraham Flexner worked as an investigator and executive, first for the Carnegie Foundation for Higher Education and then for the Rockefeller Foundation. Working through philanthropic foundations, these men had an enormous impact on the development of the health care state. As medical historian Daniel Fox put it, "the closest analog to the Ministry of Health in the United States was the philanthropic foundation."[89]

The third foundational effect was the realization by scientific and civic leaders that the mass public could be mobilized around particular diseases. Biggs, for example, started a massive tuberculosis educational campaign in New York City, distributing leaflets in multiple languages designed to reach different ethnic groups, and, through lectures and exhibitions, using media to mobilize support for the work of the health department.[90]

Lessons from TB campaigns were used to mobilize for other diseases, such as the distribution of the diphtheria antitoxin. For example, the *New York Herald* conducted a campaign to raise money for antitoxin treatment for the poor. The *Herald* put in $1,000, and several other major donors in the city contributed, as well as many middle- and working-class people who had lost a loved one to diphtheria. One letter to the *Herald* read:

> Please accept $1.00 for your antitoxin fund from a father who lost a dear boy, five years old, and his baby girl, two years old, inside of one week from the dreadful diphtheria.[91]

In 1907, the TB Association started the now-famous Christmas Seals fundraising campaign. That first year it raised a phenomenal $3,000, and is known as one of the first efforts to raise money from the public around a single disease.[92] These early

*Illustration 1.3* Cover of Journal for American Medical Association, 1912. *Source:* JAMA, 1912, vol. 6.

efforts created an impression that disease-based voluntary organizations did not receive public funding, but instead received their funding from foundations or charities.

These foundational effects are important because the impact of TB associations on the U.S. health care system did not end with tuberculosis. The growth of voluntary groups in the United States around specific diseases was enormous and unique. Europe had a few disease-based organizations, but no where near the size and influence to those found in the United States.[93] These disease-based associations, eventually called National Health Agencies, emerged out of the public health movement and were often led by same physician-scientists running other voluntary organizations (e.g., associations and foundations). They worked in concert with local, city, and state health departments. As a result, the establishment of numerous disease-based associations happened quickly: the American Cancer Society was founded in 1913, the National Committee for the Prevention of Blindness in 1915, the American Society for Hard of Hearing in 1919, the National Society for Crippled Children in 1921, the American Health Association in 1924, and the list continues.[94]

In sum, disease-based associations were able to spread quickly across the United States due to the strength of the public health network: the scientific authority of physician-scientists, the moneyed power of foundations, the support of voluntary organizations to carry out the work, and a mass public that confirmed its importance. And the public health care state grew largely because there was an active coalition of powerful actors that supported the voluntary sector and collaborated closely with all levels of government to increase the state's role in public health.

## Federated Marriage Shapes the Health Care System

In 1904, the National Tuberculosis Association specified four main objectives for building "the best delivery system" to prevent and treat tuberculosis:

1. **Research.** Research into the social, as distinct from the medical, aspects of tuberculosis. For example, into the relations between the disease and overcrowding, infected tenements, and unhealthy occupations, and also into the influence upon recovery of improved diet and hygienic living.
2. **Education.** The publication of leaflets and pamphlets, the giving of lectures, and promulgation in every possible way of the fact that tuberculosis is a communicable and *preventable* disease; the *widest distribution* of the results of *scientific research* in this field, and of the results of modern *treatment*, both in sanatoria and at home.
3. **Building Facilities.** The encouragement of movements for suitable *public and private sanatoria*, both for advanced and for incipient cases; for adults and for children; for *free care and also for the care of those who can pay moderate fees.*
4. **Indigent Care.** The relief of indigent consumptives by the provision of suitable food and medicine, by the payment of rent when this is necessary to secure adequate light and air, and by transportation and maintenance at a distance, when, in the judgment of the Committee, this is essential.[95]

While the National TB Association initially set these objectives, their application was not restricted to tuberculosis. Rather, these objectives set the stage for how the public health state, and its impact on the delivery system, would grow and expand more broadly.[96] Objective number one signaled an attempt to distinguish its role as separate from curative medicine. Thus, while this group called for a significant increase in research funding to study the medical aspects of tuberculosis, they also wanted funding to understand the social aspects of disease. Even in this early period, the movement advocated for understanding the potential impact of personal hygiene (diet and lifestyle behavior) on disease. Moreover, this first objective—investing in research—became a foundational notion of what government *should* do for American medicine.[97]

Second, investing in educational campaigns was widely supported as necessary to improving individual health and maintaining a healthy state. Voluntary health organizations pursued educational campaigns with a central purpose to instill in the American mind a sense of responsibility for one's own health.[98] In this way, the voluntary health movement prodded the government to increase public funding and simultaneously promoted a conservative ideology of individual responsibility.

Objectives three and four—government investment in building facilities and providing indigent care—are critical because they succinctly define the role of public and private actors in developing the health care delivery system. These objectives develop a logic and argument for government investment in the health care system—specifically to build hospitals (or sanatoria for the care of tuberculosis)—while at the same time detailing access to care according to individual means: tax-supported public facilities for the poor and voluntary-sector facilities for the masses referred to within the objectives as "persons of moderate means." In sum, the public health network promoted these four objectives, which served to shape how the U.S. health care system approached the question of indigence and access to medical care.

While the establishment of local tuberculosis associations spread rapidly across the country—from less than 30 in 1904 to 1,500 in 1919—so too did the infrastructure (outlined in objectives three and four) to treat the disease. In 1905, there were 32 tuberculosis dispensaries and 96 sanatoria and special hospitals in the United States. In 1914, just nine years later, there were 400 dispensaries, 550 sanatoria and special hospitals, and 250 open-air schools.[99] The federated structure of the National Tuberculosis Association, working in partnership with the federated public health care state, was key to advocating successfully for infrastructure investments at the state and local level.

In Wisconsin, for example, tuberculosis legislation was enacted practically every year starting in 1903 through 1915 (see Table 1.2). The *American Journal of Public Health* credited the Wisconsin Anti-Tuberculosis Association for

*Table 1.2*  **Tuberculosis Related Legislation in Wisconsin, 1904–1916**

| Year | Jurisdiction | Appropriation & Purpose |
|------|--------------|-------------------------|
| 1903 | State | Commission to study sanatorium feasibility |
| 1905 | State | $2,000: Print & distribute Commission Report |
| 1905 | State | $25,000: Establish state sanatorium |
| 1907 | State | $30,000 Construction<br>$40,000 Maintenance |
| 1907 | State | Reporting regulation mandating physician reporting of cases |
| 1909 | State | Permanent livestock board established |
| 1911 | State, County | Authorize counties to establish sanatoria<br>$20,000 per year to aid county sanatoria; established a payment rate of $3.00 per week per indigent patient |
| 1913 | State, County | Amendment to county sanatorium law raising state aid to $5 per week providing the appropriation of $50,000 per year |
| 1913 | State, County | Authorize counties to appropriate money for visiting nurses; salary and expenses taken from liquor license funds |
| 1913 | State | Vacuum cleaners only for dry sweeping of public buildings |
| 1913 | State, County | Compulsory commitment after careless consumptives |
| 1913 | State | Camp for convalescent consumptives established on state forest reserve; charge of $3.50/week |
| 1913 | State | County and city boards can employ visiting nurses |
| 1913 | State | Board of Health; no one with tuberculosis can attend schools (except open-air schools) |
| 1913 | State | Proper disposal of sputum required |
| 1913 | State, County | County board of supervisors authorized to establish an institution to treat TB. |
| 1913 | State | Provision for segregation, care, and treatment of insane TB patients |
| 1913 | State | Use of common drinking cup in public places prohibited |
| 1915 | State, County | State aid raised to $100,000 for first year, $125,000 for second year<br>Incipient and early-stage also to be cared for |

*Table 1.2* **Continued**

| Year | Jurisdiction | Appropriation & Purpose |
|------|-------------|-------------------------|
| 1915 | State, County | Care of indigent person should be paid for by the county of his or her residence, not the county of the institution |
| 1915 | State, County | Counties are authorized to band together to build a sanatorium; expenses will be shared, with the treasurer from the sanatorium's county managing funds for construction and maintenance |
| ? | City (Lacrosse) | Public nurse with assistants who visits and treats when possible; examination of sputum and sputum cups are free |
| ? | City (Madison) | Board of Health regulation requires disinfection of premises |
| 1905 | City (Milwaukee) | City prohibits spitting; maintains TB sanatorium; 5 TB dispensaries; 1 open-air school; 9 visiting nurses; free examinations of sputum; distributes literature, sputum cups, food, clothing, etc. |
| 1910 | City (Oshkosh) | City prohibits spitting; maintains TB sanatorium; 1 open-air school; 1 visiting nurses; free examinations of sputum; aids very poor patients |
| ? | County, City (Racine) | County maintains sanatorium; 2 open-air schools; 1 visiting nurse; free examination of sputum |
| 1910 | City (Superior) | Anti-spitting ordinance; TB included on list of infectious diseases to be reported; $7,000 appropriated for a TB hospital |

increased appropriations at the state, county, and municipality levels to fight tuberculosis. Editors of the journal wrote that "it might be mentioned that largely through [the Wisconsin Anti-Tuberculosis Association's] efforts $153,666 have been appropriated ... since last June."[100]

Moreover, the objectives of the National TB Association—education, hospital and clinic construction, and funds for indigent care—are evident in the progression of legislation in Wisconsin. The state began by studying the feasibility of constructing sanatoria, and it established the first state-owned sanatorium two years later. In 1907, the state approved funding for maintenance and additional construction of sanatoria. By 1911, the state had established formal grant-in-aid relationships with counties to build sanatoria, as well as a formal reimbursement scheme for the poor ($3.00/per week per

indigent). In addition, Wisconsin wrote into state legislation the specific language and treatments advocated by the National Tuberculosis Association
concerning the different types of consumptives—"careless," "convalescent,"
"incipient," and "insane"—a move emulated by other state legislatures across
the country.

New York City also invested heavily in tuberculosis infrastructure-building.
In 1911, appropriations increased by $231,000, and the city built eight new
clinics staffed with 34 staff physicians and 137 tuberculosis nurses. The incorporation of government funding for both public and voluntary organizations was advocated as the "most efficient" approach.[101] As a testament to
state sanitarians' support for this state-voluntary partnership, the Executive
Committee of the State Charities Aid Association's Committee on Tuberculosis
and Public Health wrote, upon Biggs's death, that "Dr. Biggs saw the whole
field of public health in due proportion and appreciated the necessity of the
fullest participation by both public and voluntary organizations in the local,
state and national fields."[102] Indeed, the list of organizations that passed special resolutions in honor of Biggs upon his death—from government agencies,
foundations, voluntary service organizations, and voluntary disease-based
associations—provides a perfect illustration of the state-voluntary coalition
(see Table 1.3).

In this way, the voluntary sector—along with the financial backing of wealthy
philanthropists and bureaucratic support—shaped the early contours of what
became the public-private health care state. This specific "public-private" delivery model distinguished between patients according to the severity of their
medical condition, their demographics (age, gender, and often race), and their
financial means. In addition, each hospital type had particular case requirements.
For example, "incipient cases" should be the most severely quarantined, whereas
"ambulant early favorable cases" were considered most appropriate for "work
hospitals." While the appropriate facility for particular conditions was discussed
in scientific terms, the actual decision and logic were often based on notions of
welfare deservedness rather than science. "Work hospitals," where patients were
assigned some form of work in return for services rendered, were supported for
"early favorable cases" under the argument that these patients could more easily
integrate back into the labor force upon discharge.[103] Moreover, patients were
often segregated according to demographic characteristics—most notably by
race, but also by gender and age—and an investigation of the financial condition
of patients was conducted to determine eligibility.[104] Health departments used
public health nurses to determine financial eligibility, and in this way they used
public health providers to act as gatekeepers to publicly funded medical care.[105]

Importantly, it was not just tuberculosis care for which this model was
advocated and developed. The same pattern was replicated across various

*Table 1.3*  **Example of a Public Health Network: The Group of Organizations That Adopted Special Resolutions upon the Death of Hermann Biggs**

*Quasi-Public: Independent Commission/Committee*

1. Public Health Council
2. International Health Board
3. National Committee for Mental Hygiene

*Foundations*

4. Board of scientific directors of the Rockefeller Institute
5. Advisory Council of the Milbank Memorial Fund

*Scientific Committees, Provider Groups, Voluntary Health Agencies*

6. Council of New York University
7. Society of Alumni of Bellevue Hospital
8. Advisory Council of the Henry Phipps Institute
9. Board of Directors of the Tuberculosis Preventorium for Children
10. Committee on Nursing of the Henry Street Visiting Nurse Service
11. Directors of Stony Wald Sanatorium
12. Alumni of Bellevue Hospital Medical College, Class of 1888

*Voluntary Associations*

13. American Social Hygiene Association
14. Board of Directors of the New York Tuberculosis Association
15. Executive Committee of the State Charities Aid Association's Committee on Tuberculosis and Public Health
16. Executive Committee of the National Tuberculosis Association
17. Board of Directors of the National Organization for Public Health Nursing
18. Executive Committee of the New York Association for Improving the Condition of the Poor

*Source:* C. -E. A. Winslow, The Life of Hermann M. Biggs, M. D., D. SC., LL D., Physician and Statesman of the Public Health (Philadelphia: Lea & Febiger, 1929).

diseases as each diseased-based voluntary association developed a federated structure and attached itself to the public health care state.[106] These diseased-based associations favored the same objectives as those for TB: states investing in research, education, building facilities, developing personnel, and expanding treatment for the indigent. As a result, there was a ready-made interest-group infrastructure across the American states. This board-based coalition advocated for government investments in the different disease-related functions of public health, and for access to preventive and curative health services to stave off their particular disease.

## The Federal Role

The tuberculosis movement was successful at federated state-building in part because the federal Public Health Service (PHS) continued to expand during this same time. In 1912, all three major political parties—Republican, Democratic, and Progressive—called for an increase in funding to uphold the work of public health.[107] Given this widespread support, it is not surprising that the PHS was established that same year. Dr. Rupert Blue was chosen as the new Surgeon General to lead this newly organized and expanding agency. His goals for the PHS mirrored the four objectives specified by the National TB Association.

First, the PHS emphasized education and standardization across the United States. It used federal funds as incentives to work with local and state health departments on the implementation of proper public health methods for particular diseases. For example, soon after his appointment, Surgeon General Blue took steps to address the severe malaria problem in the South. He started investigations in 1912, and by 1920 the disease was practically eliminated in many sections of the South. While the PHS provided education and training to the local authorities to eliminate malaria, systematic segregation and racism prevented complete eradication, and the disease continued to disproportionately impact Blacks in the South.[108]

Second, the PHS took immediate steps to work with foundations, voluntary organizations, and local health departments to implement programs in the South and across the country. The implementation of programs entailed administering funding for building health care facilities and providing preventive and curative care to those who could not afford services.

Third, the federal PHS also began conducting numerous nationwide research studies. In 1914, for example, the PHS collected information to determine the sanitary conditions in factories throughout the United States. When unsanitary conditions were found, the PHS made recommendations and worked with factories, so remedial measures were taken. And in 1917, appropriations were increased to $300,000 ($5.6 million in 2010 dollars) to further this work.[109] Moreover, additional appropriations were made to the Hygienic Laboratory in Washington, DC, to expand research on improving and informing public health work.

Finally, and most importantly, it was clear that the PHS supported a decentralized public health care state. Blue defined the federal government's role in health administration in an article he wrote for *JAMA* in 1912 as improving "state and local health agencies, in the extension of their powers and the increase of their appropriations."[110] He also pleaded for mutual dependence between government and the medical profession, which would encourage standardization.[111] The PHS began in earnest to establish ties with state and local governments to create standardization of local and state health departments across the country. There is ample evidence of these efforts—from the PHS's publication of its *Public Health Notes* encouraging local departments to follow specific "proven" and standardized procedures, to almost every issue of the *American Journal of Public Health* (*AJPH*), published by the American Public Health Association, filled with articles providing information about local practices and documenting the need to establish uniformity. In 1912, the *AJPH* reported on a survey of city health departments, and concluded with meticulous recommendations of precisely how health departments should be organized, with a detailed diagram of hierarchical roles within the department, their jurisdiction, what staff were needed, and what their pay grade should be.[112] Importantly, the PHS supported these standardization efforts by the APHA and provided the same recommendations in their documents for state and local dissemination.

The National TB Association used the newly structured PHS to advocate for federal legislation to create a special PHS Division of Tuberculosis in 1919. The association advocated and essentially wrote the bill for a new division of tuberculosis assistance within the federal government. It worked closely with PHS staff and had the support of the Surgeon General.

In its letter to Congress supporting the Tuberculosis Division, the National TB Association made four main arguments. First, private efforts alone are insufficient, and the need for government investment is paramount. Second, members of the association are the scientific leaders of the country, and therefore have authority to speak and should be selected to serve on the TB advisory council (as specified in the bill). Third, the Federal Division should not replace the TB Association and its federated structure, but should provide authority and rank over state efforts. Finally, they reiterated their four-pronged approach: that they primarily support federal research and dissemination of information, but nonetheless praise the efforts of state governments to invest in TB hospitals and programs and care for the indigent. They argued that TB programs should be implemented by local tuberculosis associations, working in concert with clinics and hospitals—some public, some private—to assure access to care.

All four arguments were successfully written into the legislation for a new federal TB Division within the Public Health Service. The creation of the division increased government funding, but it was clear that the distribution of this funding would go to state and local governments to support the development of a mixed state-voluntary system. Moreover, the structure of the division married the federated efforts of the public health care state and the voluntary sector.

Following the National TB Association's lead, other disease-based voluntary associations copied its approach, and over time several disease-specific divisions with the same structure emerged within the PHS. For example, the American Cancer Society, established in 1913, eventually secured a Cancer Division within

PHS. The Venereal Disease Association developed the PHS Division of Venereal Diseases in 1919. Similar to TB, public funding for Cancer and VD increased substantially after Congress created the federal divisions. The Chamberlain-Kahn Act, which created the VD Division, appropriated $1.2 million to control venereal disease, to be used in cooperation with the states and voluntary organizations.[113]

## Conclusion: A Federated Marriage Sets the Stage for Grow and Hide

Some have said that the relative success of public health state-building is due to its population-based approach and its rejection of class-specific policies.[114] While public health clearly had some population-based goals, such as fighting epidemic diseases, this definition of public health as solely focused on population health is based more on the profession's own strategic telling of history than on reality. The public health movement including scientist physicians, municipal officials, businessmen, and civic leaders, to coalesce under the banner of sanitary science. While this coalition shared concerns about the indigent, they usually advocated for separate solutions.[115]

Indeed, the development of health care facilities along strictly segmented categories had important implications in developing the U.S. health care delivery system. This network of public-health reformers supported a separate system of care for the indigent and people of color, and, for the rest of the population, reliance on the voluntary sector. To this day, the U.S health care system relies on a separate delivery system for the poor. Moreover, the focus of the voluntary sector on specific diseases helps explain the fragmented nature of growth. And this peculiar state-voluntary coalition also planted the seeds of grow-and-hide: the voluntary sector expanded disease by disease due in large part to the provision of public funds; however, because the voluntary sector was not considered government, the role of the state was hidden.

While the focus on sanitation and bacteriology in the late 1800s and early 1900s increased health departments' scientific authority and widespread acceptance, its next move into the treatment of communicable diseases and personal hygiene raised numerous questions about the state's proper role. As the state-voluntary coalition continued to push the boundaries of public health into new realms, they were confronted with growing opposition from physicians who were particularly worried about state infringements on private practice. This opposition did not result in a dismantling of state and local health departments, or even long-term retrenchment, as many have suggested, but instead marks the beginning of the grow-and-hide strategy.

# Expanding Public Health Boundaries

*The old public health was concerned with the environment, the new is concerned with the individual. The old sought the sources of infectious disease in the surroundings of man; the new finds them in man himself. . . . The new public health seeks these sources—and finds them—amongst those infective persons whose excreta enter, usually by the mouth, the bodies of other persons.*

—H.W. Hill, 1912[1]

The passage of New York's Metropolitan Board of Health Act in 1866 marked the beginning of significant state investment in building public health infrastructure with relatively little opposition, at least until the early 1910s. While private practice physicians raised concerns about state reporting requirements and about the development of new serums and antitoxins that the state was advising them to use, they were not well organized, and in this early period they did not have the support of the American Medical Association. As state-building continued after 1910, and as the definition of public health began to change and the boundaries of public health expanded, conflict emerged on two fronts.

First, as certain forms of sanitation, such as garbage collection, became more widely understood and practiced, local politicians saw an opportunity to use such positions for political favor. As garbage collection began to consume an ever-larger proportion of health department budgets, the influence of local politicians increased, so public health leaders wanted to separate garbage collection from what they now claimed were more legitimate scientific activities of a municipal health department. This shifting of some public health activities away from the health department to other government agencies helped to bolster public health's mission to maintain scientific authority and independence from political interference. But its separation also marks the beginning stage of institutional fragmentation in public health, and as both the "old" and "new" forms of public health continued to grow, it became one mechanism of Grow and Hide.

*Grow and Hide*. Colleen M. Grogan, Oxford University Press. © Oxford University Press 2023.
DOI: 10.1093/oso/9780199812233.003.0003

Second, as public health expanded to consider the health of individuals—as the quote from Hill notes—this necessarily moved public health into the domain of medical treatment. As this happened, private practice physicians emerged as a key opponent of what they called "state medicine." The term "state medicine"—though typically deployed as a negative—was used *very* carefully in writing and public policy discourse, because state medical societies and the AMA were not against *all* forms of state medicine. Instead, they wanted to draw a clear line to distinguish between public health and private practice. Determining where and how to draw this line is where tensions emerged.

The purpose of this chapter is to document how public health state-building continued amid this intense and growing opposition. Two crucial rhetorical devices were used to placate the opposition: (1) claiming that state public health efforts were within the accepted domain of prevention—not treatment; and (2) claiming that when health departments or publicly funded voluntary agencies provided treatment, such care was only extended to the indigent. When public health activities included treatment (not just prevention) for groups beyond a narrow definition of indigency, their efforts were hidden through the same structural mechanisms that established the public health care state: (1) reliance on a combined federated public health and voluntary sector, and (2) using intergovernmental financing. These efforts to hide public health care's expanded reach are the original seeds of Grow and Hide.

## Institutional Fragmentation Builds a New Public Health

Sanitation, in particular waste collection and disposal, was one of the most important public health activities of the 19th century. However, as its function became viewed as so essential and basic for local governments, and as new knowledge pushed the field toward focusing instead on communicable diseases, public health leaders sought to shift the responsibility of sanitation out of local health departments so they could make the case for building a new modern public health department. Over time, as sanitation became more popularly known as garbage collection, few still conceive of this occupation as public health. However, if we hold on to these original functions of public health, we can clearly see the extent of state-building, and—at the same time—we see a part of the Grow-and-Hide approach at play: because administrative authority and budgetary allocations were often diffused across multiple agencies, the real growth in public health has been hidden.

A Public Health Service report summarizing budgetary allocations in Toledo, Ohio, in 1914 provides an excellent illustration of this point.[2] If we just look at

*Table 2.1* **Budgetary Allocations for "Ordinary Maintenance" Toledo, Ohio, 1915**

| Department | Allocation Amount | |
|---|---|---|
| | 1915 dollars | Percent of total |
| Service | $157,442 | 36.1% |
| Safety | 205,364 | 47.0 |
| Health | 21,201 | 4.9 |
| University | 10,663 | 2.4 |
| Library | 2,885 | 0.7 |
| General | 16,183 | 3.7 |
| Parks and Boulevards | 19,445 | 4.5 |
| Hospital Purposes | 3,513 | .8 |
| **Total** | **$436,697** | |

*Source:* Carroll Fox, *Public Health Administration in Toledo*, USPHS, Reprint No.284, *Public Health Reports*, June 25, 1915 (Washington DC: Govt. Print. Off., 1915), 61.

allocations to the health department, city investment in health appears meager, at about 5% (see Table 2.1). However, looking more closely at the report reveals much larger support. First, the largest and most basic function of public health is sanitation, and that was administered in Toledo by the Department of Service. Garbage collection, street cleaning, and comfort stations received a budgetary allocation of $157 million—a whopping 36% of the city budget.

Second, special appropriations to address epidemic diseases were reported separately. For example, when there was a smallpox outbreak in 1914, the health department was given an additional $46,350 in emergency expenditures—over twice the amount of the department's annual appropriation—to treat and contain the spread of the disease. Third, budgetary allocations for hospitals ($3,513) were also reported separately, even though the administration of hospitals was under the health department.

This process of unbundling the functions of the health department and folding them into other line items or under the authority of other city departments was a common practice across almost all large- and medium-sized cities. While street cleaning came under the jurisdiction of health departments in all cities during the 19th century, by 1912 only one city's health department—that of Louisville, Kentucky—still did this work. In many cities (about 20) the Department of Public Works took on street cleaning, while in other cities it fell to the Engineering

Department, Highway Department, Sanitary Department, or various other departments.[3] Similarly, by 1912, the 19th-century "public health" task of removing dead animals from city streets remained under the control of the health authorities in 48 cities, but in the remaining U.S. cities it was delegated to other departments. And we find the same pattern for waste collection and disposal: it was handled by health departments in 28 cities, the Department of Works in 11 cities, and under other department titles in the remainder.[4] What this means is that while state-building for public health had expanded dramatically by 1910, its various tasks were already diffusing across multiple levels of government and different agencies within the same level of government, making its growth difficult to track.[5]

Shifting sanitation tasks out of municipal health departments was advocated by public health researchers. Carroll Fox, a researcher from the federal Public Health Service, conducted numerous studies of public health administration across U.S. cities,[6] detailing existing organizational patterns but also making recommendations for reform based on the thinking of public health leaders at the time. Fox wrote that the sanitary inspector should "devote his entire time to the elimination of those nuisances which are really important from a public health standpoint, such as surface privies and surface wells, accumulations of manure, and mosquito breeding centers, and to the enforcement of the requirement that householders provide themselves with garbage cans."[7] Fox clarified that the new public health officer should, in contrast, focus on elimination of communicable diseases by overseeing public health nurses, school health programs, child welfare stations, dispensaries, the municipal laboratory, and the collection of vital statistics.[8]

While shifting old public health functions out of the health department allowed public health leaders to argue for a new vision of what public health departments should do, it also allowed leaders to argue that too little was allocated to public health relative to other city functions. For example, in 1915, when Fox documented and compared city health departments across the country, he wrote:

> The amount received by the school department is over 55 per cent of the total budget of the city. While this amount is not too much, considering the work done by the public schools, it is mentioned to emphasize the proportionately small amount allowed for public-health purposes.[9]

Interestingly, the Toledo Health Department received a substantial increase after the smallpox outbreak and lobbying efforts—$42,400 in 1915, up from $24,840 in 1914.[10] Nonetheless, the department—and Fox's report—argued that this increase was insufficient: "The increase has been very helpful, but considering the large organization necessary to adequately handle all of the public health problems more money is needed."[11]

This method of reporting these new functions as part of the "true" health department budget became standard practice. Administrative standardization was pushed by public health leaders starting in the 1910s, and it continued well into the middle of the 20th century.[12] The Russell Sage Foundation was one of the first foundations to provide funding to understand the status of health department work, by conducting a survey of municipal health departments across the country. This study surveyed 227 cities that had populations greater than 25,000 in 1913.[13] The first set of questions on the survey asked about the department's annual appropriation. Although the total appropriation was reported, the researchers argued that many expenditures were of "no special hygienic significance" and should be deducted from the total so that "the remaining expenditure should represent with considerable accuracy the amount devoted to *actual preventive* measures."[14] Items considered inappropriate to incorporate into municipal health department budgets included "hospitals and sanitoria; plumbing inspection and street cleaning; the removal or disposal of dead animals, refuse, garbage, or night soil; and any other unusual undertakings."[15] What were once standard operating procedures were now discussed as "unusual undertakings."

Yet the amount spent for these unusual undertakings was substantial. In the New England, Mountain, and Pacific states, it represented nearly half of total expenditures (see Table 2.2). This is significant because although health

*Table 2.2* **Health Department Appropriations: Total and "Corrected," 1913**

| Group of States | Cities Reporting | Aggregate Population (in 1,000s) | Appropriation | | |
|---|---|---|---|---|---|
| | | | Total (in 1,000s) | "Corrected" (in 1,000s) | Ratio of "corrected" to total |
| New England | 39 | 3,344 | $1,585 | $939 | 59.2% |
| Mid-Atlantic | 55 | 11,541 | 5,847 | 4,716 | 80.7% |
| South Atlantic | 17 | 1,853 | 786 | 601 | 76.5% |
| East North Central | 44 | 6,717 | 2,142 | 1,656 | 77.3% |
| West North Central | 17 | 1,850 | 467 | 358 | 76.7% |
| East South Central | 8 | 852 | 330 | 267 | 81.1% |
| West South Central | 9 | 838 | 299 | 230 | 77.0% |
| Mountain | 5 | 463 | 307 | 164 | 53.4% |
| Pacific | 12 | 2,029 | 1,392 | 718 | 51.6% |
| Total | 206 | 29,488 | $13,156 | $9,651 | 73.4% |

*Source:* Franz Schneider Jr, "A Survey of the Activities of Municipal Health Departments in the United States," *American Journal of Public Health*, 6, no. 1 (January 1, 1916): 1–17. Table on p. 4.

departments still provided sanitation and built and maintained hospitals and sanitoria (and clinics), in official reports of health department activities this work was hidden. For example, although the total and "corrected" appropriations were both reported in the first table of the article published in the *American Journal of Public Health*, all remaining tables showed only the corrected (or "true prevention") appropriation.

This was the first step in what proved to be a decades-long project, with backing from the American Public Health Association (APHA), the federal PHS, and financial support from major foundations, as well as collaborations with private business through the U.S. Chamber of Commerce and with officials from the Metropolitan Life Insurance Company.[16] In essence, the public health network and the most prominent public health leaders were in full force behind this effort to standardize and embed the new public health.[17] The APHA established the Committee on Municipal Health Department Practice in 1920, and the federal PHS provided a full-time staff member, Dr. Lewis Thompson, for 10 weeks of field work, as well as five PHS staff located in various regions around the country.[18]

The APHA viewed the work of this new committee as essential not only for standardizing activities across health departments in the United States, but also for determining appropriate health department budgets, including adequate salary levels.[19] Dr. Haven Emerson, a member of the committee and commissioner of New York City Health Department, presented a "standard budget" at the annual APHA meeting in 1919, which was also published in the *American Journal of Public Health*.[20] Similarly, Dr. Ernest Meyer published "Methods for the Defense of Public Health Appropriations" in 1920.[21] Shortly after the committee was constituted, the APHA proclaimed that its work was the most important priority for the association,[22] and formally adopted the committee's recommended objectives for the study of public health administration:

> The objectives of the Association should be the preparation, study, standardization, and presentation of scientific public health procedures, the best method by which such knowledge can be given to the public, and the expression to the public of professional opinion in regard to such procedures.[23]

Noteworthy in this statement are the phrases "scientific public health procedures" and "knowledge . . . given to the public." Leaders of the public health network knew that leveraging their scientific authority and disseminating their message to the public would be crucial in their efforts to increase investments in public health. Although an increase in investments was never their stated objective, appropriation data was collected, and every report concluded that appropriations needed to be increased to insure the public's health.[24]

In 1923, when the Committee on Municipal Health Department Practice completed its first study of health department expenditures in 83 cities across the United States, *Time* magazine published an article summarizing its findings. *Time* noted in the article's lead sentence, "Fifty-one and six-tenths cents ($0.52) per capita is what the average American city of 100,000 population or more spends on health—that is, for strictly defined health services, and not including hospitals, morgues, sewerage and sewage disposal, garbage and refuse disposal.*" The asterisk in the article explains that "[t]hese functions are, of course, essential to public welfare, but should not legitimately be charged against a modern health department." Note that the removal of these functions allows the same type of advocacy evident in 1915 in Toledo and in the 1916 report of municipal health departments. The *Time* magazine reporter compared on a national scale the average city's health expenditures with other city-service expenditures: "It lavishes $6.11 on education, $1.88 on highways, $1.56 on fire prevention, $1.28 on police protection. And this expenditure for health purposes, parsimonious though it looks, increased 95% on the average between 1910 and 1920."[25] This is Grow and Hide in action: reporting significant growth and frugalness at the same time.

Particularly noteworthy is how the committee's assessment of an appropriate per capita figure for a "modern department" changed rapidly. In 1915, the committee set the figure at 50 cents.[26] Yet when the average American city reached this goal in 1923 (adjusting for inflation), this was not hailed but rather highlighted as again inadequate.[27] Indeed, a year later, in the committee's write-up of an "Ideal Health Department" for a city of 100,000 population, it advocated for four times the average allotment ($1.95 per capita).[28] This is not unusual behavior, but common practice across policy domains and within departments and agencies; it is nevertheless important to see the strategy and statecraft across the federated public health network increasing expenditures at the local level.

But why was this Grow-and-Hide argumentation pursued? One might logically conclude that agencies with large budgetary allocations became more powerful and would therefore not want to rescind their control over multiple functions. But public health leaders at the time viewed the issue differently. Not only did large budgets make their arguments of "limited government and only prevention" less legitimate, but worries about patronage politics loomed large. Public health scientists saw the inclusion of basic sanitary functions as compromising their claims to scientific superiority.

Public health researcher Wilson George Smillie noted in his 1955 book on the historical development of public health administration that when a large part of the local health department budget was allocated to sanitation, and a great proportion of its personnel were employed as street cleaners and nuisance abators, the inevitable happened: "the health department fell into the hands of politicians."

> It was generally recognized that a political retainer who was *too stupid* to be appointed as a policeman and *too awkward* to be a good fireman, could at least be utilized in the sanitary department as a street cleaner, and thus add to the voting strength of the party in power. For this reason, garbage and waste disposal became more and more a center of political intrigue, with the result that the health department was subjected to strong political pressure which forced it to employ *incompetents* and *laggards*.[29]

Himself a trained public health scientist, Smillie's description of why sanitation "fell into the hands of politicians" is telling. There is plenty of evidence that sanitation's growth was associated with patronage politics, and this political problem was of grave concern to the leaders of the public health movement.[30] And as this function became a larger part of the health department's budget, it became increasingly difficult to claim reputational uniqueness as a highly skilled scientific department. Indeed, as new techniques to deal with waste were developed, cities continued to increase their investments in garbage services. The increases over a very short time were striking: In 1869, Milwaukee had no separate line item for garbage disposal expenditures; just 10 years later, garbage costs consumed 34 percent of the department of health's budget. By 1902, when a municipal plant was built and needed to be maintained, garbage monopolized the health department budget at nearly 70 percent. At this point, there was a push to shift the responsibility for garbage from the health department to the department of public works.[31] Milwaukee, as well as other cities, shifted this function to a separate agency. Looking at the growth in Milwaukee Health Department expenses—a 343% increase from 1910 to 1920—using "corrected" appropriations seems to have been a good strategy. Indeed, despite *Time* magazine's report of parsimony (and as the increase in per capita spending suggests), every city the committee surveyed increased its public health expenditures between 1910 and 1920; 24 cities increased their public health budgets over 100% during this time period (see Table 2.3).

By 1923, most cities had moved the responsibility for garbage disposal out of their municipal health department. However, for those that had not (19 of the cities surveyed), the Committee on Municipal Health Department

*Table 2.3* **Per Capita Public Health Expenditures Average Increase from 1910–1920 by City, in Rank Order**

| City | Average Increase |
|------|------------------|
| Bridgeport | 104.9 |
| Yonkers | 93.9 |
| Flint | 88.2 |
| Pittsburgh | 81.3 |
| Savannah | 76.3 |
| Jacksonville | 74.8 |
| Salt Lake City | 73.4 |
| Detroit | 72.3 |
| Buffalo | 71.4 |
| Milwaukee | 69.8 |
| New York | 69.0 |
| Newark | 67.3 |
| Syracuse | 66.3 |
| Jersey City | 65.5 |
| Memphis | 64.7 |
| Seattle | 63.4 |
| Rochester | 62.9 |
| Grand Rapids | 61.5 |
| San Diego | 61.2 |
| Dallas | 59.2 |
| Akron | 58.2 |
| Schenectady | 57.8 |
| New Bedford | 54.5 |
| Baltimore | 53.1 |
| Toledo | 52.9 |
| Tacoma | 52.3 |
| Los Angeles | 52.2 |

*Source:* "Medicine: Health is Purchasable," *Time*, October 1, 1923.

*Table 2.4a*  **Health Department Expenditures for Garbage Disposal, 1923**

| City | Expenditure | Per Capita (cents) |
|------|-------------|--------------------|
| Albany (1924) | $30,225.00 | 25.8 |
| Allentown | $22,732.90 | 26.1 |
| Bridgeport | $174,871.00 | 121.5 |
| Duluth (1924) | $17,355.00 | 16.4 |
| Kansas City, Mo | $136,400.00 | 38.8 |
| Lawrence | $255,805.27 | 262.5 |
| Lowell | $47,562.66 | 41.3 |
| Oklahoma City | $66,875.00 | 66.3 |
| Omaha (1922) | $82,821.82 | 40.5 |
| Pittsburgh | $1,377,000.00 | 222.0 |
| Providence | $90,933.34 | 37.5 |
| San Francisco | $3,701.20 | 0.7 |
| Seattle | $77,010.93 | 151.0 |
| Tulsa | $40,000.00 | 39.2 |
| Waterbury | $27,383.00 | 27.8 |
| Wichita | $35,304.42 | 44.6 |
| Wilmington | $69,730.00 | 59.3 |
| Worcester | $5,589.50 | 2.9 |
| Youngtown | $24,382.63 | 16.2 |

*Source:* United States Public Health Service and American Public Health Association, Committee on Administrative Practice, *Municipal Health Department Practice for the Year 1923* (Washington, DC: Govt. Print. Off., 1926.

Practice was again careful in its own accounting to separate out these expenses (see Table 2.4). Several cities were similar to Milwaukee, where the per capita expenses for garbage collection were substantial (e.g., Pittsburgh, PA; Lawrence, KS; Seattle, WA) and overwhelmed the other services public health officials wanted to highlight as more truly essential to a modern health department.[32]

The public health network—not just municipal health departments and physician-scientists, but business and voluntary groups as well—were also in favor of this standardization effort. The committee was renamed the Committee on Administrative Practice (CAP), since it no longer only focused on municipalities. And the Metropolitan Life Insurance Company continued to

*Table 2.4b* **Health Department Expenditures for Hospitals, 1923**

| City | Expenditure | Per capita (cents) | City | Expenditure | Per capita (cents) |
|------|-------------|--------------------|------|-------------|--------------------|
| Akron | $13,100.00 | 6.3 | Milwaukee | $90,141.44 | 31.3 |
| Albany (1924) | $2,240.00 | 1.9 | New Bedford | $96,078.91 | 18.6 |
| Atlanta | $13,031.28 | 5.9 | New Orleans | $19,673.49 | 73.5 |
| Baltimore | $47,442.44 | 6.1 | New York | $1,760,473.68 | 4.8 |
| Boston | $15,964.72 | 2.1 | Norfolk | $9,401.60 | 29.7 |
| Bridgeport | $64,029.00 | 44.6 | Oklahoma City | $11,170.00 | 5.9 |
| Cambridge | $51,888.19 | 46.7 | Omaha (1922) | $16,879.00 | 11.0 |
| Camden | $52,000.00 | 41.8 | Paterson | $53,124.59 | 8.2 |
| Chicago | $325,641.94 | 11.2 | Peoria | $14,928.58 | 38.0 |
| Columbus | $10,706.87 | 4.1 | Pittsburgh | $207,917.39 | 18.7 |
| Dallas | $21,100.00 | 11.6 | Portland | $27,556.47 | 33.5 |
| Denver | $18,480.00 | 6.8 | Rochester | $41,527.87 | 10 |
| Des Moines | $696.00 | .5 | St. Joseph | $9,327.33 | 13.1 |
| Detroit | $877,766.00 | 88 | St. Paul | $6,193.00 | 2.6 |
| Duluth (1924) | $24,980.00 | 23.6 | Salt Lake City | $7,534.00 | 6.0 |
| Elizabeth | $15,008.59 | 14.4 | San Diego | $27,045.64 | 31.1 |
| El Paso | $14,105.84 | 14.7 | San Francisco | $912,269.05 | 169 |
| Erie | $7,950.00 | 4.2 | Schenectady | $6,405.56 | 6.5 |
| Evansville | $3,214.16 | 7.1 | Scranton | $17,341.11 | 12.3 |
| Fall River | $36,000.00 | 3.5 | Seattle | $274,899.34 | 87.0 |
| Grand Rapids | $115,910.00 | 29.8 | Somerville | $18,000.00 | 18.2 |
| Hartford | $72,631.00 | 79.2 | Spokane | $25,294.19 | 19.0 |
| Indianapolis (1924) | $373,024.00 | 47.8 | Springfield | $53,170.33 | 36.8 |
| Jersey City | $625,259.00 | 108.7 | Syracuse | $51,637.50 | 28.0 |
| Kansas City, Mo | $748,573.16 | 202.1 | Tacoma | $14,245.00 | 14.0 |

(*continued*)

*Table 2.4b* **Continued**

| City | Expenditure | Per capita (cents) | City | Expenditure | Per capita (cents) |
|------|-------------|--------------------|------|-------------|--------------------|
| Knoxville | $5,674.00 | 213.0 | Toledo | $59,244.44 | 22.0 |
| Lawrence | $748,573.16 | 6.4 | Tulsa | $3,850.00 | 3.8 |
| Los Angeles | $5,674.00 | 50.9 | Wichita | $1,627.22 | 2.1 |
| Lowell | $49,555.70 | 1.6 | Worcester | $154,311.48 | 80.4 |
| Lynn | $89,069.03 | 43.1 | Yonkers | $79,981.85 | 74.4 |
| Manchester | $25,565.03 | 86.8 | | | |

*Source:* United States Public Health Service and American Public Health Association, Committee on Administrative Practice, *Municipal Health Department Practice for the Year 1923* (Washington, DC: Govt. Print. Off., 1926).

finance the work of the CAP, as did collaborative financing from the American Red Cross and the United States Public Health Service. The CAP also received funding from the Milbank Memorial Fund, the Commonwealth Fund, the W.K. Kellogg Foundation, and the Rockefeller Foundation. And, as coverage in *Time* magazine suggests, the CAP did not just produce arcane reports that only scientists cared about. Business was particularly interested in rewarding cities that invested in health. In 1929, the U.S. Chamber of Commerce sponsored the first Health Conservation Contest—with funds provided by a group of life insurance companies—to reward the best municipal health departments. In 1934, with funding from the Kellogg Foundation, the contest idea expanded to county health departments.[33] The chairman of the committee, C.-E. A. Winslow, viewed this contest as a major achievement of the CAP's work. Winslow remarked that after nearly 10 years of the committee collecting data, formulating standards, and devising methods of appraisal, the Health Conservation Contest "marked its first comprehensive effort . . . to raise the general level of health practice throughout the country."[34]

## The New Public Health and Medical Insurgency

As early as 1905, Charles Chapin recognized when studying the proper role of state health boards that the states were getting involved in multiple aspects of controlling communicable diseases that included diagnosis *and treatment*, creating "the need to build and maintain hospitals, construct sanatoria for quarantine, build and maintain bacteriological laboratories to aid physicians in the diagnosis of various diseases, and to manufacture and freely distribute vaccines and antitoxins."[35] While supportive of the new public health, he prophetically warned that "some will surely question the diagnostic activities and dispensing of needed drugs."[36] And just as Chapin had warned, as public health more clearly moved into the domain of medical treatment, private practice physicians pushed back.

As Peter Swenson notes in his book *Disorder: A History of Reform, Reaction, and Money in American Medicine*, resentment among the rank and file of private practice physicians "percolated into open insurgency against the rising progressive forces in organized medicine."[37] The AMA's support of certain aspects of public health's mission, especially physician licensure requirements, caused disgruntlement among private physicians. As Swenson describes, mobilization among the rank and file—against what they saw as "elite physicians" pushing for progressive state reforms in state medical societies and the AMA—began in 1906 and spread quickly. By 1924, "[t]en years after the insurgency toppled the progressive leadership" of the Illinois Medicaid Society, the insurgents were able to remove medical progressivism."[38]

The "old guard"—or "aristocrats" as they were also sometimes called—those insurgents wanted to replace were "mostly elite physicians and especially surgeons who were educators and public health enthusiasts," who advocated for a strong role of the state in medicine, usually to improve the quality of care.[39] For example, Charles S. Bacon, a prominent surgeon, educator, and scholar, and a member of the Chicago Medical Society's Council, argued in 1893 that "medicine should become a function of the state largely for preventive purposes."[40]

One of the initial leaders of the insurgents, Charles J. Whalen, focused his advocacy on the "abuses of medical charities." In 1909, hospitals and clinics provided free care to indigents in most cities across the United States. Whalen argued that medical facilities in Chicago, where he practiced, were too generous, providing free care to patients who had the ability to pay. Whalen and his fellow insurgents were successful in creating the Committee on Abuse of Medical Charities, which pressured facilities to investigate patients' ability to pay.[41] Indeed, public health activities became a major area of contention for the insurgents. In Chicago, where the opposition movement began, the public health commissioner, William A. Evans, became a target for making vaccines freely available to the public during epidemics, and was eventually let go.

Swenson and other medical historians describe the actions of these insurgents as successfully impeding public health development in the United States.[42] While this mobilized opposition hindered an open embrace of the state's role, it did not stop the state's involvement from growing.

# Ambiguity, Federalism, and the Voluntary Sector Hide Expansion

If sanitation was shifted out to other agencies, and spending on hospitals and clinics was not considered prevention, what were the new modern health departments doing with increased budgets for "defined health services"? The APHA's Committee on Administrative Practice (CAP) described clearly how every "ideal health department" should be organized, which bureaus and divisions should be included, and what services should be provided under each division, and it also detailed appropriate budgets (see Table 2.5).

For several areas of the ideal health department, the CAP described the necessity of providing treatment, and the response when controversy emerged. In what follows I discuss the Grow-and-Hide process for three areas: health department laboratories, venereal disease, and maternal and child health (MCH).

Table 2.5 **Suggested Organization of the "Ideal" Health Department**

1. Bureau of Administration
   A. Division of Administration
   B. Division of Public Health Education

2. Bureau of Sanitation

3. Bureau of Foods
   A. Division of Milk
   B. Division of Food

4. Bureau of Communicable Disease Control
   A. Division of Epidemiology
   B. Division of Tuberculosis
   C. Division of Venereal Diseases

5. Bureau of Child Hygiene
   A. Division of Infant Hygiene
   B. Division of School Hygiene

6. Bureau of Nursing

7. Bureau of Laboratories

8. Bureau of Vital Statistics

Source: C.-E. A. Winslow and H. I. Harris, "An Ideal Health Department for a City of 100,000 Population," Section II from the Report of the Committee on Municipal Health Department Practice, American Journal of Public Health 12, no. 11 (1922): 891–907. See pp. 892–93.

## Translating Lab Discoveries into Treatment

To understand one of the first crucial turning points for how public health expanded to include treatment, it is useful to return to the New York City Health Department and Hermann Biggs's development of health department laboratories. The spread of laboratories across the American states was important because it moved the state from implementing public health laws and regulations to developing and distributing health care products. Government production of drugs quickly catapulted the state into decisions regarding the appropriate distribution of drugs.[43] In 1895, when Biggs secured legislation to produce the diphtheria antitoxin, he also secured authority for "authorizing the Department of Health to produce, use and distribute diphtheria antitoxin and other antitoxins and to sell any surplus products, and proceeds from the sales to constitute a special fund."[44]

Despite growing concern among practicing physicians, there was enormous support for furthering the development of research laboratories in New York City. In 1905, a new six-story laboratory research building was opened for the health department. In just eight years, the laboratory staff more than doubled, from 1,000 to 2,466, and the budget nearly tripled, from $1.3 million to $3.1 million.[45] New York City continued to expand its investment in research so significantly that by 1910 it had by far the largest group of laboratories in the world.[46]

For Biggs, however, this was not enough, because he believed strongly that the implications of laboratory work should be translated out into the community. In 1911, Biggs—then the chief medical officer of the New York City Department of Health—advocated for a new division called "Specific Therapy and Preventive Medicine," housed within the Bureau of Laboratories. The stated purpose of the new division was "to make practically available in the smaller hospitals of the city and in tenement houses the most recent discoveries in bacteriology as applied to the *treatment* of disease."[47] With newly allocated funds, the laboratories substantially expanded their scope of activities. In a 1911 article in the New York Health Department's *Monthly Bulletin*, Dr. Parks, the director of the new division, summarized its expanded focus:

1. *Cerebro-spinal meningitis.* The **production, distribution and administration** of anti-meningitis serum. The performance of lumbar puncture for the diagnosis of cases of suspected meningitis.
2. *Trachoma, and other communicable eye diseases.* A systematic investigation of the etiology and infectiousness of these diseases, with special reference to microscopic diagnosis.
3. *Syphilis.* A study of the Wassermann reaction, as a preliminary to **making this test available for physicians, hospitals and dispensaries, in cases where**

**patients are unable to pay** for having the test made by private laboratories. The Laboratory is at present ready to receive a limited number of specimens of serum for examination.

4. *Gonorrhea*. An investigation of gonorrheal vaginitis among young girls in hospitals and other public institutions for children. The **preparation and clinical application** of vaccines for gonorrheal infections.

5. *Streptococcus and Pneumococcus Sera*. The production of these sera and an investigation as to their clinical value, with a view of improving their therapeutic efficiency. These sera will be **supplied for use in suitable cases**, where bacteriological examinations can be made.

6. *Vaccines*. The **production and distribution of vaccines** for various specific infections, and the investigation of their therapeutic value.[48]

Parks's summary of the laboratory's activities illustrates not just that the breadth of government involvement in diseases had expanded, but also how the nature of government involvement in each disease was conceptualized (and practiced). The health department was no longer only dealing with just "epidemic" diseases, but also more focused diseases that could be prevented if diagnoses were scientifically perfected and appropriate serums or vaccines were widely distributed.

As the next decade unfolded, the necessity of investing in diagnostic laboratories became commonplace. By 1923, health departments in all large cities had expenditures devoted to laboratory services. Across the United States, cities were spending about seven cents per capita on laboratories. According to the CAP at the time, the ideal health department should have a Bureau of Laboratories, which would render the following new public health services: "The bacteriological examination of cultures for diagnosis and release in diphtheria, tuberculosis, typhoid fever, malaria, syphilis, gonorrhea, pneumonia, and in southern cities, hookworm and other intestinal parasitic diseases."[49] CAP also included examination of public water supply and private wells, but these "old" public health functions were listed only after laboratory testing for communicable diseases. While government investment in laboratories was not controversial, the increase in diagnostic testing for communicable diseases raised crucial questions about where positive cases would receive treatment. This question became especially paramount for venereal disease.

## Venereal Disease: Prevention and Hidden Treatment

In 1912, along with laboratory research on venereal disease (VD), the New York City Department of Health launched its "Control of Venereal Disease" plan, where they proposed a reporting mandate that all physicians report VD cases to the health department. Along with mandated reporting, the department asked for appropriations to establish clinics for diagnosis and treatment of VD. A storm of protest by practicing physicians ensued. Various county medical societies had meetings to "discuss" the plan, which primarily amounted to strong statements against the proposed government action.[50] The Commission of the New York Academy of Medicine on Budgets and Hospitals (made up primarily of practicing physicians) also held meetings on the VD clinics, and disapproved the New York City Board of Health's request for clinics to diagnose and provide treatment. Yet just one year later, in 1913, Biggs's same plan was essentially approved. This time, however, the health department downplayed treatment and focused on prevention. Nonetheless, the details of the VD plan included treatment for VD within the clinics if necessary to stop the spread of the disease.[51]

But these expansions were not unique to New York City. While it is true that New York City had the highest appropriations devoted to its health department and was often a forerunner in developing new programs, the surveys conducted on municipal health departments across the country reveal that the establishment of VD clinics was already fairly common.[52] In 1915, 83 cities reported free diagnosis, and six cities offered treatment for positive cases.[53] Given that treatment was available, and that the disease spread quickly if left untreated, more and more cities moved toward treatment.

**Federal Intergovernmental Funding.** The federal government passed the Chamberlain-Kahn Act in 1918, providing grants-in-aid to states to address the spread of VD, and propelling state investment in VD.[54] For example, in Biggs's new role as state commissioner of health, he was behind passage of a bill to create a state Bureau of Venereal Disease, taking advantage of federal funding. The passage of Chamberlain-Kahn made the financing conditions for the bureau particularly favorable: the federal government contributed $99,000 toward VD control on top of a state appropriation of $30,000. This new state-level bureau continued the march toward public health state-building on the local level, with the creation of rules and regulations for control of VD in 37 municipalities, the establishment of clinics in a total of 17 cities, and an extensive education campaign distributing 146,000 pamphlets.[55]

By 1920, most states had obtained federal grant-in-aids funds for VD, and in just two years there were 43 VD clinics functioning in 38 cities. Most importantly, despite public health leaders' claims that these clinics only provided preventive medicine, they in fact provided over 110,000 treatments within 24 months.[56]

Again, this steady march—combining prevention with treatment—occurred throughout many U.S. cities and in many state health departments. In 1922, the

CAP recommended that the "ideal health department" for a city of 100,000 or more should have a Division of VD with free laboratory diagnosis, and almost all 83 large cities had such a service.[57] With regard to treatment, the committee wrote:

> Since the great majority of venereal disease cases are ambulatory treatment cases, and early detection, followed by efficient intensive treatment, is vitally important not only for the welfare of the patient, but for the protection of the public through terminating or shortening the infectious period of the case, health departments should stimulate and in so far as may be necessary actually operate clinics for venereal diseases under such conditions of free and pay service as may be practicable. . . . [Because there were already a number of treatment clinics in existence the committee went on to specify that] . . . treatment clinics operated by a competent paid staff in a city of 100,000 population may be expected to care for as many as 1,500 cases a year.[58]

The number quoted above is particularly significant because the report also estimated that a city of 100,000 population "should show at least 1,500 cases per year."[59] Hence, an ideal health department is diagnosing 1,500 cases and investing in treatment clinics with capacity to service 100% of those cases.

After conducting several surveys of health departments in cities across the United States, in 1932 Hiscock summarized the findings and described the ideal health department as having a VD disease control division, which would include laboratory service for diagnosis and medical service for treatment. The rationale for medical service was stated as follows:

> The early detection of venereal diseases, followed by efficient treatment, is vitally important for the welfare of the patient and for the protection of the public through terminating or shortening the infectious period of the case as promptly as practicable. Health departments should, therefore, stimulate the medical profession and, in so far as it may be necessary to supplement hospital and clinical facilities, actually operate clinics for venereal diseases under such conditions of free and part-pay services as local circumstances warrant.[60]

Despite saying that the health department would attempt to "stimulate the medical profession," Hiscock went on to write that

> serious attention must be given to keeping in touch with all cases, to prevent lapse of treatment, to the study of family problems and to the

prevention of recurrent infections. For this purpose, adequate follow-up and study are necessary. This should be the function of trained social workers or public health nurses, or both. Adequate efforts should be made to secure the return to physicians or clinics of cases after they have lapsed.[61]

Again, we see the dance of claiming to give preference of treatment to physicians while also acknowledging the important role of health departments and public health personnel filling the gaps, but without exactly defining the size of the gaps—at least not in the same paragraph. For, on the next page, Hiscock wrote that, "in addition to private practice cases, there may be expected approximately 800 registrants at clinics per 100,000 population, and under an effective system, these should average at least 15 visits per case accepted for treatment annually. The necessary drugs and other supplies for the treatment of cases should be freely and immediately available."[62]

## Hidden Health Services for Healthy People: Maternal, Infant, and Children's Health

Along with programs for contagious diseases, maternal and child health (MCH) became a major focus of city and state health departments. Given the sheer size of the problem, few questioned state involvement. In the 1890s, 40% of all deaths in New York City occurred among children under five.[63] Similar to tuberculosis and other diseases described in Chapter 1, voluntary organizations were crucially important in expanding access to maternal and child health services.[64] The Association for Improving the Condition of the Poor (AICP) in New York, and other private child health agencies, created volunteer-run summer camps and milk stations to provide free or low-cost pure milk to poor families. In 1905, the AICP organized the New York Milk Committee to improve the milk supply and educate mothers on infant care.

In 1910, for example, with the help of private funds from philanthropist Mrs. J. Borden Harriman, Dr. Josephine Baker of the New York City Health Department set up baby health stations. These health stations sold bottled pasteurized milk, at the cost of a few cents less than grocery store milk, and also provided health education on the care of infants. Although private philanthropy funded 30 milk centers in New York City in 1911, there was a strong collaboration between these voluntary agencies and the city health department.[65]

**Public Health–Voluntary Sector Collaboration**. Collaboration was easy, in part because many individuals worked concurrently for the voluntary sector and the city health department. For example, although the AICP organized the New York Milk Committee, Dr. Baker was a key leader and original founding member of the Committee and, as mentioned above, also worked for the New York City Health Department. In her role at the Health Department, Dr. Baker requested municipal funds to establish child health centers and was able to secure $1.3 million in city appropriations.[66] In 1912, Dr. Baker convinced various infant welfare groups to join the Baby Welfare Association; in turn, the health department strongly supported the association with increased funds, and provided it with a central office and a secretary. The main purpose of the association, which was subsequently renamed the Children's Welfare Association, was to *coordinate* the activities of the child health centers (under the city health department) and the various volunteer groups.[67] Gradually, the city health department assumed control of the milk stations, but it continued to work collaboratively with voluntary organizations to staff the stations and provide the services. By 1914, only seven milk stations were still under the control of voluntary associations. While New York City still provided funding assistance to these remaining seven, the city operated 56 milk stations.[68]

A typical three-step programmatic progression for maternal and child health practice included (1) instituting milk stations to provide population-wide access to a clean milk supply, (2) establishing well-child clinics providing preventive examinations, and (3) developing health education campaigns to encourage good health behavior.[69]

Once well-child clinics were established, it became very difficult for the clinic to *only* dispense preventive care. Thus, the area of maternal and child health is another example where the progression from prevention to treatment became quite commonplace. Important expansions occurred along these lines in 1909 under Baker's new Division of Child Hygiene. Fifty-four educational centers—each with a medical inspector and nurse, as well as clinics for mothers and babies—were established throughout the city.[70] In 1912, Baker's new division opened six Children's Medical Clinics, "designed for the *actual treatment* of those children whose parents were unable to pay the necessary medical care indicated by the routine exam."[71]

These expansions in infant and maternal health were not confined to New York State. The survey of municipal health departments in the United States revealed that by 1915 almost all large cities (17 out of 18) and two-thirds of medium-sized cities (100,000–300,000 population) had a "complete" infant hygiene program in place, which included "milk inspection, and nurses and infant welfare stations to follow up births and educate mothers."[72] In Pennsylvania, for example, there were 460 well-baby centers in 1922, which were paid for by community taxation and made possible by cooperation from the State Department of Health, the Red Cross, and the Anti-Tuberculosis Society.[73]

When city and local departments and voluntary agencies continued to expand their practices in this area, members of local medical societies became increasingly irate. Practicing physicians viewed voluntary organizations as an extension of the state and as a threat to private practice. In 1913, Dr. Federick Green of the AMA represented the association's concern about the extent to which voluntary health agencies were involved in public health and called a conference of agency executives to discuss "mutual cooperation" and the appropriate division of labor, with a view toward eliminating "unnecessary" organizations.[74]

When the Babies' Welfare Association of NYC issued a directory of agencies available for infant, maternal, and child health, the enormity of the list (194 pages of text and 30 pages of index) raised the ire of physicians. At a meeting of the New York State Medical Society, physicians spoke out against these organizations: "To practically all these organizations, physicians are giving more or less time. Probably there is not a physician present who is not asked from time to time to undertake work that he is well aware is useless [because it is duplicative or] interferes with private practice."[75]

In response to these claims, most voluntary agency and health department officials argued that they were only providing preventive care or care for the indigent. However, some public health leaders argued further that *if* health departments were moving into the area of treatment, it was due to lack of initiative on the part of the medical profession. For example, Pennsylvania Health Department commissioner Edward Martin stated in defense of his department's actions that it treated those with tuberculosis and venereal disease "only because these are transmissible diseases."[76] He went on to say that if the medical profession was willing to take over this role by making the clinics "an active center of control, [then] the state will gladly transfer these clinics."[77] However, he hardly endorsed a full transfer of department responsibility over to the medical profession. He made clear that there were worthy and well-qualified physicians that the department should cooperate with, but also unworthy and unqualified physicians that the department should shun:

> The profession of medicine is made up of three groups: an upper third—leaders in research, thought and helpful action, self-immolating altruists, the flower of civilization; a middle third-strong, able, clear minded men, who follow the lead of the upper third; and a lower third—prejudiced, ignorant, self-centered, whose approbation is undesirable. The sanitarian must have the upper two thirds with him; the lower third against him.[78]

This quote illustrates how real (and perceived) differences between physician-scientists and private practice physicians shaped the discourse around health reform during this period. As documented in Chapter 1, paramount to why government investment in public health grew was a strong belief in the scientific integrity of the health departments and their unique ability to solve pressing health problems. These scientific departments were repeatedly defended as apolitical.

Despite the federal structure of public health, the relationship of health departments to local medical societies varied across the states. For example, physicians in Alabama applauded the public health department, noting that "The State [Medical] Society is the State Department of Health, and the County Societies are the County Boards of Health. All health officers are appointed by the censors of the medical societies and are responsible to them. Surely a medical Utopia."[79] This quote highlights an important reality: while private physicians felt outside of the state apparatus and wanted more control, they were not anti-statist, as their rhetoric sometimes claimed. They did not want to stop the growth of state investment in health, but rather wanted the state to develop in particular ways—namely ways that would give them a monopoly over other medical sects and access to favorable patients (i.e., those they knew how to treat and those who could pay for their services). When private physicians called for more control, physician-scientists and the rest of the public health network assured them that state investment would be developed as private physicians desired.

In 1916, the New York State Department of Health received appropriations to supervise the aftercare of patients diagnosed with polio. The law specified that the supervision of aftercare could only be done "with the consent and at the request of the family physician." Interpreting the law's implications, it is tempting to conclude that private physicians exerted their power over the health department. But if we look more closely, we see two important factors, which were common in most legislation passed during this period. First, the law specified that the aftercare should be conducted "under the direction of an orthopedic surgeon on the staff of the department who holds special clinics with the aid of staff nurses or of the local physicians and nurses." But these were often salaried public health physicians. Second, although there were provisions for private physician consent, there is no documentation showing that consent was obtained. What we do know is that most polio cases in New York (208 out of 260 patients in 1922, for example) came under state care. Interestingly, these data were presented in the 1922 volume of the *New York State Journal of Medicine* as "evidence of the interest which the physicians have taken and of their appreciation of the work which has been done by the State Department in the aftercare of poliomyelitis during the past five years."[80] The local medical society thanked the state for taking on difficult cases.

While physicians welcomed the state taking care of the poor and other "diffi-cult" cases, tension emerged in trying to figure out where to draw the boundaries around public health. Similar to VD and infant hygiene, the work of school-based health clinics was an illustration of this tension. As early as 1904, the concept of school medical inspection was already broadening from a narrow focus on de-tection of contagious diseases to complete examinations to promote health.[81] By 1915, nearly 80 percent of U.S. cities (over 25,000) provided medical inspections of school-aged children.[82] Lillian Wald, best known for her work with the Henry Street Settlement in New York City and for founding the Visiting Nurse Service, was also a visionary for school nursing. She argued that school nursing should not only promote health through diagnostic examinations but must necessarily provide treatment. In her view, it was wasteful to spend money on disease detec-tion without then providing treatment to address the identified illness.[83]

While the public health network continued to advocate for expansions in school health clinics under the banner of "health promotion and health educa-tion services," the clinics' day-to-day activities were more consistent with Wald's advocacy. In Duffy's history of public health, he focuses on the role of school-based clinics and suggests that treatment was clearly provided and eventually extended into dental care, immunizations, and in some cases surgery to remove adenoids and tonsils.[84] In Duffy's account he notes that local medical societies were especially concerned about school-based clinic activities around the re-moval of tonsils and adenoids. In 1914, the New York City Health Department ran five school-based nose and throat clinics for the poor. The New York Academy of Medicine called these programs "socialism," objecting on the grounds that the surgery should be performed in operating rooms backed up by convalescent wards. The academy recommended that the health department should close the clinics, writing, "the functions of the Department of Health should be re-stricted to the prevention of disease and that no therapeutic activities should be undertaken." Duffy concludes that "the health department bowed to the medical argument and closed the nose and throat clinics."[85]

However, as of 1915, the health department still operated nine other clinics providing free medical treatment for school children. Another interpretation is that the department was strategic in its response: capitulating to the medical so-ciety in the moment, while still maintaining free clinics and eventually building new ones. This occurred in the infant hygiene area as well. For example, in 1920, despite opposition from private physicians, the New York Bureau of Child Hygiene continued to operate 68 baby health stations.[86]

Again, this development of school-based clinics was not unique to New York City, but rather was normal practice in the vast majority of municipal health departments across the country. The ideal health department was instructed to have a Bureau of Child Hygiene, under which two divisions—Infant Hygiene

*Table 2.6*  **Total and Per Capita Expenditures for Specified Health Services for 100 Cities, 1923**

| Item | Expenditures | Per capita (cents) | Percent of Total |
|---|---|---|---|
| Administrative | $1,926,830.99 | 5.99 | 10.15 |
| Vital statistics | $491,801.50 | 1.53 | 2.59 |
| Communicable disease | $2,632,484.12 | 8.19 | 13.87 |
| Tuberculosis | $1,273,770.56 | 3.96 | 6.71 |
| Venereal disease | $472,925.88 | 1.47 | 2.49 |
| Maternal and child hygiene | $1,698,557.68 | 5.28 | 8.95 |
| School health service | $4,228,079.80 | 13.15 | 22.28 |
| Public health nursing | $447,054.79 | 1.39 | 2.36 |
| Laboratory | $1,291,648.04 | 4.02 | 6.81 |
| Control of milk | $1,014,637.17 | 3.16 | 5.36 |
| Control of other foods | $1,386,116.76 | 4.31 | 7.30 |
| Sanitary inspection | $2,110,676.39 | 6.56 | 11.13 |
| **Total** | **$18,974,583.68** | **59.01** | **100.00** |

*Source:* United States Public Health Service and American Public Health Association, Committee on Administrative Practice, *Municipal Health Department Practice for the Year 1923* (Washington, DC: Govt. Print. Off., 1926), Table IV, p. 43.

and School Hygiene—would reside. To prevent infant mortality and childhood diseases, treatment was considered a necessary part of the ideal health department, which should have "[a] system of infant welfare stations for medical *examination* and hygienic supervision of infants and young children."[87] And each school-based clinic should provide school examinations, follow-up in the homes, and dental health.[88] By 1923, focusing just on school-based health, expenditures for these services consumed almost a fourth of municipal health department budgets—22% on average across all health departments in 100 cities across the United States (see Table 2.6).[89]

Beyond school-based health, the CAP's ideal health department also promoted district-wide health programs. Each large city was instructed to have a staff of 30 public health nurses to provide treatment across each of the essential health services, but most notably TB, VD, infant and child welfare, and school health. For example, each nurse was instructed to "have an average of 350 to 400 school children under her charge."[90] Indeed, one of the most important shifts in thinking about the ideal role of the health department was its inclusion of preventive care for "supposedly well persons,"[91] in contrast to its prior focus on communicable disease, which dealt "primarily with the sick."[92] This was the beginning of the idea of frequent medical examinations of healthy people to prevent illness. The ideal health department would provide "an average of 15 visits per year . . . [for] each infant under one year of age."[93] and this wasn't just for poor mothers and infants. The proposal specified that these infant welfare stations would "ideally include the registration of 50 percent of all infants born."[94] Ideally "all children should be kept on the records until they enter school and pass under the care of the school physicians."[95] Clinics and home supervision would be provided for children ages one to five. Clearly, public health leaders saw the need for medical care and advocated for money to provide such care in health department clinics—50% of the ideal MCH budget should be devoted to "clinical medical service."[96]

**Federal Intergovernmental Funding.** Similar to the Chamberlain-Kahn Act's funding for VD, the Sheppard-Towner Act of 1921 provided substantial grant-in-aid funds from the federal government to the states for maternal and child health services. While most correctly identify the New Deal as the period for substantial growth in federal subsidies to the states, it is important to note the foundational effects of federal subsidies prior to 1935. In the early 1900s, the federal government adopted the grant-in-aid approach, which offered states matching federal funds for every dollar of state spending in specific areas. While the federal grant-in-aid mechanism does not require states to accept federal funds, the allure of federal funds was amazingly effective (especially given the newness of federal intervention) in stimulating state spending. Over a 15-year period, the growth in federal subsidies was phenomenal, from a mere $8 million in 1912 to over $135 million in 1927 (see Figure 2.1). By 1928, every state in the union was spending state resources and accepting federal supervision in return for federal funds.[97]

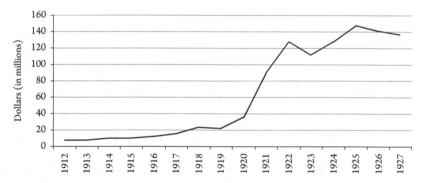

*Figure 2.1* Federal Aid Payments to the States, 1912–1927. *Source:* Austin F. MacDonald, *Federal Aid: A Study of the American Subsidy System* (New York: T.Y. Crowell, 1928), 6.

In his 1928 analysis of the federal subsidy system, political scientist Austin Macdonald offered the following as an explanation for why states were so eager to accept federal funds:

> The states, for their part, have welcomed federal financial assistance at any price. In many states federal aid has helped to solve a most perplexing problem. The voters have clamored loudly for better standards of service.... At the same time they have voiced no less insistently their demand for lower taxes. State legislators, fearing equally the wrath of the Better-What-Not organizations and the fury of the taxpayers, have cast about for new sources of revenue. One of the richest funds has been the federal treasury. Millions of federal dollars are available annually for state use. And so the states accept the offer of federal funds, accepting also perforce a measure of federal supervision over local activities.[98]

Just as Macdonald's argument suggests, MCH funding through the Sheppard-Towner Act continued at a steady upward pace until it was discontinued after 1927 (see Figure 2.2).

The Children's Bureau was given over $1 million annually, and during the seven years administering Sheppard-Towner, the bureau coordinated a nationwide program that helped to establish 2,978 prenatal centers, and visits to over 3 million homes.[99] Because Sheppard-Towner was so effective at distributing needed maternal and child health care services across the local communities in the United States, rank-and-file private practice physicians targeted the act as another example of state interference. The AMA did not take an official oppositional stance before Sheppard-Towner was passed, but as the insurgents continued to gain power in the 1920s across state medical societies and the national AMA, the opposition against the act became more intense and effective over time.[100]

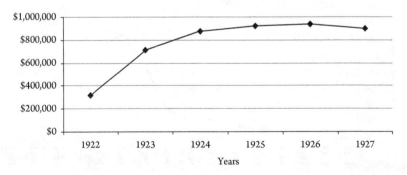

*Figure 2.2* Federal Maternity and Infancy Funds to States, 1922–1927. *Source:* Austin F. MacDonald, *Federal Aid: A Study of the American Subsidy System* (New York: T.Y. Crowell, 1928), 229.

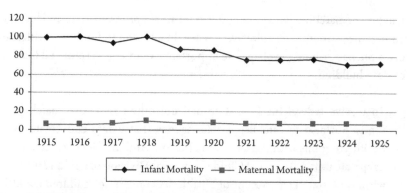

*Figure 2.3* U.S. Infant and Maternal Mortality Rates, 1915–1925. *Source:* Austin
F. MacDonald, *Federal Aid: A Study of the American Subsidy System* (New York: T.Y. Crowell.
1928), 233.

The insurgents argued that the women providing these services were ill-prepared
and the program could not adequately provide maternal and child health care
services. The data on infant and maternal mortality, which was collected and
printed while these debates were occurring, did not support their claims. To the
contrary, there was a substantial decline in mortality rates during the period of
Sheppard-Towner programs (see Figure 2.3).

Like the AMA and local medical societies, the federal PHS was against continuation of Sheppard-Towner, and that opposition might have also contributed
to the act's demise. The leaders in the PHS opposed the administrative responsibility of Sheppard-Towner funds going to the Children's Bureau, and argued
that—given its jurisdiction over public health—the PHS should administer the
program.[101] Because the Children's Bureau used local health departments and
public health nurses to implement the program, arguments to shift MCH activities under the authority of the PHS may have been political and patriarchal,[102]
but not illogical. Whereas the AMA wanted the provision of MCH services to
shift to the private doctor's office, this was not the desired position of the PHS.
Although the PHS and other public health leaders repeatedly stated in public
forums and public documents that it was strongly in favor of physician control,
the public health coalition was also raising questions about whether the distinction between prevention and treatment made sense under the emerging focus of
the new public health.

As the previous description of municipal health departments attests, the
PHS had encouraged—and local health departments had been in the business
of providing—maternal and child health programs in collaboration with voluntary groups (who also worked closely with the Children's Bureau) since the
early 1900s. The baby health stations served as models for infant programs
implemented under Sheppard-Towner.[103] Most importantly, because of the

structure of matching funds under the grant-in-aid program, state and local government investments were already in place. In addition to funding, medical historian Sheila Rothman explains the importance of intergovernmental financing for state-building:

> To receive federal funds, a state had not only to approve matching funds, but also to establish a state agency that would coordinate its health programs with the Children's Bureau. And this agency had to be a separate unit, a Bureau of Child Hygiene or Division of Child Welfare, within the state Department of Health. Its concern for children could not be diluted with any other responsibility. Further, this agency had to spawn county agencies, mini-departments of child hygiene to administer the funds. All of this was intended to bring into being a powerful and pervasive network of governmental bodies whose exclusive concern was child welfare.[104]

Thus, while federal funds were sorely missed after Sheppard-Towner ceased, the bulk of MCH funding still came from state and local governments, the infrastructure was still in operation, and given the widespread support for MCH programs, there was never any discussion about termination of MCH funding.[105] The progression of infant and child hygiene services in Indiana, described in the *American Journal of Public Health* in 1932, illustrates this point:

> Prior to 1919 sporadic attention was given to child hygiene, but in that year growing interest in the child culminated in the establishment of the Division of Child Hygiene [in the State Board of Health]. From the very first a comprehensive plan of organization was followed. . . . In July, 1922, federal assistance, under the Sheppard-Towner Act, was made available. For 7 years the Division of Child Hygiene carried out a consistent program that reached every county and township in the state. When the federal subsidy ceased, the momentum created by widespread health education and trained direction of child hygiene carried the activities through 3 trying years with but little slowing-up.[106]

In 1931, the Division of Child Hygiene employed five field physicians, six field nurses, five field assistants, one secretary, two stenographers, an artist-stenographer, and a statistician.[107]

Indeed, in writing a retrospective on the progress of the *public health*—note, not MCH or Children's Bureau—grant-in-aid programs, the PHS's Assistant Surgeon General at the time, Joseph Mountin, pointed out that "[t]he Sheppard-Towner Act . . . was one of the most important stimulants to State and local health departments prior to passage of the Social Security Act."[108] He went on to discuss how this funding was continued and stimulated again under the New Deal programs (discussed in more detail in Part II).

While the PHS favored a continuation of Sheppard-Towner MHC *practices*, public health leaders assured the AMA that the provision of public MCH services would not infringe on private practice. As discussed for VD and school-based services, this was a common rhetorical device used by public health leaders in the first half of the 20th century. Without ever defining the boundaries of public and private, the PHS and state and local health departments were able to repeatedly demonstrate a need for public health care investment. What the public health care state did—but did not advertise—was provide medical care to promote and improve health.

## More Growth: Public Health State-Building

With municipal health departments well established, the biggest advances in public health administration during the 1920s were made at the state and county levels. In 1915, only 10 states had divisions of communicable disease control or full-time epidemiologists. By 1925, 33 states provided these disease control functions. The transfer of tuberculosis work from voluntary associations to public agencies continued, and by 1925, 31 states had various levels of responsibility in the control of tuberculosis. State laboratory work also grew rapidly from 1915 to 1925. While public health nursing in state health agencies barely existed in 1915, by 1925 only two state health departments had no public health nursing activities.[109] In sum, state health agencies took on executive functions, encouraged the development of local health activities, set standards for health services and personnel, and collected vital statistics and data on outbreaks of reportable disease. The appropriation of funding by state legislatures reflects this increasing responsibility: the average per capita appropriation more than tripled, from $.036 in 1915 to $.118 in 1930.[110]

Similarly, the movement for county health departments started to gain momentum in 1917, and significantly expanded in the 1920s. By 1934, 70% of U.S. counties had continuously functioning local health units during this time.[111] This substantial increase in county health units could not have occurred without significant efforts from the PHS and the Rockefeller Foundation, which provided not only money but expertise to stimulate the growth of county health units. Although counties themselves met about 70% of their expenses, the "professionalized" expertise of the PHS and volunteer organizations was crucially important in creating standardized notions of "professional" health units. By 1934, one-fourth of all counties in the United States had employed a full-time

health officer and, for at least part of the time, usually a nurse and a sanitary inspector as well.[112] State governments also invested in county health units—over
$1 million in 1929 alone.[113]

# Conclusion

The most significant outcome of state-building in public health during this time
period was the development of the concept of an "ideal health department,"
which promoted an expanded notion of public health much beyond the traditional domain of sanitation. As the boundaries of public health expanded,
health departments extended prevention to also include medical treatment.
As Mountin said before a room of Health Officers in 1933, "It is now being
recognized that preventive and curative measures are closely related and that
each scientific advance necessitates a larger amount of personal service in administrative practice."[114]

The enormous increases in state and local health department activities, which
expanded under a coordinated state-voluntary federal structure, created—
then and in the years to come— crucial debates about the proper role of "state
medicine." Although leaders from the public health network used rhetorical
devices to hide growth, when Mountin was talking among colleagues (in this
case the foot soldiers who would provide the government-funded health services) the broader vision was revealed. Indeed, Mountin concluded his talk
boldly: "[Those] concerned with public administration as a whole take the view
that the community might profit if the health department were given administrative and budgetary responsibility for those governmental services which are
designed to promote or restore health since they are equipped to do so."[115] While
this support for state medicine is not surprising among public health leaders in
charge of running state-funded health departments, three noteworthy aspects
will become clear in the chapters to follow. First, there are numerous examples
of public health leaders admitting to the larger role of public health in providing
curative medicine; second, it was not just public health leaders who support this
expanded role, but the broader public health coalition as well; and third, when
the political climate became more conducive, public health leaders would explicitly argue in support of expanding state medicine. In short, we will see in the
next two chapters that Mountin's view was not an aberration.

# 3

# Public Health Planning

*Hope for a Unified Public-Private System*

Throughout the 1910s and 1920s, leaders in the public health network often proclaimed that all persons should have access to medical care. This did not mean, however, that those leaders supported national health insurance or any particular health insurance scheme. While some health leaders were aligned with insurance reform movements in this early period, overall these leaders were, much more concerned about the rational development of a health care system that would provide prevention *and treatment*. More importantly, they were adamant that the provision of care under such a system could be provided under public and private auspices. Indeed, as the system developed, they not only hid the extent to which public health departments provided medical treatment, but also hid the growing subsidies to the private voluntary sector, especially to the voluntary hospital system. Although these private voluntary health service organizations were heavily subsidized by government funds, this public financing was not discussed. Instead, popular discourse depicted the voluntary sector as being privately funded with minimal government involvement. This is how the Grow-and-Hide strategy worked, using the rhetoric of classic liberalism while expanding the role of government.

To see how the Grow-and-Hide strategy became embedded in the American health system, look no further than the most seminal health policy event of this period: the final recommendations of the Committee on the Costs of Medical Care (CCMC). The publication of the CCMC's recommendations is important because these ideas were not hidden away in agency memos in the PHS or in state health departments, but on full display as part of the intellectual currency of the time. The CCMC's research documents and final report planted the seeds of Grow and Hide in three major ways: first, by continuing the push to merge prevention and treatment, especially among the public health and voluntary organizations; second, by continuing to build on federalism and privileging local

*Grow and Hide.* Colleen M. Grogan, Oxford University Press. © Oxford University Press 2023.
DOI: 10.1093/oso/9780199812233.003.0004

responsibility to hide a growing public health care state; and third, by calling for continued public investment while remaining agnostic on the provision of health care services, whether by public or private organizations.

In this chapter, I discuss the substance of CCMC's recommendations to pin point where consensus existed, and show how consensus emerged out of previous public health state-building and allowed for continued growth. I also highlight the areas that were left equivocal, explain why, and detail the implications. But first, I provide background to explicate why the CCMC reports and final recommendations are considered so influential.

## The Hope: A Unified Health Care System for All

> *If you have been able to show us how adequate medical care may be made available for the entire population, with its tragic differences in ability to pay for the costs of such care; if you have set up a goal toward which the citizen and the government, the voluntary agency and the professional group, all may coordinate their efforts in a planned progress whose only consideration is the common good—then I, as an American citizen, am honored in this occasion to thank you for it.*
>
> —Franklin D. Roosevelt, 1932[1]

New York Health Commissioner Dr. Thomas Parran read the above statement on behalf of President-Elect Roosevelt at the opening session of a conference held to discuss the CCMC's final report. Roosevelt's statement makes clear three important points: first, that extending adequate medical care was considered of utmost importance; second, that the goal was access for the *entire* population; and third, that the central players to sit at the table should be the state, the voluntary sector, and the profession. Note that the players are exactly that network of actors—as discussed in the previous chapters—so instrumental in building up the public health care state.

A day-long conference at the New York Academy of Medicine, attended by "leaders in medicine, public health, industry, labor and women's organizations, educators, economists and others,"[2] and including a statement from the president-elect, illustrates clearly the importance of this long-awaited report. Its release was seminal for three reasons.

First, the stature of the committee members gave notice: these were the leaders who had been involved in building up the public health care state in the first quarter of the 20th century. They were exactly the leaders that public officials looked to for advice about health policy in the United States. Jennifer Klein notes in her influential 2003 book on the rise of employer-based health insurance in the United States that "the personnel who dominated the CCMC's final recommendations formed a network that linked universities, foundations and government; their movement among these institutions remained fluid. . . . They generally held Ph.D.'s in public health, medical sociology, or economics or MDs."[3]

The second reason the report was influential was the financial support behind the CCMC. Eight foundations and two other organizations (the Carnegie Corporation, the Josiah Macy Jr. Foundation, the Milbank Memorial Fund, the New York Foundation, the Rockefeller Foundation, the Julius Rosenwald Fund, the Russell Sage Foundation, the Twentieth Century Fund, the Social Science Research Council, and the Vermont Commission on Country Life) provided an unprecedented combined donation of $1 million for the committee to conduct research over a five-year period.[4] This extensive foundation-sponsored research linked business elites to state institutions such as the PHS, and eventually to the New Deal's Committee on Economic Security and the subsequent Social Security Board (the New Deal and subsequent developments will be discussed in Part II).[5]

And third, due to the amount of funding, the scope and volume of the studies was similarly exceptional.[6] The CCMC was the first public body to approach the entire problem of producing, delivering, and financing health services for the American people. Historians have called CCMC's final report (as well as the 28 volumes that preceded it and provided evidence supporting its recommendations), one of the most influential health policy documents in the development of U.S. health care policy.[7]

In virtually every telling of America's struggle for the enactment of national health insurance, the CCMC's studies and its final report and recommendations are discussed as setting the stage for America's long trajectory of engagement with voluntary (or what today is simply called "private") health insurance, and the rejection of compulsory (or national) health insurance.[8] The two most controversial recommendations released by the CCMC included support for voluntary health insurance and for the formation of group practice models for the delivery of medical care (see Table 3.1, recommendations #1 and #3). Not surprisingly, these controversial recommendations were the focus for the majority of discussion and debate following the release of the final report, as well as subsequent writings about the history of American health care. There were, as some have noted, areas of agreement between the majority and minority reports. And although most of the attention has been on the areas of disagreement, the areas of agreement are crucially important, as these were the provisions that most readily found their way into legislation at the local, state, and federal level.

The three recommendations with nearly unanimous agreement were strengthening public health services, coordinating medical services, and implementing basic educational improvements (see Table 3.1, recommendations #2, #4, and #5). CCMC Minority Report Number One, which was signed by nine

**Table 3.1 Committee on the Cost of Medical Care, Final Report Recommendations 1–5**

| *Description of Recommendation* | *Support for Recommendation* |
| --- | --- |
| 1. Organization of Medical Services<br>*The Committee recommends that medical service, both preventive and therapeutic, should be furnished largely by organized groups of physicians, dentists, nurses, pharmacists, and other associated personnel.* (p. 109).[1] | Dissent from 2 minority reports. |
| 2. Strengthening of Public Health Services<br>*The Committee recommends that extension of all basic public health services—whether provided by governmental or non-governmental agencies—so that they will be available to the entire population according to its needs. Primarily this extension requires increased financial support for official health departments and full-time trained health officers and members of their staffs whose tenure is dependent only upon professional and administrative competence* (p. 118). | Consensus |
| 3. Group Payment for Medical Services<br>*The Committee recommends that the costs of medical care be placed on a group payment basis, through the use of insurance, through the use of taxation, or through the use of both these methods. This is not meant to preclude the continuation of medical service provided on an individual fee basis for those who prefer the present method* (p. 120). | Dissent from 2 minority reports. |
| 4. Coordination of Medical Services<br>*The Committee recommends that the study, evaluation, and coordination of medical service be considered important functions for every state and local community, that agencies be formed to exercise these functions, and that the coordination of rural with urban services receive special attention* (p.134–35). | Minor dissent from first minority report. |
| 5. Basic Educational Improvements<br>*The Committee makes the following recommendations in the field of professional education: (A) teaching of health and the prevention of disease; that more effective efforts be made to provide trained health officers; that the social aspects of medical practice be given greater attention; that specialties be restricted to those specially qualified; and that postgraduate educational opportunities be increased* (p. 138); (B) through (G) related to educational training for dentists, pharmacists, nurses, nurse-midwives and hospital and clinic administrators. | Consensus |

[1] Italicized recommendations are taken verbatim from CCMC's final report.

*Source:* Committee on the Cost of Medical Care, *Medical Care for the American people* (Chicago: University of Chicago Press, 1932), 120–24.

private practice physicians, clearly states its agreement with recommendations #2 and #5—strengthening of public health services and basic educational improvements—and mentions only minor quibbles with #4—the coordination of medical services.[9] CCMC Minority Report Two begins by stating that it is "in accord with the main position of the majority of the committee."[10] Similar to Minority Report One, its main concern was "emphasizing the necessity of maintaining professional standards and the position of the general practitioner."[11] That is, the minority of the committee demanded protection of clinical autonomy from state regulations. Although they were not explicitly against the group practice recommendations, they were clear in calling for professional control of such practices and distinguishing between professional control from control by the apex of hierarchies in medical schools and teaching hospitals. This concern stems from previous tensions between private practice physicians and physician-scientists (discussed in Chapters 1 and 2), and from emerging ideas around what a "unified health system" would look like (to be discussed in more detail later in this chapter).[12]

Finally, there was also support for these recommendations from the two members who abstained from signing the majority report and wrote separate statements. Walter H. Hamilton, an economist from Yale University, wrote a separate statement mainly to advocate for compulsory health insurance, but also to provide support for the majority recommendations related to state-led infrastructure building and public health investments.[13] The other abstaining member, Edgar Sydenstricker, was unclear regarding his support for these three recommendations, writing only that he could not sign the final report because it did not "deal adequately with the fundamental economic question [of how to control health care costs] which the Committee was formed primarily to study and consider."[14] However, from Sydenstricker's other writings as an employee of the PHS and as the research director of the Milbank Fund, we know that he was a strong supporter of investments in public health. Indeed, his concern about cost control was related to his view that there was inadequate investment in cost-effective public health measures.[15]

It is clear in the final report that there was unanimous agreement around these three recommendations. This is significant because it means that even physicians on the committee representing the AMA and private practice physicians agreed that public health services should be expanded (recommendation #2), and that government planning (run by the public health network) was crucial to expand the coordination and availability of health care services and personnel, even if they did not pursue the group practice model in name. Considering the prevailing view presented by public health historians—that investments in public health were rife with controversy during this period[16]—it is particularly important to note that, as one might predict based on the resulting consensus, all levels of government continued to invest in the public health care state, just as the report recommended.

## Consensus: Public Health Expansion, Local Control, and Government Funding

The CCMC final report recommended "the extension of all basic public health services—whether provided by *governmental or non-governmental agencies*— so that they will be available to the entire population according to its needs. Primarily this extension requires increased *financial support* for official health departments and full-time trained health officers and members of their staffs whose tenure is dependent only upon professional and administrative *competence*."[17] Note that the minority report was "in full and hearty accord with the majority in its recommendations for 'the strengthening of public health services.'"[18]

There are three important points to note in this recommendation. First, there was unanimous agreement on expanding public health through increases in state financing. Second, one part of the statement, "whether provided by *governmental or non-governmental agencies*," illustrates that the recommendation is ambiguous on which type of organizational entity—public or private voluntary—should provide public health services. What the committee was not ambiguous on— and this is the third point—was the scientific and administrative competence of the appointed public health agency; it was of utmost importance that the agency not be *politically* influenced in any way.

That almost all the members agreed on this expansion in 1932 is perhaps not surprising, considering the statement of purpose the CCMC laid out in volume one at the beginning of its research in 1928. In outlining the scope and focus of its five-year inquiry, the CCMC reported in the first volume, that the committee was "not committed to any theories and policies, but committed to defining the problem as the field of *curative and preventive* medicine."[19] This principle—that any solution should include both curative and preventive medicine—was clearly stated at the outset and throughout all 28 volumes. The opening paragraph of the first report issued by the committee explained the creation and purpose of the CCMC and then defined two critical terms: "sanitarians" and "medical service." In clarifying the definitions, the members argued that both terms fit in public health, and that the field should clearly encompass curative and preventive services.[20]

This principle is consistent with the position of the APHA's Committee on Administrative Practices (CAP), led by Winslow and Chapin (as discussed in the previous chapter), which had been advocating for a redefinition of health department responsibilities since the mid-1910s. CCMC's recommendation in

1932 called for expanding public health administration both outward to new geographic areas and inward by expanding the scope of services offered. Given that the definition of public health's domain had been actively contested for more than 20 years prior to this report, it is important that little discussion occurred on this point. The majority report stated that "there is nearly universal agreement that the following are 'proper public health functions' ":

(a) The collection and analysis of vital statistics;
(b) The control of water, milk, and food supplies;
(c) The control of sanitation;
(d) The control, through quarantine and supervision, of communicable diseases; and
(e) The provision of laboratory service.

In addition to these the Committee believes that the following activities are also proper public health activities:

(f) The promotion of maternal, infant and child hygiene, including medical and dental inspection and supervision of school children;
(g) The popular health instruction;
(h) The provision of preventive dental care for children, and
(i) The provision of special services for the prevention, diagnosis, and treatment of patients with tuberculosis, venereal diseases, malaria, hookworm, or any other disease which constitutes a special health problem in the community that cannot be solved adequately and effectively by the other available medical and health agencies.[21]

In this first report, prevention was discussed as saving money: "Through the prevention of disease further increases in the total cost of medical service can best be avoided."[22] Five years later, in the final majority report, the disproportionate argument was presented again: "The United States spends only $1 per capita for public health services to every $29 for other medical services (see Illustration 3.1). As a consequence, public health service in the United States—both governmental and non-governmental—is far from adequate."[23] The authors of the CCMC's many volumes used the disproportionate argument repeatedly to request an increase in public health funding. For example, CCMC's final report includes a figure showing many more people dying due to preventable diseases than dying in battle during World War I (see Illustration 3.2). What's more, the majority report argued that a "satisfactory [public health] service calls for much higher appropriations—from $1.79 to $2.13 per capita expenditures."[24] While this argument was persuasive, it was also ironic, as public health leaders were at this same time increasingly claiming that the separation of prevention and treatment was a false dichotomy.

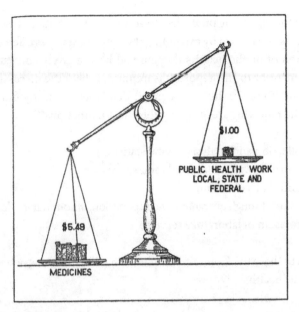

*Illustration 3.1* CCMC Depiction of Comparable Costs. *Source:* Committee on the Cost of Medical Care, *Medical Care for the American People* (Chicago: University of Chicago Press, 1932), 111.

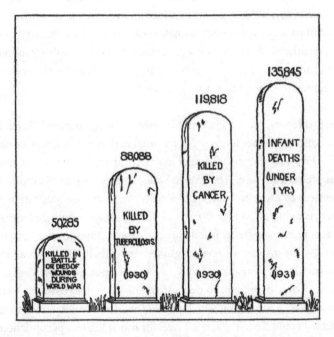

*Illustration 3.2* CCMC Depiction of Preventable Deaths. *Source:* Committee on the Cost of Medical Care, *Medical Care for the American People* (Chicago: University of Chicago Press, 1932), 148.

Not only were public health leaders and the writers of the CCMC reports adamant that prevention and curative care should be merged, and that the public health care state should be expanded, they were equally insistent that public and private entities could develop and provide a unified health system. The CCMC specified in the final report that as long as health care standards were set prior to determining availability of services, there was "no reason to separate [public and private] forces."[25] Consistent with this view, the majority report called for private physicians, under the group practice recommendation, to assume responsibility in providing needed "preventive medical services [where] . . . complete groups would contain physicians, both general practitioners and specialists, dentists, nurses, pharmacists, medical social workers, and all the needed technicians and assisting personnel."[26] Although this was discussed as the "group practice model," the concept was built off the health center movement that had grown throughout the 1920s. I briefly discuss the health center movement here to show how it helped create support for public health's role in planning, and aided the grow-and-hide approach.

## Health Center Movement

As Chapter 2 made clear, by 1921 the federated public health and voluntary agencies had a fair amount of experience in providing medical treatments. Thus, it was not a major leap for the public health network to argue for the development of a new delivery model to fully integrate preventive and curative medicine, and to coordinate public and private activities. Several leaders started to promote the idea of coordinated health centers, which would bring all the separate health and social welfare activities of voluntary agencies and public health departments together under one roof. This was called the "health center" model. Michael Davis, for example, wrote about how long waiting times was particularly detrimental to providing adequate access to health services for immigrant mothers, because the mothers had no one to care for their children.[27] In response, health centers provided child care and other social services at the place of health provision (see Table 3.2). As different health-related programs expanded (for maternal and child health, for VD, TB, etc.), public health leaders also advocated for the health center idea as a way to increase coordination, reduce duplication, and increase efficiency.[28]

From 1910 to 1920, health centers developed in many U.S. cities, including New York, Buffalo, Boston, Pittsburg, Philadelphia, Cincinnati, and Milwaukee.[29] They often grew out of child health centers or tuberculosis programs, where they were already engaged at the local community level and providing needed medical care. In Cincinnati in 1917, Wilbur Phillips and Elsie Cole Phillips started

*Table 3.2* **East Harlem Health Center Services, 1921**

| Services within the Center | Affiliated Services in Neighboring Buildings |
|---|---|
| Tuberculosis Clinic | Dental Service |
| General Medical Examinations | Children's Examination Clinic |
| Baby Health Station | Nutrition Classes |
| Eye Clinic | Social and Educational Service |
| Vaccination and Schick Tests | Infant and Child Welfare Substations |
| Heart Clinic | Infant and Preschool Clinics |
| Prenatal Clinic | Prenatal Clinics |
| Psychiatric Clinic | Nutrition Classes |
| Health Shop: Community Health Education | Home Visiting Nursing Service |
| Health Information Bureau | |
| Home Visiting Nursing Service | |
| Social and Family Welfare | |

*Source:* Michael Marks Davis and United Hospital Fund of New York, *Clinics, Hospitals and Health Centers* (New York and London: Harper & Brothers, 1927).

a health center demonstration that included prenatal and antepartum care, well child care for infants and preschool children, anti-tuberculosis work, dental examination of school children, nursing service, medical care during the influenza epidemic of 1918, and periodic examination of adults. They called the center "The Social Unit," based on their earlier health center work in Milwaukee, which applied a consciously self-governing model.[30] Although several publications at the time described broad public support for the Social Unit experiment, political opposition did emerge, primarily from the newly elected mayor, other conservative lawmakers, and the local medical society. The opposition charged the Phillips with creating a "Red Plot"—a particularly fraught scare tactic at the end of World War I—and city funding for the project was withdrawn. Opposition from local medical societies was particularly vehement. As Edward Ochsner from the Illinois Medical Society (and a leader of the practicing physicians' opposition to "state medicine") put it: "Before Compulsory Health Insurance went into coma or expired, the beast gave birth to a litter of vicious pups answering to the name of State or County Subsidized Community Health Centers."[31]

In 1971, medical historian George Rosen described how the development of several health center experiments in the early 1920s became controversial and resulted in the demise of the health center movement.[32] Nonetheless, while opposition was strong and the more radical health center ideas—especially self-governing democratic forms—did die off, important ideas and associated practices emerged from the health center movement: health centers were instrumental in building the public health profession's view of its administrative role as tantamount to planning the U.S. health care system; and because the health center model and its association with health care planning was controversial, public health leaders assured a prominent role for private provision. As a result, the American Public Health Association's Committee on Administrative Practice (CAP)—the same committee discussed in Chapter 2 that developed the "ideal health department"—continued its work to present a more politically palatable version of health centers.

In 1919, Winslow, the chair of the CAP, acknowledged that there was a health center movement afoot, but also suggested that it was a natural outgrowth of the broader public health movement: "The most striking and typical development of the public health movement of the present day is the health center."[33] The CAP collected data on the administration of health centers and reported that "thirty-three are managed entirely by the public authorities and that twenty-seven are managed entirely under private auspices, while sixteen are or will be under control of both public and private administration."[34] This became a common tactic—to assure private practice physicians that public health leaders would only play a coordinating role and would not threaten private provision of medical care. For example, Michael Davis, who headed up several research projects for CCMC, also highlighted this idea in his study of clinics, hospitals, and health centers (published in 1927):

> Many different models came under the rubric of "health center" . . .
> we cannot say that so-called "therapeutic" services do not belong in a
> health center. Nor can we specify a particular form of organization, ad-
> ministrative [function]. . . . All health centers do, however, usually pre-
> sent two factors in common: first, selection of a definite population,
> or district unit, with the aim of reaching all therein who need the serv-
> ices; and second, co-ordination of services within this area, embracing
> both its own facilities or services and those of other agencies, whether
> for health or for general social welfare. The definition might be stated
> thus: *A Health Center is an organization which provides, promotes, and
> co-ordinates medical service and related social service for a specified district*
> (italics in original text).[35]

At the American Health Congress, held in Atlantic City in May 1926, the CAP led the discussions on "community health organization," recommending plans of organization suitable for communities of different sizes.[36] Following the

Atlantic City congress, the CAP sponsored a book on community health organization, first published in 1927, which "specified the need for planning and cooperative action in the field of public health administration." Indeed, the book "was to serve as a manual for the active public health administrators."[37] By 1928, the activities of the CAP had expanded so substantially that the leadership decided to reorganize the CAP to explicitly include health system planning in separate subcommittees, including those that focused on "model health ordinances" and the "relationship to the American Medical Association (AMA)." In 1929, the CAP published a progress report on model health ordinances, and proposed that they should specify the powers, duties, and obligations of the local board of health.[38]

Several foundations served an important function in advancing health centers. The Milbank Memorial Fund, for example, played a prominent role in promoting the idea of health centers in New York. In collaboration with leaders of government and voluntary organizations, the fund organized demonstration projects in communities of differing sizes: a rural area (Cattaraugus County), a medium-size city (Syracuse), and a large city (a section of Manhattan called Bellevue-Yorkville). Initially the demonstrations intended to focus on tuberculosis prevention, but the technical board and advisory council strongly urged the fund to take a much more comprehensive approach.[39]

Hermann Biggs, the commissioner of the New York State Department of Health, also advocated for the health center idea. There was a push by several state health departments—with encouragement from the PHS—to focus more attention on developing health services in rural areas, and to use the community health center idea to do so. In his annual report to Governor Smith in 1920, Biggs advocated the development of health centers in all counties throughout New York as the most scientifically sound way to organize medical services. He played a key role in developing the 1921 NY Health Center bill, which called for state aid to counties for the development and operation of health centers and local community hospitals.[40] The report emphasized how the bill was necessary not only for residents in rural areas, but also for practicing physicians who were isolated and lacked facilities to help keep up with the latest medical developments. Biggs and his colleagues used the leverage of their scientific expertise to argue that the quality of care would be improved with the passage of the bill, much to the chagrin of private practice physicians.

Not surprisingly, New York's state and local medical societies opposed the bill, using what became familiar arguments: "too much power to the laity and too little to the medical profession," "a step toward centralization of government and paternalism," "a measure which leads us closer to state medicine."[41] Largely because of physician opposition, the bill failed passage in the New York legislature. But despite the failure of the Health Center bill, Biggs was able to secure another piece of legislation during the same session, which gave counties the authority to create their own health district with its own board of health. This received little fanfare, but was striking because it allowed counties to create county health units that might (and did) resemble health centers. Indeed, with encouragement from the Milbank Memorial Fund and public health leaders, a comprehensive health center (beyond the demonstration project) was set up in Cattaraugus County in New York.

However, missing from this legislation was any commitment of government financing. To address this problem, Biggs and other public health leaders (through the State's Public Health Council) argued again in 1922 for passage of a Health Center bill. And again, local medical societies balked and argued even more vehemently that this was an attempt at "state medicine," and the bill failed.[42]

In 1923, the state of New York successfully passed a bill that did not use the term "health center" but which fulfilled the objectives originally set forth in the Health Center bill. This bill provided state aid to counties "for the construction, establishment or maintenance [of] a county, community, or other public hospital, clinic, dispensary or similar institution . . . for the improvement of the public health, or any public health work undertaken."[43] Although this language is difficult to decipher, it meant that state grants were available to counties who wanted to create a health center model. In 1928, a health center in Cattaraugus County secured more than half its funding from a combination of county funds, state funds, and $52,000 from the Milbank Memorial Fund.[44]

Colleagues involved in passage of this bill commented on Biggs's political genius, noting that he sacrificed the name of the bill to secure its substance: state aid to develop rural health services at the county level. Alluding to this political maneuver and its farsightedness, the Public Health Council wrote in its memorial tribute to Biggs later that year that "[i]f further advances were blocked in one direction, he sought opportunities of moving forward in other directions."[45] Although they didn't call it this, the Public Health Council saw the strategy behind Grow and Hide: expanding public health's domain while hiding its reach, both in rhetoric (via changing the name) and in structure (through intergovernmental financing and voluntary sector collaboration).

Importantly, if we look at research from Ira Hiscock about the development of health centers over the 1920s, he reports significant stability.[46] As of 1930, there were over 1,500 health centers distributed throughout the country,[47] and 80% had been in existence since 1910.[48] The centers were divided equally between those run by government (729)—either county or municipal departments of health—and those run by voluntary agencies (725), including, for example, hospitals, child health organizations, and tuberculosis associations. Consistent with the ownership form, public funds supported half of the centers' budget, with "the remainder being received through community chests, or from private or voluntary funds."[49]

The public health network was amazingly successful at building up the public health care state and creating new delivery models, while at the same time strategically avoiding the question of financing and claiming outright that the state can remain agnostic on whether private or public entities should carry out public health responsibilities. Thus, in 1932, when the functions of the community medical center under recommendation #2 in the final CCMC report included "various clinical, therapeutic, and preventive services which [at the time were] provided by official health agencies,"[50] it was not surprising that the majority report called for a massive merging of treatment and preventive services through this new organizational form. Indeed, that is what public health leaders had been fighting for throughout the 1920s. While the committee came out against for-profit entities, it strongly favored the use of private voluntary agencies and official public health agencies to run these new community organizations.

## Back to CCMC Consensus: A Public-Private Approach.

The same type of private-public combined approach was suggested in the other two consensus recommendations (see Table 3.1, recommendations #4 and #5). CCMC's recommendation #4 called very broadly for the "coordination of medical care," and argued that the creation of planning agencies (or councils or committees) was necessary at both the local and state level.[51] Here, one might think the role of government was clear, as the committee explicitly argued for a governance structure to plan for the rational development of health services and the financing of care at the local level: "In each community, permanent, local agencies should be established to evaluate and to coordinate the existing preventive and curative medical services, to eliminate services not needed, and to stimulate the provision of additional services which are needed."[52] This recommendation emerged in response to what the CCMC viewed as the "principal defect" in the provision of medical care, "that there is, in most communities, no competent agency to evaluate, supplement, or coordinate the medical services of the community on the basis of unbiased and thorough knowledge."[53]

At this time, the concern about bias and incompetence was directed at local government. Thus, although the committee recommended a governing body, their distrust of government and the vices of patronage steered them toward significant private representation. The report was explicit in calling for the inclusion of all vested interests and private governing bodies. "They should include representatives of the public, the medical professions, the health agencies, the hospitals, and the social agencies. . . . Funds or services may be provided by

community chests, chambers of commerce, and local governmental or voluntary health agencies."[54] This is the same public-voluntary coalition (described in
Chapters 1 and 2) that had been building the public health care state since the
early 1900s. As such, this recommendation was a natural outgrowth of the public
health movement and the public health network's involvement in building up
the public health care state prior to 1932.

Finally, the CCMC's recommendation #5 also enjoyed widespread consensus and similarly called for state investment in building up the private health
care state. The benign title of the fifth recommendation—"Basic Educational
Improvements"—hints at why a consensus could easily form around this innoc-
uous call for more training of medical personnel.[55] While the committee was
clear about which types of medical personnel should be encouraged—nurses,
social workers, public health, general practitioners—and that the rapid increase
in specialists should be kept in check, they were silent on who should pay and
what the distribution of investments should look like. This was not because the
committee had not thought about these issues or had no data. A member of the
committee, Michael Davis, and a key staff member, Rufus Rorem, oversaw the
studies on hospital development and capital investment for the committee, and
also looked into workforce development issues. As Rorem commented years
later in an interview, it was clear to him as a staff member, and to many on the
committee, that government invested heavily in facilities and medical personnel,
though unequally:

> The primary problem facing society in providing medical care was the
> effective utilization of capital investments in facilities and personnel.
> At that time the average hospital had an investment of about a million
> dollars. The average public investment in a physician was approximately
> $10,000. The average investment in a nurse was zero, since she worked
> her way through nursing school, making a personal investment from
> the day she entered the institution's premises.[56]

In the details behind these consensus recommendations for public health
expansions, planning committees, and workforce development, one can
see the roots of America's peculiar hidden health care state. In each of these
recommendations, the need is clear for government regulation and financing
and the general authority of the state. Yet underneath each recommendation, the
inclusion of the private sector is unrelenting: there are repeated calls for experi-
mentation with multiple organizational forms where private provision of public
funds is claimed to be equally if not more appropriate; and time and again the
involvement of the private sector in decision-making is presented as paramount.
Because this report is of such strong historical significance, it is important to

note the unanimous support for the ideas presented therein—we can see the roots of grow-and-hide beginning to deepen and take hold.

Finally, it is also important to recognize the agreement regarding the role of government, an agreement located within the two recommendations that experienced the most controversy.

### Consensus within Dissensus: Support Voluntary Insurance and Tax Funding to Address Its Limits

Despite recommending voluntary health insurance, the majority report clearly understood the limitations. The United States had enough experience with voluntary health insurance even by 1932, and the committee extensively studied these experiences, which made the committee particularly concerned that voluntary insurance, if implemented, should be closely attached to their group practice recommendation. In particular, the final majority report argued that the best hope for adequate coverage was for people to purchase insurance from a community medical center.[57] The committee believed the problems of poor quality of care, inadequate reserves, and low payments to providers could be "obviated in part if all voluntary health insurance were offered by community medical centers, with financial control by representatives of the public and professional control by participating practitioners."[58]

It is important to note that CCMC was not the first time Americans debated the merits of health insurance and alternatives to compulsory health insurance. In 1906, a group of academic reformers—primarily progressive labor economists—formed the American Association of Labor Legislation (AALL). Initially, AALL's major causes were focused on workmen safety concerns, such as the elimination of poisonous phosphorus in match factories, and workmen's compensation. However, it is primarily remembered for being the first organization to mount a nationwide campaign for compulsory health insurance.[59] Even then leaders in the public health network viewed investing in public health and planning a unified health system as more important than focusing on health insurance. I turn now to the role of public health leaders in debates over compulsory insurance in this early period, since it helps to explain the positions taken in CCMC's final report.

### Public Health's Focus on Planning the Health System

The AALL's "standard bill" for compulsory health insurance was designed for adoption by individual states—not the country as a whole—and only for full-time workers. Many needy groups were intentionally excluded from coverage: workers earning less than $1,200 annually, agricultural and domestic workers, dependents, and the unemployed. Many states took on a formal review of the legislation and some put versions of the standard bill up for a vote (e.g., New York, Wisconsin, Ohio, California). However, not one state moved forward with what was called "worker's health insurance."[60]

Many historians have analyzed why the proposals failed, and tend to point to three main factors: first, although initially the AMA and many local medical societies were in favor of compulsory worker's insurance, a shift toward opposition by the local medical societies was instrumental in scaring many local politicians away from supporting the bill; second, the nationalistic zeal during World War I and its aftermath certainly changed the sense of political feasibility for state intervention, especially since many claimed that worker's insurance was a German idea (and therefore bad in the new political climate); and finally, numerous critics pointed out the shortcomings of the bill, insisting that it left out many people, and would thus only solve a small piece of the problem.[61]

It was this latter concern that leaders of the public health network worried about. They were not necessarily opposed to compulsory health insurance—indeed a number of individuals endorsed it—but it was not their preferred approach, and it was in their view of minor importance compared to creating better health systems to provide care directly to people in need of it. Most scholars have blamed public health leaders' competition and turf issues for the lukewarm reception to compulsory insurance. Perhaps, but state-building creates a larger consistent logic, one that can supersede competition or jealousy. By the time the labor economists were offering insurance to workmen, the public health movement was in a mature stage, and state-building was well established. In this light, it is not surprising that public health leaders recognized the limited insurance proposed in the AALL's Standard Model as a minor solution to the major problems of ill health in America.

Moreover, the AALL made no effort to attach insurance schemes to any particular delivery model reforms. As noted earlier, public health leaders believed strongly in the need for coordinated health care delivery, encouraging collaboration between social services and health and emphasizing prevention along with treatment, which private practitioners were not doing at all in the late 1910s and the 1920s. As such, it is no wonder they were not particularly interested in the AALL's proposal. Not only did they believe it wouldn't address the real issues related to care for illnesses, but worse—and perhaps somewhat prophetically—they worried that it would embed and encourage reimbursement for a dysfunctional delivery system, one that only emphasized curative care.

Some have noted that the Public Health Service was supportive of compulsory insurance, pointing to support for the idea in a 1915 publication written by the Assistant Surgeon General of the PHS, B. S. Warren, and another PHS staff member, Edgar Sydenstricker.[62] However, if we look closer at the entire document, it is clear that Warren and Sydenstricker did not provide a simple endorsement of the AALL's "standard bill," but rather of their own, weighing in on exactly what such a scheme should look like. Their support for compulsory insurance—or what they referred to as "sickness insurance"—was contingent upon a very strong role for local and state health departments.

The article begins by stating that the purpose of sickness insurance is to "prevent sickness and death." Notice how rather than focusing on protection against financial loss, as most AALL economists did, they focused on its potential benefits to the health of individuals and communities. After describing in detail how the funding and benefits of a sickness insurance scheme should be structured, they discuss the financial responsibilities of employers, employees, the state, and communities. Importantly, they focus on how financial policies should be structured so that each player has an incentive to focus on prevention and improve health. Indeed, by recommending employers pay a weekly contribution toward a sickness fund, they envisioned a direct benefit to public health departments: "It will give each a financial incentive to prevent sickness, and instead of opposing public-health legislation employers will insist on more efficient health departments, and they will want their places of employment studied by expert sanitarians in order to advise them as to improvements."[63]

In the next section of the article, they insist that the relationship of insurance to public health must be strong:

> Sickness insurance will be a failure unless it results in sickness prevention. . . . The American municipality is responsible for sickness no less than the employer. It is not likely to engage in work of prevention unless it is driven to do so. Health preservation must become an issue in municipal elections. One way of achieving it is to make the city contribute a part of the sickness fund. Still better results could be obtained by providing that the State shall refund to the city a part or all of its contributions in case the sick rate has been reduced in like proportion by efforts of the municipality. If this be done, it will result in the party in power "pointing with pride" to its success in reducing the sick rate and thereby reducing the city's compulsory contribution to the sickness fund, and the party not in power will promise still greater reductions.
>
> It can not be denied that physicians are able to do more than they are doing at present for the prevention of sickness. They are not doing it to the full extent of their ability on account of inertia. This inertia can best be overcome by an economic incentive. If the physicians are paid a per capita for each insured person, and if that per capita is made to rise

when the sick rate falls, or made to fall when the sick rate rises, prevention will acquire powerful promoters.[64]

I provide this quote at length for several reasons. First, it is clear that they are staking out a claim for how insurance can—and must—work within the broader political, economic, and medical system. They clearly specify how the incentives of all the major players—employers, employees, communities, the state, and physicians—must be aligned so that prevention and health improvement is valued above all else. Amazingly, they argue not only that the state should have an interest in rewarding prevention, but that the local community should be rewarded for good health outcomes, thus incentivizing political parties to build their policy agendas around preventive care. They also argue that physicians should have a "health outcomes" incentive built into their payment structure.[65]

In addition to these financial incentives, they recommend that the insurance fund hire "medical staff or a corps of efficient full-time medical men, skilled in preventive medicine, and closely related to the State and local health departments."[66] Obviously, this sounds exactly like the PHS commissioned health officer corps that the agency was extremely proud of and believed was much better trained than private practice physicians. So, here too, they envisioned significant public health state-building not just passively happening alongside the development of sickness insurance, but actively directing the insurance program and developing a financial scheme to promote health and prevent death and disease. Although this sounds very radical today, it was not an aberration at the time—it was consistent with the central mission of PHS.

Some have argued that the PHS shifted gears after opposition to the AALL bills emerged, especially the pushback from the AMA, and after legislation failed across the American states.[67] They point to a statement in another publication from Warren and Sydenstricker in 1919 in which they stated the "probability of sickness insurance acts endangering the very existence of state health departments by absorbing all of the funds available for health work."[68] But Warren and Sydenstricker do not, as that quote misleadingly suggests, argue against insurance in this article. Instead, they argue for the importance of structuring insurance by explicitly including health departments in its design so that it can be called *health* insurance and not *sickness* insurance. Indeed, the subtitle in the section where this quote is found reveals this position: *"Methods of Adequate Prevention of Sickness—Plan for Making Sickness Insurance Actually Health Insurance."*[69] More importantly, this worry about leaving out health departments was not a new worry of PHS leaders. The 1915 article raised exactly the same concerns: namely, that unless insurance was organized in close collaboration with local and state health departments, inefficiencies would increase and incentives would encourage payments for sickness rather than for health promotion and prevention. Note that the sentence immediately following the quote above reads: "Our statesmen and lawmakers must therefore be careful that proper and ample provisions are made for health machinery in any sickness insurance act."[70]

Most importantly, this telling of the story gives too much importance to the AALL's effect on the development of health care policy in the United States. As the public health care state was increasing capacity, it was conducting multiple forms of statecraft on many fronts: from the health center movement, to expansions in maternal and child health, to fighting disease epidemics and building up rural health infrastructure, to fundamental questions about the ability of people to pay for medical care. On each front, the public health network operated at multiple levels—local, state, and federal—and strategically anticipated opposition: from private practice physicians worried about public health moving into medical treatment rather than just prevention; from the private practice physicians and conservatives worried about public provision overtaking private; and from conservatives concerned about the growing power of the federal government, especially through the grants-in-aid mechanism. Although many public health leaders supported insurance, it was always contingent on it fitting into their larger fight to restructure the health care system. And at that time, there had been enough public health state-building for many to begin to envision the possibility of a federally coordinated public health infrastructure, under which insurance would not be needed and all persons would have access to care.[71]

This argument begins to take shape in another article that same year, this time by just B. S. Warren, calling for a *Unified Health Service*.[72] Alan Derickson[73] discusses this article as a pivot for the PHS—moving away from "pure" prevention and support of compulsory insurance toward a new radical position in favor of combining prevention and curative medicine in support of universal care. Derickson provides important evidence for this claim. He shows that many public health leaders openly voiced support for combining prevention with curative medicine to truly promote health, and openly acknowledged that, on the ground, the divide between these services was often artificial. This is true, and I show in more detail later in this chapter (and in Chapter 4) how actors in the public health network did become more emboldened in their claims, but also show that when and how they made these claims depended on their audience. They made what might appear to be "radical" claims, but which emerged very logically from years of statecraft and state-building, and at the same time they made important rhetorical retreats when forced to dance around the opposition.

For example, in the "Unified Health Service" article, Warren clearly laid out the case for a federated public health service. The title may appear radical, but a close examination of the article reveals a very similar structure to other articles in circulation at the time, which promoted the "ideal health depart-ment." It discusses the need for standard budgets in the development of health departments at both the local (rural and municipal) and state levels, the juris-diction of services by level, and the need for coordination and workforce ex-pertise. This was not a pivot, but an extension. And in the same article we see the rhetorical dance: this published article was read before the Civic League in Birmingham, Alabama; given that it was addressed to a city in a southern state with staunch concerns about protecting state and local rights, one can see the argument crafted to address opposition on this front. Warren begins by pointing to building of the Panama Canal under the leadership of PHS officer William Gorgas, who was from Alabama, highlighting the canal's significant benefit to Alabama, and how it couldn't have been done without significant help from and coordination with local governments and local voluntary agencies, such as the Red Cross. In explaining the Unified Health Service, he is quick to illustrate how this is merely what they already know—stressing the autonomy of local and state health departments, with the federal government providing only funding and coordination support.[74]

Returning to the AALL's fight for compulsory insurance, it is important to note that it wasn't just public health leaders who viewed the proposal as a partial solution. Most of the leading social workers of the day—Jane Addams, *Survey* editor Edward Devine, and many others—were advocates of compulsory insur-ance, because they saw the strong connection between poverty and sickness and believed insurance would at least provide some financial protection from the medical costs of illness. But because they worked in the field with poor families, they understood the need for greater access to care, and had long been advocates for more public health infrastructure and "preventive services." They advocated for the AALL's bill, but it wasn't the only social reform on their agenda. As discussed in Chapter 2, many of the leading feminists of the day were social workers with a hefty agenda of their own: suffrage, creating well-baby stations and maternal and child health clinics, fighting for the Children's Bureau and mothers' pensions. Considering that the male economists running the AALL insisted on limiting insurance benefits to industrial workers and not extending benefits to dependents or to fields of labor dominated by women, it is no wonder that social workers, though supportive, did not work in full force behind this ini-tiative. Business, too, was more enamored with investments in public health than insurance. For example, in discussions with the Boston state legislature in 1918, members of the National Industrial Conference Board (NICB) were more inter-ested in investing in direct health improvements through public health initiatives than in relieving the costs of medical care through insurance.

In sum, because leaders of the public health network were involved on an ongoing basis with implementing new programs (notably the health center movement) and new policies at local and state levels, where they were often met with opposition, the leaders continued to expand, but did so through a Grow-and-Hide strategy. The strategy invested the leaders with a particular view of health care policy; namely, one that emphasized the development of health care delivery first, with concerns about health care insurance to follow. This central tension in health care reform debates—whether to focus on health care delivery reform or health insurance coverage—began in this early period, and we see it again a decade later in CCMC's many studies and its final report.

### Back to CCMC's Consensus within Dissensus: Promoting Delivery Model Reforms and Public Subsidies to Fill in the Gaps of Voluntary Insurance

Just as one can see the roots of America's peculiar hidden health care state in the details behind the consensus recommendations for public health expansions, planning committees, and workforce development (#2, #4, and #5, see Table 3.1), so too are these roots visible under the more controversial recommendations. While much of the dissent focused on the CCMC's recommendation #1 to reorganize medical services, there was agreement in the details of this recommendation that reorganization[75] should focus on private voluntary health care facilities (see Table 3.3). Despite significant public health state-building, the inclusion of the private sector is constant and accepted. Even when tax dollars are mentioned, they are specified to go to private clinics and hospitals.

And like public health leaders' reaction to AALL's proposal, their support for voluntary health insurance was always contingent on connecting health insurance to their preferred delivery model reforms. Also, in keeping with federated public health state-building, the CCMC promoted the principles of federalism throughout its recommendations, as a way to make suggestions for delivery model reforms and various insurance schemes without recommending anything that could be construed as a federal mandate. For example, the strong belief in local control was so paramount for some CCMC members that it undergirded their support for both compulsory *and* voluntary insurance. Five members[76] of the majority report crafted a separate statement in opposition to the majority recommendation that voluntary insurance be tried first before the adoption of any compulsory plan based on the logic of federalism:

> Fortunately, we have retained in this country a wholesome local responsibility for medical service. This fact means that opportunities exist for trying out many plans under various and variable conditions. . . . We believe that experimentation along the lines of both voluntary and required

*Table 3.3* **Committee on the Cost of Medical Care, Final Report Recommendation 1: Organization of Medical Services**

**Main Recommendation**

*The Committee recommends that medical service, both preventive and therapeutic, should be furnished largely by organized groups of physicians, dentists, nurses, pharmacists, and other associated personnel. Such groups should be organized, preferably around a hospital, for rendering complete home, office, and hospital care. The form of organization should encourage the maintenance of high standards and the development or preservation of a personal relation between patient and physician.*[1,2]

| Details of Recommendation | Ownership/Source of Payment |
|---|---|
| 1A. Community Medical Centers | *Existing* (**private and public**) *hospitals may become community medical centers; coordinated with some plan of group payment.* |
| 1B. Industrial Medical Service | **Private ownership**/*private voluntary payment: Complete medical service paid for jointly by employees and employers.* |
| 1C. University Medical Service | *In "college towns" extend university medical services into a community medical center which serves townspeople as well as students.* |
| *Additional Recommendations for Supplementary or Temporary Use* | |
| 1D. Utilization of Subsidiary Personnel | *Utilize trained nursing attendants and nurse-midwives as appropriate.* |
| 1E. Private Group Clinics | *Further development of* **private** *group medical service, independent of public aid.* |
| 1F. Pay Clinics | **Voluntary or Tax Funds** *to extend the development of* **pay clinics** *to aid patients who are not indigent but unable to meet prevailing fees.* |
| 1G. Middle-Rate Hospital Service | *Further development in* **existing (voluntary) hospitals** *of middle-rate programs to assist "persons of moderate means" by creating a unified and limited bill and helping the patient devise a plan to pay for it (p. 113).* |
| 1H. Physicians' Private Offices in Hospitals | *As a first step general hospitals may make space available in their buildings for providers to hold office hours for paying ambulatory patients.* |

*(continued)*

*Table* 3.3 **Continued**

| 1I. Organized Nursing Service | *Home visiting nursing should be more widely available and therefore paid for under organized group practice plans.* |
|---|---|
| 1J. County Medical Society Clinics | *In rural areas and small towns, county medical societies may* **establish clinics** *to provide care for persons unable to pay the current fees of private practitioners.* **Taxation**: *"Services should be paid for by the county or city authorities reasonable sums" (p. 114).* |

1. Italicized recommendations are taken verbatim from CCMC's final report.
2. Endorsed by 35 of the 36 members who signed the majority report.

*Source:* Committee on the Cost of Medical Care. *Medical Care for the American People* (Chicago: University of Chicago Press, 1932), 120–24).

health insurance, along with the other experiments in the group purchase of medicine should be promoted and carried on. . . . In all likelihood, in certain areas of the country and for certain population and economic groups, required health insurance will be found to be more feasible and practicable than voluntary health insurance and vice versa.[77]

Importantly, even though the CCMC majority report recommended pursuing voluntary health insurance, they still acknowledged numerous problems inherent to the voluntary model. First, in the final report, the CCMC mentioned the potential political problems that would likely emerge if the United States pursued the incremental strategy of delaying compulsory insurance and investing in voluntary insurance:

Most European countries, one after another, have gone from a voluntary to a required system of insurance, but many of the evils of the voluntary system are carried over to the compulsory plan. Vested interests are built up under voluntary insurance which are very difficult to dislodge, even though they seriously hamper effective work. While it is true that the United States has few cooperative societies which could administer compulsory health insurance, this is a fortunate rather than an unfortunate circumstance. In European countries, such societies have almost completely outgrown their usefulness, so far as health insurance is concerned; but they still remain to clutter and confuse administration, and to prevent insurance statistics from being useful for public health purposes.[78]

This quote demonstrates remarkable foresight by seeing how initial investments in voluntary insurance could change the political dynamics in the future. Second, in addition to understanding how the emergence of new political interests could make future reform more difficult, the CCMC also understood the political implications of increasing government funding for voluntary reform without having the commensurate regulatory structures in place: "Governmental participation and regulation will undoubtedly be almost as necessary for voluntary as for compulsory insurance, if the worst abuses are to be avoided."[79]

Third, they also noted the lack of efficacy of voluntary insurance: "[F]amilies with low or irregular incomes, even if they are self-supporting while employed, cannot usually be covered by any form of voluntary insurance. . . . [Moreover] persons employed in small businesses or self-employed are also unlikely to enter a voluntary plan. . . . For these reasons, voluntary health insurance has been succeeded by compulsory insurance in most of the countries of western Europe."[80]

Fourth, the committee recognized that affordable voluntary insurance was particularly problematic in less-populated rural areas, and acknowledged the likelihood of still needing state subsidies or compulsory insurance in such areas.[81] Not surprisingly, the eight members who signed the majority report— but who disagreed with this particular recommendation in favor of compulsory insurance—also made these two points in their statement against voluntary insurance, though stating more emphatically that "voluntary insurance will *never* cover those who most need of its protection."[82] These members saw this as a serious moral and logistical failing: "[A]ny plan that helps those with less serious needs and does not reach those whose needs are sorest does not solve the fundamental problems of providing satisfactory medical service to all." But the dissenters also viewed voluntary insurance as ultimately more expensive and less efficient, because state subsidies would still be needed, which would cause further duplication and fragmentation. They argued that there would be more of a tendency to create overlapping agencies and to duplicate capital investment under voluntary schemes.[83] They worried that a voluntary approach could potentially create *more* demand for state funding because of the duplication of effort for different schemes—private voluntary insurance and publicly subsidized schemes.

Indeed, it was clear to all members of the committee that it was precisely *because* they had recommended the voluntary approach that publicly subsidized access to health care services needed to continue. While the debate emerging from the final report focused on the recommendation for voluntary health insurance, it is important to realize that this was only one of five parts to recommendation #3 (see Table 3.4). The other four parts of the recommendation focused on how the state should cover or supplement the cost of medical care. The final

*Table 3.4* **Committee on the Cost of Medical Care, Final Report**
**Recommendation 3: Organized Payments for Medical Care**

*The Committee recommends that the costs of medical care be placed on a group payment basis, through the use of insurance, through the use of taxation, or through the use of both these methods.[1]*

| Details of Recommendation | Source of Payment |
| --- | --- |
| 3A. *Voluntary Cooperative Health Insurance* | Private payments (prepaid fees or premiums); voluntary coverage |
| 3B. *Required Health Insurance for Low-Income Groups*[2] | Private payments (or **taxation**); compulsory coverage |
| 3C. *Aid by Local Governments for Health Insurance* | **Taxation** to supplement private health insurance payments—seen as necessary by the majority whether voluntary (3A) or required (3B) insurance is chosen |
| 3D. *Salaried or Subsidized Physicians in Rural Areas (or those of low economic resources)* | **Taxation** to subsidize physicians or employ salaried physicians to furnish general medical service to residents of the area |
| 3E. *State and Federal Aid* | **Taxation** from State and Federal government to aid local communities with low per capita incomes |
| *Additional Recommendations for Supplementary or Temporary Use* | |
| 3F. *Voluntary Hospital Insurance* | Individuals or groups paying agreed annual sums and receiving hospitalization when needed without further charge; voluntary |
| 3G. *Tax Funds for Local Hospital Service* | **Taxation** from cities or counties to provide hospital service—either construction of new hospitals or extension of existing, well-managed institutions |
| 3H. *Tax Funds for Medical Care of Indigent and Necessitous* | **Taxation** for general medical care—including medical, dental, and nursing care, given in hospitals, clinics, or homes—for the indigent |
| 3I. *Public Support for the Care of Chronic Diseases* | **Taxation** from local and state governments to insure hospitalization and other medical service for patients suffering from tuberculosis, mental disease, venereal disease, arthritis, and other chronic conditions |

[1] Italicized recommendations are taken verbatim from CCMC's final report.

[2] Not endorsed by the full majority. There were a total of 48 members on the Committee, 36 signed the majority report; however, 8 members disagreed with recommendation 3A and favored 3B; 5 additional members believed both 3A and 3B should be promoted and local governments should decide what is best suited for their needs; the remaining 23 members signing the majority report believed voluntary insurance should be tried first.

*Source:* Committee on the Cost of Medical Care, *Medical Care for the American People* (Chicago: University of Chicago Press, 1932), 120–24.

report reveals that much of the committee's discussion around payments for medical care focused on whether health insurance should be voluntary or compulsory (Table 3.4, recommendations 3A or 3B), because that is where the key disagreement was. However, interestingly, even the 23 members who favored the initial promotion of voluntary insurance wrote that the eventual adoption of compulsory insurance was likely because voluntary insurance would not help all people secure financial access to care. More importantly, there was no disagreement about the three other parts of the recommendation that called for taxation to provide adequate coverage for medical care (Table 3.4, recommendations 3C–3E).

Note that these were not minor provisions for the very poor. The average cost for a hospital visit in 1930 was $140 per case, and the average hospital bill at this time broke down as follows: 39% to hospitals, 45% to physicians, 8% to special nurses, and 8% for other services and supplies. The recommended voluntary insurance design only covered the hospital portion of the bill. As a result, hospital bills—even with insurance—imposed a special burden on the middle class, "who can ordinarily meet the costs of minor, brief or non-hospitalized illnesses, but who cannot pay much more [because] nowhere in this country . . . [were] the entire costs of hospitalization for the whole population above the level of indigency met from patients' fees or insurance payments."[84]

The committee's response to this problem was to recommend the extension of tax support. Because they knew that many gaps would remain if only voluntary hospital insurance was pursued, they called for a multipronged government approach: to subsidize the purchase of private health insurance, to subsidize physicians practicing in rural areas, and to subsidize whole communities with relatively low resources. Under recommendation #3, the majority report also called for four additional supplementary recommendations, of which three again depended on government funding: tax funds for local hospital service, for general medical care for the poor, and for care of chronic diseases (see Table 3.4, recommendations 3G–3I). Even as the CCMC discussed the need to keep the profession at the center, and to try voluntary insurance first, the committee's report acknowledged that "the principal supplementary support [for hospital expenditures was] from *tax funds*."[85] The majority report clarified in the discussion section that this tax support would not "replace voluntary general hospitals but merely that tax funds shall be used to build supplementary institutions or assist existing ones. The extension of hospital insurance and of tax support could well go hand-in-hand, each method supplementing the other."[86]

In sum, if we look at recommendation #3 as a whole—not just the disagreement regarding voluntary versus compulsory health insurance—we find widespread agreement: first, that the state will have to fill in the gaps; second, that the state will fill in the gaps through supplementing the hospital directly (because hospital insurance does not cover costs) (rec. 3G), supplementing medical services in rural areas or areas of low economic status (rec. 3D); and third, that the state will have to provide subsidies for the indigent. These were not new ideas—due to state-building in the first quarter of the 20th century, there was already significant government investment in hospitals, in rural and low-income communities, and for the so-called indigent. But what became clear from the 27 volumes of CCMC reports was the extent of government involvement in health, and how much of it had already taken place—primarily through public health departments and government support of hospitals and clinics. As one member of the committee noted explicitly in his statement:

> And state enterprise, whether or not we approve, has already marked out for itself areas in the ancient domain. In fact, almost every type of control known to society is to be found somewhere within "the medical order."[87]

Previous chapters documented the growth in government's investment in public health departments and its subsidy of low-income communities and indigents. But there was also significant government investment in hospitals prior to the CCMC's final report in 1932. Because access to hospital care had emerged as crucially important for the cure and treatment of many sicknesses, and because hospital care was already extremely expensive for most Americans, government's role in financing hospital infrastructure and access to hospital services was already substantial, and yet was also hidden from view. I turn now to explain that important development—how government's investment in hospitals was made transparent in CCMC studies, and yet hidden in its final report.

## More Hidden Funding: Government Investment in Hospitals

In 1932, the role medical institutions, endowed foundations, and taxpayers played in the massive investment in hospitals was clear to committee members and the broader public health network.[88] Indeed, in the CCMC's first report published in 1928, in which the committee stated its purpose and provided an overview of the studies to come, it was apparent that the members had a good understanding of government's investment in hospitals, and that they wondered about its return. For example, by 1928, $5 billion had already been invested in hospitals, and millions more spent each year to cover operating costs. Moreover, as for-profit hospitals began to grow a bit in the 1920s, the committee demanded

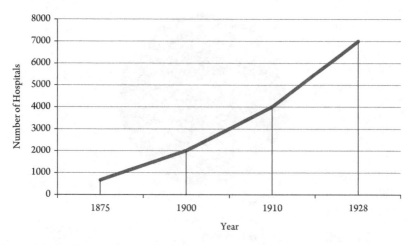

*Figure 3.1* Total Hospital Growth over Time. *Source:* Committee on the Cost of Medical Care, *Medical Care for the American People* (Chicago: University of Chicago Press, 1932), Volume 1, p. 13.

to know to what extent hospitals were operated as for-profits and whether this ownership form should be encouraged.[89]

CCMC research on hospitals came at a time when the hospital as an institution was a relatively new phenomenon. Each decade witnessed phenomenal growth: in 1875 there were 661 hospitals in the United States, by 1900 there were just over 2,000, in 1910 there were well over 4,000, and by 1928 there were almost 7,000 hospitals in the country (see Figure 3.1). From the very beginning there were different types of hospitals, with distinct roles, purposes, and ownership statuses. As described in the CCMC final report, 14% of the nation's annual medical bill was paid for through taxation, and covered "[m]ost of the hospital care of persons with mental disease, or with tuberculosis and other communicable diseases, and all work of health departments ... [and] the care of military and naval personnel, of inmates of prisons and other wards of the state and is theoretically true of general medical care of so-called 'indigent' persons."[90] According to the report, these were "accepted forms of 'state medicine'"—a term the committee used "to cover the provision of medical care *by* the government."[91] The committee was, however, quick to note in its final report that this definition of "state medicine" did not include tax funds used to supplement private provision of medical care.

At that time, the major tax outlay for medical care was for hospital service. In 1932, nearly three out of every four occupied hospital beds were government-owned. This was largely due to long stays by mentally and physically disabled patients—all of which were paid for by federal, state, or local governments. In 1930, government paid $303 million for hospital operating costs, which represented almost half (46%) of the total operating costs of all hospitals.

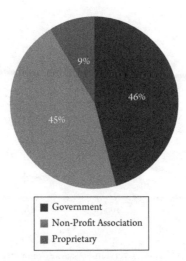

*Figure 3.2* Capital Investment by Payer Source, 1928. *Source:* C. Rufus Rorem, *Capital Investment in Hospitals: The Place of "Fixed Charges" in Hospital Financing and Costs,* Publication of the Committee of the Costs of Medical Care, Number 7 (Chicago: University of Chicago Press, 1930), 19.

Even a substantial number of short-term stays received government funding. While 60% of operating expenses went toward hospital care for tuberculosis and mental disease, the remainder, $118 million, went toward general hospital service.[92]

In addition to direct government outlays, many voluntary hospitals received payments from cities and counties for services rendered to the poor. However, the real hidden story was the government's role in hospital capital investment. Even in 1928, before the depression hit, 91% of capital investment was provided in equal amounts by government and nonprofit associations, representing a total capital investment of more than $3 billion (see Figure 3.2). By 1930, given the extent of investment in hospitals, health care was already recognized as a business—indeed, as an industry. The CCMC report compared hospital investment to other industries listed in the 1919 Bureau of the Census, and noted that only five other industries exceeded investment in the hospital sector: iron, steel, textiles, chemicals, and food. It is noteworthy that even at this nascent stage of hospital development, its capital investment exceeded that of lumber, paper, and printing. Given the relative size of these hospital investments, their impact on local economies was significant and conspicuous. The report noted that in 1928 a typical 200-bed hospital represented a capital investment of $1 million and employed at least 150 full-time skilled and unskilled workers. "In smaller cities . . . the payroll distribution of a local hospital was often the more important business establishment in the community."[93]

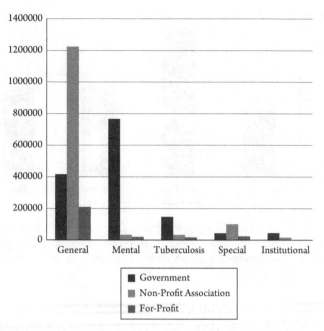

*Figure* 3.3  Capital Investment (in 1,000s) in Hospitals Registered in 1928. *Note:* Number of registered hospitals in 1928 = 6, 852. *Source:* I. S. Falk, C. Rufus Rorem, and Martha D. Ring, *The Costs of Medical Care: A Summary of Investigations on the Economic Aspects of the Prevention and Care of Illness* (Chicago: University of Chicago Press, 1933), 312–13.

Not surprisingly, given "state medicine's" assigned role, most of the government's capital investment was for chronic long-term care hospitals. Government assumed 95% of investment costs in building hospitals for the mentally ill and 75% for tuberculosis, whereas nonprofit hospitals dominated capital investment in general hospitals (see Figure 3.3). However, despite this general breakdown, it is important to note that government was also investing significantly in general acute-care hospitals—nearly 37% of capital investment in general acute-care beds in 1928 was government-funded. But investment in government-owned hospitals differed from voluntary hospitals early on: In 1928, average investment per general hospital bed in a government-owned hospital was $3,613, whereas for voluntary hospitals it was $6,202 per bed. The CCMC report did not mention this, but investments in voluntary hospitals were clearly much more expensive, and it is not clear that this level of capital investment gave the American people the bang for the buck they would have wanted. From the very beginning, capital expenditures represented a trend toward heavy emphasis on hospital improvements (e.g., acquiring new technology and private room amenities) rather than significantly expanding access to new hospitals. From 1908 to 1928 there was an average per-year increase of 20,000 beds, but most of this increase came from existing hospitals expanding bed supply. Of the 85 hospital construction projects conducted in 1929, only 24

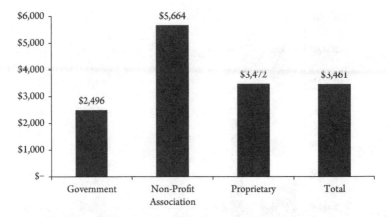

*Figure 3.4* Investment-per-bed by Type of Hospital Ownership, 1928. *Source:* C. Rufus
Rorem, *Capital Investment in Hospitals: The Place of "Fixed Charges" in Hospital Financing and Costs,*
Publication of the Committee of the Costs of Medical Care, Number 7 (Chicago: University of
Chicago Press, 1930), 22.

represented new hospital construction.[94] Moreover, in 1929 alone, $200 million
in investment resulted in less than 15,000 beds, and most of these resided in state
mental institutions.

This focus on hospital improvement rather than bed expansion is illustrated
in the steady increase in investment-per-bed figures. Investments in 13 New York
and Brooklyn hospitals resulted in an almost $3,000 increase in investments-
per-bed from 1912 to 1927. Similarly, in Pennsylvania, investments in 141 nonprofit "state-aided" hospitals resulted in an increase of investment-per-bed of
$1,000 over just a four-year period from 1923 to 1927.[95] Importantly, this rising
intensity of investment did not occur equally across all types of hospitals. The
increase was concentrated in acute-care general hospitals, where the capital
investment costs per bed were significantly higher among voluntary hospitals
than government-owned hospitals (see Figure 3.4). Indeed, the average per-
bed-investment in new acute-care hospitals in 1928 ranged from $3,000 to
$10,000.[96]

Government's role in capital investment is crucially important to understand
for two reasons. First, because the government already played a substantial financial role in building up the hospital industry, it should have—on behalf of
the American public—asked for a clear accounting from nonprofit hospitals on
what value was gained from higher-priced beds, but it did not. No government
body asked for an accounting, and although the CCMC was charged specifically
with studying the cost of medical care, it made little out of the price differential. Instead, the CCMC report commented on the significant role of voluntary hospitals in serving the needs of Americans with acute-care illnesses and
highlighted that philanthropy "supplied two-third of the investment in general

hospitals."[97] The CCMC attributed the increase in costs of hospital construction to "rising *standards* of hospital services,"[98] but there was no evidence of higher quality. It was simply assumed that greater value would result from these higher investment prices.

Second, not only did government and the authors of the CCMC reports accept the arguments of leaders of voluntary hospitals regarding increasing investment prices, they also encouraged a new inflationary form of hospital finance, which connected capital investment to hospital charges. Because capital investments supported expensive high-intensity care and fixed costs represented the interest and depreciation on capital investments, this method led to much higher fixed charges, and subsequently increased payments per patients. C. Rufus Rorem, the author of the CCMC report, argued that "[i]nterest on invested capital and depreciation on plant and equipment are costs of hospital service, even though they may be met by the general public through taxation or voluntary contributions."[99]

But why? It is important to note that there were no tax-exempt bonds at this point (that came much later). Instead, most hospital capital investments were covered by the government and philanthropic contributions (90%), for which voluntary hospitals did not have to pay interest. Why, then, did Rorem insist that hospitals consider the "whole cost of care," including fixed costs with interest, when determining patient fees? Rorem's logic arguably double-charged the public, since through taxation they already paid for capital investment, and were then being charged again for interest payments (calculated in the fixed costs), which the private hospital never assumed in the first place.

This notion of hospital financing was not simply some arcane argument hidden away in a CCMC report. In his role as director of research for the Rosenwald Fund, Michael Davis headed up a series of studies on hospital administration from 1928 through 1932.[100] And as a member of the CCMC, Davis was also asked to investigate the question of hospital finance and capital investment. In 1929 he met Rorem, who was teaching accounting at the University of Chicago at the time; impressed by his capabilities, Davis asked if he would work on these studies for the CCMC. Davis explained to Rorem that there had been no previous studies on this topic, and so the inquiry would include all primary data collection. Rorem described the research as follows:

> An interesting part of the capital investment study was that many facts and data were obtained by personal visits to institutions. I would ask each hospital for a copy of its financial statement. During the winter of 1928–1929 the first hospital I visited was the Huggins Memorial Hospital in Wolfeboro, New Hampshire which had 24 beds, and second was the Massachusetts General Hospital in Boston which had

24 operating rooms. At neither place was there any record of capital investment. For purposes of insurance, some records were maintained, but neither hospital kept a plant ledger, and management was surprised that anyone should ask for such information.

After a few weeks, and after visiting a dozen more institutions, I found that instead of asking questions I was answering questions. This was a field in which I knew very little, but in which the hospital representatives knew nothing. Within a month I became an expert on capital investments in hospitals and began writing on the subject. There was no literature. If I wanted to read something about capital investment, I had to write it myself.[101]

As a result of this research, Rorem published a book with the University of Chicago Press in 1930 titled *The Public's Investment in Hospitals*. Rorem's own explanation for choosing the title is crucially important. He explained that the title emerged out of his main finding, "that hospital capital had come from *public sources* (rather than from private investors) which expected neither repayment of the original capital nor a return in the form of interest."[102] By the author's intent, the title of the book clearly conveyed that the development of the American hospital system up to 1930 was primarily due to public investment. Yet despite his bold title and explicit statements laying bare the extent of public investment in hospitals, Rorem insisted on applying traditional financing principles to determine charges, and this idea was met with little dissent.

The book received a lot of praise and attention among hospital executives. At the annual convention of the American Hospital Association (AHA) in 1929, one of the hospital representatives on the CCMC, Dr. Winfred H. Smith, praised the work. At the next convention in 1930, Julius Rosenwald "quoted widely from the galley proofs of the forthcoming book." Notably, the 1931 annual convention focused specifically on the book's findings regarding hospital finance. At the conference, Rorem presented a paper titled "Cost Analysis—An Aid to Hospital Financing," thus infusing the field with principles of hospital finance.[103] Because it was a new field, Rorem and Davis, with the CCMC's authority and blessing, wielded enormous influence in shaping initial practices and thinking, and, more importantly, in delineating a hospital's social obligations in light of public investments. Rorem saw a clear connection between the concepts of group hospitalization plans (also called voluntary hospital insurance) and the public's role in hospital investment. In a presentation at the 1933 AHA annual meeting, he said:

> The function of group hospitalization is not to make easier the problems of the superintendent, but to solve the problems of the individual and of the public who own the hospitals.[104]

Yet he posed the "real" problem as "what proportion of the total costs are to be met through patients' fees, and how much through compulsory or voluntary contribution."[105] This question redirects attention from what was a very publicized debate at the time—voluntary versus compulsory insurance (and what became the CCMC's recommendation #3)—and focuses implicitly on what *additional* costs the public should pay for access to hospital care. In so doing, it stated as if by scientific fact that the public must pay interest and depreciation despite footing a good deal of the bill in the first place, and it hid the truly essential question: What is a fair return on what the public has *already* invested in hospitals?

At least two logical responses to this question were raised but never debated. The first response is that a fair return would guarantee some amount of "charity care." Despite the rhetoric, even in this early period, that nonprofit hospitals were benevolent and provided charity care, Rorem was clear that "the term 'charitable' does not imply that all patients are accepted as objects of charity for most of these hospitals accept paying patients."[106] The CCMC report also noted that nonprofit hospitals enjoyed tax-exempt status in most states, but did not comment on what obligations this status might entail. Medical historian Rosemary Stevens's research on hospitals confirms that nonprofit hospitals in Pennsylvania received as much money from the state government as they did from private philanthropists, and that "the amounts given by the state were not tied to expectations that any set amount of care would be given to the state's poor without charge, nor were there searching studies of the institution's financial needs. Many, if not most, of the new hospitals were not predominantly 'charitable' if the term is limited to the provision of free care."[107] Despite this reality, the public campaigns to raise money for local hospitals, "if not frankly promising, certainly implied the use of the funds for care of the sick poor."[108] These public pronouncements of charity make the logic of requiring a certain amount of charity care all the more reasonable, and make the lack of charitable provision all the more difficult to stomach.[109]

The second logical response would have been to claim that the public should not be charged for interest the nonprofit hospital did not owe. William Welch, a medical and public health powerhouse, did in fact raise this point in his response to Rorem's book at the 1932 AHA convention. Welch was especially disturbed by the reasons for the dramatic increases in nonprofit hospital charges during the 1920s, which he described (and other studies reviewing growth during this period confirmed)[110] as:

a. New institutions were over-built, thus increasing overhead.
b. Planning was poor, thereby decreasing efficiency of operation, yet the capital cost per bed previously averaging around $4,500 rose to new high levels, even reaching the unbelievable figure of $15,000.

c. Accommodations were not of a type most suitable from the standpoint of ability to pay for the clientele.

d. Construction and mechanical equipment, although enormously costly, were too often so unsuitable as to entail extraordinary maintenance charges.

e. Old plants, even though still utilizable at low cost, were wrecked and larger and more expensive institutions replaced them.[111]

Welch thus described a system that encouraged over-building of hospitals in certain areas and inappropriate building of "costly and luxurious private room hospitals from funds raised by public campaigns."[112] Not surprisingly, when the Depression hit, hospital occupancy rates decreased by 30% and "full-pay" occupancy rates decreased over 50%, and yet nonprofit hospitals continued to charge high prices. Welch was particularly concerned that nonprofit hospitals were not acting like eleemosynary institutions, and explicitly argued that it was "inequitable for the endowed institution to charge pay patients of moderate means interest on capital that has been donated."[113] Yet, despite Welch's stature, his recommendation regarding fixed charges was not reflected in CCMC's final report and never made its way into common hospital practices.

One of Welch's recommendations, however, was reflected in the CCMC final report: recommendation #4—the coordination of medical care (see Table 3.1). Welch called for a "certificate of public convenience and necessity prior to the inauguration of a hospital project . . . whereby new hospitals might be forced to plan, build, and equip in a manner suitable to the specific needs . . . [an agency would dictate] that no new hospital shall be established until the question of public convenience and necessity had been passed upon."[114] However, the CCMC only called for some agency to plan the coordination of medical care. This vague CCMC recommendation with no regulatory teeth was acted upon, and, as Stevens concluded, "the state acted as if it were a modern foundation. It acknowledged the public role of hospitals and a willingness to fund requests. However, it took no responsibility for the provision of hospital care throughout the state. The legislature was a granting agency and grants were given with few strings attached. There was no incentive to plan, to control, or to regulate."[115] As mentioned earlier, recommendation #4 suggested that some local agency should plan and regulate, and the final report stated that a "governmental agency can set minimum standards for hospital administration and practice."[116] However, upon closer scrutiny, the committee was mixed on this point. On the one hand, it called for the necessity of government supplementation of private hospital services for the poor and the need to set standards and conditions for such subsidies. On the other hand, it ended this section of the report by acknowledging that "many persons hesitate to approve governmental provision or support of hospitalization, because they believe that governmental effort, more frequently than comparable private effort is associated with waste, extravagance, and incompetence. This belief, however, at present rests far more on impressions than it does on adequate factual proof."[117] This contradiction—a belief in the necessity of government support alongside a belief in governmental incompetence—is the underpinning of the Grow-and-Hide approach. Indeed, in the CCMC report, we see most clearly the hidden health care state and the accompanying Grow-and-Hide strategy. In the report, the tables clearly show government funding, even while the text repeatedly emphasizes the dominant and stellar role of the private voluntary sector, and yet at the same time makes a plea for continued government supplementation.

## Concluding Reality: A Growing Health Care State that Hides Government Subsidies to the Private Sector

The CCMC carried over the language of "science" from the public health movement, but also the worries about political corruption. The leaders of the CCMC (some of them the same people—Emerson, Winslow, Davis) similarly supported more federated public health state-building and developing the federated voluntary health care infrastructure, yet still argued strongly that "politics" needed to stay out of any public health developments. Like those in the Progressive Era, they were adamant that preventive and curative health services be provided, but agnostic about whether they were provided through public or private provision. Indeed, if any stated bias prevailed it was a preference for the private voluntary sector.

On the one hand, they worried about free, unfettered market competition in medical care, and were especially worried about competition within the profession. On the other hand, they worried greatly about political corruption and incompetence in the public sector. This is somewhat ironic, because most of the public health leaders were quite proud of the PHS, as well as the development of state boards of health, local health departments, and county health units. Yet they were insistent that these entities be led and staffed by a scientific workforce, and they worked stridently against forces at all levels that attempted to infiltrate the authority of this federated bureaucracy rife with political appointments.

Given these worries about private for-profit competition and political involvement, combined with a strong believe that state involvement in the form of government funding was essential, the CCMC believed support of the private voluntary sector was the best alternative to deliver scientifically sound medical care for individuals and society while at the same time minimizing the role of politicians. In other words, they sold the following policy design: a scientific state would provide "objective" funding to "scientifically" sound practices carried out by the private not-for-profit sector. The details of this policy design were eventually lost, but the strategy of cultivating government funding while declaiming antigovernment rhetoric took full hold, and is still with us today.

# PART II

# THE RISE OF GROW AND HIDE

## 1930–1965

The public health leaders advocating for the National Health Program back in 1938 envisioned a federal oversight and coordinating role, administered by the PHS, that would eventually make the components of the plan work in harmony. Some voiced concerns about this incremental method, but the majority involved in the development of health policy at this time supported the National Health Program approach— implemented as separate components by all levels of government over a decade—because they also envisioned it to be more comprehensive and more attuned to improvements in the delivery system, and thus a better alternative to national health insurance. Often overlooked in historical debates about health care reform is the fact that further investment in "state medicine" (as it was called at the time)—where health services were provided essentially free (or heavily subsidized) at facilities funded by the government—was as much a legitimate policy alternative as NHI or voluntary private health insurance, if not more. Because National Health Program proponents envisioned significant government funding of hospitals to mean a public bed was available to a sick person when it was needed, even if the person was unable to pay, the argument for NHI was diminished. Understanding this debate is crucial because it reveals the incentives of public health leaders to continue to incrementally grow and hide the health care system, even when the system became more fragmented, and why they offered only tepid support for NHI. Chapter 4 shows this preference in relation to debates about compulsory insurance during the New Deal period from 1932 to 1940. It also documents significant public health state building that emerged out of the New Deal Legislation and how it built consistently on federalism and therefore in a completely decentralized and fragmented fashion.

Chapter 5 details the impact of the postwar political backlash on health policy discourse, the rise of a "volunteerism" rhetoric used by private actors, and its impact on building the American health care state, namely significant public expenditures for private, voluntary provision. At first, hospital leaders aggressively sought state grants, and they publicly referred to this funding as supporting public beds or providing needed social benefits. Over time, however, as hospital administrators fought for reimbursement of nonpaying patients, they switched to calling this "charity care," even though they received substantial public subsidies for the care. As a result, the framing of public funding to private, nonprofit facilities shifted from "state medicine" (or "public beds" or "social benefits") to "funding for charity care" in private facilities. Hidden rhetoric in relation to public investments in voluntary disease-based organizations also occured, and is described in chapter 5.

The strategies of private stakeholders were successful in redefining how Americans think about this public investment. Public funding for treatment and public investments in health care infrastructure did not change; what changed was how elites talked about it and the meaning they attached to it. When the public discourse changed, the vision for a National Health Program was lost. Grasping why this vision was lost is crucial to understanding U.S. health policy today. Allowing the term "charity care" to become part of the national health care lexicon helps explain why nonprofit hospitals in the United States still today indirectly receive public funding to provide services to the uninsured, yet claim they do not. The history of this strategic framing helps explain the absence of any regulation requiring hospitals to provide non-emergency services to uninsured patients, despite these subsidies.

Because government expenditures had by 1950 already increased significantly under an extremely fragmented and unequal system, the structure of this complicated system made it difficult to see the whole of government expenditures, even if one were specifically looking. In Chapter 6, I document how extensively the government's role was hidden under this peculiar health care state before 1965. I detail four main areas where the government's role was already substantial and yet completely obscured: reporting national health expenditures as primarily private, the extent of medical treatment under the rubric of public health policy, government subsidies for hospital construction, and showing payments for the indigent as public and residual while hiding government's reach to the nonpoor. By 1960, the U.S. government had established, in deep collaboration with the voluntary sector, all the key components of a National Health Program, but was still described—legitimately so—as a nonsystem.

# 4

# The New Public Health Deal

## An Alternative to Insurance

Descriptions of debates leading up to the New Deal suggest that in the health security realm, the main issue at hand was whether the federal government should devise a plan for compulsory health insurance. Indeed, Abraham Epstein's *Insecurity: A Challenge to America* (1933) and Isaac Max Rubinow's *The Quest for Security* (1934) are now considered classic texts making a case for compulsory health insurance. There was also a grass-roots organization—The Townsendites—which mobilized the public for compulsory health insurance. In addition, the Committee on Economic Security (CES) that wrote the New Deal legislation spent considerable energy studying compulsory health insurance early in the process. This early attention stirred significant debate before 1935 and, as many others have already explained, considerable opposition from the American Medical Association and other stakeholders.[1]

But alternative voices coming from the public health network called for a continuation of funding for public health care services during this period. Their recommendations were adopted from the CCMC report and put into practice in three main ways. First, the emergency relief and public works programs started under the New Deal provided extensive funding for medical care services and building health care facilities. Second, the Social Security Act created grant-in-aid funding, significantly increasing public health spending to state and local governments. And, third, federal committee work emerging out of the New Deal developed the framework for a National Health Program.[2]

In this chapter, I detail debates surrounding the New Deal legislation to show how many leaders in the public health network were more interested in building up health care services and providing direct access to care than they were in insurance—whether voluntary or compulsory. Consistent investments building up the federated public health care state in the quarter-century before the Social Security legislation in 1935 created a rational logic that a federated

*Grow and Hide*. Colleen M. Grogan, Oxford University Press. © Oxford University Press 2023.
DOI: 10.1093/oso/9780199812233.003.0005

health service was a better alternative to insurance. Public health leaders also favored this approach because they believed it was more politically feasible, and they honestly thought it would have a more significant impact on improving the health of the American public. Sometimes this alternative was called "state medicine," and other times it was called "socialized medicine" or simply "the public health system." At one point, it came under the banner of a "National Health Program" (where they included compulsory insurance as one of five main recommendations). If we recognize the same program proposed under different terms, this alternative to insurance becomes clear. Recognizing this alternative is essential because it redirects our attention to this question: Why did the New Deal invest in a comprehensive (though extremely fragmented) federated health service, and how was this hidden?

I detail the emergence of this system and argue that it remained largely hidden for three reasons: first, intergovernmental administration and financing—a federated health service system—hides the true extent of government's role; second, the reliance on private provision of publicly funded services hides the role of government in helping that private system exist; and, third, this complexity makes it politically feasible to conceal the role of government rhetorically.

A critical strategic dance began among leaders of the public health network during this time. In some venues, public health leaders would adamantly argue that public health funds were only being used (and would only be used) for preventive work. However, these same leaders would attempt to lay bare the true extent of government involvement in medical care in other venues. Why would they do this? They reasoned that if the public understood the extent to which government was already involved in financing health care, they would not be afraid of an abstract label such as "socialized medicine" but supportive of the system they already knew. As a result, public health leaders began to promote a Federated Public Health Service more actively as an alternative to insurance and as the country's more critical and pressing issue. There were hints of this in the 1920s from Winslow and Chapin and others (see Part I), but the leaders in the decade following the New Deal began to take a bolder stance on what public health truly was and on their vision of what it should become for the nation.

## New Deal Programs Adopt Public Health

One of Roosevelt's first major acts—the creation of the Federal Works Agency (FWA)—had an enormous impact on the economy, providing a significant stimulus at the height of the Great Depression. Not only did it infuse substantial amounts of money into local economies and put millions of Americans to work, it also had a lasting impact on America's public infrastructure.[3] The FWA worked closely with the Works Progress Administration (WPA) and the Public Works Administration (PWA), which provided extensive public health infrastructure investments, including sewage treatment facilities, stream pollution control, and significant local hospital construction. Before the depression, from 1919 to 1929, municipalities invested an average of $119 million a year in new waterworks. After the Depression hit, this decreased to an average of $47 million by 1933. However, with significant federal aid through PWA, the average increased to $85 million between 1933 and 1939. In addition, the WPA embarked on an extensive program to improve hospital capacity. By 1938, the WPA had built 100 new hospitals and renovated 1,422.[4]

The federal PHS worked in close cooperation with the FWA to improve community sanitation and environmental health and control the spread of infectious diseases. Construction of sanitary privies was a significant project, and by 1939 over $2 million was spent to build sanitary privies, of which nearly all of the funding came from WPA funds. Under these programs, the PHS also provided technical support and loaning supervisory personnel to state health departments.[5]

These investments resulted in a dramatic reduction in disease-specific mortality within a short time after implementation. For example, in Mississippi, typhoid fever decreased from 161 deaths in 1933 to only 77 deaths in 1937. And, in Tennessee, deaths reduced from 308 in 1932 to only 148 in 1937 (see Table 4.1).

Aside from more "traditional" sanitation public health works, the WPA also invested heavily in increasing the supply of health care personnel. WPA workforce projects extended across the country and into every facet of health work. First, WPA funds supplemented wages to cover personnel costs in health

*Table 4.1* **Reductions in Typhoid Fever Attributed to Public Health Work**

| States | 1932/33 | | 1937 | | Percent Decline in Deaths |
|---|---|---|---|---|---|
| | Cases | Deaths | Cases | Deaths | |
| Mississippi | 917 | 161 | 349 | 77 | 52% |
| Tennessee | 1898 | 308 | 763 | 148 | 52% |
| Kentucky | * | 337 | * | 160 | 53% |
| West Virginia | 1265 | 218 | 350 | 78 | 64% |

Note: Missing data for total number of typhoid cases, but have death rate per 100,000 population, which declined from 12.9 to 5.5 in the same years listed.

Source: J. M. Carmody, "The Federal Works Agency and Public Health," *American Journal of Public Health* 30, no. 8 (1940), 891.

*Table 4.2*  **Number of Personnel in New York City Bureau of
School Hygiene by Source of Salary Payment, 1937**

| Title | Civil Service (NYC) | WPA |
|---|---|---|
| Acting Director (M.D.) | 1 | 0 |
| Medical Supervisors | 12 | 0 |
| School Physicians | 100 | 77 |
| Ophthalmologists | 14 | 0 |
| Cardiologists | 2 | 0 |
| Chief of Dental Division | 1 | 0 |
| Dental Supervisors | 6 | 0 |
| Dentists | 37 | 98 |
| Dental Hygienists | 48 | 46 |
| Stenographers | 2 | 1 |
| Clerks | 1 | 9 |
| Total | 224 | 231 |

Source: J. M. Carmody, "The Federal Works Agency and Public Health," *American Journal of Public Health* 30, no. 8 (1940), 893.

departments across the country. Even in New York City, one of the most established health departments by this time, over half of the personnel was paid for by WPA (see Table 4.2).

Second, the WPA also supplemented clinical staff at hospitals across the country. For example, it hired nurses, laboratory assistants, attendants, and unskilled workers to work within private voluntary hospitals. Third, the WPA provided staff for a diverse array of outpatient clinics across the country, including maternal and child health clinics, tuberculosis prevention clinics, venereal disease clinics, and dental clinics. By 1938, WPA-staffed dental clinics had treated more than 3.5 million patients. Fourth, in addition to personnel, the WPA also funded health departments, medical schools, and institutes to conduct laboratory and research studies. Finally, the WPA health program also initiated new projects, such as nursery school programs and school lunch programs to address the problem of malnutrition in children.[6]

Taken together, these federal WPA investments in public health infrastructure on top of public health state-building before the Depression meant that what some called state or socialized medicine was not a far-off vision but a current reality in the 1930s. Given this reality, it was rational for public health leaders to view health infrastructure investments as a much more viable alternative to proposals for health insurance—whether compulsory or voluntary.

In 1933, for example, Pierce Williams, a Western Relief Supervisor for the Federal Emergency Relief Administration (FERA), wrote an article published in the *American Academy of Political and Social Science* titled "Alternatives to Compulsory Public Health Insurance" in response to Rubinow's essay in favor of compulsory insurance and AMA representatives Leland and Simons's essay against compulsory insurance.[7] This article is important because it reflects the views of bureaucrats in federal agencies administering the new relief recovery programs and shows how the thinking was built on programs already in effect at the state and local levels.

First, based on his reading of the Committee on the Costs of Medical Care (CCMC) final report, Williams argued that disagreement on the committee focused on the means of reform, not "on the need for a different method of financing medical service."[8] He argued further that based on the strong reactions to compulsory insurance, as an option specified in the final report of the CCMC, the insurance approach was not politically feasible, and he suggested consideration of alternatives approaches:

> During the past fifteen months, I have been continuously engaged in Federal relief administration in eleven Rocky Mountain and Pacific Coast states. My work has brought me into frequent contact with governors and state legislatures. In none of these states is there the least sign of any interest in compulsory health insurance. . . . The chances in favor of the enactment of compulsory health insurance laws are slim. This is all the more reason for seriously considering at this time the possible alternatives to compulsory health insurance.[9]

Williams's description of the position of state legislatures is critical. Since all proposals called for federal funding for compulsory insurance to be a state option, getting support from state governments would have been necessary. Given this lack of interest at the state level, Williams made the following assessment:

> Evidently two alternatives to compulsory medical insurance are possible: (1) extensive voluntary medical insurance; and (2) socialized medicine. The first term needs no definition; the second does. By "socialized medicine" I mean the remuneration of physicians and hospitals on an agreed-upon basis, out of public (i.e., tax) funds. . . . Both of these developments would be entirely logical and strictly within the framework of existing American institutions. Medical care for indigents is the recognized responsibility of government in the United States, and in

practically all states of the Union, it is an established principle long an-
tedating the present depression that the "indigent sick" are entitled to
medical and hospital care at public expense. The effect of the depression has been to increase the number of those entitled to such care from
a relatively insignificant fraction of the population to something like 17
per cent of it. The Federal Relief Administrator's published rule that
medicine, medical supplies, and medical attendance may be paid for out
of Federal funds merely confirms formally a practice of long-standing
and extends the principle to nearly one-sixth of our population.[10]

I quote Williams at length because it is essential to understand that public
health leaders did not view infrastructure investments as a stop-gap measure
until insurance was both politically feasible and, in their view, a sound alternative. Because leaders in the public health network had been building up the federated public health system for the past thirty years, they had faith that a logical
system could be created, especially with more federal funding and regulatory
control. For example, in 1934, state and local health officers voted unanimously
to support the grants-in-aid approach to states with a stronger federal health
role, giving authority to the PHS to allocate funds on an annual basis. Most noteworthy was their recommendation that, in addition to eradicating the spread of
epidemic and communicable diseases, the funds should be used to "permit the
support of necessary health service without aid from other sources."[11]

The health officers were not as explicit as Williams to label this approach
"state medicine" or call for tax-supported funds for indigent medical care and
care for the medically needy. Still, they similarly wanted to use public funding
(through a federal public health allocation) to finance health services. All public
health leaders voiced support for the grant-in-aid approach, and most specifically mentioned the need to include funding for health services—not just sanitation and infrastructure. However, because the system was already sufficiently
complex (diffused across levels of government and public and private sectors),
it was difficult even to describe what this alternative to compulsory insurance
was and what label to give it. But the complexity cut both ways: while it made
it difficult to clarify or label this approach and galvanize support for a comprehensive plan, it also made it easy to hide the government's role when opposition
rose against it.

## Social Security Adopts Public Health

This public medical service alternative was not a residual idea but central to developing the New Deal. An executive order enacted in June 1934 created the

Committee on Economic Security (CES) to develop a comprehensive set of proposals to provide a plan for long-term economic security to the American people in response to the Great Depression. Secretary of Labor Frances Perkins chaired the CES, and Edwin Witte, a labor economist from the University of Wisconsin, was appointed the executive director. Old-age insurance, old-age assistance, and unemployment insurance were the key issues considered by the CES. However, because the CES was also concerned about the dangers of economic instability arising out of illness, it created the Technical Committee on Medical Care with Edgar Sydenstricker as its chairman.[12]

Sydenstricker appointed Isadore S. Falk, and, initially, they focused on devising a plan for compulsory insurance. However, because they met shortly after the Committee on the Costs of Medicare Care (CCMC) released its final report (see Chapter 3), CES' Technical Committee broadened their mandate to include the other recommendations in the CCMC report, creating two additional advisory committees on hospitals and public health. In response to growing opposition from the AMA and state medical societies, Sydenstricker convinced Witte to set up a Medical Advisory Board under which all members had medical degrees. Witte appointed the soon to be Surgeon General, Thomas Parran, President Roosevelt's private physician, Ross McIntire, neurologist Harvey Cushing of Yale University (and father of Roosevelt's daughter-in-law), Emory University's Steward Roberts from Georgia, AMA president Walter Bierring, and Cleveland Clinic's George Crile.[13]

Many of the same leaders that were part of the CCMC were also members of these committees, including Sydenstricker, Michael Davis, and Isidore Falk. And, not surprisingly, many of the same CCMC recommendations emerged from these committees: funding for public health and maternal and child health, funding for hospital construction, and tax-supported medical care for the indigent. Given this, it is also not surprising that the same fault lines that emerged from the CCMC report took root; namely, disagreement over compulsory insurance and consensus over the other items. Most notable was that the AMA and the American Hospital Association (AHA) supported federal funds to supplement state and local investments in three areas: hospital construction, reimbursement for indigent care, and public health work. In Falk's recollections of the AMA, he opined that as their opposition to insurance intensified, their support for public health grew stronger.[14]

In the early planning stages of the Social Security Act, before dropping the health insurance proposal, the medical advisory board proposed two methods to finance medical care for the American people: federal grant funding to support medical care for the indigent through general taxation, and support for compulsory insurance through a payroll tax deduction for the non-indigent. Similar to previous proposals (e.g., AALL and CCMC), members of the committee believed that compulsory insurance was appropriate for working Americans of "moderate means." In contrast, state or locally based tax-supported public medical services were considered more suitable for indigents. Sydenstricker's question to the Committee at a meeting in January 1935, illustrates the depth of this consensus.

> Chairman Sydenstricker: Now I realize fully that our object is the provision of medical care to people who can't pay for it. That is the purpose of the study. Suppose the state doesn't want health insurance. Will it let any medical care from tax funds of the Federal Government at all? It might be considered by some that that plan is a sort of bludgeon to force the state to come into the health insurance plan. That is one way of doing it. Another way of doing it, of course, is to *consider public medical service so far as aided by the Federal Government as a thing distinctly apart from health insurance*, so that if a state has the need for Federal assistance in supplying medical care of one kind or another, it can apply to the Federal Government for that and not be compelled to have health insurance. . . . *I would like to get your judgement as to whether they shall be considered as one or separate.*

Given the strong presence of the public health network on CES advisory boards and their understanding of the extent to which public medical services had expanded in the United States—well beyond what might strictly be called "indigent"—it was not illogical for him to wonder (similar to Williams) if states should be allowed to use federal funds to expand public medical services rather than adopting insurance. Yet the conversation that ensued among committee members—primarily practicing physicians—made it clear that many did not even understand Sydenstricker's question. When Sydenstricker asked the committee to consider whether federal funding for public medical services should be combined with compulsory health insurance, Dr. Roberts's lengthy response is particularly telling:

> Dr. Roberts: In the minority report of the Committee on Costs of Medical Care, which represented the opinion of the leaders in organized medicine on that Committee, the first statement said: "that we are in favor of the Government or government agencies taking over the care of and practice for the indigent." . . . This thing of public medical service taking over the indigent already has the approval of organized medicine, for which I speak, and it should have it. To that end . . . I am highly in favor of separating health insurance from public medical services. It is the only possible way to avoid friction, and it is the only possible way to meet the good will and the approval of the medical profession. . . .

You will never, in my judgment, get the approval of organized medicine in this country . . . if we mix up health insurance with the care of the indigent and public health officer.

May I say a word about the public health officer and his department? . . . the public health official had grown up under the approval of medicine. Well, he has, but he has had a terrible fight on his hands. . . . We have got to allow preventive medicine to grow up with health insurance, and in the eyes of the public, public health is just a childish toddler here in the medical world. Dr. Parran will have to forgive me for that, but it is true.

Dr. Parran: Quite right.[15]

The response from Dr. Roberts, who was at Emory University, is quoted at length for several reasons. First, Roberts clarifies that organized medicine was firmly in favor of government control of indigent care, though—as was typical—he never defines indigence. Second, although Roberts refers to public health as "preventive medicine," his understanding of the term is publicly supported indigent care, even though the South, particularly at that time, benefitted enormously from broad universal public health works, such as the building of privies, and widespread eradication of waterborne diseases. Thus, when Dr. Roberts says that "public health is just a childish toddler here in the medical world," he only grasps one aspect of public health. But this is precisely the message that public health leaders had been giving to private physicians for several decades. Finally, it is also significant that Dr. Roberts addresses Dr. Parran, whom President Roosevelt appointed to take over as the U.S. Surgeon General the following year. Dr. Parran readily agrees with Dr. Roberts, despite knowing the much more expansive role public health was playing and his advocacy for public health to play a more prominent role. Unfortunately, he was in the company of leaders in private medical practice, and, in this context, public health leaders capitulated and portrayed public health as residual.[16]

Nonetheless, it is crucial to recognize Sydenstricker's question as part of a parallel strategic path that attempted to push the public health discussion to a different level. His question highlights the proposed alternative—that federal funds could be used to develop public medical services *instead* of compulsory health insurance. Most importantly, this alternative was not invoked this one time and dropped. Instead, public health leaders proposed the alternative repeatedly and strategically, such as when they introduced the public health titles in the Social Security Act as "prevention only."

When the first witness, the executive director of CES, Edwin Witte, presented the Social Security Act to the House Committee on Ways and Means on January 21, 1935, he outlined the bill as dealing with four distinct subjects: (1)

unemployment compensation, (2) old-age security, (3) security for children, and (4) extension of public-health services. He then said that "the fifth subject, health insurance," would be dealt with at a later date.[17] Witte's testimony described public health Title VI as follows:

> It is to be used for the development of State health services, including the training of personnel for state and local health work, for aid to counties and local governments in maintaining adequate public health services. Two million dollars more is to be expended directly by the United States Public Health Service for investigation of diseases and the problems of sanitation.[18]

To add legitimacy to the recommendation, Witte quoted from the Medical Advisory Board, which he described as "a group composed of eminent medical men from all parts of the country, medical men who differ widely on the subject of health insurance but who join in a unanimous recommendation" to increase public health spending.[19]

In discussing the public health provisions in the bill, Witte was quick to argue that the proposed spending did "not represent a new departure in Federal policy." Yet he also acknowledged that the proposal "represents a very material increase in public health services by the federal government."[20] Indeed, the recommended and approved appropriation was twice the amount provided for public health in 1935. Because the Roosevelt administration held off on the question of health insurance, Witte led Congress to believe that the New Deal legislation did nothing in the area of health care. After Witte finished his statement, the first question from Harold Knutson, a Republican congressman from Minnesota, cut straight to the underlying issue at hand:

MR. KNUTSON: Mr. Witte, is it your thought that the money that this bill proposes to allocate to the Public Health Service be used for preventive rather than curative work?

MR. WITTE: Entirely, sir, for preventive work, for public-health services.

MR. KNUTSON: It is not the thought of your Committee that we should socialize medicine and hospitalization?

MR. WITTE: Most certainly not.[21]

Consistent with the rhetoric used for several decades, when the boundaries of public health were questioned, public health leaders used the "prevention only" tagline. Assistant Secretary of the Treasury Josephine Roche used a similar rhetorical response the next day when testifying with Surgeon General

Dr. Cumming. They both emphasized that the proposal built on what the PHS was already doing. For example, Surgeon General Cumming said this:

> It is not entering upon any new ground for the Federal Government at all. It is well-tried ground, something that we have entered into in this country a good many years ago in an experimental way. The experiment has proven such a success, Mr. Chairman that other countries have sent over here and have studied this Federal "grant-in-aid" to use an English expression, to local communities. Basing my opinion on some 40 years' work in public health and having had an opportunity to observe public health work not only here but abroad, I think that is the wisest part of the bill."[22]

Congressman Carl Vinson, a Democrat from Georgia, asked for clarification on the function of a county health unit. Dr. E. E. Waller, the Assistant Surgeon General in charge of the PHS's "cooperative" work with the states, and the person who would therefore be in charge of administering the Public Health Title, responded:

> DR. WALLER: With respect to the functions of a county health unit, I should like to say, in the beginning, that the work of a county health unit is preventive in character. It is not for the purpose of providing medical care. In that respect it does not interfere in the slightest degree with the medical profession.
> MR. TREADWAY: The local medical profession?
> DR. WALLER: The practicing physician. In fact, it has the opposite effect. The educational activities of a county health unit make more work for the practicing physician in that they bring out needs for medical care that otherwise would not be discovered and direct cases into the hands of the private physicians.[23]

Waller describes the county health department's role as purely prevention and suggests it is merely a handmaiden to private physicians. However, Representative Vinson was a real fan of PHS and county health units, because he experienced firsthand what these investments meant for improving health conditions in rural Georgia. As a result, he was dissatisfied with Waller's bland, residual description of county health units, and pushed back:

> MR. VINSON: I wanted you to tell this Committee and the House just how they operate in these county health units. I should like the Committee to know how they get into their automobile and travel out into the school districts and hold

a clinic out there for these vaccinations and inoculations. They go through
the districts and get samples of the water supply, and all that sort of thing.
Those are the things that actually do the work. . . . Not only do they do these
things, but they make examinations of children who otherwise would not be
examined for physical defects, and call that condition to the attention of their
parents. . . . Not only is the child improved when the defect is corrected, but
you have the happiness of parents, all growing out of that activity.

DR. WALLER: Exactly.

THE CHAIRMAN: In that connection, it is also part of their work frequently to
look after the dental needs of the children, is it not?

DR. WALLER: That is an important part of the health program of these units in
the schools.[24]

Notice how Waller starts with a very narrow description of public health as
"only prevention" when he thinks the program might be under threat. But, when
encouraged, he ends up describing a much fuller on-the-ground reality of a
combined curative/preventive program that provides exceptional health care
value. Yet no one ever loops back to Waller's original statement. Instead, potential opponents are pleased to hear that these funds will only be used for "prevention," and proponents are delighted to fund the programs they like no matter
what label PHS bureaucrats (or other congressmen) give it.

## Post–Social Security Act: State Medicine Is Still an Alternative to Compulsory Insurance

Aware of the opposition to compulsory insurance, Sydenstricker advocated for
an expanded concept of public health in an article published in 1935, just after
the passage of the SSA. He notes that before 1935 public health had never been
the state's first concern, and he asks, "Why is that?"

> We are somewhat accustomed to accuse the politicians of lack of un-
> derstanding, the medical profession of failure to cooperate, employers
> of unenlightened selfishness, trade unions of insistence upon measures
> not directly related by even inimical to health, and so on. If there is any
> blame to be attached to any one group, *the professional sanitarian should
> come in for his share, since the public looks to him to define the scope of
> public health. The trouble lies deeper. The prevailing concept of public health
> responsibilities has been and is too narrow.* It is restricted to a few activi-
> ties such as community sanitation, water supplies and food inspection,
> control of infectious diseases, education in hygiene, the medical care of

the tuberculosis and mentally diseased, and the medical care of the indigent. A newer concept which many sanitarians are coming to accept is much broader and far more sound ... public health is being looked upon more as a major social objective, not as merely sewage disposal, or the prevention of infectious diseases, or popular instruction in hygiene.[25]

In Sydenstricker's writing emerges the concerted effort to broaden the notion of public health, especially after the Social Security grant-in-aid title had been passed, but also an acknowledgment that the problem public health leaders faced was partly because the profession itself promoted a narrow definition of what public health entails.

This call for an expanded concept of public health was not restricted to journal articles. Thomas Parran, as the new Surgeon General and president of the American Public Health Association (APHA), asked in his presidential address in October 1936, "What is the place of public health in modern life?"

> Public health in the light of present scientific knowledge goes far beyond environmental sanitation. It necessarily must be concerned with all factors, which make for healthful living—the prevention, alleviation, and cure of disease by all methods known to science.[26]

Parran was clear that he viewed 1936 as a critical time for public health workers to start changing tactics on the ground. With the grant-in-aid funds in place, state health departments could begin to broaden their roles. As Parran put it, "the wisdom we show in dealing with those tasks will determine largely the future of public health in our time."[27] In his view, this was the chance to make public health services the natural alternative.[28]

In an address before the American Public Health Association in 1937, Josephine Roche, assistant secretary of the U.S. Treasury, which oversaw the PHS, also advocated for expanding the boundaries of public health:

> With the traditional task of public health far from completed, with so much yet to be done throughout the country in "leveling up" those preventive services long accepted as a definition of public health functions, it is quite understandable that the first reaction of public health workers to a function directly concerned with individual care should be one of hesitancy. "Better do our familiar and long-accepted task well and not get into new controversial fields" is the way I have heard this first reaction expressed. Rarely, however, have I heard this position maintained after a full and open-minded examination of today's facts and conditions which clearly and overwhelmingly reveal that medical care as a public

function is not so much a new function which public health must take on as an extension of the function and services which public health leaders and workers have long claimed as their own and given their lives to advancing.[29]

Notice how Roche's address, similar to Sydenstricker, reveals the narrow strategic framing of public health from the profession, while at the same time pointing out the reality that "medical care as a public function is not . . . a new function." As Roosevelt's appointed leader to develop a national health plan, it is highly significant that she supported an expanded role for public health. She hoped to make that role more transparent and viewed it as critical for building the health service system to meet the needs of the American people.[30]

In addition to calling for an expanded vision of public health, leaders in the public health network also began to reveal the true extent of public spending in the U.S. health care system. For example, Michael Davis, the director of medical services for the Julius Rosenwald Fund, published a book in 1937 titled *Public Medical Services: A Survey of Tax-Supported Medical Care in the United States.* He wrote the book in memory of Edgar Sydenstricker, who died unexpectedly in 1935. President Roosevelt asked Sydenstricker to prepare a report to help guide the committee's consideration of health security. Interestingly, when Davis took over the task, he organized the report into three major sections: public health work, public medical services, and health insurance. This was one of the rare times that public health work—as population health and prevention—was distinguished from public medical services, which most writings and speeches defined as care for indigents, but which, as the report makes clear, reaches far beyond indigents. Because Sydenstricker was no longer around to do it, Davis wrote this book to make the latter point crystal clear. As the title implies, the book's purpose was to document the extent of public (tax-supported) medical care.

Understanding the origins of this book is essential. It was not an academic book, but a work that emerged out of the first committee Roosevelt assigned to study the issue of health security and therefore shaped what became known as the National Health Program. In the first paragraph of the introductory chapter, Davis writes, "Public medical services grew up as ancillary to poor relief, i.e., medical care was provided in serious illness for persons for whose maintenance governmental authorities had already accepted responsibility. Its advance beyond that point during the last twenty years has been remarkable both in respect to the medical care furnished and in the range of the population served."[31]

Through eight chapters, Part I of the book details the myriad of ways that the state (including all levels of government) already paid for medical services by 1937. Then, in Part II, Davis develops a total estimate of publicly financed medical expenditures. He then compares this amount with three other main methods of paying for medical care: individual out-of-pocket payments, insurance, and charity care (see Table 4.3).

When presenting this table, Davis highlights three points. First, he notes that less than 20% of public funds supported public health departments, and therefore concludes that the vast majority of public funds "were expended for public medical services of the 'curative' type."[32] Notice how he puts the word "curative" in quotes to signify that the term is ambiguous and the concept of separating curative and preventive is suspect. Yet, at the same time, he wants to emphasize that much of the tax dollars paid were already going to "curative" medical services that physicians claimed were under their "private" jurisdiction.

Second, these tax dollars were especially significant for people of low to moderate means. As with the CCMC, persons of moderate means—not the indigent—were the primary focus of the discussions around health security. At that time, there was widespread agreement that public health (or state medicine) should take care of the poor,[33] and at issue was what to do about the high cost of medical care for persons of moderate means. Davis combines low- to moderate-income Americans to illustrate that they make up 85% of the population. His analysis highlights both the large size of this group and that government is

*Table 4.3* **Expenditures for Medicare Care in 1929 from Various Sources (in Millions)**

| Source | For Total Population | For Persons of Moderate & Low Income (85% of Population) |
| --- | --- | --- |
| Out-of-Pocket Payments (Fees) | $2,830 (79%) | $1,300 (65%) |
| Taxation (Public/ Government) | $500 (14%) | $450 (23%) |
| Insurance (Private) | $170 (5%) | $150 (8%) |
| Charity | $100 (3%) | $100 (5%) |
| Total Expenditures (physician donated services not included) | $3,600 (100%) | $2,000 (100%) |

*Source:* Michael Davis, *Public Medical Services* (Chicago: University of Chicago Press, 1937), 123.

already covering a significant amount of this group's medical care: "nearly one-quarter was borne by taxation in 1929."[34]

Finally, since he used data from 1929, he argues that the amount coming from tax funds in 1936 had almost certainly increased, and concludes that, "thus, in the United States taxation is at present much the most important method of distributing the costs of medical care over groups of people and over a period of time."[35]

Davis's book is important for three reasons. First, given that he used 1929 data, it confirms my point—and the arguments of many public health leaders—that the extent of government investment in the U.S. health care system before the New Deal programs was already substantial. In other words, by 1929 there was already significant public health state-building. Second, the fact that Sydenstricker collected these data for presentation to the Medical Advisory Committee and the CES confirms my argument that key leaders shaping the New Deal—and intentionally leaving out compulsory insurance—understood the extent of the government's role. Finally, because the figures from Davis's book were often quoted in discussions around the development of the NHP, it shows how leaders used state-building to make political claims of a "long-standing tradition" that the American public had come to accept.

And, as Davis also pointed out, there was every reason to believe that public medical services would continue to increase. For example, the Social Security grant-in-aid programs for public health and maternal and child health had just been passed, and many of the relief programs were still in existence or had jump-started other state and local initiatives. In 1937, for example, the Resettlement Administration was reorganized under the Department of Agriculture and renamed the Farm Security Administration (FSA). While the FSA adopted many of the earlier New Deal programs, the bulk of the FSA's budget focused on providing two types of long-term, low-interest loans to individual farmers: (1) "rehabilitation" loans allowed low-income farmers to keep their farms, and (2) "tenant purchase" loans allowed tenants and sharecroppers to become small farm owners. In administering these loan programs, and conducting research to understand farm failures, the FSA staff realized that poor health was a major cause of farm failure. In response to this finding, the FSA hired Ralph C. Williams from the PHS as its first chief medical officer and began the development of FSA health plans.[36]

Although the rationale for the health plans was stated as wanting to create a more stable loan program to improve the rural economy, administrators had a strong interest in creating a sound and effective health program to show that this approach could be extended. With Williams at its helm, it is not surprising that the FSA recruited the assistance of key leaders in the public health network. For example, Michael Davis and several medical officers from the field—notably

Frederick Mott and Milton Roemer (who became key advocates for health care reform in the 1940s)—were officially "on loan" to the FSA from the PHS.[37]

Within just three years, 26 state medical societies had agreed to the FSA medical programs. As of September 30, 1939, there were 441 medical programs across the country. Once state and county medical societies worked out the terms, implementation across the states was typically swift. In Georgia, for example, in 1938, there were five county plans, which increased to 108 plans just one year later. The FSA negotiated with each state medical society about how best to structure the prepayment program. Most plans were structured around two main principles: farmers paid a flat monthly fee (about $15–$30 per month in 1940) to pool the risk for medical services, and the physicians agreed to a payment of reimbursement for charges. Some programs even agreed to physician salaries rather than reimbursement.[38]

The AMA's and the AHA's support for federal funding of public health and its implementation through the Social Security Act, combined with widespread calls for an expanded vision of what public health should entail, and the development of prepaid health care programs with the cooperation of county medical societies, all set the stage for a general belief among leaders in the public health network that the United States was ripe for significant change. Yet for those on the ground involved in implementing these reforms, it also created a realization that significant changes were already occurring. Although public health network leaders supported federal legislative reform, they also saw what incremental steps without comprehensive reform could do. Look at what Thomas Parran said shortly before becoming the U.S. Surgeon General of PHS about the public health provisions in the Social Security Act:

> One of the most significant events in the history of public health in this nation [occurred] when President Roosevelt signed a bill appropriating money to launch the Social Security program. . . . Most people think of social security in terms of unemployment insurance and old-age pensions, yet the law includes provisions through which, for the first time, *we get a start on a national program* to protect and promote the health of the people.[39]

## Developing the National Health Program

After the passage of the Social Security Act in August 1935, President Roosevelt ordered the formation of the Interdepartmental Committee to Coordinate Health and Welfare Activities. The committee's purpose was threefold: first, to specify the details of the entire National Health Plan; second, to explain how the provisions already passed under the SSA fit into the National Health Plan; and third, to clarify how each component of the National Health Plan could be sufficient on its own if further expanded.[40]

The public health network had a strong influence in shaping the National Health Program (NHP). First, three of the five members of the Technical Committee on Medical Care, which developed the plan's details, were from the PHS: Joseph Mountin, MD, George St. John Perrott, and Clifford E. Waller, MD. The other two members—Martha Elliot, MD, from the Children's Bureau, and I. S. Falk, PhD, from the Social Security Board—had long worked within the public health network on studying and developing programs. Second, among the 171 participants at the conference, the public health network—public health leaders, voluntary sector, and business/labor—was well represented (see Table 4.4).

*Table 4.4* **Delegates at the National Health Conference by Affiliation**

| *Affiliation* | *Number (Percent)* |
|---|---|
| Public health agencies | 20 (12%) |
| Social and Welfare agencies | 20 (12%) |
| Labor | 20 (12%) |
| Journalism | 11 (6%) |
| Hospital management and organizations | 9 (5%) |
| Local, State and Federal government officials (exclusive of public health and hospitals) | 9 (5%) |
| Industry | 9 (5%) |
| Agriculture | 8 (5% |
| Women's organizations | 8 (5%) |
| Economists | 4 (2%) |
| Educators | 4 (2%) |
| Nursing | 3 (1.5%) |
| American Legion | 3 (1.5%) |
| Dentistry | 3 (1.5%) |
| Foundations | 2 (1%) |
| Miscellaneous organizations | 10 (5%) |
| Total Delegates | 171 |

Notes:
53 (31%) delegates had an M.D. degree.
35 (21%) delegates were identified with the American Public Health Association as Fellows or members.

Source: Reginald Atwater, "National Health Conference—A Review," *AJPH* 28 (September 1938): 1103–13.

Given this influence, it is not surprising that the NHP recommendations were nearly identical to those offered in the CCMC final report in 1932. Recommendation I called for expanding existing public health and maternal and child health services (already passed in the Social Security Act). Not one delegate spoke against this recommendation, and numerous delegates emphasized public health as the most important part of the NHP. I could not locate one review article about the NHP that criticized this aspect of the plan—not even its suggested increase in appropriations (see Table 4.5). Even business representatives spoke in favor of taxation for the public health provisions. For example, Charles W. Taussig, head of an industrial corporation, said "the expenditure of $850,000,000 per public health does not frighten business. Business bears a far greater financial burden now, due to our neglect of inadequate health control than its share of the tax burden will be under the proposed plan. The annual toll of preventable illness measured in terms of money runs into billions. Progressive business will regard an adequate health service as a subsidy to industry—not a burden."[41]

Recommendations II, III, and IV—expansion of hospital facilities, medical care for the medically needy, and insurance against financial loss due to disability—all received widespread support. One might think that coverage for the medically needy would have been controversial, especially because the report (and most other writings at that time) defined the medically needy as a fairly large group. While some writings, such as the book by Davis, estimated this group to be 85% of the population, the NHP recommendations defined the group as "probably 40 million persons—almost one-third of our population—living in families with annual incomes of less than $800."[42] In the NHP recommendations, they lumped the low-income medically needy in with public assistance recipients:

> It is proposed that the Federal Government, through grants-in-aid to the States, implement the provision of public medical care to two broad groups of the population: (1) To those for whom the local, State, and Federal governments, jointly or singly, have already accepted some responsibility through the public assistance provisions of the Social Security Act, through the work relief program or through provision of general relief; (2) to those who, though able to obtain food, shelter, and clothing from their own resources, are unable to procure necessary medical care.[43]

The designers of the NHP envisioned the program for indigents and the medically needy to work alongside the first two recommendations—public health, MCH, and more government-funded hospital and health care facilities. However, "the use of nongovernmental hospital beds for medically needy

*Table 4.5* **Appropriations for Health Purposes under the Social Security Act (1939) and Appropriations Proposed to Be Authorized by the NHP (S. 1620)**

| Purpose | Authorization under the SSA in 1939 | Proposed Authorization under NHP for FY 1940 |
|---|---|---|
| Title V | | |
| Pt. 1: Maternal and Child health services | $3,800,000 | $8,000,000 |
| Pt. 2: Medical services for children, including crippled children | $2,850,000 | $13,000,000 |
| Pt. 5: Administration, Investigations and demonstrations | $425,000 | $2,500,000 |
| Title VI—Public Health work and Investigations | | |
| Pt. 1: <br> -Payments to States <br> -Admin, Studies, Demonstrations | $8,000,000 | $15,000,000 <br> $1,500,000 |
| Pt. 2: Investigations | $2,000,000 | $3,000,000 |
| Title XII | | |
| Grants for general hospitals | | $8,000,000 |
| Grants for mental and tuberculosis hospitals | | * |
| Administration <br> -Public Health Service <br> -Public Works Administration | | $1,000,000 <br> * |
| Title XIII | | |
| -Grants for medical care | | $35,000,000 |
| -Administration | | $1,000,000 |
| Title XIV | | |
| -Grants for temporary disability compensation <br> -Administration | | $10,000,000 <br> $250,000 |
| Total | $17,015,000 | $98,250,000 |

*Note:* * The amount was left undetermined/unspecified. Written instead: "A sum sufficient to carry out the purposes of (this part of) this title."

*Source:* Abel Wolman, "The National Health Program—Present Status" *American Journal of Public Health* 30, no. 1 (1940), 4.

persons, paid for on a proper basis by public funds, [was also] presumed as a part of this program."[44] Despite the estimated size of this population and acknowledged government reimbursement, it is noteworthy that even the AMA, though entirely consistent with its previous positions, backed this recommendation.[45]

The diverse groups participating in the conference, from labor, agriculture, welfare, and health, gave broad approval to the five recommendations. The AMA and the AHA opposed the compulsory insurance option under Recommendation IV, but they endorsed all the other recommendations.[46] Although there was opposition to compulsory insurance, it is noteworthy that this was only one part of Recommendation IV. The other part included funds for more state medicine: "Federal grants-in-aid to the States toward the costs of a more general medical care program."[47] As distinct from Recommendation III—grants for the medically needy, the purpose of IV was "to help self-supporting people meet the problems of medical costs" and "to acknowledge that government must assume larger responsibilities than it has carried in the past if it is to help."[48] While acknowledging an increased role of government, the architects of the NHP called for states to decide how "costs [are] distributed among groups of people and over periods of time through the use of taxation, or through insurance, or through a combination of the two."[49] The taxation approach called for the expansion of public medical services in the states. Given today's discourse, one might think that there would have been significant opposition to this approach, but there was minimal reference to it. Instead, those opposed to government involvement focused on compulsory insurance, and those in favor focused on how familiar the public medical care approach already was. In introducing the recommendation to expand public medical services, the Technical Committee wrote: "It has been pointed out that tax-supported public medical services already involve annual expenditures of about $500,000,000 to $600,000,000. The use of tax-funds to pay for medical services, of course, a very old method of distributing the costs."[50]

Even Edwin Witte, the executive director of the Committee on Economic Security in 1935, who was instrumental in deciding not to pursue compulsory health insurance under the Social Security Act, emphasized the extent to which government was already involved in health care when defending the NHP in 1939:

> The National Health Program is an unambiguous term and no one will dispute the meaning I am giving to this expression. The National Health Program is a proposal for greatly increased federal aid to the states for state and local health services. . . . A bill based upon the [NHP] was introduced in February by Senator Wagner and is popularly known as the "Wagner Health Bill." . . . What is meant by the other term in the title of my address—"socialized medicine"—is much

more debatable. Many people apply the term "socialized medicine" to every development in the health field which they do not like . . . such a usage renders the term meaningless and serves only the purposes of propaganda. No worthwhile discussion of socialized medicine is possible unless the term is used in its generally accepted scientific meaning. "Socialized medicine" is . . . medical care and other health services which are provided at public expense. . . . It is properly applied to all health services which are paid for from the public treasury—that is from tax funds. It includes the long established federal, state, and local public health services; the hospital care and medical treatment furnished employees, wards, and pensioners of the government—the Army—[other] public institutions; hospital and medical care and related services furnished indigents and others, wholly or partly at public expense; hospitalization and treatment in public institutions of such expensive diseases as mental diseases, venereal diseases, and tuberculosis; publicly supported hospitals and subsidies from tax funds to private hospitals; travelling and permanent clinics for maternal and child health and in fact care; public health nursing; physical examinations of school children and immunization treatments; and many other types of health services which are customarily or occasionally furnished at public expense.

When thus used in its proper meaning, socialized medicine is not a bugbear but a very familiar phenomenon. . . . Socialized medicine has long constituted a very considerable part of the total health services rendered in the United States.[51]

Six years after Pierce Williams's article in 1933, we still see a tortured attempt to clarify the meaning of a demonized term—not by explaining its intrinsic value, but by arguing that the United States already had socialized medicine.

Numerous speakers at the proceedings emphasized how the NHP built on existing practices and frequently argued that the NHP did not have to be enacted all at once or in its entirety. For example, the Introductory Statement to the Proceedings of the National Health Conference to discuss the National Health Program included this statement: "Each recommendation deals with a certain phase of the problem. In some important respects, the five present *some alternative choices*, especially in respect to the scope of a program to be undertaken."[52]

It is clear upon a close read of the conference proceedings that many participants viewed the recommendations as alternatives and emphasized some over others.

Take Joseph Slavitt, MD, chairman of the American League for Public Medicine, who emphasized state medicine over insurance and said in his statement:

> The alternative plan to insurance medicine is really based on principles stressed throughout the Technical Committee report, the plan for the expansion and retention of public health services and publicly provided medical care. Call it public medicine, like public education, like all other public services. Already in our United States Public Health Service, in our Army, Navy, and other departmental medical services, in our State and local health departments, in our city, county and State hospitals, clinics, health centers, et cetera, we have laid an extensive basis for a system of public medicine, both preventive and curative. This should be further expanded, extended, and developed till it reaches full fruition in a health service for all the people of America without distinctions or limitations of any kind. Public medicine is the long-range plan on which all planning should be based.[53]

Others were less explicit but clearly saw the recommendations as possible alternatives and stressed that insurance was only one part (or no part) of the larger package of reform. C.-E. A. Winslow said, "This is not a program of health insurance, it is not a program for the extension of public medical service, it is not a program for hospital construction. It is a coordinated, complete, interlocking, dove-tailing health program for the Nation, in which all these things have their just and proper part."[54]

Because the Wagner Bill emerged out of the NHP and failed to even make it out of committee for a vote, it is logical to conclude that there was little support for the bill.[55] However, in light of widespread endorsement of NHP at the conference among multiple stakeholders—including the AMA and AHA for the bulk of the NHP, it is not correct to say the bill—as a whole—lacked support. The Wagner Bill went against Roche's suggestion to view the recommendations as possible alternatives, and the larger strategy of the Interdepartmental Committee, which suggested that it was not practicable to immediately enact the maximum recommendations. Rather, it recommended "a gradual expansion along well planned lines with a view to achieving operation on a full scale within about 10 years."[56]

In his opening statement to the conference, which Chairwoman Roche read, President Roosevelt also highlighted that enactment and implementation of the NHP should be gradual and incremental, and should build on a federated, public-private approach: "We cannot do all at once everything that we should do. But, we can advance more surely if we have before us a comprehensive, long-range program, providing for the most efficient cooperation of Federal, State, and local governments, voluntary agencies, professional groups, mediums of public information, and individual citizens."[57]

Leaders in the public health network were used to working incrementally and within a federal system where reforms would start locally, be modified and adjusted, and often then disseminated across the country with the help of federal funding (see Part I). PHS funding to state and municipal health departments and county health units were good examples of this approach. Thus, while others viewed the Wagner Bill as another example of health reform failure, the bureaucrats in charge of implementing the components of the NHP viewed it as the beginning of a long-range plan in which each component would slowly be adopted and disseminated across the United States. For example, in reviewing progress of the NHP a year after the Wagner Bill failed in 1940, the previous APHA president, Abel Wolman, wrote:

> In reviewing the present status of the National Health Program, it is surprising to discover the number and variety of steps, which have been taken during the past year to extend and to facilitate public health and medical care practices by official and nonofficial agencies. A number of the states have developed administrative procedures in the fields of public health, medical care, and hospitalization, particularly for the medically needy, which represent advances in a single year comparable with those made in several decades preceding. . . . [This review] discloses that the national health program has advanced far and fast in the characteristically democratic experimental fashion with which we are familiar in this country.[58]

In the same address he gave to managers of private practice clinics in Wisconsin, Edwin Witte also predicted that "this trend toward an increasing percentage of socialized medicine is likely to continue *whether or not* the National Health Program becomes law."[59] Moreover, Harold Maslow, a staff member of the New York Committee to Formulate a Long Range Health Program, noted in his review of the Wagner Bill that, despite claims of revolutionary change from the AMA, the components of the bill built on what already existed: "[P]ublic health and hospital construction titles of the Bill are merely another step, albeit a long step, in the orderly development of existing federal health work, while the federal grants for medical care, and the disability compensation program, cannot be thought of as radical innovations, for they, too, have a broad body of precedent."[60]

# Building a Federated Health Service System

Although dramatic increases in public health state-building occurred in the first three decades of the 20th century,[61] these increases paled in comparison to expansions ignited under the Social Security Act and other New Deal programs. Even at the time, the scale of change was apparent to leaders in the public health network, and they described the changes as monumental. Joseph Mountin, the Assistant Surgeon General of PHS in the 1940s, and described as the "architect of modern public health,"[62] wrote in 1941 "that no decade in the history of public health work has witnessed more far-reaching changes in organization and scope of service than the period between 1930 and 1940."[63] While there was widespread agreement that public health services had increased over the decade, no one knew much about the details of this expansion, due to the decentralized nature of public health governance. Thus, similar to surveys conducted in 1925 and 1930,[64] the PHS set out in 1940 to survey states to document what states were doing regarding public health.

However, quite distinct from the data collection effort just one decade earlier, leaders in the PHS realized—and explicitly stated—that the nature of what states were doing under the label of public health had changed. Joseph Mountin was the leader of this new PHS study and explained that "during the past ten years there has been envisioned a broader scope of public responsibility for health measures than had previously prevailed. Many health departments are now participating in programs, which in 1930 would have been regarded as outside the realm of public health concern."[65] As a result of this expanded definition, the study shifted from only collecting data on state health departments, as they had done in 1930, to collect data on all state agencies' health activities.[66] The PHS asked about 35 different services (see Table 4.6) and inquired which

*Table 4.6* **Categories Recognized as State Public Health Activities by the PHS**

| |
|---|
| Vital statistics |
| Acute communicable disease control |
| Tuberculosis control (prevention and treatment—including hospitalization) |
| Venereal disease control |
| Maternity hygiene |
| Infant and preschool hygiene |
| School health services |

(*continued*)

*Table 4.6* **Continued**

Industrial hygiene

Workingmen's compensation

Sanitation of water supplies and sewage disposal facilities

Housing control

Plumbing control

Smoke, fumes, and odors control

Rodent control

Garbage collection and disposal

Shellfish sanitation

Milk sanitation

Malaria control

Pest mosquito control

Supervision of hotels, restaurants, tourist camps, and other facilities for the travelling public

Food and drug control

Mental hygiene (prevention and treatment–including hospitalization)

Care of crippled children

Cancer control

Prevention and care of blindness

Vocational rehabilitation

Pneumonia control

Hookworm control

Health services for migratory labor

General medical care of the needy

Dental services

Laboratory services

Health education

Research activities

Licensure of professions and agencies significant to the public health

*Source:* Joseph W. Mountin and Evelyn Flook, "Distribution of Health Services in the Structure of State Government. Chapter I: The Composite Pattern of State Health Services." Reprinted by U.S. Public Health Service (Washington DC) 1943. Reprint No. 2306, p.4. From the *Public Health Reports*, 56(34), August 22, 1941: 1673–1698, https://books.google.ht/books?id=hs1kCPvqH28C&printsec=frontcover&hl=fr&source=gbs_ge_summary_r&cad=0#v=onepage&q&f=false.

state agency administered the service. This process allowed them to follow each public health activity "through the entire structure of State government, regardless of where administrative responsibility had been placed."[67]

Mountin wrote a massive report (with his co-author Evelyn Flook) released in 10 parts over three years based on the study findings. They estimated that state governments across the country spent over 285 million dollars in 1940 on health-related activities. Of course, it is impossible to compare this to the 1930 study because they so drastically expanded the definition of what was included in state health expenditures; nonetheless, this 1940 figure, compared to a total of $13 million in 1930, must have appeared shocking.[68]

Mountin and Flook documented new public health activities and the provision of health services, and—for the first time—made transparent across all 10 reports the extent to which hospital services and medical care were provided in "traditional" public health domains. Take tuberculosis, for example; because it is a communicable disease, it had always been accepted as a primary responsibility of public health departments (see Chapter 2). In the late 1910s, when leaders of the public health network attempted to standardize the appropriate jurisdiction of responsibility for state and local health departments, they were explicit that hospitals and sanitoria (as well as sanitation) should not be included in municipal health department budgets. The rational was stated clearly in 1916 that these expenditures were of "no special hygienic significance" and should be deducted from total health department expenditures because "the remaining expenditure should represent with considerable accuracy the amount devoted to actual preventive measures."[69] In 1940, Mountin and Flook completely reversed this strategy and made every effort to include all the state government activities related to tuberculosis, including hospitals and sanitoria. Indeed, when describing the content of state tuberculosis programs in 1940, they emphasized how state programs' "paramount interest centers on operation of direct service programs. Conducting special case-finding surveys and maintaining diagnostic clinics, sanatoria, and pneumothorax stations overshadow other functions. Likewise, financial subsidy of local facilities is a more prominent measure in the eradication of tuberculosis than in many other public health performances."[70]

In 1939, the same year that the Wagner Act failed, President Roosevelt created the Federal Security Agency (FSA) and moved the PHS from the Treasury Department to the FSA, with a 30% increase in federal appropriations, from $8 million to over $10 million, to distribute to the states.[71]

Four years later, a 1943 law reorganized the PHS internally by consolidating its programs into four subdivisions: the Office of the Surgeon General, the National

Institute of Health, and two new entities, the Bureau of Medical Services and the Bureau of State Services. The creation of a new Bureau of State Services, which oversaw all "cooperative policies" with the states, highlights the importance of the grant-in-aid programs. Indeed, the 1944 Public Health Service Act significantly expanded public health action by establishing five additional categorical grant-in-aid programs: venereal disease, tuberculosis, mental health, cancer, and heart disease.[72] Before 1944, these programs were included under the "general" public health grant. However, after the 1944 Act, states received a separate allocation for each program while still maintaining the general health grant.

Although the grant-in-aid funds were crucial for instigating spending in this area, the federal portion was small (only 6%) relative to the entire national health budget, and small compared to state expenditures, which increased from $12.9 million in 1930 to $18.7 million in 1940 and up to $37 million in 1946.[73] Every state showed a sizable increase in per capita spending on health from 1935 to 1946: from an average of 10.5 cents per capita in 1935, to 15 in 1941, to 26 in 1946.[74] Mountin and colleagues were explicit that much of the state expenditures used at the local level were for the provision of health services—not just prevention but also treatment. For example, they highlighted how "free diagnostic laboratory services were provided in 48 states." And states used grant-in-aid funds "to purchase about 165 modern X-ray units and considerable amounts of equipment and supplies"—all for diagnostic and treatment purposes. Thirty-nine states distributed "curative" drugs to public clinics, and the other nine states also distributed drugs to "private practitioners, hospitals, or other treatment institutions."[75]

The PHS Bureau of State Services (directed by Mountin) used the regulatory guidance of the grants-in-aid program to improve the quality of local public health services by encouraging states to use their funds for improving the organization of services and hiring quality personnel in state health departments. The PHS also encouraged states to use the grants to support "local health units, laboratories, and special health projects operated by counties, cities, or other political subdivisions."[76] Not only were grant funds distributed downward to local health units, but states used aid to support "full-time local health units which meet specified requirements."[77] To the PHS, an important measure of quality was having a full-time health officer working in all local health units, and this did increase substantially. The number of counties with a local health unit employing a full-time health officer increased from 762 counties in 1935 to 1,828 by 1942.

Numerous publications attributed the increase in state expenditures and personnel to the strong stimulus of federal grants.[78] The amount of annual health department expenditures increased dramatically over the decade, from $45 million in 1940 to $159 million in 1950. Expenditures increased for health departments across all the states, though the increase in 21 states was over 200 percent.[79] Milton Roemer, who worked for the PHS, wrote an article titled "Government's

Role in American Medicine," and after documenting the long-standing role of the government in medicine, he wrote: "The greatly expanded federal subsidy for state and local public health activities that came with the New Deal and the social security program after 1935 has altered the picture a great deal. . . . Increasingly, government has widened its sphere of responsibility for both the prevention and the care of illness. So far as public health services alone are concerned, the line of division between therapeutic medicine under private auspices and prevention medicine under public auspices is rapidly being obliterated."[80]

A special conference was held in September 1940 among federal PHS leaders, its health officers across the states and territories, and representatives from the AMA and AHA.[81] Surgeon General Parran made clear in his opening statement at the conference that severe manpower and facilities shortages were evident, and he declared that "the federal government has planned a closer coordination of health activities to promote national defense than we have ever known before."[82] At this conference they began to lay out a plan for wartime preparedness that contributed significantly to the expansion of the PHS's programs and personnel. Following passage of the Selective Service and Training Act in 1941, PHS personnel doubled in size from 1940 to 1945.[83] Due to concerns about a shortage of nurses during wartime, Congress also passed the Nurse Training Act of 1943. This act created the Cadet Nurse Corps, which provided tuition scholarships in exchange for wartime service. This program was administered by the PHS, and was significant not only because it trained over 124,000 nurses, but also because it marked the beginning of PHS involvement on a large scale in funding the training of health professionals. In other words, it institutionalized and created acceptance that the federal government would set health manpower policies for the country.[84]

For example, when wartime production revealed numerous unmet needs, the PHS provided federal public health personnel for local communities, and recruited medical and dental personnel for the armed forces. Moreover, under the Procurement and Assignment Service set up by the War Manpower Commission, an equitable distribution of civilian medical personnel across the United States was also attempted. Although this attempt to create a more equal distribution was not very successful, it established the principle that the federal government would play a role in developing medical manpower policies to effect the supply and distribution of medical personnel.[85]

Crucially important was the development of the Emergency Maternity and Infant Care (EMIC) Program administered by the Children's Bureau, which made relatively large sums available to provide obstetrical and pediatric care for wives and infants of enlisted men in the armed forces. At the end of World War II, by June 30, 1946, EMIC had provided care for more than a million wives and infants.[86]

In 1946, two additional legislative acts also had a significant impact on the
PHS. The National Mental Health Act greatly expanded the involvement of the
PHS in the area of mental health, by supporting research, training personnel,
and providing state grants to assist in the establishment of clinics and treatment
centers. As part of this act, the National Institute of Mental Health (NIMH) was
created in 1949.[87]

Mountain and Flook's approach also allowed them to show how the proportion
of expenditures were broken down by public health activity and across agencies.
State health departments, which were considered the primary administrative
entities for providing public health activities, only consumed one-fifth (18.5%) of
total state expenditures. The largest share of expenditures were distributed by special boards or commissions (25%) followed by departments of welfare (21.3%).[88]
Special boards and commissions were typically given control over dispensing
funds to cover the costs of hospitalization services, and state welfare department
expenditures typically included funds for medical care for the needy.[89]

By presenting the data in this way, Mountin and Flook were doing something very radical and important: they were, for the first time, including public
subsidies for hospital care and medical care for the needy along with all the other
forms of public health activity to make a claim that these should all fall under
the rubric of public health services, and under the administrative purview of the
PHS. As Witte foresaw, without passing the Wagner Act, states were moving forward (with the help of the federal government) on their own. Indeed, despite
inclusion of public health and maternal and child health grants in the Social
Security Act, states actually spent more of their expenditures on hospital and
care for the needy (items not included under the SSA) than they did on "traditional" public health activities.

State and local governments had assumed the responsibility of paying for
the sick poor in public and nonprofit hospitals, and also maintaining hospitals
for "special conditions" such as tuberculosis and mental illness long before the
New Deal. What is less well known is the PHS's role in building up hospitals
and how this effort was necessarily tied to health care reform in the eyes of
PHS leaders.[90]

**Hospital Construction.** Nonprofit voluntary hospitals were the hardest hit
during the Depression, and the federal government responded to the crisis. The
Public Works Administration and the Works Progress Administration provided
hospital construction funds as part of its re-employment programs. In 1933
alone, the PWA provided 51,000 hospital beds. The program also provided
grants to local government bodies for hospital construction. From 1933 to 1936,
the PWA allocated $75 million for hospital construction. The WPA also focused
on hospital construction, mostly by providing labor, and 101 new hospitals were
built and 1,422 renovated from 1935 to 1938.[91]

President Roosevelt attempted to separate out hospital construction in another legislative proposal rhetorically called his "tiny rural hospital bill" because it offered less than $10 million to the PHS to construct fifty hospitals.[92] Nonetheless, it started a process of separately expanding each component of the NHP. Wartime expansions did the same. The Community Facilities Act of 1940 (also known as the Lantham Act) served as another public works program administered by the Federal Works Agency, which provided federal assistance to build hospitals and health centers in defense areas. Over five years, from 1941 to 1946, $121 million was spent on 874 hospital and health-related projects.[93]

Although this legislation was limited, it also set a precedent that the *federal* government[94] would continue to support the private voluntary hospital sector beyond the New Deal emergency relief programs to enable growth in this sector. And yet it also set an important precedent that the federal government would allow the sector complete autonomy to define what obligations—if any—were tied to this notion of a "community non-profit hospital." Therefore, when Congress passed the Hill-Burton Act in 1946, it allowed the federal PHS to grant funding to local communities for hospital construction *almost* carte blanche. Over the next 25 years, the federal government disbursed nearly $4 billion, asking for no commitment in return, to assure access to health or hospital care for the American people.

I emphasize *almost carte blanche*, because the one area that federal PHS leaders wanted accountability in return for subsidized hospital construction was in requiring communities to survey existing health care facilities (including hospitals and health centers), and based on this survey to present an organized plan for facility construction.[95] The PHS played a central role in promoting the importance of planning an organized system of care, in which they endorsed a very detailed conceptualization of the health delivery service system referred to as "regionalism."[96] Although George Bugbee, the American Hospital Association's (AHA) executive director and the main Washington lobbyist for the voluntary hospital sector, was an instigating force for the entire Hill-Burton legislation, Surgeon General Parran and Vane Hoge in the PHS worked closely with leaders form the AHA to write the legislative details.[97] What Daniel Fox refers to as "hierarchical regionalism" was the concept of a coordinated hospital-service plan that specified the number of beds necessary for a given population, and the number and types of hospitals that should be built in each geographic area, with highly specialized academic medical centers providing tertiary care at the center supporting community hospitals in the periphery, with coordinated links to public health agencies and community health centers, which would focus on newly expanded notions of public health—namely, mental health, chronic disease, maternal and child health, and dental services.[98]

A central element of hierarchical regionalism and its promotion in Hill-Burton was the notion of *scientific* hospital care. "The modern hospital, said Surgeon General Parran, is a 'complex technical machine, employing the latest scientific diagnostic aids, preventative and curative measures, and professional skills.'"[99] The notion of growth was embedded in this concept of hospital science—the more the better. It is important to understand how the parallel development of federal support for biomedical research through the newly created National Institute of Health (also run by the PHS) created a perfect storm: not only would the federal government build hospitals, but it would invest in scientific research and discovery in academic medical centers—the pinnacle of scientific hospital care under the concept of regionalism, which would transmit out to all other hospitals and health centers—thereby requiring and growing hospital care that was "scientifically planned."[100]

This was a dream come true for public health leaders across the country. First, hospital construction—and, more importantly, community hospital *planning*—would be administered and overseen by the PHS. This is something they had advocated for since the 1910s,[101] when Surgeon General Warren and Edgar Sydenstricker promoted a unified health system for the country. It wasn't exactly the regionalism concept as specified in the 1940s, but it supported the idea of planning a federated—and unified—health service system across the United States, which would be overseen by the PHS. Similar to Warren, who argued that the AALL insurance scheme had to be implemented within a broader plan for a unified health service delivery system, Parran in 1944 argued that an organized system of regionalism had to be in place before any program of compulsory health insurance could be implemented. In fact, he warned that passing compulsory health insurance without systemic planning would stimulate and further embed the complex and fragmented system that already existed.[102]

Second, Hill-Burton gave substantial influence to state health departments to assist in the central elements of health care planning within each state. In Parran's mind, state health departments were the ideal administrative unit because they had local familiarity and would be run by health officers highly trained in the PHS commissioned corps; such officers could be trusted to implement the larger unified vision of coordinated preventive and curative health services. Of course, as Daniel Fox and others have documented, this version of hierarchical regionalism did not work out as planned.

While there was no opposition to hospital construction, and it was definitely a bipartisan issue, there was disagreement as to whether the bill would be a starting point or end point. Taft and other conservatives in Congress believed strongly that by passing Hill-Burton along with voluntary insurance for the middle and upper class, and grants to states for the medically indigent, the problem of access to medical care would be solved. Others, especially those favoring compulsory insurance in the SSA, were against this decoupling of the NHP and believed they should hold ground until the NHP could be passed as a whole. Even early on there were voices raised arguing that separating out the components of the NHP was foolhardy because it would create the strong possibility that the United States would build a health care delivery system without ever securing the means for all Americans to afford health care. For example, when Roosevelt signaled out hospital construction into a separate bill after the Wagner Act failed in 1940, Dr. John Peters from Yale University, a longtime advocate of universal coverage, called the proposal "vicious" because hospitals would be built in poor rural areas where residents could least afford to pay for it, and he asked pointedly, "[H]ow can we approve something we declare impossible?"[103] Several years later after Hill-Burton was passed, another liberal academic, Dr. Channing Frothingham, also warned that the nation should not be lulled into believing that the health care problem had been solved.[104]

This worry made sense given that proponents of Hill-Burton often claimed the American people would have access to care. The bill's co-sponsor, Senator Lister Hill, when discussing the significant need for hospital construction in his opening remarks at the Senate hearings, said that we "have not yet organized our efforts to the end that scientific health care is readily available to all our people."[105] Thus, he implied that once the legislation was passed, such "scientific health care" would be readily available to all Americans. Of course, exaggerated claims about a bill's potential to solve a problem is not uncommon when trying to pass legislation; however, after the bill was passed, Republican congressmen were explicit in claiming that the health care problem was largely solved. For example, during the 1948 Senate hearings on the Wagner-Murray-Dingell bill for the NHP, Senator Allen Ellender said, in discussing the need for compulsory insurance, "Personally, I would much prefer that we devote some time in trying to find a voluntary method, rather than to have the government have its hands in it. I would want us to be as far removed from Government control as possible. . . . That is why I was so insistent on the Congress providing funds [under Hill Burton] so as to build a system or a chain of hospitals and clinics throughout the country, and let that be the extent of our obligation."[106]

## Build State Programs for the Poor and Medically Needy

When the Congress rejected the Wagner Bill in 1940, 38 states (75%) had general medical care programs for the needy in place. Thus, the third component of the Wagner Bill had already spread across most states without passage of the National Health Program. Almost all (35) of these states set up their own grant-in-aid funds to local units to provide general relief for home and office-based care and/or hospital care, and the majority of states (35) also operated direct medical service programs, including general clinic services for ambulatory patients (26 states) or general hospital services (22 states), and vocational rehabilitation (26 states).[107]

On top of these general medical care programs for the needy, all states provided medical care programs for children with physical disabilities (what was called the "Crippled Children's" program at that time), and the blind. States also developed programs around particular diseases: 34 states operated medical care programs for cancer patients, and 40 states operated programs for pneumonia. While all the states provided prevention services for these diseases, half the states also provided diagnostic services and treatment. State level investment in these programs was extensive. In total, state expenditures equaled $36.2 million—not including the 7.6 million spent on disabled children.[108]

States were also quick to further develop their maternal and child health (MCH) programs: spending over $6 million, all states had MCH programs in place by 1940, and most provided health services—not just prevention—for maternal care, infants, young children, and school-age children.[109]

The federal government required that only money payments could be used to pay for public assistance recipients' medical care.[110] In other words, states could not use the federal grant funds to pay providers or facilities directly for care rendered. Because the federal government also set payment maximums on the amounts states could give public assistance recipients, even if states wanted to include the cost of medical care in their monthly payments, the maximum levels restricted them from truly accounting for the cost of medical care.[111]

This restriction was a major shift from the FERA program, which paid doctors, nurses, dentists, and druggists directly for the services or goods they provided to recipients. This "method of payment" was the predominant practice at that time.[112] Because this was the predominant method, states continued such programs for their general assistance programs. And many states paid hospitals directly for the care of public assistance recipients out of "state-only" funds.

Especially because of how the public assistance groups were defined, a large proportion of recipients—especially the elderly and blind—were in poor health or disabled.[113] As a result, there was growing attention on the medical aspects of public assistance in the states. By the early 1940s, many states had eliminated the maximums on individual payments to accommodate the need to assist in paying for medical expenses. Not surprisingly, however, the wealthier states were best positioned to make more generous payments, and inequities in state payments for public assistance recipients grew early on and quickly after 1935, resulting in wide variations in medical care provisions across the states.[114] According to a study of state medical care plans for public assistance recipients conducted in 1946 by the U.S. Bureau of Public Assistance in the Federal Security Agency, "[t]hey ranged from well-organized state-wide plans furnishing comprehensive services to plans in which local officials have established their own standards [to other states] only [providing coverage for] physicians' services and drugs."[115]

As previously indicated, many states separated out the cost of hospital care and paid hospitals directly for services rendered. Just as the AHA had wanted, and their joint statement specified, many states set up arrangements with government-owned (state, county, or city) hospitals as the primary place where recipients should receive care, with private voluntary hospitals as a last resort. For example, in 1946, hospital care requirements in Connecticut's medical care program stated that "care may be furnished in other hospitals when the State-aided hospital has no bed available or does not give the type of treatment required, or when treatment is urgent and the distance to a State-aided hospital involves too great a medical risk."[116]

As one might expect given the vast variation among the states in terms of health service delivery infrastructure, cost-of-living, and state wealth, the state medical programs varied substantially in terms of how and how much they paid hospitals and providers. Some states employed physicians to give care to recipients, and other states made lump-sum payments to a group of physicians, such as a county medical society.[117] In some states, such as New York, the organizational method varied by locality—some counties paid providers a set amount for services to the indigent, others authorized fee schedules under agreements between the agency, practitioners, and hospitals.[118] Kansas developed prepayment plans with county medical societies.

Although the Social Security Board recommended compulsory health insurance in its Ninth Annual Report, "many of the public and other groups directly concerned [with public assistance programs], including State legislatures, the Council of State Governments, and the American Public Welfare Association, [had] long urged that the existing public assistance programs be strengthened and that Federal grants-in-aid be extended to general assistance."[119] In addition, provider groups were also pushing for expanding existing programs and for more generous payments. The AHA and the AMA advocated for building up a federated health service system and favored financing care for the indigent and medically needy—also a state-level responsibility—to exist alongside that system. These major pressure groups also acknowledged the need for federal financing, especially for low-resourced states. This is important, because not only was there a strong constituency fighting for a federated health service system, but they were lobbying for a two-part financing system as well—voluntary insurance, which many have written about, and state medical care programs for the poor and medically needy.

Indeed, after Truman's efforts to pass compulsory health insurance failed, the Congress passed the Social Security Act Amendments of 1950 (Public

Law 734—81st Congress), in which general medical care programs for "needy individuals" were expanded. For the first time, the act authorized the use of federal aid to states for the direct purchase of medical care for assistance recipients—those covered under the public assistance provisions of the Social Security Act, which included needy persons age 65 and over, the blind, and dependent children. The amendments also added a fourth group of needy persons: "the permanently and totally disabled."[120]

The state medical care programs were often discussed as residual and not considered a real threat to compulsory insurance. But they were much larger than proponents of compulsory insurance were willing to acknowledge. As the Joint Committee on Medical Care of the American Public Health Association (APHA) and the American Public Welfare Association (APWA) described the 1950 amendments: "Even though the federal share of funds authorized under the 1950 amendments remains limited, many states are revising their present medical care programs, exploring the possibilities of expanding their programs under the new law, and considering how state and federal resources may best be used to meet the medical requirements of needy people."[121] Because these programs—now with federal financial aid—played this important (though wholly incomplete) supplementary role, it allowed private insurance to grow in numbers while still providing very thin coverage to the majority (discussed in more detail under Chapter 5).

## Conclusion

From 1930–1946, each component of the NHP was either expanded or enacted, except compulsory insurance. Many actors in the public health network supported the idea of compulsory health insurance, but they also knew that it wasn't the only approach, and they were familiar with much less controversial methods—namely, building and expanding public medical services. Many worried about growing fragmentation and complexity, but they remained hopeful—rightly or wrongly—that as public medical services continued to grow, American public support would grow and solidify around this more rational efficient system. As Wolman predicted in a speech in 1939 titled "The National Health Program, How Far? How Fast?," "Within 10 years the major elements of the national health program will be in effect, because the people want it, can pay for it, and are entitled to it." While he believed tax-supported subsidies for medical care for the medically needy and public assistance groups and voluntary insurance would be adopted, he predicted that compulsory insurance would eventually be enacted after several decades. In Wolman's view, and many other public health leaders, the United States would ultimately adopt a compulsory insurance scheme, because the failure of voluntary health insurance was self-evident. Most noteworthy, he did not view this failure as problematic, but as necessary "before we learn to avoid."[122]

It is very important that public health leaders kept using the phrase "National Health Program." They continued to push ahead with NHP by moving pieces of legislation. At the 50th anniversary of the Centers for Disease Control and Prevention (CDC), Milton Roemer gave a speech honoring Joseph Mountin because, among all his other accomplishments, he was the director of a program to control malaria in the southern states in 1942, and under his leadership this program expanded to become the Communicable Disease Center in 1946. Roemer's speech highlighted that "Mountin's health work was directed to the strengthening and improvement of all five components of the U.S. health system."[123] Roemer pointed out that although observers of U.S. health care often called it a "non-system" because it was complicated and fragmented, Roemer argued that it was a system with main components, which could still be analyzed, despite its complexity, and "by recognizing its main components, strategies can be designed for social change."[124] This point is important because Roemer worked under Mountin in the 1940s, which gave him a unique insight into how Mountin thought about the mission and work of the PHS. As the above quote suggests, Mountin worked on all the major components of the NHP, and he thought strategically about how to approach each component to bring about social change.

Roemer provided a model of the components of the U.S. national health system (see Illustration 4.1). We can observe each component of the NHP in the model Roemer provided nearly fifty years later. His point was to show how Mountin, and thereby the PHS, played a role in building up each major component. It is clear that under the box "resource production" we see the "manpower" policies that began with the war effort, and the "facilities" that began earlier on but with a major federal commitment under Hill-Burton in 1946; "commodities" were not discussed in this Chapter, but the Food and Drug Administration emerged out of the PHS during this time.[125] "Knowledge" is government investment in research, which was represented in the NIH and CDC (to be discussed in more detail in Chapter 6). The "management" box portrays government policies and regulations over the "organization of programs" (the next box down). In this "organization of programs" box we see the federated public-private health system clearly represented, and a multipronged financing approach to support that system ("economic support" box), which includes individual out-of-pocket costs (personal households), charity, private insurance, Social Security, and taxation (government revenues). Note how all of those financing sources were present in the 1940s as Mountin and others at the PHS were helping to orchestrate the building of the U.S. health care system. Some

Model of the components of a National Health System, showing their relationships to health status

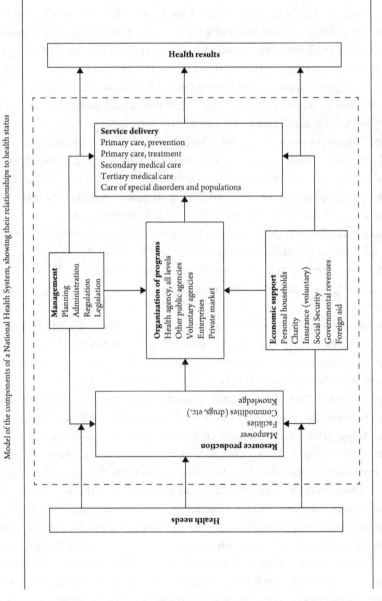

*Illustration 4.1* Depiction of How Mountin's Work Led to the Modern U.S. Health Care System. *Source:* Milton I. Roemer, "Joseph W. Mountin, Architect of Modern Public Health," *Public Health Reports* 108, no. 6 (1993): 727–35. Model on p. 728.

hoped that despite experimenting with multiple forms, the best approach would become clear and chosen. Others believed a multipronged approach could work and would flow into supporting an organized service delivery system, which is the last box, clearly denoting the concept of regionalism (even in 1993).

Even though Mountin, similar to Parran, advocated for compulsory insurance, he was careful to insist that the reform should represent a "comprehensive and closely coordinated national health program. No single method or approach will do the job." He was also clear that any nationwide program of medical care, should fall under the official auspices of PHS, to assure adequate medical care for all the people.[126]

> The Public Health Service would like to see this program assure medical services to 100 percent of the population. We believe that this would be not only more equitable but also less complex administratively and, in the long run, more economical.[127]

Other, more conservative public health leaders, such as Wilson George Smillie, a professor from Cornell, did not favor compulsory insurance and felt strongly that the American people were not ready for it, and therefore "the development of the national plan should be gradual, and along experimental lines." A national plan, he argued, "must win the approval of the people. . . . There must be free discussion, and stumbling experiments. Foolish mistakes will be made. Out of this confusion will evolve a method that will meet the needs of the people and satisfy their requirements. When the American people want a nation-wide plan of universal sickness insurance, it certainly will evolve."[128] Unfortunately, as we will see in Part III, the politics that emerges from a hidden health care state, which is fragmented and highly unequal, is one largely defined by interest groups, and a political discourse that is largely directed by private actors, and therefore perpetuates public confusion rather than enlightenment.

As the New Deal programs expanded and wartime programs were put in place, it became clear that federal employees in charge of administering these programs came to view them as a "dry-run" for national health insurance. Fredrick Mott and Milton Roemer, who oversaw and were instrumental in setting up the FSA medical care programs across the country were convinced that these programs provided evidence that government subsidized health care programs could work. One crucial lesson they learned from their experience was that the voluntary nature of the FSA programs were its biggest downfall, and therefore for programs to work well, it would have to be compulsory. As time went on, they became more emboldened in making this argument explicit, despite known opposition from the AMA. For example, in testimony at a Senate hearing considering the 1945 Wagner-Murray-Dingell bill, Mott, after reviewing the success of the FSA programs, pointed out the limitations of voluntary programs and concluded that the only way to overcome existing problems would be a "universal program for the whole population.[129] An FSA colleague of Roemer's is quoted as saying, "I can remember having a long argument on a trip with Milton Roemer in which he anticipated that within a year after the war was over we would have national health insurance."[130]

In addition to the rural medical care programs, leaders in the FSA also pointed to the federally administered and financed EMIC program that provided health services to the spouses of U.S. servicemen and their children during World War II, as well as the expansions in public medical services at the state and local levels, as evidence that compulsory health insurance could work. But these expansions occurred under a sympathetic executive and a Democratically controlled Congress. While few supported compulsory insurance in Congress, there was an atmosphere of support for the New Deal programs, and for the idea of using existing mechanisms to expand access to care. Under this environment, public health leaders felt emboldened to point out what public expenditures were already doing in terms of providing support for access to health care. It was a measured discourse for many, and they rarely stated support for compulsory insurance, since many favored public medical services, but they did attempt to lay bare what government was already doing, and therefore what it could do.

# The Voluntary Approach Hides the Role of Government

## Introduction

Publicly funded health care expenditures continued to increase throughout the 1950s. This is not surprising, with the public health and maternal and child health Titles still in place since the passage in the Social Security Act of 1935, the passage of federal grant-in-aid funding for hospital construction in the 1946 Hill-Burton Act, and medical vendor payments for the poor passed under the Social Security Amendments of 1950. And yet the public discourse at the time suggested otherwise. Instead of more open and transparent talk about the extent of government involvement and its role in the health care system, there was a reversal back to hiding the government role.

This reversal initially happened as a response to Republicans winning the majority in both the Senate and the House in the 1946 midterm elections, which resulted in a strong political backlash against the policies of the New Deal. This retaliation targeted federal employees in the Federal Security Agency (FSA), which oversaw the administration of public health programs (as well as food and drug safety, education funding, and the Social Security old-age pension plan). The backlash especially targeted those who had supported compulsory health insurance, but also those employees who openly supported a more expanded role for government. The goals for compulsory health insurance shifted in the early 1950s to a strategy of compromise, expanding health insurance only to the elderly through the Social Security Act—which eventually became Medicare—passed in 1965.[1] But there was little serious discussion about Medicare until the 1960s, when Democrats regained control of the executive branch and Congress. Instead, the dominant health policy discourse in the 1950s was centered around the principle of "private democratic volunteerism," and this concept was infused throughout the three main areas of the U.S. health care system: voluntary health

*Grow and Hide*. Colleen M. Grogan, Oxford University Press. © Oxford University Press 2023.
DOI: 10.1093/oso/9780199812233.003.0006

insurance, voluntary hospitals, and voluntary health agencies. Because the main contours of the U.S. health care system were still being developed, volunteerism discourse and its associated policy designs had an enormous and lasting impact on the U.S. health care state and Americans' understanding of it. The political transformation of the American health care state was most dramatic during this period not because public expenditures skyrocketed (though of course they did), but because this increase in taxpayer support was politically constructed as private voluntary expenditures that would enable freedom, choice, and access to high-quality medical care.

This chapter begins by explaining the extent of the political backlash against compulsory health insurance and, by association, the term "National Health Program." Understanding this political environment is integral to grasping why there were so few voices against the "voluntary approach," and why people stopped even discussing the more popular National Health Program. But while discussion of the program faded, expansion of the program's actual components persisted. Indeed, crucially important about this period is that the Grow-and-Hide strategy re-emerged and was helped by federalism's growing complexity and fragmentation. This time, however, the discourse was led by groups outside of—and rhetorically hostile to—government: the hospital industry, business, and the voluntary sector. I say "rhetorically hostile" because despite their persistent claims that government was inefficient, unresponsive, and provided low-quality services, all three groups needed and used an enormous amount of government expenditures to bolster their American Voluntary Way.[2]

## Political Backlash against Government

Harry Truman proposed National Health Insurance almost immediately after becoming President upon Roosevelt's passing, and encouraged a second Wagner-Murray-Dingell bill that was introduced in Congress in 1945. As described in the previous chapter, several leaders in the FSA who had worked on various aspects of building up the National Health Program since the New Deal—Frederick Mott and Milton Roemer running the rural FSA medical care programs; Falk and Cohen in the Social Security Administration, who had been studying various health insurance schemes in the United States and abroad; Martha Elliot from the Children's Bureau, who oversaw not only MCH programs and programs for crippled children, but also the EMIC wartime program; and Parran and Mountin who oversaw the public health grant-in-aid programs, and expansions in hospital services—testified in favor of compulsory insurance. Although labor organizations (the CIO and AFL) were supportive of compulsory insurance, they had not mobilized their grass roots and were starting to shift their energy to industry plans and negotiating employee benefits under voluntary health insurance.[3] Of course, business and the major provider groups—the AMA and AHA—favored voluntary health insurance. As a result, the main supporters and advocates for compulsory insurance came from within the federal government.[4] Given Truman's effort to pass compulsory health insurance, it was particularly ironic that he also issued Executive Order 9806, establishing the President's Temporary Commission on Employee Loyalty in November 1946. This was an overt political move to placate conservatives after the Republican congressional election victory, but it also served to completely undermined the federal employees who were Truman's main supporters for national health insurance.[5]

Following the midterm elections, when Republicans gained control of Congress, the supportive New Deal atmosphere in the federal government changed fairly quickly. Truman passed another executive order[6] that created the loyalty program for federal employees in 1947, and although he won the presidency and Democrats regained the Congress in 1948, the lid on compulsory health insurance remained tightly shut. The witch hunt against communism that many associate with Senator Joseph McCarthy started under Truman with the federal loyalty program at the FBI—administered under J. Edgar Hoover—targeting (among many others) those who were supportive of the New Deal programs. As Lieutenant Colonel Randolph testified to the Loyalty Commission, "A liberal is only a hop, skip, and a jump from a Communist. A Communist starts as a liberal."[7] This program created loyalty review boards, which questioned thousands of federal employees' loyalty to the U.S. government, specifically targeting staff members who had ever stated support for compulsory insurance in the Public Health Service (PHS), the Children's Bureau, and the Social Security Board under the Federal Security Agency. These members included the major actors within the federal government who worked on developing the National Health Program since the New Deal: I. S. Falk, Altmeyer, and Wilbur Cohen from the Social Security Board, and Surgeon General Parran, Joseph Mountin, George Perrott, and Milton Roemer from the PHS, to name just a few of those targeted.[8]

The loyalty investigations persisted over several years and were clear attempts to not only question the moral integrity of the person being reviewed, but also their scientific merit. For example, when Falk was targeted, he was subjected to a multiple-day investigative hearing interrogating the scientific rigor of his research activities and writings, as well as his previous work while employed at the University of Chicago. A central focus of the hearing was a report titled "Blueprint for the Nationalization of Medicine," in which Falk and Michael Davis were written up as the masterminds behind a nationalization plot to impose a government-run health system on the American people. It was written by a former employee of Falk's, Marjorie Shearon, and included personal attacks on

Falk and his associates. Shearon included a list of individuals who were involved in the "plot against America," in order of influence: Falk, Davis, Altmeyer, Parran, Cohen, Boas, Perrott, Mountin, Mott, and Roemer. Indeed, a few years later, a loyalty review board investigated Mott and Roemer.[9] Shearon worked with Republican senators Robert Taft of Ohio and Forrest Donnell of Missouri, who questioned Falk and others from the PHS. Simultaneous hearings in the House of Representatives, led by Republican Forest Harness of Indiana, also took up these charges of bureaucratic overreach and conspiracy to impose communist ideas. Not surprisingly, since it had long equated compulsory insurance with communism and socialism, the AMA also joined the investigation, publishing a poster entitled "The House of Falk and Davis" demonizing the two reformers as being part of a conspiracy to nationalize medicine.[10] J. Edgar Hoover, director of the FBI, reached out to the medical profession to ask for their assistance in weeding out the nation's communist threat in a *Journal of the American Medical Association* editorial titled "Let's Keep America Healthy."[11]

The loyalty program gave authority to the attorney general to list organizations considered "totalitarian, Fascist, Communist, or subversive," and although disloyalty was never defined, membership in organizations on the list resulted in "almost automatic grounds for dismissal." Even association with members of "subversive" organizations was grounds for suspected disloyalty. Federal employees were not allowed appeal if found guilty by a loyalty review board. By 1958, it was estimated that 13.5 million Americans came within the scope of the loyalty program, of which 2.3 million were in the federal civil service. Just during the time of the Truman administration, 1,210 federal employees were dismissed and about 6,000 resigned.[12]

As mentioned, the Public Health Service was one of the agencies targeted by the loyalty program. Surgeon General Parran approved a fact-finding study of New Zealand's national health care system, sending PHS health officer Jacob Fischer to conduct the study. This study and subsequent nationwide information sessions about the national health program were highly criticized as promoting propaganda for socialized medicine. Fischer was also investigated by the FBI and summoned before the House Un-American Activities Committee (HUAC). Also reviewed by the federal loyalty board were Assistant Surgeon General Joseph Mountin and George St. John Perrott, both highly influential in promoting the adoption of the medical care section within the APHA in 1944, which was strongly criticized by the AMA as evidence that the public health profession had moved beyond its "proper role."[13]

The AMA House of Delegates passed a resolution condemning the "dereliction of duty, political and partisan activities on the part of officers of the United States Public Health Service, including its Surgeon General, and recommends that steps be taken to prohibit political activity on the part of the United States

Public Health Service, and that further steps be taken to restore the prestige of this important department of our government in the scientific field for which it was created, organized and financed."[14] As if following the orders of the AMA, Truman did not reappoint Parran as Surgeon General for his second term. Some have argued that Parran's dismissal was due to a disagreement with Oscar Ewing,[15] whom Truman appointed as the head of the Federal Security Agency, which oversaw PHS. This certainly contributed, but with all the controversy surrounding the PHS, it also seems likely that Parran was forced out due to his association with compulsory health insurance, no matter how tempered Parran's support and despite Truman's stated support for such a plan. For the next Surgeon General, Truman appointed Leonard Scheele, a traditional commissioned health officer aligned with the "old guard," emphasizing PHS's role overseeing the NIH and CDC and bringing PHS back in line with, as the AMA put it, its "scientific field."[16]

This was a period of true anti-communist hysteria that went on for at least a decade, and it had an impact on what was considered acceptable health policy discourse. Given the extent to which the loyalty program touched federal employees, this environment had a predictably huge effect on morale within the federal government. Researcher Marie Jahoda surveyed federal employees who were *not* subject to investigations and found that the morale of the entire civil service was undermined. She reported that in every bureaucracy (including the FSA and PHS), employees described a rather strict (and deeply troubling) code of what was considered appropriate behavior:

> You should not discuss the admission of Red China to the U.N.; you should not advocate interracial equality; you should not mix with people unless you know them very well; if you want to read *The Nation* you should not take it to the office; if you bring it to the office, you should explain in considerable detail why you have it with you; you should take certain books off your private bookshelves; and so forth.[17]

Because the cost of an investigation was severe, many employees were extremely careful not to do anything that would raise suspicions.[18]

The anti-communist hysteria did not just affect health policy discourse at the federal level; it had an impact across the country. Even a decade after Truman's first executive order, a relatively minor bill—proposed in 1956 to establish mental health care services in Alaska—got labeled as part of a communist plot. Indeed, it is worth reviewing the brief history of this bill to paint a picture of the troubled discourse in health policy at this time.

In 1955, there were literally no mental health services in the territory of Alaska. A mentally ill person in Alaska could be admitted for treatment only after being taken before a lay jury and tried in a criminal proceeding, at which time this person was judged to be either guilty of insanity or innocent of insanity. If found insane, the person was brought to the local jail, and subsequently taken to a private mental hospital in Portland, Oregon. Many patients never saw a doctor until they reached the state of Oregon, by which point the patient was likely far from any support system they may have had. Naturally, given this horrendous standard of treatment, there was a push in Alaska for mental health reforms. The 1956 bill proposed a 10-year plan with federal grants-in-aid to provide Alaska with its own mental health care facilities, and to reform the procedures for admitting patients to treatment. The bill passed unanimously in the House and seemed ready for easy passage in the Senate until the anti-communist groups at the grass-roots level became aware of it.[19]

During this time of postwar American conservatism, a number of local voluntary clubs and organizations across the country took on anti-communism as part of their mission. Both federal and state governments encouraged mostly middle- and upper-class white women to join anti-communist organizations. Formed in 1949, the Minute Women of the U.S.A. formed groups all around the country to engage in discussions, track political developments, and network to identify and eliminate all dissenters.[20] To the Minute Women, dissenters included the New Dealers, who, in their view, favored socialized medicine and the provision of "evil" mental health services. A chapter in Burbank, California, was particularly active in lobbying against mental health legislation. A year prior, in 1955, this group claimed success in defeating a bill in the California legislature to establish state mental health clinics in local communities. The fervor from the organizations on the right against the bill for the clinics became so intense that California governor Goodwin Knight came out against the bill.[21]

The Minute Women and other anti-communist groups were also extremely anti-Semitic and often claimed that Jews were "known communists." For example, in this case, they claimed that the building of mental health services in Alaska, as proposed in the federal bill, was part of a Zionist communist plot, which would diagnose anti-Semites to be mentally ill and ship them off to Alaska—similar to Stalin's Siberia. Newsletters were distributed around Santa Ana bearing headlines such as "Mental Health Propaganda Preparing Way for Jailing Anti-Communists as Mental Cases" and "Siberia U.S.A."[22] The story spread across the country and many other right-wing groups picked it up in their publications, denouncing the bill as a communist threat. Most "mainstream" provider groups came out in favor of the bill, including the AMA and the National Association for Mental Health. However, the Association of American Physicians and Surgeons (AAPS) joined the attack. Formed in 1943 to fight against socialized medicine, the AAPS had physician committees in 45 states and a membership of 10,000 physicians and surgeons. Even though other provider groups asked AAPS to retract its position, a top AAPS official wrote to explain why they would not: "[W]hen you are in a war you have to take what allies you can find."[23]

Opposition groups showed up in force to testify before the Senate subcommittee. After listening to protesters before a standing-room-only crowd, presiding senator Alan Bible exclaimed, "It is abundantly clear . . . that no one possibly could be sent out of any state to Alaska and committed to a mental hospital there."[24] His claim fell on deaf ears, and to placate the opposition the Senate actually had to consider an alternative compromise bill from conservative Republican senator Barry Goldwater. The compromise bill authorized the building of mental hospitals for Alaska, but did nothing about modernizing commitment procedures.[25]

I provide the details of the attempt to pass the Alaskan mental health bill to illustrate the difficulty of passing during this time period any health care bill that could be associated with government overreach and policies that did not fit the hegemonic themes of the period. Given this restrictive political environment, it is not surprising that leaders in the public health network reverted back to the discourse under the Grow-and-Hide strategy familiar in the pre–New Deal period. What is new in this period, however, is the dominance of the volunteerism principle. Although the voluntary sector had long played an important role (see Chapter 2), with its increasing prominence came a more vehement antigovernment tone. Paradoxically, it is under this increasingly zealous rhetoric in this increasingly restrictive political environment that we see a larger expansion in government health expenditures than in any previous period.

## Volunteerism as the American Way

The voluntary approach was offered up on three major fronts: voluntary health insurance, voluntary hospitals, and voluntary health agencies. Many have told the important story of the rise of voluntary health insurance in the United States, arguing that the embrace of voluntary health insurance by corporate leaders, unions, and the major provider groups—including the AMA and AHA—explains why compulsory health insurance failed.[26] While this opposition was certainly a driving force, I argue further that another crucially important factor was the government's multipronged effort to prop up the private sector by supplementing and paying for health services, and that the two other components of the voluntary approach provided the language and strategy to make this happen. In 1950, when the number of Americans signed up for voluntary health insurance was minimal (less than 45% of Americans had private coverage, and this was only for hospital benefits), it was especially imperative to offer another part of the voluntary story to those without coverage (or with minimal coverage).

Health insurance was still a relatively new idea; the American public wanted affordable access to health care, but not health insurance per se. As late as 1940, public opinion surveys were still defining "health insurance" in the question, rather than just using the term. When insurance was defined as making a *mandatory* contribution of 25 cents per week for those earning $25 a week, just over two-thirds of Americans approved of the plan.[27] However, when they were asked three years later whether "the government should provide free medical care for all who need it and can't afford it," 83% favored the idea.[28] Indeed, Americans were clear that they wanted help paying for medical care, but prior to 1946 they were fairly agnostic about what particular type of solution might work best to alleviate health costs. In a 1944 public opinion survey asking if it was a good idea to increase the amount taken out of their payroll checks by 2.5 percent, 66% thought having Social Security solve the problem was a good idea, and 72% of those in favor still thought it was a good idea even when paired with a payroll tax increase.[29] When private insurance was pitted against Social Security in the same survey, support for private insurance was low (16%) relative to Social Security (59%).[30]

But although support for private health insurance was low, responses to other questions asked in the same survey reveal that the American public was not strongly committed to any one approach. Since the New Deal, people had been exposed to a multitude of approaches: some in rural areas experienced the farm medical care programs, some had voluntary hospital insurance, others received care from their local health department or (government) subsidized care from their local hospital or voluntary health agency. Thus, while there was support for Social Security, there was also support for many differing approaches. Even two years later, in 1946, as a major campaign promoting voluntary health insurance and arguing against compulsory insurance was beginning, when the public was asked "What do you think should be done to provide for payment of doctor, dentist and hospital bills for people in this country?," it is evident that the National Health Program's multipronged approach since the New Deal had become familiar: 17% said voluntary health insurance; 15% said government health insurance; 6% said government aid for medical care for the needy; 6% said private charity and agencies; 5% said government-subsidized or free hospitals and clinics; 2% said national health program.[31]

This list suggests that while people were increasingly aware of voluntary health insurance as an option, the public as a whole did not feel strongly about any one approach. Moreover, there were already hints of confusion about the role of government funding behind the voluntary approach. The fact that 5% of the public believed the voluntary health agencies could "provide for the payment of doctor, dentist and hospital bills for people in the US" is not an accident. Health care services provided by voluntary health agencies provided the approach labeled "private charity" because there was a campaign—with the AMA, AHA, and private business behind it—to present it as voluntary private charity; thus, it is likely the public was parroting back in surveys the frame they were given. The frame was misleading, because in providing services for their particular diseases—cancer, tuberculosis, heart disease, and polio, for example—these organizations worked closely with state and local health departments and received government funding.

Nonetheless, they did conduct massive public fundraising campaigns for their "charities," and the majority of Americans contributed to and were very aware of these organizations and their health causes. But it was not pure charity that allowed voluntary health agencies to accomplish what they did. Most of these voluntary health agencies focused on specific diseases and received funding from the categorical grant-in-aid programs.

Similarly, the 5% who said "free" hospitals and clinics—without specifying whether the hospitals would be privately or publicly owned—likely believed this approach would work because of the campaign around the Hill-Burton Act for hospital and clinic construction, which promised that it would provide access to medical care for the American public (see Chapter 4). In sum, the responses to the national survey question reflect in part the incremental and fragmented strategy that had been implemented over the decade prior, and in part the framing of what these approaches should mean.

Organized medicine, hospitals, and the voluntary health agencies recognized that it was important to promise access to care and to promote the idea that only the voluntary sector could offer quality health care. Thus, the voluntary approach offered three principles: democracy through volunteerism; the voluntary sector being able to respond to patient needs with no governmental interference; but, at the same time—and this is crucial—government responsibility to support the voluntary approach on behalf of the American public.

Prior to the New Deal and throughout expansions under the New Deal, voluntary hospitals and voluntary health agencies were strongly encouraged and incorporated into the provision of health services. But in the post-WWII period, the framing of what the voluntary sector stood for took a new turn. The new framing often did not specify *how* voluntary groups should be included, but the rhetoric was unrelenting, and it came from all angles. Voluntary hospitals, voluntary insurance, and voluntary health agencies would constitute the main arteries of the U.S. health care system. Scholars such as Peter Dobkin Hall and Elizabeth Clemens have noted how the nonprofit sector (or the voluntary sector, as it was called at this time) was a political construction. I extend this notion in the next section to show how the organized interests behind voluntary hospitals and voluntary health agencies constructed an antigovernment narrative, which ironically encouraged government financial support for the voluntary sector while simultaneously hiding this government funding.[32]

## Framing Voluntary Health Agencies

The voluntary health movement was more a health care industry movement than a citizen's movement. Most disease-based voluntary health agencies were started by physician specialty groups. This was true of the first voluntary health agency, the National Tuberculosis Association, as well as agencies dedicated to helping those with polio, heart disease, and cancer, to name just a few. Indeed, the cooperation with government and organized medicine was so well established that when the American Heart Association created its national voluntary health agency in 1946, at the association's annual scientific meeting, Dr. William Shepard presented "the time-tested principles which have made the other great voluntary health agencies so successful."[33]

Shepard's advice for how to best organize the American Heart Association's "voluntary public health agency" (as he put it) was based on his role as a member of the Advisory Committee of the National Health Council, which had just completed a three-year study of voluntary health agencies.[34] Although the council's report raised a number of concerns about lack of coordination among the growing number of national voluntary health agencies, its criticisms were raised in the spirit of wanting to maintain and promote the voluntary sector.[35] And while I draw on Shepard's address for illustration here because it is a perfect summary both of how *professionals* framed the Voluntary Way and of the strategic thinking behind this framing, his address is indicative of many professional writings about and by voluntary health agencies at the time.[36]

Shepard argued that the following four characteristics are common to all successful voluntary health agencies:

1. They are nonpolitical, that is nonpartisan, joining together with remarkable success members of all political parties, members of all religious faiths, people of differing social strata, and people of widespread geographic location.
2. They are guided by people who are natural leaders in their community and generally recognized as such. They are people of prestige and influence within their circle and their community. Their motives are unquestioned. No elected official can long oppose the principles for which they stand.
3. The voluntary health agencies obtain an amazing amount of time, skill, and services, given generously by these key people in their respective communities.

4. If the agency is successful, it practically always consists of a partnership between medical and nonmedical leaders.[37]

These characteristics of "successful" voluntary health agencies offer several
important insights. First, it is extremely important that the first characteristic is
for the voluntary organization to be nonpolitical and nonpartisan. This idea was
promoted as voluntary health agencies were repeatedly presented as offering scientific facts and legislation based on those facts. Of course, lobbying—lobbying
for an increase in research funding for a particular disease and for funding for
public health services and education for this disease—is fundamentally political, but Shepard's point about the popularity and success of voluntary health
agencies resting on claims of being nonpartisan and nonpolitical is exactly right.
Throughout this period, the literature explaining what voluntary health agencies
do[38] or making the case for their continued importance argued that voluntary
health agencies supported what was *right* to promote health in the American
people. These statements were presented as self-evident and based on scientific fact.

Of course, the second characteristic—that influential leaders are necessary
so no elected official can oppose them—is especially interesting in light of the
first. It is clear that the success of voluntary health agencies was measured by
their ability to influence legislation, and yet they must also be recognized as
"nonpolitical."

The fourth characteristic provides insight into the role of organized medicine
and the health care industry behind these voluntary health agencies. As Shepard
put it, the "close working relationship, a partnership in fact as well as in name,
between medical and nonmedical community leaders is characteristic of the voluntary health agencies and would almost seem a *sine qua non*."[39] Shepard, along
with the National Health Council report, argued that the most successful partnership occurred when physicians suggest *what* to do and rely on their nonmedical
partners in the voluntary agencies to determine *how* to do it. Obviously, the key
to this statement that made the partnership particularly useful to stakeholders
in the health care industry is the idea that providers maintain control by determining what the voluntary agencies advocate for, but can leverage the ability of
nonmedical leaders and staff to conduct successful fundraising.

Shepard's third characteristic gets to the heart of why the health care industry was so intent on promoting the voluntary health movement: the voluntary health agencies were incredibly successful at raising private contributions
from individuals. By 1950, all of the voluntary health agencies combined raised
well over $100 million. Especially in the post-WWII period, health donations
increased rapidly.[40] Not only did the voluntary agencies have a connection to

the public through membership and volunteering, but, as their organizations grew, they also employed sizable staffs. In 1950, 10,000 Americans worked full-time for voluntary health agencies, and another 5 to 10 million people served on its various committees. In Shepard's words, "This is indeed big business! The American Heart Association is the newest of the large national voluntary health agencies. It must do its job well."[41] Perhaps they did do their job well, since by1954, 64% of Americans had heard of the American Heart Association's campaign to fight heart disease. Even these agencies' particular campaigns were becoming household names: In the same 1954 survey, 83% had heard of the National Foundation for Infantile Paralysis's March of Dimes.[42]

Access to the American public was important to galvanize and shape public opinion around what this voluntary approach meant. The message was three-fold: First, it promoted the view that a relationship with government was nec-essary, but that government as a provider was slow and incompetent. In 1950, the "official health agencies" were the state and local health departments and the other arms of the state that provided public health services. In writings about the relationship between voluntary health agencies and official health agencies, there is an assumption of the necessity of public health departments—of gov-ernment funding and legislation to back it up—but also an insistence that vol-untary organizations are better prepared to do the work. For example, Shepard writes: "The wheels of government move slowly. The voluntary agency can be prompt and timely."

Second, crucially important to the message was the notion that voluntary agencies provide public voice and, therefore, are more democratic than govern-ment agencies. The National Health Council's report devoted an entire chapter to "the Democratic Process at Work.[43] Echoing this theme, Shepard writes,

> Time and experience have shown that the voluntary health agency is al-most essential to the complete success of the official health agency. The health department cannot operate without public support and under-standing. The voluntary agency is best equipped to provide this public support and understanding.

This connection between volunteerism and democracy is essential because it allows the health care industry to also claim the reverse—that government-run programs are undemocratic.

> The official health agency needs contact with the people to avoid the evils of bureaucracy, and there is no agency to which it can turn which is better equipped to keep it in step with public opinion than the vol-untary health agency. Thus the voluntary agencies, local, state, and

national, become valuable advisors to the official agency, such as the U.S. Public Health Service and its [NIH] National Heart Institute, state health departments and city and county health departments.

And third, Shepard is clear that it is not just access to public officials that agencies want, but supportive legislation and the allocation of funds:

> [T]he official agency is peculiarly handicapped in obtaining funds. The lone voice of the health officer or even of the Surgeon General is not enough. It is too often suspected by the appropriating body that the official director of health has an ax to grind when he asks for more money to give him more staff or to increase his own importance. The voluntary agencies speak for people, both *professional* and lay. They have no ax to grind; they have no selfish motives; they make a unique impression on elected officials for this very reason.[44]

Notice how Shepard is open about the voluntary agency's influence as a veiled front for professional interests. What makes this relationship so important to the mission of the voluntary approach is the ability of professional organizations and health care institutions (hospitals and drug companies) to use voluntary health agencies to directly influence the state under the guise of democracy.

## Framing the Voluntary Hospital

Since the early 1930s, the AHA had been promoting the idea that all hospitals across the country should use uniform cost accounting procedures. Initially, the move toward uniform accounting practices was discussed as necessary because the number of hospitals had grown so much that they represented a large industry and needed to begin acting like a "responsible business" (see Chapter 4). However, with major new hospital construction under the Hill-Burton program, increasing enrollment in Blue Cross voluntary hospital insurance, and the passage of federal medical vendor payments to assist states in covering the cost of medical care for public assistance recipients, the push for uniform accounting became more urgent. In its main journal and at its annual conference, the AHA focused substantial effort on three main topics: third-party reimbursement, cost accounting practices, and public relations. A review of the AHA's journal, *Hospitals*, from 1950 to 1960 reveals that over a fourth of its articles were centered on these issues, with many of the articles addressing all three topics.

Similar to the early 1930s, the AHA's main concern in the 1950s was making sure voluntary hospitals accounted for the *full* costs of care. The AHA's focus on this matter was partially based on wanting reliable data to compare costs across hospitals. The primary reason, however, was ensuring that hospital administrators and their allies could, in a uniform way, show to third-party payers and state governments the *full* cost of care provided. This point was particularly important because the rates state governments paid hospitals for care rendered to public assistance recipients were below rates paid by private insurance companies, and hospitals wanted to use these cost figures to convince the public that voluntary hospitals were being underpaid by state governments. The accounting associate of the Hospital Council of Philadelphia mentioned that due to growing economic pressure on hospitals there had been "an enormous increase in interest in hospital cost accounting," and explained why:

> The costs of *services for which charges are made* to patients are extremely useful data in determining hospital regular charges and the composite amount to be paid by third parties, such as Blue Cross and government agencies, for services to their constituents. These cost figures also can be used effectively in telling the hospital's story to the public.[45]

In the postwar period, the number of state hospital associations spread quickly across the American states, from only three full-time associations in 1944, to 18 in 1953. By 1953, only Nevada had no state hospital association whatsoever.[46] State hospital associations devoted their energy to persuading state, county, and local governments to increase their payments for indigent patients in voluntary hospitals. In a 1952 survey of state hospital association activities, 30 associations reported major initiatives toward this goal, and an additional seven said these had become routine efforts. All state associations said the focus on lobbying state, county, and local governments had received an increasing amount of emphasis every year since the war.[47]

As part of this effort, state associations saw uniform accounting as going "hand in hand with the problem of governmental reimbursement for indigent care," and reported a substantial increase in association attention on training and stressing the importance of uniform accounting with their member hospitals. Prior to 1948, only six state associations devoted any significant effort to uniform accounting, but by 1952, 21 associations reported this as a major project.[48]

The AHA saw this increased lobbying activity of their state hospital associations as vital to the development of the voluntary hospital movement in the United States, writing in 1953 that "[w]hen the history of hospitals is written, the postwar growth of the state association principle will go down, along with the Hill-Burton Act and the growth of the American Hospital Association itself, as one of the significant hospital trends of the century."[49] Of course, the AHA helped develop this three-pointed focus on uniform accounting, reimbursement rates, and public relations/lobbying in state hospital associations. At the AHA's annual conventions and business meetings, major emphasis was placed on the activities of its member state hospital associations. For example, at its midyear business meeting in 1950, the first session focused on "the problem of financing indigent care." In this meeting the members agreed to appoint a special commission to work with state hospital associations "to *present solutions to the problem to state legislatures*. Methods to create *public awareness* also were discussed."[50]

The AHA published numerous stories about how state hospital associations were successful in increasing rates for indigent care. The articles provided detailed how-to guidelines that included the importance of cost accounting to make an "evidence-based" case to state legislators, and specifics on how to conduct successful public relations campaigns. For example, the executive director of the Connecticut Hospital Association, Hiram Sibley, presented a paper at the AHA annual conference in 1950, subsequently published in *Hospitals*, which outlined Connecticut's successful campaign to increase its state's reimbursement rate for public assistance recipients from $5 per day to $10 per day. It is noteworthy that he starts the article by blaming the government for the financial difficulties threatening voluntary hospitals, stating that "a great many voluntary hospitals face financial bankruptcy unless means are found for collecting the costs of service from government agencies . . . of all groups purchasing hospital service, the most reluctant to recognize these factors of increased expense are welfare agencies and the legislative bodies responsible for their appropriations."[51]

Despite this introduction, he provides "good news" to AHA members by detailing the three keys to his state's success. First, "uniform cost accounting was crucial to convince state legislators what the 'true cost' of indigent care was."[52] The Connecticut Hospital Association calculated the amounts lost due to "payment under costs" as almost $200,000, or 9.4 percent of that year's total operating expense. Connecticut's coalition of hospitals was also able to convince the governor's committee to accept the cost formula recommended under the cost accounting process spelled out by the AHA.[53] The AHA published Sibley's story as exemplary for all state associations across the country, and it was one of many such stories.[54] From 1950 through 1959, the AHA published 90 articles on the importance of adopting uniform cost accounting, and another 63 articles on using the uniform rate formula—which incorporated "full costs"—for reimbursement.[55] Sibley was a perfect spokesman for the cause: "All necessary revisions have been made in the accounting manual of the Connecticut Hospital Association to bring it into line with Section 1 of the 'Handbook on Accounting, Statistics and Business Office Procedures for Hospitals.' Published in Feb 1950 by the AHA—and I recommend whole-heartedly that this be adopted without delay by all voluntary and religious hospitals."[56]

Sibley's second key to success was, in keeping with the AHA's framing, a "nonpolitical" public relations strategy. When Kenneth Williamson was appointed the executive director of the Health Information Foundation (a foundation focused on research for voluntary hospitals and voluntary health insurance), he "emphasized the fact that the foundation will be a *nonpolitical* organization. The two important goals will be to get the proper facts to the people and *get communities to help themselves*."[57] Somehow, such a clear value statement about the role of government was considered "nonpolitical." And communicating the "proper facts" to the public was a major focus of the AHA. Over the decade, the AHA published nearly 200 articles in *Hospitals* on the importance of public relations and how to conduct successful campaigns.[58] When Williamson later became associate director of the AHA and director of AHA's Washington Service Bureau, which lobbied Congress, he said successful public relations should include (1) all hospital executives lobbying government officials through their state associations, (2) engaging with hospital voluntary groups (namely the women's hospital auxiliaries), (3) engaging with their trustees to advocate on the hospitals' behalf; and (4) working with news media. Williamson asserts that the payoff for these efforts is a marked increase in public expenditures.[59]

Sibley's description of Connecticut's success includes all these components: "The governor and political leaders of both parties [were] approached. . . . Public education in support of hospital legislation began with a conference of more than a hundred hospital trustees from every part of Connecticut. . . . Members of the general assembly [were] invited by the [hospital] board president to visit the hospital and learn firsthand of its financial situation."[60] The Connecticut Hospital Association also worked closely with local newspapers. For example, the public relations director of St. Francis Hospital in Hartford, Connecticut, reported that "[b]oth Hartford newspapers are cooperative and work closely with hospital public relations officers. A newsworthy story is given excellent space; photographers often are sent to the hospitals, and the editors are on the lookout for human interest stories and anecdotes."[61] The AHA published numerous articles on the importance of engaging the local media, contending that "it is well worth any hospital administrator's time to spend an afternoon or day at one of the local newspapers . . . newspapers can be, through the administrator's own efforts, one of the most successful mediums of interpreting the hospital's story to the public."[62]

The content of "the story" was very important, and the AHA had an ongoing campaign to educate hospital executives and staff about how to "tell its story." For example, hospitals were instructed to celebrate National Hospital Day every year, and were given a "kit"—Kit No. 4, in fact—as part of the AHA's public relations series, "Telling Your Hospital's Story." The kit contained detailed information for planning publicity, and provided specific methods to "inform the community."[63]

A very important part of the story was explaining why hospital costs kept increasing. This was considered an essential role of any public relations strategy, such as the one pursued in Connecticut:

> Explanation and interpretation of rising hospital costs have been among the chief objectives of the public relations council since its inception. This has been accomplished through articles in hospital bulletins and releases in the local newspapers. These releases do not deal with costs as such but prove their point by discussing new equipment, measuring its cost in terms of value to the patient, by describing hospital expansion and what it will mean to the community, and by showing how medical developments must be reflected in the patients' bills.[64]

This approach came from the AHA's worry that the general public could not understand the "complexity" of hospital costs. As the executive director of AHA, George Bugbee, surmised, "I wonder, frankly, if the general public will *ever* understand hospital costs.... We must accept the fact that the complexity of the modern hospital defies comprehension by the average person."[65] Due to this "complexity," he advised member hospitals on how to frame the story:

> [T]ell your public what medical care in their hospital means to them. Don't apologize for costs. These costs permit offering the kind of care the public wants. Exploit the exciting and dramatic results that are occurring virtually right before their eyes, . . . [they get more services, in a shorter stay, with four-times the value—that is why it costs more].[66]

They also focused on what mechanisms could best tell the story. Connecticut developed a series of posters that were used in conjunction with talks given across the state. According to Sibley, "The success of these posters led to a reproduction of them in leaflet form, and these leaflets were distributed widely throughout the state." Pictures of each page of the pamphlet were also reproduced in the AHA article detailing Connecticut's approach (see Illustrations 5.1 and 5.2 for a few examples of pamphlet illustrations).[67]

What is most striking about "the story" presented through the pamphlet is that the government is blamed not just for paying below "true" costs, but also for being the culprit behind increasing costs. For example, after showing the difference between costs and state payments, they ask "[W]hy are these figures (cost and state payments) so far apart?" The answer provided is twofold: "Because 1—hospital costs have been soaring; 2—because revisions in state payments have borne no relationship to these costs." Then comes the question at the heart

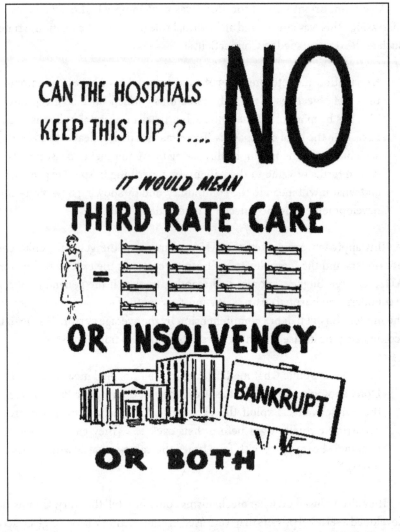

*Illustration 5.1* Poster Used as an Aid to Tell the Connecticut Hospitals' "Story". *Note:* Quote from article to describe use of the poster: "As an aid in their "argument," Connecticut hospitals used in conjunction with brief talks the posters reproduced on these pages. These posters were so successful that they were later reproduced in the form of leaflets, which were then distributed state-wide," p. 45. *Source:* Hiram Sibley, "Government Agencies Can Be Persuaded to Pay Costs for Indigent Care," *Hospitals: The Journal of American Hospital Association* 25, no. 2 (February 1951): 45–46.

# WHY DO HOSPITALS STAND FOR IT ?

Are they legally bound to accept state cases for a third the cost of their care.?

*Legally... NO*

*Morally...*they cannot refuse care to the sick, even if the cost of care is ruinous . . .

Illustration 5.2 Poster Used as an Aid to Tell the Connecticut Hospitals' "Story".
Note: Quote from article to describe use of the poster: "As an aid in their "argument," Connecticut hospitals used in conjunction with brief talks the posters reproduced on these pages. These posters were so successful that they were later reproduced in the form of leaflets, which were then distributed state-wide," p. 45. Source: Hiram Sibley, "Government Agencies Can Be Persuaded to Pay Costs for Indigent Care," Hospitals: The Journal of American Hospital Association 25, no. 2 (February 1951): 45–46.

of the story: "[C]an the hospitals keep this up?" The answer is an obvious "no," because state payments below costs would either lead to low quality care or to hospital bankruptcy (see Illustration 5.1). Thus, if low quality occurs or the hospital deficits increase, it will be the fault of government. Because hospitals, the story continues, are moral institutions that care for the sick even when they are not legally bound to do so, and even when it might lead to financial ruin (see Illustration 5.2).

The message conveyed in the pamphlet became the standard story hospitals across the country were supposed to sell. For example, several years later, Rufus Rorem, then the executive director of the Hospital Council of Philadelphia, encouraged widespread use of BCBS and other private insurance and promoted "legislation to achieve governmental payment of full costs for hospital and medical services to public assistance beneficiaries." He argued "the full assumption of responsibility by government for service to its beneficiaries would, in turn, permit lower costs and larger enrollment in group prepayment plans."[68] Thus, at the same time government was blamed for the high cost of health care expenditures, it was asked to pay more to reduce—essentially subsidize—the rates of private subscribers.

Another dramatic change in this short period of time was "the organization and development of women's hospital auxiliaries," and the AHA instructed hospitals to work closely with them.[69] Again, prior to 1948, only four state hospital associations reported devoting significant attention to women's auxiliaries, whereas by 1952 this was a major activity of 20 state associations.[70] A key reason hospitals were encouraged to work with the women's auxiliaries is that the auxiliaries were quite successful at raising funds for the many capital campaigns conducted across the country,[71] but also because they could help shape public opinion.

As hospital costs kept increasing, the public was still carrying a large burden of the expense through out-of-pocket payments, and there were growing concerns and criticisms regarding whether hospitals were acting in the best interest of the community. As an increasing number of patients had difficulty paying their hospital bills in full, hospitals often responded by creating more diligent payment collection procedures. The AHA encouraged hospitals to set up strict admissions policies related to patient finances. Admitting officers were instructed to make every effort to collect payment at the time of admission for uninsured patients.[72] The superintendent of the Wyoming County Community Hospital in Warsaw, New York, wrote about the hospital's collection procedures, stating that follow-up cards have "given us excellent results in securing payment from delinquent accounts, [and] the follow-up procedure starts the moment of the patient's admission."[73]

Patients often criticized billing and collection procedures at voluntary hospitals. An administrator of Middlesex Hospital in Middletown, Connecticut, for example, reported that although there was a reduction in unpaid bills, they began to receive "complaints from patients who said they had been 'insulted' at admission because of the way admitting officers had asked for money."[74] The AHA published an article on "Community Reactions to Bad Debt Collections," explaining the quandary for hospitals:

> Strict collection policies to prevent delinquent hospital accounts have been supported by some administrators and attacked by others for their effect on the hospital's public relations. Proponents of a policy that aims to receive part or complete payment from every patient believe that the community wants an efficiently operated hospital. The negative side of the argument holds that good collections . . . will do greater harm to the hospital's standing in the community than the few dollars it might lose because of a flexible policy.[75]

There was also a lot of disagreement among hospital staff as to what was considered a fair amount of "free service"—from none to the full amount—for those who could not pay their bills. Trustees and social workers believed substantial free-service allowances were justified, whereas admission officers and those working in collections suggested much smaller amounts. As an exercise, hospital staff were presented with the following scenario: A patient has $30 in the bank, a hospital bill of $250, is already in debt $100 for doctor and medical bills, and is billed $120 for drugs upon discharge. He will lose $720 in income while absent from work, but will receive $120 in disability benefits. The staff were then asked what they thought would be fair to charge the patient in this case. Administrators said $240; the financial group (collections and admission officers) suggested $203; trustees said $120, and social workers said $100. The staff in the financial group (who decided on charges and conducted the collection procedures) believed this amount was fair, even when the majority also believed the patient would not be able to pay the charge they suggested.[76]

To help "resolve" this dilemma for hospital administrators across the country, the AHA conducted a study of 13 hospitals to see whether rigorous collections impacted public relations. Based on this nonscientific study,[77] the AHA concluded "the statistics show that stiff policies do not harm public relations."[78] This might have been true, because the public relations strategy itself focused on shaping how the public thought about these strict collection policies. For example, in a 1957 article, a hospital administrator in South Dakota detailed their method of using bank financing to reduce unpaid accounts, from 8% in 1951 down to 1.5% in 1957. To justify the program to the public, the bank and hospital worked with the local papers to explain "the hospital's predicament." One local paper wrote:

> People of the tri-state area feel a proprietary interest in the hospital. And they should, because they are the ones who have financed that hospital through crisis after crisis—keeping it open, improving and enlarging it—that they may be guaranteed its services when they need them. . . . There are, in every community, people who never will pay their bill unless forced to do so. Yet these people become sick just the same as those who carry their share of the load. So it was easy to believe that the number of these accounts might be piling up to dangerous levels. Consequently, people accepted with relief the announcement this summer from the hospital board that the hospital was enforcing the collection of bills.[79]

Notice how conspicuously the story pits those who can pay against those in the community who cannot. The hospital also defended charging "intentionally high interest" for those who can't pay their bills, arguing that the hospital does not want to encourage this type of hospital payment, because "the patient should go to the bank rather than the hospital for this paper."[80]

In addition to collection procedures, many were concerned about the practice of turning indigent patients away from voluntary hospitals and sending them to public hospitals. Although state hospital associations and state welfare departments had an informal agreement that public assistance recipients should seek care first at public hospitals and receive care at voluntary hospitals as a last resort, members of the community were often critical of the practice—at least when it came to their own care. Hence, an intensive and sustained hospital public relations campaign was needed to shed a different light on this practice.

This is when hospital administrators realized the women's auxiliaries were well positioned to tell the hospital's story. For example, at the AHA's 1952 Institute on Public Relations in Kansas City, Missouri, the administrator of the Community Methodist Hospital in Paragould, Arkansas, presented a paper in which he gave examples of how "bad rumors about the hospital were spreading in the community," and how members of the women's auxiliary—by calling the hospital "and getting the facts right"—were able to "tell [their] fellow citizens what had happened so as to rectify the situation."[81] One of the rumors concerned "a transient from a nearby town" who claimed the hospital had turned him away:

> The auxiliary should be able to explain the rising cost of hospital care, the cost of caring for a welfare or indigent patient, hospitalization

insurance, contemplated new projects in the hospital and what the hospital's role is in the community's health program.[82]

Later that year, at the State Hospital Associations' Midyear Conference, the Council on Association Services passed a motion that "state women's hospital auxiliary organizations be included within the framework of state hospital associations." At the AHA's annual conference, women's auxiliaries figured prominently in the agenda. Many meetings at the conference were joint sessions with women's auxiliaries to determine "opportunities for hospital auxiliary service." One major topic there was "Answering Patients' Criticisms."[83]

The pages of the AHA's journal suggest that the American public did not readily accept the practices of voluntary hospitals. There were widespread criticisms about their strict collections process, and numerous exposés in local newspapers across the country about the sick being turned away from voluntary community hospitals. The AHA's response was to increase its public relations budget to better "educate" the public as to why such practices were necessary. For example, in 1957 the AHA created "A Guide to Ethical Hospital-Press-Television-Radio Relationships" because it was unhappy with critical newspaper coverage. It was critical of a Chicago newspaper reporting the following:

> On Jan 17, 1954, a child suffering from burns was brought to the emergency room of a Chicago area hospital. The child was given first aid. The mother said she did not have the money to pay a hospital bill; the intern pronounced her fit to be moved. The hospital, following established practice, referred the mother and child to a public hospital. The next day the child died.[84]

To the AHA, it was unethical for the newspaper to have published this story. The AHA guide lamented, "The hopes expressed [in the past] that we might achieve public understanding by obtaining more and better publicity, have dimmed. It seems to be expecting too much of the press that they do the job of education for us. Education is the essential element and we know we must do it ourselves."[85]

Hospitals had to increase their public relations budgets not only to address these criticisms, but also to address the lack of understanding about the high costs of hospital care (not to address the problem itself, mind you).[86] For example, hospital administrators in Minneapolis conducted a public opinion survey and reported that "[t]he public doesn't understand why costs are high, but resent it."[87] In 1957, the president of the AHA said in his annual address that there is no "greater necessity for public understanding and support than the continuing, inexorable increase in hospital costs."[88]

Hospitals were thus intent on shaping public opinion, and part of educating the public on hospital costs was to clarify (as the pamphlet mentioned above suggested) that increased expense for privately insured patients was due to two things: "charity" patients and a government that paid less than "full-costs." Both of these, according to the hospitals' narrative, required the hospital to subsidize the difference and therefore charge private patients more. And there is evidence that this framing began to take hold on the American psyche. In 1955, when a random sample of the public in New Jersey was asked if they thought hospital charges were fair, 61% said "yes" and 14% of those who said "no" said they believed high charges were due to charity patients.[89]

## Conclusion

In sum, when organized medicine and the hospital industry fought against compulsory insurance, they needed an alternative solution that gave Americans access to health care. The voluntary movement was their answer, and the voluntary health agencies were their key to reaching the public at large. Of course, behind this rosy framing of volunteerism, two great deceptions lurked: First, when the medical and hospital industries promised that all Americans would receive access to high-quality medical care, they implied that all needs would be met. This promise, however, wasn't backed by any legislative guarantee, and it said nothing on the question of equity. And second, even as the AMA and AHA aggressively pushed for government support of the voluntary sector, there was no mention of what this responsibility would (or should) add up to in terms of funding from American taxpayers.

# Solidifying the Grow-and-Hide Approach

Part I of this book illustrates that leaders in the public health network had relied on the Grow-and-Hide strategy for a long time. However, during the New Deal period, from 1930 to 1945, public health leaders advocated building a unified federated health care system, and there was less of an effort to hide government growth (see Chapter 4). The National Health Program was the public health network's grand alternative to the narrower strategy of focusing on compulsory health insurance. Several public health leaders—such as Joseph Mountin in the Public Health Service (PHS) and, working outside government, Michael Davis—explicitly documented the extensive role of government funding.

During the political backlash of the postwar period, when the PHS's scientific reputation in relation to health services was significantly harmed, public health leaders retreated to a framing that was remarkably similar to that of the pre–New Deal days. Although local health departments continued to grow, leaders reverted to describing the department's role as primarily preventive and retreated from highlighting its important role in providing treatment across the country. And although the PHS administered the Hill-Burton construction grants to build hospitals and other health care facilities across the country, the voluntary hospital industry controlled the narrative over what these investments meant. The hospital industry also took charge of the Grow-and-Hide approach around government reimbursements to hospitals for the medically needy and indigent. Meanwhile, the public health profession maintained their reputation in the scientific community by focusing on major "public health" investments for the National Institute for Health (NIH) and the Centers for Disease Control (CDC), which skyrocketed during this period.

As the push for national health reform started to regain momentum in the early 1960s, leaders from the PHS were not the major players shaping legislation.

*Grow and Hide.* Colleen M. Grogan, Oxford University Press. © Oxford University Press 2023.
DOI: 10.1093/oso/9780199812233.003.0007

By this time the health care industry had been so successful at gaining control of the health care narrative, and the strategy of hiding the role of government through fragmentation and federalism had become so pervasive, that even when the largest government health care reform to date (Medicare and Medicaid) was passed in 1965, the great extent to which all levels of government were already funding the U.S. health care system remained largely hidden to the American people.

## Hiding Government's Role in Health Expenditures

In addition to specific attacks on federal employees through the federal loyalty program discussed in Chapter 5, there were also severe reductions in federal government personnel, from 4 million employees to 2 million. The Social Security Commissioner's staff was targeted and reduced from 1,100 in 1947 to 361 in 1948, and then to 59 in 1949. Personnel in the Division for Program Research, which was responsible for collecting and reporting data on New Deal programs and publishing the *Social Security Bulletin,* was reduced from 160 to 30.[1] What is important about this attack on the federal bureaucracy is that it clearly had an impact on how data was collected and reported. Historical expenditure data published in the 1970s reveals that while personal health care expenditures covered by private health insurance were increasing during the period from 1950 to 1965, so too were expenditures covered by the government (see Figure 6.1). Because health care utilization and health care prices were both

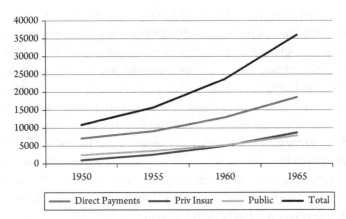

*Figure 6.1* Personal Health Care Expenditures by Source of Funds, 1950–1965 (Amounts in Millions). *Note:* "Public" does not include government public health activities. *Source:* Robert Gibson, "National Health Expenditures, 1979," *Health Care Financing Review* (Summer 1980), Tables 4 & 5, pp. 23–28.

increasing dramatically during this period, total expenditures skyrocketed, and despite increases in coverage from both private and public sources, individual out-of-pocket payments (direct payments in Figure 6.1) continued to increase, from an annual per capita average of $46 in 1950 to $101 in 1965.[2]

The dramatic increase in Americans enrolled in private health insurance plans during this period is well known. In 1948 only 41.5% of Americans had private coverage for hospital benefits, but by 1964 nearly 80% had this type of coverage.[3] Less well known, especially at the time, was how little these plans actually covered in terms of personal health care expenditures for the American public. While the percentage of total expenditures covered by private insurance increased from 1950 to 1965, the percentage covered by government remained the same during that period. And in 1965, despite 80% of Americans having private hospital coverage, public and private coverage of expenditures was essentially equal (see Figure 6.2). What this shows is that while more and more Americans were purchasing private health insurance coverage, their financial liability for health care costs was still quite high, and this increased investment through private insurance premiums did not replace what Americans were asked to pay for through taxation in terms of public coverage of health expenditures.[4] Clearly, this graph does not present a positive picture of the "Voluntary Way," but this negative picture was never presented to the American public. Instead, enrollment figures were repeatedly published to reinforce the notion that, since 80% of the public were "covered," private insurance was solving the problem of health care insecurity. Never reported were comparisons of the amount of total

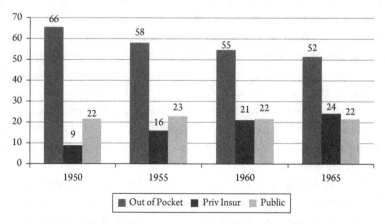

*Figure 6.2* Total Personal Health Care Expenditures by Source of Funding, 1950–1965 (Percent Distribution). *Note:* Total personal health expenditures does not include government public health activities. *Source:* Robert Gibson, "National Health Expenditures, 1979," *Health Care Financing Review* (Summer 1980), Tables 4 & 5, pp. 23–28.

health care expenditures covered by private insurance relative to public sources. Figure 6.2 shows this comparison, but I constructed it using data from 1979. No earlier publications of expenditure data allowed one to make this comparison.

The *Social Security Bulletin* started two separate series in the 1950s: one titled "Social Welfare Expenditures" that was published annually in its November issue,[5] and the other titled "Private Consumer Expenditures for Medical Care and Voluntary Health Insurance," also published annually, but in its December issue starting in 1952.[6] It was not until 1964 that elements from both series were brought into one report to "present data on total national health expenditures, public and private, giving an overall picture of expenditures . . . by type of service and sources of funds."[7] Although this 1964 report brought together public and private provision into one analysis of national health expenditures, the framing of "public" and "private" is extremely important. First, the definition of private expenditures includes a category called "consumers," which comprises both direct payments by patients and payments by private insurance plans, but the two types of payments are not broken out. By lumping the two together, the authors present "private" expenditures ($24 billion) as much more extensive than "public" ($8 billion), and highlight this distinction in the text: "consumers made 58 percent of all expenditure for hospital care, either directly or through health insurance plans, government made 40 percent, and philanthropic agencies . . . 2 percent."[8]

Searching the *Social Security Bulletin* from 1948 to 1965, only 10 articles came up under the keyword title search "health expenditures." Of these 10, only three articles were published prior to the 1960s, and all were focused on "Private Medical Care Expenditures and Voluntary Health Insurance." In these articles, all public expenditures were excluded from the totals, which allowed the percentage of expenditures covered by private insurance to look much more favorable (see Figure 6.3).[9] It is also important that these data only include private expenditures related to hospital services, which is the main benefit that private health insurance covered. Even the "physician services" shown in the graph included only those provided in hospitals, because it was only these physician services that insurance companies covered. In essence, they presented the best-case scenario for the percentage of consumer expenditures that private insurance covered. And this "best case" of course presented a clear bias in favor of private health insurance.

If we compare Figure 6.3 to Figures 6.4 and 6.5, we can observe the extent of the bias. These graphs show that while private insurance coverage of hospital services did increase substantially from 1950 to 1965, it was not nearly as substantial as the publications in the 1950s led one to believe. The "private consumer" graph from 1958 (Figure 6.3) presents private insurance as covering over half of hospital expenditures, when in 1960 it was covering only 36% of

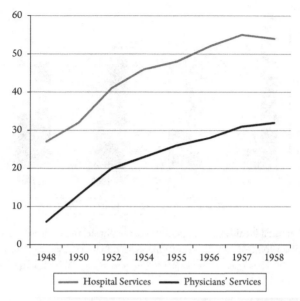

*Figure 6.3* Private Expenditures for Medical Care: Percent Met by Voluntary Health Insurance, Selected Years, 1948–1958. *Note:* Only includes expenditures related to hospital services (e.g., physician services in the hospital). "Private Expenditures" excludes expenditures made from public funds for the medical care of civilians such as "veterans and Indians and for Public Health Activities."

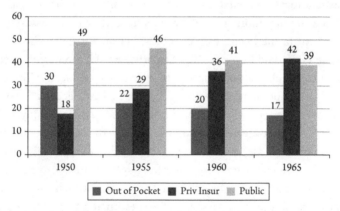

*Figure 6.4* Personal Health Care Expenditures for Hospital Services by Source of Funding, 1950–1965 (Percent Distribution). *Source:* Robert Gibson, "National Health Expenditures, 1979," *Health Care Financing Review* (Summer 1980), Tables 4 & 5, pp. 23–28.

total personal health care expenditures for hospital services (compare Figure 6.3 to 6.4). A similar pattern emerges if we consider private insurance coverage of physician services: by only considering "private hospital based expenditures," one is led to believe that private insurance covered 32% of expenditures in 1958, when it was only 28% in 1960 (compare Figure 6.3 to 6.5). Moreover,

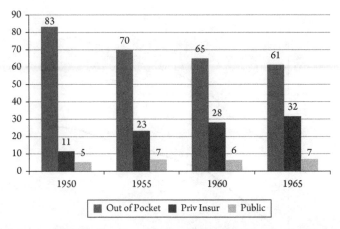

*Figure 6.5* Personal Health Care Expenditures for Physician Services by Source of
Funding, 1950–1965 (Percent Distribution). *Source:* Robert Gibson, "National Health
Expenditures, 1979," *Health Care Financing Review* (Summer 1980), Tables 4 & 5, pp. 23–28.

Figure 6.4 illustrates why it is important to include public financing in the picture. Although the percent covered by public sources decreased over this time
period, it remained quite large (39%) even in 1965, when 80% of non-elderly
American's had private health insurance.[10]

Several strong political values are hidden behind the presentation of these
health expenditure data. First, as Bruce Fetter points out about measurements
of the U.S. economy more generally at this time, they under-assessed the role
of government in the health care economy. Simon Kuznets, who with others
devised the GNP, said in 1948: "The Department of Commerce conceives the
government as an ultimate consumer rather than as a producer."[11] This comment
is especially appropriate when realizing that the Federal Security Agency (FSA)
counted government provision of health insurance to their employees (federal,
state, and local) as private health insurance because the government used private
insurance companies as the vendor, when clearly the source of this coverage was
public funding. Here, the government is portrayed as the consumer rather than
the institutional entity providing coverage. In 1959, federal health insurance for
civil-service employees was passed, and was estimated to cost $110 million in
the first year alone (in 1958, New York state spent $4.5 million for its plan).
Especially at this time, when private insurance was still getting established, the
over 8 million persons employed by federal, state, and local governments came
to represent a sizable share of "private" health insurance expenditures.[12]

Second, this framing of the data also conveyed a particular view about the
appropriate role of government. The conservative and dominant view of government in the postwar period was that government should only be used for
"welfare expenditures" and welfare was (and in many cases still is) defined as

being only for the needy. As many others have pointed out, conservatives clearly did not actually believe in this theory of government, because they constantly voted in favor of government funding for a whole host of services that benefitted middle- and upper-income Americans, such as the mortgage interest deduction policy and tax exemptions for employer-based health insurance.[13] Nonetheless, politicians were quick to call particular types of public spending "welfare." This was the welfare frame presented to the American public. Most importantly for our purposes here, during this period health service expenditure data was presented in such a way to support this same view of government.

As William Alonso and Paul Starr wrote about the politics of numbers, "Official statistics do not merely hold a mirror to reality. They reflect presuppositions and theories about the nature of society. They are products of social, political, and economic interests that are often in conflict with each other."[14] As if holding a mirror to political realities, the presentation of health care data shifted according to changing political context. After Truman's failure with health reform—from universal coverage to insurance only for the elderly—congressional leaders once in favor of compulsory health insurance shifted their strategy. Consequently, to showcase expressly the need for Medicare, the FSA's Division of Program Research began conducting surveys focusing on the health of senior citizens. It was not until 1964, in a political climate that was more favorable towards public insurance (namely Medicare), that the FSA began its series on national health expenditures in the *Social Security Bulletin*, publishing private and public health expenditures together.[15] As already discussed, however, it is noteworthy that despite putting public and private expenditures in the same article, the FSA still combined private insurance and direct payments from individuals under the heading of "private expenditures" or "consumers." This is important because in Table 1 of Reed and Rice's article in the *Social Security Bulletin*, "total private" is portrayed as 75% of the total, making government provision appear minimal, and it is impossible in this report to determine what role private insurance is playing in the system.[16]

Third, although researchers from the Public Health Service (Joseph Mountin and Evelyn Flook) made a concerted effort throughout the 1940s—and again in the 1950 survey—to convey through their survey data the extent to which state and local public health departments were providing health services (which included prevention and curative treatments—see Chapter 4), this portrayal was lost in subsequent expenditure reports in the 1950s.[17]

At the centennial meeting of the Kansas State Medical Society in 1959, Elliot L. Richardson, assistant secretary of health, education, and welfare, delivered an address titled "The Federal Role in the Nation's Health," in which he suggested that now that the infrastructure had been built, citizens expected access to health services. He argued further that the federal government was expected to be responsive to these citizen demands, in part because the federal government had already done so much: "[A]t almost every point in the spectrum which has at one end the development of new knowledge in the health field and at the other the financing of medical care, the Federal Government has already assumed some degree of responsibility."[18] His paragraph-long list of federal responsibilities is telling not only in its scope, but most importantly in the conclusion he comes to:

> We cannot, therefore—even if we were inclined to do so—start from scratch in attempting to frame legislation designed to strengthen the capacity of the Federal Government to assist in dealing with the health problems of today and tomorrow. As we see it, our function is to take . . . action . . . that will so far as possible preserve and strengthen the pattern of Federal, State, local, and private cooperation that has worked so well in the past.[19]

This quote is very important because it illustrates how by 1959 leaders heading up the PHS within the Department of Health, Education, and Welfare (HEW) already viewed the development of health policy as path-dependent. The path established significant federal investment in health care infrastructure—or what I have called here a Federated Health Service—that included medical research, subsidized training to provide adequate supply of health personnel, building health facilities, and providing direct and indirect subsidies for health care treatment. What is most striking about the description of this path is that it says nothing about the establishment of voluntary health insurance. Indeed, Richardson's talk focused primarily on how the federal government would further health infrastructure development, and only briefly discussed financing the costs of medical care. When discussing the issue of financing, he acknowledged that even after massive infrastructure development, "there remains the problem of paying for medical care."[20] Despite acknowledging that medical care costs represents a serious problem for many American families, Richardson nevertheless pointed to "voluntary health insurance [as] representing the best means of meeting the costs of medical care . . . for most people." He drew on the same statistics cited above, that 70% of the population in 1958 had "some form of health insurance," up from 37% in 1947, representing a dramatic increase in a mere nine years.[21] Notice how he used expenditure data to craft a very specific story about what the roles of the private and public sectors ought to be.

Pointing to this increase, Richardson argued that the real problem was with the elderly and their lack of coverage. He then raised the question of whether it is appropriate for the federal government to take action to address this problem. "The basic question is: should the Federal Government at this time undertake a new program to help pay the costs of hospital or medical care for the aged, or should it wait and see how effectively private health insurance can be expanded to provide the needed protection for older persons?"[22] What is very interesting here is that while he detailed the numerous and long-standing ways the federal government had assisted state and local governments in developing health care infrastructure, he ignored completely the areas in which the federal government had been involved in financing both the direct provision of health care treatment and the indirect costs of medical care. He focused on how the United States was already path-dependent on voluntary insurance, but ignored how this depend- ence was only made possible by the government, via its direct provision through public facilities and subsidies for the medically needy.

Even when public and private expenditures were brought back together in a 1964 *Social Security Bulletin* article, "government public health activities" were separated out from personal health expenditures, despite the fact that govern- ment public health activities were defined as "all health services provided by public health agencies." Taking public health activities out of the total for public health service expenditures is important for several reasons.

First, it clearly returned to an earlier message that public health activities were only "preventive" and should not be considered "medical care," despite years of public health leaders claiming otherwise.

Second, in two pie charts, one describing how public expenditures are dis- tributed and the other private expenditures, both pies included a category for "other," subdivided into "private" and "public." The category "private other" in- cluded "expenditures for the net cost of health insurance," essentially hiding the 7.1%[23] that consumers were paying private insurance companies in premiums for their coverage. Whereas "public other" included expenditures "for government public health activities, medical activities in Federal units other than hospitals, and school health services." This "public other" category made up 17% of public expenditures, representing treatment to the American public, but was hidden from view. Public health expenditures were not insubstantial, as the "other" cat- egory suggests. When we include this "public other" category as part of public expenditures for medical care, the amount covered by public and private sources in 1965 is shown to be equal: 24% (see Figure 6.6).

Finally, this removal of public health from personal health expenditure data is important because it set a precedent. Still today the data are presented separately and not counted as part of health services.[24]

In sum, although these accounting practices might seem inconsequential, they were hugely important because they altered the way health spending was seen.[25] They hid the role of government in funding, and made private insurance's expenditures look larger and its contribution more important. And because this accounting also minimized the amount that public tax dollars were paying

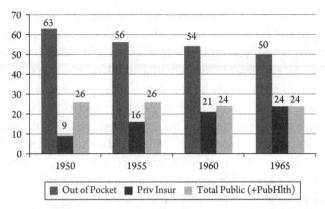

*Figure 6.6* Total Personal Health Care Expenditures by Source of Funding, 1950–1965 (Percent Distribution) *Note:* "Government public health activities" include all health services provided by public health agencies other than hospital care, research, and facilities construction (definition from Louis Reed and Ruth Hanft, "National Health Expenditures, 1950–64," Social Security Bulletin [January 1966], 9). *Source:* Robert Gibson, "National Health Expenditures, 1979," *Health Care Financing Review* (Summer 1980), Tables 4 & 5, pp. 23–28.

for health expenditures,[26] the data used to explain the U.S. health care system presented the view that the private voluntary insurance approach was working without public funding.

## Hiding Government's Role in Public Health

As discussed in Chapter 4, Joseph Mountin and his colleagues in the Bureau of State Services within the PHS conducted a major survey of the American states in 1940 to determine the distribution of health services across all state agencies. In the 1940s this survey was the most complete source of information available on total state health organization, policies, practices, personnel and expenditures. As such, it was used extensively as a basic reference for courses in public health administration—a new field in schools of public health—among those actively engaged in administrating the public health grant programs. As a result, there was demand for a 1950 update.[27] In the update, special attention was given to variation among the states in terms of types of services provided, the methods used in providing them, and in the extent of expansion of health services during the previous decade.[28] As in 1940, when there was already extreme variation among the states in terms of the agencies participating in health activities and the particular functions for which each agency was responsible, the goal of the 1950 study was to trace for each area of health activity (about 24) "everything being done for a particular problem by any organizational unit of the entire state governmental structure."[29] This extensive methodology allowed Mountin and colleagues to show the significant expansion both in the extent and variety of health services from 1940 to 1950.

Most significantly, the 1950 survey revealed that states were spending nearly a billion dollars a year for all health activities. This amount was over three times as large as that spent in 1940.[30] Because the responsibility for the provision of and payment for hospitalization and medical care were more often granted to agencies other than the health department, official health agencies made up only 16% of total state expenditures. In sharp contrast, almost half of total expenditures were administered by Departments of Welfare (20.6%) and special boards and commissions (28.6%). In some states this disparity was even more dramatic. For example, in New York and Massachusetts, special boards and commissions oversaw the allocation of over 60% of total state expenditures. In other states, the vast majority of their expenditures were administered by the Department of Welfare, notably Illinois (65.5%), Ohio (74.8%), and Pennsylvania (60.3%).[31] Moreover, as early as 1950, nearly all the states (43 of the 48 states) had some form of general enabling legislation for the establishment of full-time local health units, and specified how those departments should be financed.[32] Mountin et al. concluded that "two striking developments are revealed by the data collected for this study: (1) There has been tremendous growth in the kinds and volume of health services provided by State governments and, (2) there has been increased dispersion of responsibility for health functions within the structure of state governments."[33]

What is crucially important about this report is *how* the expansions are described. Despite the fact that a very small proportion of the expenditures came from public health departments, Mountin et al. refer to these increases in government expenditures as a "recent expansion of public health,"[34] and they explain the increase thus: "Currently, public health activity includes not only a wider array of personal health services than at any previous time in our history, but also additional services for improvement of the physical and social environments." They note important "changes in the character of public health activities" over the previous decade and attributes the change to

> the success of early public health programs in reducing the occurrence of and deaths from infectious diseases . . . Today, programs for the control of typhoid fever and diarrhea and enteritis consist principally of maintaining an environment in which these diseases do not exist . . . an aggressive campaign for eradication is no longer necessary . . . Because of these gains, however, it has been possible to turn

attention to the promotion and development of new health programs without abandoning the old. Services for controlling the effects of cancer, heart disease, diabetes, arthritis, and rheumatism are examples of the newer field of health activity into which official State agencies are now entering. . . . Rehabilitation and nutrition services and mental hygiene activities have shown marked development in recent years, as have programs for the expansion and improvement of hospitals, nursing homes, and health centers. Home accident prevention, stream pollution control, and improvement of housing are additional examples of the kinds of health programs to which State agencies are beginning to address themselves.[35]

Mountin and his colleagues present this expansive definition of the domain of public health as if they are simply reporting the activities that state governments are already involved in. Clearly, the activities listed above do impact the public's health, and there is a strong argument to be made that this list fits within the domain of public health. But, in the context of 1950, when the question of *public responsibility* was hotly contested, it is important to realize that they are making a political claim, especially when they provide a list of activities queried in their survey because they "reflect the current concept of public responsibility for health matters" (see Table 6.1).

*Table 6.1*  **Categories of Activity That Reflect the Current Concept of Public Responsibility for Health Matters, 1950 Survey**

| |
| --- |
| 1. Records and statistics |
| 2. Health education |
| 3. Laboratory services |
| 4. Expansion and improvement of hospitals and health centers |
| 5. Licensure for health reasons of individuals, agencies, establishments, and enterprises serving the public |
| 6. Nursing |
| 7. Nutrition services |
| 8. Training of health personnel |
| 9. Supervision and promotion of local health services |
| 10. General communicable disease control |
| 11. Tuberculosis control |
| 12. Venereal disease control |

*Table 6.1* **Continued**

**13. Chronic disease control**

   a. Cancer

   b. Heart disease

   c. Diabetes

   d. Arthritis and rheumatism

   e. Hygiene of the aging

14. Maternity health services

15. Infant and child (preschool) health services

16. School health services

17. Crippled children's services

**18. Mental disorders**

   a. Mental health services

   b. Hospitalization of mental patients

19. Dental services

20. Vocational rehabilitation (restorative measures)

21. General medical care

22. Human blood and blood derivatives programs

23. Health services for migratory labor

24. Prevention and care of blindness

25. Mosquito and other insect control

26. Rodent control

27. Garbage collection and disposal

28. Water pollution control

29. Control of sewage disposal facilities

30. Control of water supplies

31. Control of recreational bathing places

32. Plumbing control

33. Hygiene of housing

34. Food and drug control

35. Control of hotels, camps, and other facilities for the traveling public

36. Occupational health services

37. Accident prevention

*Source:* Joseph W. Mountin, Aaron W. Christensen, Evelyn Flook, Edward E. Minty, Rubye F. Mullins and Georgie B. Druzina, "Distribution of Health Services in the Structure of State Government, 1950," Public Health Service Bulletin no. 184 (Washington, DC: U.S. Government Printing Office, 1954); Table replicated from list on pp. 3–4, emphasis added.

The passage of the National Mental Health Act of 1946, and the other disease-based health legislation (e.g., National Heart Act, National Cancer Act), expanded services in local health departments. While these acts provided funding for training personnel in the various disciplines, and a tremendous increase in funds for disease-specific research, included in the acts were provisions for grants-in-aid to states enabling them to initiate community disease-based services, such as community mental health programs.[36] I argue that this list does reflect the areas to which state (and federal and local) governments had committed public tax dollars, but the list does not necessarily reflect the "current concept of public responsibility," because stakeholders in the health care industry framed these activities as a private voluntary responsibility, leaving silent the sources of payment.

Notice, for example, how Mountin lists "expansion and improvement of hospitals and health centers" as a public responsibility (see Table 6.1). But, as explained in Chapter 4, this activity was enacted under the Hill-Burton Act in 1946, and representatives from the hospital industry were adamant that this investment represented the Voluntary Way—only through private voluntary hospitals would improvements in health be made. Similarly, Mountin lists "chronic disease control" as a public health activity, but the voluntary health agencies control the narrative around these services as well, wherein these services are not portrayed as a government responsibility but rather the public's responsibility to support the voluntary sector. He also lists "general medical care," but it is almost comical to think Mountin believed, in the 1950s political climate, that the public viewed general medical care as a public responsibility. However, if you consider his statement based on the amount of public dollars devoted to general medical care in the states—even in 1950—it is not crazy to say that in a democracy this must on some level reflect the will of the people. He notes, for example, that many of the activities on the list are new commitments: "mental hygiene activities, programs directed toward control of the chronic diseases, and expansion and improvement of hospitals and health centers are the most conspicuous."[37] It is also not crazy when you consider that Mountin was likely doing a bit of his own statecraft.

Despite Mountin's efforts to depict all health activities at the state level as "public health," the state and local health departments were still the most clearly associated with public health, and their administration of particular programs is significant because their staffs were trained in public health. Obviously, Mountin could refer to public assistance medical care programs as "public health," but almost all the states had their welfare departments administer these programs, and because of that they brought a "public assistance" orientation to the work. Of course, this concern about administrative control was not lost on Mountin. Although the health departments in all the states had some responsibility for 15 out of the 36 activities queried, their administration over the allocation of total state funding was quite small (see Figure 6.7). The reason was that hospital

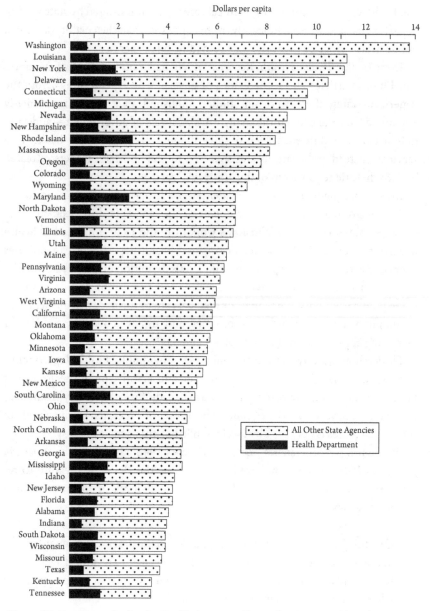

*Figure 6.7* Per Capita Outlay for Health Services Allocated to State Health Departments Compared to All Other State Agencies, 1950 Survey. *Source:* (Mountin, 1951, p.38).

and health care expenditures for medical care were administered by state welfare departments, and were significantly more expensive than the cost of traditional public health programs—even those providing health services.[38]

Even in the *Public Health Reports*, which had published all of Mountin and Flooks's articles about the extent of government expenditures across the American states, there were no studies published after 1950 that similarly attempted to make explicit the many ways all levels of government—and multiple agencies within each level of government—were providing health care services. Instead, publications and speeches by public health leaders retreated back to rhetoric reminiscent of the pre-New Deal days.

Most subsequent articles in the *Public Health Reports*, for example, narrowed their focus to state and local health departments, such as Isadore Seeman in the early 1950s, who extended Winslow's work from the 1920s on the ideal health department. In particular, Seeman compared health department expenditures over time across 11 large cities using the 1920s definition of "public health." By using this narrow definition, which only discusses prevention and does not include public payments to hospitals or medical care to the needy, he presents per capita public health expenditures for cities, and argues in a similar fashion for increasing appropriations (see Chaptes 2 and 3).[39]

Notice how quickly the transparency regarding public health departments' offerings had changed since 1945, when even conservative public health expert Harry Mustard (who said the public wasn't ready for compulsory insurance) wrote that "the vast majority of routine health service received by the people of the United States is delivered by local [public health] agencies."[40]

The new Surgeon General Leonard Scheele's 1948 editorial in the *American Journal of Public Health* similarly illustrates how the PHS felt pressure to re-establish itself (and public health departments at all levels of government) as a scientific agency:

> One thing which we have jealously guarded in the past must be guarded
> in the future; the Public Health Service must remain a technical agency
> with broad authority, and must not in any sense be placed in a position
> where it can be guided by party or politics.[41]

In this address he made clear that "one of [his] first concerns as Surgeon General is to improve the efficiency of the Public Health Service." He appointed a committee almost immediately after taking office to study the organizational structure of the PHS, and the committee's first area of inquiry was the grant-in-aid programs. Scheele argued that categorical grants, which had expanded from one general health grant to six different grant-in-aid programs, were inefficient, but he also argued—in keeping with the political rhetoric of the day—that the PHS had strayed from the intent of the grants under the Social Security Act:

> When the Social Security Act was passed in 1935, providing specifically for the development of local health services—but not for particular disease categories—[proponents of local health departments] thought the battle was at least half won. The Public Health Service, with its colleagues from the states and territories, supported these principles: Grants-in-aid should be general; the budget structure should be simple; there should be reasonable latitude for administrative discretion in the use of funds appropriated for public health work.... Since that time, the proponents of ... full-time local health service have been ... swimming upstream against the strong current of categorical appropriations and programs.

Further on in the talk, however, it becomes clear that Scheele also believes in a very expanded vision of public health, but similar to the pre–New Deal Grow-and-Hide rhetoric, he tells it slant. For example, he focuses on making the grant-in-aid programs more efficient by increasing the general health grant and eliminating the disease-based grants, allowing him to be consistent with the political rhetoric of the day but also to make the case for a massive expansion in local health departments. Indeed, this is the same case Mountin and others were making throughout the 1940s. He recalls in a politic manner the missionary spirit from 40 years prior, when the " 'Shoe-leather Epidemiologist' sent his boys from house to house preaching the gospel of the sanitary privy ... his aim was what is now the Number 1 goal of public health: the modern, model, all-purpose local health unit. A unit adequately staffed with well trained physicians, public health nurses, health educators, sanitarians, technicians, and other needed specialists. A unit housed in a functional, good-looking building—the health center."[42] Notice how there is no mention of compulsory health insurance, but nonetheless public health leaders are on very familiar ground—one they never left. What's changed is the rhetoric. For in this period of attacks on the PHS for bureaucratic overreach, Scheele ends his remarks this way:

> The health policy of the United States Government, as represented by Congressional Acts and the work of the Public Health Service, and Children's Bureau, and related programs, has never been partisan, nor even bipartisan. It is non-partisan. We of the Public Health Service and our federal colleagues are going to do all in our power to keep it that way.... The Public Health Service has one sole interest: to do and to be only what is best for the health of the people. As in the past, we await their orders.[43]

While emphasizing the scientific, nonpolitical public health professional, the details of the message within are the same: a comprehensive, tax-supported health center spread across the country for all Americans to have access to.

Another perfect example of the Grow-and-Hide rhetoric is on display in Surgeon General Scheele's address at the University of Michigan, which was reprinted in the *American Journal of Public Health* under the title "Whither Public Health?" The question mark is suggestive, and the editorial board writes in their introduction that Scheele's address "is so notable that it deserves wide reading and study."[44] Most speeches do not need "study," but as the title suggests, one must read between the lines to understand its true intent.

At first it seems Scheele only favors a very traditional notion of public health: "[A] health program becomes a public health one when, because of its nature or extent, it may be solved only by systematized social action . . . The real question . . . is not . . . whether the person is well or ill, . . . rich or poor—for the rich use the sewerage system—but rather when, or if, a given problem of health and disease can no longer be solved by the unassisted effort of the citizen and the uncoordinated resources of the community."[45] Here he invokes sanitation, not medical care for the individual, as the key example of public health, and uses a type of "economic failure" argument for when public health might come into play—only when other individualized (presumably private-practice) options fail. But, later in the talk he reveals his expansive view of what "prevention" is: "Prevention no longer deals only with preventing the initial onset or occurrence of disease. It also means preventing the continuance or progress of disease which has already occurred; it means preventing the development of persistence of disability or invalidism; and of dependency, destitution, and other undesirable social effects."[46]

Clearly this definition of prevention is so broad as to essentially say there are no differences between preventive and curative medicine, but Scheele is quite careful not to say exactly that. When addressing the public health profession at the University of Michigan, Scheele called for public health departments to take up this expanded vision of public health when and if they can,[47] but in his effort to portray the PHS as "nonpartisan," his rhetoric changed depending on the audience. In 1953, at the height of McCarthyism and just after the appointment of the Commission on Governmental Functions and Fiscal Resources to "bring the Federal budget into balance and ultimately lower taxes," Scheele presented public health as "the nation's best investment." In this context, he clearly distinguished public health as separate from hospital and medical care: "[P]ublic health budgets are small in comparison with budgets for hospital and medical care."[48] Under Parran and Mountin, the PHS attempted to "own" hospital construction and NIH as a public health function, and clearly, in terms of their expenditures, they still did. The PHS's own Annual Report in 1951

and its publication "Public Health Today" in 1952 showed the full breadth of responsibilities and increases in expenditures since 1948. Of course, the major increases in expenditures were for research and hospital construction funds, but even operating funds increased, which included the grant-in-aid funding (see Figure 6.8).[49] But Scheele, again similar to pre–New Deal days, stripped these functions away from "true" public health expenditures to present a residual budget. Mountin, who was still working for the PHS before passing away in late 1952, also adopted a more cautious tone. In a publication in 1952, he discussed the importance of increasing federal grants that would go directly to local health departments. Similar to Scheele, he expressed concern that federal appropriation for the general health purposes had decreased from 1950 to 1952, while the new special categorical grants for cancer, heart disease, and mental health were increasing (Figure 6.8).[50] His valid concern was that the categorical grants were consuming funds that would otherwise go to local health departments under the general grant.

There is an important political dynamic behind the grant-in-aid programs. While conservatives at the federal level were concerned about federal overreach, the states and local governments—even conservative ones—welcomed these funds. In a survey of state officials administering the public health grants, the vast majority viewed the public health grants favorably and reported a positive relationship with federal officials: 95% said the federal grants had stimulated state activity in public health activities, 78% said federal supervision had improved

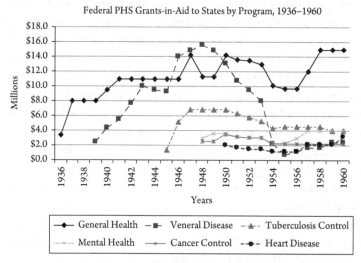

*Figure 6.8* Federal PHS Grants-in Aid to States by Program, 1936–1960. *Source:* U.S. Department of Health, Education and Welfare, Public Health Service, Background Material Concerning the Mission and Organization of the Public Health Service (U.S. House of Representatives, Interstate and Foreign Commerce Committee, April 1963).

state standards of public health administration and service, and 68% said federal aid did not lead to federal interference in state affairs in this regard.[51]

Although states generally also favored more flexibility in grant programs, which means they would favor the general health grant over the categorical grants, the voluntary health agencies and their aligned provider groups were behind the initiation of these categorical grants, making them politically more difficult to oppose, even for conservatives. As a result, despite several commission reports calling for consolidation and integration of federal grant programs, the politics encouraged more fragmentation.[52]

The effect of pressure-group politics was acknowledged in a report on "Federal Aid to Public Health" by the Commission on Intergovernmental Relations: "In recent years there has been both an absolute and a relative increase of categorical grants. The appropriation of money by the Congress for human medical research through the stimulus of pressure groups, public and congressional attitudes toward various diseases, and emotional drives should be deprecated with all vigor."[53]

The influence of the voluntary health agencies on the public health grant-in-aid programs is visible in many ways. Not surprisingly, the national associations were asked to give testimony at the various hearings held on disease-specific health bills, such as the National Mental Health Act, the National Heart Act, and the National Cancer Act, which established not only the respective research institutes but also the accompanying categorical grant-in-aid programs. The voluntary agencies were also strongly present in hearings conducted in 1949 around Truman's proposed National Health Program, in which Title V—a program for the development of local health departments—was discussed. To get a sense of the close collaboration between public health and the voluntary agencies, consider that Dr. Haven Emerson gave testimony representing "not only the American Public Health Association (as the current President), but the National Health Council (NHC, the coalition of voluntary health agencies) and particularly its National Advisory Committee on Local Health Units."[54] It is also noteworthy that all the voluntary health agencies testified in favor of increasing the general health grant under Title V (to be directed toward developing local health departments) because they saw the benefits of extending their work through an increase in public health funds.[55] Numerous representatives from the voluntary disease-based organizations came to testify in favor of increasing the general grant to build more local health units across the country. These same representatives had, of course, testified in previous hearings related to establishing the National Cancer Act, the National Heart Act, and several others during this period.

The Commission on Intergovernmental Relations was established for the stated purpose of "studying the relations between the Federal Government and the States and localities," but really it was established because at this time there was growing concern among a conservative Congress that federal aid had grown too much and was infringing on the rights and freedom of states to freely govern.[56] The Health Committee of the commission was made up of persons "representing the professional interests in the field and of members who are in a position to view these problems in terms of the general public interest."[57] It is difficult to know whether individuals from the voluntary health agencies, charities, national organizations, and provider groups were chosen for their ability to represent the public interest or their professional interests, but their views were certainly included.

First, they were favored in terms of representation on the board: of 14 board members, six were drawn from these agencies, charities, organizations, and groups, three represented business interests, and one represented labor, while only two members represented public health.[58]

Second, their views were well represented in a survey conducted to "obtain information from a wide scope of organizations, institutions and individuals who are experienced, well informed and interested in the field of health."[59] In addition to 52 state public health officers and 10 schools of public health, the study committee sent the survey to 74 national organizations, which primarily included voluntary health organizations and provider associations. Not surprisingly, this group of national organizations was split on the question of whether the grant structure should stay as is (with a plethora of categorical grants) or be reformed to largely rely on a general (noncategorical) grant.[60] The representatives from schools of public health were also split, with those favoring the approach likely doing so because they received grant funding for research on particular diseases that benefitted from the categorical grants. Only the public health officers overwhelmingly favored the block grant or "general assistance" approach, arguing, similar to PHS leaders Scheele and Mountin, that these funds should be used to develop local health departments.

Third, the voluntary agencies and professional societies also had formal representation on councils that were established to go along with each of the disease-based acts that were passed in Congress. By 1951, "to assist the Surgeon General in carrying out specific functions," Congress had created nine such councils: the National Advisory Health Council, the National Advisory Cancer Council, the National Dental Research Council, the National Advisory Heart Council, the National Advisory Mental Health Council, the Federal Hospital Council, the Water Pollution Control Advisory Board, the National Advisory Neurological Diseases and Blindness Council, and National Advisory Arthritis and Metabolic Disease Council.[61]

During the period from 1948 to 1965, almost all publications on how public health services should be developed advocated a prominent role for voluntary health agencies. In Scheele's remarks at the 150th Anniversary of the PHS, he said: "May there always be voluntary agencies to spearhead needed action! May there never come a time when only official agencies are active for the people's health! No thoughtful health officer can overlook the significance of these popular movements, devoted to the cause of particular population groups or to the conquest of a particular disease."[62]

But despite these exclamation points for the necessity of voluntary agencies to be involved and for public health departments to embrace them, Scheele hints at the underlying problem of their political power. For although Scheele suggests it is a mystery why government continued to support the categorical disease-based grants, he later references the pressure from voluntary health agencies for these grants. Indeed, it is not an accident that the disease-based grant-in-aid programs aligned almost perfectly with the five major voluntary health agencies at the time, ranked according to the support they received from the public: the American Cancer Society, the American Health Association, the National Foundation for Infantile Paralysis (better known now as the March of Dimes), the National Easter Seal Society for Crippled Children and Adults, and the American Lung Association.[63]

Nonetheless, despite questions raised by some in the PHS deep in their writings, in the post-WWII era only praise was heard in public discourse. Even in response to possible reduction in federal grant-in-aid funds to the states, Scheele wrote: "The elimination of unnecessary and low priority projects, increased State and local appropriations, and greater voluntary support should more than balance any loss of Federal grants." He also equated democracy to citizens and states being "free from any Federal paternalism that might destroy initiative in the public interest."[64]

Many scholars have written about the influence disease-based organizations have had on increasing NIH funding for research.[65] However, it was not simply that these groups were able to increase funding for a particular cause, but that they were able to influence the design of how the federal government (through the NIH and PHS) was organized, particularly special diseased-based institutes and categorical disease-based public health grants. In the PHS's 1951 Annual Report and in its 1952 publication "The Public Health Service Today," a visual depiction of the "Complete Health Structure" shows voluntary agencies as literally attached to government agencies on one side and private practitioners on the other (see Illustration 6.1).[66] The report emphasizes the federal government's main role as supporting state and local governments, but also underscores what other nonfederal agencies do—medical schools, research foundations, professional associations, and voluntary agencies.[67] Their depiction of the "ground floor of the health structure" also illustrates the important role voluntary agencies played in the health care system.

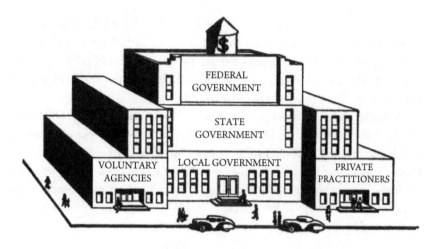

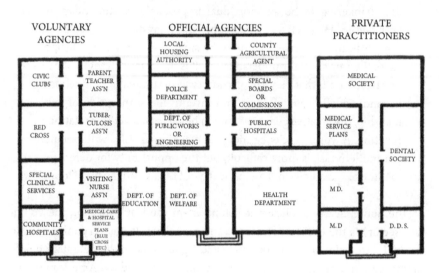

*Illustration 6.1* The Complete Public Health Structure. *Source:* Replicated from Joseph W. Mountin and Evelyn Flook, "Guide to Health Organization in the United States, 1951," Public Health Service Publication no. 196 (Washington, DC: U.S. Government Printing Office, 1953), vii–viii.

In the 1960s, despite growing confusion about how to coordinate the various roles of the numerous voluntary agencies, private stakeholders from the health care industry remained active in promoting their existence. George Bugbee, who has been called the father of the voluntary hospital movement, in 1962 was also the president of the National Health Council (a coalition of voluntary health organizations). The council's connection to the health care industry is clear in the list of the council's "sustaining members": Equitable Life Assurance Society of the United States, Metropolitan Life Insurance Company, Smith Kline & French Laboratories, and Winthrop Laboratories. The connection between the council and government agencies was similarly clear: all the federal government agencies with jurisdiction over health-related matters—the United States Bureau of Family Services, the Children's Bureau, the Department of Agriculture, the Office of Education, the Office of Vocational Rehabilitation, the PHS, and the VA—were advisory members to the NHC.

"Voluntaryism and Health: The Role of the National Voluntary Health Agency" was published in 1962, and while it critiqued the role of voluntary health agencies in the health care system, it also equated volunteerism with democracy as a clear principle (similar to voluntary hospitals). The cover of the book shows a peace sign with three equal parts: freedom of the individuals, freedom of enterprise, and freedom of association. The following quote appears on the inside page:

> This hankering to be an individual is probably greater today than ever before. Huge factories, assembly lines, mysterious mechanisms, standardization—these underline the smallness of the individual, because they are so fatally impersonal. . . . It is the unique strength of democratic methods that they can provide a way of stimulating and releasing the individual resourcefulness and inventiveness, the pride of workmanship, the creative genius of human beings whatever their station or function. A world of science and great machines is still a world of men; our modern task is more difficult, but the opportunity for democratic methods is greater even than in the days of the ax and the hand loom.[68]

The quote clearly implies that volunteerism (and by extension the voluntary sector) is the bedrock of democratic capitalism. It was very important to the NHC to maintain the importance and significance of the voluntary health movement, because it was this movement that convinced the American public that access to health care (and perhaps the achievement of health itself) was attainable through the voluntary approach. In the words of the NHC, the voluntary health agencies "have stimulated and supported great legislative and research programs. . . . Thousands of communities across the nation have new and improved health services, rehabilitation centers, and educational services as a result of their activities."[69]

Similar to the voluntary hospitals' fight for the "voluntary approach," the movement was explicit in claiming ownership over democracy. "They [the voluntary health agencies] are as American as our form of democracy. . . . Preservation of these freedoms and of our way of life must be by conscious acts on the part of the American people. . . . The future success of the national voluntary health agencies is wholly dependent on the degree to which we are willing to support and improve our free institutions."[70]

As the political context changed, so too did the focus of discourse from the U.S. Surgeon General. In 1962, Surgeon General Luther Terry published in the *Public Health Reports* an article titled "The Public Health Service Role in Medical Care Administration." According to Terry, "A quick review of our social concepts and the activities undertaken through public and private effort makes it abundantly clear that this is a complex problem."[71] After detailing the most significant legislation up to 1961 and increases in voluntary health insurance, he concluded:

[T]his history of official and voluntary action in the field of health care is not merely an anthology of action; it is an extremely important indication of what may be expected in the future. Our entire history shows a consistent public policy that finds government, either Federal, State, or local, assuming responsibility for the health care of certain groups in peculiar positions of unusual need. The major segment of the population meanwhile remains in the sector of individual or group nongovernmental programs of care.[72]

He also parroted SSA's description of how we should understand the allocation of health expenditures:

At the present time, out of the $26-billion-plus of all expenditures for medical care services, slightly more than $6 billion is from public funds. . . . Public expenditures as a percentage of total expenditures . . . has increased only from 20.8 percent in 1934–35 to 23.5 percent in 1959–60.[73]

The second lesson he said we should learn from "our history" is that the "public assumption of responsibility for high-risk or high-cost segments of the population removes them from the *community group* which otherwise must absorb their excess costs. It follows that, relieved of such adverse experience, community-rated health benefit programs can expand benefits to better serve the medical needs of their subscribers."[74] Note how this follows directly from the hospital industry's framing of private and public roles. It is hugely important that by 1961, even in a much more liberal political context, the path forward was envisioned so narrowly. But perhaps more important is the acceptance of a very tortured rhetoric that distorted the amount of public expenditures to present them as smaller than they were. And referring to private health insurance companies as "the community group" shows the extent to which the "Voluntary Way" had infused itself into American political discourse. Further evidence of this infiltration can be seen in the idea that it is fair and just that this "community group" should be relieved of the most vulnerable in society to better serve "their subscribers," because the most vulnerable would, after all, provide an "adverse experience."[75] The language is now familiar, but perhaps surprising is that it was promoted by the Surgeon General in a liberal political climate and prior to the enactment of Medicare. It shows the extent to which Americans had bought into the American Voluntary Way.[76] Also clear from Terry's statement is that by 1961 the PHS no longer hoped to be the administrative leader of the U.S. health care system. Instead, as Terry put it, the PHS "will respond to the program needs and interests of both the public and private sectors of medical care administration."[77]

Despite this language and despite no legislation targeted at local health units passing, local health departments continued to expand, as did the medical care these units provided. Although most literature on public health infrastructure suggests that public health investments declined during this period, local health departments increased from 1,239 to 1,703. Clearly this was not the increase public health advocates were hoping for, and relative to the massive investments in hospital construction, and funding to the NIH, it is logical to conclude a retrenchment of sorts occurred, or at least a clear preference toward health care services in acute-care settings. Nonetheless, by 1965 almost all the local health units in the country were providing medical care services and openly acknowledging it. That was perhaps the most significant transformation: not a systemic transformation of local health department services from preventive to curative—Parts I and II of this book have illustrated that despite what public health leaders said at various times, these local health departments and affiliated voluntary health programs had long been providing various treatments and medical services—but rather a political transformation that by 1965 allowed local health departments to openly discuss the medical services they provided. The reason for this political shift was exactly what Surgeon General Terry had advocated: local health departments taking on the bulk of responsibility for helping those that private practicing physicians did not want.

By 1965, 83% of local health units provided medical care for recipients of public assistance; 71% provided health services to "crippled children," 41% provided school health programs, 46% provided migrant health services, and 77% provided community mental health services.[78] These particular types of services were so strongly tied into existing revenue streams, and were so often for recipients for whom a limited set of providers were available, that the provision of these services by local health departments was not only politically acceptable but encouraged. It was politically acceptable because, as in the past, private practicing physicians by and large did not want to take care of patients on public assistance or patients presenting with these particular health problems, and also because there was no longer a threat that public health clinics would take away "valuable" paying patients.

In the early 1960s, before the passage of Medicare and Medicaid, and before the passage of the Comprehensive Health Planning Act of 1966,[79] there was renewed hope that the government would attain its role in creating a rational, comprehensive health care system. At the same time, ironically, because the role of local health departments had become marginalized, there was a sense that public health was not appreciated.

## Hiding Government's Role in Paying for the Medically Needy

When the Social Security Act Amendments of 1950 establishing medical vendor payments were passed, members of the Joint Committee on Medical Care—made up of the two professions in charge of administering the program: the American Public Health Association and the American Public Welfare Association—issued a joint statement calling for cooperative planning between state welfare departments and state health departments in administering public medical care programs. The committee recognized two important phenomena (in part because both had already been discussed over the previous decade): first, that there was significant fragmentation and complexity in the administration of state medical programs; and second, that the 1950 amendments would encourage expansions not only because of the federal grants-in-aid incentive, but also because the amendments' definition of "medically needy" was ambiguous. Consistent with definitions offered 30 years prior (see Chapter 4), this joint statement defined "medically needy" or "medically indigent" persons as "individuals, who are normally self-supporting," but have high medical costs relative to their income.[80] In the joint statement they highlight that "there is no sharp line of demarcation . . . between public assistance recipients and the medically needy." Because anyone is at risk of illness and medical care is sufficiently expensive, they argued, almost "any family" could shift in and out of "medical indigency." They concluded that although "a realistic approach to tax-supported medical care programs involves a recognition of limiting factors in the determination of eligibility, . . . that such limitations exist should not obscure the crucial fact that such programs are not adequate as long as any person requiring available medical care is deprived of its benefit because of inability to pay for it."[81] The seeds of the expansion of "medical indigency" are readily clear when anyone who faces an inability to pay for medical care is defined as such.

Despite these important expansionary precursors, one factor largely overlooked at the time of the bill's passage was the significance of medical vendor payments. This discounting occurred for two main reasons. The first is simply that other questions seemed more pressing. The Social Security Amendments under consideration expanded the original bill in four other ways:

- They called for substantial increases in benefits and expanded eligibility under Old-Age and Survivors Insurance (OASI).
- They created a major new category of federal-state aid to the totally and permanently disabled.
- They changed the federal matching-rate formula to use state per capita income.
- They considered extending ADC (Aid to Dependent Children) eligibility to include children with needy parents (not just single or widowed mothers).

Among the state representatives coming to testify before Congress, the vast majority focused foremost on the social insurance (OASI) expansions—this topic consumed the debate. Other issues—including medical vendor payments—were discussed only to a small extent, and even then they competed for attention among each other. Of the public welfare administrators from 20 different states who came to testify in favor of the 1950 Social Security Amendments, only a few even mentioned the medical vendor payment provision. And when they did, no discussion ensued.

The second, more important reason for the lack of attention to medical vendor payments is that proponents of national health insurance had presented amendments to public assistance as residual programs, and had argued—not necessarily in the congressional hearings, but elsewhere—that the state-level means-tested medical programs could be done away with when national health insurance was enacted. Those in favor of national health insurance did not perceive medical vendor payments as a win for their opponents (as one might presume, since conservatives tended to favor relatively small means-tested approaches); rather, they viewed this provision as a small public assistance expansion that would not harm anyone and might help some vulnerable people a little, which is why liberals were also supportive. When the lone questioner, Senator Millikin from Colorado, wondered about the potential expansionary significance of this seemingly small provision, Commissioner Altmeyer—a key proponent of national health insurance in the Truman Administration—quickly assured Millikin that any such significance could not adhere to such meager provisions for public assistance recipients:

SENATOR MILLIKIN: What control do they [states] have over the doctor or the theory of medicine?

MR. ALTMEYER: I do not think they would have any control by reason of this amendment. Many states and localities now of course have made arrangements with the local doctors of one kind or another, and they would make similar arrangements under this amendment, except that they could make payments directly to the doctors instead of including an amount in the cash assistance which is then paid to the doctors.

SENATOR MILLIKIN: But at the state level the states can make any sort of regulations that they want to make so far as the payments are concerned, can they not? . . . Would some sort of restriction on the extent of that control be desirable in connection with a bill of this kind?

MR. ALTMEYER: I do not know what restriction or control would be envisaged. I do not think it is necessary. I do not recall that it has ever been a burning question in the states. The whole problem that has vexed the welfare departments and the doctors is some way by which they can get payment as directly as possible, without a lot of red tape.

SENATOR MILLIKIN: What I am getting at is, one of the objections to the proposed social medicine plan is that in the natural tendency of governmental affairs the first thing you know the Government will be telling the doctors what medicines to prescribe and be setting up all sorts of qualifications for the doctors who receive the money, various kinds of controls, hospital rules and regulations, and so forth and so on. I am just wondering whether the same sort of objection, without discussing its merits at all, would be open to this.

MR. ALTMEYER: . . . I do not think the same question that concerns the medical profession in the case of health insurance is involved in making the necessary arrangements to pay the medical profession or the hospitals for services given to these recipients of public assistance. (U.S. 81st Congress, Senate, January 18, 1950, 57–58)

Part of the reason public assistance programs were discussed as "residual" is because they were usually viewed in relation to increasing social insurance. Indeed, every state-level public welfare administrator emphasized in their testimony that federally funded social insurance should be increased, and federal-state public assistance would then be allowed to decrease. The following statement from Loula Dunn, director of the American Public Welfare Association, illustrates this common theme:

I think the first and most important thing to do, Senator, is to extend and broaden your social insurances . . . the lack of balance which we find today in the number of people receiving public assistance and getting insurances is, one might say, almost the opposite of what we had

hoped for at the time the Social Security Act was passed. Public assistance is larger than the insurances; and in my judgment it should be
exactly the reverse. And I think if you extended your coverage and your
benefits and stepped up your rate of payments, you would find that you
would have a decline, then, of the pressures on your public-assistance
programs. (U.S. 81st Congress, Senate, January 23, 1950, 166–70)

    While many policymakers agreed with the concept of increasing social insur-
ance, there was general skepticism (even among many supporters) that a substitution effect would occur. This skepticism is illustrated by Senator Millikin's
response to Ms. Dunn:

    May I suggest that your logic is impeccable; but, if I may put out a
    thought of my own, I doubt very much, despite the good quality of
    your logic, that it will decrease public assistance $1. Because public as-
    sistance is intimately related with politics in the states and at the federal
    level. (U.S. 81st Congress, Senate, January 23, 1950, 166–70)

    Although conservatives favored the means-tested public assistance approach,
especially as a way to impede the need for national health insurance, they worried (despite their support) about increasing government expenditures under
federal grant-in-aid programs. For example, the conservative Senator Taft said
in relation to the cost of medical care: "It seems to me we are getting to a point
where there is just so much free cash going to so many millions of people that
you are getting into a very dangerous over-all situation" (Taft, U.S. 81st Congress,
Senate, January 18, 1950, 72).[82]
    Indeed, the creation of medical vendor payments did foster the type of
supply-side political pressure that Senators Millikin and Taft worried about.
While health care providers were relatively silent about the medical vendor
payment provision in the 1950 Social Security Amendments, they nonetheless
understood its significance. The Inter-Association of Health, composed of top-
ranking officials from the major provider groups,[83] submitted a statement in support of the need for earmarked funds (through medical vendor payments) to
finance medical care for public assistance recipients. Like Senator Millikin, they
understood that various financing schemes *would* influence their practice and
therefore included in their statement "the further view that any provision to finance medical care for assistance recipients . . . should have the support of those
six organizations" (statement submitted to U.S. 81st Congress, Senate Finance
Committee, January 23, 1950, 171).
    Public assistance programs continued to increase in the 1950s—despite
increases in OASI—in large part due to expansions in medical vendor payments.

Although this particular provision did not have much financial significance in the few years following its passage, the provision allowed for a series of revisions and expansions in 1953, 1956, 1958 and 1960, culminating in the passage of Medicaid in 1965.[84] In 1953, a separate federal-state matching rate for medical vendor payments (apart from cash payments) was established, and the individual medical maximums and federal matching rate for vendor payments subsequently expanded in each of the years listed above.

The 1946 Hill-Burton Act also contributed significantly to more widespread use of medical vendor payments for the elderly in need of long-term care services, because it provided funds for nursing home construction.[85] In a separate statement, the American Hospital Association also prophetically recommended that medical assistance include long-term care for chronic diseases, "because of the constantly expanding span of life of the aging population."[86] There was, however, not yet an established nursing home "industry." Though a variety of homes existed for a variety of purposes, they were of widely different standards and were almost entirely unregulated.

Meanwhile, after Truman's failure to enact national health insurance, proponents decided to restrict their goals to expanding hospital benefits only for OASI beneficiaries—in other words, elderly persons over age 65. This compromise strategy was solidified in a series of events.[87] Oscar Ewing, from the Social Security Administration (SSA), publicly proposed this limit in June of 1951,[88] and SSA's Annual Report released in April of 1952, also recommended such a limit. In April 1952, Senators Murray and Humphrey and Representatives Dingell and Celler introduced bills in Congress with this limit, and by the end of that year, in December 1952, President Truman publicly endorsed such a limit. Based on this consensus, in 1957 Senator Aime Forand introduced the original "Medicare" bill, proposing universal coverage for the elderly, with a restricted hospital-based benefit package administered and financed on a contributory basis by the federal government.[89]

In response to both the Forand bill and mounting public pressure to do something for the aged, Representative Wilbur Mills and Senator Robert Kerr proposed (similar to Senator Taft before them in the 1940s) a means-tested alternative to forestall Forand's "social insurance" scheme. In general, Republicans and conservative Democrats from the South favored the Kerr-Mills approach, while liberal Democrats favored the Forand bill.[90] This alternative passed in 1960 and came to be called the Kerr-Mills Act. Building on federal grants-in-aid for medical vendor payments, two crucial provisions were embedded in Kerr-Mills: comprehensive benefits and the concept of medical indigency. Kerr-Mills was designed to be distinct from welfare, without the latter's continuing stigma of public assistance. Under Kerr-Mills, the "medically indigent" were older persons who did not need assistance under ordinary circumstances, but only when they became sick and had large medical expenses relative to their current income. Proponents emphasized that the "medically indigent should not be equated with the totally indigent; that is, they should not be equated with those who receive cash assistance.[91] This conception of medical indigency was in keeping with the foundational principle that sickness should not cause impoverishment.

While it is unclear how much the elderly were helped under Kerr-Mills, the program had a huge impact on the growth and use of nursing homes. From 1960 to 1965, vendor payments for nursing homes increased almost tenfold, consuming about a third of total program expenditures.[92] Even at this early stage, it was increasingly difficult to view these programs as simply residual ones that would wither away under increases in social insurance. They had achieved a life and a purpose of their own. By 1960 there was already general recognition of the need for nursing homes and other chronic long-term care services. For example, in 1960, President Eisenhower's proposed alternative to Kerr-Mills also emphasized the need for chronic long-term care services for the elderly and relied on state administration.[93]

The Social Security Amendments of 1965 (the Medicare and Medicaid legislation) combined three approaches to financing medical care into a single package. While there was substantial discussion about the hospital insurance program, which became Medicare Part A, many observers were surprised when the bill also included Medicare Part B, a voluntary supplementary medical insurance program funded through beneficiary premiums and federal general revenues (similar to what the AMA had proposed—Bettercare), as well as a third layer (originally called Part C), which broadened the protections offered to the poor and medically indigent under Kerr-Mills and became what is now known as the Medicaid program.[94] The Kerr-Mills means test was liberalized in order to cover additional elderly citizens, and eligibility among the indigent was broadened to include the blind, permanently disabled, and adults in single-headed families and their dependent children.

The adoption of Medicaid in combination with Medicare (Parts A and B) in 1965 was presented as creating a limited social insurance program and "supplementing" it with an additional program for the poor. I put "supplement" in quotation marks because medical care programs were hardly supplemental for public assistance recipients, even before Medicaid was passed. State-level medical care programs were vital and grew substantially.

Despite this history, once again legislators presented Medicaid as a relatively minor piece of the 1965 Social Security legislation, of much less significance than Medicare. Government estimates of Medicaid's future budgetary costs presumed the program would not lead to a dramatic expansion of health care coverage. Even assuming that all 50 states would implement the new program, the federal government projected Medicaid expenditures to be no more than $238 million per year above what was then currently being spent on medical-welfare programs. As it turned out, this expenditure level was reached after only six states had implemented their Medicaid programs. By 1967, 37 states were implementing Medicaid programs, and spending was rising by 57% per annum.

The belief that the enactment of Medicare would result in only a small increase in Medicaid was in keeping with how policymakers, administrators, and advocates had long discussed the hoped-for relationship between public assistance and social insurance. That this substitution did not occur, however, should not have come as a surprise to anyone looking closely at medical vendor payments and the Kerr-Mills MAA (Medical Assistance for the Aged) program. The fastest-growing and most expensive component of these two public assistance programs was the cost of nursing homes for chronically ill elderly persons. By 1965, every state had medical vendor payments for public assistance recipients, and 40 states had implemented a Kerr-Mills MAA program for the medically indigent. Even though long-term care coverage was essentially ruled out under Medicare, with 40 state programs providing nursing home coverage, it would have been political suicide to withdraw such benefits from existing Kerr-Mills recipients. Indeed, Kerr-Mills and medical vendor payments were consolidated under the new program called Medicaid, and nursing home expenditures continued to increase.

While the increase in nursing home expenditures was perhaps unplanned, three points of forewarning are important to note: First, this increase in nursing home and hospital expenditures for the medically indigent was part of a larger trajectory that started 15 years before Medicaid, and yet was discussed as "residual," and as such was hidden from the public's view. Second, although many historians have described Medicaid's enactment in 1965 as an afterthought, its passage was consistent with the low-profile grant-in-aid programs passed since the New Deal: funding for public health and maternal and child health in 1935, medical vendor payments in 1950, and Kerr-Mills in 1960. All these programs were similarly described as "minor" and "residual," but all led to a substantial increase in expenditures. Third, the "afterthought" description of the enactment of Medicaid overlooks that there was a much longer precedent for means-tested, state-level medical care programs in the United States than for compulsory insurance. Thus, while Medicare built on the social insurance design for the elderly (OASI), Medicaid built on the public health/medical programs that started with the New Deal. Indeed, Senator Taft's 1945 proposal to develop a National Health Program for the poor was essentially passed in the form of medical vendor payments in 1950, and expanded to include the medically needy under Kerr-Mills in 1960. And while there were no state-level experiments with compulsory insurance, by 1965 all states had medical care programs for the poor and most for the medically needy. To say, as many have, that no policy elites saw Medicaid coming seems short-sighted. In 1955, Michael Davis wrote on his assessment of Taft's proposal that "[i]f such a scheme were actually put into effect on a large scale, it would mean national aid to state systems of poor-man's medicine, accompanied by voluntary health insurance serving primarily the middle and upper income groups." And Davis, despite calling it "poor-man's medicine," also understood the scale such a program could attain if it included the medically needy or those unable to pay the full cost of the care they needed. He noted that "a large majority of American families may be unable to pay 'full cost' on one occasion or another."[95]

As described in Chapter 5, the rhetorical shaping of these programs as residual came as much from the private medical industry as from policy elites in the public sector. Hospitals in particular were instrumental in describing the payments for public recipients as meager, well below their costs, and therefore akin to charity care. Hospitals were also influential in framing the role of government—whether it increased payments or not—as both problematic (because it was never paying enough) and minor (because voluntary hospitals and voluntary private insurance covered the bulk of Americans).

The hospitals' version of the narrative conveyed to the American public that privately insured patients deserved more than the publicly insured, and that the high cost of care that (so-called) private patients paid was the fault of government not paying enough for public patients. As an AHA executive put it when speaking from the "public's view point:

> We [Blue Cross subscribers] do not consider the ward as the baseline accommodation any more. The two-bed room now enjoys that status. We expect the hospitals and the plans to get together on that score. . . . As [for] the indigent, we hear talk about bringing them into the Blue Cross plans. That may be fine so long as it does not add a single penny to the cost of our care or increase our payments to the plan and so long as it does not in any way lessen the benefits that we, the self-payment members, receive. As we look at it, we put up the tax money to take care of the indigent, and we don't want to pay twice—once to the government and once to the plans—for the same purpose. I have heard it expressed that this group, the indigent, will use much more care than the usual participants in Blue Cross normally do. So unless a much higher premium is charged, it is going to cost the plan more, and this means we, the paying participants, will have to carry a greater load and may have less chance of enjoying increased benefits.[96]

The AHA prescribed a very confined role for government: pay full costs for the indigent, support the voluntary sector, and do not compete with the voluntary sector. While stipulating that the government should support the voluntary sector, the AHA rarely acknowledged what the government's financial role was. At the same time that the AHA was convincing the public that the price of high hospital costs reflected a high quality of care in voluntary hospitals, it was also demonizing government. As George Bugbee—the man behind the Hill-Burton Act (see Chapter 5), and who was described thusly: "to the whole postwar generation of hospital administrators, George Bugbee and the American Hospital Association are inseparable concepts, like Babe Ruth and baseball"—said in response to a question about high costs and overuse: "[I]f what we do in a public discussion is to say 'yes we can't control the situation,' what's the public going to do except turn it over to the government for control?"[97]

## Hiding Government's Role in Hospital Construction

The prior chapter describes in detail how the hospital industry framed and developed "the voluntary hospital's story." Parts of the story hidden from the American public involved the details behind how "full costs" were calculated, as well as the debate about whether the hospital should charge for depreciation and interest on capital investments. By 1950, this practice had been around for a long time (see Chapter 4) but was still not fully embraced, which is why the AHA devoted substantial effort to its widespread adoption.

The notion of charging "full costs" was also not fully accepted—especially among the payers for hospital care. Charging the government "full costs" allowed hospitals to build up a reserve to make continual investments in new technology, which they could then write off again with depreciation and interest charges. It was a very inflationary process, and average costs per patient day continued to escalate, from almost nine and half dollars a day in 1946 to nearly 22 dollars a day by 1954, an increase of 132%. AHA studies of costs explained the increases as primarily due to an increase in wages, but also "growth of health services/utilization; increased intensity and complexity; reduced length-of-stay increases cost per day; occupancy rates; and regulations."[98] Although the increase in intensity and complexity of services were built into the cost accounting and charging procedures, the AHA president and hospital administrators across the country described the cost increases as inevitable and tied to necessary increases in quality of modern medical care.[99]

In May 1951, the AHA held an invitation-only conference in Chicago to discuss the wide variation in payments across the country, variations resulting from differences in payers and differences in geography. The goal of the conference was to arrive at a standardization process for payment. Seventy persons were present, including "buyers and sellers of group hospital care ... [representation from] hospitals and hospital organizations, local, state and federal governmental agencies; Blue Cross and other prepayment plans, labor, health and welfare funds, national health societies and foundations, community welfare councils, local nonprofit health and welfare organizations."[100]

In summarizing feedback from the conference, the AHA reported that "most delegates felt that agencies purchasing hospital care should pay the 'full cost' incurred in providing the services authorized under their agreements with hospitals. 'Full cost' was not defined, however, and this is the job that must be done before complete agreement is possible."[101] It is telling that "full costs" were not defined, because the definition was exactly the point of contention. The AHA reported further that

> [a] few hospital representatives and several third-party delegates objected to the principle that interest costs on capital indebtedness should be included as an operating expense item. . . . The discussion of depreciation was accompanied by very little unanimity. The consensus was that depreciation should be included in per diem costs, but a sizable number of delegates expressed negative or indecisive opinions. A few delegates favored the principle that depreciation should be included in per diem costs only if it is funded by the hospital.[102]

It is not surprising that third-party payers, especially government agencies, were against the inclusion of interest costs on capital indebtedness as *standard* "full-cost" accounting practice, because many hospitals received interest-free grants from local governments. After Hill-Burton was passed, every issue of AHA's journal had a section devoted to hospital construction projects. In addition to detailing the plans for construction, the articles also reported on how capital funds were raised to match the federal Hill-Burton contribution. Although some articles mention bonded indebtedness, many others mentioned taxation to fund local hospital construction. Some articles mentioned a combination of taxes to fund not just construction but operating costs. For example, a rural hospital in one state was financed by a five-mill hospital tax, included in the county's property tax assessment, that was intended "to provide funds to help defray anticipated deficits." The state legislature also approved a tax levy for rural hospitals, and at the time the article was written in 1951, "[a]nother bill, pending in the legislature, would authorize a 10 percent city and county tax on all beer sold . . . funds from [these two taxes] should adequately support the hospital."[103]

The residents in Port Angeles, Washington, voted for "[l]ocal financing by the municipal corporation building [Olympic Memorial] hospital. They approved a three-mill annual tax levy and a bond authority for 1 ½ percent of the assessed value of the district." Port Angeles residents also voted for an additional statute, which allowed "bonded indebtedness up to 5 percent of assessed value."[104]

What is notable about the journal's coverage of these funding mechanisms is that the same issue could contain, for example, a description of a form of taxation to fund hospital construction, along with articles about the importance of conducting cost-accounting that instructed hospitals to include depreciation and interest on debt in their estimate of "full costs," all without any reference to how hospitals were financed in the first place.[105] The AHA also published stories of unique financing schemes by local governments, such as using surpluses from municipal utilities:

> Citizens in Frankfort, KY., will soon be paying for their hospital expansion program right along with their monthly utility bills. This unusual, practically painless method of hospital financing is the result of an agreement between the City of Frankfort, the municipally owned Frankfort Light and Water Plant, and the nonprofit organization, the Silent Workers Circle of The International Order of King's Daughters and Sons, which now operates the hospital.[106]

Even when this plan arranged for the utility plant—rather than the hospital—to pay back bonded indebtedness out of its surplus earnings, there was no suggestion that the hospital in Frankfort should perhaps not use "full-cost" accounting, or that its charges and collections process might change, since, after all, the residents of Frankfort were already paying for construction costs. Instead, by touting how "Frankfort's citizens will pay for their electricity, water, and hospital expansion in one bill," the journal effectively encouraged hospitals across the country to work with their local governments to development similar "painless" and hidden financing schemes.[107] Nonetheless, despite many local and state governments directly footing the bill for construction, hospitals still insisted on government reimbursement for their version of "full costs."[108]

One may think that hospitals' capital costs were minimal, but the value of hospital construction increased from $170 million in 1946 to $1 billion in 1960.[109] Contrary to the AHA's claim that the increase in hospital costs was largely attributable to an increase in wages (i.e., labor costs), a study conducted on hospital revenue and expenses from 1962 to 1966 found that the major contributing factors were changes in technology and investment in new equipment.[110] And on top of this increase in costs, a study conducted by the PHS suggested it would cost an additional $3.6 billion to modernize or replace obsolete urban hospital facilities.[111]

Although leaders from the hospital industry understood the importance of government as a major source of capital financing, they never referred to these funds as government subsidies. Karl Klicka, for example, in writing about the sources of capital funds for hospital construction in 1962, wrote that funding came from three major sources, each representing a third: accumulated earnings, Hill-Burton grants, and community contributions.[112] In 1965, another study of hospital construction projects similarly reported three major funding sources—"governmental, hospital, and philanthropic resources"—each contributing a third.[113]

What is particularly noteworthy about these two studies is how they belie the messiness around these categories and, more importantly, around the role of government. "Accumulated earnings," or what Jeffrey Stambaugh calls "hospital reserves," simply refers to hospitals using their own surplus revenue to fund capital investments. Of course, a hospital's ability to use "its own resources" as a source to fund capital projects is directly related to the industry's success in securing cost-based reimbursement from third-party payers—both insurance companies and government. Robert Sigmond noted that voluntary hospitals derived 35% to 40% of their total capital funds from their "own resources."[114] As noted, the main mechanism that allowed hospitals to build up reserves was funded depreciation.[115] Thus, although this was labeled and discussed as hospitals using their own revenue to fund capital projects, this revenue depended heavily on government agreeing to supply it.

Michael Davis pointed out that estimated capital invested in hospitals in 1951 was $917 million, of which 46% was from private sources and 54% percent from government.[116] Because Davis had long been intent on exposing the true role of government spending, he moved away from the categories the hospital industry had constructed—categories aggregating total government investment across all levels of government and all types of hospital ownership—to estimate the 54% public total. Note how this presentation of data offers a drastically different picture of who is investing in hospitals' technological advances: in outlining the sources of finance for capital investments, the hospitals' categories suggest an important but still more minor role for government—one-third from government, compared to two-thirds from philanthropy and the hospitals' own reserves. As Davis notes, depreciation allowances were not allowed for governmental hospitals. Instead, the usual policy at the local, state, and federal level was to "replace capital, when required, out of current tax appropriations or bond issues."[117] Thus, the $100 million paid in depreciation costs in 1951 benefitted private voluntary hospitals, much of it publicly subsidized, but was nonetheless framed as a purely private investment, superior in quality above the government-owned hospitals.[118]

As the extent to which this practice was becoming a major source in funding capital investments became more clear over time, it also became more controversial. The dissention over the reasons for the escalation in hospital costs and what to do about it had been brewing since the dramatic increases started to occur in the 1950s. However, it came to a head when the insurance commissioner of Pennsylvania issued an adjudication in 1958 on the application of the Philadelphia Blue Cross plan for a premium increase.[119] In explaining his refusal to grant the increase, the commissioner suggested widespread neglect on the part of hospitals in controlling hospital utilization and costs. The adjudication instigated a number of other official investigations across the country on the question of hospital management and costs. The hospital industry responded to this controversy with its typical voluntary-way frame: "[W]hat right did an insurance commissioner (a government bureaucrat) have to suggest that either a Blue Cross plan or a governmental agency should pry into the operation of institutions that were predominantly under local voluntary auspices?" They characterized such attacks on the voluntary hospital system as creeping socialism.[120]

Edward Springer, a government lawyer who sat on the Governor's Hospital Study Commission to study the issues raised by the adjudication and to make recommendations, responded to the hospital industry—and to the American public—that the commissioner not only had a legal right, but a duty, to oversee that "the creation of nonprofit hospital service plans shall be operated in a manner which will best serve the interest of the *whole* community."[121] Springer also pointed out that government was already funding significant aspects of hospitals' income, and therefore had a right to consider the "public's interest."[122] Because the premium increase was based on Pennsylvania's hospitals estimate of "full costs," and because a major reason for the increasing costs was investments in new technology or capital replacement, these funded depreciation costs were further scrutinized. Springer argued that instead of being charges paid by patients or third parties on behalf of patients, the following costs should be shared by the community as a whole (presumably through taxation, though he doesn't say that):

> (1) initial cost of hospital construction; (2) the amortization of hospital indebtedness and interest for initial construction and capital improvements; (3) the cost of major items of specialized equipment; (4) the repair and maintenance of the hospital plant; (5) the cost of medical research; (6) hospital costs for nurse and intern training; (7) the cost of free care; (8) the depreciation on capital investments.[123]

Springer makes a direct connection between the practice of full-cost accounting and charges to patients, and argues that if capital costs were removed from charges, hospital care could be more affordable for the patients.

What is important about Springer's argument is not whether it is "right," but rather that it raises an important question: Which aspects of hospital costs should be considered a public good, and therefore paid for out of public taxation? This question continued to be debated and became a focal point in negotiations over Medicare hospital reimbursement with the AHA. Herman and Anne Somers's history of the development of Medicare legislation describes the importance of hospital capital costs in the negotiations between hospitals and Congress: "hospitals' drive to increase funds for capital formation colored and complicated every major dispute on payments . . . and [it] proved to be the hospitals' most effective weapon in obtaining various liberalizations."[124]

Just as hospitals had fought for full-cost reimbursement with state governments, the AHA was adamant that Medicare's payments for capital expenses should include three elements: interest on borrowed capital, depreciation, and return on invested capital. There was very little discussion about interest expense, and allowance for depreciation was already accepted policy by the time the AHA started negotiations over Medicare. However, while there was agreement that the federal government would reimburse hospitals for their capital investments, there was substantial disagreement about the assets on which this allowance would be calculated. Similar to concerns raised by state governments, the Bureau of Health Insurance (BHI) within the Social Security Administration, which was charged with working on the technical details of reimbursement/payment, believed that "assets financed with Hill-Burton funds should be excluded from the base for calculating depreciation because their acquisition did not involve expenditures by recipient hospitals."[125]

In addition to debate over which assets should be counted, there was also disagreement about the amount of the allowance. The AHA argued for a depreciation allowance based on the replacement cost of assets. The BHI pointed out that an allowance based on replacement costs would be significantly higher than one based on the historical cost of assets due to inflation and changes in technology, and contended that this was inconsistent with standard accounting practices and "out of step with congressional intent."[126]

Finally, the AHA pressured Congress to include "imputed interest," which they described as "interest that could have been earned on equity capital had it not been invested in durable assets." Although SSA chief Robert Ball was, due to budget constraints, against these extra capital payments, the national AHA rallied its state hospital associations to exert more pressure, and the Department of Health, Education, and Welfare (HEW) eventually conceded, allowing payments on Hill-Burton assets and incorporating a 2% "plus factor" to allow for a return on capital. Ironically, although the Senate Finance Committee was initially critical of HEW's concessions, it ultimately agreed to an additional capital payment to proprietary institutions, largely in response to intense lobbying from the American Nursing Home Association, which was (and still is) predominantly for-profit.[127]

These concessions are enormously important in understanding the politics of the hidden health care state. Although state and federal governments funded a substantial portion of hospital capital investments—through direct grants in the first place and/or reimbursement payments that incorporated depreciation costs, interest on debt payments, and a return on investment—hospitals never acknowledged that government support was a major reason the industry as a whole was able to invest in technological advances and provide the American public with "high-quality" medical care. To the extent that the hospital industry even mentioned the government, it was most often to demonize it, either for forcing hospitals to provide low-quality care by not paying enough, or for being an overburdening regulator, stifling hospitals' private innovation.

## Conclusion: Establishing a Fragmented and Unequal System

> *From the polemic literature of the controversy, . . . one would think that the choice for America was between "voluntary and compulsory insurance." Our choice is not so simple. The forces that brought about the sixfold growth, since 1929, in the general tax revenues spent for medical care will continue to operate during the coming years. . . . The issue is "not so simple," because each alternative subdivides again. Tax-supported medical service may or may not be State Medicine; it may or may not be "poor-man's medicine"; it may be either or both of these in spots, and be something else in other spots. We observe examples of all these different "spots" today.*
> —Michael Davis, *Medical Care for Tomorrow*, 1955, 350

Because Michael Davis had been studying the development of the U.S. health care system for a long time, he knew the many "spots" that had already developed. In his 1940 study of state-level health administration, Mountin and his colleagues already noted a high degree of inequity across states, as well as fragmentation within states. By 1950, this fragmentation had magnified, and "as many as 32 agencies in a single State were participating in some activity with health aspects. . . . On a Nation-wide basis, for a single program there may be as many as 14 distinct types of agencies represented." Even the most consolidated state still had 10 different agencies involved in health activities.[128] And this was actually a fairly significant undercount, because in every state there were numerous boards and commissions overseeing each different activity—such as the tuberculosis commission for tuberculosis control services, and the dairy commission for food and drug control services—but for simplicity's sake Mountin and Flook counted them as a single state "agency."

The system was so complex that, following their 1950 study, Mountin and Flook published in 1951 a *Guide to Health Organization in the United States,* which, in their words, was needed because "the complex and divergent channels through which individuals receive health services in this country often confuse even experienced health workers."[129] This "concise pamphlet," as they called it, was over 100 pages long.

The guide is very important because it is one of the first documents (and perhaps the only one) that laid out the entire picture of the federated health service system in the United States—the functions of the federal, state, and local governments, and voluntary agencies. Although the federal role was almost always discussed as minor relative to state-level investments, the guide detailed how the federal government was involved in regulating, researching, and providing direct services in the health field. Mountin and Flook's 1951 list of 25 federal health agencies provided a sense of how much the federal role had expanded (see Table 6.2). They included a table, seven pages long, describing the range of activity and how each federal agency was engaged in health services.[130]

*Table 6.2* **Federal Health Agencies Involved with Public Health and Medical Care Activities, 1951**

| |
|---|
| 1. Federal Security Agency |
|     Public Health Service |
|     Freedman's Hospital |
|     Social Security Administration |
|     Children's Bureau |
|     Bureau of Public Assistance |
|     Office of Vocational Rehabilitation |
|     Food and Drug Administration |
|     Saint Elizabeth's Hospital |
|     Office of Education |
| 2. Department of Agriculture |
| 3. Department of Commerce |
| 4. Department of Defense |
| 5. Department of the Interior |
| 6. Department of Justice |
| 7. Department of Labor |
| 8. Department of State |
| 9. Department of the Treasury |
| 10. Atomic Energy Commission |

*Table 6.2* **Continued**

| |
| --- |
| 11. Civil Aeronautics Board |
| 12. Defense Mobilization, Office of |
| 13. Defense Production Administration |
| 14. Federal Civil Defense Administration |
| 15. Federal Trade Commission |
| 16. General Services Administration |
| 17. Housing and Home Finance Agency |
| 18. Interstate Commerce Commission |
| 19. Mutual Security Agency |
| 20. National Advisory Committee for Aeronautics |
| 21. National Academy of Sciences and National Research Council |
| 22. National Science Foundation |
| 23. National Security Resources Board |
| 24. Tennessee Valley Authority |
| 25. Veterans Administration |

*Source:* Joseph W. Mountin and Evelyn Flook, "Guide to Health Organization in the United States, 1951," Public Health Service Publication no. 196 (Washington, DC: U.S. Government Printing Office, 1953), 5.

They also summarized an exhaustive 1950 study of voluntary health insurance plans that revealed the administrative complexity of the voluntary approach.[131] Setting aside the greatly varying commercial health insurance plans, consider just the nonprofit hospital service plans: even in this infancy period, there were already 85 such plans in the United States, and each plan had its own corporate entity with its own board of directors and administrative staff, and each plan had a different benefit structure.

Federalism, too, had evolved into a more complicated and fragmented form. Politicians still insisted that American federalism was like a layer cake, with a clear division of authority between federal, state, and local; but by the early 1950s, federalist scholars and bureaucrats working in areas that relied heavily on intergovernmental financing (such as health care) were more likely to describe American federalism as a complicated, shared relationship. In 1952, Joseph McLean, from Princeton University, came up with the alternate "marble cake" metaphor:

> Most of us think of our federal system as having three layers of government...with each level assigned definite functions and responsibilities... [so] that a specific service of function generally belongs exclusively to

one layer of government. . . . Most of us fail to realize that this layer cake is much more like a marble cake. There are many combined activities—administrative, financial, and political—any public problem you can mention today involves all of the so called "layers" of government.[132]

In 1966, Morton Grodzin described the dominant feature of contemporary federalism not as "a division or power and responsibilities between the central government and the states but as a 'sharing' between them, indeed a particular style of sharing characterized by 'mild chaos.' "[133]

Perhaps because Mountin had passed away by the time the guide was published and Flook subsequently "decided to retain as nearly as possible the original format and text, for which [Mountin] was directly responsible," Mountin's description of the federal system was uncharacteristically honest and critical for a government employee: "To a person unfamiliar with a federated system of government, contradictions and exceptions seem to characterize the broad scheme of organization—if, in the mosaic, they are able to perceive any coherent pattern."[134] He highlights how public health practice varies widely across the United States, and argues that its narrow definition makes little sense:

> There is wide variation in the definition of public health, and this is reflected especially in the structure of local health organizations. In many of their operations, health departments seem to stop somewhere short of applying remedial measures. Finding a condition needing attention and bringing it to the notice of the person concerned seems, on superficial examination, to be the end and purpose of public health. The visitor from abroad has difficulty understanding why public health agencies should be divorced from such elemental health measures as removal of refuse, public housing, and various items falling within the general scope of public services.[135]

Mountin also as early as 1951 highlighted the inequities in access to medical care within the U.S. system:

> In the field of medical care the picture is equally confusing. A complete tax-supported service is provided by the Federal Government for the Indians and for veterans of wars, but medical benefits for its own workers are limited to disabilities arising out of employment. The States usually provide domiciliary care for the insane and the tuberculous, but for no others. Localities differ widely in the provision of general medical service, but they are alike in confining such provisions to the indigent.[136]

He was also clear about the inequalities resulting from the voluntary approach:

> Voluntary medical-care insurance is more common among people working in groups than among those who must be reached by individual enrollment. There is greater concentration in industrial urban areas than elsewhere of persons holding some form of medical-care insurance. Relatively twice as many people in the most urban states have some protection against the costs of hospitalization as do residents of the most rural states.

Proportionately, twice as many people in the more wealthy states had hospital insurance than those in poor states. But despite these critical statements, he ended the introduction with the beginning of an enduring myth:

> When the general scheme of health organization is first explained, the visitor or the casual observer often is amazed that it works at all. The infinite variety in program content, organizational method, and quality of performance . . . at times may seem cumbersome and inefficient. In spite of these characteristics, our form of health organization—which seeks to influence with minimum control—does work, as is well demonstrated by rather obvious and tangible results. The people of the continental United States now enjoy a level of health and well-being never before attained by any population of comparable size.[137]

This last statement is crucially important because it creates two myths that remained in the American psyche well into the 21st century: first, that the American people want minimal control and investment by government, and that is what we have; and second, that the United States can have a highly inefficient system that does not offer universal coverage, and yet still have the best system in the world. Indeed, he concludes that, "despite inequalities usually associated with medical and hospitalization services that operate on the basis of a private enterprise, the great majority of the people in this country obtain a considerable measure of medical care, at least for the more acute conditions."[138]

I quote Mountin at length here because his views encapsulate much of what the leaders in the public health network cared about and prioritized during this time period. They cared deeply about creating an organized system of care, based on the notion of hierarchical regionalism,[139] and hoped to move closer to a system of universal access to medical care. But they also believed that growth might overcome the problems of fragmentation and inequality—that through many different programs, everyone would eventually have access to a decent minimum of care. Obviously the two ideas are contradictory, which is why the leaders prioritized the creation of a "rational efficient system" over access to care. In the end, of course, Americans got neither.

By 1965, all the components of the National Health Program (NHP) were in place: there were grants for public health and maternal and child health; construction funds to build hospitals, nursing homes, and health centers across the country; grant-in-aid funds to the states for the indigent and medically needy; and private and voluntary health insurance for persons of means and social insurance for the elderly. Those advocating for an NHP back in 1938 envisioned a federal oversight and coordination that would make these five components work in harmony. Some voiced concerns about the incremental approach, but the majority involved in the development of health policy at this time supported it. The more liberal members of the public health network felt strongly that certain approaches—namely means-tested programs and voluntary health insurance— would not work, but also believed in the power of democracy to right its course. What they did not foresee was the power of the political economy, especially one that emerged under a fragmented and unequal system, to hide its failures and shift blame back on to government itself.

Many have discussed the power of the political economy in health care.[140] My contribution is to show how the actors in the health care industry created a political frame—aggressively promoting the Voluntary Way in three main areas—and successfully shaped to their favor the public's very understanding of the system. And elected officials and state agency leaders more often than not bolstered this framing by using the same language and providing data consistent with the voluntary frame. By 1950, because government expenditures had already increased significantly under an extremely fragmented and unequal system, it was difficult to see the whole of government expenditures, even if one were specifically looking. This fragmentation and inequality made the Grow-and-Hide strategy easier, and made the voluntary frame being pushed by the private sector—hiding government's role and promoting an ideology of democratic choice—more believable.

Indeed, the Grow-and-Hide Regime was well established by 1965, even before Medicare and Medicaid took off. As we will see in Part III, the logic of this perverse system persists to the present day: as public expenditures explode, they remain hidden under the rubric of a predominantly private U.S. health care system, encouraged by the fragmentation and inequities that system produces, and the American people continuing to believe they have no choice.

# PART III

## THE CONSEQUENCES OF GROW AND HIDE

### 1965–2020

*What greater power can there be than to operate namelessly?*
—George Monbiot, 2016[1]

When health reformers passed Medicare and Medicaid in 1965, millions of Americans gained coverage under public insurance, but the Grow-and-Hide Regime was left untouched. Because the structural components of the health care system were the same—with a heavy reliance on federalism (across multiple levels of government), subsidies to the nonprofit sector, and administrative responsibility across multiple government agencies—the system enabled more of the same, government money funneled into every crevice of the health care system, yet it was still persistently obscured. In Part III (chapters 7–10), I describe the three main consequences of Grow and Hide: (1) fragmentation and the demise of health care planning, (2) profiteering and the financial industry's takeover of capital investment in the U.S. health care system, and (3) growing inequality while focusing on public expenditures to the poor.

## Fragmentation: The Failure of Health Care Planning

Given the political climate in 1965, which supported more government involvement in health care, public health leaders were again hopeful that health reform would provide an opportunity for the government to plan and rationalize the U.S. health care system. This hope was logical given that two major planning policies—the Heart Disease, Cancer and Stroke Program in 1965, and the Comprehensive Health Planning Act in 1966—were passed in 1966 during the early days of the Great Society. However, because the planning acts also built on the Grow-and-Hide strategy and the same structure—federalism and public-voluntary collaboration embedded in the private sector—and the U.S. health care system was already extremely expensive, fragmented, uncoordinated, and unequal, such hopes were quickly dashed. When the largest health planning act in the United States (then and now) was passed in 1974, its ability to plan this unwieldy system effectively was considered dead on arrival. As detailed in Chapter 7, the private hospital sector was extremely influential in designing the planning acts as voluntary, local, and without government authority. Yet when planning failed, they shifted the blame back on government and reified the planning acts as "government regulation." However, rather than argue that the Voluntary Way would rationally plan the health care system as the private sector did prior to 1965, by the late 1970s they argued that a competitive health care market was the solution to governmental regulatory failure and would rationalize the system better than government planning.

## Profiteering: Hiding the Financial Industry's Takeover

By 1980, with the shift in power toward the Republican Party, there was a strong embrace of the "competitive approach." The crafted framing that government regulation in the 1970s had failed and competition was the solution to this failure (described in Chapter 7) enabled this approach. However, the rise of capital markets in the U.S. health care system provided an additional structural mechanism to continue growing and hiding the provision of public expenditures to support capital investments. Starting in the late 1960s, government policy shifted from direct government grants to fund capital construction for the voluntary hospital system, which was more explicit, to relying instead on the tax-exempt bond markets, which were (and remain) deeply obscured.

Chapter 8 explicates U.S. capital health policy from 1965 to 2008—just before the passage of the Affordable Care Act (ACA). I document how public subsidies bolstered and encouraged the private sector's reliance on capital markets and created an even more bifurcated health care system of the "must-have" and "have-not" hospitals. While some policymakers raised questions about the value and ethical uses of public subsidies to the nonprofit sector, most public subsidies for capital investments—especially those that benefited the financial sector—were not discussed and remained hidden under the rubric of competition.

## Inequality: The Conspicuous Health Care Safety Net

Because Grow and Hide strategically feeds on fragmentation and inequities, the turn toward competition and capital markets in health care made fragmentation and inequities in the health care system even more severe. However, rather than change capital health policy, the U.S. government created more transparent subsidies to support the health care safety net. Indeed, the "safety net" term's emergence in the 1980s resulted from this bifurcation. The politics of Grow and Hide creates a process whereby policymakers strategically reveal some subsidies while hiding other forms of public funding. First, conspicuous public discourse focuses on the use of public subsidies to poor/low-income Americans, reflecting a commonly understood partisan divide. Yet the continuing debate contributes to these expenditures remaining a major bipartisan focus on the political health care agenda. Second, the fragmented and unequal structure of the health care safety net creates political debates focused on the deservingness of various vulnerable groups—pitting vulnerability against vulnerability (Decribed in Chapter 9 in relation to the Medicaid program). Third, and in stark contrast to the conspicuous health care safety net, policymakers hide how public funding supports capital investments in the health care market and the affluent connected to these markets. From 1980 to the present, neither party has seriously debated capital health policy. Even around 2000, when private equity firms entering the health care space raised concerns among policymakers about the demise of publicly funded health care infrastructure, a politically polarized government acted in unison by saying little and doing absolutely nothing.

Similar to the Great Society, when health reformers passed the ACA in 2010, they also expanded coverage on top of the existing U.S. health care system. As a result, while 20 million Americans importantly gained coverage under the ACA, the logic of Grow and Hide was not only left untouched but escalated. I detail in Chapter 10 how the ills of this system perpetuate and deepen under the ACA: (1) the ACA increases fragmentation, as it continues to rely on voluntary health care planning lacking effective government regulation; (2) capital health policy continues in an even more unregulated form where private equity firms in the U.S. health care system have increased dramatically, taking advantage of public funding while remaining completely unregulated and hidden from view; and (3) the conspicuous health care safety net, most notably the Medicaid program, expands enormously but hides the true extent of its reach. Unfortunately, despite the benefits of these ACA expansions, the reform built on and extends the current inequities of the health care system.

That these three ills are allowed to fester and continue to grow and hide helps explain the power of the Grow-and-Hide Regime. George Monbiot reminds us of the power of unnamed logics, and we will see this power in the pages that follow: "[W]e respond to these crises as if they emerge in isolation, apparently unaware that they have all been either catalysed or exacerbated by the same coherent philosophy; a philosophy that has—or had—a name."[2]

# Fragmentation

## *The Failure of Health Care Planning*

When one thinks of health care legislation under the Great Society, Medicare and Medicaid quickly come to mind—as they should, since these programs extended health coverage to millions of Americans. And yet from 1965 to 1969, during President Lyndon B. Johnson's short time in office, more health legislation was passed through Congress than under all other presidents put together.[1] In Johnson's health message to Congress he referred to "20 landmark measures" and a doubling of appropriations for federal health programs to achieve "good health for every citizen to the limits of our country's capacity to provide it."[2] As Phillip Lee, the assistant secretary of health, education, and welfare (HEW) from 1965 to 1969, explained,

> There were some very large ideas in those days. . . . We were thinking
> very expansively about [health care and planning] all over the country
> for dissemination and for improving the quality of care.[3]

Similar to the National Health Program that emerged out of the New Deal (discussed in Chapter 4), these bills tended to focus on three major areas: (1) expanding direct health benefits to particular groups,[4] (2) expanding health care infrastructure in underserved areas,[5] and (3) expanding medical personnel.[6] These investments also built on the logic of Grow and Hide, where public expenditures increased dramatically but were hidden under the structure of federalism, the public-nonprofit sector collaboration, and fragmentation across multiple government agencies.

But, as discussed in Parts I and II, the public health network's mission throughout the 20th century was not just to expand the health care system, but to develop a rational and coordinated plan for it. Starting with state-level public health leaders, such as Surgeon General B. S. Warren, with his "Unified Health

*Grow and Hide*. Colleen M. Grogan, Oxford University Press. © Oxford University Press 2023.
DOI: 10.1093/oso/9780199812233.003.0008

System" proposal in 1915, and Hermann Biggs from New York, who advocated for neighborhood health centers in 1920, public health leaders had long pushed the idea that the U.S. health care system needed to be developed *and rationalized.* Even in 1915, there was concern that passing health insurance legislation before rationalizing the system would lock in a fragmented, inefficient, and costly health care system (see Chapter 3). Not surprisingly then, these public health concerns only intensified as fragmentation and health care costs continued to increase in every decade after the New Deal. While public funds increased significantly to finance expansions in health care infrastructure, no legislation was passed to plan or rationalize the growing system until 1946, when the Hill-Burton Act was enacted to provide substantial infrastructure subsidies to build hospitals across the country. Although some planning provisions were embedded in the legislation, they were weak. As a result, hospital beds flourished without any regard to planning a broader system of care.

Because those early efforts failed miserably (see Chapter 4), the calls for rationalization were loud and persistent when another major reform—the creation of Medicare and Medicaid—was on the horizon. Similar to the New Deal period, there was a brief period when discussion of government planning was more politically acceptable and rationalizing the system became a priority. Medicare and Medicaid were passed first in July 1965, and bills that sought to develop and plan the health care system were enacted quickly thereafter. Indeed, the period from 1965 to about 1974 could be labeled as a "planning panacea," because significant bills were passed, which asked and motivated stakeholders and citizens to think about how to plan a better health care system. By 1980, however, this hope in planning was dead. The voluntary, collaborative planning process of the 1970s did not improve coordination or quality or access to care, nor did it lower health care costs. Ironically, what this planning experiment did instead was further embed Grow and Hide, the then-familiar U.S. structure of hidden and significant public subsidies to private provision with little accountability. The reasons are fourfold.

First, because the planning bills were built on a fragmented system, the two major bills passed in 1965–1966 were fragmented and worked in conflict with each other. Second, the planning bills were weak, relying on voluntary action from the private sector. Third, even the more comprehensive bill passed in 1974 still relied on voluntary planning, which allowed the hospital industry to reify voluntary planning as strict government regulation, and to orchestrate the demonization of government in health policy. This demonization of government began prior to 1965 (as described in Chapters 5 and 6), but became more persistent during the 1970s and contributed to the death of planning. Fourth, because the failure of planning emboldened the conservative demonization of government, it opened up a window of opportunity for the competitive approach.

These four factors built up the Grow-and-Hide Regime, which has proven remarkably stable and difficult to overturn, largely because it has enabled providers and organizations in the health care supply chain to earn vast revenues from public expenditures. Most importantly, while public funding for expansions in coverage, personnel, and infrastructure continue up to the present day, the government lost its opportunity to rationalize that system and has never truly attempted to do so since.[7]

## Emergence of the Planning Panacea

A decade after the passage of the Hill-Burton Act of 1946, there was widespread agreement that the planning aspirations of the act—to create a rationally linked health care system where primary and secondary care was linked to tertiary care centers within geographic regions (referred to as regionalization[8])—had not been achieved. Although the leaders in the Public Health Service (PHS) and the American Hospital Association (AHA) advocated the idea of regionalism when Hill-Burton was passed (see Chapter 4), there was nothing required in the legislation to assure that type of planning occurred. While communities had to submit a planning document along with their request for hospital construction funding to the federal government, these plans tended to focus on justifying hospital construction based on community need (and demand) in relatively small geographic spaces. They rarely considered the supply of other hospitals and facilities within a larger *regional* area, nor did they consider regional capital investments to replace equipment and modernize facilities.[9] Therefore, as hospital costs continued to soar alongside growing concerns about lack of access to hospital care, there was a renewed interest in regional planning.[10]

In 1958, the PHS and the AHA developed a Joint Committee and held four regional conferences across the country for the purpose of developing a set of principles for comprehensive planning. At each meeting in four different cities— Chicago, New Orleans, Salt Lake City, and Washington, DC—they emphasized guidelines to plan for tomorrow's hospitals. When the Joint Committee issued its report, the lofty goals of regionalism remained, along with continued insistence of relying on *voluntary* planning, and in addition there were new calls for the development of area-wide planning agencies.[11]

The federal government backed this recommendation in the Community Health Services and Facilities Act of 1961, devoting funds for area-wide planning agencies throughout the country. These agencies spread quickly, increasing each year from 14 in 1961 to 80 in 1966 (see Figure 7.1), and funding also increased, reaching $13 million in 1967. In 1963, the PHS issued a manual titled *Procedures for Areawide Health Facility Planning*, which detailed the recommendations from the Joint Committee's report, and a list of 22 goals for planning agencies to follow (see Table 7.1). Consistent with the shift in focus, while goals 1 through 4 dealt with improving quality and efficiency and controlling expansion, goals 5 through 9 focused on planning in light of other facilities in the area. However, new to the list was the emphasis on community involvement in decision-making (as illustrated in goals 16, 18, 19, 21, and 22).

Because the PHS had been advocating health planning for a long time, with little success at achieving a more rationally coordinated system,[12] there were many skeptics wondering whether a new planning bill would make any difference. Consistent with the Voluntary Way approach (see Part II, especially Chapter 5), the Joint Committee and other advocates of planning emphasized the need for community-based voluntary organizations to do area-wide planning and argued that this "objective" voluntary organization would be able to focus on regional planning, because this organizational form would have no self-motivating reason to focus on one facility over another.

Given this renewed focus on planning by the PHS, it is not surprising that when the window of opportunity opened for passage of public insurance—Medicare and Medicaid—there was a sense of urgency that the health system needed to be rationalized. By then, this was a consistent pattern among public health leaders: to favor system reform prior to financing for fear that insurance would further embed a dysfunctional system of care.[13] However, consistent with the Great Society approach of pushing "all the buttons at once without much coherence among them,"[14] financing insurance and two separate health planning approaches were all passed at the same time. Essentially, the planning goals of the joint commission were segmented into two tactics: one was backed by

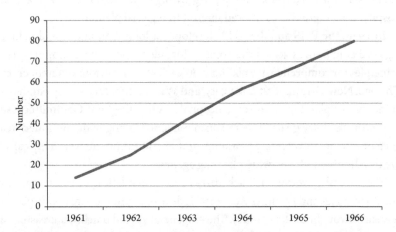

*Figure 7.1* Growth in Area-Wide Planning Agencies, 1961–1966. *Source:* Joel May, *Health Planning: Its Past and Potential* (Chicago: Center for Health Administration Studies, University of Chicago, 1967), 40.

*Table 7.1* **Consensus List Concerning Purpose and Goals of Planning Agencies**

1. Maintain and improve quality of care as economically as possible.

2. Correct deficiencies in existing facilities and services.

3. Stimulate construction of needed facilities including those for educational purposes.

4. Discourage construction not conforming to community needs.

5. Assure more effective use of community funds by avoiding unnecessary duplication of highly specialized, infrequently used, expensive facilities.

6. Improve patient care by developing more effective interrelationship of facilities.

7. Develop an orderly distribution of all facilities in keeping with expected population characteristics and overall community development.

8. Encourage individual facilities to define and carry out their objectives and projected roles in relation to other facilities, services, and community needs.

9. Stimulate facilities to recognize opportunities for better coordination of service.

10. Demonstrate the need for philanthropic and public funds through a well-developed information program.

11. Determine and project needs for services, facilities, and personnel.

12. Provide information and guidance for decision-makers.

13. Develop balance among the various categories of facilities within the area.

14. Maintain flexibility in planning.

15. Develop systematic procedures for evaluating projects.

16. Promote understanding of the planning process on the part of the public and appropriate groups.

17. Cooperate with appropriate governmental and private agencies.

18. Coordinate activities with other community planning agencies.

19. Identify the value judgments involved in the provision of adequate facilities and services and involve the community in decision-making.

20. Maintain a central storehouse for a body of knowledge and specialists which other local organizations are unable to maintain.

21. Develop broad participation in the decision-making process.

22. Analyze new trends in the organization of medical care and apprize the public and appropriate groups of their possible impact on the demand for services and facilities.

*Source:* Joel May, *Health Planning: Its Past and Potential*, Health Administration Perspectives, no. A5 (Chicago: Center for Health Administration Studies, University of Chicago, 1967), 41–42.

academic medicine and favored elite decision-making to create hierarchical regionalism; the second, backed by a much less politically powerful liberal-leaning public health group, favored community decision-making to shift the control away from physicians and hospitals toward "the people."

Although leaders in the public health network had long been involved in efforts to institute regionalism, these groups became more distinct and oppositional, emphasizing different aspects of planning and hence different ways to rationalize the health care system. Indeed, when the Johnson administration focused on reforming the health care delivery system, two groups were created that were related, but that worked in parallel lanes. One was the President's Commission on Heart Disease, Cancer and Stroke, which was chaired by Dr. Michael DeBakey, a noted cardiac surgeon from Baylor University's academic medical center in Texas. The second group was the White House Task Force on Health, chaired by George James, the commissioner of health for New York City. As William Kissick, head of the Office of Program Planning and Evaluation in the Office of the Surgeon General of the Public Health Service from 1966 to 1968, described it, these groups had the same concerns, and worked on the same problems, but from different perspectives.[15] Two drastically different bills emerged as a result, and were enacted just months apart: The Heart Disease, Cancer and Stroke Program passed in late 1965, and the Comprehensive Health Planning Act in 1966.[16]

## From Heart Disease, Cancer, and Stroke Emerged Regional Medical Programs

Shortly after President Johnson took office in January 1964, he formed the Commission on Heart Disease, Cancer and Stroke to develop "*A National Program* to Conquer Heart Disease, Cancer, and Stroke" (emphasis added). As the title of the report suggests, a systematic plan for the U.S. health care system was developed and specified in 35 recommendations (see Table 7.2). Similar to the National Health Plan proposed in 1938 (and discussed in Part II) almost every component of the plan was implemented in separate bills over several years. For example, as Secretary Anthony Celebrezze of HEW commented, "the first three recommendations of the Commission's report" were contained in a bill titled, "Regional Medical Complexes for Heart Disease, Cancer, Stroke and Other Diseases," whereas community-wide planning recommendations (#6–8), which would include local and state public health departments, were put into the Comprehensive Health Planning Act of 1966, and the manpower recommendations (#11, #19–27) were contained in the Health Manpower Act of 1968.[17]

*Table 7.2* **Recommendations from President's Commission on Heart Disease, Cancer and Stroke Report (The Commission recommends ... )**

New Institutions to Create Regionalism (#1–#4)
Regional Centers for Heart Disease, Cancer and Stroke
  Rec #1: the establishment of a national network of Regional Heart Disease, Cancer and Stroke Centers for clinical investigation, teaching and patient care, in universities, hospitals and research institutes and other institutions across the country.
Diagnostic and Treatment Stations
  Rec #2: the establishment of a national network of Diagnostic and Treatment Stations in communities across the nation, to bring the highest medical skills in heart disease, cancer and stroke within reach of every citizen.
Development of Medical Complexes
  Rec #3: a broad and flexible program of grant support be undertaken to stimulate the formation of medical complexes whereby university medical schools, hospitals and other health care and research agencies and institutions work in concert.
Development of Additional Centers of Excellence
  Rec #4: a program of developmental grants to medical schools to enable these institutions to improve their total capability for both academic and research programs for the ultimate purpose of creating a greatly increased number of true "centers of excellence" in medical education and research.
A National Stroke Program Unit
  Rec #5: the establishment of a National Stroke Program directed by an administrative unit to be created within the appropriate unit of the Public Health Service to coordinate the numerous existing and proposed activities in the field of stroke.

Develop Community-based Organizations (#6–#8)
Community Planning Grants
  Rec #6: a special program of incentive grants to communities to stimulate the development of a system for the planning and coordination of health activities.
Community Health Research and Demonstration
  Rec #7: that greatly increased emphasis and support be given to programs of community health research and research training within the Public Health Service, and that the program of demonstration projects under the Community Health Services and Facilities Act of 1961 be freed from existing appropriations ceilings, more adequately funded, and more liberally interpreted.
Support of Community Programs
  Rec #8: that appropriate units of the Public Health Service be given authority and funds for programs of project grants to community agencies, such as public health departments, voluntary agencies, and others, and that the Vocational Rehabilitation Administration launch a 5-year development program to expand its rehabilitation programs for victims of heart disease, cancer and stroke.

*(continued)*

*Table 7.2* **Continued**

Statewide Programs for Heart Disease Control

    Rec #9: that the Public Health Service be given authority and funds to establish and maintain coordinated Statewide laboratory facilities necessary for heart disease control programs.

National Cervical Cancer Detection Program

    Rec #10: the development of a national program for the early detection of cervical cancer.

Continuing Education of the Health Professions

    Rec #11: that appropriate units of the Public Health Service, and the Vocational Rehabilitation Administration, be provided with funds and any additional authority that may be necessary to spearhead a national program for the continuing education of the health professions.

Public Information on Heart Disease, Cancer and Stroke

    Rec #12: that the Federal government, primarily through the Public Health Service, recognize that public information is a primary responsibility and a major instrument for the prevention and control of disease, and that this activity be encouraged and supported on a scale commensurate with its importance.

The Development of New Knowledge

Biomedical Research Institutes

    Rec #13: the establishment of 25 non-categorical biomedical research institutes at qualified institutions throughout the country.

Specialized Research Centers

    Rec #14: the establishment of Specialized Research Centers for intensive study of specific aspects of heart disease, cancer and stroke to supplement the research and training efforts of the regional centers previously described.

Research Project Grants

    Rec #15: endorses the existing system of review of research project grants by study sections and advisory councils at the National Institutes of Health and recommends intensified and expanded support of research in heart disease, cancer and stroke.

Contracting Authority for Research and Development

    Rec #16: that existing Public Health Service authority to contract for research and development be broadened and special funds be earmarked for the use of this mechanism.

General Support for Research

    Rec #17: that the existing General Research Support grants Program of the National Institutes of Health be expanded as rapidly as possible to a level of 15 percent of the total NIH research and training budget and that the program be altered to increase its effectiveness.

    Rec #18: that the Federal Government develop a standard Government-wide policy for payment of the full costs attributable to research grant awards.

*Table 7.2* **Continued**

Education and Training of Health Manpower

Expansion of Resources for Preparation of Health Manpower

Rec #19: that legislation be sought to permit forthright support of medical education, this program to include formula grants to the health professions schools.

Recruitment for the Health Professions

Rec #20: programs designed to attract young people into the health professions and related disciplines.

Undergraduate Training in Medical and Dental Schools

Rec #21: the continuation and expansion of existing grant programs to support undergraduate training in medical schools in heart disease; undergraduate training in medical and dental school in cancer; and medical undergraduate training in rehabilitation.

Training for Research

Rec #22: that the national program of research training grants be enlarged and expanded at a rate commensurate with the training capacity of organizations so engaged and the national pool of young investigators desirous of such training.

Support of Clinical Training

Rec #23: the establishment of clinical fellowships and full-time clinical investigatorships in heart disease and stroke, the expansion of clinical training programs in cancer, and the establishment of clinical fellowships in rehabilitation.

Stabilization of Academic Positions

Rec #24: the establishment of full-time career awards in universities and other institutions, not only for research personnel but also for clinical investigators and clinical professors.

Training of Health Technicians

Rec #25: greatly increased effort and investment in the recruitment and training of health technicians and other paramedical personnel whose skills are essential to the control of heart disease, cancer and stroke.

Training of Specialists in Health Communications

Rec #26: that the Office of Information and Publications in the Office of the Surgeon General be allocated a specific annual sum of $1 million solely for training specialists in health communications.

Continuous Assessment of Health Manpower Needs

Rec #27: the establishment in the Bureau of State Services (Community Health) of the Public Health Service of a health manpower unit, comparable to the research manpower unit of the National Institutes of Health, responsible for continuous assessment of national manpower requirements for health services.

(*continued*)

*Table 7.2* **Continued**

Additional Facilities and Resources

Expanding Patient Care Facilities

Rec #28: wholeheartedly endorses the 1964 Amendments to the Hospital and Medical Facilities Construction (Hill-Burton) Act and urges their full implementation.

Strengthening the Federal Hospital Program

Rec #29: the existing Federal hospital systems administered by the Veterans Administration and the Public Health Service be given authority and funds which will enable them to augment their contribution to research, training and patient care in heart disease, cancer and stroke.

Medical Libraries

Rec #30: that the National Library of Medicine be authorized and adequately supported to serve its logical and necessary function as the primary source for strengthening the nation's medical library system.

National Medical Audiovisual Center

Rec #31: that the Public Health Service Audiovisual Facility be enlarged in scope and strengthened so that it may become a National Medical Audiovisual Center.

Statistical Programs

Rec #32: improved systems for the collection, interpretation, and dissemination of statistics essential to the understanding and efficient control of heart disease, cancer and stroke.

Animal Resources for Biomedical Research

Rec #33: additional appropriations and authority as needed to enable the Division of Research Facilities and Resources, NIH, to support an improved national program of construction of laboratory animal facilities, to contrast special regional facilities, and to support the training of specialists in the care of animals needed for biomedical research.

A Clearinghouse for Drug Information

Rec #34: endorses current proposals for the establishment of a National Drug Information Clearinghouse, in association with the National Library of Medicine, serving and supporting governmental and nongovernmental drug information units.

International Research and Training Programs

Rec #35: endorses the principle that support of research outside the United States by competent foreign nationals, collaborative research involving American and foreign laboratories, training of American scientists in foreign laboratories and of foreign scientists in American laboratories are in our national interest, and endorses programs designed to achieve such ends.

*Source:* President's Commission on Heart Disease, Cancer and Stroke, *Report to the President: A National Program to Conquer Heart Disease, Cancer and Stroke,* Vol. 1, Part I. December 1964.

While the strategy of passing multiple bills—each with a separate aim within the system—might have made passage more politically feasible, since none of these separate bills were explicitly implemented with the other bills in mind, it also (ironically, given the goals of planning) decreased coordination and increased fragmentation. This was Grow and Hide in action, because the "grand plan" was never explicitly named or acknowledged. As an AMA representative, William Ruhe, said years later in 1991, "If one tried to translate the recommendations of the [Commission's] report into the proposed legislation, one [would have] had great difficulty in tracking how one lead . . . to another."[18]

From the very beginning there was a disjuncture between what was presented on the surface as the commission's intent and what proponents hoped to achieve. For example, the commission's name, and the president and the chairman's claimed purpose for the commission, suggested promoting "better care for patients with heart disease, cancer, and stroke, and to bring to the people the latest . . . medical information available."[19] However, the final report revealed much more expansive goals. Volume I of the final report explained how the 35 recommendations were developed in two general categories: the first category included "recommendations, which were directed specifically at the three diseases in question," whereas the second category dealt much more broadly with reforming the entire medical care system:

> [H]eart disease, cancer and stroke cannot realistically be considered apart from the broad problems of American science and medicine. Therefore, the second category of recommendations—no less essential than the first—is *designed to strengthen the total national resource* for advancing scientific knowledge and providing medical services.[20]

Indeed, only six of the 35 recommendations focused on disease-specific programs. Although the first four recommendations called for new medical institutions—often with "heart disease," "cancer," and "stroke" in their titles—the details reveal that these four recommendations, taken together, called for restructuring the entire health care system along the lines of hierarchical regionalism that had long been advocated. As was envisioned under Hill-Burton, in addition to the hierarchy of regional centers, treatment stations, medical complexes, and centers of excellence, the report also recommended community-based agencies providing prevention and supporting the referral process (recommendations #6–8).

While seven recommendations (#13–18, #33) dealt with establishing or promoting biomedical research, only two of these focused specifically on heart disease, cancer, and stroke (#14 and #15). The remainder promoted research for all diseases. Similarly, ten recommendations focused on expansions for health manpower (#11, #19–27), which did not just focus on expansions for specialists related to heart disease, cancer, and stroke, but across the medical and allied health professions to staff the entire system. The commission explained its expansive focus as follows: "The diseases that fall within our purview cause over 70 percent of all deaths; consequently, we believe we cannot separate their requirements from those of the rest of medicine . . . therefore, that we must concern ourselves with the manpower needs of the entire social institutions we call health."[21]

Not only did the report call for substantial restructuring of the U.S. health care system, it also recommended "fusing the worlds of science and practice." This was a central concern of President Johnson—to not just spend more money on research in NIH, but to translate that research into real programs that could help people on the ground. As Johnson put it in his Health Message to Congress, "the American people are not receiving the full benefits of what medical research has already accomplished."[22] It is likely that Johnson's opinion about what was referred to as the "health gap" was heavily influenced by the members of the committee, which was disproportionately made up of leaders in academic medicine.[23] They believed that the science generated by NIH-funded research in the nation's medical schools was not well understood by private practice physicians, and therefore the American people were not able to benefit from their research.[24] Not surprisingly, and as will become more clear, private practice physicians did not agree with this assessment.

Similar to the 1950s, the commission report referred to voluntary agencies as the heart and center of the health care system, not only because they supported democracy, but because they engaged in "creative partnership" in support of private practice.[25] While the details of the report called for an important role for all levels of government and the need for public resources, it emphasized building on the existing private system and local and state initiatives. Observe the crafting of Grow and Hide: in Volume I's executive summary, which was widely distributed, the federal government was not even mentioned; Volume II specified the role of the federal government and other public institutions, but the chair of the commission, Dr. DeBakey, made clear that this volume was not widely distributed.[26] Moreover, even in Volume II, when state and local government support was mentioned, the committee downplayed the government's role and argued that government support would increase "personal and scientific freedom."[27]

Similar to Medicare and Medicaid, Johnson moved very quickly to leverage the democratic majorities in Congress to pass planning legislation. After the commission submitted its report to the president in December 1964, Congress drew up a bill in January, and hearings were held in February 1965. Karl Yordy, the first staff member at NIH to run the Regional Medical Program that would eventually emerge out of this legislation, remarked that

> this came along at precisely the same time as the passage of Medicare and Medicaid, which, as you know, organized medicine had strongly opposed, and they viewed that as a great defeat. Right after Medicare and Medicaid passed, the leadership of AMA came to the secretary and said, "We may have a rebellion on our hands on the part of the physicians of the country if you strike us with this second blow after Medicare and Medicaid."[28]

All the stakeholders involved in the development of this planning legislation corroborated Yordy's story, and reported that when the AMA leadership finally focused on the DeBakey Commission's report and resulting legislation, they "went ballistic."[29] Dr. Phillip Lee, who was the assistant secretary of health, education, and welfare from 1965 to 1969, also commented that "they were coming along at the same time," and the AMA was "almost more exercised about Regional Medical Programs than they were about Medicare, and that's saying quite a bit. . . . They [the AMA] were determined not to have a program that could really restructure the organization of the medical community."[30] As Lee and others explained, when the AMA looked at the details of the commission's report, they understood the enormity of the proposed changes to the health care delivery system.

Stakeholders involved in passing this legislation confirmed how politically difficult it was, and, importantly, they pointed out that it was much more politically fraught than Medicare and Medicaid. Because while these programs adopted the Blue Cross Blue Shield method of financing care, which was extremely favorable to organized medicine, the planning legislation attempted to change how the delivery system was organized.[31] What they did not say explicitly—but what nonetheless becomes clear—was that these reform efforts were marked by added political conflict from the old tension between physicians in academic medicine and physicians in private practice. Because the proposed reforms added significantly more funding and thus more power to academic medical centers, private practice physicians worried that they would have less power over how they practiced medicine.[32]

Dr. Irving Page, the editor of *Modern Medicine*, wrote, "The Senate hearings have been superficial, without regard for the long-range effects the commission report might have if enacted into law."[33] In the same issue, the AMA released a staff report, which argued that "the degree of *implicit* federalization and coercion are novel . . . in the Commission's proposal 'to reorganize medical services.' "[34] The American Academy of General Practice made a similar point: that the planning legislation would pose a much greater threat to private practice medicine than any associated with public health insurance.[35] The AMA was more "exercised" about the bill for two reasons. First, they felt tricked by Johnson due to the timing (coming immediately after the passage of Medicare and Medicaid), and second, because the bill was hidden under the title "Heart Disease, Cancer and Stroke." Even those favorable to the legislation acknowledged the title's deception. The Dean of Dartmouth's medical school wrote, "Next to Medicare, [Congress's] most significant actions were the Health Disease, Cancer, and Stroke Amendments of 1965 and the Comprehensive Health Planning and Public Health Services Amendments of 1966. The title of the former is *deceptive*; although focusing superficially on the major killer diseases, the act actually was a first step toward regionalization of the nation's health facilities and personnel."[36]

There were two major congressional hearings held on the proposed bill; in both, agency officials also attempted to hide the significance of the proposed reforms, arguing instead that the bill focused on the three major diseases.[37] For example, Secretary Celebrezze of HEW started his testimony by enumerating the "grim facts" associated with the "enormity of the toll in death, disability and economic burden exacted from the people of the United States by heart disease, cancer, and stroke." Celebrezze also emphasized local control and assured members of Congress that "[w]e are not proposing that the Federal Government operate this framework, I want to emphasize that [again]."[38]

Despite these assurances, committee members pressed to understand the proposed new organizational structure to reform the delivery system. As discussed previously (and shown in Table 7.2), the commission's report proposed an extensive list of new institutions to create regionalism, but members of Congress had a difficult time understanding how each new form fit with the others. The following exchange in the hearings was not unusual:

REP. SPRINGER (R-IL): You still have me a little vague here and I want to be crystal clear. You are talking about 30 regional centers?
DR. DEMPSEY (SPECIAL ASSISTANT TO THE SECRETARY, HEALTH AND MEDICAL AFFAIRS, HEW): Complexes.
REP. SPRINGER: Are you abandoning the 32 medical complexes?
DR. DEMPSEY: No sir; there are already a number—excuse me, I may have misunderstood. Did you ask if we were abandoning the medical complexes?
REP. SPRINGER: You are recommending 30 regional complexes?
DR. DEMPSEY: That is right.
REP SPRINGER: Are you thereby combining the regional center with the medical complex?
DR. DEMPSEY: In the centers there are complexes.

REP. SPRINGER: Are you combing the regional center with the medical complex?

DR. DEMPSEY: Yes.

REP. SPRINGER: In the recommendations of the DeBakey report for 32 medical complexes, which are separate from regional centers, you are not recommending those as being separate.

DR. DEMPSEY: The medical complexes in the DeBakey report envisioned the categorical centers as being included. We are following the DeBakey report in that combination.

REP. SPRINGER: I still don't get it . . .[39]

As a result of this confusion and AMA opposition, compromises were made[40] and the law was changed from establishing regional medical complexes with hierarchical regionalism and centers of excellence to "regional medical programs" with a network of "cooperative arrangements" *voluntarily* entered into. Also added to the bill was the following language: "To accomplish these ends without interfering with the patients, or the methods of financing, of patient care or professional practice."[41]

Even with these major compromises—to encourage rather than mandate cooperative arrangements and to not interfere with practice patterns—the bill passed by only one vote.[42] This is not surprising, as any proposal to change the health care delivery system in the United States has always been marked by enormous opposition. However, even the watered-down version that did pass remained controversial, in part because it was never entirely clear what the bill was supposed to achieve. Indeed, confusion surfaced immediately over the question of which agency should administer the program. The physician-scientists argued that the purpose of the legislation was to foster the translation and dissemination of NIH-funded research for the three major diseases out to the broader provider community (the "knowledge gap" argument). That aspect of the bill seemed appropriate for the NIH. Privately, these same scientists agreed that they wanted the program to reside in the NIH because they believed the medical schools, which they hoped would be in charge of producing regional plans and structural reforms, would be more favorable toward the program if it was in the NIH—the only true scientific agency, in their view.

The AMA also wanted the program to be in the NIH, so as to signal that the legislation would focus solely on the dissemination of research information. Despite the change in legislative language, the AMA did not trust the federal government, and was worried that if the program resided elsewhere—in the Public Health Service (PHS) arm of the Department of Health, Education, and Welfare (HEW), for example—staff might focus on changing medical practice.

This was not an unfounded concern. Although commission members argued in 1965 that they were not trying to change practice patterns, at a reconvening of key stakeholders in 1991 to reflect on the legislation and resulting Regional Medical Programs (RMPs), it was clear that changing the structure of health care delivery had been the intent. Indeed, this was a long-standing concern among private practice physicians—that academic medical centers would steal their patients. DeBakey admitted this:

> [W]hen we first conceived the program . . . we wanted to take care of patients, but as we indicated in the report, we also wanted not to interfere with the patterns of practice. Well, it became increasingly difficult to do both. You either had to interfere somewhat with the patterns of practice or you would not be able to create or implement the concept. But as soon as you started interfering with the patterns of practice, then you got a lot of objections.[43]

The director of the NIH, James A. Shannon, did not want to administer the program because it was not a research program. Nonetheless, Senator Lister Hill and Chairman DeBakey convinced Shannon that RMPs needed to be administered by the NIH to "make sure that it got off on the right foot, [and to] make sure that the relationships with the medical schools were well established."[44] Nonetheless, despite the commission's hope that giving the NIH administrative authority would have a legitimizing effect, the lack of clarity as to the RMPs' purpose persisted. By the end of the first year, even Dr. Robert Q. Marston, the first director of RMPs, admitted that while RMPs were exciting, it was "difficult to describe precisely what they did."[45] The board members who reviewed the RMP grant proposals also had drastically different perspectives about the purpose of RMP grants: some saw the program as fulfilling the goals of regionalism, while others saw the program as filling in the knowledge gap.

As a result, there was little consistency across RMPs. For example, a multistate RMP in the West focused on something close to regionalization of care.[46] Contrary to the language in the act to not change practice patterns, Dr. Hilmon Castle, who directed that RMP, described how developing centers of excellence in Utah, which changed practice patterns, was met with no resistance because Utah only had one main medical center—the University of Utah—in a large geographic area."[47] Irving Lewis described his work with an RMP in the Bronx, New York, as working on projects studying the availability of health manpower."[48]

Still others viewed RMPs as an opportunity to instill goals of equity in delivery model reforms. Board member Dr. Leonidas Berry, who was the only

African American on the 12-member advisory board and who served during a time of great transition—not only in medical care but in terms of social and racial dynamics in the United States—explained:

> The great Civil Rights movement had just achieved the Civil Rights Act of 1964 amid much turmoil and challenges of the status quo in medical human rights. Very few Black doctors were on the staffs of white hospitals in the north. None in the south. Northern medical schools had only token Black admissions. Black patients were treated mostly in public hospitals, in the several poorly funded Black hospitals or in segregated wards in white hospitals with inferior facilities. [This] describes the tenor and state of affairs for Blacks and minorities in the struggle for equality of opportunities and quality medical care as RMP had its beginning."[49]

Given this context and the fact that Berry "was already considerably in the struggle," he viewed his role on the board as "challeng[ing] grant applications from states and medical schools where there were known segregated and inferior facilities." However, while this was his main priority, he had almost no vocal support from other members on the board: "[A]fter nearly a year, Mary Bunting PhD, President of Radcliffe College was the first and only person to speak out in the council to support my challenges."[50]

While many involved in RMPs, especially those submitting grant proposals and running the programs, believed these broader goals were for the better and fit with the legislation's "original" intent, others criticized the program for its deception and lack of focus on what was, in their view, the legislation's stated goal: to improve the knowledge gap by increasing translation of knowledge to the community. However, even when RMPs did focus on closing the knowledge gap, many viewed this work as meaningless. Dr. Merlin DuVal, who ran an RMP in Arizona, and then became assistant secretary of HEW from 1971 to 1973, commented that while RMPs focused on restructuring that was important, "what emerged [instead] really [just] dealt with moving information."[51] This is how critics talked about the efforts to address the knowledge gap—as just moving information around.

## Comprehensive Health Planning (CHP)

The Comprehensive Health Planning (CHP) Act was passed at the same time as RMPs in 1966, but administered by the Public Health Service in the Department of Health, Education, and Welfare. CHP's goals originated from

Hill-Burton—to rationalize the system by conducting area-wide planning—and built explicitly on the 1961 act, which created area-wide planning agencies but with even more efforts to empower citizen decision-making around local health planning.[52] As public health scholar Lewis Polk observed in 1968, "[the] general trend ... of making Federal grants to groups even closer to the people continued."[53] When the act was first passed in 1966 it provided planning grants to state agencies, and eventually to local health departments and a plethora of other local organizations. Yet there were constant reminders that the Planning Act did not represent *government* oversight.[54] As Surgeon General William Stewart said in his speech at the 1967 National Health Forum, "it must be emphasized that comprehensive health planning does not represent the imposition of a master plan by Government upon the people. . . . As for the role of Government in the process, it is the servant and not the master."[55]

These were not hollow assurances; it was written into the bill that governmental agencies would have little authority. The CHP Act (Public Law 89-749) stipulated that "[Federal] funds will be used to supplement and ... to increase ... and not supplant non-Federal funds."[56] The Act created "A Agencies" at the state level and "B Agencies" at the regional level that were given a mandate to plan health services, at least in theory.[57] But until 1972, these agencies were virtually powerless. Despite the law's mandate to plan, the agencies in charge of planning had no authority to accomplish its mandate.[58]

As Surgeon General Stewart acknowledged, "The Act does not endow [the state health planning] agency with direct authority. [But] if it does its job well, it will certainly be influential in the fundamental decision on where the state health dollar should go, and on where a great many federal dollars would go as well."[59] He also advised that the "planning partnership" should include the "Federal government and its state and local counterparts [as well as] all health resources, public and private, individual and institutions. In this partnership each element would direct its efforts toward a common goal, rather than toward a separate objective, separately established. This concept is my interpretation of 'creative federalism' as applied to health."[60] Given the degree of fragmentation and confusion that already existed across all levels of government, one might think this Pollyannaish view of "creative federalism" suggests great naiveté on the part of Stewart. Nonetheless, he goes on to highlight the challenges by using the federal government as an example:

[H]ere in Washington, we need to look no farther than our own Department—every one of the major agencies of DHEW has a substantial health commitment. Then there are the programs of OEO, Appalachia, the new Departments of Transportation and Housing and Urban Development, the old Departments of Agriculture and

Interior—all involved to a greater or lesser extent in work related to our own. This same fragmented pattern carries over to the states, the cities and the rural areas. *It is extraordinarily difficult—as you well know—to find out who is in charge of what, spending which dollar for what purpose."*[61]

As Stewart noted, the country had arrived "at a critical moment of truth." There was a public mandate for more access to care, and for more financial protection against the high cost of that care, but at the same time there was also more fragmentation and complexity in the health care system, which encouraged increasing costs, and furthermore a planning bill that gave no authority to any entity to truly address the problems of complexity and high costs. Although Stewart's anticipation of goodwill might appear naïve, when one considers the government's lack of authority, goodwill was the only real hope.[62]

Another aspect of the CHP Act that received very little attention was the reorganization of the federal public health grant-in-aid funds that were established under the Social Security Act in 1935 (see Chapters 4 and 6 for an explanation of their significance). As described in Chapter 6, these funds became more categorical as they grew over time, requiring states to direct their local health departments to devote funding in specific areas, such as mental health, cancer, and tuberculosis.[63] In 1966, under the CHP legislation, the first block grant program was established, which consolidated nine categorical formula grant programs into a block grant for "comprehensive public health services." It was a relatively small program, never exceeding $90 million, but its development was important for several reasons. First, a critical rationale for the flexible block grant approach was to allow local preferences to have more influence over the allocation of public health resources. As such, the CHP agencies (CHPs) were supposed to include the block grant funds in their planning considerations. However, the vast majority of states reported in 1975 that their CHPs were not involved in policy decisions regarding the block grants.[64] This is important, because although CHPs were supposed to consider planning for the entire health care system at the local level, they tended to focus primarily on planning the private sector. A public health analyst writing in the *American Journal of Public Health* put it this way: "While hospitals have HSAs [Health Service Areas], state and local public health departments have nothing. Many public agencies that are supported entirely from tax funds provide little opportunity for the public to participate in the process of setting policy and priorities, or allocating resources."[65]

Nonetheless, public health officials continued to hope that the Planning Act would rationalize the private health care system, and make the entire (public and private) system more equitable. One specific hope was that public hospitals

*Table 7.3* **Recommendations of 1967 Conference Impact of Government Programs on Public Hospitals**

1. Obtain and maintain effective professional administrative and clinical leaders in each public hospital.
2. Integrate private patients into the public hospital.
3. Involve the entire community in the affairs of the hospital; include the community's influentials and users of the hospital's service.
4. Interdigitate the public hospital with the voluntary hospital system, to create a single system in each community.
5. Whenever possible, evolve interlocking managerial arrangements, both administrative and clinical, between the public hospital and an affiliated medical school.
6. Establish in the public hospital a full-time medical staff drawn from all the licensed physicians in the community and offer privileges and use of facilities to private practitioners.
7. Initiate participation of the public hospital in new programs, such as neighborhood health centers, and have the public hospital offer leadership and resources in cooperation with private hospitals.
8. Affiliate with educational programs in hospital administration, public health, administrative medicine, and public administration.
9. Establish and finance units for effective planning and evaluation and provide for research in patient care at each hospital.

*These recommendations are pertinent and applicable to all hospitals. While duality of public and private financing of health care remain and duality of administrative responsibility will continue, the trend will be toward eliminating differences in private and public hospitals to provide better service to the community.*

*Source:* Conference Report: "Impact of Governmental Programs on Public Hospitals: Directions for the Future," *Public Health Reports* 83, no. 1 (1968): 53–60; list and quote from p. 59.

would be improved to be on par with voluntary private hospitals. In June 1967, the PHS convened a conference for select invitees to discuss the issues confronting public hospitals as a result of new and expanded federal and state health programs. Twenty-one participants attended, representing heads of federal agencies and a cross-section of public hospitals across the country, as well as representatives from the AHA, and hospital planning associations.[66] The conference summary reveals that public health officials argued it was critical "to assure that financial resources available from new programs, such as Medicare and Medicaid, are used to the fullest advantage and are available to public as well as private hospitals."[67] Indeed, they specified nine recommendations for how such equity could be realized (see Table 7.3).

Three facts are noteworthy about these recommendations toward creating more equity in the U.S. hospital system. First, most of the recommendations were focused on changing the behavior of public hospitals, with no explicit mention of how private voluntary hospitals should change. Second, these represented "good faith" recommendations. No administrative unit was given authority to carry out such recommendations. Third, although following the list of recommendations is an acknowledgment of how difficult it may be to achieve the recommendations in light of the "duality in public and private financing [and administration]," no steps were recommended to eliminate this duality of treatment and the two-tiered system it created. In sum, neither planning nor a document focused on the status of public hospitals would consider changing the relationship between public and private facilities within the U.S. health system.

By 1968, it was already clear that neither the RMPs nor the CHP Act was accomplishing any of the goals related to rational planning, though for very different reasons. Additionally, the fact that the two programs were in conflict contributed to the eventual demise of government health planning in the United States.

## Conflict between RMPs and CHPs

Karl Yordy, the initial deputy director of Regional Medical Programs when it started at NIH, recalled that after the CHP legislation was proposed a good friend asked him to explain the relationship between CHPs and RMPs. "My answer, which was the honest answer, was, no, I could not. Because I don't think at that point there was, in fact, an articulated view of what the relationship was between the two."[68] Not only was there no formal relationship between the two programs, but physician-scientists across the country—especially those running RMPs—had a particularly negative view of the CHP law. Chairman DeBakey objected to the Comprehensive Health Planning program and its legislation, and even talked to President Johnson about his objections. As DeBakey explained, he "was afraid that first it would interfere with [RMPs] and, secondly, it would in time become perhaps too dictatorial."[69] The dean of Dartmouth's medical school also showed his bias when describing the RMPs in 1970 as having "the effect of stimulating fundamental dialogue and experiment pointing toward reorganization of the nation's health resources along logical lines," whereas CHP, "its companion act," was described as having "produced no dramatic results." Similar to DeBakey's comment about a tendency toward becoming "dictatorial," the dean also mentioned that CHPs have "authority for broad planning in the individual state governments," which he viewed as a negative because it was influenced by local politics.[70] Irving Lewis, who ran the RMP in the Bronx, also described the programs as completely separate:

> There were two separate worlds. . . . One was the RMP front, which created a power base for the medical schools in the health services front, but with a focus on medical care and cooperative arrangements. The other was a health planning front, with a focus on health, called the Comprehensive Health Planning legislation, which went down the route of state and local governments. There was a completely different political power base, and my feeling is that they never came together. The two power bases never joined hands.[71]

That is why in 1968, just three years after passage, when RMPs were moved from the NIH to the newly established (via reorganization of the Public Health Service) Health Services and Mental Health Administration (HSMHA) to work in closer collaboration with CHP, those involved in RMPs described it as the "kiss of death."[72] Although the director of RMPs, Robert Q. Marston, wanted the program to remain in the NIH because he wanted the program "tied to the science base of the nation," there was never much support for RMPs among other leaders within the NIH.[73] Unfortunately, there was not much support for RMPs in the HSMHA either. Six months after the program was moved over to the HSMHA, Marston was asked to be the director of the NIH, and, as Karl Yordy put it, "RMP was, in a sense, left to fend for itself in a new organizational environment that was not all entirely friendly to RMP."[74]

CHP advocates were quite negative about the administrative use of RMP funding. According to Yale University public health professor John D. Thompson, who was on the National Health Planning Board for the CHP, the CHP constituency included social planners, consumer groups, and state and local public health communities, whereas RMPs' constituency mainly relied on the medical schools and academic medical centers. The CHP constituency "screamed that the old medical schools were taking over the RMP; that the schools took the money and ran, and didn't do anything. Meanwhile they said we're out here working in the trenches for years, we were a consumer-based organization . . . involving consumers in health care decisions."[75]

While it is true that RMPs' constituency mainly included medical schools, the largesse of NIH funding was growing and becoming more integral to the political economy of the health care industry, especially in urban areas.[76] With this growth, the political power of academic medical centers was growing, too, but they cared most about NIH research and manpower funding, so when RMP was moved out of the NIH and under the purview of CHPs, RMP became marginalized even in the view of its original defenders.[77]

Shortly after the RMP reorganization, President Richard Nixon came into office in January 1969. Of course, the new administration had nothing to do with the origins of RMP, and according to Thompson he "came in with an attitude that was fairly negative to all of the products of the Great Society."[78] Nonetheless, despite the lack of support for RMP, in 1970 the combined program was amended (P.L. 91-515) to emphasize yet another renewed focused on the regionalization of health care resources, and renewed hope that the two programs could be logically coordinated. Specifically, the amendment emphasized linking primary to secondary and tertiary care with more funding for new construction and manpower for primary care in underserved areas. A requirement was also added that area-wide CHP agencies should comment on RMP grant proposals within their planning areas—a requirement RMP leaders clearly viewed as "dictatorial."[79] In 1972, the program received a significant increase in funding to support this redirection. Yet by 1973 the Nixon administration budget for FY 1974 had eliminated the RMPs, stating that the programs "have not been carried out according to any consistent theme or set of priorities." The *New York Times* reported further that "critics say the programs have been little more than continuing education programs for doctors and in some respects duplicate functions that could be carried out satisfactorily by other agencies."[80]

Not only were RMPs expansionary at a time when the national mood was beginning to change from focusing on expanding access to cost control, but, as suggested by the *New York Times*, there was concern that the money was being wasted on the medical schools. William Ruhe, who worked for the AMA, recalled that "the facts stuck in many people's craw that the government was putting up money for the continuing education of rich physicians who could easily afford to provide their own continuing education."[81] Dr. John Zapp, deputy assistant secretary for health legislation, confirmed that from the Nixon administration's perspective, "an awful lot of that money just seemed to be going to the faculties in the different health science centers."[82]

The concern about money related to the RMPs was not unfounded. Many medical schools used the RMP as a means to support their administrative costs. One evaluation reported that some medical schools devoted as much as 40 percent of RMP funds to cover administrative costs.[83] Moreover, the original legislation allocated $500 million a year to the program.[84] As Karl Yordy admitted, that was "big dollars in those days."[85] Even in 1970, when RMPs were under attack, they received $100 million in federal allocation compared to $20 million for CHPs.[86] Thus, when health care costs were becoming a massive concern of the federal government, RMPs became more problematic, because while CHPs were at least attempting to control health care costs, RMPs demanded more funding.[87]

All these factors contributed to the demise of RMPs, but the reign of Grow and Hide explains why the two planning acts that created CHPs and RMPs failed so dismally. During the period from 1964 to 1972, in addition to the passage of Medicare and Medicaid with massive accommodations to the health care industry public insurance, so many other programs were also passed that provided direct access to health care services, working in direct contradiction to cost containment and the rationalization goals of health care planning. While these direct access programs, including community health centers, community mental health centers, and migrant centers, helped fulfill the goals of increasing access, they also contributed to further fragmentation in the administration of the health care system, since "24 different Federal departments and agencies (not including state and local agencies) supported health programs" and coordination between them was minimal. A Senate study focused on the U.S. health care system revealed this fact, and it was reported in *The New York Times* under the heading: "$20 Billion Programs are Termed Uncoordinated and Unnecessarily Costly."[88]

## The Demise of Planning

In response to the failure of CHPs, Congress passed, and President Gerald Ford signed into law, the National Health Planning and Resources Development Act of 1974 (P.L. 93-641). One major new component of the law was the creation of a network of Health Systems Agencies (HSAs) across the country to conduct health planning at the local level. Each HSA had majority consumer representation, and in this way health planning would reflect the "will of the people" in local communities. The act also mandated the establishment of State Health Planning and Development Agencies (SHPDAs) and Statewide Health Coordinating Councils (SHCCs). At the federal level, a new Bureau of Health Planning and Development was established under HEW, as well as a National Health Planning Advisory Council and ten regional Technical Assistance Centers.[89] Despite the creation of all these new entities and the enormous amount of work to get them all up and running, this massive planning legislation was very quickly considered a failure, for three main reasons.

### Policy Design: Planning (Not Regulation)

First, expectations exceeded what the policy design could accomplish—this was a planning bill with weak regulatory teeth. Initially there was a sense that the 1974 act might be a more rigorous form of government regulation—as opposed to voluntary planning—primarily because it required that the new HSAs to conduct Certificate of Need (CON) evaluations for health service institutions interested in developing new capital projects or renovations, or purchasing expensive equipment. The appointed CON review board would examine the proposed hospital investment to determine whether it was really needed. This new requirement reflected the growing emphasis that planning, at least from the federal government's perspective, should focus on cost containment.[90]

By 1974, there was a strong consensus that hospitals' investment decisions resulted in unnecessary duplication of facilities, and also duplication of services across facilities. One study estimated that capital costs of major medical equipment contributed 9% to the annual rise in hospital expenditures.[91] Studies on technological adoption and diffusion revealed that hospitals tended to adopt new technologies regardless of community need. For example, although large hospitals adopted post-operative recovery rooms and intensive care units first, these new technologies quickly became standards of care in all hospitals. In 1958, less than 20% of medium-size hospitals and 10% of small hospitals had intensive care units, but by 1974, 100% and 80%, respectively, had them. Studies revealed the same upward trend for inhalation therapy facilities, radioisotope facilities, and EEGs.[92] HSAs acting as CON review boards were considered the antidote to this wasteful expansion.

The 1974 act required that any hospital or facility participating in federal programs, notably Medicare or Medicaid, must undergo CON review before adopting any new technology or undertaking any new construction.[93] However, despite requiring CON review, there was nothing specified in the federal legislation stipulating that the state must enforce the decision of the board. Similar to CHPs and RMP planning organizations, they could recommend but not enforce. To assure coordination and planning on a "proper scale," the new law prescribed significant detail on intergovernmental arrangements and HSA relationships with other regulatory agencies. Yet all this detail never gave HSAs the authority needed to follow through with a plan.[94] As Brown explained, based on his interviews with HSAs across the country, "In HSA's eyes, federal rules and guidelines are at once offensively specific and unhelpfully vague."[95]

## Democratic Representation versus "Rational" Planning

Second, there was continued confusion over what the democratic representation of HSAs was supposed to achieve versus what the experts thought should be the goal of planning. Many of the same logics that emerged out of the Voluntary Way in the 1950s (see Chapter 5) continued under the 1974 act. From the hospital industry perspective, the 1974 act was supposed to rely on voluntary

"democratic" decision-making instead of an undemocratic regulatory government. However, public health planners wanted a shift from the old Voluntary
Way to assure that HSAs were truly representative. But more inclusive decision-
making did not guarantee cost control, which was the primary aim from the
government's perspective.

Several studies showed that many consumer representatives in HSAs favored
increasing the supply of technology and health care facilities, because they were
more concerned about access problems or equity issues.[96] Although the act
stated improvements to access and quality of care and more equity as goals of
the planning program, in reality the only activities supported by the act were
around cost control—specifically putting limits on supply through the CON
requirements. Yet in many urban and rural areas, HSAs legitimately identified
expansionary needs to improve access to care, especially related to primary care
and outpatient services. But the planning law offered no direct assistance to
solve these problems.[97] In these cases, consumer participation identified needs
that remained unheard.[98]

Indeed, the focus on consumer representation as the silver bullet for "good"
planning might have actually hindered the planning program, because no level of
"perfect" representation would have overcome the other structural problems—
lack of public accountability, provider dominance, and fragmentation. As James
Morone points out, the effort to empower consumers triggered more confusion
and controversy than any other element of the program, and such efforts misled
many into believing that solving the representational problem would solve the
planning problem.[99] There were numerous amendments added to the act in 1976
and again in 1978, all in an effort to make the HSAs more democratically representative. But while these amendments added numerous detailed requirements
related to which groups should be represented, it never connected community
views to enforceable HSA decision-making.[100]

## Provider Dominance: A Preference for Planning While Calling It Regulation

Finally, the 1974 act failed because *planning* agencies with weak regulatory
authority were no match for a growing and powerful industry. Because construction and renovation projects were developed and generated by private
health care institutions, the planning agencies were always in a strictly reac-
tive posture. And, by definition, a negative posture, because they could only
determine whether expansion should occur, rather than recommending new
projects (that might have been based on ideas emerging from the community).[101] Many HSAs hoped to act as partners in the development process,
but health care institutions were not interested.[102] As Dorothy Ellenburg

concluded from her study of HSAs, planning was "a function of the provider industry, with consumers invited to make input in the provider house."[103] In the American Hospital Association's journal, a capital investment consultant to hospitals referred to the CON as a mere formality, and community participation under the HSAs "as a weapon."[104]

Often HSA recommendations did not hold, recommending against provider requests for expansion.[105] When a negative recommendation was made, state agencies would, due to provider pressure, rule against the local HSAs, or provider groups would bypass the state agencies altogether and go directly to state legislatures, the governor, or the courts.[106] Dr. James Kimmey, director of the Midwest Center for Health Planning, gave the following example at a conference on CON regulation in 1978:

> Fingers Lakes Health Systems Agency in New York worked long and hard . . . to merge some obstetrical units in the Southern part of their region. They finally succeeded. The governor came to town three days later, after everyone had agreed to the merge, and someone raised the question after a speech. He essentially said, "You don't have to worry about that. You can all have your obstetric units. Everybody should have a choice." And that was it. They all had their obstetric units and fifteen years of planning went out the window.[107]

Another study on HSAs explained a similar political bypass of the planning agencies, instead proceeding directly to the Massachusetts legislature. Kimmey confirmed this as well, stating that "if you fail to get a certificate-of-need and you have political clout, you can go to the legislature and get a special bill for the relief of [the] Hospitals, and you end up with a certificate."[108]

Hospitals also utilized the court system to avoid negative CON decisions. Although more costly, the courts often produced a favorable result because it was very hard for HSAs to prove beyond a reasonable doubt that there was insufficient need or too much duplication. What was supposed to be the will of the people in democratic voluntary agencies became in a courtroom a technical planning document expected to hold up to administrative legal review.[109]

CON programs varied substantially by state and some programs were more effective than others.[110] Despite this variation, the general consensus that emerged (and persists to this day) is that health care regulation in the United States does not work. But this conclusion did not emerge innocently from the "evidence." First, the hospital industry was adamant and successful in its lobbying efforts to assure that cost control efforts were structured as decentralized, voluntary planning across multiple local communities. Second, when this fragmented voluntary planning failed,[111] the AHA argued that *federal regulation* failed.

## Hospitals Orchestrate Distrust in Government

When the 1974 Health Planning Act was first passed, the AHA called "the concept of integrated federal, state and local planning sound."[112] Almost every issue of the AHA's journal from 1975 through 1977 had one or two articles that focused on some aspect of planning and how the hospital industry should respond. Based on their writings and conference proceedings, it is clear that the AHA's response was twofold. First, the AHA advised member hospitals to work with architects and financial consultants specializing in hospital construction to help them devise a sophisticated plan that is "rational, objective, technically sound, and of high quality" (so that it will be approved by their local HSA), and also to help them take advantage of tax-exempt bonds to finance construction projects. Second, the AHA recommended an approach to public relations that emphasized two arguments: (1) pitting cost containment against high-quality care, and (2) distrust in government.

Even though the AHA was successful in securing a planning act with no real regulatory authority, there was a strategic shift to refer to the act as regulation. This shift was visible and immediate. Just a month after the bill was passed, in February 1975, the AHA ran a special issue titled "Cost Containment in Design and Construction." The introduction warned that "this obvious expansion of *regulatory activity* continues to cause the private sector great concern."[113] In another article referring to the act, they describe a major shift in the voluntary hospital industry: "[O]ur autonomy has been greatly reduced. Our freedom of action has been severely curtailed. Our organizational prerogatives have been constrained."[114]

In April 1976, the Hospital Administration program at the University of Chicago—the top-ranked program in the country, producing many of the industry's leaders—held its Eighteenth Annual Symposium on Hospital Affairs, that year under the title "Survival in Utopia (Growth Without Expansion)." The chairman of the planning committee, Lad Grapski, explained that the rationale for this provocative title was to invoke the question: "What can a hospital do to insure its survival and visibility as an organization when funds for growth, expansion, or innovation are either cut off or severely rationed, when governmental agencies severely constrain the options and alternatives that are available to us?"[115] Participants at the conference referred to the Health Planning and Resource Development Act as the "Federal Certificate-of-Need Law."[116]

By 1976, hospitals had shifted the conversation from the planning goals of rationalizing the health care system to "rationalization of our *control system*" (emphasis added). David Kinzer, president of the Massachusetts Hospital Association, argued that from an "administrative standpoint [we] have reached the point of unmanageability." To support his point, he showed a table of 37 different regulations and controls facing hospitals in Massachusetts (see Table 7.4).

*Table 7.4* **Massachusetts Hospital Control System (Depicted by President of Massachusetts Hospital Association)**

| "Cost Provocative" | "Cost Suppressive" | "Cost Preventive" |
|---|---|---|
| 1. Hospital Licensure | 17. "Allowable Cost" Controls | 33. Growth and Development |
| 2. Health Manpower Licensure | 18. Cost Related "Inclusive Rate" Controls (Medicaid) | 34. PSRO |
| 3. Professional Education Accreditation (AMA, NLN) | 19. Industrial Accident Rate Controls | 35. Specialized Service Controls (Dialysis etc.) |
| 4. JCAH (Including SSA "Validation Surveys") | 20. Charge Controls | 36. "Appropriateness" reviews (PL-93-641) |
| 5. Hill-Burton Hospital Construction Requirements | 21. Ceiling Controls (Section 223) | 37. Benefit Controls |
| 6. Life Safety Codes (Fire, Plumbing, Sanitation) | 22. Classification Controls (Section 233) | |
| 7. Third Party Mandated Benefits | 23. Medicaid Income Sanctions | |
| 8. Hill-Burton "Charity" Regs | 24. Utilization Committee | |
| 9. Hill-Burton "Community Service" Regs | 25. Occupancy Controls | |
| 10. Minority Rights, Affirm. Action, etc. | 26. Medical Fee Controls | |
| 11. Employee Rights (Taft-Hartley, Minimum Wage Unemp. Comp., Workmen's Comp., OSHA, etc.) | 27. Blue Cross Contract Controls | |
| 12. Patients' Rights | 28. Blue Cross Premium Controls | |
| 13. Environmental Protection | 29. Patient disincentive controls (co-pay, deductibles, etc.) | |
| 14. Emergency Medical Services Regs | 30. Controls on special charges (patient records, etc.) | |
| 15. Community Mental Health | 31. MAC (Maximum Allowable Cost drug reimbursement policy) | |
| 16. Cash Flow Controls (Medicaid) | 32. Malpractice Controls | |

*Source:* Proceedings of the Eighteenth Annual Symposium on Hospital Affairs, April 1976: Survival in Utopia (Growth Without Expansion). David Kinzer, President of the Massachusetts Hospital Association, 'Straws in a Wind of Change," p. 12. Quotation marks in original. Archives from the Center for Health Administration Studies, University of Chicago.

His primary purpose was to illustrate the sheer complexity of the regulatory apparatus facing hospitals: "[W]e have reached the point where the outpouring of the laws and regulations we are getting, both state and federal, has gone far beyond the capacity of the individual hospital to cope with it." His secondary purpose was to emphasize that no one is in control of the regulations. There is no one authority that directs policy and coordinates these 37 controls, and, as a result, the controls run counter to each other, so that "one is pitted against another."[117]

But what is crucially important in Kinzer's presentation is his acknowledgment of AHA's policy and philosophy of "separating planning from certificate-of-need (regulations)." As mentioned, the AHA was instrumental in developing the planning bills at the federal level, and all the state hospital associations were influential in working with state legislatures to create their planning programs. They wanted decentralization and fragmentation, because they knew from years of experience that states were easier to influence. And they wanted voluntary planning because, of course, that meant no one entity had authority to implement a strong regulatory decision. Thus, even though it was the AHAs' successful lobbying that essentially created the byzantine regulatory mosaic shown in Kinzer's table, by 1976 (a mere two years later), he—and the AHA—blamed government for its incompetence.[118]

Kinzer highlights this important irony by pointing out that the AHA still prefers state-level regulatory control (despite his table) because "we can influence it politically more effectively"; however, he also points out that when states experience a fiscal crisis, they are much more likely to gut their state agencies:

> They [the Massachusetts government] had to fire a lot of the people who worked in the welfare department to administer the Medicaid program. The rate-setting commission was even cut down on staff. They had to freeze salaries, and some people quit. So while we have this tremendously elaborate and expensive system, the state is getting to the point where it can't afford it, [and] it is very ironic, but they can't afford to run their own controls . . . the bureaucrats that we have are so badly underpaid that it is ridiculous to compare their competence with the people they are controlling.[119]

A study of CON agencies corroborates Kinzer's story. While each staff person in Massachusetts' CON agency had to review 20 applications per year on average, the ratio was 60 to 1 in Minnesota, and 50 to 1 in Texas.[120] Thus, the extremely fragmented planning program created a paradoxical situation wherein there were a litany of federal and state approvals, checks and rules, which suggested a highly regulatory stringent government program. Yet the reality was a program with a lot of red tape but no regulatory teeth, and an extremely diminished staff in most state governments, making it exceptionally difficult to carry out the rules that were in place.[121]

During this time of "planning," the AHA emphasized the importance of investing in public relations. Every article on public relations made clear that member hospitals should use the following argument: if cost control mechanisms are imposed, health care will not be as comprehensive and lower quality will result. The AHA was very clear that the public needed to be convinced that there was a direct trade-off between comprehensive medical care and cost controls—that the public could not have both. They recommended asking community board members to set priorities and to come to an "agreement on first class care or saving money."[122] Hospital leaders were clear that the American public could not have both. As Grapski explained to a room of hospital administrators in 1975, "the public pressures us to reduce costs almost regardless of the effect [on] ... the quality of [care] ..., while at the same time society holds the utopian view of equal access for all citizens to quality health care?"[123]

While hospitals played an active role in attempting to shape public opinion about the implications of cost controls, they were also concerned about eroding public support for hospitals. Similar to concerns that emerged in the early 1960s about the behavior of voluntary hospitals (see Chapter 5), there were a number of media exposés in the early 1970s describing the greedy behavior of nonprofit voluntary hospitals. In 1972, Martin Drebin, the director of finance at Evanston Hospital in Evanston, Illinois, admonished his colleagues for having "lost all credibility with the public." He noted, "Go out to the newsstand, pick up a magazine or newspaper, and what do you find? An attack on the hospitals. *Saturday Review* has done so; the *Wall Street Journal* has done so; *Fortune, Time* and *Newsweek* published an amazing chart of the Consumer Price Index versus the hospital routine service charge. Nowhere do I see an article saying, 'The hell it is! The devil you say! We aren't that bad.' ... Even *Better Homes and Gardens* attacked you in 1970. Do you realize what a crisis you have?"[124]

At the conference there was some disagreement as to the extent to which the public liked hospitals. But Kinzer argued that support is *relative*: "I don't think the consumers love us. They just hate us less than government!"[125] Another hospital administrator noted: "[T]he Harris poll showed that medicine in general was doing an acceptable job with 42% of the public, and the government was doing an acceptable job with 8% of the public.... So we have 8 percent trying to tell 42 percent how to do it better."[126]

Thus, what changed by the mid-1970s was a recognition that public distrust in government was growing, and Kinzer, as a leader in the AHA, saw a way to exploit that distrust:

> A real fundamental change is taking place in attitudes towards government, as we all know, and it is being judged by the public more by its deeds than by its words. The game of government in Massachusetts, and at the federal level now, is denying benefits and entitlements and rights. The profound impact of this on Massachusetts is that the consumers— (and we keep in close touch with them)—the organized consumer groups are now more angry at government than they are at hospitals. This we have exploited. [We beat the cost control bill] because we kept close connections with the people who, as we told them, are going to be denied care if the governor gets his will on being able to have absolute control over the hospital system. . . . The game now is, "There is only this much money," and then we have got to say over here, "Then there is only this much care." We have got to be very aggressive about this, and we haven't been aggressive enough yet.[127]

Mr. Samuel J. Tibbitts, president of Lutheran Hospital Society of Southern California, in Los Angeles, concurred: "Our problem is with the government. . . . How do we provide all these great things that the public wants and the government doesn't want to pay for?"[128] In response to this question, there was agreement that "good, well organized hospitals" were learning how to get consumer support by "developing their own consumer movements. Their consumers are their publics."[129]

They were not only aware of public distrust, but also keenly aware that the public was *confused*. Because the health care system had become so fragmented, it was almost impossible for the average person to understand its mechanics. John M. Danielson, executive director of Capital Area Health Consortium, in Newington, Connecticut, said: "When you try to explain whole pieces of the health care system in terms of logic that the ordinary guy can understand, it is very tough to do."[130] Building on what the association's public relations department had developed in the 1950s and 1960s, the AHA had a clear strategic approach to exploit the public's confusion. The President's Report laid out a three-part strategy: (1) develop a national advertising campaign to frame hospitals as "responsible and efficient;" (2) shape opinion by holding opinion-leader seminars in key cities with physicians and local civic and business leaders on current health care issues; and (3) work with local media to get the "hospital story free of misconceptions and misinformation to the public as a whole."[131]

Of course, the purpose of shaping public opinion was to then use this influence in negotiations with policymakers. Kinzer was blunt about how to go about it:

> I met with the Governor a few weeks ago to "have a friendly discussion on cost control", and I said "I believe, Governor, you know how much money you have; I don't, and you have trouble here and I am sympathetic. But one thing you have to realize is that if you do what you want to do, we are going to have to cut services." He got mad, and said "I don't believe that." Most politicians don't believe that they can't keep their promises, which have been made abundantly, about comprehensive care for all.[132]

Another example of influence was a bill to investigate the Massachusetts Hospital Association's political action program, the salaries of chief executives of the association, and other lobbying activities, due to the concern that the association was using nonprofit money to influence state decision-making. Perhaps more important than the bill, however, was the president of the Massachusetts Hospital Association's response: "[T]his pleased me, [because] I don't know of a better testimonial to what is happening in Massachusetts and across the country and in AHA. We do have power. When we get going on it we will wield tremendous influence particularly using the hospital effectively as a political instrument."[133]

This quote illustrates how AHA members viewed their organization's political power, and their intent to use that power to yield benefits for the hospital industry. Yet it is important to emphasize that this power was not unique to the Massachusetts Hospital Association. As the quote states, this power was visible across the country and in the AHA.[134]

## Rise of the Competitive Approach

By 1978, when the 20th Symposium on Hospital Affairs was held, it was again focused on cost containment, but titled "Creative Retrenchment," a response to (in their view) "a period of retrenchment in the health services, particularly for the hospitals," and an effort to approach the problem creatively. The creative approach to retrenchment began with two economists presenting various competitive approaches to the problem of rising costs.[135] Tellingly, by this time, the CON approach was being compared to Soviet-style planning: "P.L. 93-641 [the 1974 Act] represents a fascinating attempt to impose central-planning-type planning on a largely decentralized, private health care sector."[136] Health law professor Clark Havighurst and others[137] who promoted the competitive approach argued at the conference that "planning merely provides a forum for political bargaining."[138] In contrast, the competitive approach was presented as apolitical and nongovernmental.[139] Economists who tended to favor the competitive approach concluded that government regulation was ineffective. Even those more sympathetic to national health insurance reviewed the literature on planning and concluded that government regulation failed. Although the government and planning experts were clear from the onset that the 1974 Planning Act was a voluntary effort and not regulation of the industry, the economists' review made no distinction between voluntary planning and government regulation.[140]

This review led to the natural conclusion that competition could replace planning: if HMOs are as effective as their backers hope, there is less rationale for compulsory health planning organizations.[141] Most importantly, the remaining discourse of the conference described the existing system as predominantly private and voluntary, completely ignoring the significant presence of government funding. Competition was presented as protecting the existing private sector. As Republican congressman Dan Rostenkowski (IL) said in 1978, "by all elements of the system working together we can succeed in keeping the health care system of this nation on a voluntary basis."[142]

Just as some rejected planning versus politics as a false dichotomy, others saw competition versus planning as equally false. Many pointed out how government planners would be needed to plan the market, whether that be HMOs or some other form of prepaid group practice: "Economic development planning in many societies follows the pattern of introducing free enterprise and creating markets where markets previously did not exist. I would distinguish not between a market system, however constructed, and a planned system, but rather between the planning approach and the mindless approach."[143] Nonetheless, these voices were clearly in the minority at the Creative Retrenchment conference, and the fact that they needed to remind participants that government would still be involved in a competitive approach is noteworthy.

Ironically, given that competition was supposed to replace planning, encouraging the use of competition in the health care system became one of the 17 national priorities specified in the health planning amendments of 1979. HSAs were directed to encourage market forces "wherever competition and consumer choice can constructively serve to advance the purpose of quality assurance, cost effectiveness, and access."[144] HMOs were a central component to this plan to encourage markets and competition in the 1979 amendments, which exempted large HMOs from CON requirements, with an intent to encourage their development and create more competition in the health care markets. These amendments directed HSAs to consider a combination of contradictory forces to plan a more "rational" health care system: regulation, resource development, fostering competition, improvements and access and equity, democratic processes, and more direct cost-control mechanisms.

Professor Havighurst, a strong supporter of the competitive approach, viewed the 1979 amendments as signaling a "new Congressional mood ... reflect[ing] a dramatic reversal in the unquestioning drift of public policy toward reliance on heavier regulation and other forms of centralized decision making. . . . What has happened is that Congress has reversed itself and declared competition to be the mechanism of choice, where it works, in health services."[145]

## Conclusion: The Failure of Planning Gives Way to the Market

*The committee has concluded that, if health planning is to succeed, it is necessary that those volunteers and staff people in Washington and in all fifty states be given a period of fiscal and temporal stability in which they are permitted to do their jobs. No program can succeed if it is constantly subjected to changing guidelines, altered priorities, and mixed signals. Nor is morale enhanced if the program and the repaired appropriations are constantly in jeopardy. It is possible to ensure failure by underfunding programs, harassing administrators, showing little appreciation for the thousands of citizens involved, and setting unattainable goals. It is also possible to foster a perception that government does not work and leaders cannot lead if those who enact legislation were to fail to support it and if those who oppose it, having lost, continue to try to scuttle activities. Whatever one's views are on the appropriate role for government and the private sector, surely all agree that it is unhealthy for the body politic to ask people to do a job and then create situations that make it impossible for them to succeed.*
—Rashi Fein, Chairman of IOM Report, 1981[146]

Although the decentralized, voluntary structure of the 1974 Health Planning Act certainly contributed to its demise, Rashi Fein's introduction to IOM's evaluation of the act points to a different phenomenon. He suggests that groups were actively working to discredit government and the program even before it had a chance to implement its planning activities. Many have noted that with the passage of Medicare and Medicaid came huge accommodations to providers and hospitals, and the politics of accommodation affected every aspect of government policy.[147] The politics of accommodation under Grow and Hide meant that the planning bills accommodated the preferences of private actors and allowed them to redefine what the bill represented in terms of the government's role (from planning to regulation), and to then take the decentralized, fragmented system they advocated for and use it against government itself.

Just as deception lurked behind the voluntary approach in the 1950s (see Chapter 4), it lurked behind the voluntary planning agencies in the 1970s: First, the promise that all Americans would receive access to high-quality medical care despite forestalling universal coverage yet again. Second, while government mandated planning alongside its grand goals to achieve efficiency, improve quality and access, and even democracy, there were no provisions put in place to hold private actors accountable for not achieving these goals. As in the past, this major deception allowed an explosion in public funding that was even more deeply obscured under a system that became even more unequal and fragmented despite expanding health care coverage. This explosion of public funding under the Grow-and-Hide Regime will be discussed more thoroughly in the next two chapters. But taking us back to Fein's quote, it was also deceptive because it allowed the hospital industry to shape a fragmented planning system, to control it, and to then demonize government for its failure.

# Profiteering

## The Hidden Financial Industry Takeover

With the failure of government planning, the widespread interpretation that government regulation does not work, and the election of Ronald Reagan in 1980, the competitive market approach was solidified as the next major movement in U.S. health policy. While government subsidies increased dramatically under the competitive approach, they were even more hidden than before, while increasing fragmentation and inequality and further allowing private interests to simultaneously profit from and demonize government. As such, the government's support of competition in health care turbocharged the Grow-and-Hide approach.

Before David Stockman became Reagan's director of the Office of Management and Budget, he was a Republican member of U.S. House of Representatives from Michigan, and in that capacity he co-sponsored the National Health Care Reform Act of 1981 with Rep. Richard A. Gephardt (D-MO). It was in this bill (and several other publications[1]) that he laid out his vision for a market-based "health competition" model in the United States, which would empower consumers by making the health care system more like a competitive marketplace and treating health care as an economic good. According to Stockman, the key to a competitive health care system was first to realize that "government regulation cannot work," and second to move "180 degrees in the opposite direction, where government specifies nothing."[2] But under this scheme where government specifies nothing, the private sector leverages government money more than ever.

I showed in Part II how the logic of Grow and Hide worked to build up the health care infrastructure from 1930 to 1965 by claiming a preference for private action and minimal government, while relying heavily on public funds to fuel private growth. This logic persists in the post-1965 period, but the role of the private sector changed. While the private sector relied on the "Voluntary Way" prior to 1965 to claim that the private voluntary sector was better than

*Grow and Hide*. Colleen M. Grogan, Oxford University Press. © Oxford University Press 2023.
DOI: 10.1093/oso/9780199812233.003.0009

government and to hide the use of public funds, in the post-1965 period the private sector relied on "competition" to claim that market-based planning was better than government regulation and to hide the use of public funds to support the private sector. And, just as in the past, public funding supported capital investments that build up the health care infrastructure. However, whereas government directly paid for capital investments in the pre-1965 period, its subsidies shifted toward providing incentives for health care institutions to seek funding from the financial markets for capital investments. Explicating how that occurred, how it worked under the Grow-and-Hide Regime to further obscure the role of government in funding capital investments and its consequences is the main focus of this chapter.

One of the most important ways that different levels of government in the United States promoted the competition framework was through the treatment of capital investments. Government's approach toward encouraging private capital investments is rarely discussed as health policy, but it should be not only because of the staggering amount of public expenditures committed toward securing private capital, but also because capital requirements often drive a particular type of behavior among health care institutions that reach far beyond the dollars expended and far into the future.[3]

Some have argued that part of the Republican strategy, starting most clearly with the Reagan Revolution, was to ensure that the reforms passed were not just another transitory phase of "private action" that would swing back toward "public action" the next time a Democrat was elected.[4] Political science professor Walter Dean Burnham, for example, wrote in 1984 that "[t]he basic domestic approach of Reagan's second term would be to . . . make sure that nothing like the Great Society programs could ever happen again."[5] Indeed, the conservative approach was very successful at locking in a belief that competition is necessary, and in entrenching the health care system's reliance on capital markets. Yet, importantly, the American health care state under the Grow-and-Hide Regime does not ensure that the phase of "private action" does not swing back toward "public action." It ensures instead that the two actions are indistinguishable by making public funding so deeply obscured. Because the logic of Grow and Hide needs public funding to prop up private action, in reality it almost always favors more "public action." But, muddling the distinctions between public and private is useful politically because it allows the use of "public" and "private" strategically as rhetorical labels: to obscure government under private action, and expose government under public action. In this way, the American health care state leads the American public to like private action for certain groups, and to dislike public action for other groups—and all along claiming that the United States has competition in health care (or could have it if government would get out of the way) while ignoring the outsized role of government subsidies.

Two main implications arise from the health care system's reliance on capital markets. First, while the competitive ideology highlighted the important role of consumers to hold health care providers accountable, the ideology assumed a level playing field among health care institutions, ignoring the biases of capital markets. In reality, health care institutions bifurcated dramatically during this time period into the "haves" who could demand very high prices (the price-makers) and the "have-nots" who were largely forced to be "price-takers."[6] Indeed, while public hospitals had long taken care of the poor, the "health care safety net" emerged as a new term and concept during this time period. Acknowledging the need for a health care safety net implicitly accepted the reality of a separate system of care for the poor and underserved. Yet, despite this acknowledgement, government's support of the competitive approach demanded that safety-net institutions compete for patients in the medical marketplace. Under the logic of Grow and Hide, even when the health care safety net is explicitly funded by government, it's composition is defined by the market.

Second, the central tension in public health—whether the profession and its institutions should focus on personal health care services (discussed in Part I and II)—re-emerged in the 1980s. Because health planning failed in the 1970s and was replaced by the market, and the public health infrastructure—state and local health departments and their work with public hospitals—was in demise, the whole concept of public health in America—What is it? Who controls it?—was questioned and thrown into disarray. Despite several important public health crises and worsening public health trends, which made visible the dramatic importance of public health work and the extent to which the current public health system was not up to the task, nothing was done but to invest more in the private health care sector controlled by capital markets.

## Capital Health Policy and Role of Government

In the early 1980s, U.S. capital health policy consisted of four main components. The first two, started in the late 1960s, were the major drivers: tax-exempt bonds and Medicare cost-based reimbursement, which included payments for interest and depreciation, thus assuring the cash flow needed to take on debt, and interest and principal payments.

When Medicare and Medicaid adopted the cost-based reimbursement principles of Blue Cross and the American Hospital Association (AHA), the capacity of hospitals to engage in additional capital spending was significantly augmented. By treating depreciation and interest expense as reimbursable costs, the federal government greatly expanded hospitals' capacity to carry debt.[7] This reimbursement stream allowed hospitals to build their internal reserves and increased hospital capital-spending capacity because they could use their internal reserves as leverage in the capital markets.

Other federal subsidies were also important, such as direct federal funding for hospital construction, which still existed under the Hill-Burton Act of 1946 and a mortgage insurance program under the auspices of the Federal Housing Administration.[8] Together with Medicare and Medicaid, and these other subsidy programs from the federal government, the sources of capital funding shifted significantly: by 1968, the hospital industry financed 16% of construction with equity capital and nearly 40% with debt.[9] The relative contribution of direct subsidies (philanthropic donations and government grants) declined largely due to the tax-exempt bond. As Donald Cohodes and Brian Kinkead put it, "if the impetus for capital spending and debt financing was Medicare, Medicaid, and federal capital subsidies, the vehicle that launched hospitals into the credit markets was the tax-exempt bond."[10]

Voluntary hospitals were legally entitled to use tax-exempt bonds prior to the 1970s, but only under the condition that the ownership title of the facility be passed to the local municipality upon retirement of the bond. For this reason, few hospitals made use of the instrument. But, after significant lobbying efforts by the American Hospital Association (AHA) across all states and municipalities (see Chapter 5), the creation of a "leaseback" arrangement allowed hospitals to retain ownership after debt retirement. Under this arrangement, the finance authority has temporary title to the facility for the life of the bond issue, during which time the hospital board leases the facility from the authority for a nominal rent, and upon bond retirement ownership title returns to the hospital.[11]

In their book *Hospital Capital Formation* (1984), Cohodes and Kinkead explained clearly why tax-exempt financing made debt capital so easily accessible to hospitals, increased the amount of debt capital hospitals took on, and significantly increased government subsidies of debt capital, but in a very hidden way and in direct contradiction to planning goals to harness the rapid increase in hospital technological and new plant investments.

The tax-exempt bond opened a new pool of capital to the voluntary hospital industry, because the bonds were also extremely attractive to private investment buyers. Tax-exempt bonds are attractive to lenders because they carry lower interest rates than taxable loans and all the interest earned by lenders remains disposable income. At any given interest rate, the after-tax return on investment of a tax-exempt bond is higher than that of a taxable bond, and these lower interest rates make the debt coverage requirement of lenders easier to meet. Most importantly, in the eyes of the lender, a lot more hospitals were eligible to borrow capital.

Moreover, because many of the tax-exempt bond buyers were private individuals with high incomes seeking investments that would protect their income from taxes, rules around large and recurrent borrowing that were more common among the commercial banks were less important, since these buyers tended to seek tax-exempt investments only in profitable years. In other words, investors in the tax-exempt bond market were much less risk-averse than the commercial banks. As a result, the tax-exempt bond market offered voluntary— now called nonprofit—hospitals a pool of capital with few constraints in terms of the size of the bonds and the frequency with which they were issued.[12]

Investors in the tax-exempt bond market for hospitals viewed cost-based reimbursement from Medicare as a stable revenue source for the nonprofit hospital industry. As such, private investors were willing to finance much larger portions of capital projects with a lower pledge of revenue from the hospitals. In the 1960s, the equity contribution demanded of nonprofit hospitals was 50% for commercial loans, whereas by the late 1970s, the equity contribution was only 10–20% for public bonds.[13] This created an incentive for many nonprofit hospitals to use more debt capital than, as Cohodes and Kinkead surmised, was likely "necessary."[14]

The way tax-exempt bonds were structured also took advantage of government reimbursement for the interest on debt financing. Tax-exempt bonds had tenures of up to years, whereas taxable bonds and commercial loans tended to have shorter life spans (10–15 years). This longer bond issue allowed nonprofit hospitals to capitalize on the depreciation payments of cost-based reimbursement while also allowing hospitals to earn substantial investment income from these extra payments.[15] Moreover, because interest expenses were fully reimbursable under Medicare, interest rates and expenses were relatively unimportant to hospitals with large shares of cost-based payers (i.e., Medicare), and created another incentive for more debt financing.

Most importantly, the tax-exempt bond did not magically appear. Responding to direct appeals from the nonprofit hospital industry and the investment banking industry, state legislatures created finance authorities to issue tax-exempt bonds on behalf of hospitals.[16] As Cohodes and Kinkead noted, "Considering the extent of federal government involvement in the private health care sector, it is ironic that perhaps the most important capital subsidy in the hospital industry sprang not from the federal government but from state legislatures." It is ironic, but also emerges logically from the history revealed in this book. The health care financing system was already so substantially fragmented by 1965 that when the federal government attempted to both increase subsidies to the system and rationalize the system at the same time (see Chapter 7), it is not surprising that it was completely undermined by another level of government. Moreover, it is equally unsurprising, but terribly troubling, that this major government subsidy for capital investments was hidden from public view. It is noteworthy that even Cohodes and Kinkead, scholars from the field of hospital administration and finance, observed that the move toward tax-exempt bond financing "occurred with little or no public debate or analysis of the implications for public policy objectives."[17]

In the post-1965 period, when private investment grew to a major portion of capital funding (50% by 1977), there was a sense that government's involvement in hospital capital investment, at least for the nonprofit hospital industry, was dwindling and becoming inconsequential. Despite appearances, however, "a common thread in the history of hospital capital formation is the role of *public* funds . . . the public continues to play a major, if passive, role in hospital capital formation, in the guises of exemptions from income and property taxes, the use of state and local government tax-exempt bonds, and federal mortgage loan insurance. [And] in the context of retrospective, cost-based reimbursement systems that [encouraged] capital-spending profligacy, payments for depreciation and interest expense also constitutes a public subsidy of hospital capital formation."[18]

At the same time that states opened up the capital markets to nonprofit hospitals through the tax-exempt bond, in 1969 the IRS enacted a major change in interpreting charitable care for tax-exempt nonprofit hospitals. Due to the passage of Medicare and Medicaid, the IRS accepted the AHA's claim that "they couldn't find patients to whom to give free care."[19] As part of its 1969 ruling, the IRS applied a far broader definition of "charitable" to hospitals, whereby "the promotion of health is considered to be a charitable purpose."[20] Most importantly, the IRS concluded that a hospital could be tax-exempt "even though the class of beneficiaries eligible to receive a direct benefit from its activities does not include . . . indigent members of the community."[21] This IRS ruling legally allowed nonprofit hospitals access to state-subsidized capital markets to invest in hospital renovations and new technology to distinguish themselves (as much as they could) as hospitals for the middle and upper class (by primarily accepting those with private insurance and Medicare), while leaving (and in many cases pushing) the poor and uninsured on to public hospitals.[22]

Despite their outward display of concern about "regulatory activity" in 1975, internally the AHA made clear to its member hospitals that they should continue to raise capital for new technology and construction, and strongly supported the use of tax-exempt financing.[23] Each article in the association's special issue on "Planning" focused on how to conduct a sound hospital survey, how best to secure financing, and how to hire a financial consultant.

By 1975, the increasing role of financial consultants in hospital decision-making was clearly visible. Not only were numerous articles in the association's bimonthly journal written by financial experts, but advertisements from the financial industry filled its pages. Advertisements titled "Capital Financing decisions, Are you prepared?" were commonplace (see Illustration 8.1).

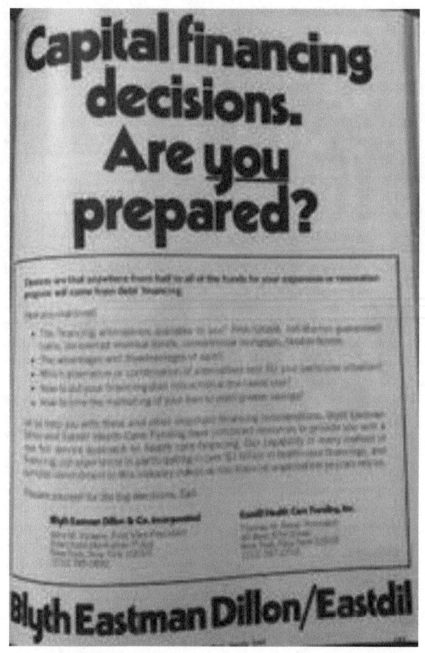

*Illustration 8.1* Sample Advertisement from Financial Companies. *Source:* Hospitals: Journal of AHA, January 16, 1975, 49(2), p.153.

In another article titled "Planning the Financing," the author, himself a financial consultant specializing in the health care industry, advised hospitals to first
hire a highly trained consultant to take the hospital through a coordinated four-
step phased approached: (1) develop a community needs assessment, (2) hire
a financial advisor/investment banker; (3) secure a certificate of need (CON),
and (4) select the best financing method. In detailing the four steps, the author
refers to the CON and informing the community as mere formalities. As long as
consultants are hired, member hospitals were told, the best financing would be
secured, and capital projects would proceed.[24]

Not surprisingly, given the clear incentives as well as pressure from the AHA, tax-
exempt debt financing continued to increase substantially during the time of "regulatory constraints." Debt financing increased from 38% of total financing for hospital
construction in 1968 to 69% in 1981.[25] The dollar volume of health care debt issues
in the tax-exempt market went from $22 billion (5.7% of total issues in 1974) to
$75 billion (12.3%) in 1982.[26] In just one year, from 1980 to 1981, hospitals and
other health care institutions borrowed over $5 billion in the long-term tax-exempt
bond market. This represented a 40% increase from the 1980 level.[27]

To reduce the dramatic increase in Medicare inpatient expenditures, the
Medicare Prospective Payment System (PPS) was passed in 1983. It changed hospital reimbursement from paying fee-for-service (FFS) to paying a fixed price per
diagnosis (Diagnosis Related Groups, or DRGs). In the beginning, the policy discourse suggested that this was part of the broader competitive reforms, because
hospitals would be asked to take on risk and would have to improve efficiencies
under a fixed payment structure.[28] In reality, it was a straightforward form of price
regulation, since the federal government's Medicare program set the price for each
diagnosis. But this rhetoric was important, because when the average length-of-
stay in U.S. hospitals reduced substantially, an average of 9 days to 7.5 days in just
two years post-PPS,[29] the conclusion was that competition "worked" by promoting
more efficiency and reducing Medicare costs.[30] It was also important because
under this increased efficiency, and so-called competition, hospitals made substantial profits. Average total profit margins increased from 2.6% in 1980 to 6.7%
in 1997. Indeed, average Medicare inpatient margins peaked at 17% in 1997.[31]

The third component of health capital policy was Medicare's return-on-
equity allowance for investor-owned hospitals. Prior to 1982, it was set at 1.5
times the rate of return earned by Medicare's Hospital Insurance Trust Fund
on its investments. Although legislation was passed in 1982 that reduced these
payments, the return-on-equity policy continued to produce a significant source
of capital, amounting to an estimated $200 million in 1984, which represented
38–40% of Medicare capital payments to investor-owned hospitals and about
7% of Medicare capital payments to hospitals.[32] Writing about the effect of
these Medicare payments, health administration scholar J. B. Silvers wrote in
2001 that "by any stretch of the imagination, this form of payment and subsidy

dramatically reduced [what lenders] required . . . to justify expansion or replace-ment . . . [and, as a result] investment was sure to boom, and it did."[33]

The fourth component of U.S. health capital policy was embedded in the tax code, which provided another source of working capital for for-profit organiza-tions in the form of investment incentives allowing companies to recover their investment costs more quickly by deferring a portion of their corporate income taxes. It is important to understand the government's deferred tax policy as an "interest-free loan from the government," especially because the subsidies from the deferred taxes were substantial.[34] The extent of the subsidy is well illus-trated in a study conducted by the Institute of Medicine, which analyzed the tax obligations of the top four investor-owned health care corporations,[35] and found that the average tax liability rate reported to shareholders was 52%. But when the subsidies for deferred taxes were taken into account, the average tax liability was only 2.5% of what was actually paid as a percentage of gross revenue.[36] The actual tax dollars deferred (or public subsidy) in 1983 ranged from about $30 million for Humana to $99 million for AMI. It is also important to realize that this tax policy created an incentive for firms to increase capital investments: if a firm's investment outlays on depreciable assets would grow from year to year (which it did), then the balance outstanding on these interest-free government loans would grow over time, and in any given year more tax would be deferred than re-paid.[37] As Cohodes and Kinkead concluded, "without those public subsidies, it is doubtful that the industry would [have been] as successful as it [was] in attracting private investment."[38]

While subsidies fueled the entire emerging competitive system, the compli-cated nature of U.S. capital health policy made understanding the role of govern-ment for even a well-informed citizen exceedingly difficult. In keeping with the logic of Grow and Hide, the government collected no information about these sources of funding for capital investments,[39] and there was no other effort to make these government subsidies transparent. This lack of data made it very difficult to study the extent of subsidies even among those who did care to understand the implications of this government policy.[40] Moreover, when analysts raised concerns about the heavy reliance on financial markets, the discourse used to de-scribe the role of government often obscured public subsidies behind the capital health policy approach. For example, in the IOM report, the first sentence from the quote below emphasizes the role of private financing and private ownership, and suggests, later in the paragraph, that there is no government funding:

> Private financing of hospital capital through the hospital's own
> revenues and through investor financing (debt or equity) parallels the
> ownership of hospitals in the United States, which also is *predominantly
> private*. However, it should not be forgotten that this pattern of owner-
> ship and financing is unique among industrialized nations . . . and that

our heavy reliance on investor financing has undeniable social and economic consequences. It may, for example, lead to more expensively equipped hospitals. If, however, *government does not wish to use its tax revenues* to supply financial capital to the health care sector, as appears to be the case, Americans must realize that the health care sector will increasingly conform to the performance expectations of the financial markets, which are interested in the rendering of services to humankind only insofar as such services yield cash revenues.[41]

While the authors of the IOM report make a very important point that U.S. capital health policy relies on the financial markets to determine future health investments with a set of motivations that likely do not match that of a democratic polity, they nevertheless suggest that the U.S. government does not provide tax revenue to support this market-based planning. It is true that in the post-1965 period, the federal government had gradually *decided* to withdraw from *direct* capital funding. As such, by 1986, private capital markets were the only realistic option for most hospitals that needed to finance a major renovation or an expansion project.[42] However, the government did not withdraw, but instead changed its capital policy to indirect, hidden subsidies, which allowed the hospital and financial industry to decide on how those public funds would be spent.

## Capital Health Policy and Health Care Inequities

The increased reliance on capital markets played a central role in creating a fundamental transformation toward the corporatization of the American health care system.[43] The implications of this shift toward corporatization were threefold.

First, reliance on capital markets encouraged the formation of multi-hospital systems. Because large organizations could support the overhead necessary to develop sophisticated financial strategies, investment advisers and bond rating agencies viewed multi-hospital systems as more financially stable.[44] As such, the credit rating of multi-institutional systems tended to be higher than single-facility hospitals. For example, while 23% and 38% of multihospital systems had a AA(+/-) and A+ rating, respectively, only 2% and 16% of single-facility providers had such ratings.[45] This higher credit rating created a strong motivation for community hospitals to join multi-hospital systems. The percentage of community hospitals affiliated with systems increased from 31% in 1979 to 53% in 2001.[46] It is important to note that these mergers and acquisitions occurred regardless of ownership: nonprofit voluntary hospitals also experienced a growing number of corporate mergers and large-scale joint ventures.[47]

Second, the shift toward reliance on capital markets created the explosive growth of proprietary hospital chains. The number of short-term acute care hospitals owned by for-profit hospital chains rose from 6% in 1977 to 10% in 1982. The five largest chains more than doubled their total beds during the same time period.[48] In 1990, 33% of system hospitals were owned by for-profit systems (about one in four hospitals beds).[49]

Third, the reliance on capital markets created an even more bifurcated two-tiered system of care in the U.S. health care system. While public subsidies made access to tax-exempt bonds easier for voluntary hospitals in the post-1965 period, public hospitals were unable to take comparable advantage of these subsidies. Because public hospitals had a higher proportion of Medicaid patients among their payer-mix, even private investors in the tax-exempt bond market with more lax rules saw them as a greater risk.[50]

It is important to point out that the lower risk rating was rooted in structural racism. Several key factors were (and still are) taken into account to determine a hospital's creditworthiness, including hospital location, hospital market share, hospital management, reimbursement system, and financial performance.[51] Each of these factors is related to economic and racial inequities in the broader U.S. society. Thus, while the federal government was insisting on desegregation of hospitals in the South through its Medicare program in the 1970s,[52] its capital health policy entrenched segregated health care use throughout the country.[53] Capital health policy was clearly biased against public hospitals with a larger Black and brown patient-base and where many public hospitals were located—in poorer Black and brown neighborhoods in urban centers.[54]

Once labeled as a bad risk, it was very difficult for public hospitals to change their risk rating. Because public hospitals had much lower capital investment, their level of payments based on debt principal was low. As a result, it was difficult to build up an internal revenue base to use as leverage. Instead, public hospitals were using a large portion of their discretionary funds to cover operating deficits, especially to meet the requirements of their mission to care for nonpaying patients. But this stopgap measure led to future problems. Since there was little capital investment, the amount of reimbursement, and thus of discretionary funds, continued to dwindle, and a downward cycle ensued. Several studies confirmed that their capital position vis-a-vis voluntary and proprietary hospitals was poor and continued to decline.[55] Already by the mid-1980s, several studies confirmed that public and nonprofit voluntary hospitals that served a disproportionate number of Black, Latino, and poor residents were very unlikely to have access to capital markets, while those hospitals that served predominately white residents with private insurance were much more likely to have access to capital markets.[56]

## Government's Fragmented Response
## to Growing Inequities

This growing bifurcation became much more visible to the American public when private hospitals began to significantly increase the practice of what became known as "patient dumping": when a private hospital transfers an emergency patient to a public hospital, refusing treatment based on the patient's inability to pay.[57] It is important to note, of course, that dumping was not a new phenomenon.[58] But the practice increased significantly, from a range of 90–125 transfers to Chicago's main public hospital (Cook County) to a range of 365–560 transfers, for example, and became the subject of numerous stories in the popular press exposing the problem across American cities. The stories detailed harrowing examples of mistreatment, such as a baby dying in childbirth in a taxi when a private hospital refused to admit the mother in labor and transferred her to a public hospital.[59]

In response, Congress passed the Emergency Medical Treatment and Active Labor Act (EMTALA),[60] which imposed a set of rules supposedly to prevent patient dumping, but in reality was only meant to prevent harmful transfers. EMTALA required private hospitals with an emergency room that participated in the Medicare program to provide emergency indigent care if a patient (of any income level or payer status) presented with an "emergency medical condition" or if a pregnant woman was in "active labor."[61] Several points are evident in how EMTALA was written—and what was not required—that are extremely important for understanding the inequality consequences of the Grow-and-Hide Regime.

First, EMTALA did not stop patient transfers based on insurance and income status. It only required hospitals to stabilize patients first; once the patient was deemed in stable medical condition, a transfer to a public hospital could be made. Second, and relatedly, EMTALA, as the name implies, only applied to emergency conditions. If a patient presents with a non-emergency condition, it was perfectly legal to refuse medical care. In sum, despite continued hope that nonprofit hospitals would provide charitable services, the details of EMTALA made clear (yet again) that charitable services never included taking care of indigent patients, or even those on public insurance.

Critics of EMTALA focused on the lack of payment for the uninsured and low levels of government reimbursement as the real problem causing patient dumping. Almost all of the news stories (and most of the health policy journal articles) identified low Medicaid payments and unpaid bills from the uninsured (what they called "bad debt") as the culprits behind this distasteful hospital behavior. For example, a story in the *Chicago Tribune* identified the new Medicaid cuts as the cause of patient dumping.[62] *New England Journal of Medicine* editor Arnold Relman focused on the problem of the uninsured: "Without more support for indigent care, hospitals caring for uninsured emergency patients will be put at a serious economic disadvantage."[63] Still others focused the combined effect of "cost cutting and management [trends] . . . on the part of Medicaid, Medicare, and private insurers [which] made it virtually impossible for hospitals to pass on the costs of indigent, unreimbursable care to other, paying patients."[64]

Most telling about constructing the problem in this way was that the locus of blame was primarily put back on government. Even when the cost-cutting measures of private insurers were mentioned, it was presented as a necessary tightening that government should respond to with more subsidies. The hospitals were largely exonerated from blame. As law professor Maria O'Brien Hylton opined, it was "not surprisingly then, [that] the 1980s saw a huge increase in patient dumping as hospitals scrambled to avoid the most undesirable of all emergency patients: those with serious, expensive-to-treat emergency conditions with no prospect for payment."[65] Given the constraints of the broader environment, in Hylton's telling, hospitals were forced to dump patients and to logically view the uninsured as "the most undesirable." Hospitals were yet again successful in shifting the blame for inadequate care back on to government. Gone from public discourse was any mention of the increase in revenues hospitals achieved during these "tightfisted times," or all the other subsidies that even well-off hospitals were already getting from the government.

Other critics argued that EMTALA was difficult to enforce due to vague statutory language.[66] In response to such concerns, amendments were passed in 1989 to improve EMTALA by providing a more detailed definition of an "emergency medical condition." The amendments specified that the definition of an "emergency medical condition" be expanded to include:

(A) a medical condition manifesting itself by acute symptoms of sufficient severity (including severe pain) such that the absence of immediate medical attention could reasonably be expected to result in:
   (i) placing the health of the individual (or, with respect to a pregnant woman, the health of the woman or the unborn child) in serious jeopardy,
   (ii) serious impairment to bodily functions, or
   (iii) serious dysfunction of any bodily organ or part; or
(B) with respect to a pregnant woman who is having contractions:
   (i) that there is inadequate time to effect a safe transfer to another hospital before delivery, or
   (ii) the transfer may pose a threat to the health or safety of the woman or the unborn child.[67]

Yet, as this excerpt makes clear, emergency care is often ambiguous, and what appears as a non-emergency at one time may appear as an emergency a short time later. Thus, rather than solve the fundamental problem of transferring "undesirable" patients when they ask for help, the EMTALA amendments only served to further exemplify the absurdity of trying to exactly define "emergency" prospectively, and the inhumanity of accepting that some patients are undesirable and therefore can be transferred if presenting as being in a non-emergency condition.

Another band-aid approach to deal with concerns about the growing profit motive in American health care was represented in two bills known as "Stark I and II," because Congressman Fortney (Pete) Stark, then chair of the House Ways and Means Subcommittee on Health, spearheaded them. These were passed first under the Omnibus Budget Reconciliation Act (OBRA) of 1990, and second under OBRA 1993. In general, these laws focused on limiting physician referral practices to entities for which the physician (or a family member) had a financial stake. The intended effect was to prevent abusive referral patterns associated with making profits off physician "self-referrals," since a study by the Office of the Inspector General found that such referrals were often found to be medically unnecessary, and yet gross and net revenues were found to be 30% to 40% higher.[68] Because a high proportion of these self-referrals were paid for by Medicare, they were targeted as another culprit of increasing health care costs. Ironically, as the competitive approach in health care was supposedly taking off, these financial arrangements created closed referral systems, which limited competition among health care providers.[69]

It is important to note that financial conflicts of interest often focused on ownership (e.g., physician-owned practices), but it was also visible in various forms of investment either through equity or debt, or in the form of a compensation arrangement between the physician (or a family member) and the entity. These other two forms of financial conflicts of interest were more difficult to observe and restrict, but no less common. As a result, the federal government then passed Stark II to address these financial complexities. Yet while Stark II attempted to regulate these other forms of investments and financial arrangements, it also established a series of exceptions to the referral ban. For example, there were exceptions to specific types of ownership and compensation arrangement if services were provided by another physician in the same group practice, or "for in-office ancillary services." Other exceptions related only to the ownership or investment prohibition or only to the compensation prohibition. All these rules, along with detailed complicated exceptions, which providers lobbied for, legitimized claims by providers of an overbearing bureaucratic state. Thus, a similar logic that emerged in the 1970s (and discussed in Chapter 7) in which the American Hospital Association lobbied for weak, fragmented, and extremely complicated regulations, and then argued that "government planning" was an example of failed government regulations, was applied again. Under Stark I and II, providers lobbied for the multiple exceptions to the rules, and then blamed government for complexity.

Neither EMTALA nor Stark I or II curbed the growing financial conflicts of interests or rising profits, nor did they reduce the growing inequalities in the U.S. health care system. Instead, their passage and the narrow focus of each on one part of the health care system were successful in advancing the illusion of increased government regulation, but with absolutely no teeth, and enhanced arguments claiming government red tape and dysfunction. Most importantly, this myopic focus kept any real discussion about restructuring capital health policy off the agenda completely.

## Entrenching the Competition Discourse
### Clinton's Health Reform Efforts and Capital Health Policy

Given clear problems in the U.S. health care system—rising costs with little evidence of increased value and an increase in the number of uninsured,[70] there was renewed interest in health care reform, though it took a distinctly conservative turn. Most Republicans in Congress (actually starting with Nixon in 1973) supported an employer mandate to offer health insurance to employees, and some also favored an individual mandate to purchase health insurance. In 1989, Stuart Butler of the conservative Heritage Foundation, for example, authored a white paper arguing that the individual mandate was essential (just as economists working for Obama would say almost two decades later), not only to achieve universal coverage but also to avoid the free rider problem.[71] In 1991, economists working for President George H. W. Bush endorsed an individual mandate under Bush's Comprehensive Health Reform Act of 1992, arguing that the mandate (along with subsidies) would allow choice of insurance and therefore "drive a competitive market and improve the efficiency of the health care system."[72]

When Bill Clinton was elected president in 1992, his administration immediately began working on health care reform and proposed the Health Security Act to Congress in 1993.[73] As discussed in the many books on the topic, although public support for reform was initially very high,[74] there was significant opposition to reform and the bill ultimately failed.[75] Central to all explanations was the enormous power of the private-sector interest groups—no longer described as just the AMA and AHA. Now pharmaceutical companies, medical device firms, and for-profit health systems, which created their own association, the Federation of American Hospitals, were just a few of the additional organizations that lobbied strongly against Clinton's plan.[76] In total, 650 groups spent $100 million working against the bill.[77] Given this opposition, one might think that Clinton proposed something akin to national health insurance (or in today's national parlance 'Medicare for All" or a "single-payer plan"). In stark contrast, but consistent with Clinton's Third Way politics, it built on prior conservative proposals, which included an individual mandate to purchase private insurance from a health care marketplace and was very similar to entities described in Bush's 1992 proposal.[78] Although there were proposed regulatory reforms pertaining to private insurance, such as getting rid of risk rating based on preexisting conditions, Clinton's proposal left the health care marketplace essentially intact, meaning that the growth of for-profit organizations, and the increase in mergers and conversions into multi-hospital systems, would likely have continued.

Nonetheless, despite this conservative approach, private actors argued that Clinton's health reform proposal would significantly reduce capital investments. Their arguments were fourfold. First, they argued that the "alliances" (what the health care marketplaces were called) would operate as a government-run monopoly that would stymie competition. Most private actors were very supportive of the overall approach to the Clinton plan, since it promoted the "managed competition" approach. For example, the CEO of Aetna (Mr. McLane, who was also the representative of a group called Alliance for Managed Competition) praised the plan in a Senate hearing on the bill: "We say bring on fundamental reform, but let it be reform that supports the progress now being made in the private marketplace and fixes what is broken."[79] But any regulation (that could legitimately be viewed as the "managed" part of competition) intended to facilitate fair operation of the marketplace or 'fix what was broken," was called out as ruining competition. For example, Jack A. Meyer, president of New Directions for Policy, argued against the plan:

> Because I believe in the managed competition approach, I don't want to see it smothered by excessively tight controls. This is not just a philosophical argument. If controls are too tight, we will not have the capital to invest in the infrastructure of managed competition—the primary care doctors, the physical expansion of HMOs and other types of alternative delivery and financing systems, the information systems, etc. For this infrastructure to develop, health plans need payment rates adequate to cover these costs on top of basic service costs."[80]

What is particularly important about Meyer's argument is that, according to his thinking, having access to capital markets *depends* on generous government payment rates. Yet, despite calling for generous public payments, the common demonization of government continued: "[W]hy would carriers risk any more scarce capital on a business that is at the discretion of a political process?"[81] Whereas regulatory policy was deemed political and damaging, their lobbying for higher rates was presented as necessary, needed, and factual to maintain access to the capital markets, and was, therefore, nonpolitical.

The second common objection emerged from a very old argument: that government should not get between the patient and the physician. This time, however, private actors argued that government should not get between the consumer and the insurer—this relationship was now deemed essential and needed to be preserved. For example, President Robert Laszewski of a Washington, DC, consulting firm, called Health Policy and Strategy Associates, whose clients included health insurers, HMOs, health plan administrators, and employers said, "Fundamentally, I have difficulty with the notion that only a Government-created bureaucracy can produce better efficiency in the distribution of health insurance, or that the service a consumer receives from an insurer can be improved by putting a Government bureaucracy between the consumer and the insurer."[82]

Third, just as the AHA argued that the Voluntary Way was more democratic than government in the 1950s (see Chapter 5), by the early 1990s this logic was replaced with democratic choice fulfilled through competition. When asked about choice under managed competition, Mr. McLane asked to include in the Congressional Record an advertisement from his organization the Alliance for Managed Competition, which detailed "10 reasons why . . . there is more choice under a reformed system that is based on managed competition"[83] (see Illustration 8.2).

They also argued that competition would somehow keep government more honest. For example, Laszewski said, "Creating monopolistic alliances would forever eliminate the potential of the market to find a better way. Indeed, a [government] monopoly would eliminate the opportunity to keep the Government itself honest."[84]

Finally, they argued that the premium caps, proposed to control the rapid rise in health expenditures, would reduce innovation because such "draconian government regulation" would create economic disincentives for new capital to enter the health care marketplace. This was by far the most important argument, because all private actors mentioned it,[85] and when the reduction in capital investments was mentioned, it was almost always connected to invoking fear that quality health care would be hindered. Laszewski's argument, for example, that a "market dominated by a single government selection body" [would create] "the economic disincentives for new capital to enter" was commonplace.[86] Aetna's McLane was also clear that what bothered him the most (after listing a series of concerns about regulations) was "that any type of premium cap or price control will inhibit capital from coming into the private sector, be it the

# WHY AMERICANS WILL HAVE
# MORE CHOICE OF HEALTH CARE PROVIDERS
# UNDER MARKET BASED MANAGED COMPETITION.

## 10.
Americans _will_ be able to change providers within their plan.

## 9.
Americans _will_ be able to switch plans.

## 8.
Americans _will_ be able to seek providers outside their plans.

## 7.
Americans _will_ be able choose from a menu of plans.

## 6.
Americans _will_ be able to have a "primary care physician" who will advise them about the selection of other providers within their plan.

## 5.
Americans will have _real information_ — a report card — about "patient satisfaction" concerning providers within their plan.

## 4.
Americans will have _real information_ — a report card — about costs when they choose a plan.

## 3.
Americans will have _real information_ — a report card — about the success of medical treatments when they choose a plan.

## 2.
Americans will _no longer_ have to choose health care providers out of a phone book.

## 1.
The essence of managed competition is _informed consumer choice_.

# REAL CHOICE. CASE CLOSED. LET'S MOVE ON.
### Let's move on in a bipartisan effort to achieve health care reform.

# THE ALLIANCE FOR MANAGED COMPETITION
### _Providing Health Coverage for 60 Million Americans_

AETNA    CIGNA    METLIFE    THE PRUDENTIAL    THE TRAVELERS

_Illustration 8.2_  Insurance Industry Advertisement for Clinton Managed Competition Reform. _Source:_ U.S. Congress, Senate Committee on Labor and Human Resources, Hearing on "Health Security Act of 1993, Part 2," October 20, 1993, hrg-1993-lhr-0058. Quote on p.321.

Harvard Community Health Plan, be it Aetna Health Plans, or be it any other health plan that you know. We are raising money in these private markets . . . in order to spend billions on what we have to do to develop networks, to develop outcome measurements, and to develop the systems and so on that need to be developed."[87]

Just a decade after the election of Ronald Reagan, the idea that the U.S. health care system must rely on financial markets for capital investments had become entrenched. With the exception of one representative,[88] I could find no other person invited to testify at the congressional hearings who advocated for a capital health policy that did not rely on the financial markets with no government regulations.[89] Instead, when comments such as those by McLane were made—we need to raise *billions* because we *have* to develop—no one challenged these assertions or offered an alternative.

Even when more liberal members of Congress expressed skepticism about relying on the managed competition approach, they were told that the competition demands reliance on capital markets. When Congressman Stark (D-CA), as the chair of the Ways and Means Subcommittee, asked how other countries fund capital allocations, Stewart Altman, chair of the Medicare Prospective Payment Assessment Commission (ProPac),[90] responded as follows:

MR. ALTMAN: I would say that every other—every country that I know of has a capital allocation system, control system, as a key component of their cost containment. And, those capital cost restrictions have worked to keep their systems much tighter than ours. We have the most excess capacity on the hospital side and high-tech side—of any country in the world. So, yes, it can and should be thought of seriously. Now the opposite is also true. If you are going to rely on the marketplace, which I know you have some concerns about and so do I, but if you are going to rely on the marketplace, I think the people who are in that camp would tell you, and I do think that they are right, they need excess capacity as the vehicle to get competition among plans. They know that the ability or willingness of hospitals to give them a discount is conditional upon excess capacity. They fear, with some justification . . . [interrupted]

MR. STARK: In other words, it won't work in a good system. It will only work in a sloppy system.

MR. ALTMAN: Well, that is exactly right. The worst of all worlds would be to have a competitive system where you squeezed out all the excess capacity before they had a chance to compete, because I think the capacity for increased rates would be very high. So it depends on which way you are going to go. If you are going on a market-oriented approach, then you need to let the market work.[91]

Note the amazing acknowledgment that the United States was creating a *sloppy* competitive health care system, but somehow more efficiency and higher quality would eventually, inevitably, emerge. And, to create this sloppy system, government must subsidize *excess* capacity. Yet the government should have no say (i.e., no regulation) in how these public funds are invested or in how the public should have access to such investments—only the market decides.

One final dimension of the public discourse evident in the congressional hearings is worth highlighting. By the 1990s, two parallel discourses emerged wherein those concerned with health equity and access to care did not discuss capital health policy in the United States, and those concerned with capital markets in health care had little to say about health equity and access.[92] Unfortunately, this perpetuated a false dichotomy and understanding that capital health policy has little to do with the uninsured and vulnerability in the U.S. health care system. Instead, financial markets are understood as squarely within the private realm absent any government role.

## Health Care Consolidations and Nonprofit Conversions

With the failure of Clinton's health care reform, the role of capital markets in directing the U.S. health care system was further secured. As one expert in health care finance concluded, by the end of the 20th century the capital markets represented such a massive investment in the health care industry that "the United States could no longer change the role of the capital markets" in health care or health policy.[93]

Indeed, even after the full phaseout of Medicare's retrospective reimbursement for capital expenses in 2001, there was by then a large industry of capital advisors—hospital consultants and investment bankers—that advised hospitals on how to gain access to capital. From 2001 to the credit crisis of 2008, hospital managers were told that the solution to easy capital was to join multi-hospital systems.[94] As a result, there was a significant rise in independent hospitals joining multi-hospital systems: from 1997 to 2009, there were 180 system acquisitions.[95]

A number of these acquisitions involved nonprofit conversions. When these conversions happened, investment bankers set the value of a nonprofit hospital for its sale to a for-profit hospital system,[96] which depends on "the hospital's existing debt, its market share in the community, and the age of the hospital's capital plant."[97] Johns Hopkins health policy and management professor Gerard Anderson pointed out that calculating the value is not an exact science and subject to many biases: "Accountants and financial consultants can manipulate earnings, taxes, depreciation, and amortization to increase or decrease the calculation of EBITDA [the value] in a given year."[98] The biases of investment bankers worked in favor of for-profits, pricing them at a much higher value than nonprofit hospitals. This gave for-profit hospital chains an enormous advantage because they could purchase a nonprofit hospital at a relatively low value, which increased significantly once it was acquired by the for-profit chain.[99]

If for-profits warranted this higher valuation, one might argue that this was fair. However, while competition proponents argued that for-profits would create more value through efficiency gains, numerous studies (by the time of these acquisitions) reported that for-profit revenue gains were not the result of greater efficiency but of higher prices and greater markups than nonprofit hospitals. In other words, the evidence suggested that their higher valuations were largely based on their ability to demand higher prices rather than creating greater substantive value.[100] Of course, it makes sense that Wall Street would care about return on investment and profit potential, but these acquisitions came with costs to the American taxpayer. As described in Chapters 5 and 6, the American nonprofit hospital system was built and developed due to public investment in the post-WWII period (through Hill-Burton funds), and renovations and expansions continued through the multiple subsidies that U.S. capital health policy provided. As Anderson points, out "the question is whether society should expect some return on its investment if society built the hospital using Hill-Burton funds, allowed donors to have a tax deduction to pay for expanding the hospital, permitted the hospital to fund expansion through earnings that were not taxed, and allowed the hospital to issue tax-free bonds to renovate its plant."[101]

Given the massive public investments in building up the U.S. health care infrastructure, one would think there would have been enormous debate about what was at stake: first, allowing investment bankers to price the value of what many thought of as a public good, and the resulting bias that led to generally low valuations on these long-term public investments; second, whether the increase in prices among for-profit hospitals was good for society at large; third, whether the loss of community control of nonprofits mattered (or if it ever existed); and, finally, whether it was fair that a small subset of shareholders should make enormous capital gains on this public investment.[102] But that debate was largely absent from public discourse.[103] Instead, the notion that the competitive approach was the right direction for the U.S. health care system had become so ingrained in the public conversation that when any concern was raised about the value and future of nonprofit hospitals, it was often labeled as "anti-competitive."

Starting in the early 2000s, there was an explosion in the number of specialty hospitals, also known as niche or boutique hospitals. While traditional acute-care hospitals provide a full range of services, specialty hospitals (as the name implies) focus on a narrow specialty, such as spinal surgeries provided by the Oklahoma Spine Hospital. Specialty hospitals were described as providing "profitable" services to highly "profitable" patients, because the margins for the services they provided, such as cardiology, neurosurgery, or orthopedics, were very high, especially relative to emergency room care or trauma care.

As a result, when specialty hospitals emerged, acute-care general hospitals— especially nonprofits, claimed that because they had a public responsibility to provide the full range of services for a community and take care of patients on public insurance or those with no insurance, specialty hospitals created a situation of unfair competition. For example, Stanley Hupfeld, CEO of a nonprofit hospital in Oklahoma, said in response to the growth of specialty hospitals in his region, "[Specialty hospitals leave us with] sick patients who have no ability to pay and it strips away from the general acute-care hospital the ability to cross-subsidize."[104] It is true that, according to the Medicare Cost Report filed to the federal government for 2002, the number of Medicare and Medicaid patients at some physician-owned specialty hospitals was significantly lower than those at traditional acute-care hospitals. For example, at Hupfeld's 548-bed hospital, Integris Baptist Medical Center, 41% of its patients were Medicare and 19% were Medicaid, with a net profit of nearly $39 million, or about $71,000 profitability per bed. Whereas Oklahoma Spine Hospital, with only 18 beds, reported that only 11% of its patients were Medicare and 0% were Medicaid, with a net profit of about $17.6 million, or nearly $1 million profitability per bed.[105]

Yet when leaders representing nonprofit hospitals complained about specialty hospitals "unfairly" taking away the profitable patients because they have no "public responsibility," executives from specialty hospitals retorted that nonprofits were "afraid of competition."[106] To which Hupfeld responded: "We're perfectly ready to compete, we compete every day with Mercy and St. Anthony and University [other full-service acute-care hospitals], there's a very competitive atmosphere and we all believe in competition, but there's competition and then there's [unfair] competition."[107]

In response to these concerns, Congress enacted an 18-month moratorium on specialty hospitals as part of the Medicare Modernization Act of 2003. As Senator Tom Carper (D-DE) described it, the purpose of the moratorium was "to serve as a sort of cooling off period during which the Congress could further study the relevant issues." After two major studies on the issue were conducted by the Federal Trade Commission (FTC) and the Medicare Payment Advisory Commission (MedPAC), the Senate held a hearing in 2005 to help inform the decision as to whether the moratorium should be lifted. The studies, and therefore the information at the hearings, focused only on whether specialty hospitals created unfair competition. As Senator Carper put it, "The focus of today's hearing is the role that specialty hospitals play in health care competition and whether this is the type of competition that we want to foster."[108]

As a Democrat, it is not surprising that Senator Carper was open to arguments and findings that for-profit specialty hospitals create unfair competition;

however, it is noteworthy that he is quite clear from the outset—as were most Democrats then and now—that competition is the preferred approach in health care. Senator Tom Coburn (R-OK), the chair of the Subcommittee on Federal Financial Management, which held the hearing, saw the purpose somewhat differently:

> The purpose of this hearing is to allow a record to be laid down in the Senate which can be used for future legislative development or to analyze current and future legislation. This hearing is intended to allow the Senate to consider arguments explaining that specialty hospitals have a pro-competitive effect on the healthcare industry, and that their elimination will reduce competition, decrease quality of medical and surgical care, and eliminate efficiencies produced by these institutions. . . . The question is not competition versus no competition, [but a] "true dose of competition."[109]

Coburn's remarks illustrate the unrelenting belief in competition, and insistence that the competitive approach would not be abandoned, regardless of evidence that would be presented in the hearing. The first testimony came from the Principal Deputy General Counsel, John Graubert, of the Federal Trade Commission (FTC), to present the agency's report, *Improving Health Care: A Dose of Competition*, which he summarized in three main points. First, that specialty hospitals "had a number of beneficial consequences for consumers who receive care from these providers;" second, because specialty hospitals have a beneficial effect, states should not restrict their entry into the health care markets; and third, that "governments should reexamine the role of subsidies in healthcare markets in light of their inefficiencies and potential to distort competition."[110]

Graubert's first point, that specialty hospitals "had a number of beneficial consequences for consumers who receive care from these providers," completely misses the concern raised about specialty hospitals—few suggested that people who receive services from specialty hospitals do not benefit. Rather, the concern was that only some people benefit at very high prices to the detriment of many others. But this question concerning equity and fairness was never addressed, or it was deemed as out of scope.

Second, even though it is legal for hospitals to lobby state governmental bodies, Graubert reminded the committee that the FTC "report concluded that market incumbents [acute care hospitals] can too easily [convince officials to use certificate of need (CON) regulations] to forestall competitors from entering an incumbent's market." He argued further that states with CON programs should reconsider whether these programs best serve their citizens' health care needs."[111] Notice how certain considerations of societal benefit are not allowed under the FTC's reasoning. If, for example, a state considers harm done to existing hospitals, particularly nonprofit hospitals, that have received public investments, under FTC's consideration this concern is illegitimate. There was no room in this paradigm of competition for the state to consider how best to protect the public's investment (in Graubert's terminology "the market incumbent") or to consider the public's return on investment.

Finally, Graubert comes to the hearings' central question:

> Medicare's administered pricing system, albeit inadvertently, can make some services very profitable and others unprofitable. [There is] concern that single specialty hospitals and ambulatory surgery centers would siphon off the most profitable patients and procedures under Medicare reimbursement policies, leaving general hospitals with less money to cross subsidize other socially valuable, but less profitable, care... allowing specialty hospitals into the market will increase competition and squeeze the profits used to cross-subsidize out of the system.[112]

At its heart, Graubert, and more importantly the FTC, argues that the Medicare program distorts the market because it sets payment rates to hospitals. These payments create cross-subsidy incentives for those hospitals with "public responsibilities" that are inefficient, and its overpayments create incentives for for-profit firms to enter the market and siphon off the profitable patients. The Medicare program is supposed to get its administered pricing "right," though it's implied that government-set prices will never work, making the tautology in the logic clear. Harvard Business School professor Regina Herzlinger, who was also invited to give testimony, concurred that the problem was not competition or specialty hospitals, but "mispricing by CMS. It is caused by a system in which a bunch of bureaucrats try to replace what the market normally does."[113]

Most importantly, Herzlinger perpetuates the myth that capital investments (on the part of specialty hospitals) are completely in the private domain and therefore costless to the public: "When it comes to healthcare, specialization has another asset that nobody has addressed and that is the infrastructure of our nonprofit community hospitals is very old. It is going to have to be replaced and it will cost the taxpayers a great deal of money to do that. Specialty hospitals are investor-owned. It will be the private sector that provides that capital and not the public sector."[114] Yet investment bankers provide capital to specialty hospitals because their finance models leverage government subsidies.

Mark Miller, executive director of MedPAC, confirmed that the primary way specialty hospitals made money was to take advantage of Medicare payments, not to increase efficiencies in a competitive hospital market: "We found that physicians are investing in specialty hospitals that focus on the type of patient that Medicare overpays. Since Medicare overpays for these less complex patients, specialty hospitals have a greater ability to earn profit whether or not they develop efficiencies. In the Commission's view, this is an unlevel playing field."[115]

Nonetheless, despite finding no evidence of "fair" competition and increased efficiency, Miller concludes: "In summary, I want to be clear. Competition and specialization are not the problem, . . . the immediate problem is that there is an unlevel playing field in Medicare reimbursement that rewards focusing on patients where Medicare overpays and discourages efficiency."[116] Although Miller acknowledged that public subsidies (through the Medicare program) were the "main stimuli in this marketplace" and drove "the development of these hospitals," no one explicitly asked what the role of for-profit specialty hospitals in a *subsidized* "competitive" market should be. Instead, when the health care market was found to be faulty, which it often was, the blame was placed back on government. In this way, the competition discourse encapsulates the central paradox in the ideology of Grow and Hide: the approach demands substantial government subsidies, yet when problems occur the cause is not market failure but public subsidies, and the government is to blame.

Other health policy scholars raised concerns about for-profit hospitals. For example, David Cutler and Jill Horwitz[117] pointed out that "for-profit hospitals make money in part by increasing reimbursement from the public sector. This is a gain for the hospital but a loss for society as a whole. And having more for-profit hospitals leads to some fragmentation of the market between rich and poor."[118] Yet when policymakers addressed concerns about fragmentation in the market between rich and poor (which was rare), they tended to focus on the behavior of nonprofit hospitals and the health care safety net, not the role of for-profits in the health care market.

This is important because discussions about health care often reflected the fragmented system. Concerns about health equity tended to focus on the problems of the uninsured and the health care safety net. Whereas concerns about for-profit providers were couched in technical terms related to reimbursement and competition. Few discussions considered the distribution of resources across the system. This is how a fragmented system works to the advantage of the Grow-and-Hide Regime: it creates the illusion that each fragmented sector has no impact on the other, that the private sector does not impact the public sector, and what the privileged pay and receive from the system does not impact how the poor and vulnerable are treated.

## Growing Inequities among Nonprofit Hospitals

At the same time that nonprofit hospitals were complaining about the rise of for-profit hospitals and increased unfair competition, there was growing awareness that nonprofit hospitals were continuing to transfer indigent patients to public hospitals. The passage of EMTALA seemed to only replace the term "patient dumping" with "emergency room diversions"—a practice whereby ambulances with patients in need of emergency care are diverted from a hospital's emergency department as a result of overcrowding.[119]

Similar to the 1980s, in the early 2000s there were numerous heart-wrenching stories of people dying on their way to an ER because they were diverted from much closer overcrowded ERs.[120] An Institute of Medicine report on the state of emergency room care in America said the "system faces an epidemic of crowded emergency departments, patients boarding in hallways waiting to be admitted, and daily ambulance diversions."[121] While this practice was not unique to nonprofit hospitals, it also did not exclude them, and was thus another example of nonprofit hospitals behaving in ways that raised serious questions about whether they were living up to their public responsibilities. But given the growing bifurcation between nonprofit hospitals—which had only continued to widen since the 1980s—it was difficult to conclude that *all* nonprofit hospitals were misbehaving.

Between 2000 and 2002, operating margins among low-performance hospitals had dropped more than 75%, while increasing about 60% among high-performance hospitals.[122] This change in operating margins was clearly reflected by the credit rating agencies: a small number of elite hospitals were upgraded to A and AA, whereas a much larger number of hospitals were downgraded to BBB or "Not investment grade" (see Figure 8.1). The differences were so stark that

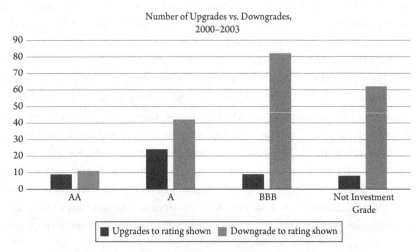

*Figure 8.1* Number of Upgrades vs. Downgrades, 2000–2003. *Source:* "How Are Hospitals Financing the Future?: The Future of Capital Access," *Healthcare Financial Management* 58, no. 5 (2004): 45-49, https://search-proquest-com.proxy.uchicago.edu/docview/196368887?accountid=14657.

health policy analysts started to refer to the high- and low-performing hospitals as the "haves" and "have-nots," and as before, these credit ratings were strongly correlated with payer mix: Medicaid was a major payer for "have-not" hospitals, whereas the opposite was true for the "haves."[123] And payer-mix was (and still is) strongly correlated with race. By 2000, people of color aged 18–64 were more likely to be uninsured, on Medicaid, and to rely on the "have-not" hospitals.[124] Newer facilities with access to capital were built in high-income areas, which limited access to the facilities by low-income patients.[125] Whereas older facilities— those with greater capital needs—were less likely to invest in renovations, new technology, and equipment.[126] And once a hospital fell behind in terms of facility renovations, it often fell into a downward financial cycle: without privately insured patients, hospitals are unable to improve cash flow, which, as Tae Hyun Kim and Michael McCue explained, "is critical to gaining access to external capital (debt) and building internal capital (cash/investment reserves). Hospitals without these sources of capital will continue to experience an aging asset base since they do not have the financing necessary to support new capital outlays (new plant and equipment, services, technology), which are needed to attract physicians and patients."[127]

In the early 2000s, more than one in four hospitals were stuck in this downward financial cycle with negative total margins.[128] This negative relationship between the age of the facility and capital investment was particularly pronounced in rural hospitals,[129] and it fueled the increase in hospital closures and health system consolidations. Between 1993 and 2003, there was a net loss of 703 hospitals, representing 198,000 beds.[130] By 2010, the top five hospitals systems accounted for 88% of market power.[131]

While many believed the for-profit hospital sector would continue to grow, by 2010, 70% of hospital beds remained in nonprofit facilities. Instead, what continued was a growing bifurcation among nonprofit hospitals, and a growing acceptance that the "haves" and "have-nots" were now firmly rooted in the national landscape.[132] Adam Reich made an in-depth study of how nonprofit hospitals in the same city had very different missions and a very different financial outlook. One nonprofit hospital was clearly a safety-net facility that cared for all patients regardless of ability to pay, and the other nonprofit hospital tailored its services to private paying patients. Referring to the former safety-net hospital, Reich wrote:

> Not only did the hospital lose money directly through its care for the poor, but its care for the poor also seemed to dissuade paying patients from using the facility—as if this care tainted the quality of the service provided there. Among the privately insured, the presence of the indigent suggested an inferior quality of care. One nurse said bluntly, "if you had a choice to stay in a room . . . that might be within a foot of some

homeless person, or to go stay at HolyCare [the other nonprofit hos-
pital] where everything's shiny and new and looks better, then—as a
paying customer—where are you going to go? [Obviously] . . . you are
going to go to somewhere nice."[133]

In 2006, Senator Chuck Grassley (R-IA) opened a congressional hearing on
the issue of charitable care in nonprofit hospitals with the following anecdote of
how nonprofit hospitals were treating the uninsured:

> Mrs. Insco was making $14,000 a year when she was hospitalized due
> to problems related to her Type II diabetes. She was charged by a non-
> profit hospital over $4,639, far more than if she had had insurance. No
> one told her about financial assistance or charity care at this hospital.
> The tax-exempt hospital went after her for debt and ultimately put a lien
> on her house. Mrs. Insco almost lost her home.[134]

After highlighting the problem, Grassley then alluded to the huge variation in
financial health and devotion to charitable activities across nonprofit hospitals:
"I think we can do better, and, I believe, so do the vast majority of tax-exempt
hospitals . . . I am confident that many nonprofit hospitals are well-intended and
do outstanding work on behalf of their communities and the poor. But I am concerned that the best practices of nonprofit hospitals are not common practices
for all, and that needs to be changed."[135]

But, in trying to figure out which hospitals were providing adequate charitable care and which were not, several senators acknowledged difficulty and
frustration in what one would think would be a straight-forwarded question.
Senator Max Baucus (D-MT) said, "In our review of nonprofit hospitals, it was
very rare to get the same answer or the same methodology to a question [of
how much charitable care they provide]. That is not to say that the hospitals that
responded gave wrong answers. It is just that this is very difficult to measure and
compare. We found that it was not even comparing apples to oranges, but more
like comparing apples to farm tractors."[136]

Professor Nancy Kane, from the Harvard School of Public Health, confirmed that it was "impossible to identify the hospitals that are doing the
good work and providing the right amount of charity care from those who are
doing nothing because there is no national data set . . . for reporting uncompensated care in a standard way." Note that "uncompensated care"—unpaid
bills from care provided to the uninsured—is one measure of charitable care,
but not the only measure, which also highlights the problem. Of course, it is
important to pause here and ask why there was no reporting requirement for
nonprofit hospitals to determine the extent of uncompensated care provided

and, more generally, whether nonprofit hospitals were meeting their public responsibility.

The answer is rooted in the inner workings of capital health policy under the Grow-and-Hide Regime. Although $20 billion was estimated to represent the value of nonprofit hospital tax exemptions in 2006, this did not include the value of the tax-exempt bond. The reason is that it is astoundingly complex to measure quantitatively, and so most estimates do not include it. Yet access to tax-exempt debt continued to be extremely valuable to nonprofit hospitals, and unequally distributed according to how capital markets determined creditworthiness. As Kane pointed out, "very large systems with lots of cash are the ones who are able to raise the debt, and the very small critical access hospitals in Montana or wherever are less able to get access to that debt because they do not have the cash and they are small. So, the tax-exempt debt is currently favoring large hospitals with lots of cash, and not necessarily creating better access to capital for some of our smaller hospitals."[137]

Ironically, Kane's description highlights that one easy way to determine whether a nonprofit hospital is attempting to meet its public responsibility is to look at its credit rating, because credit ratings are highly correlated with the types of patients a hospital serves—namely, patients who are people of color, uninsured and covered by Medicaid. Yet rather than implicate the effect of the capital markets on growing inequality in the U.S. health care system, public discourse focused on the lack of data to determine which hospitals were providing the "right amount" of charity care. And rather than change capital health policy, public policy focused instead on expanding the health care safety net. However, in keeping with the logic of the Grow-and-Hide Regime, the health care safety net expanded in an extremely fragmented and complicated way to obscure its growth.

## The Market Defines the Safety Net

The health care safety net is so complicated that even scientific studies of the sector have found it difficult to define. In 2000, an Institute of Medicine report on the topic acknowledged this: "The committee discussed at length the desirability and feasibility of identifying a specific definition of the safety net, and concluded that there is no such thing as an official health care safety net."[138] Similarly, a report on the health care safety net in 2005 called it a "meshwork," which at its core included "health centers, public hospital systems, and local health departments," but many other providers and facilities as well, including "school and church-based health clinics, private physicians and non-profit hospitals committed to serving vulnerable patients. All are lifelines in the safety net in their communities."[139] Notice how the report mentions nonprofit hospitals as part of the safety net, but not central to it, because, as the report suggests but does not explicitly say, only some nonprofit hospitals should legitimately be considered part of the safety net.

Most arguments for increased funding of the health care safety net acknowledged that part of the reason for the need to increase funding was due to "competition." For example, in discussions about increasing funding for the Consolidated Health Center Program in 2001, the Senate Committee report pointed to the "private market and public efforts to control costs [as] making it increasingly difficult for other providers to continue offering care to those without health coverage."[140] This quote begins to illustrate a crucial point—the Grow-and-Hide Regime allows the market to define the boundaries of the safety net.

## Federally Qualified Health Centers

Public investment in community health centers increased enormously over this time period. In 2001, Congress endorsed President Bush's call for a doubling of the number of Federally Qualified Health Centers (FQHCs): creating 600 new and expanded FQHCs that served over 3 million new patients.[141] From 1999 to 2004, the total number of patients served by FQHCs increased by 45%, from 9 million to more than 13 million. Over the same period, the number of uninsured persons who depend on health centers grew by 42%, or 1.6 million more uninsured patients.[142] Moreover, in 2008, Bush signed into law the Health Care Safety Net Act (Pub. L. 110-355), which provided substantial new funding and reauthorized the program for an additional four years.

Some have argued that part of the reason Bush and many Republicans in Congress supported expanding FQHCs was because conservatives came to see them as weakening pressures for systemic reform of the health care system. In other words, it is part of a longer-term strategy to build the safety net to reduce pressures to expand Medicaid or other larger reform efforts such as "Medicare for All."[143] While these are valid and logical arguments, it is also important to note how safety-net investments keep capital health policy intact and in control. Even as the Consolidated Health Center Program expanded FQHCs, the legislation put clear boundaries around its reach, "support[ing] the provision of health care services to the medically underserved—meaning those individuals living in rural and urban communities that are designated as medically underserved, or who are members of a designated medically underserved population."[144] This is a consistent pattern in U.S. health policy, where the safety net is defined by what the private sector is uninterested in.

## Hospital Emergency Departments (EDs)

By 2003, private insurance only covered about a third of emergency care payments.[145] Given that third-party reimbursement does not, on average, cover the costs associated with services provided in EDs and trauma centers, it is especially important that the financial impact of emergency and trauma care largely fell on the "have-not" (public and small nonprofit) hospitals. There was a growing gap between what hospitals would charge for ED care and their average payments. One result of this gap was the increase in ED diversions, but the other result was a significant increase in the number of nonprofit hospitals closing their EDs and trauma centers in the early 2000s,[146] leaving public hospitals with a substantial amount of safety-net care. While public hospitals represented only 2% of all hospitals in the United States, they provided nearly a quarter (24%) of all uncompensated care nationwide, which typically includes care to the uninsured and under-insured.[147] In 2007, the Institute of Medicine conducted a nationwide study on the status of emergency care, and concluded that the emergency department is the "last resort for millions of patients who are uninsured or lack adequate access to care from community providers, [and, as such, the] safety net of the safety net."[148] Note that there was no public planning to determine that EDs should be part of the nation's safety net. Government did not respond when nonprofit hospitals' closed their EDs. Instead, EDs became the "safety net of safety nets" to protect the interests of the private health care market.

## Medicaid, Nursing Homes, and Managed Care Organizations

Nursing homes provide a third example of the market defining the safety net. It is curious to note that nursing homes have never been considered (or defined) as part of the health care safety net, even though the bulk of nursing home payments come from public dollars via the Medicaid program. The reason is that the nursing homes most interested in Medicaid's business are private for-profit homes.[149] Quite simply, if private providers are interested in making money off public subsidies—even if the patients represent the poor and vulnerable—such entities are referred to as representing a part of the health care market, not the safety net. And, in these cases, the role of the safety net is called into question.

As Ronald Anderson and colleagues described, when "previously unattractive payer sources, such as Medicaid, [were] sought by private providers, both nonprofit and for-profit," it put the safety net at risk. In their view, "competition threaten[ed] the collaborative efforts of [safety net] providers for the community's well-being."[150] Yet when state governments began contracting with managed care organizations (MCOs) in the early 1990s to provide services to

Medicaid patients, a key argument for this approach was that Medicaid recipients would gain access to "mainstream" private providers. As states moved in this direction, the public discourse shifted. Whereas safety-net providers were previously viewed as good enough when the private market was not interested, under Medicaid managed care reforms private providers were defined by most state policymakers as offering more desirable care.[151]

As an IOM report described it in 2000, "This perspective [argued] that policy and program efforts targeted to the poor and uninsured should be focused on broadening access to affordable insurance rather than subsidizing a class of providers ... [and] the future viability of safety net providers should be of concern only to the extent that these providers specifically and measurably improve access to quality medical care."[152] Essentially, this view argues—and the examples presented here show how this view is often put in place—that if public insurance can sufficiently subsidize the private (credit-worthy) sector to guarantee their participation in the program, safety-net providers are only needed if the market deems them necessary. Yet, importantly, even if the market deems them necessary, the safety-net remains fragmented, vulnerable, and stigmatized.[153]

## Capital Health Policy and Private (In)Equity

Despite the continuing importance of the tax-exempt bond, the move into the capital markets opened a new world for the nonprofit hospitals' perspective on valid sources of capital. For example, shortly after the Tax Reform Act of 1986, which expanded the role of real estate investment vehicles,[154] 10% of hospitals were already using equity real estate investment trusts (REITs) as sources of capital financing.[155] In 1993, new rules in the tax law allowed nonprofit hospitals to create a Charitable Remainder Trust (CRT), which enabled wealthy hospital donors to shield their wealth while allowing the hospital to use the donation as cash revenue for interest debt.[156] And, as this hunger for access to capital continued to increase, "creative" capital financing mechanisms continued to emerge.[157]

It was around this time that private equity (PE) partnerships began to grow enormously in size and number: from a business that attracted $10 billion from investors in 1990 to $432 billion by 2006, and representing more than 680 private equity deals reaching more than $700 billion in value.[158] Private equity investments in health care also increased dramatically from 2000, when it represented about 5% of total PE leveraged buyout (LBO) activity, to 2006, when it grew to nearly 17%.[159] The number of PE deals each year increased from 78 in 2000 to 277 in 2006, representing investments totaling about $5 billion in 2000 to $75 billion in 2006.[160]

Private equity firms benefited from the ongoing trend in financial deregulation during the 1980s and 1990s, but most importantly under the 2000 Commodity Futures Modernization Act. Under this act, Congress, with the Clinton administration's support, explicitly excluded complex financial instruments from regulation, such as derivatives and credit default swaps. As a result, because these mechanisms were unregulated, there was a "massive shift of funds from the regulated financial sector to what some have called the 'shadow banking' sector," where PE investments reside.[161] As a result, unlike financial reports from publicly traded companies, the reports of PE fund advisers are confidential, and PE transactions remain private.

Private equity funds are different from venture capital and hedge funds primarily due to their use of debt to take ownership of mature operating companies (typically with a healthy cash flow) in leveraged buyouts, and then to actively manage these companies.[162] When PE funds undertake a leveraged buyout, it is typically structured with about 70% debt financing, with the remaining 30% financed by equity. This is the exact opposite of publicly traded companies, which are typically structured as 30% debt and 70% equity. A simple example of a typical leveraged buyout from a PE fund is useful to illustrate why high debt is advantageous to the PE fund. If a company is valued at $11 billion, the PE fund will borrow $9 billion from a bank (or other lender), and add $2 billion of equity from its own partners and from limited partners, who are investors in the fund.[163] The key to this arrangement is that while the PE fund secures the loan, it requires the acquired company to make the interest and principal payments from the company's cash flow, and uses the company's assets as collateral for debt (or leverage). The acquisition debt has no recourse back to the PE fund or any of its other investments. As such, this financing structure is particularly attractive to a fund's limited partners because it gives them access to the benefits of leverage while limiting the risk of that leverage. Because this structure essentially forces the acquired company to help pay for itself, it has been referred to as a "bootstrap" acquisition.[164]

To secure a high return on investment, the typical PE fund strategy is to "add value" quickly to the acquired company so that it can sell it at a higher price within five to seven years. Extending the above example, if the PE fund sells the company for $13 billion, it is able to yield $2 billion, allowing it to pay off the original loan with interest (say $.5 billion) for a remaining profit of $1.5 billion to be shared among its partners and investors. In general, this strategy has worked very well from a profit perspective: high debt has enabled enormous returns for PE funds—often around the range of 20% return on investment.[165] While the percent return depends heavily on the time frame studied, from 2005 to 2007, the S&P 500 averaged 9.9% returns, whereas private equity averaged 15.6% returns.[166]

How PE firms can achieve such high returns is complicated, but one important factor is the fund's management plan. Eileen Applebaum and Rosemary Batt (2020) describe the management structure as follows:

> Principals in the PE firm typically take seats on the board of directors of the acquired company (referred to as a "portfolio company"), [and/or] they appoint the company's board of directors. The PE firm typically works with the CEO of the acquired company to come up with a 100-day plan for how it will meet performance goals set by the PE firm. This often results in companies acquired by private equity squeezing workers—cutting hours, reducing compensation, or even firing workers. Those CEOs who either can't or won't meet the PE firm's expectations are quickly replaced with a CEO willing to follow the PE firm's strategy. PE firms typically have a cadre of executives they can turn to—whose loyalty is to the PE firm that hires them and not to the company they have been hired to manage.[167]

It is exactly because the PE firm's management plan may not be in line with improving the financial health of the acquired company, or treating its workers well, that the PE fund and its sponsor, the PE firm, must make sure that the acquired company's CEO's objectives are aligned with the fund's management plan.[168] Indeed, it is the management plans that PE firms enact for its acquired companies that makes the growth of private equity so controversial today.

Proponents of PE tend to focus on how the leveraged pressure on companies creates incentives for companies to add value by becoming more "efficient." For example, in 2008, David Haarmeyer, writing for the *Independent Review*, defined PE as a process that "creates value by moving capital, labor and technology to more valued uses . . . [by creating] much stronger incentives to manage a firm's resources productively . . . better stewardship of a company's resources, and sharper incentives to create value."[169] Notice how creating "value" in this definition is only related to whether the valuation of the company (EBITDA) increases. Under this definition, common among economists and finance scholars, it doesn't matter how the PE fund increases the price of the acquired company, it adds value as long as the price goes up.

In 2002, the Center for Private Equity and Entrepreneurship at Dartmouth's Tuck School of Business described "this 'discipline of debt' [as forcing] management to focus on certain initiatives such as divesting non-core businesses, downsizing, cost cutting or investing in technological upgrades that might otherwise be postponed or rejected outright. In this manner, the use of debt serves not just as a financing technique, but also as a tool to force changes in managerial behavior."[170]

As private equity took off in the early 2000s, these favorable descriptions of the practice might help to explain why there was relatively little concern about PE. However, the lack of regulation and transparency also played a role. Because PE funds are lightly regulated by the Securities and Exchange Commission (SEC), there was (and still is) almost no transparency about the management plan or financial structure of particular funds.[171]

Vice President Catherine Robbins and her colleagues from Cain Brothers and Company, an investment banking firm focused on serving the health care sector, confirmed that "because there was almost no regulation of private equity activity, PE firms had free reign to change health care organizations in ways that create maximum monetary value." Yet the lack of transparency laws means that PE firms' management plans are largely hidden—PE is not accountable to any entity but its own investors—which looks for value by reducing costs in ways many others view as harmful to the broader society and to patients.[172]

Robbins et al.'s second reason for why PE funds are particularly interested in the health care sector highlights how these new financial instruments are supported under the Grow-and-Hide Regime. They explain that "private equity investors gravitate toward investments in sectors where reimbursement rates and methodologies are stable or expected to be predictable, established non-profit health care services organizations will likely face increased competition in lines of business with better reimbursement and profitability."[173] Despite all the rhetoric from private sector providers in the U.S. health care system about low margins and the unpredictability of public insurance, from PE's perspective, Medicare and Medicare were viewed as stable, predictable, and profitable.

Moreover, although health policy analysts have long viewed the uncoordinated fragmentation in the U.S. health care system as hugely problematic due to its very high costs and inability to provide high-value care, PE firms viewed fragmentation and growth as opportunity. As Robbins et al. explained, "health policy analysts look at inefficiencies and inequities in health services financing and delivery and propose political, regulatory, and structural change; private equity investors look at the health care industry's challenges and see opportunity. . . . The strategy is dependent on the expectation of a large, growing health care market with room to accommodate additional competition."[174] The strategy reveals how PE would look to capitalize on the fragmented health care market through massive consolidation, and continues with the broader discourse that undergirded capital health policy in the post-1985 period—to glorify increasing competition as adding value with a promise now to force discipline on the non-profit sector.

By 2008, while PE involvement in health care received relatively little attention from the public or policymakers, PE firms had its tentacles in almost all sectors of the health care industry: acute-care hospitals, long-term care facilities, ambulatory surgery centers, dialysis centers, clinical labs, home health services, hospice care, disease management, behavioral health, and physician practice management.[175] Indeed, due to limited disclosure rules, even something as simple as studying the returns on investment to private equity funds was (and still is) difficult. Thus, while many studies suggested outsized returns, other studies suggested that returns to PE funds were roughly comparable to the S&P 500 (or even slightly under). These latter studies argued not to worry because PE incentives to maximize returns were not anymore concerning than those under publicly traded firms.[176] This is how lack of regulation under the Grow-and-Hide Regime fueled the growth of private equity, while also creating a shadow banking industry within health care that made it extremely difficult to understand its implications before it was too late.

## Conclusion

Continued dependence on the capital markets created profound changes in the health care marketplace. By 2008, the health care market granted near monopoly power to a few organizations that charged enormously high prices. Health care spending accounted for over 16% of the U.S. GDP,[177] while life expectancies were lower and infant mortality rates higher than in most other developed countries.[178] Indeed, after nearly 30 years of pursuing the competitive approach, the United States was very far away from a well-functioning competitive health care market.

But on the eve of the health care reform debate, which resulting in the passing of the Affordable Care Act in 2010, the Grow-and-Hide Regime was so entrenched that the role of capital markets in health care was never discussed in the health care reform debates, competition in the private sector was still upheld as the solution to the problems of high cost and low quality, and government was so sufficiently demonized that even when President Barack Obama signed the ACA, he was quick to tout the significant role private insurance would play. And, just as the logic of Grow and Hide would predict, despite the demonization of government, the increase in public funding continues apace while the enlarged private sector dependency on government funds remains largely hidden from public view. Instead, the private sector has an even firmer grip on how the health care system works and the discourse to describe that system.

# 9

# Inequality

## *How Medicaid Is Designed to Grow and Hide*

Most people are surprised to learn that Medicaid was America's largest health insurance program a decade before the Affordable Care Act was passed in 2010. By 2002, the number of individuals covered by Medicaid, a health care program for "the poor," surpassed Medicare—a universal program for the elderly. In 2009, Medicaid had about 62 million enrollees compared to Medicare's 45 million.[1]

But Medicaid does substantially more than provide health insurance to millions of low-income families. It plays a crucial role in providing needed long-term care (LTC) services for the elderly and disabled as well. For example, it covers 70% of the elderly residing in nursing homes and 41% of total nursing home spending, helps more than eight million elderly pay their Medicare premiums and prescription drug costs, and covers nearly nine million non-elderly people with disabilities, including paying for the bulk of services (44%) provided to AIDS patients.[2] These statistics reveal that even before the passage of the ACA, we could no longer easily describe Medicaid as a health care program for "the poor." Rather, it already was America's health care safety net for a wide range of people across various illnesses, age groups, and income levels.

The Grow-and-Hide Regime has put the Medicaid program at the center of health policy debates since its early years. Should it be a program strictly for the poor, or is Medicaid a stepping-stone toward ensuring that everyone has access to some form of health care coverage in the United States? On the one hand, when Medicaid began in 1965, there was clear evidence of defining the program as welfare medicine. The federal government required participating states to cover certain types of poor people—namely, single-headed families and the elderly, blind, and disabled receiving cash assistance. The key point to grasp about the mandatory populations is that they represented a very restricted group of people with very low-income levels relative to families' ability to afford health insurance.

*Grow and Hide*. Colleen M. Grogan, Oxford University Press. © Oxford University Press 2023.
DOI: 10.1093/oso/9780199812233.003.0010

Yet, also from the start, Medicaid's institutional design embedded under the logic of Grow and Hide—federalism and an embrace of the private sector—has allowed for an expansionary vision of the program to take root. In particular, an intergovernmental design with a generous federal matching rate and substantial state discretion has led to continual expansions and has pushed Medicaid in the middle-class direction. Not surprisingly, this gradual expansion culminated into new political conflicts even before the ACA Medicaid expansion was passed: First, partisan conflicts where conservative Republicans fight to keep a popular program from developing roots as another entrenched entitlement; second, intergovernmental conflicts where the federal government has gradually increased its financial contribution alongside programmatic requirements that many states resist; and third, state-level fiscal conflicts, since Medicaid draws general revenues in all 50 American states, and although it is a popular program, it is at the same time a budget problem in many states. While state politicians often strive to decrease Medicaid spending, state health and budget officials are caught in between when they attempt to meet state health needs and realize— ironically—that expanding Medicaid (again) often makes the most fiscal sense because they can leverage federal funds.

Nonetheless, consistent with the logic of Grow and Hide, states and the federal government continue to turn to Medicaid because of the way it is structured: federalism and optional expansions allowing state discretion and the ability to leverage federal funds to finance expansions, yet also hide what they do. These expansions, in turn, have created a political constituency for Medicaid— both provider groups and enrollees—who fight against retrenchment. Yet as program expenditures continue to increase, especially during fiscally distressed times, the partisan divide over the future direction of Medicaid becomes more stark, and the use of political discourse to hide or expose the role of government according to Medicaid deservingness becomes more commonplace.

## Medicaid's Political History

### Medicaid's Origins

Medicaid's adoption in 1965 must be understood in the context of the long struggle to adopt universal health insurance in the United States. By the late 1950s, liberal proponents of health care reform were focusing their attention on senior citizens, a clientele group that was viewed sympathetically and was already tied to the state through the Social Security system. In 1964, most political observers thought Congress would adopt one of three alternative approaches to improve access to health care for the elderly: (1) a universal hospital insurance program with limited benefits based on Social Security (the King-Anderson bills of 1963 and 1964); (2) a voluntary physician services program supported by beneficiary premiums; or (3) an expansion of the means-tested Kerr-Mills program, which offered a wide range of health care benefits to the low-income elderly. Yet, although the popular debate suggested a choice between Medicare's limited universalism or Kerr-Mills's comprehensive means-tested program, behind the scenes the chair of the powerful Ways and Means Committee, Representative Wilbur Mills, along with Wilbur Cohen, the secretary of health, education, and welfare, and President Lyndon Johnson were working out a deal to make Kerr-Mills, which they called Medicaid, a supplement to Medicare. Obviously, their plan hatched, as both Medicare and Medicaid were enacted in 1965.[3]

While the 1964 Democratic landslide provided a large enough majority to pass Medicare and Medicaid, there was a divide at the start over what this dual adoption meant for the future trajectory of health care reform. Representative Mills viewed the Medicaid supplemental strategy as a way to reduce demand for universal coverage; by providing for "worthy" groups, Mills sought to stave off claims for broader health care coverage.[4] In contrast, proponents of national health insurance (NHI) continued to view Medicare as an important first step toward universal coverage and Medicaid as a mere residual program that could be swiftly eliminated when NHI was adopted.[5]

## Early Years: Medicaid's Institutional Design Is Established

Although Medicaid was structured as a means-tested, targeted program, three crucial components of Kerr-Mills and the larger Grow-and-Hide approach— the concept of the "medically indigent," comprehensive benefits offered by private providers, and intergovernmental financing with a generous federal matching rate—were carried over into Medicaid and were the seeds for the program's expansion over time.[6] Almost immediately after the program was passed, some liberal states viewed Medicaid as an opportunity to expand coverage with federal funds. New York State was a pioneer in this regard. Using the medically needy provision, which included nonpoor people with medical needs, New York passed legislation in 1967 to set the Medicaid income eligibility requirements at a level high enough to encompass almost half its residents, thus including not only the poor but also working- and middle-class families. New York's actions called into question the fundamental purpose of the newly created Medicaid program—should it serve only as a safety net for the nation's neediest citizens, or as a stepping-stone toward universal health care coverage? Federal legislators responded to this question unequivocally by passing an amendment in 1968 that capped income eligibility for Medicaid at 133% of the state-mandated Aid to Families with Dependent Children (AFDC) eligibility line.[7]

Meanwhile, liberal reformers at the federal level focused their efforts on expanding Medicare. While logical, their complacency dashed the hopes of liberal states attempting to use Medicaid as a stepping-stone toward NHI. And, in so doing, Congress ensured that states would severely limit the expansion of coverage to citizens with incomes above state-defined cash assistance levels. Thus, early in its history, Medicaid was clearly defined as "welfare medicine."[8]

While the 1968 amendments tightened considerably the definition of medical indigency, the program nonetheless maintained the concept, which meant it had the potential to expand again in the future under the logic of Grow and Hide. The 1968 statute also expanded a series of well-child benefits for poor children, creating the Early and Periodic Screening, Diagnostic, and Treatment (EPSDT) program. The practical effect was to make the Medicaid benefit package even more comprehensive.[9]

The creation of the Supplementary Security Income (SSI) program in 1972 produced an enormous expansion of Medicaid. It consolidated five separate state-run cash assistance programs for the aged, blind, and disabled into a single, federal means-tested program.[10] Because SSI, unlike most means-tested benefits, is run as a *nationally uniform* program, a clear bifurcation among Medicaid beneficiaries was established. The elderly, blind, and disabled—who tended to be viewed sympathetically—gained Medicaid eligibility based on a *federal* eligibility standard. In contrast, with few exceptions, poor mothers and their children gained eligibility according to a (typically much lower) *state* eligibility standard.[11]

## The Middle Years: Expansionary Logic of Medicaid's Grow-and-Hide Design

Despite these contradictions in Medicaid's early history, which created a policy legacy of Medicaid as a residual welfare program, Medicaid's expansionary seeds began to take hold during the 1980s and 1990s. Medicaid's Grow-and-Hide structure of allowing state discretion over optional coverage, combined with comprehensive benefits and intergovernmental financing, prompted a series of incremental eligibility expansions for families, the elderly, and the disabled, which over time led to major growth.

### Working Families

Among the most significant changes during this period was the elimination of AFDC receipt as an eligibility requirement for poor single-parent families. Because AFDC eligibility was primarily limited to single parents with children, most uninsured two-parent families—especially those in which an adult was working—were not eligible for Medicaid. These rules began to change in the 1980s, when it became more widely recognized that most uninsured children resided in working families. Led by Representative Henry Waxman (D-CA), the federal government passed a series of policies—first as options and later as federal requirements—to expand coverage for children regardless of parental status or attachment to the labor force, which ultimately led to coverage of many children in low-income families above the federal poverty line (FPL).

The federal dynamics behind these expansions were important. The federal government was responding to state demand—in the 1980s, the National Governors Association (NGA) lobbied for expanded coverage for children— and the federal matching rate provided the incentive states needed to take up the offer.[12] Consistent with the logic of Medicaid's institutional policy design, most Medicaid expansions began modestly as optional provisions where states could expand coverage to designated groups and receive federal matching funds, but were not required to do so. Gradually, however, as more states adopted the expansion, the federal government converted optional coverage into a mandate. For example, coverage of pregnant women and infants up to 100% of the FPL was a state option in 1986 but became a federal mandate in 1988. Similarly, coverage of children age one to five up to 100% of the FPL was a state option in 1986, but the federal government mandated coverage of children up to age six at an even higher eligibility level—133% the FPL—in 1989.[13]

The reason it was politically feasible for the federal government to convert optional coverage to mandates was in large part due to state demand. Because the majority of states had already expanded coverage under the federal option, a federal mandate meant no additional cost to these states.[14] For example, when the 1988 mandate was passed to expand coverage to 100% of the FPL for pregnant women and infants, 76% of the states were already compliant. When this mandate was expanded again the following year to 133% of the FPL, 40% of states were still compliant. By at least initially allowing flexibility for state policymakers to shape their respective Medicaid programs, the federal government encouraged states through financial inducements to take the lead on transforming Medicaid eligibility and then later demanded that other states follow suit. The federal funding match meant that although states publically complained about mandates, the vast majority of states began what came to be called a "Medicaid Maximization" effort.[15] Quite simply, it became clear to states that it was cheaper to enroll many groups in Medicaid, since the state was often paying for 100% of health care expenses in their safety-net institutions, whereas even relatively wealthy states would receive a 50% federal match under Medicaid. All told, the targeted Medicaid expansions adopted from 1984 to 1990 increased the number of people receiving Medicaid benefits to 36 million in 1996, up from an average of 20 to 23 million between 1973 and 1989.[16]

## Long-Term Care for the Middle Class

These institutional components of Medicaid under the Grow-and-Hide Regime—state discretion, comprehensive benefits, and federal matching rates—also work to expand the program on the LTC side as well. Similar to that for pregnant women and children, Medicaid's role in financing services for the elderly and disabled individuals also began to grow in the late 1980s and 1990s. While Medicaid acted as the "supplement" Wilbur Mills envisioned, demand for Medicaid's supplemental services grew way beyond what Mills or others predicted. The concepts of "medically needy" and "comprehensive benefits" embedded in Medicaid's enabling legislation were sufficiently elastic that Medicaid continually filled the gaping long-term hole, as no other state or federal program covers these costs. Medicare has never covered the costs of long-term custodial nursing home care, and relatively few Americans have been able or willing to purchase private LTC insurance during their working years.[17]

As early as 1970, Medicaid had already emerged as the primary public purchaser of nursing home care. Just 10 years later, Medicaid spending on nursing home care reached $8.8 billion, equal to all other private and public sources for nursing home care combined.[18] By the 1980s, it was widely recognized that Medicaid had become America's "de facto LTC program."[19]

Senior advocacy groups believed that Medicaid's means test was stigmatizing and degrading to the elderly and therefore fought to expand Medicare—not to new groups as advocates of national health insurance had hoped—but by expanding the benefit package and reducing the out-of-pocket burdens on seniors. The old problem discussed at the time of Medicare's enactment—universal but limited benefits—came back to rear its ugly head. Congress responded to senior demands in 1988 by passing the Medicare Catastrophic Coverage Act (MCCA), which expanded Medicare's scope of services—prescription drugs, hospice, and long-term hospital care—but also required all Medicare beneficiaries to pay special premiums pegged to income. Medicaid was mandated to pay the premiums for beneficiaries with incomes below the FPL.[20] While the MCCA was repealed just one year after its enactment, MCCA provisions requiring Medicaid to pay Medicare premiums for low-income elderly remained intact.[21] Policymakers, advocates, and interest groups learned three crucial lessons from the failure of MCCA: first, despite Medicare's "favorable" politics, the program was extremely difficult to expand;[22] second, Medicaid would remain America's de facto LTC insurance program for the foreseeable future; and third, and perhaps most important, governors and state legislators understood that the federal government would continue to ask states to share in the burden of LTC coverage for the elderly and disabled.[23] Indeed, in the 1990s, Medicaid expenditures for nursing home care began to rise rapidly. By 1997, Medicaid nursing home expenditures reached $39.4 billion, representing almost half of all nursing home payments.

## Hiding Medicaid's Middle-Class Reach

When Clinton's health care reform plan failed, it brought two residual forces to bear on the Medicaid program: first, a further demonization of the federal government and a push (yet again) for policy devolution to the states; and second, a continued (unfulfilled) desire to expand health care coverage for the uninsured. During the 1990s and 2000s, there was substantial Medicaid policy activity in four main areas: the growth of Medicaid managed care in the states, expansions for elderly needing LTC services and supports, the creation and implementation of the State Children's Health Insurance Program (SCHIP), and expansions using "optional" coverage for states. Despite these significant expansions, the true expanse of the Medicaid program remained largely hidden to the American public due to discourse and institutional designs familiar to the Grow-and-Hide Regime.

## Medicaid Managed Care

In the early 1990s, policymakers readily characterized state Medicaid programs as administrative failures. To be sure, most policymakers acknowledged that Medicaid played a crucial role in providing health coverage for millions of Americans. Yet there was broad agreement—among Republican and Democratic officials alike—that Medicaid suffered from serious operational flaws. Medicaid still failed to cover many needy persons, and the health care it offered was too often of low quality and provided inefficiently. Numerous studies documented that Medicaid recipients were much less likely than Americans with private health insurance to have a relationship with a primary care doctor or to receive needed preventive care, and much more likely to receive their care in hospital emergency room settings or public clinics with long waiting lines.[24] Despite the targeted efforts to increase prenatal care and well-child-care coverage in the 1980s, a large proportion of Medicaid women received no, or only minimal, prenatal care services,[25] and many children enrolled in Medicaid were failing to receive needed immunizations.[26] Moreover, while the annual growth rate of Medicaid spending declined immediately following the retrenchment period in the early 1980s, Medicaid costs rose steadily thereafter. As the program expansions for children and pregnant women and other legislative changes for the elderly and disabled adopted in the 1980s and early 1990s were phased in, Medicaid expenditures shot up.[27]

Yet if Medicaid spending was growing rapidly in the 1990s, so too were the ranks of the uninsured. Many policymakers argued that it was inequitable to provide Medicaid coverage to the nonworking poor at a time when two-thirds of uninsured Americans came from families with at least one working parent.[28] When Medicaid was originally created, the assumption was that aid should be offered to those who could not afford health insurance because of their lack of employment.[29] By the 1990s, however, it was widely acknowledged that being employed does not guarantee affordable health insurance coverage.[30] The inability of the working poor to obtain affordable health insurance further promoted the emerging understanding that Medicaid could be expanded to low-income workers and, as such, should be thought of as a program distinct from welfare.

This new conception of Medicaid led the federal government to encourage the idea of Medicaid managed care (MMC) waivers. In 1993, President Clinton ordered the federal government to make it easier for states to use Medicaid funds to introduce new health care programs for low-income families. The federal Health Care Financing Administration (HCFA) streamlined its waiver application process so that more states could implement MMC reforms.[31] Largely because the managed care approach relied on the private sector by contracting with private managed care organizations (MCOs), national policymakers promoted the idea as a type of magic bullet solution. They promised simultaneously to reduce costs, improve access, and raise the quality of delivered services. Proponents argued that MCOs were more efficient and innovative than government. Further, because MMC would save states money, the reform enabled states to expand coverage to the uninsured under budget neutrality—a federal requirement of MMC waivers.[32] Key to promoting this solution as a panacea was repeating the long-held view and dominant frame (documented in all previous chapters) that the private sector is superior to government.

By January 1995, each of the 50 states (except Alaska) had implemented a MMC program. Nationally, total enrollment in MMC nearly doubled in 1994 and increased 51 percent again in 1995.[33] States under Democratic legislative control were just as eager to implement managed care reforms as were states under Republican legislative control. Ideological and other political factors were swamped by the rhetorical claims that the private sector would reduce costs, increase access, and improve quality of care. The only alternative states faced to adopting managed care, it seemed, was to stick with their antiquated, inefficient, state-run Medicaid programs. Outside of Medicaid managed care and the discredited status quo, no other policy options were even on the table for consideration.[34]

At the same time, state policymakers also raised concerns about the lack of physicians willing to take Medicaid patients.[35] This was not a new concern. Despite the freedom of choice provision passed in 1967, few Medicaid recipients have ever had unconstrained access to "mainstream" medical care. As early as 1972, several policy experts pointed out that the passage of Medicaid alongside Medicare perpetuated a two-tiered health care system in the United States: a lower Medicaid tier providing access to public clinics for the poor, and an upper, private-pay tier providing access to private office-based physician services for the middle and upper classes.[36] As discussed in Chapter 8, this bifurcation in the health care system intensified in the 1980s. In response to growing inequities in access to care, many state policymakers claimed that MMC would promote mainstreaming, because MCOs were structured to give physicians strong incentives to participate in the Medicaid program.[37] Even some advocates for the poor viewed MMC reform as a potential tool for ensuring more equal access to health care, believing it would serve to remove the stigma associated with the traditional Medicaid program. For example, the director of a Phoenix, Arizona, philanthropic organization said when referring to Arizona's MMC program, "Many Medicaid patients have access to mainstream private physicians whom they did not previously have access to. They don't feel like charity patients anymore."[38] Consumer advocate Geraldine Dallek, author of *Health Care for America's Poor: Separate and Unequal,* wrote in a 1996 essay that "Medicaid managed care may offer the last, best opportunity to provide integrated health care for the nation's poor."[39]

Despite these promises, state implementation of MMC did not give Medicaid recipients equal access to mainstream providers or services. Nonetheless, the prominent mainstreaming rhetoric attached to MMC continued and presented the illusion that private provision was more equitable to Medicaid recipients.[40] Part of what perpetuated this illusion was the fact that under MMC, Medicaid recipients would receive a card, which often suggested they had private coverage. For example, when Connecticut contracted with Blue Cross Blue Shield (BCBS) to provide services to Medicaid recipients, and Medicaid enrollees chose the BCBS Medicaid plan, they received a BCBS card. It had a symbol on the card designating to providers that it was a Medicaid plan, which was clearly distinct from their commercial plans, but Medicaid BCBS enrollees did not realize this— at least not initially.[41] In this way, MMC reforms were able to expand Medicaid, but hide its unequal expansion under the disguise of private provision.[42]

While some states realized cost savings through a reduction in inpatient use and improvements in quality of care through an increase in childhood immunizations, most states during the 1990s and 2000s were not able to realize substantial managed care cost savings.[43] Under budget-neutral Medicaid waivers, states that used MMC to expand eligibility found it difficult to sustain expansions. Tennessee, for example, expanded coverage under its managed care TennCare program and then rolled back coverage when savings failed to materialize, and costs exploded.[44]

Despite the lack of evidence of MMC success,[45] states continued to favor Medicaid managed care over, in their words, the "traditional, government-run, fee-for-service system." In 2006, 65 percent of the total Medicaid population in the United States was enrolled in some form of managed care, and this increased to 70 percent by the decade's end.[46] Forty out of the 50 states had over half of their Medicaid population enrolled in a managed care arrangement of one kind or another.[47] By 2010, it was clear that compared to managed care in the private sector, three key differences existed in Medicaid managed care arrangements. First, there was no longer any discussion of expanding access to "mainstream" providers, since it was clear that Medicaid managed care organizations offered much more restrictive provider networks. As had long been case, non-safety-net providers were much less likely to accept Medicaid patients, and this remained true under MMC.[48] Second, while private and Medicare MCO enrollees were more likely to choose a plan during the open enrollment period, Medicaid enrollees had a much more fragmented experience with MCO enrollment. In the majority of states, a very high percentage of Medicaid enrollees were automatically assigned to MCOs. Eventually, in the early 2000s, Congress allowed states to contract with private plans that operated exclusively in the Medicaid market. This change allowed safety-net providers (public and nonprofit hospitals, community health centers, and public health clinics)—those who had long been the providers for the vast majority of Medicaid recipients—to form their own Medicaid MCOs. Soon, a growing number of for-profit health plans operated only in the Medicaid market.[49] Thus, while private contracting was promised as the key to creating equitable access, by 2010 that promise was no longer even invoked. Instead, MMC was repeatedly described as more efficient, innovative, and less stigmatizing, with no evidence to back that up.

## Long-Term Care (LTC) for the Middle Class

After the failure of Medicare's Catastrophic Care Act resulted in additional Medicaid expansions for the elderly, middle-class reliance on the program for LTC became more politicized. In a 1990 hearing titled "Medicaid Budget Initiatives," Chairman Henry Waxman (D-CA) highlighted the middle-class aspect of Medicaid in his opening statement, but rather than an endorsement he argued—harkening back to a residual Medicaid frame—that it was unacceptable for the deserving elderly to have to rely on a stigmatized Medicaid program:

> Most people who need nursing home care eventually find themselves dependent on Medicaid. . . . It is absurd, and it is unacceptable that an individual could work hard for their entire life, set aside a fund for his or her retirement, then become—then have to be impoverished and go

on welfare in order to take advantage of facilities and services and aids that flow from the Medicaid system.[50]

The focus of this hearing was on Representative Barbara Kennelly's (R-CT) bill, which proposed demonstration projects to develop private-public partnerships to encourage middle-class elderly to use public subsidies to purchase private long-term care insurance. This was promoted as the solution to Medicaid's "inappropriate" reach. Under this bill, "if and when an individual exhausts his or her insurance and applied for Medicaid, each dollar that the insurance policy has paid out in accord with state guidelines will be subtracted from the assets Medicaid considers in determining eligibility. In other words, coverage of long-term care expenses by private insurance would count as asset spend-down for the purpose of Medicaid eligibility."[51]

Interestingly, although Waxman expressed general support for Kennelly's bill in his opening remarks, he raised concerns about whether the bill would create a new category of Medicaid eligibility—one that expanded eligibility to middle-class (or even upper-income) elderly by allowing Medicaid to be used to protect assets and to finance the transfer of wealth.[52] Kennelly's response to Waxman is revealing:

> First let me say that I think part of the reason you and I have different perspectives on this issue (whether her bill creates a new category of Medicaid eligibility) is that we start from very different points. You seem to see Medicaid solely as a means-tested entitlement for the poor. While I agree, I also see Medicaid as a program where, at least based on Connecticut figures, over 40 percent of those who receive Medicaid long-term care services did not start out poor.
>
> I hear of financial planners teaching seniors how to transfer their assets and access Medicaid benefits and I feel there ought to be a better way. . . . Our society has changed markedly in the 25 years since the enactment of the Medicaid program to the point where many of those receiving Medicaid are not included in our traditional definition of "poor."
>
> The current Medicaid long-term care program is a means-tested program in name only. The major asset most seniors possess is a house which is typically protected by Medicaid. . . . Given the political pressures associated with the aging of the population, we are likely to see even more proposals to further increase the amount of assets exempted from Medicaid.
>
> In that context, my proposal . . . may be the ONLY proposal that has the potential of actually protecting Medicaid against further erosion of its means-tested origin.[53]

This quote is important for several reasons: first, Kennelly claims that Waxman sees "Medicaid solely as a means-tested entitlement for the poor." As a Democrat who championed the 1980 Medicaid expansions, it was clear that Waxman's vision for Medicaid was not *only* as a means-tested program for "the poor." For example, just one year later he provided a much more expansive view at a hearing investigating the Medicaid program:

> Medicaid is an enormously important and enormously complex program. It is the major source of health care reform for the poor in this country, covering more than 28 million poor people, roughly half of whom are children. It is the single largest payer for maternity care. . . . It is the single largest payer for nursing home care. . . . It is the single largest payer for residential services for individuals with mental retardation. . . . (The) program has been asked to solve almost every major problem facing this society, from infant mortality to substance abuse to AIDS to the need for long-term care. . . . Despite all of the current interest in health care reform, nothing will be enacted tomorrow, . . . (and) the poor in this country, mothers and children, the disabled, the elderly will continue to rely on Medicaid for access to basic health care.[54]

Waxman's description clearly conveys support for an expanded notion of the Medicaid program. His comments regarding Medicaid's role in relation to national health care reform are also noteworthy. In sharp contrast to health care reform proposals offered in the early 1980s, where Medicaid was easily dismissed as a residual program, most health care reform bills in the early 1990s proposed expanding Medicaid to cover the uninsured (e.g., using Medicaid 1115 waivers) or expanding access to private insurance and leaving the Medicaid program intact. Very few bills, in contrast to the 1970s, proposed eliminating the program altogether. By the early 1990s, we observe a Medicaid program completely entrenched but seriously contested as to whether it already has been (or should be) expanded to the middle-class.

Nonetheless, Kennelly was right that, in general, at this time Democrats denied that middle-class elderly relied on Medicaid—or suggested that only a very small percentage of them did so. Notice how Democrats could have attempted to mobilize this middle-class Medicaid constituency, but instead, under the context of Kennelly's privatization efforts, chose not to bring attention to this middle-class reach.

The second noteworthy point related to Kennelly's quote is that it provides the perfect example of Grow and Hide: expanding public expenditures while claiming minimal government, and hiding the reach of her proposal under the banner of "private." Indeed, if we decode her quote, it is quite shocking: "the

ONLY [way of] protecting Medicaid . . . [as] its means-tested origin" (i.e., a devolved, fragmented, and unequal program) is to expand public expenditures to the middle class through the private sector.

But the lack of Democratic-led mobilization is surprising, given that what worried Kennelly (and other Republicans) the most about this middle-class incorporation was not the current level of reliance on Medicaid, but rather, as she said, "the political pressures associated with the aging of the population," which would clearly increase the generosity of Medicaid's LTC program—perhaps to the point of creating a universal program.

There were some efforts by Democrats to openly embrace a more expansive narrative revealing what the program was already doing—its true reach—and who the program should cover. President Clinton recast Medicaid as a middle-class entitlement during his budget showdown with the Gingrich-Dole Republicans in 1995–1996. Under the "Contract with America," the GOP budget package sought significant cuts in numerous social welfare programs.[55] Debate over Republican health care proposals focused almost entirely on Medicare until September 1995, when House Republicans formally unveiled their Medigrant plan, which proposed to eliminate Medicaid's entitlement in favor of a block grant.[56]

Unsurprisingly, President Clinton sought to rally public opinion against the GOP package by arguing that it would entail huge cuts in spending for Medicare, education, and environmental protection—three federal programs with obvious appeal for middle-class voters. Yet Clinton also explicitly supported Medicaid by highlighting its importance to the middle class. In particular, he emphasized that Medicaid was a key support for once-middle-class senior citizens residing in nursing homes, not an essential safety net for the economically disadvantaged. Stated Clinton in one address:

> Now, think about this — what about the Medicaid program? You hardly hear anything about Medicaid. People say, oh, that's that welfare program. One-third of Medicaid does go to help poor women and their poor children on Medicaid. Over two-thirds of it goes to the elderly and the disabled. All of you know that as well. [Commenting on Republican proposals] You think about how many middle-class working people are not going to be able to save to send their kids to college because now they'll have to be taking care of their parents who would have been eligible for public assistance.[57]

By 1995, Medicaid's long-term care role was sufficiently recognized in the health care landscape that the President of the United States pointed out its importance to middle-class Americans. Yet while Clinton exploited the fragmentation of treatment among beneficiary groups within Medicaid for political advantage by highlighting the deservingness of middle-class groups, Republicans would also exploit Medicaid's fragmented groups to pit one group against another.

## The State Children's Health Insurance Program (SCHIP), 1997

While Medicaid enrollment continued to rise through 1996, employer-sponsored health insurance declined by a greater amount. By 1997, 43 million Americans lacked health insurance.[58] In 1997, Congress passed the State Children's Health Insurance Program (SCHIP, now called CHIP) that helped make Medicaid coverage expansions—separate from cash assistance—possible. When the window of opportunity opened in 1997 for a targeted coverage expansion due to the growing economy, elected officials decided to focus—just as they had in the 1980s—on groups considered most deserving and cost-effective, namely uninsured *children* in working families.

The key debate in Congress was whether the coverage expansion should take place exclusively within Medicaid or be designed as a separate block grant. While eight major proposals were introduced, the debate quickly narrowed to two major alternatives: a major coverage expansion for children within Medicaid, and a state block grant proposal.[59]

Not surprisingly, the National Governors Association favored the new block grant approach, in large part because it offered state policymakers more control over eligibility levels and the benefit package. Many (but not all) social advocacy groups favored the Medicaid expansion approach for two reasons: First, it guaranteed benefits for individual children; in contrast, the block grant approach would have provided an entitlement to the states, but not to individual beneficiaries.[60] Second, expanding coverage for poor children through Medicaid would have further entrenched the existing Medicaid benefit package. Many were concerned (and their concerns turned out to be realized) that if states were given block grants, they might well expand coverage for children under a more restrictive benefit package, and this might create a negative policy precedent that would constrain future expansion attempts.[61]

Emphasizing federalism yet again, Congress allowed states to choose one of three options: a block grant, a Medicaid expansion approach, or a combined approach. While sixteen states opted to use their SCHIP funds for Medicaid expansions, more than half either implemented a new separate (non-Medicaid) SCHIP program (sixteen states) or created combined programs (nineteen states).[62] As expected, the main reason states implemented a separate (non-Medicaid) program was to save costs by offering a restricted benefit package.

However, many states also argued that they needed a separate program because working families would not enroll their children in Medicaid due to the welfare stigma associated with the program. There was a strong assumption that families without previous ties to TANF cash assistance (i.e., "welfare") would be unwilling to sign up for Medicaid.[63] Rhetorically, these notions of stigma were strongly associated with a government-run program.

The enactment of SCHIP coincided with the implementation of Medicaid managed care across the states, and separate SCHIP programs with restricted benefit packages were often added to existing contracts with private health insurance companies. Ironically, but quite intentionally, as Medicaid was moving away from its legacy of "welfare medicine," conservatives began attaching the language of welfare medicine to certain Medicaid recipients. In particular, under expansions to low-income families, Republicans started to argue that Medicaid reform needed to encourage "personal responsibility"—a common welfare trope. In the Medicaid context, personal responsibility meant recipients should act like a private insurance consumer: choosing a health plan; becoming literate in the language of health insurance (i.e., co-pays, cost-sharing, premiums, deductibles); and utilizing the health care system appropriately—do not use the emergency room (despite often not having adequate access to health care providers or urgent care centers).

To be fair, many policymakers—across party lines—had good intentions about wanting to destigmatize the Medicaid program. Many states streamlined the eligibility process by allowing people to mail in applications or sign up online or in places more accepting and welcoming than welfare offices, such as community centers or health care facilities. States also adopted 12-month continuous eligibility to eliminate the stigmatizing process of month-to-month redeterminations and to increase continuity of care. Finally, almost all states changed the name of their Medicaid program, especially for programs associated with SCHIP, to "user-friendly" names, such as Denali KidCare in Alaska, AllKids in Illinois, HUSKY in Connecticut, and BadgerCare in Wisconsin.[64] These new names intentionally hid the connection to Medicaid and presented a new frame that eligible recipients are deserving of private insurance. Some qualitative studies show that these rebranding efforts helped SCHIP beneficiaries carry less social stigma and perceive better treatment compared to their previous experience with Medicaid.[65] Herd, DeLeire, Harvey, and Moynihan also showed that Medicaid take-up increased after enrollment streamlining policies were put in place.[66]

Indeed, in the early years of SCHIP implementation, from 1998 to 2001, Medicaid and SCHIP enrollment grew by an average of 30% across nearly every state, declining in only three states over this time period.[67] By 2006, the average CHIP eligibility level was 220% of the FPL, and 11 states set eligibility above

300%.[68] Through Medicaid and SCHIP combined, 47% of all children were eligible, and 28 million poor and low-income children were covered in 2005.[69] By 2007, about one in four people in 13 states were covered under Medicaid, and in another 14 states one in five people were covered.[70] Obviously, these expansions were crucially important for covering uninsured children. Yet the programmatic reforms under SCHIP were also a perfect example of how programs expand under the Grow-and Hide-Regime: further privatization, further expansion and hiding for "deserving" groups, and further stigmatization of Medicaid for those who are not "truly needy."

## Expanding Coverage through Options

Since the program's inception, Medicaid legislation has allowed states the *option* to cover particular groups—namely pregnant women and infants up to 185% of FPL, children up to 200% of FPL, working parents up to 250% of FPL, elderly and disabled up to 300% of the SSI level, and "medically needy" persons— and receive federal matching dollars. States were also able to expand Medicaid to uncovered groups through a large set of optional services, such as targeted case management in 1986 and expansion of the psychosocial rehabilitation option. While these sound like wonky minor add-ons, the technical terminology hides significant expansions. For example, the psychosocial rehabilitation option allowed states cover intensive community-based supports for people with serious mental health disorders. By 2005, almost all states adopted these optional services, and targeted case management accounted for $2.9 billion in Medicaid expenditures, and the rehabilitative option accounted for another $6.4 billion.[71] People with mental health disorders constituted close to three-quarters of recipients under the rehabilitative services option and accounted for almost 80% of expenditures.[72] It is difficult to overstate the importance of these optional provisions for expanding coverage: even before the ACA was passed, optional coverage consumed about two-thirds of all Medicaid spending. This is important because while states complained about the federal Medicaid mandates, 60% of Medicaid expenditures were due to states willingly adopting optional Medicaid expansions.

## The Struggle to Redefine Medicaid and Hide Its Growth

A surprisingly diverse coalition of political actors started encouraging policymakers to use Medicaid to expand coverage. The Health Insurance Association of America and Families USA—bitter opponents during the battle over the Clinton health reform bill in 1993–1994—had both endorsed a compromise reform proposal by the end of the decade that called for Medicaid to serve as the cornerstone for expanding health access. As a precursor to the ACA Medicaid expansion, that proposal similarly would have expanded Medicaid to all persons with incomes below 133% of poverty, eliminating the categorical requirements that had long prevented single adults and couples without children from gaining Medicaid eligibility.[73] Yet while many conservatives were in favor of using Medicaid for coverage expansions, most proposals came with a catch—either a restricted benefit package and/or a block grant.

In the early 2000s, the National Governors Association offered a Medicaid reform that allowed for a substantial coverage expansion but under a restricted benefit package. And in 2003, the Bush administration proposed increasing federal spending on Medicaid by $12.7 billion over seven years to cover new constituencies, but also gave states vastly increased flexibility to redesign and restrict their benefit packages. And, like the GOP proposals in 1981 and 1995, the Bush proposal would have eliminated Medicaid's budgetary entitlement and created Medicaid block grants.[74]

The reason such reforms were considered fundamental is because conservatives, such as the Concord Coalition, clearly understood the potential political power of efforts to rebrand Medicaid as a social entitlement and to knock down categorical distinctions.[75] Notably, another development that emerged, seemingly in direct response to Democratic efforts to recast Medicaid as a social entitlement, was to return to a residual welfare notion of Medicaid. A 2003 analysis found that most proposals to help the uninsured still relied on the private health insurance market through the use of tax credits and insurance reforms.[76] Many of these proposals endorsed restricting the Medicaid program to a clearly defined "poor" or "near poor" population.[77] For example, the Congressional Health Plan, an approach developed by the Commonwealth Fund, based on input from Democratic and Republican lawmakers, relied on tax credits to subsidize private insurance and called for restricting Medicaid/SCHIP eligibility to 150% of poverty for the poor and near-poor.[78]

In February 2005, Mike Leavitt, the secretary of health and human services under President George W. Bush and former Republican governor of Utah, chose to make Medicaid the focus of his first formal speech, in which he subtly introduced the key ideological issue facing the Medicaid program: whether it would be entrenched as welfare medicine or reimagined as a mainstream social entitlement:

> Some have predicted that reform would break our commitment to our neediest and most vulnerable citizens: our mandatory populations, such as people with disabilities and children in low-income families or foster care. This is not true.[79]

Leavitt assured Americans that the federal government would maintain Medicaid's commitment to "our mandatory populations." Of course, most Americans and even many policymakers had no idea what that meant. As discussed previously, the key point to grasp about the mandatory populations is that they represent a very restricted group of people with very low income levels.[80] In Leavitt's speech and in Bush administration policy documents, there was a clear strategy for differential treatment for optional populations: either a reduced benefit package or a subsidy to purchase private health insurance. Especially since all the major coverage expansions in the decade prior to Leavitt's speech happened almost entirely through the use of optional coverage, the Bush administration's commitment only to the mandatory populations was, in short, a commitment to Medicaid as welfare medicine.

With the Bush administration clearly defining its position on Medicaid, and its support to build the safety net instead of investing in expanded Medicaid coverage (see Chapter 8), it is not too surprising that the ideological debate about Medicaid's essential purpose was at the forefront of Congress's consideration of the 2007 SCHIP reauthorization.[81] In general, the Republican position argued that the expanded SCHIP program should be a restricted to a narrowly targeted means-tested program for poor uninsured children, whereas children in families of greater economic means should be helped through the tax code to purchase private health insurance.[82] In the Bush administration's own words, opposition to the Democratic reauthorization proposal was "philosophical and ideological." The Administration and Congressional Republicans saw the plan as "big government." Senator Tom Coburn (R-OK) described it as "part of an effort to bring everyone into a socialized health care system."[83] While Republicans still wanted to use public funding by subsidizing private insurance for children in working families, their proposal would grow expenditures but hide its reach, and at the same time create more fragmentation and inequality within Medicaid.

While these statements were initially more focused on the Democrats attempt to expand SCHIP under the reauthorization bill, over time—during the summer and into the fall of 2007—Republican concerns focused on entrenching a particular vision for an *expanded* Medicaid. First, Republicans argued that Medicaid needed to focus on its original intent—to cover the "truly needy." In the SCHIP context, they claimed that many states had abandoned poor children who were the truly deserving of *public* coverage. Republicans focused on statistics suggesting that only about 60% of children in families earning less than 200 percent of the FPL were enrolled in state SCHIP programs. In response, they proposed that states should be restricted in how much they could expand eligibility (and still receive federal funding) until they could show proof of higher enrollment figures.[84] The Bush administration followed through with this proposal by issuing a federal guidance to state health officials in August 2007, which restricted state flexibility around eligibility expansions. In particular, the guidance limited states' ability to expand coverage to children with family incomes above 250 percent FPL unless states proved they had enrolled at least 95% of children below 200% FPL who were eligible.[85]

Congressional Republicans' second major argument, similar to the first, was that the target group had inappropriately expanded beyond SCHIP's original intention to cover uninsured children. Through federal waivers, states were allowed to expand coverage to groups other than children, which many states took advantage of. By 2005, about 600,000 adults were covered under SCHIP funds across states under federally allowed waiver programs.[86] Although Republicans prohibited any new waivers to cover childless adults under the Deficit Reduction Act of 2006, they fought for additional restrictions on adult coverage under the reauthorization act.

Finally, Republicans argued that some states had inappropriately used the separate SCHIP option because states had veered away from a private insurance model. In testimony, Nina Owcharenko, from the conservative Heritage Foundation, said that "administrative changes by some states have softened this private coverage model. Administrative changes, such as limiting or eliminating premiums and co-pays, diminish the correlation between SCHIP and traditional Medicaid."[87] Others worried that SCHIP crowded out private insurance. Representative Pete Sessions (R-TX), for example, said "that under the new bill, as under the old one, two million people would lose or drop private health insurance coverage and enroll in the expanded federal [SCHIP] program."[88] In response to their concern about growing "public" insurance models, Republicans proposed a new private coverage model in SCHIP, which included a more flexible premium assistance option. As Owcharenko described the proposal, "SCHIP should be a program that helps mainstream children in working families into private health care coverage, not a program that supplants it."[89]

While Democrats argued that SCHIP expansions to children in families with incomes above 200 percent of poverty should continue, it is noteworthy that they did not use Clinton's strategy a decade earlier to highlight middle-class reliance on Medicaid, or invoke an expanded social entitlement argument for why these expansions were important. Instead, consistent with a much longer history documented in this book when expansions were under threat—as they were with the SCHIP reauthorization—Democrats hid Medicaid's reach under federalism and a residual rhetoric of covering needy families (though avoiding the Republican refrain of the "truly needy").[90] Indeed, they often stated their position as one aligned with federalism and the granting of state flexibility. Testimony at a congressional hearing from the executive director of the National Academy for State Health Policy, Alan Weil, stated the preference for state actions as "a good example of 'cooperative federalism.' . . . The tremendous success and bipartisan popularity of this program is directly tied to its flexible, federal structure. Efforts to remake the program with a different vision run the risk of undermining the federal-state partnership that has allowed it to thrive."[91]

# Conclusion

Medicaid's political evolution from 1965 to 2008 illustrates the power of the Grow-and-Hide Regime to entrench an expanded Medicaid as fragmented, unequal, and strategically hidden through federalism with a heavy reliance on the private sector. Since 1965, Medicaid has developed in ways that built on its original ambiguous legislation. The failure of the 1965 act to provide precise definitions of the two concepts of medical indigence and comprehensive benefits has allowed continual debate about who is truly needy and deserving of coverage, and what type of benefits they are entitled to. While each critical juncture of expanded coverage has invited a struggle over the program's generosity and scope, it has at every turn created more fragmentation and unequal treatment between groups.

Thus, while expansion allowed Democrats to invoke an expanded vision of Medicaid as a social entitlement for the middle class at strategic times, the design of these expansions allowed an alternative frame and fostered a bifurcated political reality. The creation of SSI in 1972 led to the first clear bifurcation among Medicaid recipients: the elderly, blind, and disabled gained Medicaid eligibility based on a federal eligibility standard, while poor mothers and their children gained access through much more stringent state eligibility standards. Medicaid expansions in the 1980s further reinforced divisions among Medicaid groups by targeting special benefits to clienteles such as pregnant women and children, whom politicians viewed as both deserving and good investments. SCHIP was crucially important because it not only significantly expanded coverage but also created new delivery models for particular groups. It further enhanced private coverage with public Medicaid subsidies, while also using private insurance mechanisms to restrict coverage through premiums payments, copayments, and deductibles. And, by 2008, the vast majority of states contracted with Medicaid managed care organizations with restricted access to a narrow set of Medicaid providers, and gone were any promises that Medicaid beneficiaries would have access to the health care systems experienced by middle-class Americans. These reforms over time reveal how the Grow-and-Hide Regime expands coverage yet hides its middle-class reach by fostering fragmentation, inequality, and division within Medicaid and the larger health care system.

# The ACA Embraces Grow and Hide

The passage of the Affordable Care Act (ACA) in 2010 was a landmark political achievement. The last major reform of this proportion was the passage of Medicare and Medicaid. But, similar to the heady days of the Great Society, the ACA was also deeply ambitious. It represented the largest expansion since the passage of Medicare and Medicaid, extending coverage to 20 million Americans who were previously uninsured. It also included funding for health care infrastructure, workforce development, public health funding, and delivery model reforms.

However, the federal government passed these major reforms while leaving the Grow-and Hide-Regime untouched. As such, Grow and Hide remains as powerful as ever. Indeed, the ACA represents a set of complex and convoluted subsidies to consumers, insurance companies, large hospital systems, and the financial industry, making this reform the biggest Grow and Hide of all. The major consequences of Grow and Hide, as described in Chapters 7, 8, and 9, were not simply maintained but escalated: (1) the ACA's Medicaid expansion built on current inequities by continuing to bifurcate the program across enrollee groups and hide its true reach; (2) the ACA's attempt to create more coordination in the health care delivery system has been stymied because it relies yet again on voluntary participation lacking effective government regulation; and (3) the financial industry now reaches into every part of the health care system—physician specialty practices, hospital systems, physical therapy, behavioral health services, medical devices, telehealth, to name just a few—taking advantage of public funding to increase profits, while remaining completely unregulated and hidden from view.

## The ACA's Major Expansions

The ACA expanded coverage in two primary ways: (1) by creating health insurance marketplaces where individuals purchase health insurance from private plans during an annual open enrollment period, and (2) by expanding the

*Grow and Hide.* Colleen M. Grogan, Oxford University Press. © Oxford University Press 2023.
DOI: 10.1093/oso/9780199812233.003.0011

Medicaid program to persons up to 138% of the federal poverty level ($27,750 annual income for a family of four in 2022). The marketplace subsidies are a perfect example of complex and convoluted eligibility rules: a person (1) must not be eligible for employer-based health insurance; (2) must be a U.S. citizen or lawful resident of the United States; (3) must not be incarcerated; and (4) must have income levels between 100% and 400% of poverty to receive premium subsidies.[1]

In the early years of the ACA, the development of state-level marketplaces and the associated federal subsidies were hotly contested. Yet, compared to the tax exemption subsidies for employer-sponsored insurance (ESI) to middle- and upper-income Americans, marketplace subsidies are minuscule (see Figure 10.1). Subsidies for ESI continued under the ACA (nearly $300 billion in 2019) and will increase to over $550 billion by 2029, yet they remain hidden from public scrutiny and are not part of our health care policy debate.[2]

Despite the importance of the ACA marketplace expansions for uninsured Americans, which covered 12 million in 2021, it pales in comparison to the Medicaid program.[3] Because the ACA encouraged all uninsured Americans to sign up for health insurance, total Medicaid enrollment has increased 50% since enrollment for the ACA Medicaid expansion began in 2014. Total average monthly enrollment in Medicaid prior to the ACA was 56.5 million. By 2021, average monthly enrollment had increased to over 85 million.

Not surprisingly, a substantial increase in Medicaid spending has followed, from $498 billion in 2014 to $671 billion in 2020.[4] However, a small proportion (15%) of this spending is due to the Medicaid expansion. In addition, even states that did not expand Medicaid have increased enrollment and spending.[5] This is

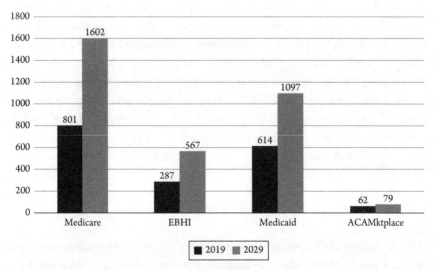

*Figure 10.1* Government Expenditures for Major Insurance Programs, 2019, and Estimated Projections for 2029 ($ billions). *Source:* Medicare data from Centers for Medicare & Medicaid Services, Office of the Actuary; all else from CBO report, *Federal Subsidies for Health Insurance Coverage for People Under Age 65: 2019 to 2029,* May 2, 2019.

due somewhat to increases in coverage during the COVID pandemic, but significant increases had occurred prior to COVID relief policy (up to $614 billion in 2019).[6] Increases in what is now called "regular Medicaid" occurred for two main reasons. First, there was a "woodwork effect" wherein expansion in coverage brought out many people who were already eligible for regular Medicaid. Second, similar to state activities prior to the ACA (as described in Chapter 9), many non-expansion states expanded regular Medicaid as much as they could (through waivers and numerous optional programs) to leverage federal funding.

Medicaid has expanded so significantly that it is the dominant form of health insurance in many states. In 2020, one-in-five non-elderly residents relied on Medicaid for coverage in half of all states. In 10 of these states, one-fourth of their residents relied on Medicaid, and in New Mexico (34%) and Louisiana (31%), nearly a third relied on the Medicaid program.[7] It is noteworthy that if the southern non-expansion states adopted the Medicaid expansion, nearly a third of their non-elderly residents would also rely on Medicaid, which helps to explain the political reluctance to expand Medicaid in these conservative states.[8]

The trend of Medicaid enrollment reaching into the middle class that started prior to the ACA has continued and expanded further. The majority (65%) of non-elderly Medicaid enrollees had incomes above the federal poverty level in 2019, up from 55% in 2008 (see Figure 10.2). One-third (32%) of non-elderly Medicaid enrollees had incomes above 200% of poverty in 2019. It is important to note that the U.S. median income level in 2019 was slightly below 300% of poverty, and about 20% of Medicaid enrollees had incomes

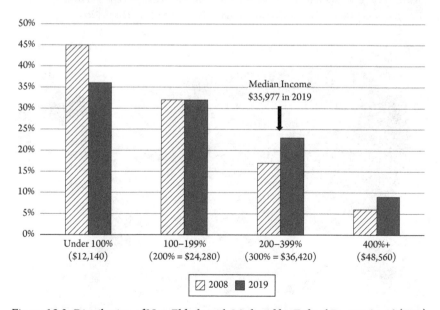

*Figure 10.2* Distribution of Non-Elderly with Medicaid by Federal Poverty Level (FPL), 2008 and 2019. *Source:* Kaiser Family Foundation, State Health Facts 2022. *Note:* Federal poverty threshold levels are for individuals (one-person household) in 2019.

above that level. While there is significant variation in the degree to which states cover Medicaid enrollees above the poverty level, it is noteworthy that even in the most restrictive states, 54% of non-elderly Medicaid enrollees have incomes above the federal poverty level (see Figure 10.3). Conversely, even several conservative, non-expansion states (e.g., Texas, Georgia, South Carolina, and Florida) cover individuals with incomes above $48,000 (above 400% FPL) for 9–12% of their Medicaid enrollees (see Figure 10.4).

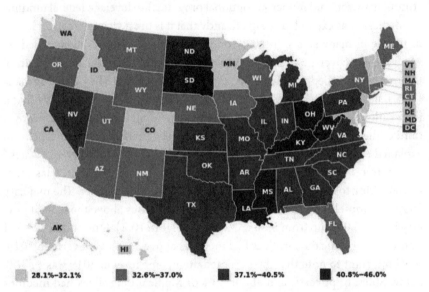

*Figure 10.3* Distribution of the Non-Elderly with Medicaid by Federal Poverty Level (FPL): Under 100%, 2019. *Source:* Kaiser Family Foundation, State Health Facts.

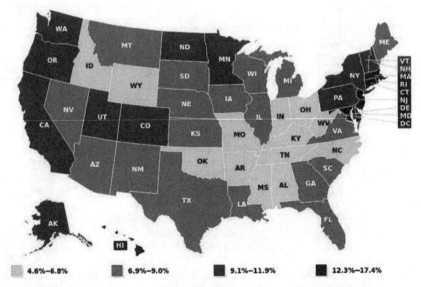

*Figure 10.4* Distribution of the Non-Elderly with Medicaid by Federal Poverty Level (FPL): 400%+, 2019. *Source:* Kaiser Family Foundation, State Health Facts.

Finally, another example of Medicaid's significant reach into America's middle class is the extent to which people have a connection to the program. In 2020, two-thirds of all Americans (66%) reported having received health insurance through the program themselves (31%), or their child (9%), or other friends or family members (26%) receiving Medicaid coverage.[9]

# Hiding Medicaid's Reach (Again)

Building on the Grow-and-Hide Regime, the ACA made the Medicaid program the main engine for expanded coverage yet hid the significant extent of these expansions through the pillars of Grow and Hide—federalism, fragmentation, private contracting, and political discourse.

## Building on Federalism, Fragmentation, and Bifurcation

While the ACA Medicaid expansion allowed Democratic-controlled states to embrace a broader ideological vision of Medicaid as a program to prevent poverty and promote health equity for low- and even middle-income Americans, it also ushered in a strong rejection of this vision. The *National Federation of Independent Business v. Sebelius* lawsuit, supported by 25 states, argued against the constitutionality of the federal ACA mandate to expand Medicaid,[10] and the Supreme Court ruled in favor of the plaintiff. This ruling emphasized the true significance of federalism under the Grow-and-Hide Regime and allowed conservative states to bargain with the federal government over how to extend and frame expanded coverage.

The ACA did not restructure the Medicaid program but added a new eligibility group on top of a complex eligibility system. From the beginning, the program has been structured differently for three main enrollment groups—the elderly, the disabled, and families who meet income eligibility cutoffs. Although the ACA Medicaid expansion expanded coverage to all individuals up to 138% of poverty, states must still go through the arduous process of figuring out which people fit into which eligibility bucket. They do this because the federal government applies different matching rates for individuals eligible through different programs, whether it is disability, "regular Medicaid," the Children's Health Insurance Program (CHIP), the ACA expansion, or many other designations. As a result, states can and do design different benefits for different eligibility groups, which means individuals within the same state Medicaid program have access to a different set of covered services and medications, a different set of providers and health care facilities, and a different set of requirements for cost-sharing and premium payments.

Despite some attempts to frame Medicaid more broadly (and accurately) as a program for millions of Americans across a spectrum of needs (as
discussed in Chapter 9), Medicaid and its constituents—even under the ACA
expansions—are often invoked differently under separate programs. For example, when the Republican Congress attempted to repeal the Medicaid expansion in 2017, several opinion pieces in the *New York Times* writing against
repeal focused on groups considered more deserving. A mother wrote one
about her "sweet son" who has autism spectrum disorder to make clear the
importance of Medicaid for middle-class families, while another stressed the
importance of long-term care services and supports (LTSS) for elderly parents
and for middle-class adults who will undoubtedly need LTSS in the future.[11]
It is noteworthy that the elderly and disabled are still drawn upon during
times of retrenchment to illustrate the clear deservingness of the program's
recipients.[12]

Equally noteworthy, conservative states have signaled out persons who
are unhoused, involved with the criminal justice system, or unemployed
as less deserving. Under the ACA, Republican-led states have expanded
Medicaid, but often under policy reforms that focus on individual behaviors
of particular Medicaid recipients with the intent to uplift "personal
responsibility."[13]

Under the Trump administration, by November 2019, seven states had
approved work requirements, which require work as a condition of eligibility for Medicaid; ten states required premium payments, including receipt of payment before coverage begins or a lockout period (e.g., six months
in Indiana) if premiums are not paid; and seven states have received waivers
to increase copays above previously allowed levels, and/or healthy behavior
incentives tied to premiums or cost-sharing.[14] The discussion around these
reforms raises questions about whether certain low-income Americans
deserve public Medicaid coverage, with the emphasis on *public* for these
individuals.[15]

Early data suggest these policy designs result in many individuals losing their
Medicaid coverage. For example, after Arkansas implemented its work requirement, 18,000 people were disenrolled from the program.[16] Other studies found
cost-related barriers due to Indiana's lockout period if required payments were
not deposited in health savings accounts. Although coverage has expanded in
the state, it's crucially important to recognize how Indiana intentionally treats
Medicaid groups differently based on individual behavior and notions of deservingness.[17] Similarly, in Wisconsin, Governor Scott Walker requested permission
to subject "the poor" who apply for Medicaid to a drug test.[18]

## Political Discourse: Parts of Medicaid Are "Not Medicaid"

Under Grow and Hide, conservative states have rejected an expanded public vision of Medicaid, even when they used public funds to expand the program. Indeed, when conservative states adopted the Medicaid expansion, they often portrayed their reform efforts as "not Medicaid" but a private initiative that demands "consumer-driven personal responsibility." Under this frame, the state's role is intentionally hidden, and public funds received from the federal government are strategically obscured.[19]

In 2011, when Democratic Governor Beebe in conservative Arkansas proposed a Medicaid waiver to adopt the ACA Medicaid expansion, he never questioned the deservingness of the uninsured to receive Medicaid coverage but argued that the private sector could do it better. At that time, the Beebe administration did not avoid arguing that Medicaid should remain intact but argued that it needed to be significantly reformed. However, as opposition in the Republican-controlled legislature increased in 2013, the administration strategically eliminated the term "Medicaid" from public statements and only referred to the expansion waiver as the "private option." The intent of this framing was clearly to portray the waiver as distinct from Medicaid and not building on the traditional program.

Iowa's Governor Terry Branstad also described the Medicaid program as broken and his Medicaid waiver as providing a "commercial-like benefits package," which demanded "shared responsibility." As Branstad described it, "If you have no skin in the game, you spend more. . . . We want to give people incentives to make the right choice."[20] Iowa's waiver reforms supported this rhetoric. The state incorporated cost-sharing, premiums, and health behavior incentives. Although these mechanisms were not new to the Medicaid program, states had never imposed cost-sharing on persons below the federal poverty level prior to Iowa's waiver.

Just a few months later, Michigan's waiver was approved, and the discourse over reform was almost identical. Although Michigan's leaders used the term "personal responsibility" instead of "shared responsibility," the emphasis was similarly on the importance of including monthly premiums and cost-sharing. It also included a health savings account so that individuals could act as "responsible health care consumers."

Under Republican governor Tom Corbett, Pennsylvania was the first state to pursue a work requirement in its waiver proposal. Initially, the discourse in favor of Pennsylvania's waiver was similar to other states by focusing on the benefits of the private sector and the virtues of the free market. However, Governor Corbett argued for the importance of connecting employment to eligibility for the Medicaid expansion waiver. In the Healthy Pennsylvania waiver proposal, any individual working less than 20 hours a week needed to demonstrate that they had completed 12 job search activities a month to remain eligible for coverage. For Corbett, the work requirement was essential to the entire waiver proposal. Jennifer Branstetter, Corbett's policy director, remarked that, for the governor, removing the employment criteria "breaks the plan as a whole."[21]

Indiana was having its Medicaid expansion waiver debate at the same time as Pennsylvania, and the discourse was very similar. Seema Verma, who became the director of the Centers for Medicare & Medicaid Services (CMS) under the Trump administration, and architect of Indiana Medicaid reforms—the Healthy Indiana Plan (HIP 2.0)—remarked that the structure of Indiana's reforms was meant to "promote the notion of consumerism," and argued that it "transforms Medicaid beneficiaries into consumers."[22] This transformation led to the most complex structure of the Medicaid expansion in any waiver state. Indiana implemented four different benefits plans, premiums for all newly insured regardless of income, cost-sharing for those below the poverty line, and an emphasis on healthy behaviors for all the newly enrolled. The central component of Indiana's plan to transform the newly eligible into health care consumers was the Personal Wellness and Responsibility (POWER) health savings account.[23]

Suzanne Mettler's book *The Submerged State* shows that hiding the role of government in various subsidized programs is part of a broader phenomenon in the American welfare state.[24] Public subsidies received through tax exemptions, such as employer-based health insurance, are so well hidden from view that many people who benefit from such programs do not believe they have ever received a public subsidy, which influences their view of government in general, and hence of public programs. Mettler's study reveals an implicit process of submerging the state's role, especially for certain groups of people, through the design of public policies.

Under Grow and Hide, the process is driven by policy design and political discourse in the American health care state. The above examples illustrate the discursive intent to alter the public's understanding of Medicaid—from a government-run and publicly funded program to one that provides access to private insurance and empowers enrollees to act as consumers in the health care marketplace.

We also find similar discourse in several states that created their own marketplace exchanges. Just as states claimed that their Medicaid expansions were not Medicaid (and not part of the ACA), states also claimed that their state-run marketplaces were not connected to the ACA, or the more politically contentious term "Obamacare." Kentucky, for example, called its marketplace "Kynect" and sought to disassociate it from the ACA. The enrollment outreach workers actively hid the connection: "When we're approaching people about getting signed up on health care, one of the first questions they have is, 'Is this

Obamacare?' So we would tell them, 'No, this is not Obamacare. This is a state-run plan.'"[25]

Because states have also intentionally created multiple types of Medicaid programs, each with a different name and set of rules for who is eligible, constituents likely feel connected to their particular program but not to Medicaid as a whole. For example, people indirectly connected to Medicaid through their elderly parents in a nursing home may only be motivated to fight against retrenchment to the long-term care side of Medicaid and not against Medicaid retrenchment for low-income families. This is the power of Grow and Hide: the regime not only creates fragmentation, inequality, and bifurcation within Medicaid, but also creates a politics and associated political rhetoric that deeply obscures the role of the state and therefore serves to further fuel fragmentation, inequality, and bifurcation.

A recent study found that people who received Medicaid coverage for their children (currently or in the past) through Medicaid's CHIP program are no more likely to support spending increases for Medicaid or adoption of the Medicaid expansion than people with no connection to the Medicaid program.[26] This finding is puzzling because most studies find that parents whose children are enrolled in CHIP report that the program is very important to them. However, the logic of Grow and Hide explains this puzzle.

First, when states eliminate Medicaid from specific program names, as in the examples discussed with the Medicaid expansion programs, and as they did with CHIP programs (e.g., AllKids in Illinois; Peach Care in Georgia), it may be (as the rhetoric and name change intended) that the people enrolled in these programs do not know they are (or were) on Medicaid. When the survey asked whether a respondent's child was covered under Medicaid, the question was worded: "Does any child under the age of 19 in your household currently have health insurance through Medicaid, also known in your state as [insert state name], or not?" However, when the survey asked respondents about support for Medicaid spending increases, the question only used the term "Medicaid"; that is, they did not follow with "also known in your state as [insert state name]." Because states make a concerted effort to distance their CHIP coverage from the Medicaid program, it is conceivable that people receiving this coverage for their children do not actually view it as Medicaid coverage. If this is the case, it is not surprising that their view about Medicaid spending and the Medicaid expansion is, all else being equal, similar to those with no connection to Medicaid.

Second, in the early 1990s, many states began reforming their Medicaid programs to contract with Medicaid managed care organizations (MCOs) to provide services primarily to non-elderly and nondisabled adults enrolled in

Medicaid (see Chapter 9). Today, almost all U.S. states contract with MCOs; almost two-thirds of states that contract with MCOs enroll 75% of their Medicaid in MCOs.[27] The use of MCOs is (and has been) especially prominent for those enrolled in CHIP (with coverage only for their child[ren]). Thus, not only do people sign up for Healthy Michigan, but they must also enroll in a health plan, such as a "Blue Cross Complete" plan, allowing another layer of confusion as to whether they are enrolled in Medicaid. Many enrollees may believe they are privately insured through their private MCO plan and have lost awareness of their status as Medicaid enrollees.

Third, it could be that people connected to Medicaid only through their children do have a more restrictive view of whom the program should be for and what its purpose should be. Perhaps because these respondents are working and only their children are eligible for coverage (by program design), and because many states often require them to pay premiums and some cost-sharing, they might feel resentment toward people on "regular" Medicaid. Health reporter Sarah Kliff's interview with a Medicaid recipient provides a good illustration of this view:

> [Kathy] had enrolled on Medicaid for a few months, right before she
> started this job. She was taking some time off to care for her husband,
> who has cancer and was in chemotherapy treatment.
> [The reporter] asked how she felt about enrolling in a program she
> sometimes criticizes.
> "Oh, no," [Kathy] said quickly. "I worked my whole life, so I know
> I paid into it. I just felt like it was a time that I needed it. That's what the
> system is set up for."[28]

The logic of Grow and Hide and the discursive tactics described here not only increase inequality within and across states under an expanded Medicaid, but also serve to fragment and bifurcate enrollment groups within Medicaid. Quotes from news stories like the one above suggest that these deservingness ideas related to Medicaid have begun to sink in among the American public. For example, a person who purchased an ACA plan on the marketplace said: "I think Medicaid is good, but I'm really having a problem with the people that don't want to work. Us middle-class people are really, really upset about having to work constantly, and then these people are not responsible." These quotes illustrate the political implications of fragmented expansion under the Grow-and-Hide Regime. Politicians have not engaged in significant cross-group mobilizing work within Medicaid, or across Medicaid and the marketplace, and different ACA enrollment groups are unable to see the potential for a broad-based coalition.[29]

# Déjà Vu: No Government Planning, ONLY Voluntary Action

Because real government-led health care planning would necessarily reform the health care delivery system, it is (and always has been) a major affront to the health care industry. The ACA continued a long-standing pattern in the United States of successfully passing coverage expansions but failing to enact any truly meaningful delivery model reforms. The ACA encouraged demonstration projects, which were all implemented by the private sector. There was no planning role with any regulatory teeth for public health or health care coverage agencies (e.g., Centers for Medicare & Medicaid Services). Instead, and again in keeping with the Grow-and-Hide pattern, the ACA provided funding in three major areas—(1) payment reform, (2) comparative effectiveness research, and (3) prevention and public health—that were intended to reform the delivery system by increasing quality and reducing health care costs, but, similar to the planning bills in the 1970s (see Chapter 7), the government centers and agencies that housed these initiatives have no regulatory power, and all private sector participation is voluntary.[30]

## ACA Payment Reforms

When the ACA was passed in 2010, many experts claimed that several cost-control provisions would "bend the cost curve." These provisions included tax breaks for high-cost employer-sponsored health insurance (the Cadillac tax), payment reforms, and an expert commission called the Independent Payment Advisory Board (IPAB) to develop recommendations for reducing excess Medicare spending growth. The assumption behind all these reforms was that health care spending in the United States was so wasteful that it was possible to reduce costs without damaging quality.[31] Indeed, all these reforms were incredibly weak from a cost-control perspective, but that didn't stop private stakeholders from rallying against them. Both the Cadillac tax and IPAB created widespread backlash and were repealed.[32] As a result, most cost-control efforts have focused on payment reform.

The ACA promoted payment reforms through the creation of the Center for Medicare and Medicaid Innovation (CMMI). CMMI was given authority to design, implement, and test new health care payment models (called Alternative Payment Models or APMs) in the Medicare and Medicaid programs. Congress allocated $10 billion over a 10-year period (from 2011 to 2019) to CMMI to focus on models that could potentially lower health care spending for Medicare and Medicaid while maintaining or enhancing the quality of care provided.[33]

Policymakers' motivations to focus on payment reform stemmed from volu-
minous studies since the 1970s showing that fee-for-service (FFS) payment is
the main culprit for high costs and overutilization of health care services in the
United States.[34] Under FFS schemes, there are incentives for providers to do
more than might be necessary, because they get paid for every service provided,
and there is evidence of "gaming," wherein providers "upcode"—submit more
intensive codes with higher reimbursement levels even though the actual care
provided represented less intensive care. These arguments provide the backbone
for CMMI's goal of moving away from FFS and towards payment models that
encourage "value-based care."

For example, the Health Care Payment Learning Action Network (HCPLAN)
is a set of committees comprising health care leaders primarily from the private
sector yet funded by the federal government's CMS to accelerate the adoption
of APMs. The network's most recent white paper argues that effective payment
reform must move away from FFS toward capitated payment linked to quality
metrics.[35]

However, it is important to note that the concern about FFS payment stems
primarily from how it operates under Grow and Hide in the U.S. system: a plethora
of fee schedules, each designed for different provider types (e.g., physicians,
hospitals, dentists), each relying on thousands of complex and minute codes
to represent minor differences in care provided (e.g., some 20 different codes
to capture the variety of primary care office visits), and each subject to interest
group lobbying.

Moreover, despite payment reform advocacy and the long-standing literature demonizing FFS, the most significant culprit for higher costs in the United
States is the incredibly high price of health care services. Cross-national health
care spending analyses show that differences in prices explain much of the difference in spending between the United States and other countries.[36] Although
price transparency has become a more important policy issue,[37] most prices remain entirely hidden from view and are so convoluted and complex that most
consumers would have no idea what their bill might be even if they tried to
figure it out prospectively. Most importantly, any discussion of regulated prices
was completely off the table under the ACA. For example, Congress gave no
authority to CMMI to address health care prices. Instead, still building on the
competition rhetoric that began in the 1980s (see Chapter 8), these new payment models under health care competition are supposed to bring down health
care spending.[38] Health law and antitrust expert Thomas Greaney described the
situation in a congressional hearing on the ACA in 2011:

> I'd like to begin with an important proposition that is sometimes lost in
> the rhetoric about health reform. The Affordable Care Act both depends

on and promotes competition in provider and insurance markets. A key point is that the new law does not regulate prices for commercial health insurance or prices in the hospital, physician, pharmaceutical, or medical device markets. Instead, the law relies on (1) competitive bargaining between payers and providers and (2) rivalry within each sector to drive price and quality to levels that best serve the public.[39]

Greaney argued that so many programs under the ACA were designed to enhance competition that "the ACA might well be rechristened as the 'Accommodation of Competition Act.' "[40] Indeed, since ACA's passage, the CMMI has been extremely active in implementing new payment models to encourage competition. By 2018, the CMMI had launched over 40 new payment models in all 50 states and the District of Columbia, involving more than 18 million patients and 200,000 providers.[41] However, the CMMI developed so many new models that several researchers have complained that rather than create innovation or competition, the plethora of models has created further complexity in an already chaotic system. Rocco Perla and colleagues' evaluation of the five early models used by the CMMI concluded: "Innovation is not always about creating new models; sometimes it is about better integrating and coordinating existing models."[42] True enough. However, this statement belies the reality of attempting payment reform under the Grow-and-Hide Regime, where the government plays the most prominent role in financing the U.S. health care system and yet has become completely marginalized as a regulator or planner. Indeed, in keeping with the historical pattern of Grow and Hide, CMMI reforms have actually increased complexity by layering new payments models on top of the FFS chassis.[43]

Moreover, while APMs apply to many sectors in the health care system, pharmaceutical prices and payment policy remain largely untouched by CMMI reforms, even though the cost of drugs now consumes nearly 10% of total health expenditures and is expected to increase 50% in the next few years.[44] Not only does the CMMI not address pharmaceutical costs, but the ACA was clear that Medicare cannot negotiate over drug prices.[45] As a result, novel medicines continue to command very high prices, and while some are highly effective, many are not aligned with value.[46]

Although the CMMI launched numerous models, the Accountable Care Organizations (ACOs) model is the most prominent. In addition to the concerns about FFS, the problem of fragmentation in the U.S. health care system was also prominent (as it had been so many times in the past) in reform discussions around the ACA. For example, a book in 2010 concluded that considerable scholarship had identified fragmentation in health care delivery as a significant source of inefficiency in the health care system but argued that the problem is not the market but government policy.[47] The CMMI's Medicare Shared Savings Program, which promoted Accountable Care Organizations (ACOs), was one of the key reforms to address fragmentation. As Greaney explains:

> An ACO must be a group of providers and suppliers that has an es-
> tablished mechanism for joint decision making and may include
> practitioners (physicians, regardless of specialty; nurse practitioners;
> physician assistants; and clinical nurse specialists) in group practice
> arrangements, networks of practices, and partnerships or joint ven-
> ture arrangements between hospitals and practitioners. The Medicare
> program will pay the ACOs a . . . share savings based on comparing
> the ACOs' cost to benchmark payments under traditional Medicare.
> To qualify, these "accountable care organizations" (ACOs) must agree
> to be accountable for the overall care of a defined group of Medicare
> beneficiaries, to have sufficient participation of primary care physicians,
> to have processes that promote evidence-based medicine, to report on
> quality and costs, and to be capable of coordinating care.[48]

The Medicare Payment Advisory Commission (MedPAC) and a group of influential health service researchers at Dartmouth endorsed the idea. What is crucially important about the ACO model is that it promotes vertical coordination across health care sectors and market competition simultaneously. In congressional testimony, Greaney promoted ACOs in relation to consolidation as follows:

> [T]here is both good consolidation and bad consolidation. Problematic
> consolidation occurs principally among horizontal combinations
> of hospitals forming monopolies and getting dominant systems, as
> well as on the insurance side. By contrast, vertical combinations be-
> tween hospitals and physicians can reduce fragmentation and help
> fix the problems of the system and encourage more competition.
> The Affordable Care Act, I believe, encourages the pro-competitive
> consolidations.[49]

The problem for Greaney and other supporters of ACOs is that even as early as 2012, when this congressional hearing took place, consolidations in the health care marketplace were on the rise, and there was growing concern about increasing prices due to monopoly power. It is noteworthy that the title of this hearing was "Healthcare Consolidation and Competition after PPACA." Republicans had taken control of both Houses for the first time in eight years and were strongly against the ACA. Not only did they argue that the ACA was unconstitutional due to the individual mandate to purchase insurance on the marketplace, but they also argued that the law reduced competition. As the Republican chairman of the subcommittee said in his opening remarks:

> The law [ACA] . . . scrambles the economics of America's health care system in a way that reduces competition. And when competition is reduced, higher prices, less innovation, and lower quality care follows. . . . We know that centralized, top-down, government run systems do not work as well as competitive markets. . . . But Obamacare places government decision making over free-market competition. . . . I expect the testimony at today's hearing will demonstrate how the administration's regulatory approach reduces competition and leads to higher medical costs and lower quality care.[50]

As with most topics connected to the ACA, the debate over the ACA and consolidation was utterly partisan. However, most importantly, even during this politically polarized time, there was agreement that market competition in health care was the goal. Democrats acknowledged that consolidation was a problem with many harmful effects but argued (as is true) that the trends were occurring before the ACA, and placed blame on a weak Department of Justice and lack of antitrust enforcement under the Federal Trade Commission.[51] Nonetheless, this hyperbolic debate over whether the ACA was the culprit made it impossible to rationally discuss how the government might approach the rise in consolidations.

Although the CMMI's ACO model was often touted as original and new, as policy fads often are,[52] its theory of care coordination and cross-sector coordination was similar to the HMOs promoted in the 1970s and the managed care models that followed. A key difference, however, was that the CMMI's ACO programs started with even weaker designs in terms of cost control. The decision to create an ACO is entirely voluntary among participating Medicare providers, and Medicare patient participation in ACOs is also voluntary, and fluid— patients can leave the ACO any time during the year. Most importantly, most of these early models only offered bonuses to incentivize change—what is called "upside risk"—and most experts argue that upside risk alone will not move the dial on either producing value or reducing costs.[53] Studies to date report modest savings for ACOs and conclude that imposing downside risk on ACOs is needed to achieve reform.[54] Under downside risk, providers agree to a set payment amount for a predetermined enrollee group. The theory is that under a set payment, providers have incentives to provide high-value, efficient care.

However, as the CMMI encourages more downside risk, ACOs are more likely to drop out of the shared-savings program. As long as provider participation is voluntary, providers will only participate in downside risk if there is evidence that the risks are relatively minimal—that is, they have good data on patients to suggest that they can reach the spending targets and quality metrics and still make money. Not surprisingly, not all providers view the CMMI's offer as a good risk, and there is no regulatory authority on the part of the CMMI to make them participate.

Indeed, some value-based payment models exacerbate inequities because payments do not adequately adjust for higher risk among vulnerable populations and, as a result, act as a disincentive to provide care to such populations.[55] For example, the CMMI's new ACO investment model recently contracted with 41 ACOs serving higher-risk patients in underserved rural areas. Although net savings occurred in the program's first three years, when these ACOs were asked to take on downside risk based on benchmarks tied to historically low payment rates, two-thirds of these ACOs exited the program.[56] To date, Medicare's implementation of its ACO AIM program has resulted in further inequities in an unequal health care system. However, despite these findings, recent Medicare CMMI reforms provide ACOs with even more incentives to select providers with lower-risk patients, thus providing opportunities for further patient bifurcation and inequities.[57]

It is also clear that ACOs work better for some sectors in the health care system than others. For example, because physicians, unlike hospitals, do not have competing profit incentives to hospitalize patients, independent physician group ACOs have a greater incentive to participate in the ACO model. In contrast, hospitals still produce the highest costs in the health care system and have little incentive to participate. Among the hospital ACOs participating, 47% left the CMMI's Shared Savings Program from 2014 to 2017.[58]

In sum, providers and plans are most interested in participating in CMMI models where the payments are high and, as a result, Medicaid savings are modest. In a parallel vein, providers have voiced much less enthusiasm for moving toward population-based capitated payments in the areas where payments are low, such as the Medicaid program. Again, we see Grow and Hide in action: if the payments are high, private actors are quickly ready to serve; private actors will call this innovative high-value care driven by the private sector; yet, under such large payments, it will be a charade to call this "value-based care" or good value for the money.

Finally, the hope that vertical consolidation under ACOs would bring about good competition has not borne fruit. Despite Greaney's early hope, he and his coauthor acknowledged in 2020 that "[h]ospital acquisitions of physician practices have escaped scrutiny, despite going on apace for years. The percentage of primary care physicians and specialists in practices owned by hospitals/ health systems nearly doubled from 2010 to 2018. Vertical integration across other sectors is common as well: insurers, hospitals, surgi-centers, pharmacies, pharmacy benefit managers and physician practices."[59] A 2016 study on health care market concentration found that 90% of Metropolitan Statistical Areas (MSAs) were highly concentrated for hospitals, 65% for specialists, 39% for primary care physicians, and 57% for insurers.[60] Considerable empirical evidence demonstrates that consolidation—horizontal and vertical integration—results in higher prices, with no improvements to quality.[61] And as health care prices increase, so too have health insurance premiums.[62] Another study reports that some hospital mergers resulted in lower wages for health care workers.[63]

## Comparative Effectiveness Research

Many countries use comparative effectiveness research (CER) to increase the use of treatments with known effectiveness. Many argue that CER is needed because there is surprisingly little information about the benefits and harms of many medical services. According to a recent literature review, 50% of all medical services actively being used are of unknown effectiveness, and an additional 9% of medical services are unlikely to be helpful or have proven ineffective or even harmful.[64] To reduce low-value spending, many experts have called for an increase in comparative effectiveness research in the United States to create the evidence base for providing effective medical technologies and treatments.[65]

The ACA created the Patient-Centered Outcomes Research Institute (PCORI) to encourage the use of effective treatments. Even though CER received bipartisan support prior to the ACA, the creation of the PCORI quickly became a political lightning rod, with the familiar claims of an overbearing government interfering in doctor-patient relationships and rationing of care. Town hall meetings equated the work of the PCORI to "death panels."[66] In response to the political hyperbole, Congress curtailed the PCORI's authority to prevent it from influencing physician decision-making. The PCORI was explicitly not housed in a government agency, but instead designed as an independent, nonprofit institute with a small budget. Unlike many OECD countries, which use cost-effectiveness methods to guide coverage decisions regarding particular treatments, PCORI-funded research on treatment effectiveness is not permitted to include health care costs in their studies. The PCORI is only allowed to present its findings in terms of effectiveness (not cost-effectiveness). Congress also barred the Centers for Medicare & Medicaid Services (CMS) from using PCORI-funded research as the basis for reimbursement decisions.[67] In sum, there is intentionally no linkage between the PCORI's research findings and public-sector spending on health care.

Nevertheless, similar to the 1970s Planning Act (see Chapter 7), under Grow and Hide, even though provider interest groups successfully created an extremely weak agency, they have used the agency's lack of efficacy against it. For example, provider groups argue that spending on the PCORI is wasteful and has not contributed to research in a meaningful way. Indeed, by design, the PCORI is a timid agency and can only offer vague or weak guidelines based on its research, and has not had any significant impact on the clinical behavior of physicians.[68] Even with no regulatory power, Ann Keller and colleagues found that PCORI often avoids researching high-cost treatments for fear of mobilizing hostile stakeholders.[69]

Moreover, and also similar to the multiple fragmented planning agencies created in the 1970s, Congress created the PCORI with no clear plan as to how it fits in with existing health research agencies—the U.S. Food and Drug Administration (FDA), Agency for Healthcare Research and Quality (AHRQ), and National Institutes of Health (NIH). As such, even though the PCORI was designed to fill a clear gap in knowledge about treatment effectiveness, provider groups launch charges of duplication and government waste.[70]

Finally, and again remarkably similar to the National Health Planning and Resources Development Act of 1974, adding the term "Patient-Centered" to the PCORI's name sent a signal about whom the institute should serve. It attempts to denote a type of democratic engagement (similar to the Health Service Agencies run by local communities), and symbolically moves the organization away from claims of attempts to control physician behavior, but naively assumes patients will support limits on access to specific treatments based on its effectiveness research.[71]

## Prevention and Public Health Fund

The ACA also created the Prevention and Public Health Fund (PPHF) to "provide expanded and sustained national investments in prevention and public health, to improve health and help restrain the rate of growth in private and public health care costs."[72] Just as in the past, a core part of PPHF's funding has bolstered the country's federated public health infrastructure by providing support directly to local, state, and federal programs (APHA 2017). In the first year alone (2011), the CDC provided 67 grants across 36 states. Most grants funded private-public partnerships across multiple sectors, including schools, transportation, private businesses, and faith-based and nonprofit community-based organizations (CDC 2017).

Politicians discussed PPHF spending in ways almost identical to the 1920s, reflecting a debate about prevention versus treatment. For example, when HHS allocated some of the funding to increase the primary care workforce, several key Democrats in Congress expressed concern, saying there was a clear idea that PPHF would not support physician workforce expansion efforts (McCarthy 2010). However, if one looks at strategies for improving health promotion and prevention and attacking chronic disease, primary, community-based care investments have always been paramount.

And that is the point: for public health to be most effective, it must be active in many spheres. But therein also lies its political conundrum. Under Grow and Hide, even in 1926, public health luminary Charles-Edward Winslow was clear that efforts to demarcate prevention and cure provided a useful political rationale but hindered practical implementation of any efforts to improve health:

> In the past [there was a] plausible attempt to draw a line between prevention and cure, by assuming that prevention is the task of the state and that treatment should be left to the private physician. This is a good phrase, and as a people, we Americans love to govern our affairs by phrases . . . [But] the habit of condemning any attempt at intelligent community action by labeling it as "socialistic" and "bureaucratic" is for example unworthy of serious-minded men. Some things are better done by the individual, some better by the state; and catchwords will not help us to determine to which class a given activity belongs. (Winslow 1926, 1082)

The extremely partisan debate over the ACA and attempts since its passage to repeal the PPHF illustrates that Americans still love to govern their affairs by phrases (U.S. Congress 2011, 2633). While the phrases have changed, the essence of the debate lurking behind prevention spending is the same, insisting on a false divide between prevention and treatment. At the root of this insistence is a political struggle about the role of government in planning and organizing the U.S. health care system. And that relates to the persistent hiding of the true extent that public funding covers expenditures in the system. Surely if the American public knew the extent, it might insist on some accountability for how private actors use that funding. That fact, of course, helps explain why funding continues and labeling prevention spending as "socialistic" and "bureaucratic" persists.

## The Financial Industry's Takeover of ACA's "Competition"

By 2020, private equity (PE) firms had moved into almost every facet of health care. Apollo Global Management, a $330 billion investment firm, owned RCCH

Healthcare Partners, an operator of 88 rural hospital campuses in West Virginia, Tennessee, Kentucky, and 26 other states. Cerberus Capital Management, a $42 billion investment firm, owned Steward Health Care, which runs 35 hospitals and a swath of urgent care facilities in 11 states. Warburg Pincus owned Modernizing Medicine, an information technology company that helps health care providers ramp up profits through medical billing and, to a lesser degree, debt collections. The Carlyle Group owned MedRisk, a leading provider of physical therapy cost-containment systems for U.S. workers' compensation payers, such as insurers and large employers.[73]

Estimated annual health care deal values increased from $41.5 billion in 2010 to nearly $120 billion in 2019, reaching approximately $750 billion over the 2010 decade.[74] In 2018, the value of PE health care assets under management reached nearly $1.5 trillion.[75] From 2011 to 2019, health care ranked among the top three industries every year in terms of return on investment for PE firms since 2011.[76]

Although public policy incentives for private capital investments in health care were well in place prior to 2010 (see Chapter 8), the ACA turbocharged these incentives due to three main factors: (1) coverage expansion under the ACA, (2) a lack of regulations over private capital and weak antitrust enforcement, and (3) the continuation of a hidden capital health policy.

## Private Equity Takes Advantage of ACA Expansions and Public Funds

Given the political volatility of Obama's health care reform, especially from 2010 through 2017, one might ask why the health care industry was so attractive to PE investment firms? An essay in Health Capital Topics identified three factors that assure investment stability: "a reliably aging population with increasing demands for healthcare services; an influx of newly insured individuals due to ACA coverage expansions; and, an increasing incidence and prevalence of chronic disease."[77]

In explaining why health care is a good investment, PE funds usually point to the reliable revenue stream that reimbursement from publicly funded programs provides. For example, increasing demand due to an aging population creates favorable investment opportunities because Medicare covers those over age 65. Moreover, as the quote suggests, the coverage expansions under the ACA provide a sure increase in demand for health care services and a revenue stream to pay for it. Kara Murphy and Nirad Jain of Bain Insights, writing in Forbes, also concur: "healthcare is a safe-haven investment—that is, one with a proven resilience to economic volatility . . . [this] holds true even when the uncertainty affects the industry itself, as it has with the acrimonious debate over the future of the ACA."[78] Indeed, by 2017, they concluded that "[h]ealthcare has long been a winning investment for PE funds."[79]

Just as the reliability of Medicare dollars created a profitable market for specialty hospitals, as did Medicaid dollars for PE investments in the nursing home industry in the early 2000s (see Chapter 8), publicly funded expansions under the ACA have been a particularly lucrative target for PE since the early 2010s. For example, due to new benefit requirements under the ACA, Medicaid coverage of behavioral health services has expanded enormously since 2010. This coverage expansion came at the same time the United States was still experiencing the opioid epidemic; thus, as Medicaid coverage expanded, there was a dramatic increase in demand for substance use disorder treatment, and PE firms pounced at the opportunity. PE investments in behavioral health increased 24% in deal volume in just one year. As *Wall Street Journal* reporters explained in an article titled "Private-Equity Pours Cash into Opioid-Treatment Sector," PE is drawn to behavioral health due to "soaring demand, expanded insurance coverage and the chance to consolidate a highly fragmented market, firms plowed $2.9 billion into treatment facilities last year (2016), up from $11.4 million in 2011."[80]

## Lack of Regulation Allows PE to Grow and Consolidate with Impunity

Although 2017 was called "the year M&A shook the healthcare landscape,"[81] health care financial analysts reported another record year in 2021 with an increase in mergers and acquisition (M&A) deals of more than 25% compared to 2020.[82] While the government views fragmentation as a problem, PE firms view fragmentation and growth as an opportunity. As a result, PE firms have provided the main source of capital to fuel the enormous growth in consolidation since 2010.[83] PE firms describe M&A deals as adding value to the health care industry; however, the overwhelming evidence on consolidations is that the price of health care has increased with no improvements in quality of care.[84]

There is also the problem of "stealth consolidation," which is "a series of vertical acquisitions that cumulatively create market power."[85] Numerous health care mergers are exempt from premerger notification to the FTC because their deal size is under the notification threshold. The logic for this exemption stems from statutes established before the 1970s, which argued that such small deals represent a small amount of market share and therefore are not a threat to competition. However, PE firms are experts at what they call "roll-ups." A roll-up strategy is a process of acquiring and merging multiple smaller companies in the same industry and consolidating them into a large company. Because the

FTC statutes do not account for roll-ups' cumulative effect, they are a perfect example of stealth consolidation. Nevertheless, studies on health care M&As are starting to reveal the harmful effects of this hidden, unregulated consolidation. Thomas Wollmann, for example, shows how a series of small deals in the US dialysis market over several decades resulted in control by two major monopoly companies, which has increased hospitalizations and mortality.[86]

## Grow and Hide Allows Financial Interests to Hide

*Wall Street investors invade its every corner, engineering medical practices and hospitals to maximize profits as if they were little different from grocery stores. At the center of this story are private equity firms, which saw the explosive growth of healthcare spending and have been buying up physicians staffing companies, surgery centers, and everything else in sight.*[87]

Taxpayers fuel this "explosive growth" in spending, yet few Americans are aware of the role of private capital behind their health care providers because it is so well hidden. Just as the American health care state expands and hides the role of government, the PE industry capitalizes on fragmentation and the growth in public financing and is able to hide its role. As *Bloomberg Businessweek* reported: "One of PE's superpowers is that it's hard for outsiders to see and understand the industry"[88]

It is hard to see and understand because private equity firms are not required to report their acquisition deals to financial regulatory authorities. Even when transactions are reported, the complex structure of private equity funds obscures their presence. Ownership data submitted to the Centers for Medicare & Medicaid Services is incomplete and often inaccurate, especially when providers are part of complex corporate structures with multiple levels and subsidiaries.[89] For example, no publicly available central database accurately reveals which health care companies are currently acquired and backed by PE capital or which companies were acquired and then sold by PE funds, and PE funds are not required to disclose deal amounts. Lack of disclosure regulation makes studying the effect of PE acquisitions extremely challenging, as MedPAC recently reported to Congress about the role of PE in health care.[90] Indeed, despite enormous growth in PE investments in health care, MedPAC reported that only "2 percent of [physician] practices were acquired by PE firms from 2013 to 2016, but that figure does not account for previous PE acquisitions and appears to have grown since then."[91] Essentially, MedPAC is forced to conclude in its report to Congress that the presence of PE in various health care sectors is minor, but at the same time acknowledges the lack of ability to say anything with confidence due to data limitations and no disclosure requirements.

Indeed, we know very little about the outcomes of PE investments because these financial mechanisms are intentionally obscure. However, what we do know is alarming. Private equity firms are behind the closing of many rural hospitals,[92] major lay-offs among staff working in the long-term care industry,[93] higher mortality in nursing homes,[94] and the surprise-billing phenomenon in emergency departments and ambulatory care services.[95] In the meantime, PE investments have also produced significant shifts in ownership in several sectors, such as behavioral health, from predominantly nonprofit to for-profit (Baker, 2016).

Health economists Richard Scheffler and colleagues detail why the incentives of PE firms are misaligned with good patient care:

> Private equity funds, by design, are focused on short-term revenue generation and consolidation and not on the care and long-term wellbeing of patients. This in turn leads to pressure to prioritize revenue over quality of care, to overburden health care companies with debt, strip their assets, and put them at risk of long-term failure, and to engage in anticompetitive and unethical billing practices. Adding to the mounting evidence of the negative impact of private equity on health care, two recent National Bureau of Economic Research studies of the nursing home and dialysis markets found that private equity ownership is correlated with worse health outcomes and higher prices.[96]

## The Grow and Hide of Finance in Health Care Politics

Despite some murmurings of the need to regulate the private equity markets, or at least how they operate in the health care industry, especially in relation to surprise billing, the industry remains almost entirely unregulated. In 2017, Senator Elizabeth Warren (D-MA) introduced a bill that would have limited payouts that private equity owners could receive from their acquired companies with significant debt,[97] and also put an end to favorable tax treatment for PE (eliminating the carried interest tax break for fund managers),[98] yet very few members of Congress showed interest in the bill.[99] Even in relation to controlling surprise billing, which has outraged the public and has support across party lines, it took two years of attempted legislation before Congress passed relatively weak legislation in December 2020.

In July 2019, the House Energy and Commerce Committee introduced a bill, called the No Surprises Act, that would have required medical providers to give patients 24-hours' notice if they were going to be treated by an out-of-network provider, and restricted how much out-of-network providers could charge. Shortly after the bill was introduced, negative television ads criticizing the bill appeared across the country. The ad campaign was paid for by Doctor-Patient Unity, which is classified as a dark-money group, meaning it did not disclose its staff or where it got its money. Nonetheless, investigative reporting revealed that PE firms funded "Doctor-Patient Unity," spending nearly $30 million on this negative advertising.

Besides using the American Investment Council to lobby heavily against any restrictions or regulations on industry, not surprisingly, PE firms also give money directly to elected officials. For example, three months before the House Ways and Means Committee introduced the surprise billing legislation, the chair of the committee, Richard Neal (D-MA), received $29,000 in donations from Blackstone Inc., one of the largest investment firms with an extensive private equity portfolio.[100] Private investment firms have become significant donors, contributing $400 million to federal campaigns—more than commercial banks or the insurance industry. In the past, the health care state was controlled by the health care industry; today, it is also controlled by the financial industry.

There is a revolving door between public sector jobs in Washington and PE firms. Cerberus Global Investments seems to have a standing policy to hire Washington insiders: former vice president Dan Quayle became chairman of Cerberus Global Investments in 1999; former treasury secretary John W. Snow joined Cerberus seven years later; and Stephen Feinberg, who has a top position in the company, was a member of Trump's Intelligence Advisory Board, an independent entity created to advise the president on national-security matters.[101] While this example points toward the Republican Party, PE firms, like any savvy lobbyist, invests to influence both parties.[102]

In 2019, *Bloomberg Businessweek* wrote in an aptly titled article, *Everything is Private Equity Now,* that the "[p]rivate equity managers won the financial crisis. A decade since the world economy almost came apart, big banks are more heavily regulated and scrutinized. . . . But the firms once known as leveraged buyout shops are thriving. Almost everything that's happened since 2008 has tilted in their favor."[103] In October 2019, just six months before the pandemic hit, the PE industry had trillions of dollars in assets under management,[104] and health care was still its most active area of investment deals, valued at $79 billion, and this is where the returns on investment were highest. Moreover, even during the COVID-19 pandemic, when the rest of the economy was experiencing one of the worst downturns since the Great Depression, PE profits continued apace because the American health care state fuels the industry.[105]

# Conclusion

## Possibilities for Change: Reveal and Mobilize

The three major consequences of Grow and Hide have deepened over time and are completely embedded in the U.S. health care system: (1) capital health policy continues, and the role of private equity firms in the U.S. health care system has increased dramatically since 2010, taking advantage of public funding and remaining completely unregulated and hidden from view; (2) the conspicuous Medicaid program continues to expand for some and retract for others, continuing a long pattern of inequality; and (3) the U.S. government continues to increase funding for the health system, but still relies on voluntary planning and reforms with an extremely weak regulatory framework. As a result, the health care system remains highly fragmented, expensive, and inequitable despite years of reforms attempting to address these exact issues.

That these three ills are allowed to fester and grow under the American health care state helps explain why the U.S. health care system responded so poorly to the COVID-19 pandemic starting in 2020. Recent policy responses to address the shortcomings that became so apparent during COVID suggest increasing the scientific integrity and autonomy of the CDC, expanding and securing more affordable health care coverage, and investing in prevention and social services to address health inequities. Yet the history I detail shows that we have focused on all three of these reforms to varying degrees in the past. They are still worthy reforms. But if that remains our focus without addressing the Grow-and-Hide Regime, the United States will continue to increase health expenditures while also increasing fragmentation and inequality. And, as complexity increases, the American health care state will keep the American public under a shroud of confusion about the government's role and the extensive reach of public financing to fund this uncoordinated, unequal, so-called private system.

*Grow and Hide*. Colleen M. Grogan, Oxford University Press. © Oxford University Press 2023.
DOI: 10.1093/oso/9780199812233.003.0012

How do we tackle the Grow-and-Hide Regime? This history makes clear that dismantling Grow and Hide is especially difficult because there are no incentives among stakeholders to dismantle the regime's central strategies. Instead, the incentives remain to increase health care expenditures but hide its reach in almost every crevice of this highly complex system. Yet this history also reveals moments in time, especially at the dawn of major reforms—the New Deal, and the Great Society programs—when actors made concerted efforts to reveal the true extent of the government's role and reach. Despite all the pain that COVID has caused, it has also pushed many to demand changes that have been needed for a long time. When a window of opportunity opens again for health care reform, we must insist on honesty regarding the true role of government. That means we need to begin now to change the discourse about the extent to which government is already funding the U.S. health care system and begin revealing the extent to which private actors benefit from this publicly funded system.

What would a transparent discourse look like? It must include three main components: (1) debunking the competition myth, (2) showing the extent to which private actors rely on public funds, and (3) revealing the true role of government.

First, because policy ideas that promote "competition" have become ubiquitous in political discourse about the U.S. health care system, a reformed discourse needs to attack false notions that we have ever had or ever will have something resembling competition without significant government involvement. Attacking the competition myth is especially important today, as policymakers and many health economists frequently raise serious concerns about the rise of consolidation in the U.S. health care system. With monopoly power on the political agenda, the typical policy solution offered to address the problem is stricter, more effective antitrust law to enhance competition. But focusing solely on antitrust law is hugely problematic for several reasons.

First, as Thomas Greaney and Richard Scheffler point out, antitrust law, especially concerning vertical mergers, which are now very common in the U.S. health care system, "is antiquated and out of step with economic learning."[1] Up until 2019, the FTC did not litigate vertical cases because antitrust law assumed vertical mergers are usually procompetitive. Although the Department of Justice and the Federal Trade Commission (FTC) developed new vertical merger guidelines a few years ago, Greaney and Scheffler's review showed that the proposed guidelines still overlook important contemporary economic learning, and "for the health care sector, the guidelines signal a green light for continued and expanded vertical consolidation." Moreover, the guidelines did nothing to prevent against stealth consolidation—the cumulation of small mergers and acquisitions (M&As) that do not meet the threshold for antitrust attention (see

Chapter 10)—and indeed actually downplayed the seriousness of this type of consolidation.

Of course, just three years later, in 2022, it is clear that vertical consolidation is a serious problem in health care.[2] Even though the FTC is currently revising the merger rules and guidelines, enforcement agencies face significant resource constraints. As merger activity has increased, merger enforcement resources have decreased, resulting in more mergers to review and fewer resources to review them. Between 2010 and 2016, FTC and DOJ funding in real terms declined, and in 2019 was 50% less than at the beginning of the Reagan administration.[3]

Finally, the FTC faces a very high evidentiary burden to prove that a merger will result in anticompetitive behavior and harm consumers.[4] With reduced staff, the FTC is no match for industry, especially the financial sector, with so much cash on hand to hire a large team of expert litigators. Moreover, in keeping with the logic of Grow and Hide (voluntary participation with no regulatory teeth), the FTC must rely on the voluntary participation of insurance companies to provide reliable claims data to develop its case of anticompetitive behavior. Not surprisingly, since insurance companies have also been interested in M&As, and do not want to strain their relationships with investors and provider groups involved in M&As, the largest insurance company—United Healthcare— backed out of this voluntary data partnership in 2019.[5] Given the demonization of government and regulatory agencies, it is foolish to think we can rely on such agencies to create the change we need.

Most importantly, the U.S. health care system has never resembled a competitive model. Most health economists agree with this statement. Richard Scheffler and his colleague from the University of California Berkeley note that, "for a significant part of the health care system, the standard competitive model now has little relevance. The hospital and insurer markets have become so concentrated that consumer choice is often limited to a few hospitals and insurers."[6] But it is not only due to the dramatic increase in consolidation over the last decade. Hopefully, this book has made abundantly clear that the U.S. government funded the creation of the U.S. health care system from the very beginning. While its funding and role have increased over time, its intentional hiding has made its role more obscure.

Yet, even health economist Mark Pauly, writing for the conservative American Enterprise Institute in 2019, acknowledged this when he asked, "[W]ill health care's immediate future look a lot like the recent past?" There will be "more public-sector funding, but more private-sector delivery and administration, too."[7] He advocates for this increase in "public subsidies to become more market-like" to provide operational efficiencies.[8] But this argument has been used since the 1980s, and market-like efficiencies have yet to be realized. Nonetheless, at least he explicitly acknowledges the role of public subsidies behind these so-called market-like policies that embolden private sector delivery with little accountability. Indeed, this acknowledgment is the second main component of a reformed discourse. We must no longer allow the exposure of selective government funds without also demanding a truthful exposure of which actors benefit from public funds.

Finally, COVID revealed how little the American public understands about the essential governmental activities of public health. Ironically, part of this is a result of public health actually working well. There is a very logical modern assumption that we should have clean water, basic sanitation, trash collection, and safe food, for example, but we do not think to thank government (the Centers for Disease Control and Prevention [CDC], local public health departments, or the Food and Drug Administration) for these services when they work well.[9] Indeed, in our everyday lives, public health services are so hidden that the scientific knowledge within such agencies is not questioned, but it is also not highly valued.[10]

When problems occurred during COVID, the lack of investment in these public health agencies was exposed. But, COVID also revealed the long-term marginalization of these once respected scientific agencies.[11] The politicization of COVID and the right-wing backlash against science make marginalized public health agencies and their staff an easy target.

Yet the history in this book shows how 19th-century medical populism was also antiscientific and antigovernment (see Chapter 1). Over time, during the 20th century, Progressives were successful in creating a public health infrastructure that spread across the entire United States. This movement and subsequent public health reformers fought against medical populism by hiding the role of government and claiming its work to be based on "pure, nonpolitical" scientific legitimacy. Parts I and II of this book show how this was a key strategy that helped to create the Grow-and-Hide Regime. Notably, public health reformers today are promoting the same strategy. Current public health reformers argue that the CDC needs to reclaim itself as a nonpolitical scientific agency, and in an effort to legitimize the nongovernmental side of public health, federalism, public-private partnerships, and programs administered by the nonprofit sector are highlighted.[12]

It is time to be honest and transparent. Government public health agencies must use scientific knowledge to create safe and effective programs. At the same time, how much the United States decides to invest in these agencies, and what these agencies are empowered to do, are fundamentally political questions about the extent to which Americans value maintaining and promoting a healthy society.

For over a century, liberal reformers have accommodated opposition by hiding the role of government in its discourse, and contracting with the nonprofit sector with the intent to compromise and pass needed reforms. But these compromises have not led, as many initially hoped, to an eventual realization among the American public that government plays an important role and is not the demon many feared. Instead, the rhetorical devil has materialized because government continues to spend more while hiding its reach and delivering little value.

The ACA is the most recent example of this hugely consequential rhetorical compromise. Bruce Vladeck, the former administrator of the federal Health Care Financing Administration (now the CMS), which runs the Medicare and Medicaid programs, and Tom Rice, a health economist at UCLA, wrote about the failure of discourse in 2009 on the eve of health care reform:

> It is a truism in the political economy of the U.S. health care sector that costs are so difficult to control because every dollar in cost savings is a dollar less income for one or more interest groups. Health reform will necessarily be redistributive. As the health reform debate heats up in the coming months and years, the likely losers from such a redistribution will seek to deflect the discussion to blaming patients, government, or each other as the source of cost [and quality] problems. We would all be better served, we believe, if the issues of who wins and who loses were made more open and more explicit.[13]

But their advice was not heeded. The ACA was the largest increase in government funding for health care in U.S. history, yet it was designed to promote and rely on competition with no meaningful regulatory oversight. Although the U.S. government significantly assisted private actors in this so-called competitive market, the prevailing discourse hid this public subsidy, and the debate focused instead on whether government spending for newly eligible Medicaid recipients was appropriate—are they "truly" vulnerable and deserving?

The most important reform going forward is changing the dominant discourse. We need a three-pronged transparent discourse, which (1) reveals the extent to which the private sector, including the financial industry, relies on (and profits from) public funding; (2) debunks the myth that health care markets exist without significant government funding; and (3) clarifies the role of government in maintaining a healthy society and crystalizes where improvements are needed. Because there are no incentives for politicians or private actors to reveal these truths, this discursive reform must come from independent sources with a wide reach to influence public opinion. We need a movement that insists on revealing the role of government and the sources of funding behind private profits. We need to start now.

# ACKNOWLEDGMENTS

When books take a long time to write, as this one surely did, there are many people to thank. So many generous colleagues and friends helped in ways vast and complex that it is impossible to capture the wealth of their guidance and the depth of gratitude here. They deserve much credit for helping me gain a deeper understanding of America's health care and health policy history, though, of course, whatever shortcomings found herein are not their responsibility but solely my own.

The early stages of this work started with a Robert Wood Johnson Foundation Investigator Award to understand the political evolution of the U.S. Medicaid program. In an effort to understand the antecedents to Medicaid, I stumbled upon *Grow and Hide*—a much larger American health care state than I was anticipating, but also glimpses of a discourse that intentionally hid the state's role. The Investigator Award was one of those rare gifts allowing a scholar to explore a topic with quite a bit of latitude. This book would not have happened if I didn't have that academic freedom—and time and funding—to explore these ideas when they started as just a hunch. For that, I'm enormously grateful to RWJF's generous support, and the University of Chicago for still encouraging deep dives into the unknown.

A conference and edited book volume (also funded by the RWJF) titled *History and Health Policy in the United States: Putting the Past Back In* was led and edited by Rosemary Stevens, Charles Rosenberg, and Lawton Burns. I thank them for their insights and for providing the opportunity to explore how the state's role in developing nursing homes led to the creation of Medicaid. Although that is a minor story in this book, the work propelled me to pursue the larger historical question. A special thanks goes to Rosemary Stevens not only because she edited my chapter, but more importantly because her incredible work has influenced my thinking so profoundly. She didn't call it Grow and Hide, but documented the phenomenon in the development of so-called Charity Hospitals at the turn of the 20th century long before me. Other historians of medicine whom I had the great fortune to meet long ago at that conference are Beatrix Hoffman, Nancy Tomes, and Keith Wailoo. Their deeply researched work on the history of medicine has also greatly shaped my thinking.

I also met Daniel Fox at that conference. After learning enormously from his work, I reached out to him several years later to ask if he would review some chapters from the book. Despite not knowing me well, Dan read the chapters in a few days, provided detailed comments, and took even more time to discuss the work. He has read numerous versions of every chapter, offering incredible insights not only from his research but his wealth of experience from working in health care and health policy in the United States. This book is immensely improved by Dan's keen eye. It is rare to find such a generous mentor, and I am enormously grateful.

My colleagues at Yale University were also there at the beginning when this book started as a kernel of an idea. Mark Schlesinger, Michael Gusmano, and Karl Kronenbusch remain good friends. I'm grateful for their encouragement and insights over the years and for putting up with my constant return to the book project. Karl read the entire book with such a sharp eye. I'm so appreciative for him both identifying ideas that struck him as novel and for his help in identifying where the arguments were weak. Michael Sparer also gave generously of his time and intellect, providing valuable feedback on early drafts of chapters.

There is also a community of scholars in health politics who have sustained me over all these years. I have learned from so many through their writing and from our yearly exchange of ideas at the American Political Science Association meetings. The health politics section started as a committee, which I joined as a newly minted PhD. Early members of this committee—Ted Marmor, Deborah Stone, Jim Morone, and Mark Peterson—have shaped my thinking in ways too numerous to list. Although Deborah and Mark did not review the book, they have reviewed and provided so much invaluable feedback over the years that their influences are here in the pages. Jim reviewed the entire book and provided the right mix of enthusiastic critical feedback that amazingly got me excited about revising the book. I am indebted to Jim for encouraging me to call the book Grow and Hide and for helping to keep the main arc of the argument in focus.

A shout out to all the reference librarians who were so incredibly helpful in tracking down historical documents. They are too many to list, but assistance from archives at the following institutions were particularly valuable: the Wisconsin State Historical Society, the New York Academy of Medicine, and the National Library of Medicine.

As I wrote the book, I was fortunate to present at different conferences and universities to try out my arguments. The book is much improved from these exchanges, and I'm so grateful to my colleagues. The list is too long but a special mention to Christy Ford, Peter Swenson, Carolyn Tuohy, Colleen Flood, Andrew Kelly, Andrea Campbell, Kimberly Morgan, Eric Patashnik, Suzanne Mettler, and Miriam Laugesen.

Although the Medicaid program is the focus of only one chapter in this book, its complex politics and policies has occupied a major focus of my scholarly career. As such, there is a group of Medicaid scholars whose work has constantly changed my thinking in such important ways that they too have found their way into the pages herein: Jamila Michener, Sara Rosenbaum, Laura Katz Olson, Heidi Allen, Larry Brown, Frank Thompson, and Heather Howard.

I'm enormously grateful to the Dean Deborah Gorman Smith and my colleagues at the Crown Family School at the University of Chicago. A special shout-out to those who have supported me in more ways than I can list over many years: Harold Pollack, Jeanne Marsh, and Robert Chaskin. Others who I have learned much from include Mark Courtney, Sydney Hans, Julie Henly, Waldo Johnson, Susan Lambert, Nicole Marwell, Jennifer Mosley, Gina Miranda Samuels, Yoonsun Choi, and Bill Sites. Crown is a special place to live out an academic career because it nurtures scholars who care deeply about research to advance a more just and humane society. I hope this book can live up to that tall order.

My current and former graduate students have patiently played with the ideas in this book when they were not fully formed, and in the process taught me so much. Special thanks to Rebecca Feinstein, Angelica Velazquillo Franco, Lauren Peterson, Sungguen (Ethan) Park, Tina Sachs, Daniel Scott, Bikki Tran Smith, and Allison Stinson. I'm grateful to Hannah MacDougall for tracking down historical data on nonprofit hospital finances, and for her own work on nonprofit hospitals' community benefits. The late David Jones and Phillip Singer worked as research assistants on projects related to the Affordable Care Act. Their smart thinking influenced me profoundly, and their energy for a reformed health care system thankfully left me with renewed hope that change can happen.

Other research projects have continued alongside this book project, and I am grateful to my colleagues, especially Amanda Abraham and Christina Andrews, who were willing to pick up the slack when I needed to focus on finishing *Grow and Hide*. Laura Botwinick kept the Graduate Program for Health Administration & Policy going smoothly when I had sabbatical to work on the book. A grant from the National Library of Medicine for Scholarly Works in Biomedicine and Health made completion of the book possible. Working with developmental editor Meribah Knight was not only enormously helpful, but fun and interesting. She helped me keep the lay reader in focus with hope that *Grow and Hide* could reach a broader audience. Marilyn Cavicchia's copyediting assistance is also greatly appreciated. Finally, I'm grateful to Editor David McBride from Oxford University Press for supporting the book for a long time, even when its focus changed over time.

My running/walking group kept me grounded in what really matters in life: Lisa Jenschke, Amy Reifert, Ruth Kmak, and Beck Benson. When the book started, we were running, but when my hip gave out and I needed a hip replacement, they stuck with me, slowing down their faster pace so I could still tag along. Ruth actually ran in the cold pool with me! I'm so grateful for their friendship, and for meeting in the early mornings right outside my door so I can just roll out of bed minutes before! Other dear friends whose support means so much include Deb Hass and Mary Stoner Saunders.

My extended family—39 and growing—has sustained me all these years. As sickness and death inevitably arrive in our midst, it's hard to articulate the comfort of a large embracing family, but it is clearly there. Just listing my siblings and their spouses to offer my gratitude for their love: James and Annie, Mike and Betty, Bob and Margaret, Brian and our dear Peggy, who passed away, and Katie and Todd. My Mom, Geri Grogan Wendt, who is the youngest 90-year-old I have ever met, has been fighter her whole life and continues to be an inspiration. My sister's friendship means more than I can articulate.

My in-laws, Marlene and Peter Grosse, have been so kind and generous to us and our children. Our family reunions with Sue, Carol, Keith, and Nathan and their families have brought so much joy into our lives and were always an important break from work. To have a sister-in-law who is also one of your closest friends is a rare and special gift.

Finally, I've dedicated this book to Michael Grosse and our daughters Adelaide, Eleanor, and Clara. This book would not have come to fruition without his loving support, and the wonderful diversion of parenting, and the pure joy today in seeing them as beautiful young adults with so much to offer the world. With all my love.

# NOTES

## Introduction

1. Transcript of speech given on March 22, 2010, just after the passage of the ACA. J. Lee, "This Is What Change Looks Like," White House blog, March 22, 2010, www.whitehouse.gov/blog/2010/03/22/what-change-looks.
2. "Trump Gets Down to Business on 60 Minutes," Interview with Scott Pelley, September 27, 2015, https://www.cbsnews.com/news/donald-trump-60-minutes-scott-pelley/.
3. Sarah Ferris, "Trump: I'll Replace Obamacare with 'Something Terrific,'" *The Hill*, July 29, 2015, https://thehill.com/policy/healthcare/249697-trump-replace-obamacare-with-something-terrific.
4. Food Safety and Inspection Service (FSIS), "About FSIS" (Washington, DC: U.S. Department of Agriculture), www.fsis.usda.gov/About_FSIS/index.asp.
5. United States Department of Agriculture (USDA), "F.Y. 2019 Budget Summary," https://www.usda.gov/sites/default/files/documents/usda-fy19-budget-summary.pdf.
6. Ibid., Table FNCS-2, 42–43.
7. Ibid., see Table FNCS-2, pp. 42–43.
8. Arthur J. Viseltear, "History of the Medical Care Section—Emergence of the Medical Care Section of the American Public Health Association, 1926–1948," *American Journal of Public Health* 63, no. 11 (1973): 986–1007.
9. C. E. Winslow, "Public Health at the Crossroads," *American Journal of Public Health* 89 (1999): 1645–48; quote on 1646, https://doi.org/10.2105/AJPH.89.11.1645. This is a reprint of the 1926 original (*AJPH* 16: 1075–85; quote on 1080).
10. For a nice summary of these classic stories, see Jill Quadagno, *One Nation Uninsured: Why the U.S. Has No National Health Insurance* (Oxford: Oxford University Press, 2003), xi, 274.
11. FDR's Statements on Social Security, available on the History page of the Social Security Administration's website, https://www.ssa.gov/history/fdrstmts.html.
12. I document this extensively in Parts I and II, but specifically for hospitals in Chapters 3, 4, and 5.
13. Jonathan Cohn, *The Ten Year War* (New York: St. Martin's Press, 2021), xx.
14. Pierre Bourdieu, "Rethinking the State: Genesis and Structure of the Bureaucratic Field," trans. Loic Wacquant and Samar Farage, *Sociological Theory* 12, no. 2 (1994): 1–18.
15. National Association of Community Health Centers (NACHC), "America's Health Centers: 2021" (Bethesda, MD: NACHC, August 2021), https://www.nachc.org/research-and-data/research-fact-sheets-and-infographics/americas-health-centers-2021-snapshot/.
16. Robert W. Mickey, "Dr. StrangeRove; or, How Conservatives Learned to Stop Worrying and Love Community Health Centers," in *The Health Care "Safety Net" in a Post-Reform World*,

ed. Mark A. Hall and Sara Rosenbaum (New Brunswick, NJ: Rutgers University Press, 2012), 21–66.
17. Ibid., 24.
18. Gwen Ifill, "Clinton Proposes Making Employers Cover Health Care," *New York Times*, September 25, 1992, A1.
19. William J. Novak, *The People's Welfare: Law and Regulation in Nineteenth-Century America* (Chapel Hill: University of North Carolina Press, 1996); Max Edling, *A Revolution in Favor of Government: The Origins of the U.S. Constitution and the Making of the American State* (New York: Oxford University Press, 2003); Sparrow, James T., Novak, William T., and Stephen W. Sawyer, *Boundaries of the State in U.S. History* (Chicago: University of Chicago Press, 2015); Morgan, Kimberly J. and Ann Shola Orloff, *The Many Hands of the State: Theorizing Political Authority and Social Control* (New York: Cambridge University Press, 2017).
20. Novak, *The People's Welfare*, Introduction, p. 7. Note, this is also consistent with Rogers Smith's recent call to seriously study how political ideas and discourse have influenced American Political Development. See Rogers M. Smith, "Ideas and the Spiral of Politics: The Place of American Political Thought in American Political Development," *American Political Thought* 3, no. 1 (Spring 2014): 126–36.
21. I am indebted to Rosemary Stevens's work for clarifying how our thinking about public beds in the early 20th century shifted from social provision to charity care. See Rosemary Stevens, "'A Poor Sort of Memory': Voluntary Hospitals and Government before the Depression," *Milbank Memorial Fund Quarterly. Health and Society* 60, no. 4 (Autumn, 1982): 551–84.

## *Chapter 1*

1. Charles E. Rosenberg, "Anticipated Consequences: Historians, History, and Health Policy," in *History and Health Policy in the United States: Putting the Past Back In*, ed. Rosemary A. Stevens, Charles E. Rosenberg, and Lawton R. Burns (New Brunswick, NJ: Rutgers University Press, 2006), 14.
2. Quote obtained from C. -E. A. Winslow, *The Life of Hermann M. Biggs, M. D., D. SC., LL D., Physician and Statesman of the Public Health* (Philadelphia: Lea & Febiger, 1929).
3. Charles Rosenberg, *The Cholera Years: The United States in 1832, 1849, and 1866* (Chicago: University of Chicago Press, 1962).
4. Peter A. Swenson, "License or Liberty: Public Health and Medical Licensure's Movers and Motives, 1870s to the 1910s," *Social Science Research Network Electronic Journal*, January 2021, https://papers.ssrn.com/sol3/papers.cfm?abstract_id=3803526.
5. Rosenberg, *Cholera Years*, 68.
6. John H. Powell, *Bring Out Your Dead: The Great Plague of Yellow Fever in Philadelphia in 1793* (Philadelphia, 1949).
7. Howard D. Kramer, "Early Municipal and State Boards of Health," *Bulletin of the History of Medicine* 24 (November-December 1950): 503–29; quote on 504.
8. Rosenberg, *Cholera Years*.
9. Ibid., 176. See also Kramer, "Early Municipal and State Boards of Health."
10. Howard D. Kramer, "The Beginnings of the Public Health Movement in the United States," *Bulletin of the History of Medicine* 21 (May–June 1947): 352–76.
11. Kramer, "Early Municipal and State Boards," 506, 507.
12. Kramer, "Beginnings," 355–56.
13. Kramer, "Early Municipal and State Boards, " 508.
14. Ibid.
15. *American Medical Times*, 1863, p. 231; VII, 1863, pp. 41–42. As quoted in Kramer, "Early Municipal and State Boards," 509.
16. *New York Times*, March 13, 1865, 8. As quoted in Kramer, "Early Municipal and State Boards, " 512. See also Stephen Smith, *The City That Was* (New York, 1911).
17. Rosenberg, *Cholera Years*. For an in-depth treatment of the role of business leaders in the public health movement, see Peter A. Swenson, *Disorder: A History of Reform, Reaction, and Money in American Medicine* (New Haven, CT: Yale University Press, 2021).
18. Kramer, "Early Municipal and State Boards, " 514.

19. Rosenberg, *Cholera Years*, 190.
20. Ibid., 193.
21. Ibid., 210. See also Swenson, "License or Liberty."
22. Rosenberg, *Cholera Years*, 209.
23. Ibid., 210.
24. J. M. Freeman, "New York City as a Mission Field," *Methodist* 6 (December 10, 1866). As quoted in Rosenberg, *The Cholera Years*, 215.
25. See Rosenberg, *Cholera Years*, especially Chapter 12, "The Gospel of Public Health."
26. John Duffy, *The Sanitarians: A History of American Public Health* (Urbana: University of Illinois Press, 1990); "Report of the Committee on Organization and Functions of Municipal Health Departments," *American Journal of Public Health* 2, no. 5 (1912): 366–83.
27. This survey includes cities in Canada and Mexico, and the article did not break down the numbers by countries, so it is impossible to ascertain the exact number for the United States. Nevertheless, the article confirms that it was the majority of U.S. cities.
28. F. B. Sanboarn, "The Work of Social Science Past and Present," *Journal of Social Science* 8 (May 1876): 25–26. As quoted in Swenson, "License or Liberty," 9.
29. Swenson, "License or Liberty," 9–10.
30. Ibid., 18–19.
31. Technically, Louisiana's was the first state board of health, in 1855; however, because it focused exclusively on maintaining quarantine in New Orleans, most historians point to Massachusetts as the first state to establish a board to oversee the multiple function of public sanitation. Charles V. Chapin, "State Boards of Health," *Proceedings of the American Political Science Association* 1 (1904): 143–51; Barbara Gutmann Rosenkrantz, *Public Health and the State: Changing Views in Massachusetts, 1842–1936* (Cambridge, MA: Harvard University Press, 1972).
32. Winslow, *The Life of Hermann M. Biggs*. See also Kramer, "Early Municipal and State Boards," 517.
33. Rosenkrantz, *Public Health and the State*
34. Chapin, "State Boards of Health."
35. Donald Alan Blubaugh, *The Impact and Evaluation of Federal Grants-in-Aid on State and Local Public Health Programs and Services* (Thesis: Dissertation, Graduate School of Arts and Sciences, University of Pennsylvania, 1965); Ira V. Hiscock, *Public Health in Norwich, Connecticut: A Survey of Problems, Resources and Opportunities Relating to Public Health, for the Year 1950* (New Haven: Yale University, publisher unidentified, 1950). Howard D. Kramer, "Early Municipal and State Boards of Health," *Bulletin of the History of Medicine* 24, no. 6: pp. 503–29 (especially p. 518). Initially, state boards of health were expected to function in an advisory capacity to local health departments. This changed after Dillon's Rule was passed in 1868, which affirmed that the ultimate decision of what powers local governments possess resides with the states.
36. These boards eventually became state departments of health.
37. Winslow, *The Life of Hermann M. Biggs*; Duffy, *The Sanitarians*.
38. P. B. P., "Domestic Correspondence: Letter from New York," *Journal of the American Medical Association* 5, no. 23 (1885): 639–42.
39. Janway was quoted in P. B. P., "Domestic Correspondence: Letter from New York," *Journal of the American Medical Association* 5, no. 23 (1885): 639–42 (quote on pp. 641–42).
40. Biggs, "The Development," 54–56.
41. Wilson G. Smillie, *Public Health: Its Promise for the Future: A Chronicle of the Development of Public Health in the United States, 1607–1914* (New York: Macmillan, 1955).
42. Biggs, "The Development," 54–56.
43. *Report of the Board of Health of the Department of Health of the City of New York for the Years 1910 and 1911* (New York City: The J.W. Pratt Co., 1912); Evelynn Maxine Hammonds, *Childhood's Deadly Scourge: The Campaign to Control Diphtheria in New York City, 1880–1930* (Baltimore, MD: Johns Hopkins University Press, 1999).
44. Elizabeth Fee and Roy M. Acheson, *A History of Education in Public Health: Health That Mocks the Doctors' Rules* (Oxford: Oxford University Press, 1991).
45. Fee and Acheson, *A History*; Caroline A. Chandler, *Famous Men of Medicine* (New York: Dodd, Mead, 1950).

46. Winslow, *The Life of Hermann M. Biggs.*
47. Winslow, *The Life of Hermann M. Biggs;* George Rosen, *A History of Public Health* (New York: MD Publications, 1958).
48. The other being "the studies of the fundamental problems of water supply and sewage disposal from the Lawrence Experiment Station" (Smillie, *Public Health*).
49. National Institutes of Health (US) and Bess Furman, *A Profile of the United States Public Health Service, 1798–1948* (Washington, DC: US Government Printing Office, 1973); Bess Furman and Ralph C. Williams. *A Profile of the United States Public Health Service, 1798–1948.* (Bethesda, MD: United States Department of Health, Education and Welfare, 1973).
50. Smillie, "The National Board of Health."
51. Smillie, *Public Health.*
52. William H. Allen, *The Rise of the National Board of Health* (Philadelphia: American Academy of Political and Social Science, 1900), 52.
53. Smillie, Public Health.
54. American Medical Association, *The Transactions of the American Medical Association, Instituted 1847,* Vol. 26 (Philadelphia: Collins, printed for the Association, 1875.
55. American Medical Association, *The Transactions;* National Institutes of Health and Furman, *Profile of the United States;* Milton Terris and Nathan A. Kramer, "Medical Care Activities of Full-time Health Departments," *American Journal of Public Health and the Nation's Health* 39, no. 9 (1949): 1129–35; Allen, *The Rise;* American Medical Association, *The Transactions.*
56. American Medical Association, *The Transactions.*
57. Smillie, "The National Board of Health," 930.
58. Furman, *A Profile,* 143.
59. See Furman, *A Profile,* 140–49, for fascinating details regarding their feud.
60. For an in-depth treatment of the AMA's early support for progressive legislation, see Swenson, *Disorder: A History of Reform.*
61. Furman, *A Profile.*
62. Allen, *The Rise,* 62. See also Margaret Humphreys, *Yellow Fever and the South* (New Brunswick, NJ: Rutgers University Press, 1992).
63. Smillie, *The National Board,* 926.
64. American Medical Association, *The Transactions;* Terris and Kramer, "Medical Care Activities."
65. Furman, *A Profile,* 149.
66. Aside from running the National Board of Health, Billings was also medical librarian for the Surgeon General of the Army and complied the Index Medicus (for which he became famous), played a central role in gathering vital statistics for the 10th decennial Census, was vice-president of the APHA and chairman of several committees of the AMA, and after designing Johns Hopkins Hospital in 1875, he was asked to act as a medical advisor to the hospital until 1889.
67. Smillie, *The National Board,* 929; Furman, *A Profile.*
68. Furman, *A Profile,* p. 194.
69. Smillie, *The National Board,* 925–30; Furman, *A Profile.* United States Public Health Service, 1963.
70. Ibid. This is what most historians describe as the origin of the National Institute of Health (NIH).
71. Furman and Williams. *A Profile.*
72. William Welch, "Relations of Laboratories to Public Health," in *Papers and Addresses,* 615–620, quote in 619 (Baltimore: Johns Hopkins Press, 1920). Report of an address delivered before the American Public Health Association, Minneapolis, October 31, 1899. Printed in original: *American Public Health Association Report, 1899* (Columbus, 1900), xxv, 460–65.
73. Furman and Williams, *A Profile.*
74. Walter W. Powell and Richard Steinberg, *The Nonprofit Sector: A Research Handbook* (New Haven, CT: Yale University Press, 2006); John A. Hall, "Trust in Tocqueville," *Policy, Organisation and Society* 5, no. 1 (1992): 16–24.
75. Bonnie Bullough and George Rosen, *Preventive Medicine in the United States, 1900–1990: Trends and Interpretations* (Canton, MA: Science History Publications/USA, 1992);

Thomas Karter, "Voluntary Agency Expenditures for Health and Welfare from Philanthropic Contributions, 1930–1955," *Social Security Bulletin* 22, no. 8 (1958): 14–18. See also Richard Carter, *The Gentle Legions: National Voluntary Health Organizations in America* (New Brunswick: Transaction Publishers, 1961; 2nd edition, 1992).

76. Alfredo Morabia, *Enigmas of Health and Disease* (New York, Columbia University Press, 2014).

77. Rosen, *A History*; Theda Skocpol, "State Formation and Social Policy in the United States," *American Behavioral Scientist* 35, no. 4–5 (1992): 559–84.

78. Given the competing congresses in the United States, the international conference was postponed until 1905 when the American's could agree on one congress to act as a US representative (Knopf, *JAMA*, 1903).

79. S. A. Knopf, "American and International Congresses on Tuberculosis and Tuberculosis Exhibits for the Years 1904 and 1905," *Journal of the American Medical Association* 41, no. 23 (1903):1421–22.

80. First quote from Sir William Osler's letter to Knopf; second quote from Dr. Frank Billings of Chicago's letter to Knopf. Both provided in National Tuberculosis Association, *Some Plans and Suggestions for Housing Consumptives* (New York: National Association for the Study and Prevention of Tuberculosis, 1909), 24–27.

81. Edwin M. Bliss, Joseph A. Hill, and John Koren, *Benevolent Institutions, 1910* (Washington, DC: Government Printing Office, 1913)

82. S. Adolphus Knopf, *A History of the National Tuberculosis Association: The Antituberculosis Movement in the United States* (New York: National Tuberculosis Association, 1922).

83. Knoph, S. Adolphus, *A History of the National Tuberculosis Association: The Anti-Tuberculosis Movement in the United States* (New York: National Tuberculosis Association, 1922).

84. Adolphus, *A History of the National Tuberculosis Association*.

85. Daniel M. Fox, "Foundations' Impact on Health Policy," *Health Affairs* 25, no. 6 (2006): 1724–29; Daniel M. Fox, *Health Policies, Health Politics: British and American Experience, 1911–1965* (Princeton, NJ: Princeton University Press, 1986); Fee and Acheson, *A History of Education*.

86. Fox, *Health Policies, Health Politics*.

87. John Ettling, *The Germ of Laziness: Rockefeller Philanthropy and Public Health in the New South* (Cambridge, MA: Harvard University Press, 1981).

88. Fox, *Health Policies, Health Politics*.

89. Fox, *Health Policies, Health Politics*; Fox, "Foundations' Impact."

90. Winslow, *The Life of Hermann Biggs*.

91. Ibid.

92. Richard Carter, *The Gentle Legions: National Voluntary Health Organizations in America* (New Brunswick, NJ: Transaction, 1992; Selskar Michael Gunn and Philip Skinner Platt, *Voluntary Health Agencies, an Interpretive Study* (New York: Ronald Press Company, 1945).

93. Winslow, *The Life of Hermann Biggs*; Ralph Martin Kramer, *Voluntary Agencies in the Welfare State* (Berkeley: University of California Press, 1981).

94. National Health Council, *Voluntaryism and Health: The Role of the National Voluntary Health Agency* (Washington, DC: National Health Council, 1962), 5; Kramer, *Voluntary Agencies*.

95. Committee objectives quoted in Winslow, *The Life of Hermann Biggs*, 202 (headings for objectives added).

96. Knopf, *A History of the National Tuberculosis Association*; Winslow, *The Life of Hermann M. Biggs*.

97. R. M. Harden, "Approaches to Curriculum Planning," *Medical Education* 20, no. 5 (1986): 458–66.

98. Smillie, *Public Health*; Carter, *The Gentle Legions*.

99. National Tuberculosis Association, *Some Plans and Suggestions*.

100. "Rural Tuberculosis," *American Journal of Public Health* 2, no. 2 (1912): 126–34 (quote on p. 127).

101. Winslow, *The Life of Hermann M. Biggs*.

102. Ibid.

103. Winslow, *The Life of Hermann M. Biggs*; Knopf, *A History of the National Tuberculosis Association*.

104. Winslow, *The Life of Hermann M. Biggs*; "The Annual Report of the Department of Health of the City of New York," 1919, 222–33.

105. "The Annual Report of the Department of Health of the City of New York," 1919, 222–33.

106. Carter, *Gentle Legions*.

107. Manfred Waserman, "The Quest for a National Health Department in the Progressive Era," *Bulletin of the History of Medicine* 49, no. 3 (1975): 353–80. Charles V. Chapin, *A Report on State Public Health Work: Based on a Survey of State Boards of health* (Chicago: American Medical Association, 1916.

108. E. Battaglia and F. Kisat, "Malaria, Race, and Inequality: Evidence from the Early 1900s U.S. South," *The Journal of Economic History* 81, no. 4 (2021): 1173–222.

109. Ibid.

110. Rupert Blue, "The Problem of the Public Health." *Journal of the American Medical Association* 59, no. 6 (1912): 413–15.

111. Ibid.

112. Anonymous, *Report of the Committee on Organization and Functions of Municipal Health Departments* (1912), 366–83.

113. Battaglia and Kisat, 2021.

114. Alfred Hyman Katz, Jared A. Hermalin, and Robert E. Hess, eds., *Prevention and Health: Directions for Policy and Practice* (New York: Haworth Press, 1986).

115. Theodore M. Brown and Elizabeth Fee, "Social Movements in Health," *Annual Review of Public Health* 35, no. 1 (2014): 385–98; Elizabeth Fee and Nancy Krieger, "Health, Politics and Power," *The Women's Review of Books* 11, no. 10/11 (1994): 4–5; Elizabeth Fee, *Disease and Discovery: A History of the Johns Hopkins School of Hygiene and Public Health 1916–1939* (Baltimore: Johns Hopkins University Press, 1987).

## Chapter 2

1. Hibbert Winslow Hill, *The New Public Health* (Minneapolis, 1912), 4.

2. Carroll Fox, *Public Health Administration in Toledo*, USPHS, Reprint no. 284, *Public Health Reports*, June 25, 1915 (Washington DC: Government Printing Office, 1915).

3. "Report of the Committee on Organization and Functions of Municipal Health Departments," *American Journal of Public Health* 2, no. 5 (1912): 366–383.

4. Ibid., 368.

5. For an excellent collection of historical articles on the building of public health infrastructure, especially related to sewage systems, see Joel A. Tarr (Joel Arthur), *The Search for the Ultimate Sink: Urban Pollution in Historical Perspective* (Akron, OH: University of Akron Press, 1996). See also, Maureen Ogle, *All the Modern Conveniences: American Household Plumbing, 1840–1890* (Baltimore: Johns Hopkins University Press, 1996).

6. See reports for the following cities: Birmingham, AL; Quincy, IL; Springfield, OH; Youngstown, OH; Baltimore, MD; Toledo, OH. See also Ralph C. Williams (Ralph Chester), *Public Health Administration in Arizona* (Washington, DC: Government Printing Office, 1922).

7. Carroll Fox and U.S. Public Health Service, *Reprint 417: Public Health Administration in Springfield, Ohio* (Washington: Government Printing Office, 1917), 6.

8. Ibid.

9. Carroll Fox, *Public Health Administration in Toledo*, USPHS, Reprint No.284, *Public Health Reports*, June 25, 1915 (Washington, DC: Government Printing Office, 1915), 61.

10. Ibid., This figure includes the allocation for hospitals in Toledo.

11. Ibid.

12. C.-E. A. Winslow and Williams Memorial Publication Fund, *The Evolution and Significance of the Modern Public Health Campaign* (New Haven, CT: Yale University Press, 1923); American Public Health Association, Committee on Municipal Health Dept. Practice, et al., *Report of the Committee On Municipal Health Department Practice of the American Public Health Association in Cooperation with the United States Public Health Service* (Washington, DC: Government Printing Office, 1923); American Public Health Association, Committee on Administrative Practice, C.-E. A. Winslow, and George T. Palmer, *Appraisal Form for City Health Work*, 3rd ed., rev. (New York: American Public Health Association, 1929); John A. Ferrell, Wilson George Smillie, Platt W. Covington, and Pauline A. Mead, *Health Departments of States and Provinces of the United States and Canada* (Washington, DC: U.S. Government Printing Office, 1929); Joseph W. Mountin, United States Public Health Service, and E. Evelyn Flook, *Devices*

*for Reducing Health Department Records and Reports* (Washington, DC: U.S. Government Printing Office, 1945).

13. Franz Schneider Jr., "A Survey of the Activities of Municipal Health Departments in the United States." *American Journal of Public Health* 6, no. 1 (1916): 1–17.

14. Ibid., 4 (emphasis added).

15. Ibid., 4.

16. "First Report of the Committee on Municipal Health Department Practice of the American Public Health Association, November, 1921," *American Journal of Public Health* 12, no. 1 (January 1, 1922): 7–15. H. F. Vaughan, "Local Health Services in the United States: the Story of the CAP," *American Journal of Public Health* 62, no. 1 (January 1, 1972): 95–111.

17. Starting with public health leader, Charles Chapin of Providence, Rhode Island, who argued for quantitative evaluation of health department practices in 1913. See Charles V. Chapin, Superintendent of Health, "How Shall We Spend the Health Appropriation?," *American Journal of Public Health* 3, no. 3 (March 1, 1913): 202–8.

18. "First Report of the Committee on Municipal Health Department Practice of the American Public Health Association, November, 1921," *American Journal of Public Health* 12, no. 1 (January 1, 1922): 7–15.

19. Carroll Fox, S. J. Crumbine, J. A. Ferrell, J. R. Phelps, Maud Wood Park, and James A. Tobey, "Report of the Committee on Salary Standards," *American Journal of Public Health* 12, no. 8 (August 1, 1922): 693–701; Haven Emerson, William C. Hanson, and Ernest C. Meyer, "Report of the Committee on Uniform Administrative Accounting for Health Departments," *American Journal of Public Health* 6, no. 7 (July 1, 1916): 746–50.

20. Haven Emerson, "A Standard Budget; The Health Officer's First Need," *American Journal of Public Health* 10, no. 3 (March 1, 1920): 221–23.

21. Ernest Meyer, "Methods for the Defense of Public Health Appropriations," *American Journal of Public Health* 10, no. 3 (1920): 201–9, https://www.ncbi.nlm.nih.gov/pmc/articles/PMC 1362778/.

22. Vaughan, "Local Health Services in the United States."

23. C.-E. A. Winslow "Fifteen Years of the Committee on Administrative Practice," *American Journal of Public Health* 25, no. 12 (December 1, 1935): 1303–16; quote on 1304.

24. Henry F. Vaughan, "Getting Public Health Needs across to Appropriating Bodies by a Municipal Health Department," *American Journal of Public Health* 22, no. 7 (July 1, 1932): 700–704; D. B. Armstrong et al. "Report of the Committee on Municipal Health Department Practice," *American Journal of Public Health* 14, no. 3 (March 1, 1924): 184–87.

25. "Medicine: Health Is Purchasable," *Time*, October 1, 1923, http://content.time.com/time/ magazine/article/0,9171,716733,00.html.

26. Schneider, "A Survey of the Activities," 17.

27. "First Report of the Committee on Municipal Health Department Practice of the American Public Health Association, November, 1921," *American Journal of Public Health* 12, no. 1 (January 1, 1922): 7–15; see p. 10.

28. C.-E. A. Winslow and H. I. Harris, "An Ideal Health Department for a City of 100,000 Population (Section II from the Forthcoming Report of the Committee on Municipal Health Department Practice)," *American Journal of Public Health* 12, no. 11 (November 1, 1922): 891–907; see p. 907.

29. Wilson G. Smillie, *Public Health: Its Promise for the Future; A Chronicle of the Development of Public Health in the United States, 1607–1914* (New York: Macmillan, 1955).

30. P. Strach, K. Sullivan, and E. Pérez-Chiqués, "The Garbage Problem: Corruption, Innovation, and Capacity in Four American Cities, 1890–1940," *Studies in American Political Development* 33, no. 2 (2019), 209–33.. See also P. Strach and K. Sullivan, "Dirty Politics: Public Employees, Private Contractors, and the Development of Nineteenth-Century Trash Collection in Pittsburgh and New Orleans," *Social Science History* 39, no. 3 (2015), 387–407.

31. Judith Walzer Leavitt, *The Healthiest City: Milwaukee and the Politics of Health Reform* (Princeton, NJ: Princeton University Press, 1982).

32. United States Public Health Service and American Public Health Association, Committee on Administrative Practice, *Municipal Health Department Practice for the Year 1923* (Washington, DC: Government Printing Office, 1926).

33. C.-E. A. Winslow, "Fifteen Years of the Committee on Administrative Practice," *American Journal of Public Health* 25, no. 12 (December 1, 1935): 1303–16; quote on 1304.
34. Ibid., 1305.
35. Charles V. Chapin, "State Boards of Health," *Proceedings of the American Political Science Association* 1 (1904): 143–51.
36. Ibid, 147.
37. Peter A. Swenson, *Disorder: A History of Reform, Reaction, and Money in American Medicine* (New Haven, CT: Yale University Press, 2021), 318.
38. See Swenson, *Disorder*, 318. I agree with Swenson's argument that the loss of medical progressivism from the AMA was not largely due to the AMA's dalliance with compulsory health insurance in 1917, but rather started earlier and had more to do with state health department legislation that regulated private practice or were perceived to move into the realm of private practice. As I detail in Chapter 3, most public health leaders, which included the elite physician scientists he refers to, were not strongly supportive of compulsory health insurance unless they had administrative control.
39. Swenson, *Disorder*, 318–19.
40. As quoted in Swenson, *Disorder*, 319.
41. Swenson, *Disorder*, 320.
42. Swenson, *Disorder*; John Duffy, *The Sanitarians: A History of American Public Health* (Urbana: University of Illinois Press, 1990).
43. Daniel Carpenter, *Reputation and Power: Organizational Image and Pharmaceutical Regulation at the FDA* (Princeton, NJ: Princeton University Press, 2010).
44. Hermann M. Biggs, "The Development of the Research Laboratories," *Monthly Bulletin of the Department of Health in the City of New York* 1 (1911): 54–56.
45. C.-E. A. Winslow, *The Life of Hermann M. Biggs, M.D., D. SC., LL. D., Physician and Statesman of the Public Health* (Philadelphia: Lea & Febiger, 1929).
46. Biggs, "Development of the Research Laboratories," 54–56.
47. Winslow, *The Life of Hermann M. Biggs*, 230.
48. William Hallock Park, "The New Activities of the Research Laboratory of the Department of Health," *Monthly Bulletin of the Department of Health in the City of New York* 1 (1911): 56–65.
49. Winslow and Harris, "Ideal Health Department," 905.
50. Winslow, *The Life of Hermann M. Biggs*, 235.
51. Winslow, *The Life of Hermann M. Biggs*.
52. Franz Schneider, *A Survey of the Activities of Municipal Health Departments in the United States* (New York: Dept. of Surveys and Exhibits, Russell Sage Foundation, 1916).
53. Ibid.
54. Alexandra M. Lord, "'Naturally Clean and Wholesome': Women, Sex Education, and the United States Public Health Service, 1918–1928," *Social History of Medicine* 17, no. 3 (2004): 423–41,
55. Winslow, *The Life of Herman M. Biggs*.
56. Ibid.
57. Winslow and Harris, "Ideal Health Department," 905.
58. Ibid., 900.
59. Ibid., 900.
60. Ira V. Hiscock and American Public Health Association, Committee on Administrative Practice, *Community Health Organization: A Manual of Administration and Procedure for Cities of 100,000, With Suggested Modifications for Larger and Smaller Urban Units* (New York: Commonwealth Fund, 1932), 78.
61. Ibid., 78.
62. Ibid., 79.
63. Duffy, *The Sanitarians*.
64. Skocpol's *Protecting Soldiers and Mothers* provides substantial support for this point. See Theda Skocpol, *Protecting Soldiers and Mothers: The Political Origins of Social Policy in the United States*. (Cambridge, MA: Belknap Press of Harvard University Press, 1995).
65. Duffy, *The Sanitarians*.

66. Duffy, *The Sanitarians*. See also, Commissioner of Health, Ernst J. Lederle, *Four Years in the Department of Health* (Department of Health of the City of New York, Reprint Series No. 14, January 1914).
67. Duffy, *The Sanitarians*.
68. Duffy, *The Sanitarians*; Winslow, *The Life of Herman M. Biggs*.
69. George Rosen, *A History of Public Health* (New York: MD Publications, 1958).
70. Winslow, *The Life of Hermann M. Biggs*.
71. Ibid., p. 234.
72. Schneider, *A Survey of the Activities*, 6.
73. Edward Martin, "Next Step for State Health Departments: III," *American Journal of Public Health* 12, no. 12 (1922): 1005–8.
74. Carl Bakal, *Charity U.S.A.: An Investigation into the Hidden World of the Multi-Billion Dollar Charity Industry* (New York: Times Books, 1980).
75. Louis Curtis Ager, "The Official Relation of the State Medical Society to Child Welfare Activities," *New York State Journal of Medicine* 22, no. 2 (1922): 62–63; quote on 62.
76. Edward Martin, "Symposium on the Next Step for State Health Departments: III," *American Journal of Public Health* 12, no. 12 (1922): 1005–8; quote on 1006.
77. Ibid., 1006.
78. Ibid., 1006.
79. Ager, "The Official Relation," 63.
80. "State Department of Health: After-Care of Poliomyelitis," *New York State Journal of Medicine*. 22, no. 2 (1922): 78.
81. Winslow, *The Life of Hermann M. Biggs*.
82. Schneider, *A Survey of the Activities*, 7.
83. Lillian D. Wald, *The House on Henry Street* (New York: Holt, 1915), 60.
84. Duffy, *The Sanitarians*.
85. Ibid.
86. Alfred Hyman Katz, Jared A. Hermalin, and Robert E. Hess, eds., *Prevention and Health: Directions for Policy and Practice* (New York: Haworth Press, 1986).
87. Winslow and Harris, "Ideal Health Department," 901, emphasis added.
88. Winslow and Harris, "Ideal Health Department," 903.
89. United States Public Health Service, and American Public Health Association, Committee on Administrative Practice, *Municipal Health Department Practice for the Year 1923* (Washington, DC: Government Printing Office, 1926); data on p. 43.
90. Winslow and Harris, "Ideal Health Department," 903–4.
91. Ibid., 901.
92. Ibid., 901.
93. Ibid., 901.
94. Ibid., 901.
95. Ibid., 901.
96. Ibid., 901.
97. Austin F. Macdonald, *Federal Aid: A Study of the American Subsidy System* (New York: Arno Press, 1978), 3.
98. Macdonald, *Federal Aid*, 5.
99. Skocpol, *Protecting Soldiers and Mothers*, Kindle location 5732 of 8724.
100. Ibid., Kindle location 5942 of 8724. See also Theda Skocpol, "State Formation and Social Policy in the United States," *American Behavioral Scientist* 35, no. 4–5 (1992): 559–84; Sheila M. Rothman, *Woman's Proper Place* (New York: Basic Books, 1978), 139–41.
101. B. S. Warren, "A Unified Health Service," *Public Health Reports* 34, no. 9 (1919): 377–85.
102. Rothman, *Woman's Proper Place*; Katz, Hermalin, and Hess, *Prevention and Health*, 143.
103. Rothman, *Woman's Proper Place*, 139–41.
104. Ibid., 140–41.
105. W. M. Schmidt, "The Development of Health Services for Mothers and Children in the United States," *American Journal of Public Health* 63, no. 5 (May 1, 1973): 419–27.
106. "Child Hygiene," *American Journal of Public Health* 22, no. 3 (March 1, 1932): 330–31; quote on 330.

107. Ibid.
108. Joseph W. Mountin, Emily K. Hankla, and Georgie B. Druzina, *Ten Years of Federal Grants-in Aid for Public Health, 1936–1946* (Washington, DC: Federal Security Agency, Public Health Service, 1948), 27.
109. John A. Ferrell et al., *Health Departments of States and Provinces of the United States and Canada*, Public Health Bulletin Number 184 (Washington DC: Government Printing Office, 1929), 26.
110. E. L. Bishop, "Modern Trends in Public Health Administration," *American Journal of Public Health* 24, no. 6 (1934), Part I, 591–93.
111. Joseph W. Mountin et al., *Experience of the Health Department in 811 Counties, 1908–1934*, Public Health Bulletin Number 230 (Washington DC: Government Printing Office, 1936), 7–8
112. Ibid.
113. Bishop, "Modern Trends in Public Health Administration," 592.
114. Joseph W. Mountin, "Modern Trends in Public Health Administration: County Health Work," *American Journal of Public Health*, July 1934, 715–21; quote on 721.
115. Ibid., 721.

## Chapter 3

1. "Socialized Medicine Is Urged in Survey: Wilbur Committee Advocates Community Centres to Treat and Prevent Illness," *New York Times*, November 30, 1932, A1, A10.
2. As reported in the *New York Times* article "Socialized Medicine Is Urged in Survey," p. A1.
3. Jennifer Klein, *For All These Rights: Business, Labor, and the Shaping of America's Public-Private Welfare State* (Princeton, NJ: Princeton University Press, 2003), 120.
4. The equivalent of nearly $13 million in 2013 dollars.
5. Klein, *For All These Rights*, 120.
6. Lewis E. Weeks, Editor. "C. Rufus Rorem. In First Person: An Oral History," *Hospital Administration Oral History Collection* (Chicago, IL: American Hospital Association and Hospital Research and Educational Trust, 1983).
7. I. S. Falk "The Committee on the Costs of Medical Care—25 Years of Progress I. Introductory Remarks," *American Journal of Public Health and the Nation's Health* 48, no. 8 (1958): 979–82; Rosemary A. Stevens, "History and Health Policy in the United States: The Making of a Health Care Industry, 1948—2008," *Social History of Medicine* 21 (2008): 461–83.
8. Falk, "The Committee on the Costs of Medical Care"; Klein, *For All These Rights*; Stevens, "History and Health Policy"; Daniel M. Fox, *Health Policies, Health Politics: British and American Experience, 1911–1965* (Princeton, NJ: Princeton University Press, 1986). Paul Starr, *The Social Transformation of American Medicine* (New York: Basic Books, 1982).
9. Committee on the Cost of Medical Care (CCMC), *Medical Care for the American People: The Final Report of the Committee on the Cost of Medical Care, adopted October 31, 1932* (Washington, DC: U.S. Department of Health, Education, and Welfare, Community Health Service), 152–53).
10. Ibid., 184.
11. Ibid.
12. See Daniel M. Fox, "The Consequences of Consensus: American Health Policy in the Twentieth Century," *Milbank Quarterly* 64, no. 1 (1986): 76–99, for detail on the origins of hierarchical regionalism, which started at this time.
13. CCMC, *Medical Care for the American People*, 189–200.
14. Ibid., 201.
15. Daniel M. Fox, "The Significance of the Milbank Memorial Fund for Policy: An Assessment at Its Centennial," *Milbank Quarterly* 84, no. 1 (2006): 5–36.
16. John Duffy, *The Sanitarians: A History of American Public Health* (Urbana: University of Illinois Press, 1990); George Rosen, *A History of Public Health* (New York: MD Publications, 1958.
17. CCMC, *Medical Care for the American People*, 118; emphasis added.
18. Ibid., 152.

19. Committee on the Cost of Medical Care, *The Five-year Program of the Committee on the Costs of Medical Care: Adopted February 13, 1928*, Vol. 1 (Washington, DC, 1929), 11; emphasis added.
20. Ibid., 10.
21. CCMC, *Medical Care for the American People*, 119.
22. CCMC, *The Five-year Program of the Committee on the Costs of Medical Care*, 42. Also visible in this list is how the distinction between curative and preventive care remained murky even in attempts to officially define the jurisdiction of public health functions.
23. CCMC, *Medical Care for the American People*, 118.
24. Ibid., 13.
25. Ibid., 29.
26. Ibid., 114.
27. Michael Marks Davis, *Immigrant Health and the Community* (New York: Harper & Brothers Publishers, 1921). See also Ralph E. Pumphrey, "Michael Davis and the Transformation of the Boston Dispensary," *Bulletin of the History of Medicine*, 49, no. 4 (Winter 1975): 451–65.
28. George Rosen, "Public Health: Then and Now: The First Neighborhood Health Center Movement—Its Rise and Fall." *American Journal of Public Health* 61, no. 8 (1971): 1620–37; M. I. Roemer, "Resistance to Innovation: The Case of the Community Health Center," *American Journal of Public Health* 78, no. 9 (September 1, 1988): 1234–39.
29. Rosen, "Public Health."
30. Ibid., 1626.
31. Edward H. Ochsner, "Our Medical Economics Problems," *Illinois Medical Journal* 42, no. 5 (November 1922): 366. For a detailed account of opposition from rank-and-file physicians and its impact on the AMA, see Chapter 12, "Insurgency," in Peter A. Swenson, *Disorder: A History of Reform, Reaction, and Money in American Medicine* (New Haven, CT: Yale University Press, 2021), 317–59.
32. George Rosen, "The First Neighborhood Health Center Movement—Its Rise and Fall," *American Journal of Public Health* 61, no. 8 (1971): 1620–37.
33. C.-E. A. Winslow, "Public Health and Public Welfare: Administrative Medicine, Organized Health Service," *The Nation's Health* 1, no. 4 (1919): 327..
34. Winslow, "Public Health and Public Welfare," 214.
35. Michael Marks Davis and United Hospital Fund of New York, *Clinics, Hospitals and Health Centers* (New York and London: Harper & Brothers, 1927); quote on 357.
36. H. F. Vaughan, "Local Health Services in the United States: The Story of the CAs," *American Journal of Public Health* 62, no. 1 (January 1, 1972): 95–111, see p. 98.
37. Ibid., 98.
38. Vaughan, "Local Health Services," 100.
39. Fox, "The Significance of the Milbank Memorial Fund."
40. Winslow, *The Life of Herman M. Biggs*.
41. Ibid., 355.
42. Ibid.
43. Chapter 662, Acts of 1923. New article II-B added to Chap. XLIX of the Laws of 1909; quoted in Winslow, *The Life of Hermann M. Biggs*, quote on p. 368.
44. I. V. Hiscock, "Health Department and Other Reports," *American Journal of Public Health* 17, no. 5 (1927): 507–11.
45. Winslow, *The Life of Herman M. Biggs*, 370.
46. Ira Hiscock, "Human Nature: A Guide to Its Understanding," *American Journal of Public Health* 25, no. 2 (1935): 228; Marian Hart Ewalt and Ira V. Hiscock, *The Appraisal of Public Health Activities in Pittsburgh, Pennsylvania, 1930 and 1933* (Pittsburgh: Bureau of Social Research, Federation of Social Agencies of Pittsburgh and Allegheny County, 1935).
47. There were 1,511 centers to be exact, and Hiscock described them as major and minor health centers. The important point, however, is that they all incorporated this idea of providing "comprehensive preventive services," which included the concept of an ideal health department and breaking down the divisions of prevention and treatment that Winslow and Chapin advocated.
48. Hiscock, "Human Nature," 50.

49. Hiscock, "Human Nature," 51.
50. CCMC, *Medical Care for the American People*, 110.
51. Ibid., 135–36.
52. Ibid., 135.
53. Ibid., 134.
54. Ibid., 135–36.
55. Ibid., 137.
56. Weeks et al., *Hospital Administration Oral History Collection*, 328.
57. CCMC, *Medical Care for the American People*, 124–25.
58. Ibid., 125.
59. John Gee, "Twilight of Consensus: The American Association for Labor Legislation and Academic Public Policy Research," *Penn History Review* 19, no. 2 (2012): 44–70.
60. Beatrix Rebecca Hoffman, *The Wages of Sickness: The Politics of Health Insurance in Progressive America* (Chapel Hill: University of North Carolina Press, 2001); Ronald L. Numbers, *Almost Persuaded: American Physicians and Compulsory Health Insurance, 1912–1920* (Baltimore: Johns Hopkins University Press, 1978); Swenson, *Disorder*.
61. Numbers, *Almost Persuaded*; Swenson, *Disorder*.
62. Daniel Sledge, *Health Divided: Public Health and Individual Medicine in the Making of the Modern American State* (Lawrence: University Press of Kansas, 2017); Daniel S. Hirshfield, *The Lost Reform: The Campaign for Compulsory Health Insurance in the United States from 1932 to 1943* (Cambridge, MA: Harvard University Press, 1970); Alan Derickson, *Health Security for All: Dreams of Universal Health Care in America* (Baltimore: Johns Hopkins University Press, 2005).
63. B. S. Warren and Edgar Sydenstricker, *Health Insurance: Its Relation to the Public Health* (Washington, DC: Government Printing Office, 1916), 94.
64. Warren and Sydenstricker, *Health Insurance*, 96.
65. As will be discussed in Chapter 10 of this book, this exact same manifesto, sans the political incentive, was—amazingly and ironically—reproduced about a hundred years later in the Affordable Care Act under the rubric of "value-based payments."
66. Warren and Sydenstricker, *Health Insurance*, 96.
67. Derickson, *Health Security*.
68. Warren and Sydenstricker, *Health Insurance*, 786; Derickson, *Health Security*, 29.
69. Warren and Sydenstricker, *Health Insurance*, 786.
70. Ibid., 786.
71. This argument will become clearer in the remainder of this chapter and in Part II.
72. B. S. Warren, "A Unified Health Service," *Public Health Reports* 34, no. 9 (1919): 377–85.
73. Derickson, *Health Security*.
74. Warren, "A Unified Health Service."
75. This was actually the beginning stages of recommendations to organize the U.S. health care system according to hierarchical regionalism. This is discussed in more detail in Part II. For an excellent comparative US-UK history of hierarchical regionalism, see Fox, *Health Policies, Health Politics*.
76. Committee members included Haven Emerson, MD (public health), Mary M. Roberts, RN (provider institutions and special interests), William J. Schieffelin, PhD (the public), John Sundwall, MD (Public Health), Henry C. Taylor, PhD (Social Sciences).
77. CCMC, *Medical Care for the American People*, 127–28.
78. Ibid., 131.
79. Ibid., 132.
80. Ibid., 127.
81. Ibid., 127.
82. Ibid., 131; emphasis added.
83. Ibid., 131–32.
84. Ibid., 132–33.
85. Ibid., 133; emphasis added.
86. Ibid., 133.
87. CCMC Final Report, Statement by Walton H. Hamilton, who abstained from signing majority or minority reports, p.192.

88. CCMC, *Medical Care for the American People*, 12.
89. Ibid., 13.
90. Ibid., 52.
91. Ibid., 52; emphasis added.
92. E. H. L. Corwin, *The American Hospital* (New York: Commonwealth Fund, 1946).
93. C. Rufus Rorem, *The Public's Investment in Hospitals* (Chicago: University of Chicago Press, 1930), 10.
94. Ibid., 26.
95. Ibid., 16, 26.
96. Ibid., 26.
97. Ibid., 22.
98. Ibid., 26; emphasis added.
99. Ibid., 27.
100. And later became the founder of the first program in the country to focus on hospital administration in the Business School at the University of Chicago in 1934.
101. Weeks, "C. Rufus Rorem," *Hospital Administration Oral History Collection*, 10–11.
102. Ibid., 9; emphasis added.
103. Ibid..
104. Ibid., 22.
105. Rorem, *The Public's Investment in Hospitals*, 29.
106. Ibid., 14.
107. Rosemary Stevens, "'A Poor Sort of Memory': Voluntary Hospitals and Government before the Depression," *Milbank Memorial Fund Quarterly: Health and Society* 60, no. 4 (1982): 551–84. Rosemary Stevens, "Sweet Charity: State Aid to Hospitals in Pennsylvania, 1870–1910," *Bulletin of the History of Medicine* 58, no. 3 (1984): 287–314.
108. William Henry Welch, "The Relation of the Source of Capital Investment Funds to the Cost of Hospitalization," *Transactions of the American Hospital Association* 34 (1932): 638–48; quote on 639.
109. Of course, an extensive legal literature on community obligations required of nonprofit hospitals eventually emerged, but it was nonexistent at this time.
110. I. S. Falk, C. Rufus Rorem, and Martha D. Ring, *The Costs of Medical Care: A Summary of Investigations on the Economic Aspects of the Prevention and Care of Illness* (Chicago: University of Chicago Press, 1933); Corwin, *The American Hospital*.
111. Welch, "The Relation," 640.
112. Ibid., 639.
113. Ibid., 644.
114. Ibid., 644.
115. Stevens, "Sweet Charity," 301.
116. CCMC, *Medical Care for the American People*, 90.
117. Ibid.

## Chapter 4

1. See Hacker, 2002; Klein, 2003; Quadagno, 2005; Rick Mayes, *Universal Coverage: The Elusive Quest for National Health Insurance* (Ann Arbor: University of Michigan Press, 2004); Colin Gordon, *Dead on Arrival: The Politics of Health Care in Twentieth-Century America* (Princeton, NJ: Princeton University Press, 2003). For a direct statement in opposition to compulsory health insurance from an AMA representative at the time, see R. G. Leland and A. M. Simons, "Do We Need Compulsory Public Health Insurance? No," *Annals of the American Academy of Political and Social Science* 170, Social Insurance (November 1933), 121–27.
2. The Social Security Act also established the public assistance titles, namely Old Age Assistance, Aid to the Blind, and Aid to Dependent Children, which were significant for starting public medical programs specifically for these eligible groups in the states (discussed in more detail in Chapter 6).
3. Jason Scott Smith, *Building New Deal Liberalism: The Political Economy of Public Works, 1933–1956* (New York: Cambridge University Press, 2006).

4. J. M. Carmody, "The Federal Works Agency and Public Health," *American Journal of Public Health* 30, no. 8 (1940), 887–94; see p. 890.

5. Ibid. See also Daniel Sledge, *Health Divided: Public Health and Individual Medicine in the Making of the Modern American State* (Lawrence: University Press of Kansas, 2017); Elizabeth Fee, "History and Development of Public Health," in *Principles of Public Health Practice*, 2d ed., ed. F. Douglas Scutchfield and C. William Keck (Florence, KY: Cengage Learning, 2002).

6. Carmody, "The Federal Works Agency," 893–94.

7. Pierce Williams, "Alternatives to Compulsory Public Health Insurance." *Annals of the American Academy of Political and Social Science* 170 (1933):128–40.

8. Ibid., 128.

9. Ibid., 129.

10. Ibid., 129.

11. E. L. Bishop, "Integration of Federal, State and Local Agencies—Report of the Committee on Federal Relations of the State and Territorial Health Officers." *American Journal of Public Health*, June 1934: 637.

12. Edwin Emil Witte, *The Development of the Social Security Act: A Memorandum on the History of the Committee on Economic Security and Drafting and Legislative History of the Social Security Act* (Madison: University of Wisconsin Press, 1963); Daniel S. Hirshfield, *The Lost Reform: The Campaign for Compulsory Health Insurance in the United States from 1932–1943* (Cambridge, MA: Harvard University Press, 1970.

13. Because Sydenstricker had been diagnosed with a heart condition and his health was failing, he requested that the CES retain his colleague from the Milbank Fund, I. S. Falk, as a staff member for the Technical Committee on Medical Care. According to Hirshman's interview of Falk, "Dr. Falk soon came to carry the major burden of the Technical Committee's work." See Witte, *Development of the Social Security Act*, 12–13, 27–41; and Hirshman, *Lost Reform*, 44–46 and endnote #8. See also Sledge, *Health Divided*.

14. I. S. Falk and Harlan B. Phillips, *Reminiscences of Isidore Sydney Falk*, Health Sciences Project, 1963.

15. Edwin Witte Papers, Wisconsin State Historical Society, Folder 303, Medical Advisory Board, transcript from Meeting January 1935.

16. Ibid. It is essential to note the larger context of Dr. Roberts's comments. He was providing his perception of medicine and public health in the state of Georgia, in which he makes a clear connection between race, indigency, and public health services. He proposes advancing insurance within a segregated system: *"I think in this next great move of medicine in America, preventive medicine has got to be allowed to grow up with health insurance as its twin brother, but separate from it, united in purpose, as Booker Washington said, as a hand itself, but as separate as the fingers of the hand."* Thus, when Parran agrees, he is, in part, also accepting without protest this segregated picture of health services in the South. Parran was not unusual in this regard. There was widespread acceptance of racially segregated health care facilities in the North and the South.

   The intersection of race and class has always been paramount in the United States, which explains why even "liberal" proposals treated racial minorities and the poor as "other." See Jill S. Quadagno, *The Color of Welfare: How Racism Undermined the War On Poverty* (New York: Oxford University Press, 1994); Robert C. Lieberman, *Shifting the Color Line: Race and the American Welfare State* (Cambridge, MA: Harvard University Press, 1998); David Barton Smith, *Health Care Divided: Race and Healing a Nation* (Ann Arbor: University of Michigan Press, 1999).

17. U.S. Congress, Hearing, 74th Cong., HR 4120, p. 4.

18. Ibid., 166–67.

19. Ibid., 167.

20. Ibid., 167.

21. Ibid., 167–68.

22. Ibid., 328–39. Katherine Lenroot, Chief of the Children's Bureau, also testified to present Title VI of SSA, which provided federal grants-in-aid for Maternal and Child Health and Crippled Children. She made a case for increasing appropriations, similarly emphasizing that there was nothing new in federal responsibilities in this area.

23. Ibid., 316.

24. Ibid., 316–17.

25. Edgar Sydenstricker, "The Changing Concept of Public Health," *Milbank Memorial Fund Quarterly* 13, no. 4 (1935): 301–10; quote on 304–5, 310; emphasis added.

26. Thomas Parran, "Reporting Progress." Presidential Address delivery before the APHA at the 65th Annual Meeting in New Orleans, LA., October 20, 1936. Reprinted in *American Journal of Public Health* 26, no. 1: 1071–76; quote on 1071. Note Parran's definition was even broader: "the promotion of the physical and mental status of the race; the provision of decent housing, healthful working conditions, facilities for recreation, food adequate in amount and kind for proper nutrition; a standard of living compatible with normal family life and the up-bringing of children" (1071).

27. Ibid., 1071.

28. See C.-E. A. Winslow, "The Public Health Aspects of Medical Care: From the Standpoint of Public Health," *American Journal of Public Health* 29 (1939):16–19.

29. Josephine Roche, "Medical Care as a Public Health Function," *American Journal of Public Health* 27 (1937): 1221–26; quote on p.1221.

30. Ibid.

31. Michael M. Davis, *Public Medical Services: A Survey of Tax-Supported Medical Care in the United States* (Chicago: University of Chicago Press, 1937), 1.

32. Ibid., 124.

33. Ibid.; Interdepartmental Committee to Coordinate Health and Welfare Activities, "Proceedings: National Health Conference" (Washington, DC: U.S. Government Printing Office, 1938), viii.

34. Ibid., 125.

35. Ibid., 125.

36. R. C. Williams, "Development of Medical Care Plans for Low Income Farm Families: Three Years Experience," *American Journal of Public Health* 30, no. 7 (1940): 725–35. See also Thomas R. Clark, "The Limits of State Autonomy: The Medical Cooperatives of the Farm Security Administration, 1935–1946," *Journal of Policy History* 11, no. 3 (1999): 257–82.

37. Ibid.

38. Williams, "Development of Medical Care Plans."

39. Thomas Parran, "Health Security." Read before the New York Tuberculosis and Health Association, in New York, NY, February 25, 1936, and reprinted in *American Journal of Public Health* 26 (April 1936): 329–35. Quote on p. 329 (emphasis added).

40. Interdepartmental Committee to Coordinate Health and Welfare Activities, "Proceedings: National Health Conference" (Washington, DC: U.S. Government Printing Office, 1938), viii. (Hereafter referred to as "Proceedings.")

41. "Proceedings," 86.

42. Ibid., 49–54; quotes on 53 and 54.

43. Ibid., 49–54; quotes on 53 and 54.

44. Ibid., 53.

45. Ibid., see statement by Olin West representing the AMA, 26–28.

46. Ibid., 26–28.

47. Ibid., 58.

48. Ibid., 58.

49. Ibid., 58.

50. Ibid., 58.

51. Edwin E. Witte, "Socialized Medicine and the National Health Program," address to the Fourteenth Annual Conference of the National Association of Clinic Managers, Eau Claire, Wisconsin, September 29, 1939. Witte Papers, Box #301.

52. "Proceedings," ix (emphasis added).

53. Ibid., 142. In Daniel Hirshfield's book *The Lost Reform: the Campaign for Compulsory Health Insurance in the United States from 1932 to 1943*, he discounts Joseph Slavitt's statement saying he was the "leader of a tiny socialist-oriented American League for Public Medicine, urged a system of state medicine in which all forms of medical care would be provided free by the state" (113). He implies that Slavitt was on the fringe and recommending something no one else mentioned. But, as the quote above (and a close read of his statement) reveals, Slavitt

emphasizes (as many others did at the National Health Conference) what was already being done in the area of public medical services to make the case that this alternative was more familiar and superior to compulsory insurance. This was not a fringe suggestion, but part of Recommendation IV as specified by the Technical Committee.

54. "Proceedings," 50.
55. Hirshfield, *Lost Reform*; Hacker, 2002; Quadagno, 2005.
56. Reginald M. Atwater, "National Health Conference: A Review," *American Journal of Public Health* 28, no. 9 (1938): 1103–13; quote on 1105.
57. Proceedings, 1.
58. Abel Wolman "The National Health Program—Present Status," *American Journal of Public Health* 30, no. 1 (January 1, 1940): 1–8; quote on p.6–7.
59. Witte, "Socialized Medicine and the National Health Program."
60. See Harold Maslow, "The Background of the Wagner National Health Bill," *Law and Contemporary Problems* (Fall 1939): 606–18; quote on 618. See also Chapter 5 herein for more details on this point.
61. Joseph Mountin and Evelyn Flook, "Distribution of Health Services in the Structure of State Government. Chapter 1: The Composite Pattern of State Health Services," *Public Health Reports* 56, no. 34 (August 1941): 1673–722. Surveys described on p. 1673. For report of changes from 1915 to 1925 see John Ferrell, *Health Departments of States and Provinces of the United States and Canada*, Public Health Bulletin 184 (Washington, DC: U.S. Public Health Service, 1932). See also Part I herein for details on growth before 1930, and Charles V. Chapin, "State Health Organization," *JAMA* LXVI, no. 10 (1916): 699–703.
62. M. I. Roemer, "Joseph W. Mountin, Architect of Modern Public Health," *Public Health Reports* 108, no. 6 (1993): 727–35.
63. Joseph Mountin and Evelyn Flook, "Distribution of Health Services in the Structure of State Government. Chapter 1: The Composite Pattern of State Health Services," *Public Health Reports* 56, no. 34 (August 1941): 1673–1722; quote on 1674.
64. John Ferrell, *Health Departments of States and Provinces of the United States and Canada*, Public Health Bulletin 184 (Washington, DC: U.S. Public Health Service, 1932).
65. Mountin and Flook, "Distribution of Health Services: The Composite Pattern," 1674.
66. Ibid., 1675.
67. Ibid., 1676.
68. Ferrell, *Health Departments of States and Provinces*, 23.
69. Franz Schneider Jr., "A Survey of the Activities of Municipal Health Departments in the United States," *American Journal of Public Health* 6, no. 1 (1916): 4
70. Joseph Mountin and Evelyn Flook, "Distribution of Health Services in the Structure of State Government. Chapter III: Tuberculosis Control of State Agencies," *Public Health Reports* 57, no. 65 (1942): 68–69.
71. Joseph P. Harris, "The Future of Federal Grants-in-Aid," *Annals of the American Academy of Political and Social Science* 207, no. 1 (1940): 14–26; Advisory Commission on Intergovernmental Relations, *Periodic Congressional Reassessment of Federal Grants-in-Aid to State and Local Governments* (Washington, DC: U.S. Government Printing Office, 1961); John L. Parascandola, "Public Health Service," in A Historical Guide to the U.S. Government, ed. George Thomas Kurian (New York: Oxford University Press, 1998), 487–93.
72. Mountin and Flook, "Distribution of Health Services," 1942.
73. Joseph W. Mountin, Emily K. Hankla, and Georgie B. Druzina, "Ten Years of Federal Grants-in-Aid for Public Health," *Public Health Bulletin* (1948): 1–84, see p. 2, 11; Harris, "The Future of Federal Grants-in-Aid," 15.
74. Mountin, Emily K. Hankla and Druzina, "Ten Years of Federal Grants-in-Aid," 1948, 8.
75. Ibid., 16, 18–19.
76. Ibid., 8.
77. Ibid., 8.
78. F. W. Kratz, "Status of Full-Time Local Health Organization at the End of the Fiscal Year 1941–1942," *Public Health Reports (1896–1970)* 58, no. 9 (1943): 345–51; See also Morton Grodzins, *The American System* (Chicago: Rand McNally, 1966).

79. Joseph W. Mountin, Aaron W. Christensen, Evelyn Flook, Edward E. Minty, Rubye F. Mullins, and Georgie B. Druzina, *Distribution of Health Services in the Structure of State Government, 1950* (Washington, DC: U.S. Government Printing Office, 1954), data from Table 9, p. 45.

80. Milton Irwin Roemer, "Government's Role in American Medicine: A Brief Historical Survey," *The Bulletin of the History of Medicine* 18, no. 2 (July 1945): 146–68; quotes on pp. 153, 166.

81. *Transactions of the Special Conference of State and Territorial Health Officers with the United States Public Health Service*, September 16–17, 1940 (Washington, DC: Federal Security Agency, Public Health Service, 1940). .

82. Ibid., 2.

83. Mountin, Hankla, and Druzina, 1948.

84. Parascandola, "Public Health Service."

85. Roemer, 1945.

86. Mountin, Hankla, and Druzina, 1948, 27. See also Beatrix Hoffman, "Health Care at War," in *Health Care for Some: Rights and Rationing in the United States since 1930* (Chicago: University of Chicago Press, 2012).

87. Parascandola, "Public Health Service." Joseph Mountin had his hand in the early 1940s in the development of mental health services as well. As Roemer described it, "as head of the wartime Emergency Health and Sanitation Program, later as Associate Chief of the Bureau of State Services, Dr. Mountin had considerable freedom to assign personnel to explore new ideas . . . he took advantage of his positions to be innovative. His strategy was to support young PHS officer to explore and develop new public health ideas. One such appointment was Dr. Vane Hoge in the hospital field; others were Dr. Robert Felix in mental hygiene [who became the Director of NIMH] . . . Colleagues spoke of these men as 'Mountin's boys,' and most became the chief actors in programs that were subsequently implemented" (Roemer, "Joseph W. Mountin, Architect," 731).

88. Mountin and Flook, "Distribution of Health Services: The Composite Pattern," 1690.

89. Indeed, according to Mountin and Flook these estimates probably did not reflect the full cost of care provided since grant-in-aid funds by state welfare departments to counties for general medical care of the needy was often not separated from expenditures for general relief and therefore were not counted in the estimates.

90. Daniel M. Fox, *Health Policies, Health Politics: The British and American Experience, 1911–1965* (Princeton, NJ: Princeton University Press, 1986; Rosemary Stevens, In Sickness and in Wealth: American *Hospitals in the Twentieth Century* (New York: Basic Books, 1989).

91. Commission on Hospital Care, *Hospital Care in the United States* (Cambridge, MA: Harvard University Press, 1957).

92. Stevens, *In Sickness and in Wealth*: 198.

93. Stevens, *In Sickness and in Wealth,* 209.

94. As described in Chapter 4 (and by Stevens, 1989), a precedent had already been set for state and local governments' investment in hospital construction for quite some time.

95. Stevens, *In Sickness and in Wealth*, xx; Parascandola,"Public Health Service."

96. Daniel Fox writes the best account of the development of this concept of regionalism in both the United States and the United Kingdom. See Fox, *Health Policies, Health Politics*, 1986). Rosemary Stevens's *In Sickness and in Wealth* is the definitive history of the development of hospitals in the United States. She also discusses the importance of volunteerism. This section draws heavily from their work.

97. Stevens, *In Sickness and in Wealth,* 216.

98. Fox, *Health Policies, Health Politics,* 1986.

99. Quoted in Stevens, *In Sickness and in Wealth,* 219–20.

100. Stevens, *In Sickness and in Wealth,* 220.

101. See Fox, *Health Policies, Health Politics,* 1986. See also Chapter 4 herein.

102. Stevens, *In Sickness and in Wealth,* 220.

103. Quoted in Engel, 2002, 183.

104. Starr, 1982, 274.

105. Quoted in Stevens, *In Sickness and in Wealth,* 217.

106. Ibid., 159.

107. Joseph Mountin and Evelyn Flook, "Distribution of Health Services in the Structure of State Government. Chapter VI: Medical and Dental Care by State Agencies," *Public Health Reports* 57 (1942): 1195 (August 14) and 57 (1942): 1235 (August 21). Reprint No. 2395. Data from Table 4.

108. Ibid.

109. Ibid.

110. For explanation for how this came about, see Robert Stevens and Rosemary Stevens, *Welfare Medicine in America: A Case Study of Medicaid* (New York: Free Press, 1974); and Colleen M. Grogan, "A Marriage of Convenience: The History of Nursing Home Coverage and Medicaid," in *Putting the Past Back In: History and Health Policy in the United States*, ed. Rosemary A, Stevens, Charles E. Rosenberg, and Lawton R. Burns (New Brunswick, NJ: Rutgers University Press, 2006).

111. A. J. Altmeyer, "Medical Care for Persons in Need," *Social Security Bulletin* 8, no. 5 (May1945): 3. United States Bureau of Public Assistance, Social Security Board, Federal Security Agency, *Public Assistance Report*, no. 10 (Washington, DC: U.S. Bureau of Public Assistance, 1946), 1.

112. U.S. Bureau of Public Assistance, *Public Assistance Report*, 1.

113. Ibid., 2.

114. Altmeyer, "Medical Care for Persons in Need"; U.S. Bureau of Public Assistance, *Public Assistance Report*, 2.

115. U.S. Bureau of Public Assistance, *Public Assistance Report*, 2.

116. Ibid., 5.

117. Public Assistance: Statistics for the United States for January 1939. *Social Security Bulletin* 1, no. 1/3 (March 1938): 35–36.

118. Ibid., 36.

119. Altmeyer, "Medical Care for Persons in Need," 5.

120. Joint Committee on Medical Care of the American Public Health Association and the American Public Welfare Association, "Tax-Supported Medical Care for the Needy." A Statement of the Joint Committee on Medical Care of the American Public Health Association and the American Public Welfare Association. *American Journal of Public Health* 42 (October 1952): 1310–27.

121. Ibid., 1311.

122. Abel Wolman, "The National Health Program: How Far? How Fast?," *American Journal of Public Health* 29, no. 6 (1939): 628–632; quote on 632. The following quote in Witte's 1939 speech also supports this view of public opinion: "A concept is developing among the American people that everyone has a right to necessary medical care and that it is a responsibility of the government to establish conditions under which this right will become an actuality. Two of the most concrete expressions of this developing concept are the *furnishing of medical care at public expense for the medically indigent* and the *extension of preventive public health services* . . . which medical men agree . . . must go beyond education to include actual treatment" (pp. 4–5, emphasis added).

123. Milton I. Roemer, "Joseph W. Mountin, Architect of Modern Public Health," *Public Health Reports* 108, no. 6 (1993): 727–35. Quote on p. 727.

124. Ibid., 727.

125. Daniel P. Carpenter, *Reputation and Power: Organizational Image and Pharmaceutical Regulation at the FDA* (Princeton, NJ: Princeton University Press, 2010).

126. J. W. Mountin, "Statement," in US Senate, Committee on Education and Labor, *National Health Program: Hearings... on S. 1606*, 79th Cong., 2d sess., 1946 (Washington: Government Printing Office, 1946), 137 (quotation), 134–68.

127. Ibid., 142.

128. Wilson George Smillie, *Preventive Medicine and Public Health* (New York: Macmillan, 1948): 576–77.

129. Michael R. Grey, *New Deal Medicine: The Rural Health Programs of the Farm Security Administration* (Baltimore: Johns Hopkins University Press, 1999), chapter 6, quote on p. 160.

130. Grey, *New Deal Medicine*. Quote is from John Newdrop, who Grey interviewed on February 3, 1984, for his research on the FSA. See p. 156, endnote #14.

## Chapter 5

1. Theodore R. Marmor and Jan S. Marmor, *The Politics of Medicare* (Chicago: Aldine, 1973).
2. Rothman uses the term "American Way" to refer to the strategy pursued by Blue Cross. I adapt it a bit to emphasize the importance of the voluntary sector in their political strategy. See David. J. Rothman, "The Public Presentation of Blue Cross, 1935–1965," *Journal of Health Politics, Policy and Law* 16, no. 4 (Winter 1991): 671–93; and David J. Rothman, "Blue Cross and the American Way in Health Care," in *Beginnings Count: The Technological Imperative in American Health Care* (New York: Oxford University Press), chapter 1. Of course, this is also draws directly from the American Way billboards from 1937–1940.
3. Jacob S. Hacker, *The Divided Welfare State: The Battle over Public and Private Social Benefits in the United States* (New York: Cambridge University Press, 2002); Jennifer Klein, *For All These Rights: Business, Labor, and the Shaping of America's Public-Private Welfare State* (Princeton, NJ: Princeton University Press, 2003); Marie Gottschalk, *The Shadow Welfare State: Labor, Business, and the Politics of Health-Care in the United States* (Ithaca, NY: ILR Press, 2000).
4. Alan Derickson, "The House of Falk: The Paranoid Style in American Health Politics," *American Journal of Public Health* 87, no. 11 (1997):1836–43; Marjorie Shearon, "Blueprint for the Nationalization of Medicine" (n.p., 1947); Reprinted in U.S. Senate, Committee on Labor and Public Welfare, Subcommittee on Health, "National Health Program: Hearings . . . on S. 545 . . . and S. 1320, 80th Cong., 1st Sess., 1947–1948," 5 vols. (Washington, DC: U.S. Government Printing Office, 1947–1948); see Vol. 4, pp. 1706–29. J. T. H. Connor, "'One Simply Doesn't Arbitrate Authorship of Thoughts': Socialized Medicine, Medical McCarthyism, and the Publishing of Rural Health and Medical Care (1948)," *Journal of the History of Medicine and Allied Sciences* 72, no. 3 (2017): 245–71.
5. Derickson, "The House of Falk."
6. Executive Order 9835.
7. David Caute, *The Great Fear: The Anti-Communist Purge Under Truman and Eisenhower* (New York: Simon & Schuster, 1978). See chapter 13, "The Federal Civil Service." Quote on p. 269.
8. Derickson, "The House of Falk"; Jane Pacht Brickman, "'Medical McCarthyism': The Physicians Forum and the Cold War," *Journal of the History of Medicine and Allied Sciences* 49 (July 1994): 380–418.
9. Derickson, "The House of Falk." See Appendix 6.A for a copy of Roemer's letter from the Loyalty Review Board. I acknowledge James Connors for bring this document to my attention, from the Roemer Papers, Yale University.
10. Derickson, "The House of Falk," 1838–39; Michael R. Grey, *New Deal Medicine: The Rural Health Programs of the Farm Security Administration* (Baltimore, MD: Johns Hopkins University Press, 1999), 163.
11. J. Edgar Hoover, "Let's Keep America Healthy," *Journal of the American Medical Association* 144, no. 13 (1950): 1094–95.
12. Caute, *The Great Fear*, 269–75. Looking at the decade, from 1947 to 1956, there was a total of 2,700 dismissals and 12,000 resignations as a result of investigations into subversive activities. Quote on p. 269.
13. Derickson, "The House of Falk"; Shearon, "Blueprint for the Nationalization of Medicine,"; J. T. H. Connor, "'One Simply Doesn't Arbitrate Authorship of Thoughts': Socialized Medicine, Medical McCarthyism, and the Publishing of Rural Health and Medical Care (1948)," *Journal of the History of Medicine and Allied Sciences* 72, no. 3 (2017.): 245–71.
14. "Organization Section: Resolution on Prohibition of Political Activity on Part of the United States Public Health Service," *JAMA* 132, no. 10 (1946): 584–87; quote on 584.
15. Daniel Sledge, *Health Divided: Public Health and Individual Medicine in the Making of the Modern American State* (Lawrence, KS: University Press of Kansas, 2017).
16. Mott and Roemer also resigned and went to work in Canada for several years. See Grey, *New Deal Medicine*, 164. It is also noteworthy that many health officers in the PHS believed Parran was let go for political reasons. Whether true or not, this perception that the head of their agency, which health officers were groomed to feel proud of as a scientific agency, was dismissed under a cloud of political character assassination, had an important impact on their morale. See Bess Furman Papers, National Library of Medicine.

17. Marie Jahoda, "Morale in the Federal Civil Service," *Annals of the American Academy of Political and Social Science* 300 (July1955): 110–13; quote on 111. For a description of how the loyalty-security program operated for federal civil service employees, see Ralph S. Brown, "The Operation of Personnel Security Programs," *Annals of the American Academy of Political and Social Science* 300 (1955): 94–101. See also Lloyd K. Garrison, "Some Observations on the Loyalty-Security Program," *University of Chicago Law Review* 23, no. 1 (1955): 1–11.

    For a more extensive overview of the program, see Eleanor Bontecou, *The Federal Loyalty-Security Program* (Ithaca, NY: Cornell University Press, 1953).
18. The costs included: salary suspended during investigation before verdict was reached, reputations attacked, job opportunities outside of the government were undercut by the publicity of security investigations. See Jahoda, "Morale in the Federal Civil Service," 112.
19. Robert A. Smith, "Siberia, U.S.A.," *Reporter Magazine*, June 28, submitted as part of the Congressional Record—Appendix, "Alaska Mental Health Facts and Fantasies" Extension of Remarks of Hon. Edith Green, Representative of the House, D-Oregon. Wednesday, July 18, 1956, p. A5641–3. In submitting this article to the record, Rep. Green said: "Mr. Speaker, so much nonsense and absurdity has been peddled about the Alaska mental health bill that it seems necessary, once again, patiently to state the facts that are obscured by all this fantasy. I know no better or more objective statement of the facts than the article by A. Bert Smith."
20. Peg A. Lamphier and Rosanne Welch, eds. *Women in American History: A Social, Political, and Cultural Encyclopedia and Document Collection* (Santa Barbara, CA: ABC-CLIO, 2017), "Volume 4: Cold War America to Today, Anticommunist Women's Organizations," p. 8. Mary C. Brennan, "Who Were These Women?," in *Wives, Mothers, and the Red Menace: Conservative Women and the Crusade against Communism* (Denver: University Press of Colorado, 2008), 31–58.
21. Smith, "Siberia U.S.A."
22. Inside the newsletter they claimed that this was part of a "Zionist power movement . . . to make anti-Semitism a crime and to brand all opponents (bigots and anti-Semites, as they call their opponents) as mental cases and send them to insane asylums." See Smith, "Siberia, U.S.A.," A5642.
23. Ibid., A5643.
24. Ibid., A5642.
25. Actually, this latter responsibility was given over to the Alaska legislature so the objectives of the bill were eventually largely achieved. Smith, "Siberia, U.S.A.," A5643.
26. See, for example, Hacker, *The Divided Welfare State*, and Klein, *For All These Rights*, though there are many others as well.
27. People's Research Survey, January 1940 [survey question]. USPR.45.R07. People's Research [producer]. Ithaca, NY: Roper Center for Public Opinion Research, Cornell University, iPOLL [distributor], accessed March 29, 2018. The question wording was as follows: "It has been suggested that every family earning $20 a week or less be made to contribute 25 cents every week to take care of doctor and hospital bills in case of accident or illness. Would you approve or disapprove such a plan?"
28. Office of Public Opinion Research Roosevelt Survey, Mar, 1943 [survey question]. USOPOR.43-004.Q15. Office of Public Opinion Research [producer]. Ithaca, NY: Roper Center for Public Opinion Research, Cornell University, iPOLL [distributor], accessed March 29, 2018. The exact question wording was: "After the war do you think the government should provide free medical care for all who need it and can't afford it?"
29. National Opinion Research Center, University of Chicago. Hospital and Medical Insurance, August 1944 [survey question]. USNORC.440226.R19B. National Opinion Research Center, University of Chicago [producer]. Ithaca, NY: Roper Center for Public Opinion Research, Cornell University, iPOLL [distributor], accessed March 29, 2018.
30. National Opinion Research Center, University of Chicago. Hospital and Medical Insurance, August 1944 [survey question]. USNORC.440226.R19C. National Opinion Research Center, University of Chicago [producer]. Ithaca, NY: Roper Center for Public Opinion Research, Cornell University, iPOLL [distributor], accessed March 29, 2018. Exact question wording: "Would you rather have the Social Security law handle the insurance that would pay

for people's doctor and hospital care, or would you rather have it handled through some private insurance plan?"

31. Gallup Organization. Gallup Poll, Apr, 1946 [survey question]. USGALLUP.052046.RT14. Gallup Organization [producer]. Ithaca, NY: Roper Center for Public Opinion Research, Cornell University, iPOLL [distributor], accessed March 29, 2018. It is noteworthy that only 2% mentioned National Health Program given that it was the major proposal just six years prior and many people active in health policy reforms had continued to refer to the term. However, the list reflects the incremental and fragmented strategy that was actually pursued, despite the larger goal of creating a "national health program."

32. Peter Dobkin Hall, "Scope and Dimensions of the Nonprofit Sector," in *The Nonprofit Sector*, ed. Walter W. Powell and Richard Steinberg (New Haven, CT: Yale University Press, 2006); Elizabeth Clemens, "Scope and Theory of Government-Nonprofit Relations," in *The Nonprofit Sector*, ed. Walter W. Powell and Richard Steinberg (New Haven, CT: Yale University Press, 2006); See also J. Steven Ott, *The Nature of the Nonprofit Sector* (Boulder, CO: Westview Press, 2001).

33. W. P. Shepard, "The American Health Association as a National Voluntary Public Health Agency," *Circulation* 2 (1950): 736–41; quote on 736.

34. M. Gunn Selskar and Philip S. Platt, *Voluntary Health Agencies: An Interpretive Study* (New York: Ronald Press, 1945). The National Council's Executive Committee and Advisory Committee was a "who's who" of the leaders in public health and health system reform at that time, including Geo. St. John Perrott from the U.S. PHS, C.-E. A. Winslow from Yale University, Ray Lyman Wilbur, chancellor of Leland-Stanford University and chair of the CCMC some twenty years prior. In addition to Shepard, there were two others from Life Insurance companies on the Committee.

35. Ibid.

36. In addition to Gunn and Platt's *Voluntary Health Agencies*, see also Robert H. Hamlin, *Voluntary Health and Welfare Agencies in the United States* (New York: Schoolmasters' Press, 1961); Richard Carter, *The Gentle Legions: National Voluntary Health Organizations in America* (New Brunswick, NJ: Transaction, 1961). In public health textbooks at the time, voluntary health agencies were mentioned and described as essential to the organization of public health services. See Hugh Rodman Leavell and E. Gurney Clark, *Preventive Medicine for the Doctor in His Community: An Epidemiological Approach* (New York: McGraw-Hill, 1953); Murray Grant, *Handbook of Preventive Medicine and Public Health* (Philadelphia: Lee & Febiger, 1967).

37. W. P. Shepard, "The American Health Association as a National Voluntary Public Health Agency," *Circulation* 2 (1950): 736–41; quote on 737.

38. See Gunn and Platt, *Voluntary Health Agencies*; chapter 2 is devoted to defining what voluntary agencies do and their types.

39. Ibid., 737; emphasis in original text.

40. Gunn and Platt, *Voluntary Health Agencies*.

41. Shepard, "The American Health Association," 737.

42. Gallup Organization. National Health Survey, February 1954 [survey question]. USGALLUP. POS352.R26A. Gallup Organization [producer]. Ithaca, NY: Roper Center for Public Opinion Research, Cornell University, iPOLL [distributor], accessed March 29, 2018.

43. Gunn and Platt, *Voluntary Health Agencies*, 121–49.

44. Shepard, "The American Health Association," 738–39.

45. A. C. Eglin, "A Direct Expense Report for Departmental Costs," *Hospitals* 24 (April 1950): 73–74; quote on 73 (emphasis in original).

46. American Hospital Association, "The State Association: In Profile," *Hospitals* 27 (May1953): 49–51; see p. 49.

47. Ibid., 48.

48. Ibid., 49.

49. Ibid., 51.

50. American Hospital Association, "Association Business: State Activities on Mid-Year Program," *Hospitals* 24 (March 1950): 117 (emphasis added).

51. Hiram Sibley, "Government Agencies Can Be Persuaded to Pay Costs for Indigent Care," *Hospitals* 25 (February 1951): 43–46, quote on 43.

52. Ibid., original emphasis.
53. This was part of the AHA's accounting handbook, but for another good example of how this was used for proposing a rate formula, see Charles G. Roswell "A Detailed Formula for Setting Hospital Rates," *Hospitals* 25, Part I (June 1951): 64–65.
54. For example, see G. C. Long, "How Alabama Hospitals Helped Win State Aid for Medical Indigents," *Hospitals* 32 (February 16, 1958): 45–46; John Bigelow, "State Hospital Association Campaigns Among Legislative Candidates," *Hospitals* 31 (April 1, 1957): 45–46.
55. Based on my own content analysis research of all articles published in *Hospitals* from January 1950 through December 1959. A total of 168 issues were reviewed. The journal was published monthly from 1950 through 1955. In January 1956, the series switched to a bimonthly, 24 issues per year format.
56. Hiram Sibley, "Government Agencies Can Be Persuaded to Pay Costs for Indigent Care," *Hospitals* 25 (February 1951): 43–46, quote on 44.
57. American Hospital Association, "Association Business: Health Information Foundation Head," *Hospitals* 24 (April 1950): 125 (emphasis added).
58. Based on authors content analysis research. The total was 190 articles.
59. Kenneth Williamson, "The Hospital and Government," *Hospitals* 31 (April 16, 1957): 45–46.
60. Sibley, "Government Agencies," 45.
61. Katherine Zahronsky, "Better Public Relations through United Efforts," *Hospitals* 24 (March 1950): 57–58; quote on 57.
62. William B. Meytrott, "The Value of a Friendly Press," *Hospitals* 24 (January 1950): 54–55; quote on 55. David Rothman also discusses the importance of using the media to gain subscribers for Blue Cross—the hospitals' insurance plan. See Rothman, "The Public Presentation of Blue Cross"; and Rothman, "Blue Cross and the American Way."
63. American Hospital Association, "Association Business: State Activities," 120.
64. Zahronsky, "Better Public Relations," 57.
65. George Bugbee, "Is Our Cost Story Understandable?," Hospitals 26 (May 1952): 52, 78, 80; quote on 52. (emphasis in original).
66. Ibid., 80.
67. Reproductions of the pamphlet were obtained from an original copy in the Michael Davis papers, New York Academy of Medicine, Rare Books Rooms.
68. Rufus C. Rorem, "What Hospitals Can Do about Rising Costs," *Hospitals* 31 (March 1, 1957): 35–36.
69. Most of the 190 articles on public relations over the decade mentioned the importance of working with the hospital's local auxiliary. See, for example, Donald W. Cordes and Mrs. James Enyart, "Dynamic Partners: The State Association and Women's Auxiliaries," *Hospitals* 27 (October 1953): 73–74, 166. Written by the president of Iowa Hospital Association and Iowa Hospital Auxiliary about how best to organize the hospital-auxiliary relationship to maximally effect the hospital. See also F. Ross Porter, "Hospital-Auxiliary Relations: Activate Your Good Intentions," *Hospitals* 31 (February 1, 1957): 35–36.
70. Ibid., 49.
71. Lynn C. Wimmer, "Auxiliaries Know How to Raise Money," *Hospitals* 24 (March 1950): 43–44. This article notes that there were 250,000 women working with hospital auxiliaries in 1950.
72. Howard S. Pfirman, "The Evolution Stages of an Admitting Procedure," *Hospitals* 24 (January 1950): 65–68.
73. Robert A. Anderson, "A Simple Collection Aid for the Small Hospital," *Hospitals* 24 (February 1950): 39–41.
74. Ibid., 65 (emphasis in original text).
75. American Hospital Association, "Community Reactions to Bad Debt Collections," *Hospitals* 24 (October 1950): 52.
76. Rufus Rorem, "The Case of Mr. X," *Hospitals* 27 (May 1953): 78, 80; quote on 78.
77. Clearly, a sample size of 13 was not large enough to meet the standards of randomization necessary to make such claims.
78. Rorem, "The Case of Mr. X," 52.
79. Jack L. Rogers, "Bank Financing to Reduce Unpaid Accounts," *Hospitals* 31 (April 1, 1957): 47–49.

80. Ibid., 49. For other examples, see J. A. Connelly, "Social Factors Play a Part in the Collection Policy," *Hospitals* 25 (January 1951): 58–59; American Hospital Association, "Opinions: On Trends in Accounts Receivable," *Hospitals*, 24 (April 1950): 30, 32, 154.
81. Eugene Lopez, "Our Potential Ambassadors—Auxiliaries," *Hospitals* 26 (June 1952): 59–60; quote on .60.
82. Ibid., 60.
83. American Hospital Association, "The Fifty-Fourth Convention: The Association Year in Review," *Hospitals* 26 (September 1952): 70–75, quote on 75.
84. Delbert L. Price and David Kinzer, "Cooperation is the Keystone of New Chicago Hospital-Press Code," *Hospitals* 31 (February 1, 1957): 28–32, 96; quote on 28.
85. Ibid., 96.
86. Alex Dworkin, "A Public Relations Budget Needs Some Public Relations of Its Own," *Hospitals* 30 (November 1, 1956): 40–41. Michael Reese Hospital in Chicago tripled its public relations budget in five years.
87. Earl G. Dressre and Frank R. Briggs, "How Do You Feel about Your Hospitals?," *Hospitals* 28 (January 1953): 76–78, 168. See also William S. McNary, "Don't Fence the Community Out," *Hospitals* 29 (December 1955): 61–63, 156.
88. Albert W. Snoke, "President's Address," *Hospitals* 31(October 16, 1957): 41–44, 132; quote on 42.
89. Robert A. Loder, "The Public Evaluates New Jersey's Hospitals," *Hospitals* 29 (September 1955): 78–80, 208–10.

## Chapter 6

1. Bruce Fetter, "Origins and Elaboration of the National Health Accounts, 1926–2006," *Health Care Financing Review* 28 (Fall 2006): 53–67, see 56.
2. Robert M. Gibson, "National Health Expenditures, 1978," *Health Care Financing Review* 1, no. 1 (Summer 1979): 1–36. See Table 7, p. 32.
3. Louis S. Reed, "Private Health Insurance in the United States: An Overview," *Social Security Bulletin* 28 (December 1965): 3–21, 48. See Table 2, p. 15. Note enrollment figures were much lower for other more comprehensive coverage plans, which explain why the depth of coverage was so sparse. See Tables 3 and 4, p. 17.
4. The average family living in an urban area in 1950 spent 5% of its $4,000 in annual income on medical care, and families with high medical expenditures ($1,000 or more) spent on average more than 20% of its income on medical care. See Selma Mushkin, "Characteristics of Large Medical Expenses," *Public Health Reports* 72, no. 8 (1957): 697–702.
5. In general this is true, but the title of the series changed slightly over the years, and actually started in the February issue of 1953: Ida C. Merriam, "Social Welfare Programs in the United States," *Social Security Bulletin* 16 (February 1953): 3–12.
6. The title of the series changes slightly over the years. It starts as "Voluntary Insurance against Sickness: 1948–51 Estimates," *Social Security Bulletin* 15, no. 3 (1952).
7. Louis S. Reed and Dorothy P. Rice, "National Health Expenditures: Object of Expenditures and Source of Funds, 1962," *Social Security Bulletin* 27 (August 1964): 11–21; quote on 11.
8. Ibid., 13. The ubiquitous use of the term "consumer" in the health care context even by this time is also noteworthy. For a history on the creation of the American health care consumer, see Nancy Tomes, *Remaking the American Patient: How Madison Avenue and Modern Medicine Turned Patients into Consumers* (Chapel Hill: University of North Carolina Press, 2016). The only text I could find from this time period that questioned the use of the term "consumer" and its measurement is in Michael Davis, *Medical Care for Tomorrow* (New York: Harper & Brothers, 1955); see especially pp. 306–310.
9. Actually, the search generated 11 articles, but one was about voluntary agency expenditures for health and welfare, so that was excluded. The three articles prior to 1960 are: Agnes W. Brewster, "Voluntary Health Insurance and Medical Care Expenditures, 1948–58," *Social Security Bulletin* 22, no. 12 (December 1959): 3–9; Agnes W. Brewster and Simon Dinitz, "Health Insurance Protection and Medical Care Expenditures: Findings from Three Family Surveys," *Social Security Bulletin* 19, no. 11 (1956): 3–10; Agnes W. Brewster, "Voluntary

Health Insurance and Medical Care Expenditures: A Ten-Year Review," *Social Security Bulletin* 21, no. 12: 8–15.

10. Actually, there was one article published in 1964 stating that the amount covered by private insurance might be "subject to misinterpretation unless the relationship of consumer expenditures to total national expenditures for these purposes is borne in mind." It then went on to present this comparison based on total expenditures, identical to that which I present in Figure 6.6. As I discuss, they even include public health expenditures, making the percentage covered by public and private equal at 24%. However, it is noteworthy that these data are never shown in a table or figure, and this point is made on the last page of the article. And, most importantly, despite this acknowledgment of a "misinterpretation" this accounting approach—not directly comparing private and public based on total health expenditures—continued until the late 1970s. See Louis S. Reed, "Private Consumer Expenditures for Medical Care and Voluntary Health Insurance, 1948–63," *Social Security Bulletin* 27, no. 12 (1964): 1–22; quote on 22.

11. Fetter, "Origins and Elaboration," 57. Fetter describes how the National Income and Product Accounts (NIPA) devised in 1947 also presented three separate tables—personal consumption expenditures, gross private domestic investment, and government purchases of goods and services—making it very difficult to compare the government's role relative to private investments. Moreover, NIPA lumped medical care together with death expenses (e.g., funerals, cemeteries, and tombstones), and other tables combined all categories of social spending. Finally, NIPA also did not distinguish between what private insurance paid for health service versus what the consumer paid for directly. In sum, NIPA's presentation of data made it very difficult to understand what the United States was spending (and how) for health care services at this time. For more information about Simon Kuznets and the politics associated with the creation of national accounts, see Mark Perlman, "Political Purpose and the National Accounts," in *The Politics of Numbers*, ed. William Alonso and Paul Starr (New York: Russell Sage Foundation, 1987),133–52.

12. Brewster, "Voluntary Health Insurance," 8. Fox and Fronstin raise this concern about counting government contributions to employee health insurance as private expenditures in national health expenditures accounts in 2000. As I discuss in Part III, these accounting practices, despite concerns raised initially by Brewster in 1959 as to their appropriateness, set the United States on a particular path of describing "private expenditures" that still continues. See Daniel M. Fox and Paul Fronstin, "Letter to the Editor: Public Spending For Health Care Approaches 60 Percent," *Health Affairs* 19, no. 2 (2000): 271–73.

13. See Jacob S. Hacker, *The Divided Welfare State: The Battle over Public and Private Social Benefits in the United States* (New York: Cambridge University Press, 2002); Christopher Howard, *The Hidden Welfare State: Tax Expenditures and Social Policy in the United States* (Princeton, NJ: Princeton University Press, 1997).

14. Alonso William and Paul Starr, eds., *The Politics of Numbers* (New York: Russell Sage Foundation, 1987), 1.

15. Reed and Rice, "National Health Expenditures," 1964.

16. Ibid., Table 1, p. 4. See also Fetter, "Origins and Elaboration," 58.

17. Joseph W. Mountin and Evelyn Flook, "Guide to Health Organization in the United States, 1951," Public Health Service Publication no. 196 (Washington, DC: US Government Printing Office, 1953). The role of public health in the provision of health services remains a reality in the US health care system, but its portrayal is still largely lost today, which will be discussed in more detail in Part III.

18. Elliot L. Richardson, *Federal Role in the Nation's Health* (archival materials, National Library of Medicine, 1959). Quote on pp. 661–62.

19. Ibid., 662.

20. Ibid., 666.

21. Ibid., 666.

22. Ibid., 666.

23. The "private other" category also included private expenditures for voluntary health agencies and health services in industrial plants, so it is impossible from this article to know the exact amount consumers were paying in premiums.

24. Louis S. Reed and Ruth S. Hanft, "National Health Expenditures, 1950–64," *Social Security Bulletin* 29 (January 1966): 3–19; see Chart 1, p. 5 and Table 9, p. 13. To witness continuation of these trends in data presentation and interpretation, see Dorothy P. Rice and Barbara S. Cooper, "National Health Expenditures, 1950–66," *Social Security Bulletin* 31 (April 1968): 3–22; Dorothy P. Rice and Barbara S. Cooper, "National Health Expenditures, 1950–67," *Social Security Bulletin* 31 (January 1968): 3–20; Barbara S. Cooper, Nancy L. Worthington, and Paula A. Piro, "National Health Expenditures, 1929–73," *Social Security Bulletin* 37 (March 1974): 3–19, 48; Marjorie Smith Mueller and Robert M. Gibson, "National Health Expenditures, Fiscal Year 1975," *Social Security Bulletin* 39 (February 1976): 3–20, 48. Robert M. Gibson, "National Health Expenditures, 1978," *Health Care Financing Review* 1, no. 1 (Summer 1979): 1–36.
25. Fetter, "Origins and Elaboration," 58.
26. Note that I have not even discussed yet the revenue lost due to the tax exemption for health insurance offered to employers, which is another important (and very large) form of a hidden public subsidy. This will be discussed in Part III.
27. Joseph W. Mountin, Aaron W. Christensen, Evelyn Flook, Edward E. Minty, Rubye F. Mullins, and Georgie B. Druzina, "Distribution of Health Services in the Structure of State Government, 1950," Public Health Service Bulletin no. 184 (Washington, DC: U.S. Government Printing Office, 1954).
28. Ibid. The survey covered the 48 states, the District of Columbia, and the Territories of Alaska, Hawaii, Puerto Rico, and the Virgin Islands. This was a very extensive methodological process. Rather than rely on mail surveys, they interviewed "state agency personnel responsible for any activity contributing to the conservation or improvement of human health." PHS personnel in 10 regional offices of the FSA conducted the interviews in each state of their respective regions. For details on methods see p. 2. Quote on p. 2.
29. Ibid., 2.
30. Ibid., 37.
31. Ibid., 39–40, see Table 7.
32. Ibid., 33–4.
33. Ibid., 64.
34. Ibid. This is a subheading in the executive summary on p. 3.
35. Ibid., 3.
36. Julian G. Hanlon, "The Role of the Mental Health Service in the Local Health Department," *Public Health Reports* 72, no. 12 (December 1957): 1093–97.
37. Ibid., 4.
38. Ibid., 17.
39. Isadore Seeman, "Expenditures of Health Departments in Large Cities," *Public Health Reports* 67, no. 3 (1952): 279–86. Indeed, this author even reverts to the famous "Public Health is Purchasable" phrase first used by Hermann Biggs in 1912 (see Chapter 2 and 3).
40. Harry S. Mustard, *Government in Public Health* (New York: Commonwealth Fund, 1945).
41. Leonard A. Scheele, "Letters to the Editor," *American Journal of Public Health* 38, no. 11 (1948): 1579–80; quote on 1579.
42. Leonard A. Scheele, "Anniversary Program—150th Year U.S. Public Health Service: The Past and Future of the Public Health Service," *American Journal of Public Health* 39, no. 3 (1949): 293–302; quotes on 294–97.
43. Ibid., 301–2.
44. "Whither, Public Health," *American Journal of Public Health* 40, no. 8 (1950): 1006–8; quote on 1006.
45. Ibid.
46. Ibid.
47. Ibid. The AJPH editorial board start the essay as follows: "An address delivered last winter at the Michigan School of Public Health by Surgeon-General Leonard A. Scheele, is so notable that it deserves wide reading and study" (1006).
48. Leonard A. Scheele, "Public Health Today—The Nation's Best Investment," *Public Health Reports* 68, no. 2 (1953): 771–77; quote on 772.
49. Ibid. Figure 7.7 is a replica of the figure shown on p. 707.

50. Joseph W. Mountin, "Financing Local Health Services: Federal Participation," *Public Health Reports* 67, no. 10 (1952): 944–49.

51. "Federal Grants-in-Aid," The Committee on Federal Grants-in-Aid of the Council of State Governments, 1949. See Appendix A, pp. 273–281. There were ten questions in all, to which the majority of state public health officials responded positively.

52. Commission reports included: "Federal Grants-in-Aid," 1949 (see Chapter 12, "Public Health," pp.180–98, recommendation on p. 197); "Federal Aid to Public Health," 1955, A Study Committee on Federal Aid to Public Health submitted to the U.S. Commission on Intergovernmental Relations.

53. "Federal Aid to Public Health," 1955, 29.

54. U.S. Congress, Hearings on H.R. 4312 and H.R. 4313 and H.R. 4918. "National Health Plan." Subcommittee of the Committee on Interstate and Foreign Commerce, House of Representatives, 81st Congress. July 6, 1949, 968.

55. Ibid.

56. "Federal Aid to Public Health," 1955, 31.

57. Ibid.

58. Ibid., ii. The other two members included Angier Goodwin, a U.S. representative from Massachusetts, and Franklin Murphy, the chancellor of the University of Kansas. Business interests included the Indianapolis Chamber of Commerce, president of Winthrop Stearns, and president of State Mutual Life Insurance Co.

59. Ibid., 31.

60. Ibid., 34.

61. Mountin and Flook, "Guide to Health Organization in the United States, 1951," 19.

62. Scheele, "Anniversary Program," 298.

63. Originally, and still at this time in the 1950s, the American Lung Association was the National Tuberculosis Association. Selskar Michael Gunn, Philip Skinner Platt, and National Health Council, Committee for the Study of Voluntary Health Agencies, *Voluntary Health Agencies: An Interpretive Study* (New York: The Ronald press company, 1945); Richard Carter, *The Gentle Legions* (New York: Doubleday, 1961), 133.

64. Scheele, "Public Health Today," 775.

65. For excellent contemporary review of the literature on disease-based organizations and health movements, see Steven Epstein, "The Politics of Health Mobilization in the United States: The Promise and Pitfalls of 'Disease Constituencies'," *Social Science and Medicine* 165 (September 2016): 246–54. See also Rachel Kahn Best, "Disease Campaigns and the Decline of Treatment Advocacy," *Journal of Health Politics, Policy and Law* 42, no. 3 (2017): 425–57.

66. It is also important that there was a strong regional bias in the influence of voluntary health agencies, which deserves further study. These agencies were more active in urban communities than in rural areas, and they were much more prolific in New England. Indeed, hidden public health services were most significant in the New England region because local health departments contracted out to voluntary health agencies to provide health services. It is difficult to obtain data on the amount of public health expenditures contracted out to voluntary agencies in New England at this time, but according to Mountin and Flook, "a large proportion of public health personnel were employed by voluntary health agencies, which also sponsor a great number of health facilities and services." See Mountin and Flook, "Guide to Health Organization in the United States, 1951," 68. See also Mountin et al., "Distribution of Health Services in the Structure of State Government, 1950," 1954, p. 132 and Table 3 starting on p. 134 for an example of how voluntary agencies were involved in providing services for tuberculosis at the state level.

67. "The Public Health Service Today" (Public Health Service Publication no. 165), 1952. Annual Report of the Public Health Service, Federal Security Agency, 1951. See also a synopsis of these reports: "The Public Health Service in 1952," *Public Health Reports* 67, no. 7: 705–708; Figure 7.7 on p. 708.

68. National Health Council, *Voluntaryism and Health: The Role of the National Voluntary Health Agency* (New York: National Health Council, 1962). Quote on front inside page from David Lilienthal, *Words to Live By*, edited by William Nichols (New York: Simon & Schuster, 1948).

69. The NHC wrote on p. 23 that the voluntary movement "has been of deep and significant import to the health of the nation."

70. National Health Council, "Voluntaryism and Health," 23.

71. Luther Terry, "The Public Health Service Role in Medical Care Administration," *Public Health Reports* 77, no. 2 (1962) : 93–96; quote on 93. See also U.S. Department of Health, Education, and Welfare, *Medical Care in the United States: The Role of the Public Health Service*, Public Health Publication no. 862 (Washington, DC: U.S. Dept. of Health, Education, and Welfare, Public Health Service, 1961)..

72. Terry, "The Public Health Service Role," 94.

73. Ibid.

74. Ibid., 94 (emphasis added).

75. Ibid. This is the beginning of that language which Deborah Stone so aptly describes in Deborah A. Stone, "The Struggle for the Soul of Health Insurance," *Journal of Health Politics, Policy and Law* 18, no. 2 (1993): 287–317.

76. Federal employee Elizabeth Wickenden's review of the role of voluntary agencies in the *Social Security Bulletin* also illustrates this dogma: "The fact that it has consistently served as a dynamic force in the development and expansion of the governmental programs of social security has in no way served to limit the horizons of its own challenge or to dry up the well-springs of its own ingenuity . . . whereas the governmental programs by their nature tend toward the broad and universal, voluntary programs ten toward the diverse and particular . . . Voluntarism is a built-in device through which democratic society protects itself against monolithic universality and static resistance to change. In this sense American voluntary welfare, by its very detachment from the social security complex, plays an essentially constructive role in its functioning and warrants a place of honor in this quarter-century celebration of its achievements" (106).

77. Terry, "The Public Health Service Role," 94.

78. Beverlee A. Myers, Bruce J. Steinhardt, Mary L. Mosley, and John W. Cashman, "The Medical Care Activities of Local Health Units," *Public Health Reports* 83, no. 9 (1968): 757–69.

79. This act will be discussed in more detail in Chapter 7 of the book. The exact title is Public Law 89-749: Comprehensive Health Planning and Public Health Services Amendments of 1966. See Arthur Jacobs and Richard Froh, "Significance of Public Law 89-749—Comprehensive Health Planning," *New England Journal of Medicine* 279 (December 12, 1968): 1314–18.

80. Joint Committee on Medical Care of the American Public Health Association and the American Public Welfare Association, "Tax-Supported Medical Care for the Needy," A Statement of the Joint Committee on Medical Care of the American Public Health Association and the American Public Welfare Association, *American Journal of Public Health* 42 (October 1952): 1310–27; quote on 1311.

81. Joint Committee, "Tax-Supported Medical Care for the Needy," 1311–12.

82. For a discussion about the important influence of financial concerns during this period, see Eric Patashnik and Julian Zelizer, "Paying for Medicare: Benefits, Budgets, and Wilbur Mills's Policy Legacy," *Journal of Health Politics, Policy and Law* 26, no. 1 (2001): 7–36.

83. The six organizations: American Medicaid Association, American Hospital Association, American Nurses Association, American Dental Association, American Public Health Association, and American Public Welfare Association.

84. Robert Bocking Stevens and Rosemary Stevens, *Welfare Medicine in America: A Case Study of Medicaid* (New York: Free Press, 1974); Harry S. Truman and Monte M. Poen, *Strictly Personal and Confidential: The Letters Harry Truman Never Mailed* (Boston, MA: Little Brown, 1982).

85. For a discussion of how SBA and FHA construction loans encouraged the building of private for-profit nursing homes, see Martha Holstein and Thomas R. Cole, "The Evolution of Long-term Care in America," in *The Future of Long-term Care: Social and Policy Issues*, ed. Robert H. Binstock, Leighton E. Cluff and Otto Von Mering (Baltimore, MD: Johns Hopkins University Press, 1996).

86. See Holstein and Cole (1996) for a discussion of how SBA and FHA construction loans encouraged the building of private for-profit nursing homes.

87. Colin Gordon, *Dead on Arrival: The Politics of Health Care in Twentieth-century America* (Princeton, NJ: Princeton University Press, 2003); Theodore R. Marmor, *The Politics of Medicare*, 2nd ed. (New York: A. de Gruyter, 2000).

88. At Press Conference, June 25, 1951, 2:30 p.m., Room 5246, Federal Security Agency, 330 Independence Avenue, SW, Washington, DC.

89. Marmor, *The Politics of Medicare*, 2000.

90. Interestingly, President Eisenhower offered what could be defined as a slightly more generous proposal, but did not gain much attention.

91. Sydney Fein, "The Kerr-Mills Act: Medical Care for the Indigent in Michigan, 1960–1965," *Journal of the History of Medicine and Allied Sciences* 53, no. 3 (1998): 285–316.

92. Bruce C. Vladeck, *Unloving Care: The Nursing Home Tragedy* (New York: Basic Books, 1980).

93. Fein, "The Kerr-Mills Act" 1998.

94. Marmor, *The Politics of Medicare*, 2000; Stevens and Stevens, *Welfare Medicine*, 1974.

95. Davis, *Medical Care for Tomorrow*, 362. Quotes around "full costs" are in the original texts illustrating Davis's skepticism as to the meaning of full costs.

96. Snoke, President of the AHA: *Hospitals* 31 (October 16, 1957): 41–44, 132, Quote on 44.

97. American Hospital Association, "An Interview with George Bugbee," *Hospitals* 33 (January 1, 1959): 32–36; quote on 36.

98. Ray E. Brown, "The Nature of Hospital Costs," *Hospitals* 30 (April 1, 1956): 36–41.

99. Ray E. Brown, "Your President Reports," *Hospitals* 30 (March 1, 1956): 45; Robert H. Reeves, Albert G. Proseus, and Frederick C. Morgan, "Annual Administrative Reviews: Accounting and Financial Management," *Hospitals* 32 (April 16, 1958): 28–30; American Hospital Association, "The 1955 Convention in Review," *Hospitals* 29 (October 1955): 81–96.

100. American Hospital Association, "The Principles of Third-Party Payment for Hospital Care," *Hospitals* 25 (July 1951): 37–39; Quote on 37.

101. Ibid., 37 (emphasis in original text).

102. Ibid., 38.

103. M. B. Shroyer, "A Year-Old Modern Rural Hospital Reports," *Hospitals* 25 (July 1951): 43–46; quote on p.46.

104. American Hospital Association, "A Cross Section of Hospital Construction," *Hospitals* 25 (April 1951): 49–72, see pp. 61–62.

105. Only one article made this connection; see Edward L. Springer, "The Community and Hospital Financing: Who Should Foot the Bill?," *Hospitals* 33 (April 1, 1959): 28–29.

106. Harris B. Jones, "A Painless Method of Hospital Financing," *Hospitals* 27 (August 1953): 71–72; quote on 71. This is an amazing story because the nonprofit hospital had to transfer its title to the City of Frankfort in order for the city to float a revenue bond issue and to make formal application for the Hill-Burton matching funds, yet despite taxpayers paying for the construction and the interest payments, when all bonds were paid off, the law stipulated that the title of the hospital would return to the nonprofit.

107. Ibid., 72. See also William B. Meytrott, "'Hidden Dollars'—A Source of Extra Hospital Income," *Hospitals* 25 (May 1951): 64–65.

108. Charles G. Roswell, "A Detailed Formula for Setting Hospital Rates," *Hospitals* 25, Part I (June 1951): 64–65; American Hospital Association, "Nationwide Survey of Rates in General Hospitals," *Hospitals* 25 (December 1951): 62; Harry Becker, "Four-Point Study on Financing Hospital Care," *Hospitals* 26 (April 1952): 53–55.

109. Jack C. Haldeman, "Goals for the Sixties in Health Facilities Construction," *The Modern Hospital* 98, no. 3 (1962): 93.

110. Karen Davis, "Community Hospital Expenses and Revenues: Pre-Medicare Inflation," *Social Security Bulletin* 35, no. 10 (October 1972): 3–19.

111. Delbert J. Kenny, "Financing Hospital Capital Requirements," *Hospitals* 34 no. 5 (1960): 28.

112. Karl S. Klicka, "Hospital Financing in the Future," In *Guides to Capital Financing of Hospitals*, American Hospital Association Report Series, no. 1 (Chicago: American Hospital Association, 1962).

113. Jeffrey Lynn Stambaugh, "A Study of the Sources of Capital Funds for Hospital Construction in the United States," *Inquiry* 4, no. 2 (1967): 3–22.

114. Robert, M. Sigmond, "Hospital Capital Funds: Changing Needs and Sources," *Hospitals* 39, no. 16 (1965): 54. For a discussion of how internal reserves substantially enhanced hospital capital spending capacity, see Donald R. Cohodes and Brian M. Kinkead, *Hospital Capital Formation in the 1980s* (Baltimore, MD: The Johns Hopkins University Press, 1984), especially pp. 17–18.
115. Stambaugh, "A Study of the Sources," 7.
116. Davis, *Medical Care for Tomorrow*, 120.
117. Ibid., 439.
118. Ibid., 313.
119. F. R. Smith, "Adjudication in the Matter of the Filing of the Associated Hospital Service in Philadelphia (Blue Cross)" (Harrisburg, PA: Insurance Commissioner of the Commonwealth of Pennsylvania, April 15, 1958), 8.
120. Max Shain and Milton Roemer, "Hospitals and the Public Interest," *Public Health Reports* 76, no. 5 (1961): 401–410; quote on 401.
121. Edward L. Springer, "A Government Lawyer Looks at Health Protection and Hospital Income," *American Journal of Public Health* 50, no. 5 (1960): 661–69; quote on 662 (emphasis added).
122. Shain and Roemer, "Hospitals and the Public Interest."
123. Springer, "A Government Lawyer," 666.
124. Herman M. Somers and Anne R. Somers, *Medicare and the Hospitals: Issues and Prospects* (Washington, DC: Brookings Institution, 1967), 177. As quoted in Brian M. Kinkead, "Medicare Payment and Hospital Capital: The Evolution of Policy," *Health Affairs* 3, no. 3 (1984): 49–74.
125. Kinkead, "Medicare Payment and Hospital Capital," 51.
126. Ibid., 51.
127. Ibid., 52–53. See also Judith M. Feder, *Medicare: The Politics of Federal Hospital Insurance* (Lexington: MA: D.C. Health, 1977).
128. Mountin et al., 1954, 64.
129. Mountin and Flook, "Guide to Health Organization in the United States, 1951," iii.
130. Ibid., 5, and Table 1 (pp.6–13).
131. *Health Insurance Plans in the United States, Report of the Committee on Labor and Public Welfare United States Senate*, Part 1, Washington, DC, 1951.
132. Thomas J. Graves, "IGR and the Executive Branch: The New Federalism," *The Annals of the American Academy of Political and Social Science* 416 (1974): 40–51. Quote on p. 46.
133. Morton Grodzins, *The American System* (Chicago: Rand McNally, 1966). Quotes on pp. 11–12, 316.
134. Mountin and Flook, "Guide to Health Organization in the United States, 1951," 1.
135. Ibid., 1.
136. Ibid., 1.
137. Ibid., 3.
138. Ibid., 2.
139. See Chapter 6 and Daniel M. Fox, *Health Policies, Health Politics: The British and American Experience, 1911–1965* (Princeton, NJ: Princeton University Press, 1986) who developed this term.
140. See Vladek, *Unloving Care*, 1980; Fox, *Health Policies, Health Politics*, 1986; James A. Morone, *The Democratic Wish: Popular Participation and the Limits of American Government* (New Haven, CT: Yale University Press, 1998); Marmor, *The Politics of Medicare*, 2000; Kimberly J. Morgan and Andrea Louise Campbell, *The Delegated Welfare State: Medicare, Markets, and the Governance of Social Policy* (New York: Oxford University Press, 2011); Jacob S. Hacker, *The Divided Welfare State: The Battle over Public and Private Social Benefits in the United States* (New York: Cambridge University Press, 2002).

## Part III

1. George Monbiot, "Neoliberalism—The Ideology of the Root of All Our Problems," *The Guardian*, April 15, 2016, https://www.theguardian.com/books/2016/apr/15/neoliberalism-ideology-problem-george-monbiot.
2. Ibid.

## Chapter 7

1. Obviously, the president does not pass legislation through Congress. However, I wrote this intentionally, because as Blumenthal and Morone (2009) discuss, Johnson was a master legislator and played a very active role in ushering the major pieces of health legislation through the Congress. David Blumenthal and James A. Morone, *The Heart of Power: Health and Politics in the Oval Office* (Berkeley: University of California Press, 2009). See also National Library of Medicine, Regional Medical Programs Collection, Bethesda, MD. A number of the oral interviews also describe Johnson as very involved with health legislation. See, for example, interviews with Phillip Lee and Michael DeBakey. Karen Tumulty, "The Great Society at 50," *Washington Post*, May 17, 2014 (see interactive graph which lists key pieces of Great Society legislation enacted between 1963 and 1968, which also shows the significance of health-related bills in green. Website: https://www.washingtonpost.com/sf/national/2014/05/17/the-great-soceity-at-50/?utm_term=.306ad5dcaff3, accessed May 9, 2019).
2. U.S. President, "Advancing the Nation's Health," Special Message to Congress, January 7, 1965, Public Papers of the Presidents, 1965, Vol. I (Washington, DC: U.S. Government Printing Office, 1966), 20.
3. National Library of Medicine, Regional Medical Programs Collection, Bethesda, MD; oral interview with Phillip Lee on December 6, 1991.
4. Examples include: Benefits for Disabled Veterans Bills passed in August 1965; Vocational Rehabilitation Act Amendments of 1967; Child Health Program in 1965; Narcotics Rehabilitation Act; Mental Health Amendments of 1967.
5. Examples include, e.g., Community Mental Health Centers Act Amendments of 1965; Community Health Services Extension Act in August 1965.
6. e.g., Nurse Training Act, passed in September 1964, Health Professions Educational Assistance Amendments in October 1965; Health Manpower Act in August 1968. There were numerous environmental acts passed as well, which at the time were considered as part of public health and were under the jurisdiction of PHS until the Environmental Protection Agency (EPA) was created in 1970. This is another example of shifting public health functions out of departments of health when the boundaries became too large.
7. This may seem too bold a statement given the delivery model reforms included under the Affordable Care Act of 2010. However, as I will make clear in Chapter 10, because the United States still fails to do anything about capital health policy (a policy path I explicate in Chapter 8) and the ACA expanded coverage on top of existing inequitable structures (as described in Chapter 9), the health care system is no closer to a rational and/or equitable system than was discussed and envisioned by many in the 1970s. And all of the delivery model reforms passed under the ACA rely again on voluntary action from the private sector.
8. Dan Fox refers to this planning concept that emerged in the United Kingdom and the United States as "hierarchical regionalism," which is an apt description. However, because the stakeholders involved in promoting this idea just use the term "regionalism" to refer to the concept, for consistency—since I quote them and want to highlight the significance of their language—I also use this term. See Daniel M. Fox, *Health Policies, Health Politics: The British and American Experience, 1911–1965* (Princeton, NJ: Princeton University Press, 1986).
9. Joel May, *Health Planning: Its Past and Potential*, Health Administration Perspectives, no. A5 (Chicago: Center for Health Administration Studies, University of Chicago, 1967). For example, when the Pennsylvania Economy League asked 32 hospital administrators whether they considered what other hospitals in the area do when doing their own planning, only one said he discussed plans with the hospital council. See Pennsylvania Economy League, *Coordinated Planning for Hospitals* (Pittsburgh: The League, February 1959).
10. May, *Health Planning*. May provides data on the number of journal articles devoted to the topic of planning as an indicator of this resurgent interest. The number of articles increased from 11 during the period 1954–1957 to 103 from 1958 to 1961 and 188 from 1962 to 1965. See p. 21.
11. Daniel M. Fox, David Rosner, and Rosemary A. Stevens, "Between Public and Private: A Half Century of Blue Cross and Blue Shield in New York," *Journal of Health Politics, Policy and Law* 16, no. 4 (1991): 643–50.

12. See Daniel Fox's historical account of hierarchical regionalism. Daniel M. Fox, *Health Policies, Health Politics: The British and American Experience, 1911–1965* (Princeton, NJ: Princeton University Press, 1986).

13. Lindberg interview with William Kissick; NLM, NIH, Bethesda, Maryland, September 13, 1991.

14. National Library of Medicine, NIH, Regional Medical Programs Collection, Retrospective Conference, remarks by Karl Yordy, December 6, 1991.

15. Lindberg interview with William Kissick; NLM, NIH, Bethesda, Maryland, September 13, 1991.

16. The Partnership for Health Amendments of 1967 also fit the latter approach, but that will be discussed later in this chapter.

17. U.S. Congress, House Committee on Interstate and Foreign Commerce, Regional Medical Complexes for Heart Disease, Cancer, Stroke, and Other Diseases. Hearings. 89th Congress, 1st session, on H.R. 3140. U.S. Government Printing Office, July 20, 1965. Quote on p. 11.

18. National Library of Medicine, Regional Medical Program Collection, Oral Interview. Lindberg interview with William Ruhe, 1991.

19. National Library of Medicine, Regional Medical Program Collection, Oral Interview with Dr. Michael DeBakey, August 17, 1991.

20. President's Commission on Heart Disease, Cancer and Stroke, *Report to the President: A National Program to Conquer Heart Disease, Cancer and Stroke*, Vol. I, December 1964, p. viii (emphasis added).

21. President's Commission Report, Vol. II, 1964, p. 269.

22. The President's Commission on Health Disease, Cancer and Stroke, "Report to the President: A Program to Conquer Heart Disease, Cancer and Stroke," Vol. I, December 1964 (Appendix C, "The Formation of the Commission"), p. 87. See also Whaley interview with Lewis, 1991, from Regional Medical Program Collection, National Library of Medicine. Irving Lewis in his interview with Whaley also confirmed that this was of interest to Johnson: "[T]here was a feeling that there was a lot of information which was locked up in the laboratories which hadn't yet made its way out into the world of medical care, and that's what the President was trying to achieve." Regional Medical Program Collection, National Library of Medicine.

23. Including the chair, there were 28 members, of which 16 were from university academic medical centers (57%). Of the remaining members, 7 were from business interests. There was one representative from the AMA and a surgeon on the commission.

24. See many of the interviews from the Regional Medical Program Collection, National Library of Medicine.

25. President's Commission Report, Vol. I, 1964, xii.

26. President's Commission Report, Vol II, 1964, v.

27. President's Commission, Vol. I, 1964, xii–xiii.

28. Whaley interview with Karl Yordy, 1991.

29. Strickland, p. 18. This is confirmed by looking through the interviews of the National Library of Medicine, Regional Medical Program Collection.

30. National Library of Medicine, Regional Medical Program Collection, Retrospective Conference on RMPs, Remarks by Dr. Phillip Lee, Assistant Secretary of Health, Education and Welfare from 1965 to 1969. Conference date: 1991.

31. See Kissick interview for specific statement about BCBS, 1991, in the National Library of Medicine, Regional Medical Program Collection. Marston, DeBakey and Yordy interviews also confirm the political difficulties. See Carleton Chapman and John M. Talmadge, "Historical and Political Background of Federal Health Care Legislation," *Law and Contemporary Problems* 35 (Winter 1970): 334–47 for a similar statement to Kissick about this being more difficult than the passage of Medicare and Medicaid.

32. This is confirmed by William Ruhe. See RMP Historical Collection, Profiles in Science, Library of Medicine. Letter from C.H. William Ruhe to Donald A.B. Lindberg, August 5, 1991. Box HMD 6.

33. "Evolution or Revolution in American Medicine," *Modern Medicine* (Special Report), June 21, 1965, 16.

34. Ibid., emphasis added.
35. *Modern Medicine*, Special Report, June 21, 1965, 16. This view was illustrated in the hearings as well. See U.S. Congress, House Committee on Interstate and Foreign Commerce, Regional Medical Complexes for Heart Disease, Cancer, Stroke, and Other Diseases. Hearings. 89th Congress, 1st session, on H.R. 3140. U.S. Government Printing Office, July 20, 1965. Testimony from Dr. Appel from the AMA (p. 293) and general practitioner Dr. Townsend (p. 214).
36. Chapman and Talmadge, "Historical and Political Background," 345–46 (emphasis added).
37. U.S. Congress, House Committee on Interstate and Foreign Commerce, Regional Medical Complexes for Heart Disease, Cancer, Stroke, and Other Diseases. Hearings. 89th Congress, 1st session, on H.R. 3140. U.S. Government Printing Office, July 20, 1965. These principals were clearly espoused by Anthony Celebrezze, secretary of HEW, in his opening testimony (see pp. 10–11). It is noteworthy that he presenting his testimony with Dr. James Shannon, director of the NIH, and Dr. Luther Terry, Surgeon General of PHS, since after the bill was passed there was significant debate as to which agency (NIH or the Health Services Division under HEW) should implement the program. This debate is reflective of the confusion about whether this bill was about research dissemination (more in the realm of NIH) or delivery model reform (more in line with service side of PHS).
38. U.S. Congress, House Committee on Interstate and Foreign Commerce, Regional Medical Complexes for Heart Disease, Cancer, Stroke, and Other Diseases. Hearings. 89th Congress, 1st session, on H.R. 3140. U.S. Government Printing Office, July 20, 1965. Quote on p.11.
39. Ibid.
40. For details on the political compromise with the AMA, see the Whaley interview with Karl Yordy, 1991 in the National Library of Medicine, Regional Medical Program Collection.
41. Public Law 89–239, 89th Congress, 3.596. October 6, 1965. See also Strickland, p. 19–20.
42. National Library of Medicine, Regional Medical Program Collection, Oral Interview by Lindberg with Dr. Michael DeBakey, August 17, 1991.
43. Ibid.
44. Whaley interview with Karl Yordy, September 4, 1991. National Library of Medicine, Regional Medical Programs Collection. I wrote "convinced," but according to DeBakey, Shannon had no choice because Senator Hill insisted on NIH administering the program.
45. National Library of Medicine, Reginal Medical Programs Collection, Retrospective Conference on RMPs, Quote from Dr. Robert Q. Marston, first director of RMPs, December 6, 1991.
46. They were part of a special panel reflecting on specific RMPs at 1991 conference.
47. Stephen P. Strickland, *The History of Regional Medical Programs: The Life and Death of a Small Initiative of the Great Society* (Lanham, MD: University Press of America, 2000).
48. Whaley interview with Lewis, 1991.
49. NLM Regional Medical Programs Collection, Letter from Leonidas Berry to Mr. John Parascandola, Chief History of Medicine, dated December 2, 1991. Quote on p. 1.
50. Ibid., quote on p. 2.
51. National Library of Medicine, Regional Medical Program Collection, Oral Interview with Dr. Michael DeBakey, August 17, 1991. Interviewer Dr. Donald A.B. Lindberg's summary of his interview with Duval.
52. William Kissick commented that CHPs emerged out of Mountin's 1945 report to Congress on regionalism, which addressed coordinated hospital and health services. This was the basis of Hill-Burton program, and Kissick observed that the CHP continued the concept of decentralization and voluntary initiative within the communities and services. See Lindberg interview with Kissick, 1991.
53. Lewis D. Polk, "The Comprehensive Health Planning Laws from the Local Viewpoint: Philadelphia's Experience," *Public Health Reports* 84, no. 1 (1968): 86–90; quote on 87.
54. William H. Stewart and James H. Cavanaugh, *Partnership for Planning* (Washington, DC: Public Health Service, 1967. Extension of remarks before the National Advisory Council on Regional Medical Programs, Nov. 27, 1966; and the Surgeon General's joint conference with state and territorial health authorities, mental health authorities, hospital and medical facilities

construction authorities, and mental retardation construction authorities, Washington, DC, December 6, 1966, p. 2.

55. William H. Stewart, "Comprehensive Health Planning," address to the National Health Forum of the National Health Council, Chicago, March 21, 1967, p. 11.

56. U.S. Public Health Service, *Information and Policies on Grants for Comprehensive Areawide Health Planning*. Section 314(b), Public Health Service Act, as amended by Public Law 89-749 (Office of the Surgeon General, Office of Comprehensive Health Planning, Bethesda, MD, August 30, 1967), p. 6.

57. E. Richardson, "Address to the Institute of Medicine," Washington, DC, May 10, 1972.

58. Lawrence D. Brown, "Some Structural Issues in the Health Planning Program," in *Health Planning in the United States: Selected Policy Issues*, Vol. 2 (Washington, DC: National Academy Press, 1981).

59. Stewart, "Comprehensive Health Planning," 11. It was not just Stewart who referred to the importance of a partnership. The Comprehensive Health Planning Act was referred to more broadly as the "Partnership for Health" and introduced as such by Senator Lister Hill. See Advisory Commission on Intergovernmental Relations (ACIR), *The Partnership for Health Act: Lessons from a Pioneering Block Grant* (Washington, DC, #A-56, January 1977), 10.

60. Stewart, "Comprehensive Health Planning," 3.

61. Stewart, "Comprehensive Health Planning," 6 (emphasis added).

62. The substantial increase in publications and educational programs focused on health system planning also suggests this hope in rational planning extended beyond the federal PHS. A National Commission on Community Health Services, for example, conducted the Community Action Studies Project with the goal to "translate community plans into the kind of action that will result in providing better health services for all citizens." See their report, titled *Action-Planning for Community Health Services* (Washington, DC: Public Affairs Press, 1967), quote from the foreword.

63. Starting in the 1950s, there was growing criticism among conservatives that federal grant-in-aid programs were coercive and, due to the strong inducement of federal funding, "forced" states to spend money in certain areas they would not otherwise. Conservatives began to call for reformulating federal funding to the states into block grants to allow for more state flexibility. Critics of block grants questioned their usefulness as instruments for national policy; because they allowed so much state discretion, there was less ability to focus on high-priority problem areas, and they worried about the lack of adequate accountability related to state spending of block grant funds. See Advisory Commission on Intergovernmental Relations, *The Partnership for Health Act*, 1.

64. Ibid., 50–51.

65. C. A. Miller, "Issues of Health Policy: Local Government and the Public's Health," *American Journal of Public Health* 65 (1975): 1330–34; quote on 1330.

66. Conference Report: "Impact of Governmental Programs on Public Hospitals: Directions for the Future," *Public Health Reports* 83, no. 1 (1968): 53–60.

67. Ibid., 58.

68. National Library of Medicine, Reginal Medical Programs Collection, Storm Whaley interview with Karl Yordy, September 4, 1991. Several interviews confirmed the lack of an articulated administrative relationship between the two programs, as well as animosity between the programs. The original director of RMPs, Marston, mentioned that Jim Cavanaugh was the head of Comprehensive Health Planning at that time, and "probably is the single person who tried to articulate the relationship between the two programs for people." Marston interview, 1991.

69. DeBakey on panel at 1993 Conference.

70. Chapman and Talmadge, "Historical and Political Background."

71. National Library of Medicine, Regional Medical Programs Collection, Interview with Irving J. Lewis, NLM, Bethesda, Maryland. Interviewer: Storm Whaley. September 6, 1991.

72. All the interviews confirmed this view, though this particular phrase came from the interview with William Ruhr. See RMP Historical Collection, Profiles in Science, Library of Medicine. Letter from C. H. William Ruhe to Donald A.B. Lindberg, August 5, 1991. Box HMD 6.

73. Interviews with Marston, DeBakey, and Kissick all confirm this point about the reorganization at HEW and the swap. The quote comes from Marston on a panel at the 1991 conference.

74. Whaley interview with Karl Yordy, 1991.

75. Strickland interview of Joseph Thompson, 1993.

76. Daniel M. Fox, "From Piety to Platitudes to Pork: The Changing Politics of Health Workforce Policy," *Journal of Health Politics, Policy and Law* 21, no. 4 (1996): 823–42; Irving J. Lewis and Cecil G. Sheps, *The Sick Citadel: The American Academic Medical Center and the Public Interest* (Cambridge, MA: Oelgeschlager, Gunn and Hain, 1983).

77. Fox, "From Piety to Platitudes," 1996; Lewis and Sheps, *The Sick Citadel*, 1983. These two studies confirm that leaders of academic medical centers face political incentives that lead to maximizing NIH grants and clinical revenue being the highest priority; neither education or the community benefit. DeBakey's interview confirms this, but also Joe Thompson's interview with Strickland argues that medical schools became completely uninterested in RMPs, especially when the program was moved and brought under the authority of CHPs. He additionally argues that when the 1974 act moved more aggressively toward including consumer groups, medical schools wanted nothing to do with consumer-based planning.

78. Strickland interview of Joseph Thompson, 1993.

79. Congressional Research Service (CRS), National Health Planning and Resources Development Act of 1974, P.L. 93-641. RA 11 U.S., 75–58. Edited by Jennifer O. Sullivan, February 24, 1975.

80. Harold M. Schmeck Jr., "Congress Is Resisting the Nixon Administration's Orders for Elimination of Regional Medical Programs," *New York Times*, April 16, 1973.

81. RMP Historical Collection, Profiles in Science, Library of Medicine. Letter from C. H. William Ruhe to Donald A.B. Lindberg, August 5, 1991. Box HMD 6.

82. Lindberg interview with Dr. John Zapp; NLM, NIH, Bethesda, Maryland, September 23, 1991.

83. Lindberg interview with DeBakey, 1991.

84. Although much was made of this amount appropriated to RMPs—in congressional hearings and by others involved in the process as described below—it is important to point out that this amount paled in comparison to all the federal funds allocated to health services during the same period. As Ostow and Brudney note in their review of RMPs, "in its peak year, 1973, RMP was appropriated $140 million, compared to $9.5 billion expended for Medicare and $5 billion for Medicaid. (Medicaid received an additional $4 billion of State and local funds.)" See Miriam Ostow and Karen Brudney, "Regional Medical Programs," in *Regionalization & Health Policy*, DHEW Pub No. 77-623 (Washington, DC: Government Printing Office, 1977): 60–70; quote on 64.

85. Lindberg interview with Karl Yordy, 1991.

86. Institute of Medicine, *Health Planning in the United States: Selected Policy Issues: Report of a Study*, Vol. 11 (Washington, DC: Institute of Medicine, January 1981), 37.

87. Ibid. See also Whaley interview with Karl Yordy, 1991, where he describes being asked by his superiors at HEW via the Office of Management and Budget to cut the RMP budget, and wrote back that costs would probably increase.

88. "U.S. Healthcare Called Muddled in Senate Study: $20-Billion Programs Are Termed Uncoordinated and Unnecessarily Costly," *New York Times*, March 17, 1970, 1.

89. Arthur A. Atkisson and Richard M. Grimes, "Health Planning in the United States: An Old Idea with a New Significance," *Journal of Health Politics, Policy and Law* 1, no. 3 (1976): 295–318; Drew Altman, "The Politics of Health Care Regulation: The Case of the National Health Planning and Resources Development Act," *Journal of Health Politics, Policy and Law* 2, no. 4 (1978): 560–80.

90. Atkisson and Grimes, "Health Planning," 1976; Altman, "The Politics of Health Care Regulation," 1978; Brown, "Some Structural Issues in the Health Planning Program," 1981.

91. Abt Associates, Inc., *Incentives and Decisions Underlying Hospitals' Adoption and Utilization of Major Capital Equipment*, Report for NCHSR, HRA Contract HSM-110-73-513 (Cambridge, MA: Abt Associates, Inc., 1975)

92. Ibid.

93. Louise Russell, "The Diffusion of New Hospital Technologies in the United States," *International Journal of Health Services* 6, no. 4 (1976): 557–80; John T. Tierney, William J. Waters, and William H. Rosenberg, "Certificate-of-Need: No Panacea but Not without Merit," *Journal of Public Health Policy* 3, no. 2 (1982): 178–81; Alan B. Cohen and Donald R. Cohodes, "Certificate of Need and Low Capital-Cost Medical Technology," *Milbank Memorial Fund Quarterly. Health and Society* 60, no. 2 (1982): 307–28.

94. Lawrence D. Brown, "Some Structural Issues in the Health Planning Program," in *Health Planning in the United States: Selected Policy Issues*, Vol. 2 (Washington, DC: National Academy Press, 1981), 1–53.

95. Ibid.

96. Ibid. See also James A. Morone, "The Real World of Representation: Consumers and the HSAs" pp. 257–89 in the same volume; Theodore R. Marmor and James Morone, *HSAs and the Representation of Consumer Interests: Conceptual Issues and Litigation Problems, Final Report* (Washington, DC: Government Printing Office, 1978.

97. Drew Altman, "The Politics of Health Care Regulation," 578.

98. James A. Morone, *The Democratic Wish: Popular Participation and the Limits of American Government* (New York: Basic Books, 1990).

99. James Morone, "Models of Representation: Consumers and HSAs," in *Health Planning in the United States: Issues in Guideline Development*, Vol. 2 (Washington, DC: Institute of Medicine, 1981), 225–56.

100. IOM Report, Vol. 2, 1981, p. 3.

101. George Bugbee Symposium on Hospital Affairs, "Creative Retrenchment," Proceedings of the Twentieth Annual Symposium on Hospital Affairs, 1978. James Kimmey, "The Health Services Agencies and Hospital Costs," pp. 19–24, https://bpb-us-w2.wpmucdn.com/voices.uchicago.edu/dist/e/439/files/2017/08/Creative-Retrenchment-1suyu6t.pdf. See also IOM Report, Vol. 2, 1981. The entire volume applies; however, see in particular chapters by Brown, Sapolsky, and Morone.

102. Ibid. See also Altman, "The Politics of Health Care Regulation."

103. Dorothy Ellenburg, "Special Interests vs. Citizen Control: Who Owns Planning," in *Health Planning in the United States: Issues in Guideline Development?*, Vol. 2 (Washington, DC: Institute of Medicine, 1980), 204–24, quote on 223.

104. Alvin E. Wanthal, "Planning the Financing," *Hospitals* 49, no. 3 (1975):103–118, quote on p.118. Note that Wanthal was a partner in charge of management services for Touche Ross and Co., in the Southeast region. In 1975, he was responsible for more than 40 feasibility studies for revenue bond financing of health care facilities, ranging from $750,000 to $37.5 million (in 2019 dollars, a range of 3.5 million to 176.5 million). See also "Rush to Debt," *Hospitals* 49, no. 3 (1975): 87, which encouraged hospitals to rely on debt financing.

105. Altman, "The Politics of Health Care Regulation"; Morone, *The Democratic Wish*.

106. A number of studies confirmed the influence of interest groups, especially local hospitals, on CON decisions. See volume 2 of the IOM Report cited above.

107. Proceedings, 1978, "Creative Retrenchment," Kimmey, 22.

108. Ibid., 22. See also James Morone, "The Real World of Representation: Consumers and HSAs," in *Health Planning in the United States: Issues in Guideline Development*, Vol. 2 (Washington, DC: Institute of Medicine, 1981), 257–89; see p. 285–86.

109. Morone's study of HSAs also illustrates the extent to which the courts became involved. See James Morone, "Models of Representation," in *Health Planning in the United States* (National Academy Press, 1981), 251–53.

110. Daniel Cohodes, "Interstate Variation in Certificate of Need Programs: A Review and Prospectus," in *Health Planning in the United States: Issues in Guideline Development*, Vol. 2 (Washington, DC: Institute of Medicine, 1981), 54–88. Cohodes show how the effectiveness of the CON varied not just by state laws, but by the strength of the state hospital industry. See pp. 57–61 in particular.

111. The IOM's overview of health planning in the United States also makes this point regarding confusion between planning and regulation, especially among those promoting

the competitive approach. See National Academy of Sciences, Institute of Medicine, *Health Planning in the United States: Issues in Guideline Development*, Vol. 1 (1980), 11–13.

112. Robert H. Cathcart, "Planning a Priority," *Hospitals* 49, no. 1 (1975): 36–43, quote on 40.

113. American Hospital Association, Introduction to Special Issue: "Cost Containment in Design and Construction," *Hospitals* 49, no. 3 (1975): 61 (emphasis added).

114. American Hospital Association, Forward to Special Issue: "Cost Containment in Design and Construction," *Hospitals* 49, no. 3 (1975): 2 (is forward written by Logan and Clayton??).

115. "Introductory Remarks," in *Proceedings of the Eighteenth Annual Symposium on Hospital Affairs: Survival in Utopia (Growth Without Expansion)* (Chicago: Archives from the Center for Health Administration Studies, University of Chicago, April 1976), 1.

116. Logan and Clayton, 1975, p.2.

117. Proceedings, 1976. See in particular, David Kinzer, President of the Massachusetts Hospital Association, "Straws in a Wind of Change," 12.

118. Proceedings, 1976. See in particular, Kinzer, "Straws in a Wind of Change." Kinzer clearly states these two aspects of AHA policy on p. 14.

119. Proceedings, 1976. See in particular, Kinzer, "Straws in a Wind of Change," 14.

120. Daniel Cohodes, *Interstate Variation in Certificate of Need Programs: A Review and Prospectus* (Baltimore, MD: Johns Hopkins Medical Institutions, Center for Hospital Finance and Management, 1980). See Table 3 on p. 63.

121. The IOM Report, Vol. 1, p. 32, also makes light of this paradoxical situation. See National Academy of Sciences, Institute of Medicine, *Health Planning in the United States: Selected Policy Issues*, Vol. 1, chapter 3, "National, State and Local Roles and Relationships" (Washington, DC: Institute of Medicine, 1981), 31–52.

122. Gordon W. Epperson and R. F. Juedeman, "Accounting to the Community," *Hospitals* 49, no. 3 (1975): 83–84, 87–88, 90–91, quote on p.87.

123. "Introductory Remarks," in *Proceedings of the Eighteenth Annual Symposium on Hospital Affairs: Survival in Utopia (Growth Without Expansion)* (Chicago: Archives from the Center for Health Administration Studies, University of Chicago, April 1976), 1.

124. "Public Control and Hospital Operations," in *Proceedings of the Fourteenth Annual Symposium on Hospital Affairs*, May 1972 (University of Chicago, CHAS Archives). Quote on p. 51.

125. Proceedings, 1976. See in particular, Kinzer, "Straws in a Wind of Change," 24.

126. Proceedings, 1976, "Discussion with Danielson, Tibbits, Mungerson, Kinzer, Anderson and Wilmot." Quote on p. 46. See also John L. McKnight, "Hospitals Must Work to Change Image," *Hospitals* 49, no. 10 (1975): 72–74.

127. Proceedings, 1976. See in particular, Kinzer, "Straws in a Wind of Change," 15.

128. Proceedings, 1976, "Discussion with Danielson, Tibbits, Mungerson, Kinzer, Anderson and Wilmot." Quote on p. 46.

129. Proceedings, 1976. See in particular, Kinzer, "Straws in a Wind of Change," 15.

130. Proceedings, 1976, "Discussion with Danielson, Tibbits, Mungerson, Kinzer, Anderson and Wilmot." Quote on p. 50.

131. "The AHA President's Report," *Hospitals* 49, no. 6 (1975): 79–86, quote on p.84.

132. Ibid.

133. Proceedings, 1976. See in particular, Kinzer, "Straws in a Wind of Change," 16–17.

134. Several sources document the political power of the hospital industry. See, for example, the IOM Report, 1981, Vol. 2. The entire volume supports this conclusion. Cohodes also creates measures of the strength of the hospital industry in selected states. See Table 1 on p. 58 and text on pp. 75–77.

135. "Creative Retrenchment," In *Proceeding of the Twentieth Annual Symposium on Hospital Affairs* (Chicago: Graduate Program in Hospital Administration and Center for Health Administration Studies, Graduate School of Business, University of Chicago, 1978). From the CHAS Archives; see Introduction, and presentations by Laurence Seidman and Carl Stevens, pp.1–18.

136. Ibid., 14.

137. In the Proceedings, proponents of competition included, for example, Guido Calabrese, Mark Pauly, and Richard Posner.

138. Havighurst, p. 44, in Proceedings, 1974.

139. Clark C. Havighurst, ed., *Regulating Health Facilities Construction: Proceedings of a Conference on Health Planning, Certificate of Need, and Market Entry* (Washington, DC: American Enterprise Institute for Public Policy Research, 1974), Remarks during Discussion: Planning's Role in Relation to the Market, quote on p. 41.

140. Joesph P. Newhouse and Jan P. Acton, "Compulsory Health Planning Laws and National Health Insurance," in *Regulating Health Facilities Construction: Proceedings*, ed. Clark C. Havighurst, pp. 217–31. From Conference on Health Planning, Certificates of Need, *and Market Entry* (Washington, DC: American Enterprise Institute for Public Policy Research, 1974);Clark C. Havighurst and American Enterprise Institute for Public Policy Research, *Regulating Health Facilities Construction: Proceedings* (Washington: American Enterprise Institute for Public Policy Research, 1974).

141. Newhouse and Acton, "Compulsory Health Planning Laws." See also many others in Havighurst, *Regulating Health Facilities Construction*.

142. Newhouse and Acton, "Compulsory Health Planning Laws." As quoted by Howard Gindele, the president of the Blue Cross Association of Western Pennsylvania, p. 27.

143. Remarks by Robert Grosse, professor, School of Public Health, University of Michigan, during "Discussion: Planning or Politics's Role in Relation to the Market," quote on p. 44. In Havighurst, *Regulating Health Facilities Construction* .

144. Institute of Medicine, *Health Planning in the United States: Issues in Guideline Development*, Vol. 1 (Washington DC: National Academy Press, 1980); quote on p. 15.

145. Clark C. Havighurst, "Statement of Dissent," in *Health Planning in the United States: Issues in Guideline Development*, Vol. 1 (Washington, DC: National Academy Press, 1980); quote on p. A2, A4.

146. Institute of Medicine, *Health Planning in the United States: Selected Policy Issues*, Vol. 1 (Washington, DC: National Academy Press, 1981); quote by Rashi Fein, Preface, pp. ix–x.

147. See, most notably, Paul Starr, *Social Transformation of American Medicine* (New York: Basic Books, 1982). See Book Two, Chapter 2, "The Triumph of Accommodation," and Chapter 3, "The Liberal Years." See p. 376 specifically for this statement.

## Chapter 8

1. See, for example, David A. Stockman, "Premises for a Medical Marketplace: A Neoconservative's Vision of How to Transform the Health System," *Health Affairs*, 1, no. 1 (1981): 5–18; Stockman, "Rethinking Federal Health Policy: Unshackle the Health Care Consumer," *National Journal* 11 (1979): 934–36.

2. Stockman, "Premises for a Medical Marketplace," 12–14.

3. Jonathan Betz Brown and Richard B. Saltman, "Health Capital Policy in the United States: A Strategic Perspective," *Inquiry* 22 (1985): 122–31. See also Jonathan Betz Brown and Stephen R. Thomas, *Health Capital Financing: Structuring Politics and Markets to Produce Community Health* (Ann Arbor, MI: Health Administration Press, 1988).

4. This cyclical pattern alternating between "public action" and "private action" was argued by Albert O. Hirschman in his book *Shifting Involvements*. I attribute the connection of these trends to health policy to William Shonick, "Recapitulation and Reflections," in *Government and Health Services: Government's Role in the Development of U.S. Health Services, 1930–1980* (New York: Oxford University Press, 1995), 475–88.

5. Walter Dean Burnham, "The Election and After," *New York Review of Books*, August 16, 1984. This comment was made at a discussion sponsored by the Institute for National Strategy on the future of American politics held in New York in between California governor Edmund G. Brown, Walter Dean Burnham, Kevin Phillips, and Arthur Schlesinger Jr. In this same essay Arthur Schlesinger argued that Reagan was just part of a broader cyclical pattern in the United States of shifting from private action to public action and back again. Burnham's essay presents a remarkably accurate 1984 prediction of the future United States.

6. Robert Berenson, "Addressing Pricing Power in Integrated Delivery: The Limits of Antitrust," *Journal of Health Politics, Policy and Law* 40, no. 4 (August 2015): 711–44.

7. Donald R. Cohodes and Brian M. Kinkead, *Hospital Capital Formation in the 1980s* (Baltimore: Johns Hopkins University Press, 1984), 18.

8. Eleanor D. Kinney and Bonnie Lefkowitz, "Capital Cost Reimbursement to Community Hospitals under Federal Health Insurance Programs," *Journal of Health Politics, Policy and Law* 7, no. 3 (1982): 648–66.

9. *Journal of Hospital Capital Finance*, First Quarter, 1986, p. 8. Data source used: AHA Survey of Sources of Funding for Hospital Construction, 1968.

10. Cohodes and Kinkead, *Hospital Capital Formation*, 19.

11. Ibid., 19.

12. Ibid., 19

13. Ibid., 19–20.

14. Ibid., 20.

15. Ibid., 20.

16. D. Hee, M. Gray, and M. Hernandez, "Tax-Exempt Hospital Revenue Bonds: A Database," *Healthcare Financial Management*, 10 (October 1980): 15.

17. Cohodes and Kinkead, *Hospital Capital Formation*, 19.

18. Ibid., 19.

19. Daniel C. Schaffer and Daniel M. Fox, "Tax Administration as Health Policy: The Tax Exemption of Hospitals, 1969–1990," *Tax Notes* October 21, 1991, 217. This article offers an excellent summary of the history of the hospital charitable tax exemption from its beginnings. See also: Daniel M. Fox and Daniel C. Schaffer, "Tax Administration as Health Policy: Hospitals, the Internal Revenue Service, and the Courts," *Journal of Health Politics, Policy and Law* 16, no. 2 (1991): 251–79.

20. Ibid.

21. IRS Revenue Ruling 69–545.

22. As described in more detail in Chapter 8, this statement is not completely right. Over time, a strict demarcation between public and nonprofit voluntary hospitals did not emerge. Due to their heavy reliance on Medicaid, nonprofit community hospitals located in areas with large minority populations and rural areas across the country also became part of what came to be called the "health care safety net." They similarly suffered from low credit ratings and did not have access to capital markets.

23. Richard W. Logan and Norris V. Clayton, "Cost Savings through Areawide Planning," *Hospitals* 49, no. 3 (1975): 65–71; quote on 70–71.

24. Alvin E. Wanthal, "Planning the Financing," *Hospitals* 49, no. 3 (1975): 103–18; quote on p.118. Note that Wanthal was a partner in charge of management services for Touche Ross and Co., in the Southeast region. In 1975, he was responsible for more than 40 feasibility studies for revenue bond financing of health care facilities, ranging from $750,000 to $37.5 million (a range of 3.5 million to 176.5 million in 2019 dollars). See also "Rush to Debt" *Hospitals* 49, no. 3 (1975):, which encouraged hospitals to rely on debt financing.

25. AHA Survey of Sources of Funding for Hospital Construction, 1968, 1981. Cohodes and Kincaid figures are a little different, but the general trend is the same. They report that by 1981, approximately 80% of hospital construction funding was debt-financed, with tax-exempt bonds accounting for about four-fifths of capital borrowed that year. See Cohodes and Kincaid, *Hospital Capital Formation*, 22.

26. Cohodes and Kincaid, *Hospital Capital Formation*, 22.

27. Donald R. Cohodes, "Which Will Survive? The $150 Billion Capital Question," *Inquiry* 20, no. 1 (1983): 5–11.

28. For more detail on the history and politics of Medicare reimbursement schemes (both for physicians and hospitals), see Mirium Laugesen, *Fixing Medical Prices: How Physicians Are Paid* (Cambridge, MA: Harvard University Press, 2016); Rick Mayes and Robert A. Berenson. *Medicare Prospective Payment and the Shaping of U.S. Health Care* (Baltimore: Johns Hopkins University Press, 2006).

29. K. G. Manton, M. A. Woodbury, J. C. Vertrees, and E. Stallard, "Use of Medicare Services before and after Introduction of the Prospective Payment System," *Health Services Research* 28, no. 3 (1993): 269–92; see Table 2, p. 280. Several other studies also confirmed that hospital

length of stay (LOS) decreased and post-acute care use increased with few adverse effects. See S. DesHarnais, E. Kobrinski, J. Chesney, M. Long, R. Ament, and S. Fleming, "The Early Effects of the Prospective Payment System on Inpatient Utilization and the Quality of Care," *Inquiry* 24, no. 1 (1987): 7–16; L. I. Iezzoni, "Change in the Health Care System: The Search for Proof," *Journal of the American Geriatrics Society* 24, no. 8 (1987): 615–17; K. G. Manton and K. Liu, "Recent Changes in Service Use Patterns of Disabled Medicare Beneficiaries," *Health Care Financing Review* 11, no. 3 (1990): 51–66.

30. Ibid.
31. S. Gutterman, *Putting Medicare in Context: How Does the Balanced Budget Act Affect Hospitals?*, Urban Institute Working Paper (Washington, DC: Urban Institute, 2000). Although PPS payments were very generous, the extent to which hospitals could take advantage of the payment rates varied by hospital type. Hospitals that provided a relatively high proportion of their services to the poor, and were located in low-income neighborhoods that served predominantly people of color, had on average negative Medicare inpatient margins. Because they served a higher-risk population, the margins of a fixed diagnosis payment were not as generous. Thus, one important critique is that PPS served to further differences between the have and have-not hospitals. For more on this point, see J. B. Silvers, "The Role of Capital Markets in Restructuring Health Care," *Journal of Health Politics, Policy and Law* 26, no. 5 (2001):1019–30.
32. Institute of Medicine, Committee on Implications of For-Profit Enterprise in Health Care, and B. H. Gray, eds., *For-Profit Enterprise in Health Care* (Washington, DC: National Academies Press, 1986; quote on p. 51 (in chapter 3 on capital investments).
33. Silvers, "The Role of Capital Markets." See also Kinney and Lefkowitz, "Capital Cost Reimbursement."
34. Institute of Medicine and Gray, *For-Profit Enterprise in Health Care*, 52–53.
35. These were AMI, Humana, HCA, and NME.
36. Institute of Medicine and Gray, *For-Profit Enterprise in Health Care*, see Table 3.5 on p. 53.
37. Ibid., 54. Moreover, it is important to recognize the multiple forms of inflationary aspects under U.S. capital health policy. For example, depreciation reimbursement also helped fuel increases in new capital investment. See Kinney and Lefkowitz, "Capital Cost Reimbursement."
38. Cohodes and Kinkead, *Hospital Capital Formation*, 25–26.
39. Ibid., 55.
40. Ibid., 55.
41. Institute of Medicine and Gray, *For-Profit Enterprise in Health Care*, pp. 55, 57 (emphasis added).
42. Jonathan Betz Brown and Richard B. Saltman, "Health Capital Policy in the United States: A Strategic Perspective," *Inquiry* 22 (Summer 1985): 122–31, see p. 123.
43. Bradford Gray, ed., *The New Health Care for Profit: Doctors and Hospitals in a Competitive Environment* (Washington, DC: National Academy Press, 1983). See also Richard B. Siegrist, "Wall Street and the For-Profit Hospital Management Companies," in same volume; Dan Ermann and John Gabel, "Multihospital Systems: Issues and Empirical Findings," *Health Affairs* 3 (Spring 1984): 50–64.
44. Brown and Saltman, "Health Capital Policy in the United States," 124.
45. IOM Report, Chapter 3, p. 61, Table 3.8. Source: Kidder, Peabody & Co., Health Finance Group, Hospital Database (Hernandez and Henkel, 1982).
46. Gloria J. Bazzoli, "The Corporatization of American Hospitals," *Journal of Health Politics, Policy and Law* 29, no. 4–5 (2004): 865–905.
47. Gray, *The New Health Care for Profit*. See also Richard B. Siegrist, "Wall Street and the For-Profit Hospital Management Companies," in same volume; Ermann and Gabel, "Multihospital Systems."
48. Gray, *The New Health Care for Profit*. See also Richard B. Siegrist, "Wall Street and the For-Profit Hospital Management Companies," in same volume; Ermann and Gabel, "Multihospital Systems"; Arnold S. Relman, "The New Medical-Industrial Complex," *New England Journal of Medicine* 305 (July 2, 1980): 41–45.
49. Gloria J. Bazzoli, "The Corporatization of American Hospitals," *Journal of Health Politics, Policy and Law* 29, no. 4–5 (2004): 865–905; see p. 890

50. W. O. Cleverley and P. C. Nutt, "The Decision Process Used for Hospital Bond Rating—And Its Implications." *Health Services Research* 19, no. 5 (1984): 615–37.
51. Cohodes and Kinkead, *Hospital Capital Formation*, 7–8.
52. David Barton Smith, *The Power to Heal: Civil Rights, Medicare, and the Struggle to Transform America's Health Care System* (Nashville. Vanderbilt University Press, 2016).
53. Brown and Saltman, "Health Capital Policy in the United States," 1985, p. 124; Judith M. Feder and Jack Hadley, *Cutbacks, Recession and Care to the Poor: Will the Urban Poor Get Hospital Care?* (Washington, DC: Urban Institue, 1983); Arthur Schatzkin, "The Relationship in Inpatient Racial Composition and Hospital Closure in New York City," *Medical Care* 22 (May 1984): 379–87.
54. Brown and Saltman, "Health Capital Policy in the United States," 1985.
55. Kinney and Lefkowitz, "Capital Cost Reimbursement," 653; Cleverley and Nutt, "The Decision Process."
56. Brown and Saltman, "Health Capital Policy in the United States," 124; Feder and Hadley, *Cutbacks, Recession and Care to the Poor*; Schatzkin, "The Relationship in Inpatient Racial Composition."
57. See Emily Friedman, "The 'Dumping' Dilemma: The Poor Are Always with Some of Us," *Hospitals* 56 (September 1, 1982): 51, 52.
58. David A. Rosner, *Once Charitable Enterprise: Hospitals and Health Care in Brooklyn and New York* (New York: Cambridge University Press, 1982); Robert Bocking Stevens and Rosemary Stevens, *Welfare Medicine in America: A Case Study of Medicaid* (New Brunswick, NJ: Transaction, 2003); Beatrix Hoffman, "Emergency Rooms and Epidemics," in *Health Care for Some: Rights and Rationing in the United States Since 1980* (Chicago: University of Chicago Press, 2012), Chapter 8; See also Chapter 4.
59. See the opening story in Maria O'Brien Hylton, "The Economics and Politics of Emergency Health Care for the Poor: The Patient Dumping Dilemma," *Brigham Young University Law Review* 4 (1992): 971–1034. See also a summary in Hoffman, "Emergency Rooms and Epidemics," 169. Examples of newspaper stories include: Fern Schumer and R.C. Longworth, "Country Hospital at the Brink," *Chicago Tribune*, May 2, 1982, 33, 40; Margaret Engel, "Hospitals Refusing to Admit Poor; Patients Transferred to DC General," *Washington Post*, October 15, 1984, B1; Bard Lineman, "Some Hospitals Turn Away Uninsured Sick People," *Miami Herald*, April 22, 1985, 2.
60. EMTALA was passed under the Consolidated Omnibus Budget Reconciliation Act (COBRA) of 1985 and became effective on August 1, 1986.
61. See 42 U.S.C. § 1395dd0b)(1) (1988).
62. Fern Schumer and R. C. Longworth, "County Hospital at the Brink," *Chicago Tribune*, May 2, 1982, 33, 40.
63. Quoted in Hoffman, "Emergency Rooms and Epidemics," 175.
64. Hylton, "The Economics and Politics of Emergency Health Care," 977.
65. Ibid.
66. Karen J. Treiger, "Note, Preventing Patient Dumping: Sharpening the COBRA's Fangs," *N.Y.U. Law Review* 61 (1986): 1186–87.
67. 42 U.S.C. § 1395dd(a) (2012); see text for law on website: https://uscode.house.gov/view.xhtml?req=granuleid:USC-1994-title42-section1395dd&num=0&edition=1994#amendment-note (accessed on March 15, 2023).
68. Morey Kolber, "Stark Regulation: A Historical and Current Review of the Self-Referral Laws," *HEC Forum: An Interdisciplinary Journal on Hospitals' Ethical and Legal Issues* 18 (2006): 61–84; Jennifer O'Sullivan, "Medicare: Physician Self-Referral ('Stark I and II')," CRS Report for Congress (Order Code RL32494), September 27, 2007.
69. O'Sullivan, "Medicare: Physician Self-Referral."
70. Betty Leyerle, *The Private Regulation of American Health Care* (Armonk, NY: M.E. Sharpe, 1994).
71. Jill Quadagno, "Right-Wing Conspiracy? Socialist Plot? The Origins of the Patient Protection and Affordable Care Act," *Journal of Health Politics, Policy and Law* 39, no. 1 (2014): 35–56.

72. Ibid., 39. Quote is from Mark Pauly, Patricia Damon, Paul Feldstein, and John Hoff, "A Plan for Responsible National Health Insurance," *Health Affairs* 10, no. 1 (1991): 5–25; quote on 8.

73. H.R. 3600, 103D Conf. 1st Sess. [1993].

74. Nearly all (98%) Americans said health care was a very important issue (79%) or somewhat important issue (18%) to them in deciding how to vote in the November 1992 elections. Moreover, while Americans said the economy was the most important issue in their decision to support a candidate in 1992, the second most commonly mentioned issue was health care. Henry J. Kaiser Family Foundation, Commonwealth Fund. Kaiser Family Foundation/Commonwealth Health Insurance Survey, January 1992 [survey question]. USHARRIS.92KAI.RA1. Louis Harris & Associates [producer]. Ithaca, NY: Roper Center for Public Opinion Research, Cornell University, iPOLL [distributor]. See https://ropercen ter.cornell.edu/ipoll/study/31105752/questions#b1a542e6-5caf-4d0d-a951-26e788c4b 15e (accessed April 6, 2020).

75. See, for example, Jacob Hacker, *The Road to Nowhere* (Princeton, NJ: Princeton University Press, 1997); Jill Quadagno, *One Nation, Uninsured: Why the US Has No National Health Insurance* (New York: Oxford University Press, 2005); Theda Skocpol, *Boomerang: Health Care Reform and the Turn against Government* (New York: Norton, 1996).

76. Quadagno, *One Nation, Uninsured.*

77. Quadagno, *One Nation, Uninsured.*

78. And, as Jill Quadagno points out, similar to the ACA marketplaces. See Quadagno, "Right-Wing Conspiracy?"

79. U.S. Congress, Senate, Committee on Labor and Human Resources, Hearing, "Health Security Act of 1993, Part 2," October 20, 1993, hrg-1993-lhr-0058. Quote on p. 324.

80. U.S. Congress, House of Representatives, Committee on Ways and Means, 103rd Cong., 1st Sess. Hearing, "Health Care Cost Containment under H.R. 3600, The Health Security Act," December 16, 1993, p. 84.

81. Ibid.

82. Ibid., Laszewski Testimony, p. 60.

83. Ibid., 342.

84. Ibid., 61.

85. This assertion is based on a review of all the congressional hearings that considered the Clinton health reform proposal.

86. In conducting a search of all the House and Senate hearings pertaining to the Health Security Act of 1993, 90% of the times that capital investments were raised by witnesses invited to give testimony, they mentioned concerns about reduced quality of care. Note that six hearings were reviewed, and there were a total of 227 mentions. See, for example, testimony from Chip Kahn, executive vice president of the Health Insurance Association of America (HIAA) (p. 364, 371); Robert Tedoldi, Association of Health Insurance Agents and president of the National Association of Life Underwriters (p. 406–7); Lodewifk de Vink, president and chief operating officer of the Warner-Lambert Company, "a worldwide company devoted to quality health care and consumer products," and Parke-Davis, their pharmaceutical division. For Laszewski's quote, see U.S. Congress, Senate, Committee on Labor and Human Resources, Hearing, "Health Security Act of 1993, Part 2," October 20, 1993, hrg-1993-lhr-0058. See "Prepared Statement of Robert L. Laszewski," p. 63.

87. U.S. Congress, Senate, Committee on Labor and Human Resources, Hearing, "Health Security Act of 1993, Part 2," October 20, 1993, hrg-1993-lhr-0058. Testimony from McLane, p. 323.

88. Ibid., See Sara Nichols from Public Citizen's Congress Watch, pp. 336–38.

89. Note that there were health policy experts who made these claims, but they were not invited to testify and their voices were not part of the public discourse.

90. Formed to advise Congress on Medicare hospital payments.

91. U.S. Congress, House of Representatives, Committee on Ways and Means, 103rd Cong., 1st Sess. Hearing, "Health Care Cost Containment under H.R. 3600, The Health Security Act," December 16, 1993, p. 38.

92. This segregated discussion is evident in numerous congressional hearings. When I searched on the term "capital," discussions focused on access to capital markets for organizations in the health care system with no discussion of access or equity, and when I search on the terms "equity" and "access," there was no mention of capital markets or access to capital.

93. J. B. Silvers, "The Role of the Capital Markets in Restructuring Health Care," *Journal of Health Politics, Policy and Law* 26, no. 5 (2001): 1020–30; quote on 1028.

94. Nathan W. Carroll, Dean G. Smith, and John R. C. Wheeler, "Capital Investment by Independent and System-Affiliated Hospitals," *Inquiry: The Journal of Health Care Organization, Provision and Financing* 52 (2015): 1–9.

95. Carroll et al., "Capital Investment," p. 3, Table 1.

96. To determine the value of a nonprofit hospital, investment bankers use a formula, called EBITDA, which stands for the hospital's "earning before interest, taxes, depreciation, and amortization," and considers the data on these items for 12 months prior to valuation. EBITDA is then multiplied by a factor to calculate the value of the hospital (e.g., if a hospital's EBITDA is $10 million and the multiple is 6, the investment bankers would value the hospital at $60 million).

97. Gerard F. Anderson, "The Role of Investment Bankers in Nonprofit Conversions," *Health Affairs* 16, no. 2 (1997): 144–47; quote on 144.

98. Ibid., 144. Relying on financial information about the previous year can also distorts and creates a myopic view of a hospital's value, if that represents a weak financial year in what might be an otherwise healthy long-term financial picture, which can seriously undervalue a hospital. See Daniel M. Fox and P. Isenberg, "Anticipating the Magic Moment: The Public Interest in Health Plan Conversions in California," *Health Affairs* 15, no. 1 (Spring 1996): 202–9.

99. Anderson, "The Role of Investment Bankers," 145.

100. Ibid; J. M. Watt et al., "The Comparative Economic Performance of Investor-Owned Chains and Not-for-Profit Hospitals," *New England Journal of Medicine* 314, no. 2 (1986): 89–96; B. Arrington and C. C. Haddock, "Who Really Profits from Not-for-Profits?," *Health Services Research* 25, no. 2 (1990): 291–304; VHA, Inc., *Florida Hospital Analysis* (Irving, TX: VHA, 1995).

101. Anderson, "The Role of Investment Bankers," 146.

102. One research study found the following costs associated with hospital systems acquiring independent hospitals: substantial transaction costs, higher market prices for hospital services, and a loss of community control. Ironically, they also found that while access to capital increased in the first five years of the acquisition, it then was no different from prior to joining the system. See Carroll et al., "Capital Investment." Also see G. Melnick and E. Keeler, "The Effects of Multi-Hospital Systems on Hospital Prices," *Journal of Health Economics* 26, no. 2 (2007): 400–413; B. Herman, "How Much Did Hospitals Pay to Find a Partner? A Case Study," *Becker's Hospital Review*, March 4, 2014, http://www.beckershospitalreview.com/hospital-transactions-and-valuation how-much-do-hospitals-pay-to-find-a-partner-a-case-study.html.

103. There were some research studies on conversions, but even Cutler and Horwitz wrote in 2000 that "despite these large changes [in the hospital industry], there has been almost no empirical research on the reasons for and the effects of conversions." See David M. Cutler and Jill R. Horwitz, "Converting Hospitals from Not-for-Profit to For-Profit Status: Why and What Effects?," in *The Changing Hospital Industry: Comparing For-Profit and Not-for-Profit Institutions*, ed. David M. Cutler (Chicago: University of Chicago Press, 2000), 45–90.

104. Heidi R. Centrella, "General Acute-Care Hospitals Compete with Specialty Hospitals for Profitable Patients," *Journal Record*, June 21, 2004, 1, https://search-proquest-com.proxy.uchicago.edu/docview/259460509?accountid=14657.

105. Centrella, "General Acute-Care Hospitals."

106. Ibid. See also Ronette King, "Healthy Competition?: Small Specialty Hospitals Are Increasingly Reaching for the Same Patients that Community Hospitals Serve, and They're Denting the Profits of Their Larger Competitors," *Times-Picayune*, March 27, 2005, https://search-proquest-com.proxy.uchicago.edu/docview/415919791?accountid=14657; Sean Parnell, "As You

Were Saying . . . A Dose of Healthy Competition," *Boston Herald,* June 11, 2005, https://sea rch-proquest-com.proxy.uchicago.edu/docview/400383982?accountid=14657.

107. Centrella, "General Acute-Care Hospitals."
108. U.S. Congress, Subcommittee on Federal Financial Management, Government Information, and International Security; Committee on Homeland Security and Governmental Affairs. U.S. Senate. S. Hrg. 109-140. Hearing, "Overview of the Competitive Effects of Specialty Hosptials," May 24, 2005. Quote on p. 3.
109. Ibid., 2.
110. Ibid., 5–6.
111. Ibid.
112. Ibid.
113. Ibid., 21.
114. Ibid., 21.
115. Ibid., 7.
116. Ibid., 8.
117. Actually, David Cutler is a health economist and Jill Horwitz is a health legal scholar.
118. Cutler and Horwitz, "Converting Hospitals," 78.
119. Institute of Medicine, *Hospital-Based Emergency Care: At the Breaking Point* (Washington, DC: National Academies Press, 2007).
120. For excellent account of ER diversions in cities across the country in the early 2000s, see Jonathan Cohn, *Sick: The Untold Story of America's Health Care Crisis and the People Who Pay the Price* (New York: HarperCollins, 2007). Some newspaper stories include: Andy Miller, "Too-Crowded Hospitals Play Diverting Game," *Atlanta Journal-Constitution,* June 15, 2001; Diane Solov and Regina McEnery, "Hospital Ambulance Diversions Keep Climbing," *Plain-Dealer* (Cleveland), May 6, 2001.
121. Institute of Medicine, *Hospital-Based Emergency Care,* 1.
122. "How Are Hospitals Financing the Future?: The Future of Capital Access," *Healthcare Financial Management* 58, no. 5 (2004): 45–49, https://search-proquest-com.proxy.uchic ago.edu/docview/196368887?accountid=14657.
123. IOM Report, 2000, 58.
124. D. Gaskin and J. Hadley, "Population Characteristics of Safety Net and Other Urban Hospitals' Markets," *Journal of Urban Health: Bulletin of the New York Academy of Medicine* 76, no. 3 (1999): 351–70. Of course, because racial composition varies dramatically across the United States, these proportions vary substantially by place. In New York City, minority patients accounted for 90% of outpatient visits and 88% of admissions among the city's public hospitals. See B. Siegel, *Public Hospitals—A Prescription for Survival* (New York: The Commonwealth Fund, 1996).
125. G. J. Bazzoli, A. Gerland, and J. May, "Construction and Expansion Activity in U.S. Hospitals," *Health Affairs* 25, no. (20063):783–91.
126. R. A. Hirth, Michael E. Chernew, and S. M. Orzol, "Ownership, Competition, and the Adoption of New Technologies and Cost-Saving Practices in a Fixed-Price Environment," *Inquiry* 37, no. 3 (2000): 282–94; R. Barniv, K. Danvers, and J. Healy, "The Impact of Medicare Capital Prospective Payment Regulation on Hospital Capital Expenditures," *Journal of Accounting and Public Policy* 19, no. 1 (2000): 9–40; Tae Hyun Kim and Michael J. McCue, "Association of Market, Operational, and Financial Factors with Nonprofit Hospitals' Capital Investment," *Inquiry* 45, no. 2 (Summer 2008): 215–31; quote on 226.
127. Ibid.
128. "How Are Hospitals Financing the Future?: The Future of Capital Access," *Healthcare Financial Management* 58, no. 5 (2004): 45–49.
129. Kim and McCue, "Association of Market, Operational, and Financial Factors."
130. Institute of Medicine, *Hospital-Based Emergency Care* .
131. David M. Cutler and Fiona Scott Morton, "Hospitals, Market Share, and Consolidation," *JAMA* 310, no. 18 (2013): 1964–70.
132. Ron Anderson, Peter Cunningham, Paul Hofmann, Wayne Lerner, Kevin Seitz, and Bruce McPherson. "Protecting the Hospital Safety Net," *Inquiry* 46, no. 1 (2009): 7–16.

133. Adam, D. Reich, "Contradictions in the Commodification of Hospital Care," *American Journal of Sociology* 119, no. 6 (2014): 1576–1629; quote on 1600.

134. U.S. Congress, Committee on Finance. U.S. Senate. S. Hrg. 109-967. Hearing, "Taking the Pulse of Charitable Care and Community Benefits at Nonprofit Hospitals," September 13, 2006. Quote on p. 2.

135. Ibid., 2–3.

136. Ibid., 2.

137. Ibid., 28.

138. Institute of Medicine, *America's Health Care Safety Net: Intact but Endangered* (Washington, DC: National Academies Press, 2000); quote on p. 22. Grogan and Gusmano also found that because it was such a patchwork of organizations, which varied by state and localities, very little was known about what organizations within the safety net or how the so-called health care safety-net fit together. See Colleen M. Grogan and Michael K. Gusmano, "How Are Safety-Net Providers Faring under Medicaid Managed Care?," *Health Affairs* 18, no. 2 (1999): 233–37.

139. Catherine Hoffman and Susan Starr Sered, *Threadbare: Holes in America's Health Care Safety Net* (San Francisco: Kaiser Commission on Medicaid and the Uninsured, Kaiser Family Foundation, 2005), 1.

140. United States Congress, Senate Committee on Health, Education, Labor and Pensions. "Health Care Safety Net Amendments of 2001." 107th Congress, 1st Sess., Rpt 107-83. Quote on p. 2. For examples of difficulty defining the health care safety net in states, see Grogan and Gusmano, "How Are Safety-Net Providers Faring?"; Lynn A. Blewett and Timothy J. Beebe, "State Efforts to Measure the Health Care Safety Net," *Public Health Reports* 119, no. 2 (2004): 125–35.

141. Robert W. Mickey, "Dr. StrangeRove; or, How Conservatives Learned to Stop Worrying and Love Community Health Centers," in *The Health Care Safety Net in a Post-Reform World*, ed. Mark A. Hall and Sara Rosenbaum (New Brunswick, NJ: Rutgers University Press, 2012), 21–66.

142. Hoffman and Sered, *Threadbare*, 6.

143. Robert Mickey makes this argument specifically about increases in FQHCs. See Mickey, "Dr. StrangeRove." Others make a similar argument about investments in small programs to prevent mobilization for larger reforms. See Paul Pierson and Theda Skocpol, "American Politics in the Long Run," in *The Transformation of American Politics: Activist Government and the Rise of Conservatism*, ed. Paul Pierson and Theda Skocpol (Princeton, NJ: Princeton University Press, 2007), 3–16; Brian J. Glenn and Steven M. Teles, *Conservatism and American Political Development* (New York: Oxford University Press, 2009).

144. United States Congress, Senate Committee on Health, Education, Labor and Pensions, "Health Care Safety Net Amendments of 2001." 107th Congress, 1st Sess., Rpt 107-83. Quote on p. 2.

145. Institute of Medicine, *Hospital-Based Emergency Care*, 64.

146. S. Lambe, D. L. Washington, A. Fink, K. Herbst, H. Liu, J. S. Fosse, and S. M. Asch, "Trends in the Use and Capacity of California's Emergency Departments, 1990–1999," *Annals of Emergency Medicine* 39, no. 4 (2002): 389–96; C. D. Dauner, "Emergency Capacity in California: A Look at More Recent Trends," *Health Affairs Web Exclusive* (2004): W4–152–154; W. W. Fields, "Emergency Care in California: Robust Capacity or Busted Access?" *Health Affairs Web Exclusive* (2004): W4–143–145; A. L. Kellermann, "Emergency Care in California: No Emergency?" *Health Affairs Web Exclusive* (2004): W4–149–151; Glen Melnick, A. Nawathe, A. Bamezai, and L. Green, "Emergency Department Capacity and Access in California, 1990–2001: An Economic Analysis," *Health Affairs Web Exclusive* (2004): W4–136–142.

147. J. Huang, J. Silbert, and M. Regenstein, *America's Public Hospitals and Health Systems, 2003: Results of the Annual NAPH Hospital Characteristics Survey* (Washington, DC: National Association of Public Hospitals and Health Systems, 2005).

148. Institute of Medicine, *Hospital-Based Emergency Care*, 42. See also J. Haughton, "Emergency Services: Part of the Safety Net?," *Journal of Public Health Policy* 26, no. 3 (2005), 282–85.

149. The reason for this is complex and emerges from a unique history regarding long-term care and nursing homes. See Colleen M. Grogan, "A Marriage of Convenience: The History of Nursing Home Coverage and Medicaid," in *Putting the Past Back In: History and Health Policy in the United States*, ed. Rosemary A. Stevens, Charles E. Rosenberg, and Lawton R. Burns (New Brunswick, NJ: Rutgers University Press, 2006); Bruce C. Vladeck, *Unloving Care: The Nursing Home Tragedy* (New York: Basic Books, 1980).

150. R. J. Anderson, S. Pickens, and P. J. Boumbulian, Toward a New Urban Health Model: Moving beyond the Safety Net to Save the Safety Net—Resetting Priorities for Healthy Communities, *Journal of Urban Health: Bulletin of the New York Academy of Medicine* 75, no. 2 (1998): 367–78; see p. 374.

151. Grogan and Gusmano, "How Are Safety-Net Providers Faring?"

152. Institute of Medicine, *America's Health Care Safety Net*, 27–28.

153. A number of reports about the status of the safety net reveal this constant state of shortages and fragmentation, and therefore lack of coordination, across safety net providers. For example, a report from the Kaiser Family Foundation in 2005 concluded that, even after funding increases, the safety net still fell short. "An estimated 929 counties lack a health center, a number that accounts for almost a third of all counties and more than half of all poor counties. About 20 million persons live in these counties and more than 40% have family incomes below twice the federal poverty level." See Hoffman and Sered, *Threadbare*, 8; M. Proser, P. Shin, and D. Hawkins, *A Nation's Health at Risk* (Washington, DC: NACHC, 2005), https://publichealth.gwu.edu/departments/healthpolicy/CHPR/downloads/poorcountiesSTIB9.pdf. See also Gay Becker, "Deadly Inequality in the Health Care 'Safety Net': Uninsured Ethnic Minorities' Struggle to Live with Life-Threatening Illnesses," *Medical Anthropology Quarterly* 18, no. 2 (2004), 258–75; Louis Rubino and William J. French, "Re-engineering the Los Angeles County Public Health Care Safety Net: Recommendations from a Blue Ribbon Health Task Force," *Journal of Health and Human Services Administration* 27, no. 1 (2004): 56–79.

154. David M. Einhorn, "Unintended Advantage: Equity REITS vs. Taxable Real Estate Companies, *The Tax Lawyer* 51, no. 2 (1998): 203–28.

155. Stephen M. Monroe and Paul R. Peach, "Are Healthcare REITs a Cheap Source of Capital?," *Healthcare Financial Management* 41, no. 4 (1987): 88–92, https://search-proquest-com.proxy.uchicago.edu/docview/196353386?accountid=14657.

156. Therese L. Wareham, "A Capital Idea: Bonds and Nontraditional Financing Options," *Healthcare Financial Management* 58, no. 5 (2004): 54–62, https://search-proquest-com.proxy.uchicago.edu/docview/196370975?accountid=14657.

157. George C. Koutsakos, Cyril Chern, and Gregory N. Bonn, "Charitable Remainder Trusts Provide a Creative Source of Cap," *Healthcare Financial Management* 49, no. 3 (1995): 40–2, 44, 46, https://search-proquest-com.proxy.uchicago.edu/docview/196367130?accountid=14657.

158. David Haarmeyer, "Private Equity: Capitalism's Misunderstood Entrepreneurs and Catalysts for Value Creation," *Independent Review* 13, no. 2 (2008): 245–88.

159. Eileen Applebaum and Rosemary Batt, "Private Equity Buyouts in Healthcare: Who Wins, Who Loses?" Working Paper no. 118 (Washington, DC: Center for Economic and Policy Research, March 15, 2020), 14. See Figure 2.1.

160. Ibid., 15. See Figure 2.2.

161. Eileen Applebaum and Rosemary L. Batt, *Private Equity at Work: When Wall Street Manages Main Street* (New York: Russell Sage Foundation, 2014), 30.

162. For excellent overview of the private equity industry, see Appelbaum and Batt, *Private Equity at Work*. They also provide an excellent history on the origins of private equity and why the prior managerial business model worked. As part of this history they point out how leveraged buyouts (LBOs) in the 1980s were the precursors to Private Equity LBOs. See chapter 2: "Institutional Change and the Emergence of Private Equity."

163. This example is from the Wikipedia page on private equity. See https://en.wikipedia.org/wiki/Private_equity. Appelbaum and Batt also have a very useful description of the classic private equity business model starting. See Applebaum and Batt, "Private Equity Buyouts in Healthcare," 6.

164. "Note on Leveraged Buyouts" (Hanover, NH: Tuck School of Business at Dartmouth: Center for Private Equity and Entrepreneurship, 2003), see p. 2. https://www.tuck.dartmouth.edu/uploads/centers/files/LBO_Note_(1).pdf.

165. Ibid, 2. This point is made on page 2, but supported throughout the entire document. Also, this is not a controversial point; it is well known fact that part of what makes PE firms so attractive is the lack of SEC regulation.

166. Haarmeyer, "Private Equity," 247. His source is Joseph McCafferty, "The Buyout Binge," *CFO Magazine*, April 1, 2007, http://www.cfo.com/article.cfm/8909971/c_8910395?f=singlepage.

167. Applebaum and Batt, "Private Equity Buyouts in Healthcare," 6.

168. Dartmouth's Center for Private Equity reported in 2002 that "[p]rivate equity firms typically invest alongside management, encouraging (if not requiring) top executives to commit a significant portion of their personal net worth to the deal. By requiring the target's management team to invest in the acquisition, the private equity firm guarantees that management's incentives will be aligned with their own." See "Note on Leveraged Buyouts."

169. Haarmeyer, "Private Equity," 247. Kaplan and Strumberg's work on PE is highly cited, and they define PE value in similar ways by looking at EBITDA and ROI. See Steven N. Kaplan and Per Strömberg, "Leveraged Buyouts and Private Equity" (Social Science Research Network, June 2008).

170. Note on Leveraged Buyouts."

171. Ibid, 2. This point is made on page 2, but supported throughout the entire document. Also, as noted in endnote #166 above, this is not a controversial point, it is well known fact that part of what makes PE firms so attractive is the lack of SEC regulation.

172. More detailed examples are given in Chapter 10, but see Applebaum and Batt, *Private Equity At Work*, for numerous examples in PE more generally; and Applebaum and Batt, "Private Equity Buyouts in Healthcare," for more examples of PE's involvement in health care.

173. Robbins, 2008, p.1394.

174. Ibid., p.1394. Applebaum and Batt, *Private Equity at Work*; Applebaum and Batt "Private Equity Buyouts in Healthcare." Studies of PE behavior also confirm that PE firms look to capitalize on fragmented markets.

175. Applebaum and Batt, "Private Equity Buyouts in Healthcare."

176. Robert S. Harris, Tim Jenkinson and Steven Neil Kaplan, *How Do Private Equity Investments Perform Compared to Public Equity?* (June 15, 2015). Darden Business School Working Paper No. 2597259, Available at SSRN: https://ssrn.com/abstract=2597259 or http://dx.doi.org/10.2139/ssrn.2597259.

177. A. Catlin, C. Cowan, M. Hartman, S. Heffler, and the National Health Expenditure Accounts Team. "National Health Spending in 2006: A Year of Change for Prescription Drugs," *Health Affairs*27, no. 1 (2008):14–29..

178. George B. Moseley, "The U.S. Health Care Non-System, 1908–2008," *Virtual Mentor* 10, no. 5 (May 2008): 324–31.

## Chapter 9

1. This chapter draws from the following published articles from Grogan and co-authors: Colleen M. Grogan, "Medicaid: Designed to Grow," in *Health Politics and Policy*, ed. James Morone and Daniel Ehlke, 5th ed. (Stamford, CT: Cengage Learning, 2013), 142–63; Colleen M. Grogan and Christina Andrews, "The Politics of Aging within Medicaid," in *The New Politics of Old Age Policy*, ed. Robert B. Hudson, 2nd ed. (Baltimore: Johns Hopkins University Press, 2011); Colleen M. Grogan and Elizabeth Rigby, "Federalism, Partisan Politics, and Shifting Support for State Flexibility: The Case of the U.S. State Children's Health Insurance Program, *Publius: The Journal of Federalism* 39 (2009): 47–69; Colleen M. Grogan and Vernon Smith, "From Charity Care to Medicaid: Governors, States, and the Transformation of American Health Care," in *A More Perfect Union*, ed. Ethan Sribnick (Philadelphia: University of Pennsylvania Press, 2008); Colleen M. Grogan, "Medicaid: Health Care for You and Me?," in *Health Politics and Policy*, ed. James Morone, Theodor Litman, and Leonard Robins, 4th

ed. (New York: Delmar Thompson, 2008), 329–54; Colleen M. Grogan and Eric Patashnik, "Between Welfare Medicine and Mainstream Program: Medicaid at the Political Crossroads," *Journal of Health Politics, Policy and Law* 28, no. 5 (2003): 821–58.

2. Kaiser Family Foundation, *Medicaid: A Primer* (San Francisco: Kaiser Family Foundation, 2010), http://www.kff.org/medicaid/upload/7334-04.pdf.

3. D. Blumenthal and J. A. Morone, *The Heart of Power: Health and Politics in the Oval Office* (Berkeley: University of California Press, 2009).

4. Ibid.

5. Ibid., See also E. M. Patashnik and J. E. Zelizer, "Paying for Medicare: Benefits, Budgets, and Wilbur Mills's Policy Legacy," *Journal of Health Politics, Policy and Law* 26, no. 1 (2001): 7–36.

6. R. B. Stevens and R. Stevens, *Welfare Medicine in America: A Case Study of Medicaid* (New York: Free Press, 1974).

7. C. Grogan and E. Patashnik, "Between Welfare Medicine and Mainstream Program: Medicaid at the Political Crossroads," *Journal of Health Politics, Policy and Law* 28, no. 5 (2003): 821–58.

8. Stevens and Stevens, *Welfare Medicine in America*.

9. S. Rosenbaum and C. A. Sonosky, "Child Health Advocacy in a Changing Policy Environment," paper presented at conference on the "Roles of Child Advocacy Organizations in Addressing Policy Issues," Urban Institute, Washington, DC, December 13–14, 1999.

10. J. S. Quadagno, *The Transformation of Old-Age Security: Class and Politics in the American Welfare State* (Chicago: University of Chicago Press, 1988).

11. S. D. Watson, "Medicaid Physician Participation: Patients, Poverty, and Physician Self-Interest," *American Journal of Law & Medicine* 21, no. 2–3 (1995): 191–220.

12. L. K. Olson, *The Politics of Medicaid* (New York: Columbia University Press, 2010).

13. Congressional Research Service, "Medicaid Rehabilitation Services" (Washington, DC: Congressional Research Service, 2008), 36, http://aging.senate.gov/crs/medicaid13.pdf; Teresa A. Coughlin, Leighton Ku, and John Holahan, *Costs, Coverage, and the Shifting Alliance between the Federal Government and the States* (Washington, DC: Urban Institute Press, 1994), 48–51.

14. Colleen M. Grogan, "The Influence of Federal Medicaid Mandates on State Medicaid and AFDC Decisionmaking," *Publius: The Journal of Federalism* 29, no. 3 (1999):1–30.

15. Grogan and Smith, "From Charity Care to Medicaid"; J. Buck, "The Looming Expansion and Transformation of Public Substance Abuse Treatment under the Affordable Care Act," *Health Affairs* 30, no. 80 (2011): 1402–10.

16. S. R. Melnick, "The Unexpected Resilience of Means-Tested Programs," paper prepared for delivery at the 1998 Annual Meeting of the American Political Science Association, Boston, Massachusetts, September 3–6, 1998, 31.

17. T. R. Konetzka and Y. Luo, "Explaining Lapse in Long-Term Care Insurance Markets," *Health Economics* 20, no. 10 (2011): 1169–83.

18. Olson, *The Politics of Medicaid*.

19. D. Justice, L. Etheredge, J. Luehrs, and B. Burwell. *State Long Term Care Reform: Development of Community Care Systems in Six States, Final Report* (Washington, DC: United States Department of Health and Human Services and National Governors Association, 1988), http://aspe.hhs.gov/daltcp/reports/strfrm.htm#execsum.

20. J. Oberlander, *The Political Life of Medicare* (Chicago: University of Chicago Press, 2003).

21. R. Himelfarb, *Catastrophic Politics: The Rise and Fall of the Medicare Catastrophic Coverage Act of 1988* (University Park: Pennsylvania State University Press, 1995).

22. Oberlander, *The Political Life of Medicare*.

23. C. Grogan and E. Patashnik, "Universalism within Targeting: Nursing Home Care, the Middle Class, and the Politics of the Medicaid Program," *Social Service Review* 77, no. 1 (2003): 51–71.

24. S. Davidson and S. Somers, eds., *Remaking Medicaid: Managed Care for the Public Good* (San Francisco: Jossey-Bass, 1998).

25. Don Colburn, "Pregnant Women on Medicaid Get Less Care Than Others," *Washington Post*, October 29, 1991, Z5.

26. Gordon Slovut, "Many Kids under 5 Lack Shots, HMO Says," *Star Tribune* (Minneapolis), June 28, 1991, 3B.

27. Coughlin, Ku, and Holahan, *Costs, Coverage*, 48–51; Diane Rowland, Judith M. Feder, and Alina Salganicoff, eds., *Medicaid Financing Crisis: Balancing Responsibilities, Priorities, and Dollars* (Washington, DC: AAAS Press, 1993); Teresa A. Coughlin, Sharon Long, and John Holahan, "Reforming the Medicaid Disproportionate Share Program in the 1990s," *Inquiry– Blue Cross and Blue Shield Association* 38 (2001):137–58.

28. Glenn Beamer, *Creative Politics: Taxes and Public Goods in a Federal System* (Ann Arbor: University of Michigan Press, 1999).

29. U.S. Senate, Committee on Finance, Social Security Amendments of 1967, Part 3. 90th Cong., 1st sess., 20–22 and 26 September, p. 1547.

30. Robert J. Blendon, John T. Young, and Catherine M. DesRoches, "The Uninsured, the Working Uninsured, and the Public," *Health Affairs* 18, no. 6 (1999): 203–11.

31. Thomas L. Friedman, "President Allows States Flexibility on Medicaid Funds," *New York Times*, February 2, 1993, A1.

32. Robert E. Hurley and Stephen A. Somers, "Medicaid and Managed Care: A Lasting Relationship?," *Health Affairs* 22, no. 1 (2003): 77–88.

33. Jane Horvath and Neva Kaye, *Medicaid Managed Care: A Guide for States*, 2d ed. (Portland, ME: National Academy for State Health Policy, 1995); Colleen M. Grogan, "The Medicaid Managed Care Policy Consensus for Welfare Recipients: A Reflection of Traditional Welfare Concerns," *Journal of Health Politics, Policy and Law* 22 (1997): 815–38.

34. Grogan, "The Medicaid Managed Care Policy Consensus."

35. John Holahan, Stephen Zuckerman, Alison Evans, and Suresh Rangarajan, "Medicaid Managed Care in Thirteen States," *Health Affairs* 17, no. 3 (1998):43–63.

36. Stevens and Stevens, *Welfare Medicine in America*.

37. Holahan et al., "Medicaid Managed Care in Thirteen States."

38. John K. Iglehart, "Health Policy Report: Medicaid and Managed Care," *New England Journal of Medicine* 332, no. 25 (1995):1727–31.

39. Geraldine Dallek, "A Consumer Advocate on Medicaid Managed Care," *Health Affairs* 15, no. 3 (1996):174–77; quote on 174.

40. Colleen M. Grogan and Michael K. Gusmano, *Healthy Voices/Unhealthy Silence: Advocacy and Health Policy for the Poor* (Washington, DC: Georgetown University Press, 2007).

41. Grogan and Gusmano found reports of Medicaid recipients' disappointment when they realized their card only gave them access to "the same old Medicaid providers" they had prior to the MMC reform. See Grogan and Gusmano, *Healthy Voices/Unhealthy Silence*.

42. For explanations of similar phenomenon of hiding expansion under private provisions under employer-based health insurance and Medicare managed care (Medicare Advantage) programs, see Jacob Hacker, *The Divided Welfare State* (New York: Cambridge University Press, 2002); Kimberly J. Morgan and Andrea Louise Campbell, *The Delegated Welfare State: Medicare, Markets, and the Governance of Social Policy* (New York: Oxford University Press, 2011).

43. Stephen M. Davidson and Stephen A. Somers, eds., *Remaking Medicaid: Managed Care for the Public Good* (San Francisco: Jossey-Bass, 1998).

44. G. Bonnyman, "TennCare—A Failure of Politics, Not Policy: A Conversation with Gordon Bonnyman, Interview by Robert E. Hurley," *Health Affairs* 25, no. 3 (2006.): 217–25.

45. Project, No. 23 (September), The Robert Wood Johnson Foundation, https://www.rwjf.org/ en/library/research/2012/09/medicaid-managed-care.html (accessed on August 12, 2020).

46. Medicaid and CHIP Payment and Access Commission (MACPac, U.S.), *Report to the Congress: the Evolution Of Managed Care in Medicaid* (2011); L. Ku, M. Ellwood, S. Hoag, B. Ormond, and J. Wooldridge, "Evolution of Medicaid Managed Care Systems and Eligibility Expansions," *Health Care Financing Review* 22, no. 2 (2000): 7–27.

47. Centers for Medicare & Medicaid Services, *Medicaid Managed Care Report*, June 30, 2006; Hurley and Somers, "Medicaid and Managed Care."

48. L. C. Baker and A. B. Royalty, Medicaid Policy, Physician Behavior, and Health Care for The Low-Income Population. *Journal of Human Resources* 35, no. 3 (2000), 480–502; J. Bisgaier,

K. V. Rhodes, and D. Polsky, "Factors Associated with Increased Specialty Care Access in an Urban Area: The Roles of Local Workforce Capacity and Practice Location," *Journal of Health Politics, Policy and Law* 39, no. 6 (2014), 1173–11; S. L. Decker, "Changes in Medicaid Physician Fees and Patterns of Ambulatory Care," *Inquiry* 46 (2009), 291–304; MACPac, *Report to the Congress.*

49. Michael Sparer, *Medicaid Managed Care: Costs, Access, and Quality of Care*, The Synthesis Project: New Insights from Research Results, Research Synthesis Report No. 23. ISSN 2155-3718, September, 2012, https://www.cancercarediff.org/wp-content/uploads/2020/12/managed-care-rwjf.pdf (accessed March 15, 2023).

50. U.S. Congress, 101-206, Waxman, September 10, 1990, p. 2.

51. U.S. Congress, 101-206, Kennelly, September 10, 1990, p. 23.

52. This is taken from Kennelly's testimony and prepared statement for the record, where she responds to Chairman Waxman's questions and concerns about her bill.

53. U.S. Congress, 101-206, Kennelly, September 10, 1990, p. 23.

54. U.S. Congress 102-91, Waxman, p. 3–4.

55. Paul Pierson, "The Deficit and the Politics of Domestic Reform," in *The Social Divide: Political Parties and the Future of Activist Government*, ed. Margaret M. Weir (Washington, DC: Brookings Institution Press, 1998), 126–79.

56. Peter G. Gosselin, "House GOP Proposes Medicaid as Payment to States under Plan, Mass. Would Get Less Aid Than Weld Sought," *Boston Globe*, September 20, 1995, A7; Elizabeth Shogren, "GOP Nursing Home Plan Holds Perils, Democrats Say," *Los Angeles Times*, October 13, 1995, A1.

57. U.S. Newswire, September 15, 1995.

58. John Holahan and Mary Beth Pohl, "Changes in Insurance Coverage: 1994–2000 and Beyond," *Health Affairs* 21, Suppl. 1 (2002).

59. Alice Sardell and Kay Johnson, "The Politics of EPSDT Policy in the 1990s: Policy Entrepreneurs, Political Streams, and Children's Health Benefits," *Milbank Quarterly* 76, no. 2 (1998):175–205.

60. Actually, there is some disagreement about the official status of block grants as budgetary entitlements, but the important point here is that advocates believed that both legally and politically there was a significant difference between the two alternatives. For different views on this debate see Rosenbaum and Sonosky, "Child Health Advocacy," and Jerry L. Mashaw and Dylan S. Calsyn, "Block Grants, Entitlements, and Federalism: A Conceptual Map of Contested Terrain," *Yale Law and Policy Review* 14, no. 2 (1996): 297–324.

61. Rosenbaum and Sonosky, "Child Health Advocacy."

62. Cindy Mann, David Rousseau, Rachel Garfield, and Molly O'Malley, *Reaching Uninsured Children through Medicaid: If You Build It Right, They Will Come* (Washington, DC: Kaiser Commission on Medicaid and the Uninsured, 2002).

63. Ibid.

64. J. M. Snow, "Overcoming Barriers to Enrollment: A 50-State Assessment of Outreach and Enrollment Simplification Strategies for the State Children's Health Insurance Program (SCHIP)," *Journal of Public Affairs Education* 9, no. 1 (2003): 63–73.

65. P. Ketsche, E. K, Adams, K, Minyard, and R. Kellenberg, "The Stigma of Public Programs: Does a Separate S-CHIP Program Reduce It?," *Journal of Policy Analysis & Management* 26, no. 4 (2007): 775–90.

66. P. Herd, T. DeLeire, H. Harvey, and D. P. Moynihan, "Shifting Administrative Burden to the State: the Case of Medicaid Take-Up," *Public Administration Review* 73, no. S1 (2013): S69–S81, https://doi.org/10.1111/puar.12114.

67. Mann et al., *Reaching Uninsured Children.*

68. Grogan and Rigby, "Federalism, Partisan Politics."

69. D. C. Ross and L. Cox, *Enrolling Children and Families in Health Coverage: The Promise of Doing More* (Washington, DC: Kaiser Commission on Medicaid and the Uninsured, 2002).

70. See Henry J. Kaiser Family Foundation Website: http://www.statehealthfacts.org/compare bar.jsp?ind=877&cat=1 (accessed on July 24, 2011).

71. C. Shirk, *Medicaid and Mental Health Services* (Washington, DC: National Health Policy Forum, October 23, 2008), 19, https://hsrc.himmelfarb.gwu.edu/sphhs_centers_n hpf/208/.

72. J.S. Crowley and M. O'Malley, "Medicaid's Rehabilitation Services Option: Overview and Current Policy Issues," Issue Brief (Washington, DC: Kaiser Commission on Medicaid and the Uninsured, 2007), 24, https://www.kff.org/medicaid/issue-brief/medicaids-rehabilitat ion-services-option-overview-and-current/.

73. Charles N. Kahn and Ronald F. Pollack, "Building a Consensus for Expanding Health Coverage," *Health Affairs* 20, no. 1 (2001): 40–48.

74. Melanie Nathanson and Iris J. Lav, *The Bush Administration's Medicaid Proposal Would Shift Risks and Costs to States* (Washington, DC: Center on Budget and Policy Priorities, 2003). Extracted from CBPP website at www.cbpp.org/2-12-03health.htm; Robert Pear, "Medicaid Proposal Would Give States More Say on Costs," *New York Times*, February 1, 2003, A1.

75. "It's Time to Say No to Medicaid for the Middle Class," Facing Facts Alert no. 14, February 19 (Arlington, VA: Concord Coalition, 1996), https://www.concordcoalition.org/issues/fac ing-facts/facing-facts-alert-14.

76. Ted Halstead, "To Guarantee Universal Coverage, Require It" (op-ed), *New York Times*, January 31, 2003.

77. Jeanne M. Lambrew and Arthur Garson, *Small but Significant Steps to Help the Uninsured*, Commonwealth Fund Pub. no. 585 (New York: Commonwealth Fund, 2003).

78. Karen Davis, "Strategic Issues and Options: Expanding Insurance Coverage," presentation for the Michael Reese Health Trust, Chicago, January 21, 2003.

79. Mike Leavitt, Secretary of Health and Human Services, Speech to World Health Care Congress, Marriott Wardman Park Hotel, Washington DC, Tuesday, February 1, 2005.

80. Colleen M. Grogan, "Chapter 15. Medicaid: Health Care for You and Me?" in *Health Politics and Policy*, 4th ed., ed. James Morone, Theodor Litman, and Leonard Robins (New York: Delmar Thompson, 2008), 329–54.

81. Robert Pear, "A Battle over Expansion of Children's Insurance," *New York Times*, July 9, 2007. The Reauthorization bill renamed SCHIP to simply CHIP. See John Reichard, "Here's the Deal on SCHIP . . . Er, CHIP," Newsletter Article, September 21, 2007, https://www.commonwealthf und.org/publications/newsletter-article/heres-deal-schip-er-chip (accessed March 15, 2023).

82. Colleen M. Grogan and Elizabeth Rigby, "Federalism, Partisan Politics, and Shifting Support for State Flexibility: The Case of the U.S. State Children's Health Insurance Program," *Publius: The Journal of Federalism* 39 (2009): 47–69.

83. Pear, "A Battle over Expansion."

84. Congressional Budget Office, "The State Children's Health Insurance Program," U.S. Congress (May 2007), p. ii.

85. Kaiser Commission on Medicaid and the Uninsured, "SCHIP Reauthorization: Key Questions in the Debate. A Description of New Administrative Guidance and the House and Senate Proposals," Issue Brief (San Francisco: The Henry J. Kaiser Family Foundation, August 29, 2007).

86. Congressional Budget Office, "The State Children's Health Insurance Program"; Kaiser Commission, "SCHIP Reauthorization."

87. Nina Owcharenko (Senior Health Care Policy Analyst for the Heritage Foundation), Testimony before U.S. Senate Finance Subcommittee on Health Care: "States' View of Children's Health Insurance Program," November 16, 2006.

88. Robert Pear, "House Defies Bush and Passes Insurance Bill," *New York Times*, October 26, 2007.

89. Owcharenko, Testimony before U.S. Senate Finance Subcommittee.

90. Pear , "A Battle over Expansion"; John D. Dingell, "Statement of John D. Dingell, Chairman Committee on Energy and Commerce." Remarks prepared for Center for American Progress SCHIP event, Washington, DC, March 29, 2007.

91. Alan Weil (Executive Director, National Academy for State Health Policy [NASHP]), Testimony before U.S. House Energy and Commerce Subcommittee on Health: "Covering the Uninsured through the Eyes of a Child," March 1, 2007.

## Chapter 10

1. Julia James, "Health Policy Brief: Premium Tax Credits," *Health Affairs*, August 1, 2013, https://www.healthaffairs.org/do/10.1377/hpb20130801.398718/full/healthpolicybrief_97-1554749982904.pdf (accessed March 15, 2023).
2. While the EBHI exclusion is not shown in National Health Expenditure Accounts, the CBO does estimate the spending amounts due to tax exemption.
3. Katie Keith, "Health Affairs Forefront: Marketplace Enrollment Tops 12 Million for 2021," *Health Affairs*, April 22, 2021, https://www.healthaffairs.org/do/10.1377/forefront.20210422.65513/ (accessed March 15, 2023).
4. Centers for Medicare & Medicaid Services (CMS), National Health Expenditure Tables, Table 3: National Health Expenditures: Levels and Annual Percent Change, by Source of Funds: Selected Calendar Years, 1960–2020, https://www.cms.gov/Research-Statistics-Data-and-Systems/Statistics-Trends-and-Reports/NationalHealthExpendData/NationalHealthAccountsHistorical (accessed June 9, 2022).
5. Kaiser Family Foundation, State Health Facts, Medicaid Expansion Spending, 2018, https://www.kff.org/medicaid/state-indicator/medicaid-expansion-spending/?currentTimeframe=0&sortModel=%7B%22colId%22:%22Location%22,%22sort%22:%22asc%22%7D (accessed June 9, 2022).
6. CMS, NHE Tables, Table 3.
7. These data include those relying on Medicaid only and those dually enrolled in Medicaid and Medicare and Medicaid and private health insurance. Kaiser Family Foundation, State Health Facts, "Health Insurance Coverage of Nonelderly 0-64, Multiple Sources of Coverage (CPS)," 2021, https://www.kff.org/other/state-indicator/health-insurance-coverage-of-nonelderly-0-64-multiple-sources-of-coverage-cps/?currentTimeframe=0&sortModel=%7B%22colId%22:%22Location%22,%22sort%22:%22asc%22%7D (accessed April 6, 2022).
8. See Kaiser Family Foundation, "Health Insurance Coverage of Nonelderly." Based on Current Population Report projections and estimates of the uninsured by state."
9. Kaiser Family Foundation, "Data Note: 5 Charts about Public Opinion on Medicaid," February 28, 2020.
10. Kaiser Family Foundation, "States' Positions in the Affordable Care Act Case at the Supreme Court," State Health Facts, 2019, www.kff.org/health-reform/state-indicator/state-positions-on-aca-case/?currentTimeframe=0andsortModel=%7B%22colId% 22:%22Location%22,%22sort%22:%22asc%22%7D (accessed November 24, 2019).
11. D. Grabowski, J. Gruber, and V. Mor, "You're Probably Going to Need Medicaid," *New York Times*, June 13, 2017, https://www.nytimes.com/2017/06/13/opinion/youre-probably-going-to-need-medicaid.html; K. O'Brien, "Trump's Budget Takes Aim at My Sweet Son," *New York Times*, May 24, 2017, https://www.nytimes.com/2017/05/24/opinion/trump-budget-autism-special-needs-medicaid.html.
12. C. M. Grogan and C. Andrews, "Medicaid," in *Governing America: Major Decisions of Federal, State, and Local Governments from 1789 to the Present*, ed. P. J. Quirk and W. Cunion (New York: Facts on File Press, 2011); C. M. Grogan and E. Patashnik, "Between Welfare Medicine and Mainstream Entitlement: Medicaid at the Political Crossroads," *Journal of Health Politics, Policy and Law* 28, no. 5 (2003): 821.
13. C. M. Grogan, P. M. Singer, and D. K. Jones, "Rhetoric and Reform in Waiver States," *Journal of Health Politics, Policy and Law* 42, no. 2 (2017): 247–84; Madhulika Vulimiri, William K. Bleser, Robert S. Saunders, Farrah Madanay, Connor Moseley, F. Hunter McGuire, Peter A. Ubel, Aaron McKethan, Mark McClellan, and Charlene A. Wong, "Engaging Beneficiaries in Medicaid Programs That Incentivize Health-Promoting Behaviors," *Health Affairs* 38, no. 3 (2019): 431–39.
14. Kaiser Family Foundation "Approved Section 1115 Medicaid Waivers" (San Francisco: Kaiser Family Foundation, 2019), www.kff.org/other/state-indicator/approved-section-1115--medicaid-waivers/?current Timeframe=0andsortModel=%7B%22colId%22:%22Location% 22,%22sort%22:% 22asc%22%7D.
15. Grogan, Singer, and Jones, "Rhetoric and Reform."

16. Robin Rudowitz, MaryBeth Musumeci, and Cornelia Hall, "February State Data for Medicaid Work Requirements in Arkansas" (San Francisco: Kaiser Family Foundation, March 25, 2019), www.kff.org/medicaid/issue-brief/state-data-for-medicaid-work-requirements-in-arkansas/.

17. Seth Freedman, Lilliard Richardson, and Kosali I. Simon, "Learning from Waiver States: Coverage Effects under Indiana's HIP Medicaid Expansion." *Health Affairs* 37, no. 6 (2018): 936–43; Benjamin D. Sommers, Carrie E. Fry, Robert J. Blendon, and Arnold M. Epstein, "New Approaches in Medicaid: Work Requirements, Health Savings Accounts, and Health Care Access," *Health Affairs* 37, no. 7 (2018): 1099–1108.

18. Dee J. Hall, "Scott Walker to Propose Drug Tests for Medicaid, Food Stamps," Madison.com, January 23, 2015, https://madison.com/news/local/govt-and-politics/scott-walker-to-prop ose-drug-tests-for-medicaid-food-stamps/article_3e8daab4-31e9-55b7-802b-8d981d6c1 f24.html (accessed November 10, 2019).

19. Grogan, Singer, and Jones, "Rhetoric and Reform"; Damon Mayrl and Sarah Quinn, "Beyond the Hidden American State: Classification Struggles and the Politics of Recognition," in *The Many Hands of the State*, ed. Kimberly J. Morgan and Ann Shola Orloff (New York: Cambridge University Press, 2017), 58–80.

20. Jason Noble, "Branstad Promises Changes to IowaCare Program to Improve Health-Care Delivery," *Des Moines Register*, February 26, 2013, blogs.desmoinesregister.com/dmr/index. php/2013/02/26/branstad-promises-changes-to-iowacare-program-to-improve-health-care-delivery.

21. Associated Press, "Pennsylvania Awaits Ruling on Proposal to Link Work Requirements to Medicaid Benefits," *PBS NewsHour*, April 27, 2014.

22. Mitchell Roob and Seema Verma, "Indiana: Health Care Reform amidst Colliding Values," *Health Affairs Blog*, May 1, 2008, healthaffairs.org/blog/2008/05/01/indiana-health-care-reform-amidst-colliding-values/.

23. Grogan, Singer, and Jones, "Rhetoric and Reform."

24. Suzanne Mettler, *The Submerged State: How Invisible Government Policies Undermine American Democracy* (Chicago: University of Chicago Press, 2011).

25. S. Kliff, "Why Obamacare Enrollees Voted for Trump," Vox, December 13, 2016, http://www.vox.com/science-and-health/2016/12/13/13848794/kentucky-obamacare-trump.

26. Colleen M. Grogan and Sunggeun Park, "The Politics of Medicaid: Most Americans Are Connected to the Program, Support Its Expansion, and Do Not View It as Stigmatizing," *Milbank Quarterly* 95, no. 4 (2017): 749–82.

27. Lina Stolyar, Elizabeth Hinton, Natalie Singer, and Robin Rudowitz, "Growth in Medicaid MCO Enrollment during the COVID-19 Pandemic" (San Francisco: Kaiser Family Foundation, June 24, 2021), https://www.kff.org/coronavirus-covid-19/issue-brief/gro wth-in-medicaid-mco-enrollment-during-the-covid-19-pandemic/.

28. Kliff, "Why Obamacare Enrollees Voted for Trump."

29. Grogan and Park, "The Politics of Medicaid." See also Colleen M. Grogan and Sunggeun Park, "Medicaid Retrenchment Politics: Fragmented or Unified?" *Journal of Social Policy and Aging* 30, no. 3–4 (2018): 372–99.

30. Mary Crossley, "Health and Taxes: Hospitals, Community Health and the IRS," *Yale Journal of Health Policy, Law, and Ethics* 16, no. 1 (2016), Article 2: 51–110; see pp. 54–56.

31. Eric Patashnik, "Comparatively Ineffective? PCORI and the Uphill Battle to Make Evidence Count in American Medicine," *Journal of Health Politics, Policy and Law* 45, no. 5 (2020): 787–800.

32. Jonathan Oberlander and Steven B. Spivack, "Technocratic Dreams, Political Realities: The Rise and Demise of Medicare's Independent Payment Advisory Board," *Journal of Health Politics, Policy and Law* 43, no 3 (2018): 483–510; Peter Suderman, "Congress Repealed Major Elements of Obamacare and Almost No One Noticed." *Reason*, January 7, 2020, reason.com/2020/01/07/congress-repealed-major-elements-of-obamacare-and-almost-no-one-noticed/.

33. Michael E. Chernew, Patrick H. Conway, and Austin B. Frakt, "Transforming Medicare's Payment Systems: Progress Shaped by the ACA," *Health Affairs* 39, no. 3 (2020): 413–20.

34. Ibid.

35. HCPLAN, *Alternative Payment Model Framework: Refreshed for 2017* (McLean, VA: The MITRE Corporation, 2017), http://hcp-lan.org/workproducts/apm-refresh-whitepaper-final.pdf.

36. I. Papanicolas, I. R. Woskie, and A. K. Jha, "Health Care Spending in the United States and Other High-Income Countries," *JAMA* 319, no. 10 (2018): 1024–39.

37. See the Centers for Medicare & Medicaid Services' Hospital Price Transparency Rule, at https://www.cms.gov/hospital-price-transparency (accessed on June 5, 2022).

38. See Point-Counterpoint with Joseph White and Jonathan Skinner: Joseph White, "Prices, Volume, and the Perverse Effects of the Variations Crusade," *Journal of Health Politics, Policy and Law* 36, no. 4 (2011): 775–90; Jonathan Skinner, "Understanding Prices and Quantities in the U.S. Health Care System," *Journal of Health Politics, Policy and Law* 36, no. 4 (2011): 791–801.

39. Healthcare Consolidation and Competition after PPACA: Hearing before the Subcommittee on Intellectual Property, Competition, and the Internet of the Committee on the Judiciary, House of Representatives, 112th Congress, Second Session. Testimony from Thomas L. Greaney, p. 19.

40. Thomas L. Greaney, "The Affordable Care Act and Competition: Antidote or Placebo?," *Oregon Law Review* 89 (2011): 811–45; quote on 812.

41. Kaiser Family Foundation, "What is CMMI? and 11 other FAQs about the CMS Innovation Center" (San Francisco: Kaiser Family Foundation, February 27, 2018), https://www.kff.org/medicare/fact-sheet/what-is-cmmi-and-11-other-faqs-about-the-cms-innovation-center/.

42. Rocco J. Perla, Hoangmai Pham, Richard Gilfillan, Donald M. Berwick, Richard J. Baron, Peter Lee, C. Joseph McCannon, Kevin Progar, and William H. Shrank, "Government as Innovation Catalyst: Lessons from the Early Center for Medicare and Medicaid Innovation Models," *Health Affairs* 37, no. 2 (2018): 213–21.

43. Chernew et al., "Transforming Medicare's Payment Systems," 415.

44. Rena M. Conti, Ani Turner, and Paul Hughes-Cromwick, "Projections of US Prescription Drug Spending and Key Policy Implications," *JAMA Health Forum* 2, no. 1 (2021): e201613, doi:10.1001/jamahealthforum.2020.1613.

45. Victoria D. Lauenroth, Aaron S. Kesselheim, Ameet Sarpatwari, and Ariel D. Stern, "Lessons from the Impact of Price Regulation on the Pricing of Anticancer Drugs in Germany," *Health Affairs* 39, no. 7 (2020): 1185–93.

46. N. R. Augustine, G. Madhavan, and S. J. Nass, eds., *Making Medicines Affordable: A National Imperative* (Washington, DC: National Academies Press, 2018); I. Hernandez, A. San-Juan Rodriguez, C. B. Good, and W. F. Gellad, "Changes in List Prices, Net Prices, and Discounts for Branded Drugs in the US, 2007–2018," *JAMA* 323, no. 9 (2020): 854–62.

47. Einer R. Elhauge, "Why We Should Care about Fragmentation," in *The Fragmentation of US. Health Care*, ed. Einer R. Elhauge (New York: Oxford University Press, 2010), 11.

48. Greaney, "The Affordable Care Act and Competition," 833.

49. Healthcare Consolidation and Competition after PPACA: Hearing before the Subcommittee on Intellectual Property, Competition, and the Internet of the Committee on the Judiciary, House of Representatives, 112th Congress, Second Session, 2012. Testimony from Thomas L. Greaney, p. 15.

50. Hearing before the Subcommittee on Intellectual Property, Competition, and the Internet of the Committee on the Judiciary, House of Representatives, 112th Congress, Second Session, 2012. *Healthcare Consolidation and Competition after PPACA*. Statement from Chairman Lamar Smith (R-TX); quote on p. 5.

51. Hearing before the Subcommittee on Intellectual Property, Competition, and the Internet of the Committee on the Judiciary, House of Representatives, 112th Congress, Second Session, 2012. *Healthcare Consolidation and Competition after PPACA*. See statements from Reps. John Conyers, Jr. (D-MI) and Melvin L. Watt (D-NC) on pp. 1–8.

52. Theodore R. Marmor, *Fads, Fallacies and Foolishness in Medical Care Management and Policy* (Hackensack, NJ: World Scientific, 2007).

53. The first round of ACOs was called the Pioneer Model. One study reports that subsequent rounds of ACO participation in the Medicare Shared Savings Program did not benefit from

favorable selection and yet the savings were still modest. See Austin Frakt, "Results Lag in Medicare Innovation Programs," *New York Times*, September 24, 2019; Carrie Colla and Jonathan Skinner, "Déjà Vu All Over Again: Healthcare Spending Back on the Rise," *The Hill*, November 10, 2019, thehill.com/opinion/healthcare/469780-deja-vu-all-over-again-health-care-spending-back-on-the-rise. See also HCPLAN, *Alternative Payment Model Framework*.

54. Michael J. McWilliams, Laura A. Hatfield, Bruce E. Landon, and Michael E. Chernew, "Savings or Selection? Initial Spending Reductions in the Medicare Shared Savings Program and Considerations for Reform," *Milbank Quarterly* 98, no. 3 (2020): 847–907.

55. W. H. Shrank, N. A. DeParle, S. Gottlieb, S. H. Jain, P. Orszag, B. W. Powers, and G. R. Wilensky, "Health Costs and Financing: Challenges and Strategies for a New Administration," *Health Affairs* 40, no. 2 (2021): 235–42. See p. 237.

56. Matthew J. Trombley, J. Michael McWilliams, Betty Fout, and Brant Morefield, "ACO Investment Model Produced Savings, but the Majority of Participants Exited When Faced with Downside Risk," *Health Affairs* 41, no. 1 (2022): 138–46. See also K. E. Joynt and A. K. Jha, "Characteristics of Hospitals Receiving Penalties under the Hospital Readmissions Reduction Program," *JAMA* 309, no. 4 (2013): 342–43.

57. McWilliams et al, "Savings or Selection?"

58. Chernew et al., "Transforming Medicare's Payment Systems," 416.

59. Thomas L. Greaney and Richard M. Scheffler, "The Proposed Vertical Merger Guidelines and Health Care: Little Guidance and Dubious Economics," *Health Affairs Blog*, April 17, 2020.

60. Brent D. Fulton, "Health Care Market Concentration Trends in the United States: Evidence and Policy Responses." *Health Affairs* 36, no. 9 (2017): 1530–38.

61. Brady Post, Tom Buchmueller, and Andrew M. Ryan, "Vertical Integration of Hospitals and Physicians: Economic Theory and Empirical Evidence on Spending and Quality," *Medical Care Research and Review* 75, no. 4 (2018): 399–433.

62. Jessica Van Parys, "ACA Marketplace Premiums Grew More Rapidly in Areas with Monopoly Insurers than in Areas with More Competition," *Health Affairs* 37, no. 8 (2018): 1243–51.

63. Elena Prager and Matthew Schmitt, "Employer Consolidation and Wages: Evidence from Hospitals," Working Paper Series 29 (Washington, DC: Washington Center for Equitable Growth, 2019).

64. Frakt, "Results Lag in Medicare Innovation Programs."

65. Gail R. Wilensky, "Developing a Center for Comparative Effectiveness Information," *Health Affairs Web Exclusive*, November 7, 2006, w-572-w-585; Carol M. Ashton and Nelda P. Wray, *Comparative Effectiveness Research: Evidence, Medicine, and Policy* (New York: Oxford University Press, 2013).

66. Ashton and Wray, *Comparative Effectiveness Research*; Corinna Sorenson, Michael K. Gusmano, and Adam Oliver, "The Politics of Comparative Effectiveness Research: Lessons from Recent History," *Journal of Health Politics, Policy and Law* 39, no. 1 (2014): 139–70.

67. Ann C. Keller, Robin Flagg, Justin Keller, and Suhasini Ravi, "Impossible Politics? PCORI and the Search for Publicly Funded Comparative Effectiveness Research in the United States," *Journal of Health Politics, Policy and Law* 44, no. 2 (2019): 221–65.

68. Patashnik, 2020; Keller et al., "Impossible Politics?"

69. Ann C. Keller, Robin Flagg, Justin Keller and Suhasini Ravi, "Impossible Politics? PCORI and the Search for Publicly Funded Comparative Effectiveness Research in the United States," *Journal of Health Politics, Policy and Law* 44, no. 2 (2019): 221–65.

70. Keller et al., "Impossible Politics?"

71. Patashnik, 2020; Keller et al., "Impossible Politics?"

72. Centers for Disease Control and Prevention (CDC), "Prevention and Public Health Fund," https://www.cdc.gov/funding/pphf/index.html (accessed March 15, 2023).

73. Gretchen Morgenson and Emmanuelle Saliba, "Private Equity Firms Now Control Many Hospitals, ERs and Nursing Homes. Is It Good for Health Care?" NBC News, May 13, 2020, https://news.yahoo.com/private-equity-firms-now-control-095518241.html.

74. Richard M. Scheffler, Laura M. Alexander, and James R. Godwin, *Soaring Private Equity Investment in the Healthcare Sector: Consolidation Accelerated, Competition Undermined, and Patients at Risk* (American Antitrust Institute and University of California Berkeley Petris Center, 2021).

75. Ibid.; See also PitchBook Data, Inc., 2019, which shows an increase of total healthcare assets under PE management increased by $600 billion from 2006.
76. "Private Equity and Venture Capital Funds Underperformed Public Markets During Q3 2016," Cambridge Associates, April 5, 2017, https://www.cambridgeassociates.com/press-release/private-equity-and-venture-capital-funds-underperformed-public-markets-during-q3-2016/ (accessed November 27, 2017); Kara Murphy and Nirad Jain, "How Private Equity Picks Healthcare Winners" (Bain and Company, June 20, 2017), https://www.for bes.com/sites/baininsights/2017/06/20/how-private-equity-picks-healthcare-winners/#57db2fc12490 (accessed December 10, 2017).
77. Jessica L. Bailey-Wheaton, ed., "Valuation of Healthcare Service Sector Enterprises for Purposes of Private Equity Investment: Introduction (Part 1 of a 3 Part Series)," Health Capital Topics 10, no. 11 (2017.): 1, https://www.healthcapital.com/hcc/newsletter/11_17/PDF/PE.pdf.
78. Murphy and Jain, "How Private Equity Picks Healthcare Winners."
79. Ibid.
80. Jeanne Whalen and Laura Cooper, "Private-Equity Pours Cash into Opioid-Treatment Sector," Wall Street Journal, September 2, 2017.
81. Kaufman Hall, 2017 M&A in Review: A New Healthcare Landscape Takes Shape (Chicago: Kaufman Hall, 2017).
82. Heather Landi, "The Top 10 Healthcare M&A Deals of 2021," Fierce Healthcare, December 14, 2021, https://www.fiercehealthcare.com/special-report/top-10-healthc are-m-a-deals-2021.
83. Scheffler et al., Soaring Private Equity Investment in the Healthcare Sector .
84. Brady Post, Tom Buchmueller, and Andrew M. Ryan, "Vertical Integration of Hospitals and Physicians: Economic Theory and Empirical Evidence on Spending and Quality," Medical Care Research and Review 75, no. 4 (2018): 399–433.
85. Thomas G. Wollmann, "Stealth Consolidation: Evidence from an Amendment to the Hart-Scott-Rodino Act," American Economic Review: Insights 1, no. 1 (2019): 77–94.
86. Thomas G. Wollmann, "How to Get Away with Merger: Stealth Consolidation and Its Effects on US Healthcare," NBER Working Paper Series (Cambridge, MA: National Bureau of Economic Research, 2020, Revised July 2021), https://www.nber.org/system/files/wor king_papers/w27274/w27274.pdf.
87. Heather Perlberg, "How Private Equity is Running American Health Care," Bloomberg Businessweek, May 20, 2020, https://www.bloomberg.com/news/features/2020-05-20/private-equity-is-ruining-health-care-covid-is-making-it-worse.
88. Ibid.
89. Medicare Payment Advisory Commission (MedPAC), "Congressional Request: Private Equity and Medicare," in Report to the Congress: Medicare and the Health Care Delivery System (MedPAC, June 2021), file:///Users/cgrogan/Dropbox/Private%20Equity%20-%20Laura%20and%20Miriam/Sources%20-%20cross-cutting%20topics/HC%20Consolidation%20and%20private%20ownership/medpac_report_to_congress_chapter%203.2021.pdf (accessed on May 12, 2022).
90. Ibid.
91. Ibid., 72. See also L. P. Casalino, R. Saiani, S. Bhidya, D. Khullar, and E. O'Donnell, "Private Equity Acquisition of Physician Practices," Annals of Internal Medicine 170, no. 2 (2019), 114–15, https://doi.org/10.7326/M18-2363; J. Bruch, D. Zeltzer, and Z. Song, "Characteristics of Private Equity–Owned Hospitals in 2018," Annals of Internal Medicine 174, no. 2 (2021), 277–79.
92. About 80 rural hospitals have closed or eliminated inpatient services since 2010, and many more are vulnerable to closure (see A. Ellison, A State-by-State Breakdown of 80 Rural Hospital Closures, 2017).
93. Amy Abdnor and Alexandra Spratt, "Hotspots for COVID Deaths, Nursing Homes Have Long Been Targeted—And Gutted—By Private Equity" (Washington, DC: Arnold Foundation, September 8, 2020), https://www.arnoldventures.org/stories/hotspots-for-covid-deaths-nursing-homes-have-long-been-targeted-and-gutted-by-private-equity/.
94. A. Gupta, S. T. Howell, C. Yannelis, and A. Gupta, "Does Private Equity Investment in Healthcare Benefit Patients? Evidence from Nursing Homes," Working Paper 28474

(Cambridge, MA: National Bureau of Economic Research, February 2021), https://www.nber.org/system/files/working_papers/w28474/w28474.pdf.

95. Z. Cooper, F. S. Morton, and N. Shekita, "Surprise! Out-of-Network Billing for Emergency Room Services in the U.S.," Working Paper (New Haven, CT: Yale University, March 2018), https://isps.yale.edu/sites/default/files/publication/2018/03/20180305_oon_paper2_tables_appendices.pdf. See also J. D. Bruch, S. Gondi, and Z. Song, "Changes in Hospital Income, Use, and Quality Associated with Private Equity Acquisition," *JAMA Internal Medicine* 180, no. 11 (2020), 1428–35, https://jamanetwork.com/journals/jamainternalmedicine/article-abstract/2769549?guestAccessKey=87f981c4-d66d-4901-b869-43f3489dfb8a&utm_source=For_The_Media&utm_medium=referral&utm_campaign=ftm_links&utm_content=tfl&utm_term=082420.

96. Scheffler et al., *Soaring Private Equity Investment*, 2.

97. Lauren Coleman-Lochner and Eliza Ronalds-Hannon, "Buyouts Push Companies to the Limit. Or Over It," *Bloomberg Businessweek*, October 8, 2019, https://www.bloomberg.com/news/features/2019-10-03/how-private-equity-works-and-took-over-everything. For an excellent expose that revealed enormous payouts to private equity owners after the PE fund loaded its acquired company with significant debt (and thus the reason why Sen. Warren and others were concerned), see Jesse Barron, "How America's Oldest Gun Maker Went Bankrupt: A Financial Engineering Mystery," *New York Times Magazine*, May 1, 2019, https://www.nytimes.com/interactive/2019/05/01/magazine/remington-guns-jobs-huntsville.html.

98. Sahil Kapur, "Elizabeth Warren Declares War on Private Equity 'Vampires' in 2020 Plan," Bloomberg, July 18, 2019, https://www.bloomberg.com/news/articles/2019-07-18/warren-declares-war-on-private-equity-vampires-in-2020-plan.

99. Lynnley Browning and Saleha Mohsin, "Mnuchin Says No Plan to Change Carried Interest Tax Treatment," *Bloomberg Businessweek*, May 22, 2019, https://www.bloomberg.com/news/articles/2019-05-22/mnuchin-says-no-plan-to-change-carried-interest-tax-treatment.

100. Sheelah Kolhatkar, "How Private-Equity Firms Squeeze Hospital Patients for Profits," *New Yorker*, April 9, 2020.

101. Barron, "How America's Oldest Gun Maker Went Bankrupt."

102. Heather Perlberg and Benjamin Bain, "Private Equity Wields More Power Than Ever as Warren Picks Fight," *Bloomberg Businessweek*, October 3, 2019, https://www.bloomberg.com/news/articles/2019-10-03/private-equity-flexes-muscle-in-washington-as-warren-picks-fight.

103. Jason Kelly, "Everything Is Private Equity Now," *Bloomberg Businessweek*, October 8, 2019, https://www.bloomberg.com/news/features/2019-10-03/how-private-equity-works-and-took-over-everything.

104. Barron, "How America's Oldest Gun Maker Went Bankrupt."

105. Morgenson and Saliba, "Private Equity Firms Now Control Many Hospitals, ERs and Nursing Homes."

## Conclusion

1. Thomas L. Greaney and Richard M. Scheffler, "The Proposed Vertical Merger Guidelines and Health Care: Little Guidance and Dubious Economics," *Health Affairs Blog*, April 17, 2020.

2. Cory Capps, David Dranove and Christopher Ody, "Physician Practice Consolidation Driven by Small Acquisitions, So Antitrust Agencies Have Few Tools to Intervene," *Health Affairs* 36, no. 9 (2017): 1556–63.

3. Rebecca Kelly Slaughter, "Remarks of Commissioner: Antitrust and Health Care Providers Policies to Promote Competition and Protect Patients," Center for American Progress, May 14, 2019 (Washington, DC: Federal Trade Commission, 2019).

4. Cory Capps, Laura Kamitch, Zenon Zabinski, and Slava Zavats, "The Continuing Saga of Hospital Merger Enforcement," *Antitrust Law Journal* 82, no. 2 (2019): 441–96.

5. Slaughter, "Remarks of Commissioner."

6. Richard M. Scheffler and Daniel R. Arnold, "Insurer Market Power Lowers Prices In Numerous Concentrated Provider Markets," *Health Affairs* 36, no. 9 (2017): 1539–46; quote on 1545.

7. Mark V. Pauly, *Will Health Care's Immediate Future Look a Lot Like the Recent Past?* (Washington, DC: American Enterprise Institute, June 2019), https://www.aei.org/research-products/report/health-care-public-sector-funding/. Quote on cover page.

8. Pauly, *Will Health Care's Immediate Future Look a Lot Like the Recent Past?*, 4.

9. L. D. Brown, "The Political Face of Public Health," *Public Health Review* 32 (2010): 155–73.

10. Ibid., Harold Pollack, "We Need a Public Health Revolution," *Democracy Journal*, August 21, 2020, https://democracyjournal.org/arguments/we-need-a-public-health-revolution/.

11. Nason Maani and Sandro Galea, "COVID-19 and Underinvestment in the Public Health Infrastructure of the United States," *Milbank Quarterly* 98, no. 2 (2020): 250–59.

12. Michael Lewis, *The Premonition: A Pandemic Story* (New York: W. W. Norton, 2021); Pollack, "We Need a Public Health Revolution."

13. Bruce C. Vladeck and Thomas Rice, "Market Failure and the Failure of Discourse: Facing Up to the Power of Sellers," *Health Affairs* 28, no. 5 (2009): 1305–14; quote on 1314.

# INDEX

For the benefit of digital users, indexed terms that span two pages (e.g., 52–53) may, on occasion, appear on only one of those pages.

Note: Tables and figures are indicated by t and f following the page number

focus on public health expansion
    planning, 102–8
Grow-and-Hide and, 193, 199, 208–9, 214, 217
institutional fragmentation, 58–68, 61t
introduction to, 16, 17
planning panacea and, 244, 245–48, 247t
tuberculosis and, 54–56
public health state-building
    challenges to, 70–85, 70t
    Division of Child Hygiene, 76, 84–85
    garbage collection, 57, 58–59, 64–66, 66t
    growth of, 85–86
    health department laboratories and, 36,
        70, 71–72
    hospital expenditures, 67t
    institutional fragmentation, 15, 58–68, 61t
    introduction to, 57–58
    maternal and child health and, 70, 75–85, 80t,
        81f, 82f, 83f
    medical insurgency, 68–69
    New Public Health Deal, 153–64
    summary of, 86
    venereal disease and, 70, 72–75, 77
*Public Medical Services: A Survey of Tax-Supported
    Medical Care in the United States* (Davis), 142
*The Public's Investment in Hospitals* (Rorem), 120
Public Works Administration (PWA), 130–31

quarantine, 32–33, 35, 37, 38, 40, 41–42, 44, 52,
    68–69, 93, 371n.31
Quarantine Act, 40
Quayle, Dan, 358
*The Quest for Security* (Rubinow), 129

Reagan, Ronald, 279, 280, 297
real estate investment trusts (REITs), 310
Regional Medical Programs (RMPs), 254–55,
    257–60, 263–66
Reich, Adam, 305–6
residual public assistance programs, 164, 220, 221,
    224, 225–26, 317
Rice, Tom, 363
Richardson, Elliot L., 199–200
Robbins, Catherine, 313
Roberts, Stewart, 135, 136–37
Roche, Josephine, 138–39, 141–42
Rockefeller Foundation, 85–86, 89
Rockefeller Institute for Medical Research, 46
Roemer, Milton, 165–68, 170–71
Roosevelt, Franklin Delano, 10–11, 88
Roosevelt, Theodore, 42
Rorem, C. Rufus, 119–21
Rorem, Rufus, 101
Rosen, George, 96–97
Rosenau, Milton J., 42
Rosenberg, Charles, 28, 32–33
Rosenwald Fund, 119, 142

Rostenkowski, Dan, 276
Rothman, Sheila, 83–84
Rubinow, Isaac Max, 129
Ruhe, William, 253
Russell Sage Foundation, 61, 89

sanitary reforms, 12–14, 23, 28–33, 33t, 131–32,
    131t, 132t
*Saturday Review,* 272–73
scarlet fever, 33–34
Scheele, Leonard, 172–73, 208–11
Scheffler, Richard, 357, 360–61
Section on State Medicine and Public Hygiene
    (1872), 37–38
Securities and Exchange Commission (SEC), 313
Sedgwick, William, 37
Sedgwick, William T., 43
Selective Service and Training Act (1941), 157
self-referrals, 292
Senate Finance Committee, 232–33
Sessions, Pete, 333
Shannon, James A., 258
Shearon, Marjorie, 171–72
Shepard, William, 178–81
Sheppard-Towner Act (1921), 81, 82–85
Sibley, Hiram, 183–84, 185
sickness insurance, 103–6, 167
Slavitt, Joseph, 151, 383–84n.53
Smillie, Wilson George, 63–64, 167
Smith, Stephen, 31–32, 37, 38
Smith, Theobald, 45–46
Smith, Winfred H., 120
Snow, John, 30
socialized medicine, 129–30, 132–34, 149–50,
    152, 172, 174–75
Social Science Research Council, 89
Social Security Act (1935), 10–11, 84–85,
    134–40, 261
Social Security Act Amendments (1950), 163–64,
    219–20, 224
Social Security Administration (SSA), 223
Social Security Board, 89
*Social Security Bulletin,* 194–95, 196, 199, 201
Special Supplemental Nutrition Program
    for Women, Infants, and Children
    (WIC), 6–7
Springer, Edward, 231–32, 256–57
Stambaugh, Jeffrey, 230
Stark, Fortney (Pete), 292, 297
Starr, Paul, 199
State Children's Health Insurance Program
    (SCHIP), 321, 328–30
State Health Planning and Development Agencies
    (SHPDAs), 266
state medicine, 17, 19, 37–38, 58, 86, 95–96,
    98–99, 115–18, 125–26, 129–30, 134,
    140–45, 151, 383–84n.53